THE CIVILISATION

OF THE

RENAISSANCE IN ITALY

BY JACOB BURCKHARDT

AUTHORIZED TRANSLATION

BY

S. G. C. MIDDLEMORE

KONECKY&KONECKY

Konecky & Konecky
72 Ayers Point Rd.
Old Saybrook, CT 06475

ISBN: 1-56852-446-3

Printed in the USA

PREFACE.

DR. BURCKHARDT'S work on the Renaissance in Italy is too well known, not only to students of the period, but now to a wider circle of readers, for any introduction to be necessary. The increased interest which has of late years, in England, been taken in this and kindred subjects, and the welcome which has been given to the works of other writers upon them, encourage me to hope that in publishing this translation I am meeting a want felt by some who are either unable to read German at all, or to whom an English version will save a good deal of time and trouble.

The translation is made from the third edition of the original, recently published in Germany, with slight additions to the text, and large additions to the notes, by Dr. LUDWIG GEIGER, of Berlin. It also contains some fresh matter communicated by Dr. BURCKHARDT to Professor DIEGO VALBUSA of Mantua, the Italian translator of the book. To all three gentlemen my thanks are due for courtesy shown, or help given to me in the course of my work.

In a few cases, where Dr. GEIGER'S view differs from that taken by Dr. BURCKHARDT, I have called attention to the fact by bracketing Dr. GEIGER'S opinion and adding his initials.

THE TRANSLATOR.

CONTENTS.

PART I.

THE STATE AS A WORK OF ART.

CHAPTER I.

INTRODUCTION.

CHAPTER II.

THE TYRANNY OF THE FOURTEENTH CENTURY.

CHAPTER III.

THE TYRANNY OF THE FIFTEENTH CENTURY.

CHAPTER IV.

THE PETTY TYRANNIES.

CHAPTER V.

THE GREATER DYNASTIES.

CHAPTER VI.

THE OPPONENTS OF TYRANNY.

CHAPTER VII.

THE REPUBLICS: VENICE AND FLORENCE.

CHAPTER VIII.

FOREIGN POLICY OF THE ITALIAN STATES.

CHAPTER IX.

WAR AS A WORK OF ART.

CHAPTER X.

THE PAPACY AND ITS DANGERS.

PART II.

THE DEVELOPMENT OF THE INDIVIDUAL.

CHAPTER I.

THE ITALIAN STATE AND THE INDIVIDUAL.

CHAPTER II.

THE PERFECTING OF THE INDIVIDUAL.

CHAPTER III.

THE MODERN IDEA OF FAME.

CHAPTER IV.

MODERN WIT AND SATIRE.

PART III.

THE REVIVAL OF ANTIQUITY.

CHAPTER I.

INTRODUCTORY REMARKS.

CHAPTER II.

ROME, THE CITY OF RUINS.

PART IV.

THE DISCOVERY OF THE WORLD AND OF MAN.

CHAPTER I.

JOURNEYS OF THE ITALIANS.

CHAPTER II.

NATURAL SCIENCE IN ITALY.

CHAPTER III.

THE DISCOVERY OF NATURAL BEAUTY.

CHAPTER IV.

THE DISCOVERY OF MAN.—SPIRITUAL DESCRIPTION IN POETRY.

CHAPTER V.

BIOGRAPHY.

CHAPTER VI.

THE DESCRIPTION OF NATIONS AND CITIES.

CHAPTER VII.

DESCRIPTION OF THE OUTWARD MAN.

CHAPTER VIII.

DESCRIPTIONS OF LIFE IN MOVEMENT.

PART V.

SOCIETY AND FESTIVALS.

CHAPTER I.

THE EQUALISATION OF CLASSES.

CHAPTER VII.

DOMESTIC ECONOMY.

CHAPTER VIII.

THE FESTIVALS.

PART VI.

MORALITY AND RELIGION.

CHAPTER I.

MORALITY.

CHAPTER II.

RELIGION IN DAILY LIFE.

CHAPTER III.

RELIGION AND THE SPIRIT OF THE RENAISSANCE.

CHAPTER IV.

MIXTURE OF ANCIENT AND MODERN SUPERSTITIONS.

CHAPTER V.

GENERAL DISINTEGRATION OF BELIEF.

PART I.

THE STATE AS A WORK OF ART.

CHAPTER I.

INTRODUCTION.

THIS work bears the title of an essay in the strictest sense of the word. No one is more conscious than the writer with what limited means and strength he has addressed himself to a task so arduous. And even if he could look with greater confidence upon his own researches, he would hardly thereby feel more assured of the approval of competent judges. To each eye, perhaps, the outlines of a given civilisation present a different picture; and in treating of a civilisation which is the mother of our own, and whose influence is still at work among us, it is unavoidable that individual judgment and feeling should tell every moment both on the writer and on the reader. In the wide ocean upon which we venture, the possible ways and directions are many; and the same studies which have served for this work might easily, in other hands, not only receive a wholly different treatment and application, but lead also to essentially different conclusions. Such indeed is the importance of the subject, that it still calls for fresh investigation, and may be studied with advantage from the most varied points of view. Meanwhile we are content if a patient hearing be granted us, and if this book be taken and judged as a whole. It is the most serious difficulty of the history of civilisation that a great intellectual process must be broken up into single, and often into what seem arbitrary categories, in order to be in any way intelligible. It was formerly our intention to fill up the gaps in this book by a special work on the 'Art of the Renaissance,'—an intention, however, which we have been able only to fulfil[1] in part.

[1] *History of Architecture*, by Franz Kugler. (The first half of the fourth volume, containing the 'Architecture and Decoration of the Italian Renaissance,' is by the Author.)

The struggle between the Popes and the Hohenstaufen left Italy in a political condition which differed essentially from that of other countries of the West. While in France, Spain and England the feudal system was so organised that, at the close of its existence, it was naturally transformed into a unified monarchy, and while in Germany it helped to maintain, at least outwardly, the unity of the empire, Italy had shaken it off almost entirely. The Emperors of the fourteenth century, even in the most favourable case, were no longer received and respected as feudal lords, but as possible leaders and supporters of powers already in existence; while the Papacy,[1] with its creatures and allies, was strong enough to hinder national unity in the future, not strong enough itself to bring about that unity. Between the two lay a multitude of political units--republics and despots—in part of long standing, in part of recent origin, whose existence was founded simply on their power to maintain it.[2] In them for the first time we detect the modern political spirit of Europe, surrendered freely to its own instincts, often displaying the worst features of an unbridled egoism, outraging every right, and killing every germ of a healthier culture. But, wherever this vicious tendency is overcome or in any way compensated, a new fact appears in history—the state as the outcome of reflection and calculation, the state as a work of art. This new life displays itself in a hundred forms, both in the republican and in the despotic states, and determines their inward constitution, no less than their foreign policy. We shall limit ourselves to the consideration of the completer and more clearly defined type, which is offered by the despotic states.

The internal condition of the despotically governed states

[1] Macchiavelli, *Discorsi*, l. i. c. 12. 'E la cagione, che la Italia non sia in quel medesimo termine, ne habbia anch' ella ò una republica ò un prencipe che la governi, è solamente la Chiesa; perchè havendovi habitato e tenuto imperio temporale non è stata si potente ne di tal virtè, che l'habbia potuto occupare il restante d'Italia e farsene prencipe.'

[2] The rulers and their dependents were together called 'lo stato,' and this name afterwards acquired the meaning of the collective existence of a territory.

had a memorable counterpart in the Norman Empire of Lower Italy and Sicily, after its transformation by the Emperor Frederick II.[1] Bred amid treason and peril in the neighbourhood of the Saracens, Frederick, the first ruler of the modern type who sat upon a throne, had early accustomed himself, both in criticism and action, to a thoroughly objective treatment of affairs. His acquaintance with the internal condition and administration of the Saracenic states was close and intimate; and the mortal struggle in which he was engaged with the Papacy compelled him, no less than his adversaries, to bring into the field all the resources at his command. Frederick's measures (especially after the year 1231) are aimed at the complete destruction of the feudal state, at the transformation of the people into a multitude destitute of will and of the means of resistance, but profitable in the utmost degree to the exchequer. He centralised, in a manner hitherto unknown in the West, the whole judicial and political administration by establishing the right of appeal from the feudal courts, which he did not, however, abolish, to the imperial judges. No office was henceforth to be filled by popular election, under penalty of the devastation of the offending district and of the enslavement of its inhabitants. Excise duties were introduced; the taxes, based on a comprehensive assessment, and distributed in accordance with Mohammedan usages, were collected by those cruel and vexatious methods without which, it is true, it is impossible to obtain any money from Orientals. Here, in short, we find, not a people, but simply a disciplined multitude of subjects; who were forbidden, for example, to marry out of the country without special permission, and under no circumstances were allowed to study abroad. The University of Naples was the first we know of to restrict the freedom of study, while the East, in these respects at all events, left its youth unfettered. It was after the example of Mohammedan rulers that Frederick traded on his own account in all parts of the Mediterranean, reserving to himself the monopoly of many

[1] C. Winckelmann, *De Regni Siculi Administratione qualis fuerit regnante Friderico II.*, Berlin, 1859. A. del Vecchio. *La legislazione di Federico II. imperatore.* Turin, 1874. Frederick II. has been fully and thoroughly discussed by Winckelmann and Schirrmacher.

commodities, and restricting in various ways the commerce of his subjects. The Fatimite Caliphs, with all their esoteric unbelief, were, at least in their earlier history, tolerant of the differences in the religious faith of their people; Frederick, on the other hand, crowned his system of government by a religious inquisition, which will seem the more reprehensible when we remember that in the persons of the heretics he was persecuting the representatives of a free municipal life. Lastly, the internal police, and the kernel of the army for foreign service, was composed of Saracens who had been brought over from Sicily to Nocera and Luceria—men who were deaf to the cry of misery and careless of the ban of the Church. At a later period the subjects, by whom the use of weapons had long been forgotten, were passive witnesses of the fall of Manfred and of the seizure of the government by Charles of Anjou ; the latter continued to use the system which he found already at work.

At the side of the centralising Emperor appeared an usurper of the most peculiar kind: his vicar and son-in-law, Ezzelino da Romano. He stands as the representative of no system of government or administration, for all his activity was wasted in struggles for supremacy in the eastern part of Upper Italy ; but as a political type he was a figure of no less importance for the future than his imperial protector Frederick. The conquests and usurpations which had hitherto taken place in the Middle Ages rested on real or pretended inheritance and other such claims, or else were effected against unbelievers and excommunicated persons. Here for the first time the attempt was openly made to found a throne by wholesale murder and endless barbarities, by the adoption, in short, of any means with a view to nothing but the end pursued. None of his successors, not even Cæsar Borgia, rivalled the colossal guilt of Ezzelino ; but the example once set was not forgotten, and his fall led to no return of justice among the nations, and served as no warning to future transgressors.

It was in vain at such a time that St. Thomas Aquinas, a born subject of Frederick, set up the theory of a constitutional monarchy, in which the prince was to be supported by an upper house named by himself, and a representative body elected by the people; in vain did he concede to the people the right of revolution.[1] Such theories found no echo outside the lecture-room, and Frederick and Ezzelino were and remain for Italy the great political phenomena of the thirteenth century. Their personality, already half legendary, forms the most important subject of 'The Hundred Old Tales,' whose original composition falls certainly within this century.[2] In them Frederick is already represented as possessing the right to do as he pleased with the property of his subjects, and exercises on all, even on criminals, a profound influence by the force of his personality; Ezzelino is spoken of with the awe which all mighty impressions leave behind them. His person became the centre of a whole literature from the chronicle of eye-witnesses to the half-mythical tragedy[3] of later poets.

Immediately after the fall of Frederick and Ezzelino, a crowd of tyrants appeared upon the scene. The struggle between Guelph and Ghibelline was their opportunity. They came forward in general as Ghibelline leaders, but at times and under conditions so various that it is impossible not to recognise in the fact a law of supreme and universal necessity. The means which they used were those already familiar in the party struggles of the past—the banishment or destruction of their adversaries and of their adversaries' households.

[1] Baumann, *Staatslehre des Thomas von Aquino.* Leipzig, 1873, esp. pp. 136 sqq.

[2] *Cento Novelle Antiche*, ed. 1525. For Frederick, Nov. 2, 21, 22, 23, 24, 30, 53, 59, 90, 100; for Ezzelino, Nov. 31, and esp. 84

[3] Scardeonius, *De Urbis Patav. Antiqu. in Grævius*, Thesaurus, vi. iii. p. 259.

CHAPTER II.

THE TYRANNY OF THE FOURTEENTH CENTURY.

THE tyrannies, great and small, of the fourteenth century afford constant proof that examples such as these were not thrown away. Their misdeeds cried forth loudly and have been circumstantially told by historians. As states depending for existence on themselves alone, and scientifically organised with a view to this object, they present to us a higher interest than that of mere narrative.

The deliberate adaptation of means to ends, of which no prince out of Italy had at that time a conception, joined to almost absolute power within the limits of the state, produced among the despots both men and modes of life of a peculiar character.[1] The chief secret of government in the hands of the prudent ruler lay in leaving the incidence of taxation so far as possible where he found it, or as he had first arranged it. The chief sources of income were: a land tax, based on a valuation; definite taxes on articles of consumption and duties on exported and imported goods; together with the private fortune of the ruling house. The only possible increase was derived from the growth of business and of general prosperity. Loans, such as we find in the free cities, were here unknown; a well-planned confiscation was held a preferable means of raising money, provided only that it left public credit unshaken—an end attained, for example, by the truly Oriental practice of deposing and plundering the director of the finances.[2]

Out of this income the expenses of the little court, of the body-guard, of the mercenary troops, and of the public buildings were met, as well as of the buffoons and men of talent who belonged to the personal attendants of the prince. The

[1] Sismondi, *Hist. de Rép. Italiennes*, iv. p. 420; viii. pp. 1 sqq.

[2] Franco Sacchetti, *Novelle* (61, 62).

illegitimacy of his rule isolated the tyrant and surrounded him with constant danger; the most honourable alliance which he could form was with intellectual merit, without regard to its origin. The liberality of the northern princes of the thirteenth century was confined to the knights, to the nobility which served and sang. It was otherwise with the Italian despot. With his thirst of fame and his passion for monumental works, it was talent, not birth, which he needed. In the company of the poet and the scholar he felt himself in a new position, almost, indeed, in possession of a new legitimacy.

No prince was more famous in this respect than the ruler of Verona, Can Grande della Scala, who numbered among the illustrious exiles whom he entertained at his court representatives of the whole of Italy.[1] The men of letters were not ungrateful. Petrarch, whose visits at the courts of such men have been so severely censured, sketched an ideal picture of a prince of the fourteenth century.[2] He demands great things from his patron, the lord of Padua, but in a manner which shows that he holds him capable of them. 'Thou must not be the master but the father of thy subjects, and must love them as thy children; yea, as members of thy body.[3] Weapons, guards, and soldiers thou mayest employ against the enemy—with thy subjects goodwill is sufficient. By citizens, of course, I mean those who love the existing order; for those who daily desire change are rebels and traitors, and against such a stern justice may take its course.'

Here follows, worked out in detail, the purely modern fiction of the omnipotence of the state. The prince is to be inde-

[1] Dante, it is true, is said to have lost the favour of this prince, which impostors knew how to keep. See the important account in Petrarch, *De Rerum Memorandarum*, lib. ii. 3, 46.

[2] Petrarca, *Epistolæ Seniles*, lib. xiv. 1, to Francesco di Carrara (Nov. 28, 1373). The letter is sometimes printed separately with the title, 'De Republica optime administranda,' e.g. Bern, 1602.

[3] It is not till a hundred years later that the princess is spoken of as the mother of the people. Comp. Hieron. Crivelli's funeral oration on Bianca Maria Visconti, in Muratori, *Scriptores Rerum Italicarum*, xxv. col. 429. It was by way of parody of this phrase that a sister of Sixtus IV. is called in Jac Volateranus (Murat., xxiii. col. 109) 'mater ecclesiæ.'

pendent of his courtiers, but at the same time to govern with simplicity and modesty; he is to take everything into his charge, to maintain and restore churches and public buildings, to keep up the municipal police,[1] to drain the marshes, to look after the supply of wine and corn; he is to exercise a strict justice, so to distribute the taxes that the people can recognise their necessity and the regret of the ruler to be compelled to put his hands in the pockets of others; he is to support the sick and the helpless, and to give his protection and society to distinguished scholars, on whom his fame in after ages will depend.

But whatever might be the brighter sides of the system, and the merits of individual rulers, yet the men of the fourteenth century were not without a more or less distinct consciousness of the brief and uncertain tenure of most of these despotisms. Inasmuch as political institutions like these are naturally secure in proportion to the size of the territory in which they exist, the larger principalities were constantly tempted to swallow up the smaller. Whole hecatombs of petty rulers were sacrificed at this time to the Visconti alone. As a result of this outward danger an inward ferment was in ceaseless activity; and the effect of the situation on the character of the ruler was generally of the most sinister kind. Absolute power, with its temptations to luxury and unbridled selfishness, and the perils to which he was exposed from enemies and conspirators, turned him almost inevitably into a tyrant in the worst sense of the word. Well for him if he could trust his nearest relations! But where all was illegitimate, there could be no regular law of inheritance, either with regard to the succession or to the division of the ruler's property; and consequently the heir, if incompetent or a minor, was liable in the interest of the family itself to be supplanted by an uncle or cousin of more resolute character. The acknowledgment or exclusion of the bastards was a fruitful source of contest; and most of these families in consequence

[1] With the parenthetical request, in reference to a previous conversation, that the prince would again forbid the keeping of pigs in the streets of Padua, as the sight of them was unpleasing, especially for strangers, and apt to frighten the horses.

were plagued with a crowd of discontented and vindictive kinsmen. This circumstance gave rise to continual outbreaks of treason and to frightful scenes of domestic bloodshed. Sometimes the pretenders lived abroad in exile, and like the Visconti, who practised the fisherman's craft on the Lake of Garda,[1] viewed the situation with patient indifference. When asked by a messenger of his rival when and how he thought of returning to Milan, he gave the reply, 'By the same means as those by which I was expelled, but not till his crimes have outweighed my own.' Sometimes, too, the despot was sacrificed by his relations, with the view of saving the family, to the public conscience which he had too grossly outraged.[2] In a few cases the government was in the hands of the whole family, or at least the ruler was bound to take their advice; and here, too, the distribution of property and influence often led to bitter disputes.

The whole of this system excited the deep and persistent hatred of the Florentine writers of that epoch. Even the pomp and display with which the despot was perhaps less anxious to gratify his own vanity than to impress the popular imagination, awakened their keenest sarcasm. Woe to an adventurer if he fell into their hands, like the upstart Doge Aguello of Pisa (1364), who used to ride out with a golden sceptre, and show himself at the window of his house, 'as relics are shown,' reclining on embroidered drapery and cushions, served like a pope or emperor, by kneeling attendants.[3] More often, however, the old Florentines speak on this subject in a tone of lofty seriousness. Dante saw and characterised well the vulgarity and commonplace which mark the ambition of the new princes.[4] 'What mean their trumpets and their bells,

[1] Petrarca, *Rerum Memorandar.*, lib. iii. 2, 66.—Matteo I. Visconti and Guido della Torre, then ruling in Milan, are the persons referred to.

[2] Matteo Villani, v. 81: the secret murder of Matteo II. (Maffiolo) Visconti by his brother.

[3] Filippo Villani, *Istorie*, xi. 101. Petrarch speaks in the same tone of the tyrants dressed out 'like altars at a festival.'—The triumphal procession of Castracane at Lucca is described minutely in his life by Tegrimo, in Murat., xi., col, 1340.

[4] *De Vulgari Eloqui*, i. c. 12: . . . 'qui non heroico more, sed plebeo sequuntur superbiam.'

their horns and their flutes; but come, hangman—come, vultures?' The castle of the tyrant, as pictured by the popular mind, is a lofty and solitary building, full of dungeons and listening-tubes,[1] the home of cruelty and misery. Misfortune is foretold to all who enter the service of the despot,[2] who even becomes at last himself an object of pity: he must needs be the enemy of all good and honest men; he can trust no one, and can read in the faces of his subjects the expectation of his fall. 'As despotisms rise, grow, and are consolidated, so grows in their midst the hidden element which must produce their dissolution and ruin.'[3] But the deepest ground of dislike has not been stated; Florence was then the scene of the richest development of human individuality, while for the despots no other individuality could be suffered to live and thrive but their own and that of their nearest dependents. The control of the individual was rigorously carried out, even down to the establishment of a system of passports.[4]

The astrological superstitions and the religious unbelief of many of the tyrants gave, in the minds of their contemporaries, a peculiar colour to this awful and God-forsaken existence. When the last Carrara could no longer defend the walls and gates of the plague-stricken Padua, hemmed in on all sides by the Venetians (1405), the soldiers of the guard heard him cry to the devil 'to come and kill him.'

The most complete and instructive type of the tyranny of the fourteenth century is to be found unquestionably among the Visconti of Milan, from the death of the Archbishop Giovanni onwards (1354). The family likeness which shows itself between Bernabò and the worst of the Roman Emperors

[1] This we find first in the fifteenth century, but their representations are certainly based on the beliefs of earlier times: L. B. Alberti, *De re ædif.*, v. 3.—Franc. di Giorgio, 'Trattato,' in Della Valle, Lettere Sanesi, iii. 121.

[2] Franco Sacchetti, Nov. 61.

[3] Matteo Villani, vi. 1.

[4] The Paduan passport office about the middle of the fourteenth century is referred to by Franco Sacchetti, Nov. 117, in the words, 'quelli delle bullete.' In the last ten years of the reign of Frederick II., when the strictest control was exercised on the personal conduct of his subjects, this system must have been very highly developed.

is unmistakable;[1] the most important public object was the prince's boar-hunting; whoever interfered with it was put to death with torture; the terrified people were forced to maintain 5,000 boar-hounds, with strict responsibility for their health and safety. The taxes were extorted by every conceivable sort of compulsion; seven daughters of the prince received a dowry of 100,000 gold florins apiece; and an enormous treasure was collected. On the death of his wife (1384) an order was issued 'to the subjects' to share his grief, as once they had shared his joy, and to wear mourning for a year. The *coup de main* (1385) by which his nephew Giangaleazzo got him into his power—one of those brilliant plots which make the heart of even late historians beat more quickly[2]—was strikingly characteristic of the man. Giangaleazzo, despised by his relations on account of his religion and his love of science, resolved on vengeance, and, leaving the city under pretext of a pilgrimage, fell upon his unsuspecting uncle, took him prisoner, forced his way back into the city at the head of an armed band, seized on the government, and gave up the palace of Bernabò to general plunder.

In Giangaleazzo that passion for the colossal which was common to most of the despots shows itself on the largest scale. He undertook, at the cost of 300,000 golden florins, the construction of gigantic dykes, to divert in case of need the Mincio from Mantua and the Brenta from Padua, and thus to render these cities defenceless.[3] It is not impossible, indeed, that he thought of draining away the lagoons of Venice. He founded that most wonderful of all convents, the Certosa of Pavia,[4] and

[1] Corio, *Storia di Milano*, fol. 247 sqq. Recent Italian writers have observed that the Visconti have still to find a historian who, keeping the just mean between the exaggerated praises of contemporaries (*e.g.* Petrarch) and the violent denunciations of later political (Guelph) opponents, will pronounce a final judgment upon them.

[2] E.g. of Paolo Giovio: *Elogia Virorum bellicâ virtute illustrium*, Basel, 1575, p. 85, in the life of Bernabò. Giangal. (*Vita*, pp. 86 sqq.) is for Giovio 'post Theodoricum omnium præstantissimus.' Comp. also Jovius, *Vitæ xii. Vicecomitum Mediolani principum*, Paris, 1549, pp. 165 sqq.

[3] Corio, fol. 272, 285.

[4] Cagnola, in the *Archiv. Stor.*, iii. p. 23.

the cathedral of Milan, 'which exceeds in size and splendour all the churches of Christendom.' The Palace in Pavia, which his father Galeazzo began and which he himself finished, was probably by far the most magnificent of the princely dwellings of Europe. There he transferred his famous library, and the great collection of relics of the saints, in which he placed a peculiar faith. King Winceslaus made him Duke (1395); he was hoping for nothing less than the Kingdom of Italy [1] or the Imperial crown, when (1402) he fell ill and died. His whole territories are said to have paid him in a single year, besides the regular contribution of 1,200,000 gold florins, no less than 800,000 more in extraordinary subsidies. After his death the dominions which he had brought together by every sort of violence fell to pieces; and for a time even the original nucleus could with difficulty be maintained by his successors. What might have become of his sons Giovanni Maria (died 1412) and Filippo Maria (died 1417), had they lived in a different country and among other traditions, cannot be said. But, as heirs of their house, they inherited that monstrous capital of cruelty and cowardice which had been accumulated from generation to generation.

Giovanni Maria, too, is famed for his dogs, which were no longer, however, used for hunting, but for tearing human bodies. Tradition has preserved their names, like those of the bears of the Emperor Valentinian I.[2] In May, 1409, when war was going on, and the starving populace cried to him in the streets, *Pace! Pace!* he let loose his mercenaries upon them, and 200 lives were sacrificed; under penalty of the gallows it was forbidden to utter the words *pace* and *guerra*, and the priests were ordered, instead of *dona nobis pacem*, to say *tran-*

[1] So Corio, fol. 286, and Poggio, *Hist. Florent.* iv. in Murat. xx. col. 290.—Cagnola (loc. cit.) speaks of his designs on the imperial crown. See too the sonnet in Trucchi, *Poesie Ital. ined.*, ii. p. 118:

"Stan le città lombarde con le chiave
In man per darle a voi . . . etc.
Roma vi chiamo : Cesar mio novello
Io sono ignuda, e l'anima pur vive:
Or mi coprite col vostro mantello," etc.

[2] Corio, fol. 301 and sqq. Comp. Ammian. Marcellin., xxix. 3.

quillitatem! At last a band of conspirators took advantage of the moment when Facino Cane, the chief Condottiere of the insane ruler, lay ill at Pavia, and cut down Giovan Maria in the church of San Gottardo at Milan; the dying Facino on the same day made his officers swear to stand by the heir Filippo Maria, whom he himself urged his wife[1] to take for a second husband. His wife, Beatrice di Tenda, followed his advice. We shall have occasion to speak of Filippo Maria later on.

And in times like these Cola di Rienzi was dreaming of founding on the rickety enthusiasm of the corrupt population of Rome a new state which was to comprise all Italy. By the side of rulers such as those whom we have described, he seems no better than a poor deluded fool.

[1] So Paul. Jovius, *Elogia*, pp. 88–92, Jo. Maria Philippus.

CHAPTER III.

THE TYRANNY OF THE FIFTEENTH CENTURY.

THE despotisms of the fifteenth century show an altered character. Many of the less important tyrants, and some of the greater, like the Scala and the Carrara, had disappeared, while the more powerful ones, aggrandized by conquest, had given to their systems each its characteristic development. Naples for example received a fresh and stronger impulse from the new Arragonese dynasty. A striking feature of this epoch is the attempt of the Condottieri to found independent dynasties of their own. Facts and the actual relations of things, apart from traditional estimates, are alone regarded; talent and audacity win the great prizes. The petty despots, to secure a trustworthy support, begin to enter the service of the larger states, and become themselves Condottieri, receiving in return for their services money and impunity for their misdeeds, if not an increase of territory. All, whether small or great, must exert themselves more, must act with greater caution and calculation, and must learn to refrain from too wholesale barbarities; only so much wrong is permitted by public opinion as is necessary for the end in view, and this the impartial bystander certainly finds no fault with. No trace is here visible of that half-religious loyalty by which the legitimate princes of the West were supported; personal popularity is the nearest approach we can find to it. Talent and calculation are the only means of advancement. A character like that of Charles the Bold, which wore itself out in the passionate pursuit of impracticable ends, was a riddle to the Italian. 'The Swiss were only peasants, and if they were all killed, that would be no satisfaction for the Burgundian nobles who might fall in the war. If the Duke got possession of all Switzerland without a struggle, his income would not be 5,000 ducats the greater.'[1] The mediæval features in the character of Charles, his chivalrous aspirations and ideals, had long become unintelligible to the Italian. The diplomatists of the South, when they saw him strike his officers and yet keep them in his service, when he maltreated his troops to punish them for a defeat, and then threw the blame on his counsellors in the presence of the same troops, gave him up for lost.[2] Louis XI., on the other hand, whose policy surpasses that of the Italian princes in their own style, and who was an avowed admirer of Francesco Sforza, must be placed in all that regards culture and refinement far below these rulers.

Good and evil lie strangely mixed together in the Italian States of the fifteenth century. The personality of the ruler is so highly developed, often of such deep significance, and so characteristic of the conditions and needs of the time, that to form an adequate moral judgment on it is no easy task.[3]

The foundation of the system was and remained illegitimate, and nothing could remove the curse which rested upon it. The imperial approval or investiture made no change in the matter, since the people attached little weight to the fact, that the despot had bought a piece of parchment somewhere in foreign countries, or from some stranger passing through his territory.[4] If the Emperor had been good for anything—so ran the logic of uncritical common sense—he would never have let the tyrant rise at all. Since the Roman expedition of Charles IV., the emperors had done nothing more in Italy than sanction a tyranny which had arisen without their help; they could give it no other practical authority than what might flow from an imperial charter. The whole conduct of Charles in Italy

[1] De Gingins, *Dépêches des Ambassadeurs Milanais*, Paris and Geneva 1858, ii. pp. 200 sqq. (N. 213). Comp. ii. 3 (N. 144) and ii. 212 sqq. (N. 218).

[2] Paul. Jovius, *Elogia*, pp. 156 sqq. Carolus, Burg. dux.

[3] This compound of force and intellect is called by Macchiavelli *Virtù*, and is quite compatible with *scelleratezza.* E.g. *Discorsi*, i. 10. in speaking of Sep. Severus.

[4] On this point Franc. Vettori, *Arch. Stor.* vi. p. 29. 3 sqq.: 'The investiture at the hands of a man who lives in Germany, and has nothing of the Roman Emperor about him but the empty name, cannot turn a scoundrel into the real lord of a city.'

was a scandalous political comedy. Matteo Villani[1] relates how the Visconti escorted him round their territory, and at last out of it; how he went about like a hawker selling his wares (privileges, etc.) for money; what a mean appearance he made in Rome, and how at the end, without even drawing the sword, he returned with replenished coffers across the Alps. Nevertheless, patriotic enthusiasts and poets, full of the greatness of the past, conceived high hopes at his coming, which were afterwards dissipated by his pitiful conduct. Petrarch, who had written frequent letters exhorting the Emperor to cross the Alps, to give back to Rome its departed greatness, and to set up a new universal empire, now, when the Emperor, careless of these high-flying projects, had come at last, still hoped to see his dreams realized, strove unweariedly, by speech and writing, to impress the Emperor with them, but was at length driven away from him with disgust when he saw the imperial authority dishonoured by the submission of Charles to the Pope.[2] Sigismund came, on the first occasion at least (1414), with the good intention of persuading John XXIII. to take part in his council; it was on that journey, when Pope and Emperor were gazing from the lofty tower of Cremona on the panorama of Lombardy, that their host, the tyrant Gabino Fondolo, was seized with the desire to throw them both over. On his second visit Sigismund came as a mere adventurer, giving no proof whatever of his imperial prerogative, except by crowning Beccadelli as

[1] M. Villani, iv. 38, 39, 44, 56, 74, 76, 92; v. 1, 2, 14-16, 21, 22, 36, 51, 54. It is only fair to consider that dislike of the Visconti may have led to worse representations than the facts justified. Charles IV. is once (iv. 74) highly praised by Villani.

[2] It was an Italian, Fazio degli Uberti (*Dittamondo*, l. vi. cap. 5—about 1360) who recommended to Charles IV. a crusade to the Holy Land. The passage is one of the best in this poem, and in other respects characteristic. The poet is dismissed from the Holy Sepulchre by an insolent Turk:

'Con passi lunghi e con la testa bassa
Oltre passai e dissi: ecco vergogna
Del cristian che'l saracin qui lassa!
Poscia al Pastor (the Pope) mi volsi far rampogna:
E tu ti stai, che sei vicar di Cristo,
Co' frati tuoi a ingrassar la carogna?

a poet; for more than half a year he remained shut up in Siena, like a debtor in gaol, and only with difficulty, and at a later period, succeeded in being crowned in Rome. And what can be thought of Frederick III.? His journeys to Italy have the air of holiday-trips or pleasure-tours made at the expense of those who wanted him to confirm their prerogatives, or whose vanity it flattered to entertain an emperor. The latter was the case with Alfonso of Naples, who paid 150,000 florins for the honour of an imperial visit.[1] At Ferrara,[2] on his second return from Rome (1469), Frederick spent a whole day without leaving his chamber, distributing no less than eighty titles; he created knights, counts, doctors, notaries—counts, indeed, of different degrees, as, for instance, counts palatine, counts with the right to create doctors up to the number of five, counts with the right to legitimatise bastards, to appoint notaries, and so forth. The Chancellor, however, expected in return for the patents in question a gratuity which was thought excessive at Ferrara.[3] The opinion of Borso, himself created Duke of Modena and Reggio in return for an annual payment of 4,000 gold florins, when his imperial patron was distributing titles and diplomas to all the little court, is

Similimente dissi a quel sofisto (Charles IV.)
Che sta in Buemme (Bohemia) a piantar vigne e fichi
E che non cura di si caro acquisto:
Che fai? Perchè non segui i primi antichi
Cesari de' Romani, e che non segui,
Dico, gli Otti, i Corradi, i Federichi?
E che pur tieni questo imperio in tregui?
E se non hai lo cuor d' esser Augusto,
Che non rifiuti? o che non ti dilegui?' etc.

Some eight years earlier, about 1352, Petrarch had written (to Charles IV., *Epist. Fam.*, lib. xii. ep. 1, ed. Fracassetti, vol. ii. p. 160): 'Simpliciter igitur et aperte . . . pro maturando negotio terræ sanctæ . . . oro tuo egentem auxilio quam primum invisere velis Ausoniam.'

[1] See for details Vespasiano Fiorent. ed. Mai, *Specilegium Romanum*, vol. i. p. 54. Comp. 150 and Panormita, *De Dictis et Factis Alfonsi*, lib. iv. nro. 4.

[2] *Diario Ferrarese*, in Murat. xxiv. col. 217 sqq.

[3] 'Haveria voluto scortigare la brigata.' Giov. Maria Filelfo, then staying at Bergamo, wrote a violent satire 'in vulgus equitum auro notatorum.' See his biography in Favre, *Mélanges d'Histoire littéraire*, 1856, i. p. 10.

not mentioned. The humanists, then the chief spokesmen of the age, were divided in opinion according to their personal interests, while the Emperor was greeted by some[1] of them with the conventional acclamations of the poets of imperial Rome. Poggio[2] confessed that he no longer knew what the coronation meant; in the old times only the victorious Inperator was crowned, and then he was crowned with laurel.[3]

With Maximilian I. begins not only the general intervention of foreign nations, but a new imperial policy with regard to Italy. The first step—the investiture of Ludovico Moro with the duchy of Milan and the exclusion of his unhappy nephew—was not of a kind to bear good fruits. According to the modern theory of intervention, when two parties are tearing a country to pieces, a third may step in and take its share; and on this principle the empire acted. But right and justice were appealed to no longer. When Louis XII. was expected in Genoa (1502), and the imperial eagle was removed from the hall of the ducal palace and replaced by painted lilies, the historian, Senarega[4] asked what after all, was the meaning of the eagle which so many revolutions had spared, and what claims the empire had upon Genoa. No one knew more about the matter than the old phrase that Genoa was a *camera imperii.* In fact, nobody in Italy could give a clear answer to any such questions. At length, when Charles V. held Spain and the empire together, he was able by means of Spanish forces to make good imperial claims; but it is notorious that what he thereby gained turned to the profit, not of the empire, but of the Spanish monarchy.

Closely connected with the political illegitimacy of the

[1] *Annales Estenses*, in Murat. xx. col. 41.

[2] Poggii, *Hist. Florent. pop.* l. vii. in Murat. col. 381. This view is in accordance with the anti-monarchical sentiments of many of the humanists of that day. Comp. the evidence given by Bezold, 'Lehre von der Volkssouverainität während des Mittelalters,' *Hist. Ztschr.* bd. 36, s. 365.

[3] Some years later the Venetian Lionardo Giustiniani blames the word 'imperator' as unclassical and therefore unbecoming the German emperor, and calls the Germans barbarians, on account of their ignorance of the language and manners of antiquity. The cause of the Germans was defended by the humanist H. Bebel. See L. Geiger, in the *Allgem. Deutsche Biogr.* ii. 196.

[4] Senarega, *De reb. Genuens.* in Murat. xxiv. col. 575.

dynasties of the fifteenth century, was the public indifference to legitimate birth, which to foreigners—for example, to Comines—appeared so remarkable. The two things went naturally together. In northern countries, as in Burgundy, the illegitimate offspring were provided for by a distinct class of appanages, such as bishoprics and the like; in Portugal an illegitimate line maintained itself on the throne only by constant effort; in Italy, on the contrary, there no longer existed a princely house where, even in the direct line of descent, bastards were not patiently tolerated. The Aragonese monarchs of Naples belonged to the illegitimate line, Aragon itself falling to the lot of the brother of Alfonso I. The great Frederick of Urbino was, perhaps, no Montefeltro at all. When Pius II. was on his way to the Congress of Mantua (1459), eight bastards of the house of Este rode to meet him at Ferrara, among them the reigning duke Borso himself and two illegitimate sons of his illegitimate brother and predecessor Leonello.[1] The latter had also had a lawful wife, herself an illegitimate daughter of Alfonso I. of Naples by an African woman.[2] The bastards were often admitted to the succession where the lawful children were minors and the dangers of the situation were pressing; and a rule of seniority became recognised, which took no account of pure or impure birth. The fitness of the individual, his worth and his capacity, were of more weight than all the laws and usages which prevailed elsewhere in the West. It was the age, indeed, in which the sons of the Popes were founding dynasties. In the sixteenth century, through the influence of foreign ideas and of the counter-reformation which then began, the whole question was judged more strictly: Varchi discovers that the succession of the legitimate children 'is ordered by reason, and is the will of heaven from eternity.'[3] Cardinal Ippolito de' Medici founded his claim to the lordship of Florence on the fact that he was perhaps the fruit of a lawful marriage, and at all events son of a gentlewoman, and not, like Duke Alessandro, of

[1] Enumerated in the *Diario Ferrarese*, in Murat. xxiv. col. 203. Comp. Pic. ii. *Comment.* ii. p. 102, ed. Rome, 1584.

[2] Marin Sanudo, *Vita de' Duchi di Venezia*, in Murat. xxii. col. 1113.

[3] Varchi, *Stor. Fiorent.* i. p. 8.

a servant girl.[1] At this time began those morganatic marriages of affection which in the fifteenth century, on grounds either of policy or morality, would have had no meaning at all.

But the highest and the most admired form of illegitimacy in the fifteenth century was presented by the Condottiere, who, whatever may have been his origin, raised himself to the position of an independent ruler. At bottom, the occupation of Lower Italy by the Normans in the eleventh century was of this character. Such attempts now began to keep the peninsula in a constant ferment.

It was possible for a Condottiere to obtain the lordship of a district even without usurpation, in the case when his employer, through want of money or troops, provided for him in this way;[2] under any circumstances the Condottiere, even when he dismissed for the time the greater part of his forces, needed a safe place where he could establish his winter quarters, and lay up his stores and provisions. The first example of a captain thus portioned is John Hawkwood, who was invested by Gregory XI. with the lordship of Bagnacavallo and Cotignola.[3] When with Alberigo da Barbiano Italian armies and leaders appeared upon the scene, the chances of founding a principality, or of increasing one already acquired, became more frequent. The first great bacchanalian outbreak of military ambition took place in the duchy of Milan after the death of Giangaleazzo (1402). The policy of his two sons was chiefly aimed at the destruction of the new despotisms founded by the Condottieri; and from the greatest of them, Facino Cane, the house of Visconti inherited, together with his widow, a long list of cities, and 400,000 golden florins, not to speak of the soldiers of her first husband whom Beatrice di Tenda brought with her.[4] From henceforth that thoroughly immoral relation between the governments and their Con-

[1] Soriano, *Relazione di Roma*, 1533, in Tommaso Gar. *Relaz. della Corte di Roma* (in Alberi, *Relaz. degli ambasc. Veneti*, ii. ser. iii.).

[2] For what follows, see Canestrini, in the Introduction to vol. xv. of the *Archiv. Stor.*

[3] For him, see Shepherd-Tonelli, *Vita di Piggio*, App. pp. viii.–xvi.

[4] Cagnola, *Archiv. Stor.* iii. p. 28: 'Et (Filippo Maria) da lei (Beatr.) ebbe molto tesoro e dinari, e tutte le giente d'arme del dicto Facino, che obedivano a lei.'

dottieri, which is characteristic of the fifteenth century, became more and more common. An old story [1]—one of those which are true and not true, everywhere and nowhere—describes it as follows: The citizens of a certain town (Siena seems to be meant) had once an officer in their service who had freed them from foreign aggression; daily they took counsel how to recompense him, and concluded that no reward in their power was great enough, not even if they made him lord of the city. At last one of them rose and said, 'Let us kill him and then worship him as our patron saint.' And so they did, following the example set by the Roman senate with Romulus. In fact, the Condottieri had reason to fear none so much as their employers; if they were successful, they became dangerous, and were put out of the way like Robert Malatesta just after the victory he had won for Sixtus IV. (1482); if they failed, the vengeance of the Venetians on Carmagnola [2] showed to what risks they were exposed (1432). It is characteristic of the moral aspect of the situation, that the Condottieri had often to give their wives and children as hostages, and notwithstanding this, neither felt nor inspired confidence. They must have been heroes of abnegation, natures like Belisarius himself, not to be cankered by hatred and bitterness; only the most perfect goodness could save them from the most monstrous iniquity. No wonder then if we find them full of contempt for all sacred things, cruel and treacherous to their fellows—men who cared nothing whether or no they died under the ban of the Church. At the same time, and

[1] Inpressura, in Eccard, *Scriptores*, ii. col. 1911. For the alternatives which Macchiavelli puts before the victorious Condottiere, see *Discorsi*, i. 30. After the victory he is either to hand over the army to his employer and wait quietly for his reward, or else to win the soldiers to his own side to occupy the fortresses and to punish the prince 'di quella ingratitudine, che esso gli userebbe.'

[2] Comp. Barth. Facius, *De Viv. Ill.* p. 64, who tells us that C. commanded an army of 60,000 men. It is uncertain whether the Venetians did not poison Alviano in 1516, because he, as Prato says in *Arch. Stor.* iii. p. 348, aided the French too zealously in the battle of S. Donato. The Republic made itself Colleoni's heir, and after his death in 1475 formally confiscated his property. Comp. Malipiero, *Annali Veneti*, in *Arch. Stor.* vii. i. 244. It was liked when the Condottieri invested their money in Venice, ibid. p. 351.

through the force of the same conditions, the genius and capacity of many among them attained the highest conceivable development, and won for them the admiring devotion of their followers; their armies are the first in modern history in which the personal credit of the leader is the one moving power. A brilliant example is shown in the life of Francesco Sforza;[1] no prejudice of birth could prevent him from winning and turning to account when he needed it a boundless devotion from each individual with whom he had to deal; it happened more than once that his enemies laid down their arms at the sight of him, greeting him reverently with uncovered heads, each honouring in him 'the common father of the men-at-arms.' The race of the Sforza has this special interest, that from the very beginning of its history we seem able to trace its endeavours after the crown.[2] The foundation of its fortune lay in the remarkable fruitfulness of the family; Francesco's father, Jacopo, himself a celebrated man, had twenty brothers and sisters, all brought up roughly at Cotignola, near Faenza, amid the perils of one of the endless Romagnole 'vendette' between their own house and that of the Pasolini. The family dwelling was a mere arsenal and fortress; the mother and daughters were as warlike as their kinsmen. In his thirteenth year Jacopo ran away and fled to Panicale to the Papal Condottiere Boldrino—the man who even in death continued to lead his troops, the word of order being given from the bannered tent in which the embalmed body lay, till at last a fit leader was found to succeed him. Jacopo, when he had at length made himself a name in the service of different Condottieri, sent for his relations, and obtained through them the same advantages that a prince derives from a numerous dynasty. It was these relations who kept the army together when he lay a captive in the Castel dell' Uovo at Naples; his sister took the royal envoys prisoners with her own hands, and saved him by this reprisal from death. It was an indication of the breadth and the range of his plans that in monetary affairs Jacopo was

[1] Cagnola, in *Arch. Stor.* iii. pp. 121 sqq.

[2] At all events in Paul Jovius, *Vita Magni Sfortiæ*, Rom. 1539, (dedicated to the Cardinal Ascanio Sforza), one of the most attractive of his biographies.

thoroughly trustworthy; even in his defeats he consequently found credit with the bankers. He habitually protected the peasants against the licence of his troops, and reluctantly destroyed or injured a conquered city. He gave his well-known mistress, Lucia, the mother of Francesco, in marriage to another in order to be free from a princely alliance. Even the marriages of his relations were arranged on a definite plan. He kept clear of the impious and profligate life of his contemporaries, and brought up his son Francesco to the three rules: 'Let other men's wives alone; strike none of your followers, or, if you do, send the injured man far away; don't ride a hard-mouthed horse, or one that drops his shoe.' But his chief source of influence lay in the qualities, if not of a great general, at least of a great soldier. His frame was powerful, and developed by every kind of exercise; his peasant's face and frank manners won general popularity; his memory was marvellous, and after the lapse of years could recall the names of his followers, the number of their horses, and the amount of their pay. His education was purely Italian: he devoted his leisure to the study of history, and had Greek and Latin authors translated for his use. Francesco, his still more famous son, set his mind from the first on founding a powerful state, and through brilliant generalship and a faithlessness which hesitated at nothing, got possession of the great city of Milan (1447–1450).

His example was contagious. Æneas Sylvius wrote about this time:[1] 'In our change-loving Italy, where nothing stands firm, and where no ancient dynasty exists, a servant can easily become a king.' One man in particular, who styled himself 'the man of fortune,' filled the imagination of the whole country: Giacomo Piccinino, the son of Niccolò. It was a burning question of the day if he, too, would succeed in founding a princely house. The greater states had an obvious interest in hindering it, and even Francesco Sforza thought it would be all the better if the list of self-made sovereigns were not enlarged. But the troops and captains sent against him,

[1] Æn. Sylv. *Comment. de Dictis et Factis Alfonsi*, Opera, ed. 1538, p. 251: Novitate gaudens Italia nihil habet stabile, nullum in eâ vetus regnum, facile hic ex servis reges videmus.'

at the time, for instance, when he was aiming at the lordship of Siena, recognised their interest in supporting him:[1] 'If it were all over with him, we should have to go back and plough our fields.' Even while besieging him at Orbetello, they supplied him with provisions; and he got out of his straits with honour. But at last fate overtook him. All Italy was betting on the result, when (1465), after a visit to Sforza at Milan, he went to King Ferrante at Naples. In spite of the pledges given, and of his high connections, he was murdered in the Castel dell' Uovo.[2] Even the Condottieri, who had obtained their dominions by inheritance, never felt themselves safe. When Roberto Malatesta and Frederick of Urbino died on the same day (1482), the one at Rome, the other at Bologna, it was found[3] that each had recommended his state to the care of the other. Against a class of men who themselves stuck at nothing, everything was held to be permissible. Francesco Sforza, when quite young, had married a rich Calabrian heiress, Polissena Russa, Countess of Montalto, who bore him a daughter; an aunt poisoned both mother and child, and seized the inheritance.[4]

From the death of Piccinino onwards, the foundations of new States by the Condottieri became a scandal not to be tolerated. The four great Powers, Naples, Milan, the Papacy, and Venice, formed among themselves a political equilibrium which refused to allow of any disturbance. In the States of the Church, which swarmed with petty tyrants, who in part were, or had been, Condottieri, the nephews of the Popes, since the time of Sixtus IV., monopolised the right to all such undertakings. But at the first sign of a political crisis, the soldiers of fortune appeared again upon the scene. Under the

[1] Pii, ii. *Comment.* i. 46; comp. 69.

[2] Sismondi, x. 258; Corio. fol. 412, where Sforza is accused of complicity, as he feared danger to his own son from P.'s popularity. *Storia Bresciana*, in Murat. xxi. col. 209. How the Venetian Condottiere Colleoni was tempted in 1466, is told by Malipiero *Annali Veneti*, *Arch. Stor.* vii. i. p. 210. The Florentine exiles offered to make him Duke of Milan if he would expel from Florence their enemy, Piero de' Medici.

[3] Allegretti, *Diari Sanesi*, in Murat. xxiii. p. 811.

[4] *Orationes Philelphi*, ed. Venet. 1492, fol. 9, in the funeral oration on Francesco.

wretched administration of Innocent VIII. it was near happening that a certain Boccalino, who had formerly served in the Burgundian army, gave himself and the town of Osimo, of which he was master, up to the Turkish forces;[1] fortunately, through the intervention of Lorenzo the Magnificent, he proved willing to be paid off, and took himself away. In the year 1495, when the wars of Charles VIII. had turned Italy upside down, the Condottiere Vidovero, of Brescia, made trial of his strength:[2] he had already seized the town of Cesena and murdered many of the nobles and the burghers; but the citadel held out, and he was forced to withdraw. He then, at the head of a band lent him by another scoundrel, Pandolfo Malatesta of Rimini, son of the Roberto already spoken of, and Venetian Condottiere, wrested the town of Castelnuovo from the Archbishop of Ravenna. The Venetians, fearing that worse would follow, and urged also by the Pope, ordered Pandolfo, 'with the kindest intentions,' to take an opportunity of arresting his good friend: the arrest was made, though 'with great regret,' whereupon the order came to bring the prisoner to the gallows. Pandolfo was considerate enough to strangle him in prison, and then show his corpse to the people. The last notable example of such usurpers is the famous Castellan of Musso, who during the confusion in the Milanese territory which followed the battle of Pavia (1525), improvised a sovereignty on the Lake of Como.

[1] Marin Sanudo, *Vita dei Duchi di Venezia*, in Murat. xxii. col. 1241. See Reumont, *Lorenzo von Medici* (Lpz. 1874), ii. pp. 324–7, and the authorities there quoted.

[2] Malipiero, *Ann. Venet.*, *Arch. Stor.* vii. i. p. 407.

CHAPTER IV.

THE PETTY TYRANNIES.

It may be said in general of the despotisms of the fifteenth century that the greatest crimes are most frequent in the smallest states. In these, where the family was numerous and all the members wished to live in a manner befitting their rank, disputes respecting the inheritance were unavoidable. Bernardo Varano of Camerino put (1434) two of his brothers to death,[1] wishing to divide their property among his sons. Where the ruler of a single town was distinguished by a wise, moderate, and humane government, and by zeal for intellectual culture, he was generally a member of some great family, or politically dependent on it. This was the case, for example, with Alessandro Sforza,[2] Prince of Pesaro, brother of the great Francesco, and stepfather of Frederick of Urbino (d. 1473). Prudent in administration, just and affable in his rule, he enjoyed, after years of warfare, a tranquil reign, collected a noble library, and passed his leisure in learned or religious conversation. A man of the same class was Giovanni II., Bentivoglio of Bologna (1462–1506), whose policy was determined by that of the Este and the Sforza. What ferocity and bloodthirstiness is found, on the other hand, among the Varani of Camerino, the Malatesta of Rimini, the Manfreddi of Faenza, and above all among the Baglioni of Perugia. We find a striking picture of the events in the last-named family towards the close of the fifteenth century, in the admirable historical narratives of Graziani and Materazzo.[3]

The Baglioni were one of those families whose rule never took the shape of an avowed despotism. It was rather a

[1] *Chron. Eugubinum*, in Murat. xxi. col. 972.

[2] *Vespas. Fiorent.* p. 148.

[3] *Archiv. Stor.* xvi., parte i. et ii., ed. Bonaini, Fabretti, Polidori.

leadership exercised by means of their vast wealth and of their practical influence in the choice of public officers. Within the family one man was recognised as head; but deep and secret jealousy prevailed among the members of the different branches. Opposed to the Baglioni stood another aristocratic party, led by the family of the Oddi. In 1487 the city was turned into a camp, and the houses of the leading citizens swarmed with bravos; scenes of violence were of daily occurrence. At the burial of a German student, who had been assassinated, two colleges took arms against one another; sometimes the bravos of the different houses even joined battle in the public square. The complaints of the merchants and artisans were vain; the Papal Governors and *Nipoti* held their tongues, or took themselves off on the first opportunity. At last the Oddi were forced to abandon Perugia, and the city became a beleaguered fortress under the absolute despotism of the Baglioni, who used even the cathedral as barracks. Plots and surprises were met with cruel vengeance; in the year 1491, after 130 conspirators, who had forced their way into the city, were killed and hung up at the Palazzo Comunale, thirty-five altars were erected in the square, and for three days mass was performed and processions held, to take away the curse which rested on the spot. A nephew of Innocent VIII. was in open day run through in the street. A nephew of Alexander VI., who was sent to smooth matters over, was dismissed with public contempt. All the while the two leaders of the ruling house, Guido and Ridolfo, were holding frequent interviews with Suor Colomba of Rieti, a Dominican nun of saintly reputation and miraculous powers, who under penalty of some great disaster ordered them to make peace—naturally in vain. Nevertheless the chronicle takes the opportunity to point out the devotion and piety of the better men in Perugia during this reign of terror. When in 1494 Charles VIII. approached, the Baglioni from Perugia and the exiles encamped in and near Assisi conducted the war with such ferocity, that every house in the valley was levelled to the ground. The fields lay untilled, the peasants were turned into plundering and murdering savages, the fresh-grown bushes were filled with stags and wolves, and the beasts grew fat on the bodies of the slain, on so-called 'Christian flesh.' When Alexander VI. withdrew (1495) into Umbria before Charles VIII., then returning from Naples, it occurred to him, when at Perugia, that he might now rid himself of the Baglioni once for all; he proposed to Guido a festival or tournament, or something else of the same kind, which would bring the whole family together. Guido, however, was of opinion, 'that the most impressive spectacle of all would be to see the whole military force of Perugia collected in a body,' whereupon the Pope abandoned his project. Soon after, the exiles made another attack, in which nothing but the personal heroism of the Baglioni won them the victory. It was then that Simonetto Baglione, a lad of scarcely eighteen, fought in the square with a handful of followers against hundreds of the enemy: he fell at last with more than twenty wounds, but recovered himself when Astorre Baglione came to his help, and mounting on horseback in gilded armour with a falcon on his helmet, 'like Mars in bearing and in deeds, plunged into the struggle.'

At that time Raphael, a boy of twelve years of age, was at school under Pietro Perugino. The impressions of these days are perhaps immortalised in the small, early pictures of St. Michael and St. George: something of them, it may be, lives eternally in the great painting of St. Michael: and if Astorre Baglione has anywhere found his apotheosis, it is in the figure of the heavenly horseman in the Heliodorus.

The opponents of the Baglioni were partly destroyed, partly scattered in terror, and were henceforth incapable of another enterprise of the kind. After a time a partial reconciliation took place, and some of the exiles were allowed to return. But Perugia became none the safer or more tranquil: the inward discord of the ruling family broke out in frightful excesses. An opposition was formed against Guido and Ridolfo and their sons Gianpaolo, Simonetto, Astorre, Gismondo, Gentile, Marcantonio and others, by two great-nephews, Grifone and Carlo Barciglia; the latter of the two was also nephew of Varano, Prince of Camerino, and brother of one of the former exiles, Ieronimo della Penna. In vain did Simonetto, warned by sinister presentiment, entreat his uncle on his knees to allow him to put Penna to death: Guido refused. The plot ripened suddenly on the occasion of the marriage of Astorre with Lavinia Colonna, at Midsummer 1500. The festival began and lasted several days amid gloomy forebodings, whose deepening effect is admirably described by Matarazzo. Varano fed and encouraged them with devilish ingenuity: he worked upon Grifone by the prospect of undivided authority, and by stories of an imaginary intrigue of his wife Zenobia with Gianpaolo. Finally each conspirator was provided with a victim. (The Baglioni lived all of them in separate houses, mostly on the site of the present castle.) Each received fifteen of the bravos at hand; the remainder were set on the watch. In the night of July 15 the doors were forced, and Guido, Astorre, Simonetto, and Gismondo were murdered; the others succeeded in escaping.

As the corpse of Astorre lay by that of Simonetto in the street, the spectators, 'and especially the foreign students,' compared him to an ancient Roman, so great and imposing did he seem. In the features of Simonetto could still be traced the audacity and defiance which death itself had not tamed. The victors went round among the friends of the family, and did their best to recommend themselves; they found all in tears and preparing to leave for the country. Meantime the escaped Baglioni collected forces without the city, and on the following day forced their way in, Gianpaolo at their head, and speedily found adherents among others whom Barciglia had been threatening with death. When Grifone fell into their hands near S. Ercolono. Gianpaolo handed him over for execution to his followers. Barciglia and Penna fled to Varano, the chief author of the tragedy, at Camerino; and in a moment, almost without loss, Gianpaolo became master of the city.

Atalanta, the still young and beautiful mother of Grifone, who the day before had withdrawn to a country house with the latter's wife Zenobia and two children of Gianpaolo, and more than once had repulsed her son with a mother's curse, now returned with her step-daughter in search of the dying man. All stood aside as the two women approached, each man shrinking from being recognised as the slayer of Grifone, and dreading the malediction of the mother. But they were deceived: she herself besought her son to pardon him who had dealt the fatal blow, and he died with her blessing. The eyes of the crowd followed the two women reverently as they crossed the square with blood-stained garments. It was Atalanta for whom Raphael afterwards painted the world-famed 'Deposition,' with which she laid her own maternal sorrows at the feet of a yet higher and holier suffering.

The cathedral, in the immediate neighbourhood of which the greater part of this tragedy had been enacted, was washed with wine and consecrated afresh. The triumphal arch, erected for the wedding, still remained standing, painted with the deeds of Astorre and with the laudatory verses of the narrator of these events, the worthy Matarazzo.

A legendary history, which is simply the reflection of these atrocities, arose out of the early days of the Baglioni. All the members of this family from the beginning were reported to have died an evil death—twenty-seven on one occasion together; their houses were said to have been once before levelled to the ground, and the streets of Perugia paved with the bricks—and more of the same kind. Under Paul III. the destruction of their palaces really took place.[1]

For a time they seem to have formed good resolutions, to have brought their own party into order, and to have protected the public officials against the arbitrary acts of the nobility. But the old curse broke out again like a smouldering fire. Gianpaolo was enticed to Rome under Leo X., and there beheaded; one of his sons, Orazio, who ruled in Perugia for a short time only, and by the most violent means, as the partisan of the Duke of Urbino (himself threatened by the Pope), once more repeated in his own family the horrors of the past. His uncle and three cousins were murdered, whereupon the Duke sent him word that enough had been done.[2] His brother, Malatesta Baglione, the Florentine general, has made himself immortal by the treason of 1530; and Malatesta's son Ridolfo, the last of the house, attained, by the murder of the legate

[1] Julius II. conquered Perugia with ease in 1506, and compelled Gianpaolo Baglione to submit. The latter, as Macchiavelli (*Discorsi*, i. c. 27) tells us, missed the chance of immortality by not murdering the Pope.

[2] Varelin, *Stor. Fiorent.* i. pp. 242 sqq.

and the public officers in the year 1534, a brief but sanguinary authority.

Here and there we meet with the names of the rulers of Rimini. Unscrupulousness, impiety, military skill, and high culture, have been seldom so combined in one individual as in Sigismondo Malatesta (d. 1467).[1] But the accumulated crimes of such a family must at last outweigh all talent, however great, and drag the tyrant into the abyss. Pandolfo, Sigismondo's nephew, who has been mentioned already, succeeded in holding his ground, for the sole reason that the Venetians refused to abandon their Condottiere, whatever guilt he might be chargeable with; when his subjects (1497), after ample provocation,[2] bombarded him in his castle at Rimini, and afterwards allowed him to escape, a Venetian commissioner brought him back, stained as he was with fratricide and every other abomination. Thirty years later the Malatesta were penniless exiles. In the year 1527, as in the time of Cæsar Borgia, a sort of epidemic fell on the petty tyrants: few of them outlived this date, and none to their own good. At Mirandola, which was governed by insignificant princes of the house of Pico, lived in the year 1533 a poor scholar, Lilio Gregorio Giraldi, who had fled from the sack of Rome to the hospitable hearth of the aged Giovanni Francesco Pico, nephew of the famous Giovanni; the discussions as to the sepulchral monument which the prince was constructing for himself gave rise to a treatise, the dedication of which bears the date of April in this year. The postscript is a sad one.[3]—'In October of the same year the unhappy prince was attacked in the

[1] Comp. (inter. al.) Jovian. Pontan. *De Immanitate*, cap. 17.

[2] Malipiero, *Ann. Venet.*, *Archiv. Stor.* vii. i. pp. 498 sqq. After vainly searching for his beloved, whose father had shut her up in a monastery, he threatened the father, burnt the monastery and other buildings, and committed many acts of violence.

[3] Lil. Greg. Giraldus, *De Sepulchris ac vario Sepeliendi Ritu*. *Opera*, ed. Bas. 1580, i. pp. 640 sqq. Later edition by J. Faes, Helmstädt, 1676. Dedication and postscript of Gir. 'ad Carolum Miltz Germanum,' in these editions without date; neither contains the passage given in the text.—In 1470 a catastrophe in miniature had already occurred in the same family (Galeotto had had his brother Antonio Maria thrown into prison). Comp. *Diario Ferrarese*, in Murat. xxiv. col. 225.

night and robbed of life and throne by his brother's son ; and I myself escaped narrowly, and am now in the deepest misery.'

A pseudo-despotism without characteristic features, such as Pandolfo Petrucci exercised from the year 1490 in Siena, then torn by faction, is hardly worth a closer consideration. Insignificant and malicious, he governed with the help of a professor of jurisprudence and of an astrologer, and frightened his people by an occasional murder. His pastime in the summer months was to roll blocks of stone from the top of Monte Amiata, without caring what or whom they hit. After succeeding, where the most prudent failed, in escaping from the devices of Cæsar Borgia, he died at last forsaken and despised. His sons maintained a qualified supremacy for many years afterwards.

CHAPTER V.

THE GREATER DYNASTIES.

In treating of the chief dynasties of Italy, it is convenient to discuss the Aragonese, on account of its special character, apart from the rest. The feudal system, which from the days of the Normans had survived in the form of a territorial supremacy of the Barons, gave a distinctive colour to the political constitution of Naples; while elsewhere in Italy, excepting only in the southern part of the ecclesiastical dominion, and in a few other districts, a direct tenure of land prevailed, and no hereditary powers were permitted by the law. The great Alfonso, who reigned in Naples from 1435 onwards (d. 1458), was a man of another kind than his real or alleged descendants. Brilliant in his whole existence, fearless in mixing with his people, mild and generous towards his enemies, dignified and affable in intercourse, modest notwithstanding his legitimate royal descent, admired rather than blamed even for his old man's passion for Lucrezia d'Alagna, he had the one bad quality of extravagance,[1] from which, however, the natural consequence followed. Unscrupulous financiers were long omnipotent at Court, till the bankrupt king robbed them of their spoils; a crusade was preached, as a pretext for taxing the clergy; the Jews were forced to save themselves from conversion and other oppressive measures by presents and the payment of regular taxes; when a great earthquake happening in the Abruzzi, the survivors were compelled to make good the contributions of the dead. On the other hand, he abolished unreasonable taxes, like that on dice, and aimed at relieving his poorer subjects from the imposts which pressed most heavily

[1] Jovian. Pontan. Opp. ed. Basileæ, 1538, t. i. *De Liberalitate*, cap. 19, 29, and *De Obedientia*, l. 4. Comp. Sismondi, x. p. 78, and Panormita, *De Dictis et Factis Alphonsi*, lib. i. nro. 61, iv. nro. 42.

upon them. By such means Alfonso was able to entertain distinguished guests with unrivalled splendour; he found pleasure in ceaseless expense, even for the benefit of his enemies, and in rewarding literary work knew absolutely no measure. Poggio received 500 pieces of gold for translating Xenophon's 'Cyropædeia.'

Ferrante,[1] who succeeded him, passed as his illegitimate son by a Spanish lady, but was not improbably the son of a half-caste Moor of Valentia. Whether it was his blood or the plots formed against his life by the barons which embittered and darkened his nature, it is certain that he was equalled in ferocity by none among the princes of his time. Restlessly active, recognised as one of the most powerful political minds of the day, and free from the vices of the profligate, he concentrated all his powers, among which must be reckoned profound dissimulation and an irreconcileable spirit of vengeance, on the destruction of his opponents. He had been wounded in every point in which a ruler is open to offence; for the leaders of the barons, though related to him by marriage, were yet the allies of his foreign enemies. Extreme measures became part of his daily policy. The means for this struggle with his barons, and for his external wars, were exacted in the same Mohammedan fashion which Frederick II. had introduced: the Government alone dealt in oil and wine; the whole commerce of the country was put by Ferrante into the hands of a wealthy merchant, Francesco Coppola, who had entire control of the anchorage on the coast, and shared the profits with the King. Deficits were made up by forced loans, by executions and confiscations, by open simony, and by contributions levied on the ecclesiastical corporations. Besides

[1] Tristano Caracciolo. 'De Fernando qui postea rex Aragonum fuit, ejusque posteris,' in Muratori XXII.; Jovian Pontanus, *De Prudentia*, l. iv.; *De Magnanimitate*, l. i.; *De Liberalitate*, cap. 29, 36; *De Immanitate*, cap. 8. Cam. Porzio, *Congiura dei Baroni del Regno de Napoli contro il re Ferdinando I.*, Pisa, 1818, cap. 29, 36, new edition, Naples, 1859, *passim;* Comines, Charles VIII., with the general characteristics of the Arragonese. See for further information as to Ferrante's works for his people, the *Regis Ferdinandi primi Instructionum liber*, 1486–87, edited by Scipione Vopicella, which would dispose us to moderate to some extent the harsh judgment which has been passed upon him.

hunting, which he practised regardless of all rights of property, his pleasures were of two kinds: he liked to have his opponents near him, either alive in well-guarded prisons, or dead and embalmed, dressed in the costume which they wore in their lifetime.[1] He would chuckle in talking of the captives with his friends, and made no secret whatever of the museum of mummies. His victims were mostly men whom he had got into his power by treachery; some were even seized while guests at the royal table. His conduct to his first minister, Antonello Petrucci, who had grown sick and grey in his service, and from whose increasing fear of death he extorted present after present, was literally devilish. At length the suspicion of complicity with the last conspiracy of the barons gave the pretext for his arrest and execution. With him died Coppola. The way in which all this is narrated in Caracciolo and Porzio makes one's hair stand on end. The elder of the King's sons, Alfonso, Duke of Calabria, enjoyed in later years a kind of co-regency with his father. He was a savage, brutal profligate—described by Comines as 'the cruelest, worst, most vicious and basest man ever seen'—who in point of frankness alone had the advantage of Ferrante, and who openly avowed his contempt for religion and its usages.[2] The better and nobler features of the Italian despotisms are not to be found among the princes of this line; all that they possessed of the art and culture of their time served the purposes of luxury or display. Even the genuine Spaniards seem to have almost always degenerated in Italy; but the end of this cross-bred house (1494 and 1503) gives clear proof of a want of blood. Ferrante died of mental care and trouble; Alfonso accused his brother Federigo, the only honest member of the family, of treason, and insulted him in the vilest manner. At length, though he had hitherto passed for one of the ablest generals in Italy, he lost his head and fled to Sicily, leaving his son, the younger Ferrante, a prey to the French and to domestic treason.

[1] Paul. Jovius. *Histor.* i. p. 14. in the speech of a Milanese ambassador; *Diario Ferrarese*, in Muratori, xxiv. col. 294.

[2] He lived in the closest intimacy with Jews, e.g. Isaac Abranavel, who fled with him to Messina. Comp. Zunz, *Zur. Gesch. und Lit.* (Berlin, 1845) s. 529.

A dynasty which had ruled as this had done must at least have sold its life dear, if its children were ever to hope for a restoration. But, as Comines one-sidedly, and yet on the whole rightly observes on this occasion, '*Jamais homme cruel ne fut hardi.*'

The despotism of the Dukes of Milan, whose government from the time of Giangaleazzo onwards was an absolute monarchy of the most thorough-going sort, shows the genuine Italian character of the fifteenth century. The last of the Visconti, Filippo Maria (1412–1447), is a character of peculiar interest, and of which fortunately an admirable description[1] has been left us. What a man of uncommon gifts and high position can be made by the passion of fear, is here shown with what may be called a mathematical completeness. All the resources of the State were devoted to the one end of securing his personal safety, though happily his cruel egoism did not degenerate into a purposeless thirst for blood. He lived in the Citadal of Milan, surrounded by magnificent gardens, arbours, and lawns. For years he never set foot in the city, making his excursions only in the country, where lay several of his splendid castles; the flotilla which, drawn by the swiftest horses, conducted him to them along canals constructed for the purpose, was so arranged as to allow of the application of the most rigorous etiquette. Whoever entered the citadel was watched by a hundred eyes; it was forbidden even to stand at the window, lest signs should be given to those without. All who were admitted among the personal followers of the Prince were subjected to a series of the strictest examinations; then, once accepted, were charged with the highest diplomatic commissions, as well as with the humblest personal services—both in this Court being alike honourable. And this was the man who conducted long and difficult wars, who dealt habitu-

[1] Petri Candidi Decembrii Vita Phil. Mariæ Vicecomitis, in Murat. xx., of which however Jovius (*Vitæ xii. Vicecomitum* p. 186) says not without reason: 'Quum omissis laudibus quæ in Philippo celebrandæ fuerant, vitia, notaret.' Guarino praises this prince highly. Rosmino Guarini, ii. p. 75. Jovius, in the above-mentioned work (p. 186), and Jov. Pontanus, *De Liberalitate*, ii. cap. 28 and 31, take special notice of his generous conduct to the captive Alfonso.

ally with political affairs of the first importance, and every day sent his plenipotentiaries to all parts of Italy. His safety lay in the fact that none of his servants trusted the others, that his Condottieri were watched and misled by spies, and that the ambassadors and higher officials were baffled and kept apart by artificially nourished jealousies, and in particular by the device of coupling an honest man with a knave. His inward faith, too, rested upon opposed and contradictory systems; he believed in blind necessity, and in the influence of the stars, and offering prayers at one and the same time to helpers of every sort;[1] he was a student of the ancient authors, as well as of French tales of chivalry. And yet the same man, who would never suffer death to be mentioned in his presence,[2] and caused his dying favourites to be removed from the castle, that no shadow might fall on the abode of happiness, deliberately hastened his own death by closing up a wound, and, refusing to be bled, died at last with dignity and grace.

His step-son and successor, the fortunate Condottiere Francesco Sforza (1450–1466, see p. 24), was perhaps of all the Italians of the fifteenth century the man most after the heart of his age. Never was the triumph of genius and individual power more brilliantly displayed than in him; and those who would not recognise his merit were at least forced to wonder at him as the spoilt child of fortune. The Milanese claimed it openly as an honour to be governed by so distinguished a master; when he entered the city the thronging populace bore him on horseback into the cathedral, without giving him the chance to dismount.[3] Let us listen to the balance-sheet of his life, in the estimate of Pope Pius II., a judge in such matters:[4] 'In the year 1459, when the Duke came to the

[1] Were the fourteen marble statues of the saints in the Citadel of Milan executed by him? See *History of the Frundsbergs*, fol. 27.

[2] It troubled him: *quod aliquando 'non esse' necesse esset.*

[3] Corio, fol. 400; Cagnola, in *Archiv. Stor.* iii. p. 125.

[4] *Pii II. Comment.* iii. p. 130. Comp. ii. 87. 106. Another and rather darker estimate of Sforza's fortune is given by Caracciolo, *De Varietate Fortunæ*, in Murat. xxii. col. 74. See for the opposite view the praises of Sforza's luck in the *Oratio parentalis de divi Francesci Sphortiæ felicitate*, by Filelfo (the ready eulogist of any master who paid him), who sung, without publishing, the exploits of Francesco in the Sforziad.

congress at Mantua, he was 60 (really 58) years old; on horseback he looked like a young man; of a lofty and imposing figure, with serious features, calm and affable in conversation, princely in his whole bearing, with a combination of bodily and intellectual gifts unrivalled in our time, unconquered on the field of battle,—such was the man who raised himself from a humble position to the control of an empire. His wife was beautiful and virtuous, his children were like the angels of heaven; he was seldom ill, and all his chief wishes were fulfilled. And yet he was not without misfortune. His wife, out of jealousy, killed his mistress; his old comrades and friends, Troilo and Brunoro, abandoned him and went over to King Alfonso; another, Ciarpollone, he was forced to hang for treason; he had to suffer it that his brother Alessandro set the French upon him; one of his sons formed intrigues against him, and was imprisoned; the March of Ancona, which he had won in war, he lost again in the same way. No man enjoys so unclouded a fortune, that he has not somewhere to struggle with adversity. He is happy who has but few troubles.' With this negative definition of happiness the learned Pope dismisses the reader. Had he been able to see into the future, or been willing to stop and discuss the consequences of an uncontrolled despotism, one prevading fact would not have escaped his notice—the absence of all guarantee for the future. Those children, beautiful as angels, carefully and thoroughly educated as they were, fell victims, when they grew up, to the corruption of a measureless egoism. Galeazzo Maria (1466–1476), solicitous only of outward effect, took pride in the beauty of his hands, in the high salaries he paid, in the financial credit he enjoyed, in his treasure of two million pieces of gold, in the distinguished people who surrounded him, and in the army and birds of chase which he maintained. He was fond of the sound of his own voice, and spoke well, most fluently, perhaps, when

Even Decembrio, the moral and literary opponent of Filelfo, celebrates Sforza's fortune in his biography (*Vita Franc. Sphortiæ*, in Murat. xx.). The astrologers said: 'Francesco Sforza's star brings good luck to a man, but ruin to his descendants.' Arluni, *De Bello Veneto*, libri vi. in Grævius, *Thes. Antiqu. et Hist. Italicæ*, v. pars iii. Comp. also Barth. Facius, *De Vir. Ill.* p. 67.

he had the chance of insulting a Venetian ambassador.[1] He was subject to caprices, such as having a room painted with figures in a single night; and, what was worse, to fits of senseless debauchery and of revolting cruelty to his nearest friends. To a handful of enthusiasts, at whose head stood Giov. Andrea di Lampugnano, he seemed a tyrant too bad to live; they murdered him,[2] and thereby delivered the State into the power of his brothers, one of whom, Ludovico il Moro, threw his nephew into prison, and took the government into his own hands. From this usurpation followed the French intervention, and the disasters which befell the whole of Italy.

The Moor is the most perfect type of the despot of that age, and, as a kind of natural product, almost disarms our moral judgment. Notwithstanding the profound immorality of the means he employed, he used them with perfect ingenuousness; no one would probably have been more astonished than himself to learn, that for the choice of means as well as of ends a human being is morally responsible; he would rather have reckoned it as a singular virtue that, so far as possible, he had abstained from too free a use of the punishment of death. He accepted as no more than his due the almost fabulous respect of the Italians for his political genius.[3] In 1496 he boasted that the Pope Alexander was his chaplain, the Emperor Maximilian his Condottiere, Venice his chamberlain, and the King of France his courier, who must come and go at his bidding.[4] With

[1] Malipiero, *Ann. Veneti*, *Archiv. Stor.* vii. i. pp. 216 sqq. 221–4.

[2] Important documents as to the murder of Galeazzo Maria Sforza are published by G. D'Adda in the *Archivio Storico Lombardo Giornale della Società Lombarda*, vol. ii. (1875), pp. 284–94. 1. A Latin epitaph on the murderer Lampugnano, who lost his life in the attempt, and whom the writer represents as saying: 'Hic lubens quiesco, æternum inquam facinus monumentumque ducibus, principibus, regibus, qui modo sunt quique mox futura trahantur ne quid adversus justitiam faciant dicantve; 2. A Latin letter of Domenico de' Belli, who, when eleven years old, was present at the murder; 3. The 'lamento' of Galeazzo Maria, in which, after calling upon the Virgin Mary and relating the outrage committed upon him, he summons his wife and children, his servants and the Italian cities which obeyed him, to bewail his fate, and sends forth his entreaty to all the nations of the earth, to the nine muses and the gods of antiquity, to set up a universal cry of grief.

[3] *Chron. Venetum*, in Murat. xxiv. col. 65.

[4] Malipiero, *Ann Veneti*, *Archiv. Stor.* vii. i. p. 492. Comp. 482, 562.

marvellous presence of mind he weighed, even in his last extremity, all possible means of escape, and at length decided, to his honour, to trust to the goodness of human nature; he rejected the proposal of his brother, the Cardinal Ascanio, who wished to remain in the Citadel of Milan, on the ground of a former quarrel: 'Monsignore, take it not ill, but I trust you not, brother though you be;' and appointed to the command of the castle, 'that pledge of his return,' a man to whom he had always done good, but who nevertheless betrayed him.[1] At home the Moor was a good and useful ruler, and to the last he reckoned on his popularity both in Milan and in Como. In former years (after 1496) he had overstrained the resources of his State, and at Cremona had ordered, out of pure expediency, a respectable citizen, who had spoken against the new taxes, to be quietly strangled. Since that time, in holding audiences, he kept his visitors away from his person by means of a bar, so that in conversing with him they were compelled to speak at the top of their voices.[2] At his court, the most brilliant in Europe, since that of Burgundy had ceased to exist, immorality of the worst kind was prevalent: the daughter was sold by the father, the wife by the husband, the sister by the brother.[3] The Prince himself was incessantly active, and, as son of his own deeds, claimed relationship with all who, like himself, stood on their personal merits—with scholars, poets, artists, and musicians. The academy which he founded[4] served rather for his own purposes than for the instruction of scholars; nor was it the fame of the distinguished men who surrounded him which he heeded, so much as their society and their services.

[1] His last words to the same man, Bernardino da Corte, are to be found, certainly with oratorical decorations, but perhaps agreeing in the main with the thoughts of the Moor, in Senarega, Murat. xxiv. col. 567.

[2] *Diario Ferrarese*, in Murat. xxiv. col. 336, 367, 369. The people believed he was forming a treasure.

[3] Corio, fol. 448. The after effects of this state of things are clearly recognisable in those of the novels and introductions of Bandello which relate to Milan.

[4] Amoretti, *Memorie Storiche sulla Vita Ecc. di Lionardo da Vinci*, pp. 35 sqq., pp. 83 sqq. Here we may also mention the Moor's efforts for the improvement of the university of Pavia.

It is certain that Bramante was scantily paid at first;[1] Lionardo, on the other hand, was up to 1496 suitably remunerated—and besides, what kept him at the court, if not his own free will? The world lay open to him, as perhaps to no other mortal man of that day; and if proof were wanting of the loftier element in the nature of Ludovico Moro, it is found in the long stay of the enigmatic master at his court. That afterwards Lionardo entered the service of Cæsar Borgia and Francis I. was probably due to the interest he felt in the unusual and striking character of the two men.

After the fall of the Moor—he was captured in April 1500 by the French, after his return from his flight to Germany—his sons were badly brought up among strangers, and showed no capacity for carrying out his political testament. The elder, Massimiliano, had no resemblance to him; the younger, Francesco, was at all events not without spirit. Milan, which in those years changed its rulers so often, and suffered so unspeakably in the change, endeavoured to secure itself against a reaction. In the year 1512 the French, retreating before the arms of Maximilian and the Spaniards, were induced to make a declaration that the Milanese had taken no part in their expulsion, and, without being guilty of rebellion, might yield themselves to a new conqueror.[2] It is a fact of some political importance that in such moments of transition the unhappy city, like Naples at the flight of the Aragonese, was apt to fall a prey to gangs of (often highly aristocratic) scoundrels.

The house of Gonzaga at Mantua and that of Montefeltro of Urbino were among the best ordered and richest in men of ability during the second half of the fifteenth century. The Gonzaga were a tolerably harmonious family; for a long period no murder had been known among them, and their dead could be shown to the world without fear. The Marquis Francesco Gonzaga[3] and his wife, Isabella of Este, in spite of

[1] See his sonnets in Trucchi, *Poesie inedite.*

[2] Prato, in the *Arch. Stor.* iii. 298. Comp. 302.

[3] Born 1466, betrothed to Isabella, herself six years of age in 1480. suc. 1484; m. 1490, d. 1519. Isabella's death, 1539. Her sons, Federigo (1519–1540), made Duke in 1530, and the famous Ferrante Gonzaga. What

some few irregularities, were a united and respectable couple, and brought up their sons to be successful and remarkable men at a time when their small but most important State was exposed to incessant danger. That Francesco, either as statesman or as soldier, should adopt a policy of exceptional honesty, was what neither the Emperor, nor Venice, nor the King of France could have expected or desired; but certainly since the battle at Taro (1495), so far as military honour was concerned, he felt and acted as an Italian patriot, and imparted the same spirit to his wife. Every deed of loyalty and heroism, such as the defence of Faenza against Cæsar Borgia, she felt as a vindication of the honour of Italy. Our judgment of her does not need to rest on the praises of the artists and writers who made the fair princess a rich return for her patronage; her own letters show her to us as a woman of unshaken firmness, full of kindliness and humorous observation. Bembo, Bandello, Ariosto, and Bernardo Tasso sent their works to this court, small and powerless as it was, and empty as they found its treasury. A more polished and charming circle was not to be seen in Italy, since the dissolution (1508) of the old Court of Urbino; and in one respect, in freedom of movement, the society of Ferrara was inferior to that of Mantua. In artistic matters Isabella had an accurate knowledge, and the catalogue of her small but choice collection can be read by no lover of art without emotion.

In the great Federigo (1444–1482), whether he were a genuine Montefeltro or not, Urbino possessed a brilliant representative of the princely order. As a Condottiere—and in this capacity he served kings and popes for thirty years after he became prince—he shared the political morality of soldiers of fortune, a morality of which the fault does not rest with them alone; as ruler of his little territory he adopted the plan of spending at home the money he had earned abroad, and tax-

follows is taken from the correspondence of Isabella, with Appendices, *Archiv. Stor.*, append., tom. ii. communicated by d'Arco. See the same writer, *Delle Arti e degli Artifici di Mantova*, Mant. 1857–59, 2 vols. The catalogue of the collection has been repeatedly printed. Portrait and biography of Isabella in Didot, *Alde Manuce*, Paris, 1875, pp. lxi–lxviii. See also below, part ii. chapter 2.

ing his people as lightly as possible. Of him and his two successors, Guidobaldo and Francesco Maria, we read: 'They erected buildings, furthered the cultivation of the land, lived at home, and gave employment to a large number of people: their subjects loved them.'[1] But not only the state, but the court too, was a work of art and organization, and this in every sense of the word. Federigo had 500 persons in his service; the arrangements of the court were as complete as in the capitals of the greatest monarchs, but nothing was wasted; all had its object, and all was carefully watched and controlled. The court was no scene of vice and dissipation: it served as a school of military education for the sons of other great houses, the thoroughness of whose culture and instruction was made a point of honour by the Duke. The palace which he built, if not one of the most splendid, was classical in the perfection of its plan; there was placed the greatest of his treasures, the celebrated library.[2] Feeling secure in a land where all gained profit or employment from his rule, and where none were beggars, he habitually went unarmed and almost unaccompanied; alone among the princes of his time he ventured to walk in an open park, and to take his frugal meals in an open chamber, while Livy, or in time of fasting, some devotional work, was read to him. In the course of the same afternoon he would listen to a lecture on some classical subject, and thence would go to the monastery of the Clarisse and talk of sacred things through the grating with the abbess. In the evening he would overlook the martial exercises of the young people of his court on the meadow of St. Francesco, known for its magnificent view, and saw to it well that all the feats were done in the most perfect manner. He strove always to be affable and accessible to the utmost degree, visiting the artisans who worked for him in their shops, holding frequent audiences, and, if possible, attending to the requests of each individual on

[1] Franc. Vettori, in the *Arch. Stor.* Append., tom. vi. p. 321. For Federigo, see *Vespas. Fiorent.* pp. 132 sqq. and Prendilacqua, *Vita di Vittorino da Feltre*, pp. 48–52. V. endeavoured to calm the ambitious youth Federigo, then his scholar, with the words: 'Tu quoque Cæsar eris.' There is much literary information respecting him in, e.g., Favre, *Mélanges d'Hist. Lit.* i. p. 125, note 1.

[2] See below, part iii. chapter 3.

the same day that they were presented. No wonder that the people, as he walked along the street, knelt down and cried: 'Dio ti mantenga, signore!' He was called by thinking people 'the light of Italy.'[1] His gifted son Guidobaldo,[2] visited by sickness and misfortune of every kind, was able at the last (1508) to give his state into the safe hands of his nephew Francesco Maria (nephew also of Pope Julius II.), who, at least, succeeded in preserving the territory from any permanent foreign occupation. It is remarkable with what confidence Guidobaldo yielded and fled before Cæsar Borgia and Francesco before the troops of Leo X.; each knew that his restoration would be all the easier and the more popular the less the country suffered through a fruitless defence. When Ludovico made the same calculation at Milan, he forgot the many grounds of hatred which existed against him. The court of Guidobaldo has been made immortal as the high school of polished manners by Baldassar Castiglione, who represented his eclogue Thyrsis before, and in honour of that society (1506), and who afterwards (1518) laid the scena of the dialogue of his 'Cortigiano' in the circle of the accomplished Duchess Elisabetta Gonzaga.

The government of the family of Este at Ferrara, Modena, and Reggio displays curious contrasts of violence and popularity.[3] Within the palace frightful deeds were perpetrated; a princess was beheaded (1425) for alleged adultery with a step-son;[4] legitimate and illegitimate children fled from the court, and even abroad their lives were threatened by assassins sent in pursuit of them (1471). Plots from without were incessant; the bastard of a bastard tried to wrest the crown from the lawful heir, Hercules I.: this latter is said afterwards (1493) to have poisoned his wife on discovering that she, at the

[1] Castiglione, *Cortigiano*, l. i.

[2] Petr. Bembus, *De Guido Ubaldo Feretrio deque Elizabetha Gonzaga Urbini ducibus*, Venetis, 1530. Also in Bembo's Works, Basel, 1566, i. pp. 529–624. In the form of a dialogue; contains among other things, the letter of Frid. Fregosus and the speech of Odaxius on Guido's life and death.

[3] What follows is chiefly taken from the *Annales Estenses*, in Murat. xx. and the *Diario Ferrarese*, Murat. xxiv.

[4] See Bandello, i. nov. 32.

instigation of her brother Ferrante of Naples, was going to poison him. This list of tragedies is closed by the plot of two bastards against their brothers, the ruling Duke Alfonso I. and the Cardinal Ippolito (1506), which was discovered in time, and punished with imprisonment for life. The financial system in this State was of the most perfect kind, and necessarily so, since none of the large or second-rate powers of Italy were exposed to such danger and stood in such constant need of armaments and fortifications. It was the hope of the rulers that the increasing prosperity of the people would keep pace with the increasing weight of taxation, and the Marquis Niccolò (d. 1441) used to express the wish that his subjects might be richer than the people of other countries. If the rapid increase of the population be a measure of the prosperity actually attained, it is certainly a fact of importance that in the year 1497, notwithstanding the wonderful extension of the capital, no houses were to be let.[1] Ferrara is the first really modern city in Europe; large and well-built quarters sprang up at the bidding of the ruler: here, by the concentration of the official classes and the active promotion of trade, was formed for the first time a true capital; wealthy fugitives from all parts of Italy, Florentines especially, settled and built their palaces at Ferrara. But the indirect taxation, at all events, must have reached a point at which it could only just be borne. The Government, it is true, took measures of alleviation which were also adopted by other Italian despots, such as Galeazzo Maria Sforza: in time of famine corn was brought from a distance and seems to have been distributed gratuitously;[2] but in ordinary times it compensated itself by the monopoly, if not of corn, of many other of the necessaries of life—fish, salt meat, fruit, and vegetables, which last were carefully planted on and near the walls of the city. The most considerable source of income, however, was the annual sale of public offices, a usage which was common throughout Italy, and about the working of which at Ferrara we have more precise information. We read, for example, that at the new

[1] *Diario Ferrar.* l. c. col. 347.

[2] Paul. Jov. *Vita Alfonsi ducis*, ed. Flor. 1550, also an Italian by Giovanbattista Gelli, Flor. 1553.

year 1502 the majority of the officials bought their places at 'prezzi salati;' public servants of the most various kinds, custom-house officers, bailiffs (massari), notaries, 'podestà,' judges, and even captains, *i.e.*, lieutenant-governors of provincial towns, are quoted by name. As one of the 'devourers of the people' who paid dearly for their places, and who were 'hated worse than the devil,' Tito Strozza—let us hope not the famous Latin poet—is mentioned. About the same time every year the dukes were accustomed to make a round of visits in Ferrara, the so called 'andar per ventura,' in which they took presents from, at any rate, the more wealthy citizens. The gifts, however, did not consist of money, but of natural products.

It was the pride of the duke[1] for all Italy to know that at Ferrara the soldiers received their pay and the professors of the University their salary not a day later than it was due; that the soldiers never dared lay arbitrary hands on citizen or peasant; that the town was impregnable to assault; and that vast sums of coined money were stored up in the citadel. To keep two sets of accounts seemed unnecessary; the Minister of Finance was at the same time manager of the ducal household. The buildings erected by Borso (1430–1471), by Hercules I. (till 1505), and by Alfonso I. (till 1534), were very numerous, but of small size: they are characteristic of a princely house which, with all its love of splendour—Borso never appeared but in embroidery and jewels—indulged in no ill-considered expense. Alfonso may perhaps have foreseen the fate which was in store for his charming little villas, the Belvedere with its shady gardens, and Montana with its fountains and beautiful frescoes.

It is undeniable that the dangers to which these princes were constantly exposed developed in them capacities of a remarkable kind. In so artificial a world only a man of consummate address could hope to succeed; each candidate for distinction was forced to make good his claims by personal merit and show himself worthy of the crown he sought. Their characters are not without dark sides; but in all of them lives

[1] Paulus Jovius, l. c.

something of those qualities which Italy then pursued as its ideal. What European monarch of the time so laboured for his own culture as, for instance, Alfonso I.? His travels in France, England, and the Netherlands were undertaken for the purpose of study: by means of them he gained an accurate knowledge of the industry and commerce of these countries.[1] It is ridiculous to reproach him with the turner's work which he practised in his leisure hours, connected as it was with his skill in the casting of cannon, and with the unprejudiced freedom with which he surrounded himself by masters of every art. The Italian princes were not, like their contemporaries in the North, dependent on the society of an aristocracy which held itself to be the only class worth consideration, and which infected the monarch with the same conceit. In Italy the prince was permitted and compelled to know and to use men of every grade in society; and the nobility, though by birth a caste, were forced in social intercourse to stand upon their personal qualifications alone. But this is a point which we shall discuss more fully in the sequel.

The feeling of the Ferrarese towards the ruling house was a strange compound of silent dread, of the truly Italian sense of well-calculated interest, and of the loyalty of the modern subject: personal admiration was transformed into a new sentiment of duty. The city of Ferrara raised in 1451 a bronze equestrian statue to their Prince Niccolò, who had died ten years earlier; Borso (1454) did not scruple to place his own statue, also of bronze, but in a sitting posture, hard by in the market; in addition to which the city, at the beginning of his reign, decreed to him a 'marble triumphal pillar.' And when he was buried the whole people felt as if God himself had died a second time.[2] A citizen, who, when abroad from Venice, had spoken ill of Borso in public, was informed on his return home, and condemned to banishment and the confiscation of his goods; a loyal subject was with difficulty restrained from

[1] The journey of Leo X. when Cardinal, may be also mentioned here. Comp. Paul. Jov. *Vita Leonis X.* lib. i. His purpose was less serious, and directed rather to amusement and knowledge of the world; but the spirit is wholly modern. No Northerner then travelled with such objects.

[2] *Diar. Ferr.* in Murat. xxiv. col. 232 and 240.

cutting him down before the tribunal itself, and with a rope round his neck the offender went to the duke and begged for a full pardon. The government was well provided with spies, and the duke inspected personally the daily list of travellers which the innkeepers were strictly ordered to present. Under Borso,[1] who was anxious to leave no distinguished stranger unhonoured, this regulation served a hospitable purpose; Hercules I.[2] used it simply as a measure of precaution. In Bologna, too, it was then the rule, under Giovanni II. Bentivoglio, that every passing traveller who entered at one gate must obtain a ticket in order to go out at another.[3] An unfailing means of popularity was the sudden dismissal of oppressive officials. When Borso arrested in person his chief and confidential counsellors, when Hercules I. removed and disgraced a tax-gatherer, who for years had been sucking the blood of the people, bonfires were lighted and the bells were pealed in their honour. With one of his servants, however, Hercules let things go too far. The director of the police, or by whatever name we should choose to call him (Capitano di Giustizia), was Gregorio Zampante of Lucca—a native being unsuited for an office of this kind. Even the sons and brothers of the duke trembled before this man; the fines he inflicted amounted to hundreds and thousands of ducats, and torture was applied even before the hearing of a case: bribes were accepted from wealthy criminals, and their pardon obtained from the duke by false representations. Gladly would the people have paid any sum to this ruler for sending away the 'enemy of God and man.' But Hercules had knighted him and made him godfather to his children; and year by year Zampante laid by, 2,000 ducats. He dared only eat pigeons bred in his own house, and could not cross the street without a band of archers and bravos. It was time to get rid of him; in 1490 two students and a converted Jew whom he had mortally offended, killed him in his house while taking his siesta, and then rode through the town on horses held in waiting, raising the cry, 'Come out! come out! we have slain Zampante!'

[1] Jovian. Pontan. *De Liberalitate*, cap. 28.

[2] Giraldi, *Hecatomithi*, vi. nov. 1 (ed. 1565, fol. 223 *a*).

[3] Vasari, xii. 166, *Vita di Michelangelo.*

The pursuers came too late, and found them already safe across the frontier. Of course it now rained satires—some of them in the form of sonnets, others of odes.

It was wholly in the spirit of this system that the sovereign imposed his own respect for useful servants on the court and on the people. When in 1469 Borso's privy councillor Ludovico Casella died, no court of law or place of business in the city, and no lecture-room at the University, was allowed to be open: all had to follow the body to S. Domenico, since the duke intended to be present. And, in fact, 'the first of the house of Este who attended the corpse of a subject' walked, clad in black, after the coffin, weeping, while behind him came the relatives of Casella, each conducted by one of the gentlemen of the Court: the body of the plain citizen was carried by nobles from the church into the cloister, where it was buried. Indeed this official sympathy with princely emotion first came up in the Italian States.[1] At the root of the practice may be a beautiful, humane sentiment; the utterance of it, especially in the poets, is, as a rule, of equivocal sincerity. One of the youthful poems of Ariosto,[2] on the Death of Lionora of Aragon, wife of Hercules I., contains besides the inevitable graveyard flowers, which are scattered in the elegies of all ages, some thoroughly modern features: 'This death had given Ferrara a blow which it would not get over for years: its benefactress was now its advocate in heaven, since earth was not worthy of her; truly, the angel of Death did not come to her, as to us common mortals, with blood-stained scythe, but fair to behold (onesta), and with so kind a face that every fear was allayed.' But we meet, also, with a sympathy of a different kind. Novelists, depending wholly on the favour of their patrons, tell us the love-stories of the prince, even before his death,[3] in a way which, to later times, would seem the height

[1] As early as 1446 the members of the House of Gonzaga followed the corpse of Vittorino da Feltre.

[2] Capitolo 19, and in the *Opere Minore*, ed. Lemonnier, vol. i. p. 425, entitled Elegia 17. Doubtless the cause of this death (above, p. 46) was unknown to the young poet, then 19 years old.

[3] The novels in the *Hecatomithi* of Giraldi relating to the House of Este are to be found, with one exception (i. nov. 8), in the 6th book, dedicated to Francesco of Este, Marchese della Massa, at the beginning of

of indiscretion, but which then passed simply as an innocent compliment. Lyrical poets even went so far as to sing the illicit flames of their lawfully married lords, *e.g.* Angelo Poli-

the second part of the whole work, which is inscribed to Alfonso II. 'the fifth Duke of Ferrara.' The 10th book, too, is specially dedicated to him, but none of the novels refer to him personally, and only one to his predecessor Hercules I.; the rest to Hercules I. 'the second Duke,' and Alfonso I. 'the third Duke of Ferrara.' But the stories told of these princes are for the most part not love tales. One of them (i. nov. 8) tells of the failure of an attempt made by the King of Naples to induce Hercules of Este to deprive Borso of the government of Ferrara; another (vi. nov. 10) describes Ercole's high-spirited treatment of conspirators. The two novels that treat of Alfonso I. (vi. nov. 2, 4), in the latter of which he only plays a subordinate part, are also, as the title of the book shows and as the dedication to the above-named Francesco explains more fully, accounts of 'atti di cortesía' towards knights and prisoners, but not towards women, and only the two remaining tales are love-stories. They are of such a kind as can be told during the lifetime of the prince; they set forth his nobleness and generosity, his virtue and self-restraint. Only one of them (vi. nov. 1) refers to Hercules I., who was dead long before the novels were compiled, and only one to the Hercules II. then alive (b. 1508, d. 1568) son of Lucrezia Borgia, husband of Renata, of whom the poet says: 'Il giovane, che non meno ha benigno l'animo, che cortese l'aspetto, come già il vedemmo in Roma, nel tempo, ch'egli, in vece del padre, venne à Papa Hadriano.' The tale about him is briefly as follows:—Lucilla, the beautiful daughter of a poor but noble widow, loves Nicandro, but cannot marry him, as the lover's father forbids him to wed a portionless maiden. Hercules, who sees the girl and is captivated by her beauty, finds his way, through the connivance of her mother, into her bedchamber, but is so touched by her beseeching appeal that he respects her innocence, and, giving her a dowry, enables her to marry Nicandro.

In Bandello, ii. nov. 8 and 9 refer to Alessandro Medici, 26 to Mary of Aragon, iii. 26, iv. 13 to Galeazzo Sforza, iii. 36, 37 to Henry VIII. of England, ii. 27 to the German Emperor Maximilian. The emperor, 'whose natural goodness and more than imperial generosity are praised by all writers,' while chasing a stag is separated from his followers, loses his way, and at last emerging from the wood, enquires the way from a countryman. The latter, busied with lading wood, begs the emperor, whom he does not know, to help him, and receives willing assistance. While still at work, Maximilian is rejoined, and, in spite of his signs to the contrary, respectfully saluted by his followers, and thus recognised by the peasant, who implores forgiveness for the freedom he has unwittingly taken. The emperor raises the kneeling suppliant, gives him presents, appoints him as his attendant, and confers upon him distinguished privileges. The narrator concludes: 'Dimostrò Cesare nello smontar da cavallo e con allegra ciera aiutar il bisognoso contadino, una

ziano, those of Lorenzo the Magnificent, and Gioviano Pontano, with a singular gusto, those of Alfonso of Calabria. The poem in question[1] betrays unconsciously the odious disposition of the Aragonese ruler; in these things too, he must needs be the most fortunate, else woe be to those who are more successful! That the greatest artists, for example Lionardo, should paint the mistresses of their patrons was no more than a matter of course.

But the house of Este was not satisfied with the praises of others; it undertook to celebrate them itself. In the Palazzo Schifanoja Borso caused himself to be painted in a series of historical representations, and Hercules kept the anniversary of his accession to the throne by a procession which was compared to the feast of Corpus Christi; shops were closed as on Sunday; in the centre of the line walked all the members of the princely house (bastards included) clad in embroidered robes. That the crown was the fountain of honour and authority, that all personal distinction flowed from it alone, had been long[2] expressed at this court by the Order of the Golden Spur—an order which had nothing in common with mediæval chivalry. Hercules I. added to the spur a sword, a gold-laced mantle, and a grant of money, in return for which there is no doubt that regular service was required.

The patronage of art and letters for which this court has

indicibile e degna d'ogni lode humanità, e in sollevarlo con danari e privilegii dalla sua faticosa vita, aperse il suo veramente animo Cesareo' (ii. 415). A story in the *Hecatomithi* (viii. nov. 5) also treats of Maximilian. It is the same tale which has acquired a world-wide celebrity through Shakespeare's *Measure for Measure* (for its diffusion see Kirchhof's *Wendunmuth*, ed. Oesterley, bd. v. s. 152 sqq.), and the scene of which is transferred by Giraldi to Innsbruck. Maximilian is the hero, and here too receives the highest eulogies. After being first called 'Massimiliano il Grande,' he is designated as one 'che fù raro esempio di cortesia, di magnanimità, e di singolare giustizia.'

[1] In the *Deliciæ Poet. Italorum* (1608), ii. pp. 455 sqq.: ad Alfonsum ducem Calabriæ. (Yet I do not believe that the above remark fairly applies to this poem, which clearly expresses the joys which Alfonso has with Drusula, and describes the sensations of the happy lover, who in his transports thinks that the gods themselves must envy him.—L.G.).

[2] Mentioned as early as 1367, in the *Polistore*, in Murat. xxiv. col. 848, in reference to Niccolò the Elder, who makes twelve persons knights in honour of the twelve Apostles.

obtained a world-wide reputation, was exercised through the University, which was one of the most perfect in Italy, and by the gift of places in the personal or official service of the prince; it involved consequently no additional expense. Bojardo, as a wealthy country gentleman and high official, belonged to this class. At the time when Ariosto began to distinguish himself, there existed no court, in the true sense of the word, either at Milan or Florence, and soon there was none either at Urbino or at Naples. He had to content himself with a place among the musicians and jugglers of Cardinal Ippolito till Alfonso took him into his service. It was otherwise at a later time with Torquato Tasso, whose presence at court was jealously sought after.

CHAPTER VI.

THE OPPONENTS OF TYRANNY.

In face of this centralised authority, all legal opposition within the borders of the state was futile. The elements needed for the restoration of a republic had been for ever destroyed, and the field prepared for violence and despotism. The nobles, destitute of political rights, even where they held feudal possessions, might call themselves Guelphs or Ghibellines at will, might dress up their bravos in padded hose and feathered caps[1] or how else they pleased; thoughtful men like Macchiavelli[2] knew well enough that Milan and Naples were too 'corrupt' for a republic. Strange judgments fall on these two so-called parties, which now served only to give an official sanction to personal and family disputes. An Italian prince, whom Agrippa of Nettesheim[3] advised to put them down, replied that their quarrels brought him in more than 12,000 ducats a year in fines. And when in the year 1500, during the brief return of Ludovico Moro to his States, the Guelphs of Tortona summoned a part of the neighbouring French army into the city, in order to make an end once for all of their opponents, the French certainly began by plundering and ruining the Ghibellines, but finished by doing the same to their hosts, till Tortona was utterly laid waste.[4] In Romagna, the hotbed of every ferocious passion, these two names had long lost all political meaning. It was a sign of the political delusion of the people that they not seldom believed the Guelphs to be the natural allies of the French and the Ghibellines of the Spaniards. It is hard to see that those who tried to profit by this error got

1 Burigozzo, in the *Archiv. Stor.* iii. p. 432.
2 *Discorsi*, i. 17, on Milan after the death of Filippo Visconti.
3 *De Incert. et Vanitate Scientiar.* cap. 55.
4 Prato, *Archiv. Stor.* iii. p. 241.

much by doing so. France, after all her interventions, had to abandon the peninsula at last, and what became of Spain, after she had destroyed Italy, is known to every reader.

But to return to the despots of the Renaissance. A pure and simple mind, we might think, would perhaps have argued that, since all power is derived from God, these princes, if they were loyally and honestly supported by all their subjects, must in time themselves improve and lose all traces of their violent origin. But from characters and imaginations inflamed by passion and ambition, reasoning of this kind could not be expected. Like bad physicians, they thought to cure the disease by removing the symptoms, and fancied that if the tyrant were put to death, freedom would follow of itself. Or else, without reflecting even to this extent, they sought only to give a vent to the universal hatred, or to take vengeance for some family misfortune or personal affront. Since the governments were absolute, and free from all legal restraints, the opposition chose its weapons with equal freedom. Boccaccio declares openly [1] 'Shall I call the tyrant king or prince, and obey him loyally as my lord? No, for he is the enemy of the commonwealth. Against him I may use arms, conspiracies, spies, ambushes and fraud; to do so is a sacred and necessary work. There is no more acceptable sacrifice than the blood of a tyrant.' We need not occupy ourselves with individual cases; Macchiavelli,[2] in a famous chapter of his 'Discorsi,' treats of the conspiracies of ancient and modern times from the days of the Greek tyrants downwards, and classifies them with cold-blooded indifference according to their various plans and results. We need make but two observations, first on the

[1] *De Casibus Virorum Illustrium*, l. ii. cap. 15.

[2] *Discorsi*, iii. 6; comp. *Storie Fiorent.* l. viii. The description of conspiracies has been a favourite theme of Italian writers from a very remote period. Luitprand (of Cremona, *Mon. Germ.*, ss. iii. 264–363) gives us a few, which are more circumstantial than those of any other contemporary writer of the tenth century; in the eleventh the deliverance of Messina from the Saracens, accomplished by calling in Norman Roger (Baluz. *Miscell.* i. p. 184), gives occasion to a characteristic narrative of this kind (1060); we need hardly speak of the dramatic colouring given to the stories of the Sicilian Vespers (1282). The same tendency is well known in the Greek writers.

murders committed in church, and next on the influence of classical antiquity. So well was the tyrant guarded that it was almost impossible to lay hands upon him elsewhere than at solemn religious services; and on no other occasion was the whole family to be found assembled together. It was thus that the Fabrianese [1] murdered (1435) the members of their ruling house, the Chiavistelli, during high mass, the signal being given by the words of the Creed, 'Et incarnatus est.' At Milan the Duke Giovan Maria Visconti (1412) was assassinated at the entrance of the church of San Gottardo, Galeazzo Maria Sforza (1476) in the church of Santo Stefano, and Ludovico Moro only escaped (1484) the daggers of the adherents of the widowed Duchess Bona, through entering the church of Sant' Ambrogio by another door than that by which he was expected. There was no intentional impiety in the act; the assassins of Galeazzo did not fail to pray before the murder to the patron saint of the church, and to listen devoutly to the first mass. It was, however, one cause of the partial failure of the conspiracy of the Pazzi against Lorenzo and Guiliano Medici (1478), that the brigand Montesecco, who had bargained to commit the murder at a banquet, declined to undertake it in the Cathedral of Florence. Certain of the clergy 'who were familiar with the sacred place, and consequently had no fear' were induced to act in his stead.[2]

As to the imitation of antiquity, the influence of which on moral, and more especially on political, questions we shall often refer to, the example was set by the rulers themselves, who, both in their conception of the state and in their personal conduct, took the old Roman empire avowedly as their model. In like manner their opponents, when they set to work with a deliberate theory, took pattern by the ancient tyrannicides. It may be hard to prove that in the main point—in forming the resolve itself—they consciously followed a classical example; but the appeal to antiquity was no mere phrase. The most striking disclosures have been left us with respect to the murderers of Galeazzo Sforza—Lampugnani, Olgiati, and

[1] Corio, fol. 333. For what follows, ibid. fol. 305, 422 sqq. 440.

[2] So in the quotations from Gallus, in Sismondi, xi. 93. For the whole subject see Reumont, *Lorenzo dei Medici*, pp. 387–97, especially 396.

Visconti.[1] Though all three had personal ends to serve, yet their enterprise may be partly ascribed to a more general reason. About this time Cola de' Montani, a humanist and professor of eloquence, had awakened among many of the young Milanese nobility a vague passion for glory and patriotic achievements, and had mentioned to Lampugnani and Olgiati his hope of delivering Milan. Suspicion was soon aroused against him: he was banished from the city, and his pupils were abandoned to the fanaticism he had excited. Some ten days before the deed they met together and took a solemn oath in the monastery of Sant' Ambrogio. 'Then,' says Olgiati, 'in a remote corner I raised my eyes before the picture of the patron saint, and implored his help for ourselves and for all *his* people.' The heavenly protector of the city was called on to bless the undertaking, as was afterwards St. Stephen, in whose church it was fulfilled. Many of their comrades were now informed of the plot, nightly meetings were held in the house of Lampugnani, and the conspirators practised for the murder with the sheaths of their daggers. The attempt was successful, but Lampugnani was killed on the spot by the attendants of the duke; the others were captured: Visconti was penitent, but Olgiati through all his tortures maintained that the deed was an acceptable offering to God, and exclaimed while the executioner was breaking his ribs, 'Courage, Girolamo! thou wilt long be remembered; death is bitter, but glory is eternal.'[2]

[1] Corio, fol. 422. Allegretto, *Diarî Sanesi*, in Murat. xxiii. col. 777. See above, p. 41.

[2] The enthusiasm with which the Florentine Alamanno Rinuccini (b. 1419) speaks in his *Ricordi* (ed. by G. Aiazzi, Florence, 1840) of murderers and their deeds is very remarkable. For a contemporary, though not Italian, apology for tyrannicide, see Kervyn de Lettenhove, *Jean sans Peur et l' Apologie du Tyrannicide*, in the *Bulletin de l' Académie de Bruxelles*, xi. (1861), pp. 558–71. A century later opinion in Italy had changed altogether. See the condemnation of Lampugnani's deed in Egnatius, *De Exemplis Ill. Vir.*, Ven. fol. 99 *b;* comp. also 318 *b*.

Petr. Crinitus, also (*De honestâ disciplinâ*, Paris, 1510, fol. 134 *b*), writes a poem *De virtute Jo. Andr. Lamponiani tyrannicidæ*, in which Lampugnani's deed is highly praised, and he himself is represented as a worthy companion of Brutus.

Comp. also the Latin poem: *Bonini Mombritii poetæ Mediol. trenodiæ in funere illustrissimi D. Gal. Marie Sfor* (2 Books—Milan, 1504), edited by Ascalon Vallis (*sic*), who in his dedication to the jurist Jac.

But however idealistic the object and purpose of such conspiracies may appear, the manner in which they were conducted betrays the influence of that worst of all conspirators, Catiline—a man in whose thoughts freedom had no place whatever. The annals of Siena tells us expressly that the conspirators were students of Sallust, and the fact is indirectly confirmed by the confession of Olgiati.[1] Elsewhere, too, we meet with the name of Catiline, and a more attractive pattern of the conspirator, apart from the end he followed, could hardly be discovered.

Among the Florentines, whenever they got rid of, or tried to get rid of, the Medici, tyrannicide was a practice universally accepted and approved. After the flight of the Medici in 1494, the bronze group of Donatello[2]—Judith with the dead Holofernes—was taken from their collection and placed before the Palazzo della Signoria, on the spot where the 'David' of Michael Angelo now stands, with the inscription, 'Exemplum salutis publicæ cives posuere 1495.'[3] No example was more popular than that of the younger Brutus, who, in Dante,[4] lies with Cassius and Judas Iscariot in the lowest pit of hell, because of his treason to the empire. Pietro Paolo Boscoli, whose plot against Guiliano, Giovanni, and Guilio Medici failed (1513), was an enthusiastic admirer of Brutus, and in order to follow his steps, only waited to find a Cassius. Such a

Balsamus praises the poet and names other poems equally worthy to be printed. In this work, in which Megæra and Mars, Calliope and the poet, appear as interlocutors, the assassin—not Lampugnano, but a man from a humble family of artisans—is severely blamed, and he with his fellow conspirators are treated as ordinary criminals; they are charged with high treason on account of a projected alliance with Charles of Burgundy. No less than ten prognostics of the death of Duke Galeazzo are enumerated. The murder of the Prince, and the punishment of the assassin are vividly described; the close consists of pious consolations addressed to the widowed Princess, and of religious meditations.

[1] 'Con studiare el Catalinario,' says Allegretto. Comp. (in Corio) a sentence like the following in the desposition of Olgiati: 'Quisque nostrum magis socios potissime et infinitos alios sollicitare, infestare, alter alteri benevolos se facere cœpit. Aliquid aliquibus parum donare: simul magis noctu edere, bibere, vigilare, nostra omnia bona polliceri,' etc.

[2] Vasari, iii. 251, note to *V. di Donatello.*

[3] It now has been removed to a newly constructed building.

[4] *Inferno*, xxxiv. 64.

partner he met with in Agostino Capponi. His last utterances in prison [1]—a striking evidence of the religious feeling of the time—show with what an effort he rid his mind of these classical imaginations, in order to die like a Christian. A friend and the confessor both had to assure him that St. Thomas Aquinas condemned conspirators absolutely; but the confessor afterwards admitted to the same friend that St. Thomas drew a distinction and permitted conspiracies against a tyrant who had forced himself on a people against their will. After Lorenzino Medici had murdered the Duke Alessandro (1537), and then escaped, an apology for the deed appeared,[2] which is probably his own work, and certainly composed in his interest, and in which he praises tyrannicide as an act of the highest merit; on the supposition that Alessandro was a legitimate Medici, and, therefore, related to him, if only distantly, he boldly compares himself with Timoleon, who slew his brother for his country's sake. Others, on the same occasion, made use of the comparison with Brutus, and that Michael Angelo himself, even late in life, was not unfriendly to ideas of this kind, may be inferred from his bust of Brutus in the Uffizi. He left it unfinished, like nearly all his works, but certainly not because the murder of Cæsar was repugnant to his feeling, as the couplet beneath declares.

A popular radicalism in the form in which it is opposed to the monarchies of later times, is not to be found in the despotic states of the Renaissance. Each individual protested inwardly against despotism, but was rather disposed to make tolerable or profitable terms with it, than to combine with others for its destruction. Things must have been as bad as at Camerino, Fabriano, or Rimini (p. 28), before the citizens united to destroy or expel the ruling house. They knew in most cases only too well that this would but mean a change of masters. The star of the Republics was certainly on the decline.

[1] Related by a hearer, Luca della Robbia, *Archiv. Stor.* i. 273. Comp. Paul. Jovius, *Vita Leonis X.* iii. in the *Viri Illustres.*

[2] First printed in 1723, as appendix to Varchi's History, then in Roscoe, *Vita di Lorenzo de' Medici*, vol. iv. app. 12, and often besides. Comp. Reumont, *Gesch. Toscana's seit dem Ende des Florent. Freistaates*, Gotha, 1876, i. p. 67, note. See also the report in the *Lettere de' Principi* (ed. Venez. 1577), iii. fol. 162 sqq.

CHAPTER VII.

THE REPUBLICS: VENICE AND FLORENCE.

THE Italian municipalities had, in earlier days, given signal proof of that force which transforms the city into the state. It remained only that these cities should combine in a great confederation; and this idea was constantly recurring to Italian statesmen, whatever differences of form it might from time to time display. In fact, during the struggles of the twelfth and thirteenth centuries, great and formidable leagues actually were formed by the cities; and Sismondi (ii. 174) is of opinion that the time of the final armaments of the Lombard confederation against Barbarossa was the moment when a universal Italian league was possible. But the more powerful states had already developed characteristic features which made any such scheme impracticable. In their commercial dealings they shrank from no measures, however extreme, which might damage their competitors; they held their weaker neighbours in a condition of helpless dependence—in short, they each fancied they could get on by themselves without the assistance of the rest, and thus paved the way for future usurpation. The usurper was forthcoming when long conflicts between the nobility and the people, and between the different factions of the nobility, had awakened the desire for a strong government, and when bands of mercenaries ready and willing to sell their aid to the highest bidder had superseded the general levy of the citizens which party leaders now found unsuited to their purposes.[1] The tyrants destroyed the freedom of most of the cities; here and there they were expelled, but not thoroughly, or only for a short time; and they were always restored, since

[1] On the latter point see Jac. Nardi, *Vita di Ant. Giacomini*, Lucca (1818), p. 18.

the inward conditions were favourable to them, and the opposing forces were exhausted.

Among the cities which maintained their independence are two of deep significance for the history of the human race: Florence, the city of incessant movement, which has left us a record of the thoughts and aspirations of each and all who, for three centuries, took part in this movement, and Venice, the city of apparent stagnation and of political secrecy. No contrast can be imagined stronger than that which is offered us by these two, and neither can be compared to anything else which the world has hitherto produced.

Venice recognised itself from the first as a strange and mysterious creation—the fruits of a higher power than human ingenuity. The solemn foundation of the city was the subject of a legend. On March 25, 413, at mid-day the emigrants from Padua laid the first stone at the Rialto, that they might have a sacred, inviolable asylum amid the devastations of the barbarians. Later writers attributed to the founders the presentiment of the future greatness of the city; M. Antonio Sabellico, who has celebrated the event in the dignified flow of his hexameters, makes the priest, who completes the act of consecration, cry to heaven, 'When we hereafter attempt great things, grant us prosperity! Now we kneel before a poor altar; but if our vows are not made in vain, a hundred temples, O God, of gold and marble shall arise to Thee.'[1] The island city at the end of the fifteenth century was the jewel-casket of the world. It is so described by the same Sabellico,[2] with its ancient cupolas, its leaning towers, its inlaid marble

[1] 'Genethliacum Venetæ urbis,' in the *Carmina* of Ant. Sabellicus. The 25th of March was chosen 'essendo il cielo in singolar disposizione, si come da gli astronomi è stato calcolato più volte.' Comp. Sansovino, *Venezia città nobilissima e singolare, descritta in* 14 *libri*, Venezia, 1581, fol. 203. For the whole chapter see *Johannis Baptistæ Egnatii viri doctissimi de exemplis Illustrium Virorum Venetæ civitatis atque aliarum gentium*, Paris, 1554. The eldest Venetian chronicler, Joh. Diaconi, *Chron. Venetum* in Pertz, *Monum.* S.S. vii. pp. 5, 6, places the occupation of the islands in the time of the Lombards and the foundation of the Rialto later.

[2] 'De Venetæ urbis apparatu panagiricum carmen quod oraculum inscribitur.'

façades, its compressed splendour, where the richest decoration did not hinder the practical employment of every corner of space. He takes us to the crowded Piazza before S. Giacometto at the Rialto, where the business of the world is transacted, not amid shouting and confusion, but with the subdued hum of many voices; where in the porticos round the square [1] and in those of the adjoining streets sit hundreds of money-changers and goldsmiths, with endless rows of shops and warehouses above their heads. He describes the great Fondaco of the Germans beyond the bridge, where their goods and their dwellings lay, and before which their ships are drawn up side by side in the canal; higher up is a whole fleet laden with wine and oil, and parallel with it, on the shore swarming with porters, are the vaults of the merchants; then from the Rialto to the square of St. Mark come the inns and the perfumers' cabinets. So he conducts the reader from one quarter of the city to another till he comes at last to the two hospitals which were among those institutions of public utility nowhere so numerous as at Venice. Care for the people, in peace as well as in war, was characteristic of this government, and its attention to the wounded, even to those of the enemy, excited the admiration of other states.[2] Public institutions of every kind found in Venice their pattern; the pensioning of retired servants was carried out systematically, and included a provision for widows and orphans. Wealth, political security, and acquaintance with other countries, had matured the understanding of such questions. These slender fair-haired men,[3] with quiet cautious steps, and deliberate speech, differed but slightly in costume and bearing from one another; ornaments, especially pearls, were reserved for the women and girls. At that time the general prosperity, notwithstanding the losses sustained from the Turks, was still dazzling; the stores of

[1] The whole quarter was altered in the reconstructions of the sixteenth century.

[2] Benedictus *Carol. VIII.* in Eccard, *Scriptores*, ii. col. 1597, 1601, 1621. In the *Chron. Venetum*, Murat. xxiv. col. 26, the political virtues of the Venetians are enumerated: 'bontà, innocenza, zelo di carità, pietà, misericordia.'

[3] Many of the nobles cropped their hair. See *Erasmi Colloquia*, ed. Tiguri, a. 1553: miles et carthusianus.

energy which the city possessed and the prejudice in its favour diffused throughout Europe, enabled it at a much later time to survive the heavy blows which were inflicted by the discovery of the sea route to the Indies, by the fall of the Mamelukes in Egypt, and by the war of the League of Cambray.

Sabellico, born in the neighbourhood of Tivoli, and accustomed to the frank loquacity of the scholars of his day, remarks elsewhere [1] with some astonishment, that the young nobles who came of a morning to hear his lectures could not be prevailed on to enter into political discussions: 'When I ask them what people think, say, and expect about this or that movement in Italy, they all answer with one voice that they know nothing about the matter.' Still, in spite of the strict inquisition of the state, much was to be learned from the more corrupt members of the aristocracy by those who were willing to pay enough for it. In the last quarter of the fifteenth century there were traitors among the highest officials; [2] the popes, the Italian princes, and even second-rate Condottieri in the service of the government had informers in their pay, sometimes with regular salaries; things went so far that the Council of Ten found it prudent to conceal important political news from the Council of the Pregadi, and it was even supposed that Ludovico Moro had control of a definite number of votes among the latter. Whether the hanging of single offenders and the high rewards—such as a life-pension of sixty ducats paid to those who informed against them—were of much avail, it is hard to decide; one of the chief causes of this evil, the poverty of many of the nobility, could not be removed in a day. In the year 1492 a proposal was urged by two of that order, that the state should annually spend 70,000 ducats for the relief of those poorer nobles who held no public office; the matter was near coming before the Great Council, in which it might have had a majority, when the Council of Ten interfered in time

[1] *Epistolæ*, lib. v. fol. 28.

[2] Malipiero, *Ann. Veneti*, *Archiv. Stor.* vii. i. pp. 377, 431, 481, 493, 530; ii. pp. 661, 668, 679. *Chron. Venetum*, in Muratori, xxiv. col. 57. *Diario Ferrarese*, ib. col. 240. See also *Dispacci di Antonio Giustiniani* (Flor. 1876), i. p. 392.

and banished the two proposers for life to Nicosia in Cyprus.[1] About this time a Soranzo was hung, though not at Venice itself, for sacrilege, and a Contarini put in chains for burglary; another of the same family came in 1499 before the Signory, and complained that for many years he had been without an office, that he had only sixteen ducats a year and nine children, that his debts amounted to sixty ducats, that he knew no trade and had lately been turned on to the streets. We can understand why some of the wealthier nobles built houses, sometimes whole rows of them, to provide free lodging for their needy comrades. Such works figure in wills among deeds of charity.[2]

But if the enemies of Venice ever founded serious hopes upon abuses of this kind, they were greatly in error. It might be thought that the commercial activity of the city, which put within reach of the humblest a rich reward for their labour, and the colonies on the Eastern shores of the Mediterranean, would have diverted from political affairs the dangerous elements of society. But had not the political history of Genoa, notwithstanding similar advantages, been of the stormiest? The cause of the stability of Venice lies rather in a combination of circumstances which were found in union nowhere else. Unassailable from its position, it had been able from the beginning to treat of foreign affairs with the fullest and calmest reflection, and ignore nearly altogether the parties which divided the rest of Italy, to escape the entanglement of permanent alliances, and to set the highest price on those which it thought fit to make. The keynote of the Venetian character was, consequently, a spirit of proud and contemptuous isolation, which, joined to the hatred felt for the city by the other states of Italy, gave rise to a strong sense of solidarity within. The inhabitants meanwhile were united by the most powerful ties of interest in dealing both with the colonies and with the possessions on the mainland, forcing the population of the latter, that is, of all the towns up to Bergamo, to buy and sell in Venice alone. A power which rested on means so artifi-

[1] Malipiero, in the *Archiv. Stor.* vii. ii. p. 691. Comp. 694, 713, and i. 535.

[2] Marin Sanudo, *Vite dei Duchi*, Murat. xxii. col. 1194.

cial could only be maintained by internal harmony and unity; and this conviction was so widely diffused among the citizens that the conspirator found few elements to work upon. And the discontented, if there were such, were held so far apart by the division between the noble and the burgher, that a mutual understanding was not easy. On the other hand, within the ranks of the nobility itself, travel, commercial enterprise, and the incessant wars with the Turks saved the wealthy and dangerous from that fruitful source of conspiracies—idleness. In these wars they were spared, often to a criminal extent, by the general in command, and the fall of the city was predicted by a Venetian Cato, if this fear of the nobles 'to give one another pain' should continue at the expense of justice.[1] Nevertheless this free movement in the open air gave the Venetian aristocracy, as a whole, a healthy bias.

And when envy and ambition called for satisfaction an official victim was forthcoming, and legal means and authorities were ready. The moral torture, which for years the Doge Francesco Foscari (d. 1457) suffered before the eyes of all Venice, is a frightful example of a vengeance possible only in an aristocracy. The Council of Ten, which had a hand in everything, which disposed without appeal of life and death, of financial affairs and military appointments, which included the Inquisitors among its number, and which overthrew Foscari, as it had overthrown so many powerful men before,—this Council was yearly chosen afresh from the whole governing body, the Gran Consilio, and was consequently the most direct expression of its will. It is not probable that serious intrigues occurred at these elections, as the short duration of the office and the accountability which followed rendered it an object of no great desire. But violent and mysterious as the proceedings of this and other authorities might be, the genuine Venetian courted rather than fled their sentence, not only because the Republic had long arms, and if it could not catch him might punish his family, but because in most cases it acted from rational motives and not from a thirst for blood.[2] No state,

[1] *Chron. Venetum*, Murat. xxiv. col. 105.

[2] *Chron. Venetum*, Murat. xxiv. col. 123 sqq. and Malipiero, l. c. vii. i. pp. 175, 187 sqq. relate the significant fall of the Admiral Antonio Gri-

indeed, has ever exercised a greater moral influence over its subjects, whether abroad or at home. If traitors were to be found among the Pregadi, there was ample compensation for this in the fact that every Venetian away from home was a born spy for his government. It was a matter of course that the Venetian cardinals at Rome sent home news of the transactions of the secret papal consistories. The Cardinal Domenico Grimani had the despatches intercepted in the neighbourhood of Rome (1500) which Ascanio Sforza was sending to his brother Ludovico Moro, and forwarded them to Venice; his father, then exposed to a serious accusation, claimed public credit for this service of his son before the Gran Consilio; in other words, before all the world.[1]

The conduct of the Venetian government to the Condottieri in its pay has been spoken of already. The only further guarantee of their fidelity which could be obtained lay in their great number, by which treachery was made as difficult as its discovery was easy. In looking at the Venetian army list, one is only surprised that among forces of such miscellaneous composition any common action was possible. In the catalogue for the campaign of 1495 we find 15,526 horsemen, broken up into a number of small divisions.[2] Gonzaga of Mantua alone had as many as 1,200, and Gioffredo Borgia 740; then follow six officers with a contingent of 600 to 700, ten with 400, twelve with 400 to 200, fourteen or thereabouts with 200 to 100, nine with 80, six with 50 to 60, and so forth. These forces were partly composed of old Venetian troops, partly of veterans led by Venetian city or country nobles; the majority of the leaders were, however, princes and rulers of cities or their relatives. To these forces must be added 24,000 infantry—we are not told how they were raised or commanded—with 3,300 additional troops, who probably belonged to the special services.

mani, who, when accused on account of his refusal to surrender the command in chief to another, himself put irons on his feet before his arrival at Venice, and presented himself in this condition to the Senate. For him and his future lot, see Egnatius, fol. 183 *a* sqq., 198 *b* sqq.

[1] *Chron. Ven.* l. c. col. 166.

[2] Malipiero, l. c. vii. i. 349. For other lists of the same kind see Marin Sanudo, *Vite dei Duchi*, Murat. xxii. col. 990 (year 1426), col. 1088 (year 1440), in Corio, fol. 435-438 (1483), in Guazzo, *Historie*, fol. 151 sqq.

In time of peace the cities of the mainland were wholly unprotected or occupied by insignificant garrisons. Venice relied, if not exactly on the loyalty, at least on the good sense of its subjects; in the war of the League of Cambray (1509) it absolved them, as is well known, from their oath of allegiance, and let them compare the amenities of a foreign occupation with the mild government to which they had been accustomed. As there had been no treason in their desertion of St. Mark, and consequently no punishment was to be feared, they returned to their old masters with the utmost eagerness. This war, we may remark parenthetically, was the result of a century's outcry against the Venetian desire for aggrandisement. The Venetians, in fact, were not free from the mistake of those over-clever people who will credit their opponents with no irrational and inconsiderate conduct.[1] Misled by this optimism, which is, perhaps, a peculiar weakness of aristocracies, they had utterly ignored not only the preparations of Mohammed II. for the capture of Constantinople, but even the armaments of Charles VIII., till the unexpected blow fell at last.[2] The League of Cambray was an event of the same character, in so far as it was clearly opposed to the interest of the two chief members, Louis XII. and Julius II. The hatred of all Italy against the victorious city seemed to be concentrated in the mind of the Pope, and to have blinded him to the evils of foreign intervention; and as to the policy of Cardinal Amboise and his king, Venice ought long before to have recognised it as a piece of malicious imbecility, and to have been thoroughly on its guard. The other members of the League took part in it from that envy which may be a salutary corrective to great wealth and power, but which in itself is a beggarly sentiment. Venice came out of the conflict with honour, but not without lasting damage.

A power, whose foundations were so complicated, whose activity and interests filled so wide a stage, cannot be imagined without a systematic oversight of the whole, without a regular estimate of means and burdens, of profits and losses. Venice

[1] Guicciardini (*Ricordi*, n. 150) is one of the first to remark that the passion for vengeance can drown the clearest voice of self-interest.

[2] Malipiero, l. c. vii. i., p. 328.

can fairly make good its claim to be the birthplace of statistical science, together, perhaps, with Florence, and followed by the more enlightened despotisms. The feudal state of the Middle Ages knew of nothing more than catalogues of signorial rights and possessions (Urbaria); it looked on production as a fixed quantity, which it approximately is, so long as we have to do with landed property only. The towns, on the other hand, throughout the West must from very early times have treated production, which with them depended on industry and commerce, as exceedingly variable; but, even in the most flourishing times of the Hanseatic League, they never got beyond a simple commercial balance-sheet. Fleets, armies, political power and influence fall under the debit and credit of a trader's ledger. In the Italian States a clear political consciousness, the pattern of Mohammedan administration, and the long and active exercise of trade and commerce, combined to produce for the first time a true science of statistics.[1] The absolute monarchy of Frederick II. in Lower Italy was organised with the sole object of securing a concentrated power for the death-struggle in which he was engaged. In Venice, on the contrary, the supreme objects were the enjoyment of life and power, the increase of inherited advantages, the creation of the most lucrative forms of industry, and the opening of new channels for commerce.

The writers of the time speak of these things with the greatest freedom.[2] We learn that the population of the city amounted in the year 1422 to 190,000 souls; the Italians were,

[1] The statistical view of Milan, in the 'Manipulus Florum' (in Murat. xi. 711 sqq.) for the year 1288, is important, though not extensive. It includes house-doors, population, men of military age, 'loggie' of the nobles, wells, bakeries, wine-shops, butchers'-shops, fishmongers, the consumption of corn, dogs, birds of chase, the price of salt, wood, hay, and wines; also the judges, notaries, doctors, schoolmasters, copying clerks, armourers, smiths, hospitals, monasteries, endowments, and religious corporations. A list perhaps still older is found in the 'Liber de magnalibus Mediolani,' in *Heinr. de Hervordia*, ed. Potthast, p. 165. See also the statistical account of Asti about the year 1250 in Ogerius Alpherius (Alfieri), *De Gestis Astensium*, *Histor. patr. Monumenta*, *Scriptorum.* tom. iii. col. 684. sqq.

[2] Especially Marin Sanudo, in the *Vite dei Duchi di Venezia*, Murat. xxii. *passim.*

perhaps, the first to reckon, not according to hearths, or men able to bear arms, or people able to walk, and so forth, but according to 'animæ,' and thus to get the most neutral basis for further calculation. About this time,[1] when the Florentines wished to form an alliance with Venice against Filippo Maria Visconti, they were for the moment refused, in the belief, resting on accurate commercial returns, that a war between Venice and Milan, that is, between seller and buyer, was foolish. Even if the duke simply increased his army, the Milanese, through the heavier taxation they must pay, would become worse customers. 'Better let the Florentines be defeated, and then, used as they are to the life of a free city, they will settle with us and bring their silk and woollen industry with them, as the Lucchese did in their distress.' The speech of the dying Doge Mocenigo (1423) to a few of the senators whom he had sent for to his bedside[2] is still more remarkable. It contains the chief elements of a statistical account of the whole resources of Venice. I cannot say whether or where a thorough elucidation of this perplexing document exists; by way of illustration, the following facts may be quoted. After repaying a war-loan of four million ducats, the public debt ('il monte') still amounted to six million ducats; the current trade reached (so it seems) ten millions, which yielded, the text informs us, a profit of four millions. The 3,000 'navigli,' the 300 'navi,' and the 45 galleys were manned respectively by 17,000, 8,000, and 11,000 seamen (more than 200 for each galley). To these must be added 16,000 shipwrights. The houses in Venice were valued at seven millions, and brought in a rent of half a million.[3] There were 1,000 nobles whose income ranged from 70 to 4,000 ducats. In another passage the ordinary income of the state

[1] See for the marked difference between Venice and Florence, an important pamphlet addressed 1472 to Lorenzo de' Medici by certain Venetians, and the answer to it by Benedetto Dei, in Paganini, *Della Decima*, Florence, 1763, iii. pp. 135 sqq.

[2] In Sanudo, l. c. col. 958. What relates to trade is extracted in Scherer, *Allgem. Gesch. des Welthandels*, i. 326, note.

[3] Here all the houses, not merely those owned by the state, are meant. The latter, however, sometimes yielded enormous rents. See Vasari, xiii. 83. V. d. Jac. Sansovino.

in that same year is put at 1,100,000 ducats; through the disturbance of trade caused by the wars it sank about the middle of the century to 800,000 ducats.[1]

If Venice, by this spirit of calculation, and by the practical turn which she gave it, was the first fully to represent one important side of modern political life, in that culture, on the other hand, which Italy then prized most highly she did not stand in the front rank. The literary impulse, in general, was here wanting, and especially that enthusiasm for classical antiquity which prevailed elsewhere.[2] The aptitude of the Venetians, says Sabellico, for philosophy and eloquence was in itself not less remarkable than for commerce and politics; but this aptitude was neither developed in themselves nor rewarded in strangers as it was rewarded elsewhere in Italy. Filelfo, summoned to Venice not by the state, but by private individuals, soon found his expectations deceived; and George of Trebizond, who, in 1459, laid the Latin translation of Plato's Laws at the feet of the Doge, and was appointed professor of philology with a yearly salary of 150 ducats, and finally dedicated his 'Rhetoric' to the Signoria,[3] soon left the city in dissatisfaction. Literature, in fact, like the rest at Venice, had mostly a practical end in view. If, accordingly, we look through the history of Venetian literature which Francesco Sansovino has appended to his well-known book,[4] we shall find in the fourteenth century almost nothing but history, and special works on theology, jurisprudence, and medicine; and in the fifteenth century, till we come to Ermolao Barbaro and Aldo Manucci, humanistic

[1] See Sanudo, col. 963. In the same place a list of the incomes of the other Italian and European powers is given. An estimate for 1490 is to be found, col. 1245 sqq.

[2] This dislike seems to have amounted to positive hatred in Paul II. who called the humanists one and all heretics. Platina, *Vita Pauli*, ii. p. 323. See also for the subject in general, Voigt, *Wiederbelebung des classischen Alterthums*, Berlin, 1859, pp. 207-213. The neglect of the sciences is given as a reason for the flourishing condition of Venice by Lil. Greg. Giraldus, *Opera*, ii. p. 439.

[3] Sanudo, l. c. col. 1167.

[4] Sansovina, *Venezia*, lib. xiii. It contains the biographies of the Doges in chronological order, and, following these lives one by one (regularly from the year 1312, under the heading, *Scrittori Veneti*), short notices of contemporary writers.

culture is, for a city of such importance, most scantily represented. Similarly we find comparatively few traces of the passion, elsewhere so strong, for collecting books and manuscripts; and the valuable texts which formed part of Petrarch's legacies were so badly preserved that soon all traces of them were lost. The library which Cardinal Bessarion bequeathed to the state (1468) narrowly escaped dispersion and destruction. Learning was certainly cultivated at the University of Padua, where, however, the physicians and the jurists—the latter as the authors of legal opinions—received by far the highest pay. The share of Venice in the poetical creations of the country was long insignificant, till, at the beginning of the sixteenth century, her deficiences were made good.[1] Even the art of the Renaissance was imported into the city from without, and it was not before the end of the fifteenth century that she learned to move in this field with independent freedom and strength. But we find more striking instances still of intellectual backwardness. This Government, which had the clergy so thoroughly in its control, which reserved to itself the appointment to all important ecclesiastical offices, and which, one time after another, dared to defy the court of Rome, displayed an official piety of a most singular kind.[2] The bodies of saints and other reliques imported from Greece after the Turkish conquest were bought at the greatest sacrifices and received by the Doge in solemn procession.[3] For the coat without a seam it was decided (1455) to offer 10,000 ducats, but it was not to be had. These measures were not the fruit of any popular excitement, but of the tranquil resolutions of the heads of the Government, and might have been omitted without attracting

[1] Venice was then one of the chief seats of the Petrarchists. See G. Crespan, *Del Petrarchismo*, in *Petrarca e Venezia*, 1874, pp. 187–253.

[2] See Heinric. de Hervordia ad a. 1293, p. 213, ed. Potthast, who says: 'The Venetians wished to obtain the body of Jacob of Forli from the inhabitants of that place, as many miracles were wrought by it. They promised many things in return, among others to bear all the expense of canonising the defunct, but without obtaining their request.'

[3] Sanudo, l. c. col. 1158, 1171, 1177. When the body of St. Luke was brought from Bosnia, a dispute arose with the Benedictines of S. Giustina at Padua, who claimed to possess it already, and the Pope had to decide between the two parties. Comp. Guicciardini, *Ricordi*, n. 401.

any comment, and at Florence, under similar circumstances, would certainly have been omitted. We shall say nothing of the piety of the masses, and of their firm belief in the indulgences of an Alexander VI. But the state itself, after absorbing the Church to a degree unknown elsewhere, had in truth a certain ecclesiastical element in its composition, and the Doge, the symbol of the state, appeared in twelve great processions ('andate')[1] in a half-clerical character. They were almost all festivals in memory of political events, and competed in splendour with the great feasts of the Church; the most brilliant of all, the famous marriage with the sea, fell on Ascension Day.

The most elevated political thought and the most varied forms of human development are found united in the history of Florence, which in this sense deserves the name of the first modern state in the world. Here the whole people are busied with what in the despotic cities is the affair of a single family. That wondrous Florentine spirit, at once keenly critical and artistically creative, was incessantly transforming the social and political condition of the state, and as incessantly describing and judging the change. Florence thus became the home of political doctrines and theories, of experiments and sudden changes, but also, like Venice, the home of statistical science, and alone and above all other states in the world, the home of historical representation in the modern sense of the phrase. The spectacle of ancient Rome and a familiarity with its leading writers were not without influence; Giovanni Villani[2] confesses that he received the first impulse to his great work at the jubilee of the year 1300, and began it immediately on his return home. Yet how many among the 200,000 pilgrims of that year may have been like him in gifts and tendencies, and still did not write the history of their native cities! For not all of them could encourage themselves with the thought: 'Rome is sinking; my native city is rising, and ready to achieve great things, and therefore I wish to relate its past

[1] Sansovino, *Venezia*, lib. xii. 'dell' andate publiche del principe.' Egnatius, fol. 50*a*. For the dread felt at the papal interdict see Egnatius, fol 12 *a* sqq.

[2] G. Villani, viii. 36. The year 1300 is also a fixed date in the *Divine Comedy*.

history, and hope to continue the story to the present time, and as long as my life shall last.' And besides the witness to its past, Florence obtained through its historians something further —a greater fame than fell to the lot of any other city of Italy.[1]

Our present task is not to write the history of this remarkable state, but merely to give a few indications of the intellectual freedom and independence for which the Florentines were indebted to this history.[2]

In no other city of Italy were the struggles of political parties so bitter, of such early origin, and so permanent. The descriptions of them, which belong, it is true, to a somewhat later period, give clear evidence of the superiority of Florentine criticism.

[1] Stated about 1470 in *Vespas. Fiorent.* p. 554.

[2] The passage which followed in former editions referring to the *Chronicle of Dino Compagni* is here omitted, since the genuineness of the *Chronicle* has been disproved by Paul Scheffer-Boichhorst (*Florentiner Studien*, Leipzig, 1874, pp. 45–210), and the disproof maintained (*Die Chronik des D. C.*, Leipzig, 1875) against a distinguished authority (C. Hegel, *Die Chronik des D. C., Versuch einer Rettung*, Leipzig, 1875). Scheffer's view is generally received in Germany (see W. Bernhardi, *Der Stand der Dino-Frage, Hist. Zeitschr. N.F.*, 1877, bd. i.), and even Hegel assumes that the text as we have it is a later manipulation of an unfinished work of Dino. Even in Italy, though the majority of scholars have wished to ignore this critical onslaught, as they have done other earlier ones of the same kind, some voices have been raised to recognise the spuriousness of the document. (See especially P. Fanfani in his periodical *Il Borghini*, and in the book *Dino Campagni Vendicato*, Milano, 1875). On the earliest Florentine histories in general see Hartwig, *Forschungen*, Marburg, 1876, and C. Hegel in H. von Sybel's *Historischer Zeitschrift*, b. xxxv. Since then Isidore del Lungo, who with remarkable decision asserts its genuineness, has completed his great edition of Dino, and furnished it with a detailed introduction: *Dino Campagni e la sua cronaca*, 2 vols. Firenze, 1879–80. A manuscript of the history, dating back to the beginning of the fifteenth century, and consequently earlier than all the hitherto known references and editions, has been lately found. In consequence of the discovery of this MS. and of the researches undertaken by C. Hegel, and especially of the evidence that the style of the work does not differ from that of the fourteenth century, the prevailing view of the subject is essentially this, that the Chronicle contains an important kernel, which is genuine, which, however, perhaps even in the fourteenth century, was remodelled on the ground-plan of Villani's Chronicle. Comp. Gaspary, *Geschichte der italienischen Literatur*. Berlin, 1885, i. pp. 361–9, 531 sqq.]

And what a politician is the great victim of these crises, Dante Alighieri, matured alike by home and by exile! He uttered his scorn of the incessant changes and experiments in the constitution of his native city in verses of adamant, which will remain proverbial so long as political events of the same kind recur;[1] he addressed his home in words of defiance and yearning which must have stirred the hearts of his countrymen. But his thoughts ranged over Italy and the whole world; and if his passion for the Empire, as he conceived it, was no more than an illusion, it must yet be admitted that the youthful dreams of a new-born political speculation are in his case not without a poetical grandeur. He is proud to be the first who had trod this path,[2] certainly in the footsteps of Aristotle, but in his own way independently. His ideal emperor is a just and humane judge, dependent on God only, the heir of the universal sway of Rome to which belonged the sanction of nature, of right and of the will of God. The conquest of the world was, according to this view, rightful, resting on a divine judgment between Rome and the other nations of the earth, and God gave his approval to this empire, since under it he became Man, submitting at his birth to the census of the Emperor Augustus, and at his death to the judgment of Pontius Pilate. We may find it hard to appreciate these and other arguments of the same kind, but Dante's passion never fails to carry us with him. In his letters he appears as one of the earliest publicists,[3] and is perhaps the first layman to publish political tracts in this form. He began early. Soon after the death of Beatrice he addressed a pamphlet on the state of Florence 'to the Great ones of the Earth,' and the public utterances of his later years, dating from the time of his banishment, are all directed to emperors, princes, and cardinals. In these letters and in his book 'De Vulgari Eloquio' the feeling, bought with such bitter pains, is con-

[1] *Purgatorio*, vi. at the end.

[2] *De Monarchia*, i. 1. (New critical edition by Witte, Halle, 1863, 71; German translation by O. Hubatsch, Berlin, 1872).

[3] *Dantis Alligherii Epistolæ*, cum notis C. Witte, Padua, 1827. He wished to keep the Pope as well as the Emperor always in Italy. See his letter, p. 35, during the conclave of Carpentras, 1314. On the first letter see *Vitæ Nuova*, cap. 31, and *Epist.* p. 9.

stantly recurring that the exile may find elsewhere than in his native place an intellectual home in language and culture, which cannot be taken from him. On this point we shall have more to say in the sequel.

To the two Villani, Giovanni as well as Matteo, we owe not so much deep political reflexion as fresh and practical observations, together with the elements of Florentine statistics and important notices of other states. Here too trade and commerce had given the impulse to economical as well as political science. Nowhere else in the world was such accurate information to be had on financial affairs. The wealth of the Papal court at Avignon, which at the death of John XXII. amounted to twenty-five millions of gold florins, would be incredible on any less trustworthy authority.[1] Here only, at Florence, do we meet with colossal loans like that which the King of England contracted from the Florentine houses of Bardi and Peruzzi, who lost to his Majesty the sum of 1,365,000 gold florins (1338)—their own money and that of their partners —and nevertheless recovered from the shock.[2] Most important facts are here recorded as to the condition of Florence at this time:[3] the public income (over 300,000 gold florins) and expenditure; the population of the city, here only roughly estimated, according to the consumption of bread, in 'bocche,' *i.e.* mouths, put at 90,000, and the population of the whole territory; the excess of 300 to 500 male children among the 5,800 to 6,000 annually baptized;[4] the school-children, of whom 8,000 to 10,000 learned reading, 1,000 to 1,200 in six schools arithmetic; and besides these, 600 scholars who were

[1] Giov. Villani, xi. 20. Comp. Matt. Villani, ix. 93, who says that John XXII. 'astuto in tutte sue cose e massime in fare il danaio,' left behind him 18 million florins in cash and 6 millions in jewels.

[2] See for this and similar facts Giov. Villani, xi. 87, xii. 54. He lost his own money in the crash and was imprisoned for debt. See also Kervyn de Lettenhove, *L'Europe au Siècle de Philippe le Bel*, *Les Argentiers Florentins* in *Bulletin de l'Académie de Bruxelles* (1861), vol. xii. pp. 123 sqq.

[3] Giov. Villani, xi. 92, 93. In Macchiavelli, *Stor. Fiorent.* lib. ii. cap. 42, we read that 96,000 persons died of the plague in 1348.

[4] The priest put aside a black bean for every boy and a white one for every girl. This was the only means of registration.

taught Latin grammar and logic in four schools. Then follow the statistics of the churches and monasteries; of the hospitals, which held more than a thousand beds; of the wool-trade, with its most valuable details; of the mint, the provisioning of the city, the public officials, and so on.[1] Incidentally we learn many curious facts; how, for instance, when the public funds ('monte') were first established, in the year 1353, the Franciscans spoke from the pulpit in favour of the measure, the Dominicans and Augustinians against it.[2] The economical results of the black death were and could be observed and described nowhere else in all Europe as in this city.[3] Only a Florentine could have left it on record how it was expected that the scanty population would have made everything cheap, and how instead of that labour and commodities doubled in price; how the common people at first would do no work at all, but simply give themselves up to enjoyment; how in the city itself servants and maids were not to be had except at extravagant wages; how the peasants would only till the best lands, and left the rest uncultivated; and how the enormous legacies bequeathed to the poor at the time of the plague seemed afterwards useless, since the poor had either died or had ceased to be poor. Lastly, on the occasion of a great bequest, by which a childless philanthropist left six 'danari' to every beggar in the city, the attempt is made to give a comprehensive statistical account of Florentine mendicancy.[4]

This statistical view of things was at a later time still more highly cultivated at Florence. The noteworthy point about it is that, as a rule, we can perceive its connection with the higher aspects of history, with art, and with culture in general. An inventory of the year 1422[5] mentions, within the compass of the same document, the seventy-two exchange offices which

[1] There was already a permanent fire brigade in Florence.

[2] Matteo Villani, iii. 106.

[3] Matteo Villani, i. 2-7, comp. 58. The best authority for the plague itself is the famous description by Boccaccio at the beginning of the *Decameron*.

[4] Giov. Villani, x. 164.

[5] *Ex Annalibus Ceretani*, in Fabroni, *Magni Cormi Vita*, Adnot. 34. vol. ii. p. 63.

surrounded the 'Mercato Nuovo;' the amount of coined money in circulation (two million golden florins); the then new industry of gold spinning; the silk wares; Filippo Brunellesco, then busy in digging classical architecture from its grave; and Lionardo Aretino, secretary of the republic, at work at the revival of ancient literature and eloquence; lastly, it speaks of the general prosperity of the city, then free from political conflicts, and of the good fortune of Italy, which had rid itself of foreign mercenaries. The Venetian statistics quoted above (p. 70), which date from about the same year, certainly give evidence of larger property and profits and of a more extensive scene of action; Venice had long been mistress of the seas before Florence sent out its first galleys (1422) to Alexandria. But no reader can fail to recognise the higher spirit of the Florentine documents. These and similar lists recur at intervals of ten years, systematically arranged and tabulated, while elsewhere we find at best occasional notices. We can form an approximate estimate of the property and the business of the first Medici; they paid for charities, public buildings, and taxes from 1434 to 1471 no less than 663,755 gold florins, of which more than 400,000 fell on Cosimo alone, and Lorenzo Magnifico was delighted that the money had been so well spent.[1] In 1472 we have again a most important and in its way complete view of the commerce and trades of this city,[2] some of which may be wholly or partly reckoned among the fine arts—such as those which had to do with damasks and gold or silver embroidery, with wood-carving and 'intarsia,' with the sculpture of arabesques in marble and sandstone, with portraits in wax, and with jewellery and work in gold. The inborn talent of the Florentines for the systematisation of outward life is shown by their books on agriculture, business, and domestic economy, which are markedly superior to those of other European people in the

[1] *Ricordi* of Lorenzo, in Fabroni. *Laur. Med. Magnifici Vita*, Adnot. 2 and 25. Paul. Jovius, *Elogia*, pp. 131 sqq. Cosmus.

[2] Given by Benedetto Dei, in the passage quoted above (p. 70, note 1). It must be remembered that the account was intended to serve as a warning to assailants. For the whole subject see Reumont, *Lor. dei Medici*, ii. p. 419. The financial project of a certain Ludovico Ghetti, with important facts, is given in Roscoe, *Vita di Lor. Med.* ii. Append. i.

fifteenth century. It has been rightly decided to publish selections of these works,[1] although no little study will be needed to extract clear and definite results from them. At all events, we have no difficulty in recognising the city, where dying parents begged the Government in their wills to fine their sons 1,000 florins if they declined to practise a regular profession.[2]

For the first half of the sixteenth century probably no state in the world possesses a document like the magnificent description of Florence by Varchi.[3] In descriptive statistics, as in so many things besides, yet another model is left to us, before the freedom and greatness of the city sank into the grave.[4]

[1] E. g. in the *Arch. Stor.* iv. (?) See as a contrast the very simple ledger of Ott. Nuland, 1455-1462 (Stuttg. 1843), and for a rather later period the day-book of Lukas Rem, 1494-1541, ed. by B. Greiff, Augsb., 1861.

[2] Libri, *Histoire des Sciences Mathématiques*, ii. 163 sqq.

[3] Varchi, *Stor. Fiorent.* iii. p. 56 and sqq. up to the end of the 9th book. Some obviously erroneous figures are probably no more than clerical or typographical blunders.

[4] In respect of prices and of wealth in Italy, I am only able, in default of further means of investigation, to bring together some scattered facts, which I have picked up here and there. Obvious exaggerations must be put aside. The gold coins which are worth referring to are the ducat, the sequin, the 'fiorino d'oro,' and the 'scudo d'oro.' The value of all is nearly the same, 11 to 12 francs of our money.

In Venice, for example, the Doge Andrea Vendramin (1476) with 170,000 ducats passed for an exceedingly rich man (Malipiero, l. c. vii. ii. p. 666. The confiscated fortune of Colleoni amounted to 216,000 florins, l. c. p. 244.

About 1460 the Patriarch of Aquileia, Ludovico Patavino, with 200,000 ducats, was called 'perhaps the richest of all Italians.' (Gasp. Veroneus. *Vita Pauli II.*, in Murat. iii. ii. col. 1027.) Elsewhere fabulous statements.

Antonio Grimani paid 30,000 ducats for his son's election as Cardinal. His ready money alone was put at 100,000 ducats. (*Chron. Venetum*, Murat. xxiv. col. 125.)

For notices as to the grain in commerce and on the market at Venice, see in particular Malipiero, l. c. vii. ii. p. 709 sqq. Date 1498.

In 1522 it is no longer Venice, but Genoa, next to Rome, which ranks as the richest city in Italy (only credible on the authority of Francesc. Vettori. See his history in the *Archiv. Stor.* Append. tom. vi. p. 343). Bandello, *parte* ii. *novello* 34 and 42, names as the richest Genoese merchant of his time Ansaldo Grimaldi.

Between 1400 and 1580 Franc. Sansovino assumes a depreciation of 50 per cent. in the value of money. (*Venezia*, fol. 151 bis.)

In Lombardy it is believed that the relation between the price of corn about the middle of the fifteenth and that at the middle of the present

This statistical estimate of outward life is, however, uniformly accompanied by the narrative of political events to which we have already referred.

Florence not only existed under political forms more varied

century is as 3 to 8. (Sacco di Piacenza, in *Archiv. Stor.* Append. tom. v. Note of editor Scarabelli.)

At Ferrara there were people at the time of Duke Borso with 50,000 to 60,000 ducats (*Diario Ferrarese*, Murat. xxiv. col. 207, 214, 218; an extravagant statement, col. 187). In Florence the data are exceptional and do not justify a conclusion as to averages. Of this kind are the loans to foreign princes, in which the names of one or two houses only appear, but which were in fact the work of great companies. So too the enormous fines levied on defeated parties; we read, e.g. that from 1430 to 1453 seventy-seven families paid 4,875,000 gold florins (Varchi, iii. p. 115 sqq.), and that Giannozzo Mannetti alone, of whom we shall have occasion to speak hereafter, was forced to pay a sum of 135,000 gold florins, and was reduced thereby to beggary (Reumont, i. 157).

The fortune of Giovanni Medici amounted at his death (1428) to 179,221 gold florins, but the latter alone of his two sons Cosimo and Lorenzo left at his death (1440) as much as 235,137 (Fabroni, *Laur. Med.* Adnot. 2). Cosimo's son Piero left (1469) 237,982 scudi (Reumont, *Lorenzo de' Medici*, i. 286).

It is a proof of the general activity of trade that the forty-four goldsmiths on the Ponte Vecchio paid in the fourteenth century a rent of 800 florins to the Government (Vasari, ii. 114, *Vita di Taddeo Gaddi*). The diary of Buonaccorso Pitti (in Delécluze, *Florence et ses Vicissitudes*, vol. ii.) is full of figures, which, however, only prove in general the high price of commodities and the low value of money.

For Rome, the income of the Curia, which was derived from all Europe, gives us no criterion; nor are statements about papal treasures and the fortunes of cardinals very trustworthy. The well-known banker Agostino Chigi left (1520) a fortune of in all 800,000 ducats (*Lettere Pittoriche*, i. Append. 48).

During the high prices of the year 1505 the value of the *staro ferrarrese del grano*, which commonly weighed from 68 to 70 pounds (German), rose to 1⅓ ducats. The *semola* or *remolo* was sold at *venti soldi lo staro;* in the following fruitful years the *staro* fetched six *soldi.* Bonaventura Pistofilo, p. 494. At Ferrara the rent of a house yearly in 1455 was 25 *Lire;* comp. *Atti e memorie*, Parma, vi. 250; see 265 sqq. for a documentary statement of the prices which were paid to artists and amanuenses.

From the inventory of the Medici (extracts in Muntz, *Prècurseurs*, 158 sqq.) it appears that the jewels were valued at 12,205 ducats; the rings at 1,792; the pearls (apparently distinguished from other jewels, S.G.C.M.) at 3,512; the medallions, cameos and mosaics at 2,579; the vases at 4,850; the reliquaries and the like at 3,600; the library at 2,700; the silver at 7,000. Giov. Rucellai reckons that in 1473 (?) he has paid 60,000

than those of the free states of Italy and of Europe generally, but it reflected upon them far more deeply. It is a faithful mirror of the relations of individuals and classes to a variable whole. The pictures of the great civic democracies in France and in Flanders, as they are delineated in Froissart, and the narratives of the German chroniclers of the fourteenth century, are in truth of high importance; but in comprehensiveness of thought and in the rational development of the story, none will bear comparison with the Florentines. The rule of the nobility, the tyrannies, the struggles of the middle class with the proletariate, limited and unlimited democracy, pseudo-democracy, the primacy of a single house, the theocracy of Savonarola, and the mixed forms of government which prepared the way for the Medicean despotism—all are so described that the inmost motives of the actors are laid bare to the light.[1] At length Macchiavelli in his Florentine history (down to 1492) represents his native city as a living organism

gold florins in taxes, 10,000 for the dowries of his five daughters, 2,000 for the improvement of the church of Santa Maria Novella. In 1474 he lost 20,000 gold florins through the intrigues of an enemy. (*Autografo dallo Tibaldone di G.R.*, Florence, 1872). The marriage of Barnardo Rucellai with Nannina, the sister of Lorenzo de' Medici, cost 3,686 florins (Muntz, *Précurseurs*, 244, i).

[1] So far as Cosimo (1433–1465) and his grandson Lorenzo Magnifico (d. 1492) are concerned, the author refrains from any criticism on their internal policy. The exaltation of both, particularly of Lorenzo, by William Roscoe (*Life of Lorenzo de' Medici, called the Magnificent*, 1st ed. Liverpool, 1795; 10th ed. London, 1851), seems to have been a principal cause of the reaction of feeling against them. This reaction appeared first in Sismondi (*Hist. des Rép. Italiennes*, xi.), in reply to whose strictures, sometimes unreasonably severe, Roscoe again came forward (*Illustrations, Historical and Critical, of the Life of Lor. d. Med.*, London, 1822); later in Gino Capponi (*Archiv. Stor. Ital.* i. (1842), pp. 315 sqq.), who afterwards (*Storia della Rep. di Firenze*, 2 vols. Florence, 1875) gave further proofs and explanations of his judgment. See also the work of Von Reumont (*Lor. d. Med. il Magn.*), 2 vols. Leipzig, 1874, distinguished no less by the judicial calmness of its views than by the mastery it displays of the extensive materials used. See also A. Castelman: *Les Medicis*, 2 vols. Paris, 1879. The subject here is only casually touched upon. Comp. two works of B. Buser (Leipzig, 1879) devoted to the home and foreign policy of the Medici. (1) *Die Beziehungen der Medicus zu Frankreich.* 1434–1494, &c. (2) *Lorenzo de' Medici als italienischen Staatsman*, &c., 2nd ed., 1883.

and its development as a natural and individual process; he is the first of the moderns who has risen to such a conception. It lies without our province to determine whether and in what points Macchiavelli may have done violence to history, as is notoriously the case in his life of Castruccio Castracane—a fancy picture of the typical despot. We might find something to say against every line of the 'Istorie Fiorentine,' and yet the great and unique value of the whole would remain unaffected. And his contemporaries and successors, Jacopo Pitti, Guicciardini, Segni, Varchi, Vettori, what a circle of illustrious names! And what a story it is which these masters tell us! The great and memorable drama of the last decades of the Florentine republic is here unfolded. The voluminous record of the collapse of the highest and most original life which the world could then show may appear to one but as a collection of curiosities, may awaken in another a devilish delight at the shipwreck of so much nobility and grandeur, to a third may seem like a great historical assize; for all it will be an object of thought and study to the end of time. The evil, which was for ever troubling the peace of the city, was its rule over once powerful and now conquered rivals like Pisa—a rule of which the necessary consequence was a chronic state of violence. The only remedy, certainly an extreme one and which none but Savonarola could have persuaded Florence to accept, and that only with the help of favourable chances, would have been the well-timed resolution of Tuscany into a federal union of free cities. At a later period this scheme, then no more than the dream of a past age, brought (1548) a patriotic citizen of Lucca to the scaffold.[1] From this evil and from the ill-

[1] Franc. Burlamacchi, father of the head of the Lucchese Protestants, Michele B. See *Arch. Stor. Ital.* ser. i. tom. x., pp. 435–599; Documenti, pp. 146 sqq.; further Carlo Minutoli, *Storia di Fr. B.*, Lucca, 1844, and the important additions of Leone del Prete in the *Giornale Storico degli Archiv. Toscani*, iv. (1860), pp. 309 sqq. It is well known how Milan, by its hard treatment of the neighbouring cities from the eleventh to the thirteenth century, prepared the way for the foundation of a great despotic state. Even at the time of the extinction of the Visconti in 1447, Milan frustrated the deliverance of Upper Italy, principally through not accepting the plan of a confederation of equal cities. Comp. Corio, fol. 358 sqq.

starred Guelph sympathies of Florence for a foreign prince, which familiarised it with foreign intervention, came all the disasters which followed. But who does not admire the people, which was wrought up by its venerated preacher to a mood of such sustained loftiness, that for the first time in Italy it set the example of sparing a conquered foe, while the whole history of its past taught nothing but vengeance and extermination? The glow which melted patriotism into one with moral regeneration may seem, when looked at from a distance, to have soon passed away; but its best results shine forth again in the memorable siege of 1529–30. They were 'fools,' as Guicciardini then wrote, who drew down this storm upon Florence, but he confesses himself that they achieved things which seemed incredible; and when he declares that sensible people would have got out of the way of the danger, he means no more than that Florence ought to have yielded itself silently and ingloriously into the hands of its enemies. It would no doubt have preserved its splendid suburbs and gardens, and the lives and prosperity of countless citizens; but it would have been the poorer by one of its greatest and most ennobling memories.

In many of their chief merits the Florentines are the pattern and the earliest type of Italians and modern Europeans generally; they are so also in many of their defects. When Dante compares the city which was always mending its constitution with the sick man who is continually changing his posture to escape from pain, he touches with the comparison a permanent feature of the political life of Florence. The great modern fallacy that a constitution can be made, can be manufactured by a combination of existing forces and tendencies,[1] was constantly cropping up in stormy times; even Macchiavelli is not wholly free from it. Constitutional artists were never wanting who by an ingenious distribution and division of political

[1] On the third Sunday in Advent, 1494, Savonarola preached as follows on the method of bringing about a new constitution: The sixteen companies of the city were each to work out a plan, the Gonfalonieri to choose the four best of these, and the Signory to name the best of all on the reduced list. Things, however, took a different turn, under the influence indeed of the preacher himself. See P. Villari, *Savonarola.* Besides this sermon, S. had written a remarkable *Trattato circa il reggimento di Firenze* (reprinted at Lucca, 1817).

power, by indirect elections of the most complicated kind, by the establishment of nominal offices, sought to found a lasting order of things, and to satisfy or to deceive the rich and the poor alike. They naïvely fetch their examples from classical antiquity, and borrow the party names 'ottimati,' 'aristocrazia,'[1] as a matter of course. The world since then has become used to these expressions and given them a conventional European sense, whereas all former party names were purely national, and either characterised the cause at issue or sprang from the caprice of accident. But how a name colours or discolours a political cause!

But of all who thought it possible to construct a state, the greatest beyond all comparison was Macchiavelli.[2] He treats existing forces as living and active, takes a large and an accurate view of alternative possibilities, and seeks to mislead neither himself nor others. No man could be freer from vanity or ostentation; indeed, he does not write for the public, but either for princes and administrators or for personal friends. The danger for him does not lie in an affectation of genius or in a false order of ideas, but rather in a powerful imagination which he evidently controls with difficulty. The objectivity of his political judgment is sometimes appalling in its sincerity; but it is the sign of a time of no ordinary need and peril, when it was a hard matter to believe in right, or to credit others with just dealing. Virtuous indignation at his expense is thrown away upon us who have seen in what sense political morality is understood by the statesmen of our own century. Macchiavelli was at all events able to forget himself in his cause. In truth, although his writings, with the exception of very few words, are altogether destitute of enthusiasm, and although the Florentines themselves treated him at last as a criminal,[3] he was a patriot in the fullest meaning of the word. But free as he was, like most of his contemporaries, in speech and morals, the welfare of the state was yet his first and last thought.

[1] The latter first in 1527, after the expulsion of the Medici. See Varchi, i. 121, &c.

[2] Macchiavelli, *Storie Fior.* l. iii. cap. 1: 'Un Savio dator di leggi,' could save Florence.

[3] Varchi, *Stor. Fior.* i. p. 210.

His most complete programme for the construction of a new political system at Florence is set forth in the memorial to Leo X.,[1] composed after the death of the younger Lorenzo Medici, Duke of Urbino (d. 1519), to whom he had dedicated his 'Prince.' The state was by that time in extremities and utterly corrupt, and the remedies proposed are not always morally justifiable; but it is most interesting to see how he hopes to set up the republic in the form of a moderate democracy, as heiress to the Medici. A more ingenious scheme of concessions to the Pope, to the Pope's various adherents, and to the different Florentine interests, cannot be imagined; we might fancy ourselves looking into the works of a clock. Principles, observations, comparisons, political forecasts, and the like are to be found in numbers in the 'Discorsi,' among them flashes of wonderful insight. He recognises, for example, the law of a continuous though not uniform development in republican institutions, and requires the constitution to be flexible and capable of change, as the only means of dispensing with bloodshed and banishments. For a like reason, in order to guard against private violence and foreign interference—'the death of all freedom'—he wishes to see introduced a judicial procedure ('accusa') against hated citizens, in place of which Florence had hitherto had nothing but the court of scandal. With a masterly hand the tardy and involuntary decisions are characterised, which at critical moments play so important a part in republican states. Once, it is true, he is misled by his imagination and the pressure of events into unqualified praise of the people, which chooses its officers, he says, better than any prince, and which can be cured of its errors by 'good advice.'[2] With regard to the government of Tuscany, he has no doubt that it belongs to his native city, and maintains, in a special 'Discorso' that the reconquest of Pisa is a question of life or death; he deplores that Arezzo, after the rebellion of 1502, was not razed to the ground; he admits in general that Italian republics must be allowed to expand freely and add to their territory in order to enjoy peace at home, and not to be

[1] 'Discorso sopra il riformar lo Stato di Firenze,' in the *Opere Minori*, p. 207.

[2] The same view, doubtless borrowed from here, occurs in Montesquieu.

themselves attacked by others, but declares that Florence had always begun at the wrong end, and from the first made deadly enemies of Pisa, Lucca, and Siena, while Pistoja, 'treated like a brother,' had voluntarily submitted to her.[1]

It would be unreasonable to draw a parallel between the few other republics which still existed in the fifteenth century and this unique city—the most important workshop of the Italian, and indeed of the modern European spirit. Siena suffered from the gravest organic maladies, and its relative prosperity in art and industry must not mislead us on this point. Æneas Sylvius[2] looks with longing from his native town over to the 'merry' German imperial cities, where life is embittered by no confiscations of land and goods, by no arbitrary officials, and by no political factions.[3] Genoa scarcely comes within range of our task, as before the time of Andrea Doria it took almost no part in the Renaissance. Indeed, the inhabitant of the Riviera was proverbial among Italians for his contempt of all higher culture.[4] Party conflicts here assumed so fierce a character, and disturbed so violently the whole course of life, that we can hardly understand how, after so many revolutions and invasions, the Genoese ever contrived to return to an endurable condition. Perhaps it was owing to the fact that nearly all who took part in public affairs were at the same

[1] Belonging to a rather later period (1532?). Compare the opinion of Guicciardini, terrible in its frankness, on the condition and inevitable organisation of the Medicean party. *Lettere di Principi*, iii. fol. 124, (ediz. Venez. 1577).

[2] Æn. Sylvii, *Apologia ad Martinum Mayer*, p. 701. To the same effect Macchiavelli, *Discorsi*, i. 55, and elsewhere.

[3] How strangely modern half-culture affected political life is shown by the party struggles of 1535. Della Valle, *Lettere Sanesi*, iii. p. 317. A number of small shopkeepers, excited by the study of Livy and of Macchiavelli's *Discorsi*, call in all seriousness for tribunes of the people and other Roman magistrates against the misgovernment of the nobles and the official classes.

[4] Piero Valeriano, *De Infelicitate Literator.*, speaking of Bartolommeo della Rovere. (The work of P. V. written 1527 is quoted according to the edition by Menken, *Analecta de Calamitate Literatorum*, Leipz. 1707.) The passage here meant can only be that at p. 384, from which we cannot infer what is stated in the text, but in which we read that B. d. R. wished to make his son abandon a taste for study which he had conceived and put him into business.

time almost without exception active men of business.[1] The example of Genoa shows in a striking manner with what insecurity wealth and vast commerce, and with what internal disorder the possession of distant colonies, are compatible.

Lucca is of small significance in the fifteenth century.

[1] Senarega, *De reb. Genuens*, in Murat. xxiv. col. 548. For the insecurity of the time see esp. col. 519, 525, 528, &c. For the frank language of the envoy on the occasion of the surrender of the state to Francesco Sforza (1464), when the envoy told him that Genoa surrendered in the hope of now living safely and comfortably, see Cagnola, *Archiv. Stor.* iii. p. 165 sqq. The figures of the Archbishop, Doge, Corsair, and (later) Cardinal Paolo Fregoso form a notable contrast to the general picture of the condition of Italy.

CHAPTER VIII.

THE FOREIGN POLICY OF THE ITALIAN STATES.

As the majority of the Italian states were in their internal constitution works of art, that is, the fruit of reflection and careful adaptation, so was their relation to one another and to foreign countries also a work of art. That nearly all of them were the result of recent usurpations, was a fact which exercised as fatal an influence in their foreign as in their internal policy. Not one of them recognised another without reserve; the same play of chance which had helped to found and consolidate one dynasty might upset another. Nor was it always a matter of choice with the despot whether to keep quiet or not. The necessity of movement and aggrandisement is common to all illegitimate powers. Thus Italy became the scene of a 'foreign policy' which gradually, as in other countries also, acquired the position of a recognised system of public law. The purely objective treatment of international affairs, as free from prejudice as from moral scruples, attained a perfection which sometimes is not without a certain beauty and grandeur of its own. But as a whole it gives us the impression of a bottomless abyss.

Intrigues, armaments, leagues, corruption and treason make up the outward history of Italy at this period. Venice in particular was long accused on all hands of seeking to conquer the whole peninsula, or gradually so to reduce its strength that one state after another must fall into her hands.[1] But on a closer view it is evident that this complaint did not come from the people, but rather from the courts and official classes, which were commonly abhorred by their subjects, while the mild government of Venice had secured for it general confidence.[2] Even Florence, with its restive subject cities, found

[1] So Varchi, at a much later time. *Stor. Fiorent.* i. 57.

[2] Galeazzo Maria Sforza, indeed, declared the contrary (1467) to the Venetian agent, namely, that Venetian subjects had offered to join him in

itself in a false position with regard to Venice, apart from all commercial jealousy and from the progress of Venice in Romagna. At last the League of Cambray actually did strike a serious blow at the state (p. 68), which all Italy ought to have supported with united strength.

The other states, also, were animated by feelings no less unfriendly, and were at all times ready to use against one another any weapon which their evil conscience might suggest. Ludovico Moro, the Aragonese kings of Naples, and Sixtus IV.—to say nothing of the smaller powers—kept Italy in a state of constant and perilous agitation. It would have been well if the atrocious game had been confined to Italy; but it lay in the nature of the case that intervention and help should at last be sought from abroad—in particular from the French and the Turks.

The sympathies of the people at large were throughout on the side of France. Florence had never ceased to confess with shocking *naïveté* its old Guelph preference for the French.[1] And when Charles VIII. actually appeared on the south of the Alps, all Italy accepted him with an enthusiasm which to himself and his followers seemed unaccountable.[2] In the imagina-

making war on Venice; but this is only vapouring Comp. Malipiero, *Annali Veneti*, *Archiv. Stor.* vii. i. p. 216 sqq. On every occasion cities and villages voluntarily surrendered to Venice, chiefly, it is true, those that escaped from the hands of some despot, while Florence had to keep down the neighbouring republics, which were used to independence, by force of arms, as Guicciardini (*Ricordi*, n. 29) observes.

[1] Most strongly, perhaps, in an instruction to the ambassadors going to Charles VII. in the year 1452. (See Fabroni, *Cosmus*, Adnot. 107, fol. ii. pp. 200 sqq.) The Florentine envoys were instructed to remind the king of the centuries of friendly relations which had subsisted between France and their native city, and to recall to him that Charles the Great had delivered Florence and Italy from the barbarians (Lombards), and that Charles I. and the Romish Church were 'fondatori della parte Guelfa. Il qual fundamento fa cagione della ruina della contraria parte e introdusse lo stato di felicità, in che noi siamo.' When the young Lorenzo visited the Duke of Anjou, then staying at Florence, he put on a French dress. Fabroni, ii. p. 9.

[2] Comines, *Charles VIII.* chap. x. The French were considered 'comme saints.' Comp. chap. 17; *Chron. Venetum*, in Murat. xxiv. col. 5, 10, 14, 15; Matarazzo, *Cron. di Perugia*, *Arch. Stor.* xvi. ii. p. 23, not to speak of countless other proofs. See especially the documents in Desjardins, op. cit. p. 127, note 1.

tion of the Italians, to take Savonarola for an example, the ideal picture of a wise, just, and powerful saviour and ruler was still living, with the difference that he was no longer the emperor invoked by Dante, but the Capetian king of France. With his departure the illusion was broken; but it was long before all understood how completely Charles VIII., Louis XII., and Francis I. had mistaken their true relation to Italy, and by what inferior motives they were led. The princes, for their part, tried to make use of France in a wholly different way. When the Franco-English wars came to an end, when Louis XI. began to cast about his diplomatic nets on all sides, and Charles of Burgundy to embark on his foolish adventures, the Italian Cabinets came to meet them at every point. It became clear that the intervention of France was only a question of time, even though the claims on Naples and Milan had never existed, and that the old interference with Genoa and Piedmont was only a type of what was to follow. The Venetians, in fact, expected it as early as 1642.[1] The mortal terror of the Duke Galeazzo Maria of Milan during the Burgundian war, in which he was apparently the ally of Charles as well as of Louis, and consequently had reason to dread an attack from both, is strikingly shown in his correspondence.[2] The plan of an equilibrium of the four chief Italian powers, as understood by Lorenzo the Magnificent, was but the assumption of a cheerful optimistic spirit, which had outgrown both the recklessness of an experimental policy and the superstitions of Florentine Guelphism, and persisted in hoping the best. When Louis XI. offered him aid in the war against Ferrante of Naples and Sixtus IV., he replied, 'I cannot set my own advantage above the safety of all Italy; would to God it never came into the mind of the French kings to try their strength in this country! Should they ever do so, Italy is lost.'[3] For the other princes,

[1] *Pii II. Commentarii*, x. p. 492.

[2] Gingins, *Dépêches des Ambassadeurs Milanais, etc.* i. pp. 26, 153, 279, 283, 285, 327, 331, 345, 359; ii. pp. 29, 37, 101, 217, 306. Charles once spoke of giving Milan to the young Duke of Orleans.

[3] Niccolò Valori, *Vita di Lorenzo*, Flor. 1568. Italian translation of the Latin original, first printed in 1749 (later in Galletti, *Phil. Villani, Liber de Civit. Flor. famosis Civibus*, Florence, 1847, pp. 161–183; passage here referred to p. 171). It must not, however, be forgotten that this earliest

the King of France was alternately a bugbear to themselves and their enemies, and they threatened to call him in whenever they saw no more convenient way out of their difficulties. The Popes, in their turn, fancied that they could make use of France without any danger to themselves, and even Innocent VIII. imagined that he could withdraw to sulk in the North, and return as a conqueror to Italy at the head of a French army.[1]

Thoughtful men, indeed, foresaw the foreign conquest long before the expedition of Charles VIII.[2] And when Charles was back again on the other side of the Alps, it was plain to

biography, written soon after the death of Lorenzo, is a flattering rather than a faithful portrait, and that the words here attributed to Lorenzo are not mentioned by the French reporter, and can, in fact, hardly have been uttered. Comines, who was commissioned by Louis XI. to go to Rome and Florence, says (*Mémoires*, l. vi. chap. 5): 'I could not offer him an army, and had nothing with me but my suite.' (Comp. Reumont, *Lorenzo*, i. p. 197, 429; ii. 598). In a letter from Florence to Louis XI. we read (Aug. 23, 1478: 'Omnis spes nostra reposita est in favoribus suæ majestatis.' A. Desjardins, *Négociations Diplomatiques de la France avec la Toscane* (Paris, 1859), i. p. 173. Similarly Lorenzo himself in Kervyn de Lettenhove, *Lettres et Négociations de Philippe de Comines*, i. p. 190. Lorenzo, we see, is in fact the one who humbly begs for help, not who proudly declines it.

Dr. Geiger in his appendix maintains that Dr. Burchhardt's view as to Lorenzo's national Italian policy is not borne out by evidence. Into this discussion the translator cannot enter. It would need strong proof to convince him that the masterly historical perception of Dr. Burchhardt was in error as to a subject which he has studied with minute care. In an age when diplomatic lying and political treachery were matters of course, documentary evidence loses much of its weight, and cannot be taken without qualification as representing the real feelings of the persons concerned, who fenced, turned about, and lied, first on one side and then on another, with an agility surprising to those accustomed to live among truth-telling people (S.G.C.M.)

Authorities quoted by Dr. Geiger are: Reumont, *Lorenzo*, 2nd ed., i. 310; ii. 450. Desjardins: *Négociations Diplomatiques de la France avec la Toscane* (Paris, 1859), i. 173. Kervyn de Lettenhove, *Lettres et Négociations de Philippe de Comines*, i. 180.

[1] Fabroni, *Laurentius Magnificus*, Adnot. 205 sqq. In one of his Briefs it was said literally, 'Flectere si nequeo superos, Acheronta movebo;' but it is to be hoped that he did not allude to the Turks. (Villari, *Storia di Savonarola*, ii. p. 48 of the 'Documenti.')

[2] E.g. Jovian. Pontan. in his *Charon*. In the dialogue between Æcus, Minos, and Mercurius (*Op.* ed. Bas. ii. p. 1167) the first says: 'Vel quod haud multis post sæculis futurum auguror, ut Italia, cujus intestina te

every eye that an era of intervention had begun. Misfortune now followed on misfortune; it was understood too late that France and Spain, the two chief invaders, had become great European powers, that they would be no longer satisfied with verbal homage, but would fight to the death for influence and territory in Italy. They had begun to resemble the centralised Italian states, and indeed to copy them, only on a gigantic scale. Schemes of annexation or exchange of territory were for a time indefinitely multiplied. The end, as is well known, was the complete victory of Spain, which, as sword and shield of the counter-reformation, long held the Papacy among its other subjects. The melancholy reflections of the philosophers could only show them how those who had called in the barbarians all came to a bad end.

Alliances were at the same time formed with the Turks too, with as little scruple or disguise; they were reckoned no worse than any other political expedients. The belief in the unity of Western Christendom had at various times in the course of the Crusades been seriously shaken, and Frederick II. had probably outgrown it. But the fresh advance of the Oriental nations, the need and the ruin of the Greek Empire, had revived the old feeling, though not in its former strength, throughout Western Europe. Italy, however, was a striking exception to this rule. Great as was the terror felt for the Turks, and the actual danger from them, there was yet scarcely a government of any consequence which did not conspire against other Italian states with Mohammed II. and his successors. And when they did not do so, they still had the credit of it; nor was it worse than the sending of emissaries to poison the cisterns of Venice, which was the charge brought against the heirs of Alfonso King of Naples.[1] From a scoundrel like Sigismondo Malatesta nothing better could be expected than that he should

odia male habent Minos, in unius redacta ditionem resumat imperii majestatem.' And in reply to Mercury's warning against the Turks, Æcus answers: 'Quamquam timenda hæc sunt, tamen si vetera respicimus, non ab Asia aut Græcia, verum a Gallis Germanisque timendum Italiæ semper fuit.'

[1] Comines, *Charles VIII.*, chap. 7. How Alfonso once tried in time of war to seize his opponents at a conference, is told by Nantiporto, in Murat. iii. ii. col. 1073. He was a genuine predecessor of Cæsar Borgia.

call the Turks into Italy.[1] But the Aragonese monarchs of Naples, from whom Mohammed—at the instigation, we read, of other Italian governments, especially of Venice [2]—had once wrested Otranto (1480), afterwards hounded on the Sultan Bajazet II. against the Venetians.[3] The same charge was brought against Ludovico Moro. 'The blood of the slain, and the misery of the prisoners in the hands of the Turks, cry to God for vengeance against him,' says the state historian. In Venice, where the government was informed of everything, it was known that Giovanni Sforza, ruler of Pesaro, the cousin of the Moor, had entertained the Turkish ambassadors on their way to Milan.[4] The two most respectable among the Popes of the fifteenth century, Nicholas V. and Pius II., died in the deepest grief at the progress of the Turks, the latter indeed amid the preparations for a crusade which he was hoping to lead in person; their successors embezzled the contributions sent for this purpose from all parts of Christendom, and degraded the indulgences granted in return for them into a private commercial speculation.[5] Innocent VIII. consented to be gaoler to the fugitive Prince Djem, for a salary paid by the prisoner's brother Bajazet II., and Alexander VI. supported the steps taken by Ludovico Moro in Constantinople to further a Turkish assault upon Venice (1498), whereupon the latter threatened him with a Council.[6] It is clear that the notorious

[1] *Pii II. Commentarii*, x. p. 492. See a letter of Malatesta in which he recommends to Mohammed II. a portrait-painter, Matteo Passo of Verona, and announces the despatch of a book on the art of war, probably in the year 1463, in Baluz. *Miscell.* iii. 113. What Galeazzo Maria of Milan told in 1467 to a Venetian envoy, namely, that he and his allies would join with the Turks to destroy Venice, was said merely by way of threat. Comp. Malipiero, *Ann. Veneti*, *Archiv. Stor.* vii. i. p. 222. For Boccalino, see page 36.

[2] Porzio, *Congiura dei Baroni*, l. i. p. 5. That Lorenzo, as Porzio hints, really had a hand in it, is not credible. On the other hand, it seems only too certain that Venice prompted the Sultan to the deed. See Romanin, *Storia Documentata di Venezia*, lib. xi. cap. 3. After Otranto was taken, Vespasiano Bisticci uttered his 'Lamento d'Italia, *Archiv. Stor. Ital.* iv. pp. 452 sqq.

[3] *Chron. Venet.* in Murat. xxiv. col. 14 and 76.

[4] Malipiero, l. c. p. 565, 568.

[5] Trithem. *Annales Hirsaug*, ad. a. 1490, tom. ii. pp. 535 sqq.

[6] Malipiero, l. c. 161; comp. p. 152. For the surrender of Djem to

alliance between Francis I. and Soliman II. was nothing new or unheard of.

Indeed, we find instances of whole populations to whom it seemed no particular crime to go over bodily to the Turks. Even if it were only held out as a threat to oppressive governments, this is at least a proof that the idea had become familiar. As early as 1480 Battista Mantovano gives us clearly to understand that most of the inhabitants of the Adriatic coast foresaw something of this kind, and that Ancona in particular desired it.[1] When Romagna was suffering from the oppressive government of Leo X., a deputy from Ravenna said openly to the Legate, Cardinal Guilio Medici: 'Monsignore, the honourable Republic of Venice will not have us, for fear of a dispute with the Holy See; but if the Turk comes to Ragusa we will put ourselves into his hands.'[2]

It was a poor but not wholly groundless consolation for the enslavement of Italy then begun by the Spaniards, that the country was at least secured from the relapse into barbarism which would have awaited it under the Turkish rule.[3] By itself, divided as it was, it could hardly have escaped this fate.

If, with all these drawbacks, the Italian statesmanship of this period deserves our praise, it is only on the ground of its practical and unprejudiced treatment of those questions which were not affected by fear, passion, or malice. Here was no feudal system after the northern fashion, with its artificial

Charles VIII. see p. 145, from which it is clear that a connection of the most shameful kind existed between Alexander and Bajazet, even if the documents in Burcardus be spurious. See on the subject Ranke, *Zur Kritik neuerer Geschichtschreiber*, 2 Auflage, Leipzig, 1874, p. 99, and Gregorovius, bd. vii. 353, note 1. *Ibid.* p. 353, note 2, a declaration of the Pope that he was not allied with the Turks.

[1] Bapt. Mantuanus, *De Calamitatibus Temporum*, at the end of the second book, in the song of the Nereid Doris to the Turkish fleet.

[2] Tommaso Gar, *Relaz. della Corte di Roma*, i. p. 55.

[3] Ranke, *Geschichte der romanischen und germanischen Völker*. The opinion of Michelet (*Reforme*, p. 467), that the Turks would have adopted Western civilisation in Italy, does not satisfy me. This mission of Spain is hinted at, perhaps for the first time, in the speech delivered by Fedra Inghirami in 1510 before Julius II., at the celebration of the capture of Bugia by the fleet of Ferdinand the Catholic. See *Anecdota Litteraria*, ii. p. 419.

scheme of rights; but the power which each possessed he held in practice as in theory. Here was no attendant nobility to foster in the mind of the prince the mediæval sense of honour, with all its strange consequences; but princes and counsellors were agreed in acting according to the exigencies of the particular case and to the end they had in view. Towards the men whose services were used and towards allies, come from what quarter they might, no pride of caste was felt which could possibly estrange a supporter; and the class of the Condottieri, in which birth was a matter of indifference, shows clearly enough in what sort of hands the real power lay; and lastly, the Government, in the hands of an enlightened despot, had an incomparably more accurate acquaintance with its own country and that of its neighbours, than was possessed by northern contemporaries, and estimated the economical and moral capacities of friend and foe down to the smallest particular. The rulers were, notwithstanding grave errors, born masters of statistical science. With such men negotiation was possible; it might be presumed that they would be convinced and their opinion modified when practical reasons were laid before them. When the great Alfonso of Naples was (1434) a prisoner of Filippo Maria Visconti, he was able to satisfy his gaoler that the rule of the House of Anjou instead of his own at Naples would make the French masters of Italy; Filippo Maria set him free without ransom and made an alliance with him.[1] A northern prince would scarcely have acted in the same way, certainly not one whose morality in other respects was like that of Visconti. What confidence was felt in the power of self-interest is shown by the celebrated visit which Lorenzo the Magnificent, to the universal astonishment of the Florentines, paid the faithless Ferrante at Naples—a man who would be certainly tempted to keep him a prisoner, and was by no means too scrupulous to do so.[2] For to arrest a powerful mon-

[1] Among others Corio, fol. 333. Jov. Pontanus, in his treatise, *De Liberalitate*, cap. 28, considers the free dismissal of Alfonso as a proof of the 'liberalitas' of Filippo Maria. (See above, p. 38, note 1.) Compare the line of conduct adopted with regard to Sforza, fol. 329.

[2] Nic. Valori, *Vita di Lorenzo;* Paul Jovius, *Vita Leonis X.* l. i. The latter certainly upon good authority, though not without rhetorical embellishment. Comp. Reumont, i. 487, and the passage there quoted.

arch, and then to let him go alive, after extorting his signature and otherwise insulting him, as Charles the Bold did to Louis XI. at Péronne (1468), seemed madness to the Italians;[1] so that Lorenzo was expected to come back covered with glory, or else not to come back at all. The art of political persuasion was at this time raised to a point—especially by the Venetian ambassadors—of which northern nations first obtained a conception from the Italians, and of which the official addresses give a most imperfect idea. These are mere pieces of humanistic rhetoric. Nor, in spite of an otherwise ceremonious etiquette, was there in case of need any lack of rough and frank speaking in diplomatic intercourse.[2] A man like Macchiavelli appears in his 'Legazioni' in an almost pathetic light. Furnished with scanty instructions, shabbily equipped, and treated as an agent of inferior rank, he never loses his gift of free and wide observation or his pleasure in picturesque description. From that time Italy was and remained the country of political 'Istruzioni' and 'Relazioni.' There was doubtless plenty of diplomatic ability in other states, but Italy alone at so early a period has preserved documentary evidence of it in considerable quantity. The long despatch on the last period of the life of Ferrante of Naples (January 17, 1494), written by the hand of Pontano and addressed to the Cabinet of Alexander VI., gives us the highest opinion of this class of political writing, although it is only quoted incidentally and as one of many written. And how many other despatches, as important and as vigorously written, in the diplomatic intercourse of this and later times, still remain unknown or unedited![3]

[1] If Comines on this and many other occasions observes and judges as objectively as any Italian, his intercourse with Italians, particularly with Angelo Catto, must be taken into account.

[2] Comp. e.g. Malipiero, pp. 216, 221, 236, 237, 468, &c., and above pp. 88, note 2, and 93, note 1. Comp. Egnatius, fol. 321 *a*. The Pope curses an ambassador; a Venetian envoy insults the Pope; another, to win over his hearers, tells a fable.

[3] In Villari, *Storia di Savonarola*, vol. ii. p. xliii. of the 'Documenti,' among which are to be found other important political letters. Other documents, particularly of the end of the fifteenth century in Baluzius, *Miscellanea*, ed. Mansi, vol. i. See especially the collected despatches of Florentine and Venetian ambassadors at the end of the fifteenth and

A special division of this work will treat of the study of man individually and nationally, which among the Italians went hand in hand with the study of the outward conditions of human life.

beginning of sixteenth centuries in Desjardins, *Négociations diplomatiques de la France avec la Toscane*, vols. i. ii. Paris, 1859, 1861.

CHAPTER IX.

WAR AS A WORK OF ART.

It must here be briefly indicated by what steps the art of war assumed the character of a product of reflection.[1] Throughout the countries of the West the education of the individual soldier in the middle ages was perfect within the limits of the then prevalent system of defence and attack: nor was there any want of ingenious inventors in the arts of besieging and of fortification. But the development both of strategy and of tactics was hindered by the character and duration of military service, and by the ambition of the nobles, who disputed questions of precedence in the face of the enemy, and through simple want of discipline caused the loss of great battles like Crécy and Maupertuis. Italy, on the contrary, was the first country to adopt the system of mercenary troops, which demanded a wholly different organisation; and the early introduction of fire-arms did its part in making war a democratic pursuit, not only because the strongest castles were unable to withstand a bombardment, but because the skill of the engineer, of the gun-founder, and of the artillerist—men belonging to another class than the nobility—was now of the first importance in a campaign. It was felt, with regret, that the value of the individual, which had been the soul of the small and admirably-organised bands of mercenaries, would suffer from these novel means of destruction, which did their work at a distance; and there were Condottieri who opposed to the utmost the introduction at least of the musket, which had been lately invented in Germany.[2]

[1] The subject has been lately treated more fully by Max Jähns, *Die Kriegskunt als Kunst*, Leipzig, 1874.

[2] *Pii II. Comment.* iv. p. 190, ad. a. 1459.

We read that Paolo Vitelli,[1] while recognising and himself adopting the cannon, put out the eyes and cut off the hands of the captured 'schioppettieri,' of the enemy, because he held it unworthy that a gallant, and it might be noble, knight should be wounded and laid low by a common, despised foot soldier. On the whole, however, the new discoveries were accepted and turned to useful account, till the Italians became the teachers of all Europe, both in the building of fortifications and in the means of attacking them.[2] Princes like Federigo of Urbino and Alfonso of Ferrara acquired a mastery of the subject compared to which the knowledge even of Maximilian I. appears superficial. In Italy, earlier than elsewhere, there existed a comprehensive science and art of military affairs; here, for the first time, that impartial delight is taken in able generalship for its own sake, which might, indeed, be expected from the frequent change of party and from the wholly unsentimental mode of action of the Condottieri. During the Milano-Venetian war of 1451 and 1452, between Francesco Sforza and Jacopo Piccinino, the headquarters of the latter were attended by the scholar Gian Antonio Porcello dei Pandoni, commissioned by Alfonso of Naples to write a report of the campaign.[3] It is written, not in the purest, but in a fluent Latin, a little too much in the style of the humanistic bombast of the day, is modelled on Cæsar's Commentaries, and interspersed with speeches, prodigies, and the like. Since for the past hundred years it had been seriously disputed whether Scipio Africanus or Hannibal was the greater,[4] Piccinino

[1] The Cremonese prided themselves on their skill in this department. See *Cronaca di Cremona* in the *Bibliotheca Historica Italica*, vol. i. Milan, 1876, p. 214, and note. The Venetians did the same, Egnatius, fol. 300 sqq.

[2] To this effect Paul Jovius (*Elogia*, p. 184) who adds: 'Nondum enim invecto externarum gentium cruento more, Italia milites sanguinarii et multæ cædis avidi esse didicerant.' We are reminded of Frederick of Urbino, who would have been 'ashamed' to tolerate a printed book in his library. See *Vespas. Fiorent.*

[3] *Porcellii Commentaria Jac. Picinini*, in Murat. xx. A continuation for the war of 1453, *ibid.* xxv. Paul Cortesius (*De Hominibus Doctis*, p. 33, Florence, 1734) criticises the book severely on account of the wretched hexameters.

[4] Porcello calls Scipio Æmilianus by mistake, meaning Africanus Major.

through the whole book must needs be called Scipio and Sforza Hannibal. But something positive had to be reported too respecting the Milanese army; the sophist presented himself to Sforza, was led along the ranks, praised highly all that he saw, and promised to hand it down to posterity.[1] Apart from him the Italian literature of the day is rich in descriptions of wars and strategic devices, written for the use of educated men in general as well as of specialists, while the contemporary narratives of northerners, such as the 'Burgundian War' by Diebold Schelling, still retain the shapelessness and matter-of-fact dryness of a mere chronicle. The greatest *dilettante* who has ever treated in that character[2] of military affairs, was then busy writing his 'Arte della Guerra.' But the development of the individual soldier found its most complete expression in those public and solemn conflicts between one or more pairs of combatants which were practised long before the famous 'Challenge of Barletta'[3] (1503). The victor was assured of the praises of poets and scholars, which were denied to the Northern warrior. The result of these combats was no longer regarded as a Divine judgment, but as a triumph of personal merit, and to the minds of the spectators seemed to be both the decision of an exciting competition and a satisfaction for the honour of the army or the nation.[4]

It is obvious that this purely rational treatment of warlike affairs allowed, under certain circumstances, of the worst atrocities, even in the absence of a strong political hatred, as, for instance, when the plunder of a city had been promised to the

[1] Simonetta, *Hist. Fr. Sfortiæ*, in Murat. xxi. col. 630.

[2] So he was considered. Comp. Bandello, parte i. nov. 40.

[3] Comp. e.g. *De Obsidione Tiphernatium*, in vol. 2, of the *Rer. Italic. Scriptores excodd. Florent.* col. 690. The duel of Marshal Boucicault with Galeazzo Gonzaga (1406) in Cagnola, *Arch. Stor.* iii. p. 25. Infessura tells us of the honour paid by Sixtus IV. to the duellists among his guards. His successors issued bulls against duelling.

[4] We may here notice parenthetically (see Jähns, pp. 26, sqq.) the less favourable side of the tactics of the Condottieri. The combat was often a mere sham-fight, in which the enemy was forced to withdraw by harmless manœuvres. The object of the combatants was to avoid bloodshed, at the worst to make prisoners with a view to the ransom. According to Macchiavelli, the Florentines lost in a great battle in the year 1440 one man only.

troops. After the four days' devastation of Piacenza, which Sforza was compelled to permit to his soldiers (1447), the town long stood empty, and at last had to be peopled by force.[1] Yet outrages like these were nothing compared with the misery which was afterwards brought upon Italy by foreign troops, and most of all by the Spaniards, in whom perhaps a touch of Oriental blood, perhaps familiarity with the spectacles of the Inquisition, had unloosed the devilish element of human nature. After seeing them at work at Prato, Rome, and elsewhere, it is not easy to to take any interest of the higher sort in Ferdinand the Catholic and Charles V., who knew what these hordes were, and yet unchained them. The mass of documents which are gradually brought to light from the cabinets of these rulers will always remain an important source of historical information; but from such men no fruitful political conception can be looked for.

[1] For details, see *Arch. Stor.* Append. tom. v.

CHAPTER X.

THE PAPACY AND ITS DANGERS.

THE Papacy and the dominions of the Church[1] are creations of so peculiar a kind, that we have hitherto, in determining the general characteristics of Italian states, referred to them only occasionally. The deliberate choice and adaptation of political expedients, which gives so great an interest to the other states, is what we find least of all at Rome, since here the spiritual power could constantly conceal or supply the defects of the temporal. And what fiery trials did this state undergo in the fourteenth and the beginning of the fifteenth century, when the Papacy was led captive to Avignon! All, at first, was thrown into confusion; but the Pope had money, troops, and a great statesman and general, the Spaniard Alboronoz, who again brought the ecclesiastical state into complete subjection. The danger of a final dissolution was still greater at the time of the schism, when neither the Roman nor the French Pope was rich enough to reconquer the newly-lost state; but this was done under Martin V., after the unity of the Church was restored, and done again under Eugenius IV., when the same danger was renewed. But the ecclesiastical state was and remained a thorough anomaly among the powers of Italy; in and near Rome itself, the Papacy was defied by the great families of the Colonna, Orsini, Savelli, and Anguillara; in Umbria, in the Marches, and in Romagna, those civic republics had almost ceased to exist, for whose devotion the Papacy had showed so little gratitude; their place had been taken by a crowd of princely dynasties, great or small, whose loyalty

[1] Here once for all we refer our readers to Ranke's *Popes*, vol. i., and to Sugenheim, *Geschichte der Entstehung und Ausbildung des Kirchenstaates*. The still later works of Gregorovius and Reumont have also been made use of, and when they offer new facts or views, are quoted. See also *Geschichte der römischen Papstthums*, W. Wattenbach, Berlin, 1876.

and obedience signified little. As self-dependent powers, standing on their own merits, they have an interest of their own; and from this point of view the most important of them have been already discussed (pp. 28 sqq., 44 sqq.).

Nevertheless, a few general remarks on the Papacy can hardly be dispensed with. New and strange perils and trials came upon it in the course of the fifteenth century, as the political spirit of the nation began to lay hold upon it on various sides, and to draw it within the sphere of its action. The least of these dangers came from the populace or from abroad; the most serious had their ground in the characters of the Popes themselves.

Let us, for this moment, leave out of consideration the countries beyond the Alps. At the time when the Papacy was exposed to mortal danger in Italy, it neither received nor could receive the slightest assistance either from France, then under Louis XI., or from England, distracted by the wars of the Roses, or from the then disorganized Spanish monarchy, or from Germany, but lately betrayed at the Council of Basel. In Italy itself there were a certain number of instructed and even uninstructed people, whose national vanity was flattered by the Italian character of the Papacy; the personal interests of very many depended on its having and retaining this character; and vast masses of the people still believed in the virtue of the Papal blessing and consecration;[1] among them

[1] For the impression made by the blessing of Eugenius IV. in Florence, see *Vespasiano Fiorent*, p. 18. See also the passage quoted in Reumont, *Lorenzo*, i. 171. For the impressive offices of Nicholas V., see Infessura (Eccard, ii. col. 1883 sqq.) and J. Manetti, *Vita Nicolai V.* (Murat. iii. ii. col. 923). For the homage given to Pius II., see *Diario Ferrarese* (Murat. xxiv. col. 205), and *Pii II. Commentarii*, *passim*, esp. iv. 201, 204, and xi. 562. For Florence, see *Delizie degli Eruditi*, xx. 368. Even professional murderers respect the person of the Pope.

The great offices in church were treated as matters of much importance by the pomp-loving Paul II. (Platina, l. c. 321) and by Sixtus IV., who, in spite of the gout, conducted mass at Easter in a sitting posture. (*Jac. Volaterran. Diarium*, Murat. xxiii. col. 131.) It is curious to notice how the people distinguished between the magical efficacy of the blessing and the unworthiness of the man who gave it; when he was unable to give the benediction on Ascension Day, 1481, the populace murmured and cursed him. (*Ibid.* col. 133.)

notorious transgressors like that Vitellozzo Vitelli, who still prayed to be absolved by Alexander VI., when the Pope's son had him slaughtered.[1] But all these grounds of sympathy put together would not have sufficed to save the Papacy from its enemies, had the latter been really in earnest, and had they known how to take advantage of the envy and hatred with which the institution was regarded.

And at the very time when the prospect of help from without was so small, the most dangerous symptoms appeared within the Papacy itself. Living, as it now did, and acting in the spirit of the secular Italian principalities, it was compelled to go through the same dark experiences as they ; but its own exceptional nature gave a peculiar colour to the shadows.

As far as the city of Rome itself is concerned, small account was taken of its internal agitations, so many were the Popes who had returned after being expelled by popular tumult, and so greatly did the presence of the Curia minister to the interests of the Roman people. But Rome not only displayed at times a specific anti-papal radicalism,[2] but in the most serious plots which were then contrived, gave proof of the working of unseen hands from without. It was so in the case of the conspiracy of Stefano Porcaro against Nicholas V. (1453), the very Pope who had done most for the prosperity of the city, but who, by enriching the cardinals, and transforming Rome into a papal fortress, had aroused the discontent of the people.[3] Porcaro aimed at the complete overthrow of the papal authority, and had distinguished accomplices, who, though their names

[1] Macchiavelli, *Scritti Minori*, p. 142, in the well-known essay on the catastrophe of Sinigaglia. It is true that the French and Spanish soldiers were still more zealous than the Italians. Comp. in Paul. Jov. *Vita Leonis X.* (l. ii.) the scene before the battle of Ravenna, in which the Legate, weeping for joy, was surrounded by the Spanish troops, and besought for absolution. See further (*ibid.*) the statements respecting the French in Milan.

[2] In the case of the heretics of Poli, in the Campagna, who held the doctrine that a genuine Pope must show the poverty of Christ as the mark of his calling, we have simply a kind of Waldensian doctrine. Their imprisonment under Paul II. is related by Infessura (Eccard, ii. col. 1893), Platina, p. 317, &c.

[3] As an illustration of this feeling see the poem addressed to the Pope, quoted in Gregorovius, vii. 136.

are not handed down to us,[1] are certainly to be looked for among the Italian governments of the time. Under the pontificate of the same man, Lorenzo Valla concluded his famous declamation against the gift of Constantine, with the wish for the speedy secularisation of the States of the Church.[2]

The Catilinarian gang, with which Pius II. had to contend[3] (1460), avowed with equal frankness their resolution to overthrow the government of the priests, and its leader, Tiburzio, threw the blame on the soothsayers, who had fixed the accomplishment of his wishes for this very year. Several of the chief men of Rome, the Prince of Tarentum, and the Condottiere Jacopo Piccinino, were accomplices and supporters of Tiburzio. Indeed, when we think of the booty which was accumulated in the palaces of wealthy prelates—the conspirators had the Cardinal of Aquileia especially in view—we are surprised that, in an almost unguarded city, such attempts were not more frequent and more successful. It was not without reason that Pius II. preferred to reside anywhere rather than in Rome; and even Paul II.[4] was exposed to no small anxiety through a plot formed by some discharged abbreviators, who, under the command of Platina, besieged the Vatican for twenty days. The Papacy must sooner or later have fallen a victim to such enterprises, if it had not stamped out the aristocratic factions under whose protection these bands of robbers grew to a head.

This task was undertaken by the terrible Sixtus IV. He

[1] *Dialogus de Conjuratione Stephani de Porcariis*, by his contemporary Petrus Godes de Vicenza, quoted and used by Gregorovius, viii. 130. L. B. Alberti, *De Porcaria Conjuratione*, in Murat. xxv. col. 309. Porcari was desirous 'omnem pontificiam turbam funditus exstinguere.' The author concludes: 'Video sane, quo stent loco res Italiæ; intelligo qui sint, quibus hic perturbata esse omnia conducat. . . .' He names them 'Extrinsecus impulsores,' and is of opinion that Porcari will find successors in his misdeeds. The dreams of Porcari certainly bore some resemblance to those of Cola Rienzi. He also referred to himself the poem 'Spirto Gentil,' addressed by Petrarch to Rienzi.

[2] 'Ut Papa tantum vicarius Christi sit et non etiam Cæsaris . . . Tunc Papa et dicetur et erit pater sanctus, pater omnium, pater ecclesiæ,' &c. Valla's work was written rather earlier, and was aimed at Eugenius IV. See Vahlen, *Lor. Valla* (Berlin, 1870), pp. 25 sqq., esp. 32. Nicholas V., on the other hand, is praised by Valla, Gregorovius, vii. 136.

[3] *Pii II. Comment.* iv. pp. 208 sqq. Voigt, *Enea Silvio*, iii. pp. 151 sqq.

[4] Platina, *Vita Pauli II.*

was the first Pope who had Rome and the neighbourhood thoroughly under his control, especially after his successful attack on the House of Colonna, and consequently, both in his Italian policy and in the internal affairs of the Church, he could venture to act with a defiant audacity, and to set at nought the complaints and threats to summon a council which arose from all parts of Europe. He supplied himself with the necessary funds by simony, which suddenly grew to unheard-of proportions, and which extended from the appointment of cardinals down to the granting of the smallest favours.[1] Sixtus himself had not obtained the papal dignity without recourse to the same means.

A corruption so universal might sooner or later bring disastrous consequences on the Holy See, but they lay in the uncertain future. It was otherwise with nepotism, which threatened at one time to destroy the Papacy altogether. Of all the 'nipoti,' Cardinal Pietro Riario enjoyed at first the chief and almost exclusive favour of Sixtus. He soon drew upon him the eyes of all Italy,[2] partly by the fabulous luxury of his life, partly through the reports which were current of his irreligion and his political plans. He bargained with Duke Galeazzo Maria of Milan (1473), that the latter should become King of Lombardy, and then aid him with money and troops to return to Rome and ascend the papal throne; Sixtus, it appears, would have voluntarily yielded it to him.[3] This plan, which, by making the Papacy hereditary, would have ended in the secularization of the papal state, failed through the

[1] Battista Mantovano, *De Calamitatibus Temporum*, l. iii. The Arabian sells incense, the Tyrian purple, the Indian ivory: 'Venalia nobis templa, sacerdotes, altaria sacra, coronæ, ignes, thura, preces, cælum est venale Deusque.' *Opera*, ed. Paris, 1507, fol. 302 *b*. Then follows an exhortation to Pope Sixtus, whose previous efforts are praised, to put an end to these evils.

[2] See e.g. the *Annales Placentini*, in Murat. xx. col. 943.

[3] Corio, *Storia di Milano*, fol. 416–420. Pietro had already helped at the election of Sixtus. See Infessura, in Eccard, *Scriptores*, ii. col. 1895. It is curious that in 1469 it had been prophesied that deliverance would come from Savona (home of Sixtus, elected in 1471) within three years. See the letter and date in Baluz. *Miscell.* iii. p. 181. According to Macchiavelli, *Storie Fiorent.* l. vii. the Venetians poisoned the cardinal. Certainly they were not without motives to do so.

sudden death of Pietro. The second 'nipote,' Girolamo Riario, remained a layman, and did not seek the Pontificate. From this time the 'nipoti,' by their endeavours to found principalities for themselves, became a new source of confusion to Italy. It had already happened that the Popes tried to make good their feudal claims on Naples in favour of their relatives;[1] but since the failure of Calixtus III. such a scheme was no longer practicable, and Girolamo Riario, after the attempt to conquer Florence (and who knows how many other places) had failed, was forced to content himself with founding a state within the limits of the papal dominions themselves. This was, in so far, justifiable, as Romagna, with its princes and civic despots, threatened to shake off the papal supremacy altogether, and ran the risk of shortly falling a prey to Sforza or the Venetians, when Rome interfered to prevent it. But who, at times and in circumstances like these, could guarantee the continued obedience of 'nipoti' and their descendants, now turned into sovereign rulers, to Popes with whom they had no further concern? Even in his lifetime the Pope was not always sure of his own son or nephew, and the temptation was strong to expel the 'nipote' of a predecessor and replace him by one of his own. The reaction of the whole system on the Papacy itself was of the most serious character; all means of compulsion, whether temporal or spiritual, were used without scruple for the most questionable ends, and to these all the other objects of the Apostolic See were made subordinate. And when they were attained, at whatever cost of revolutions and proscriptions, a dynasty was founded which had no stronger interest than the destruction of the Papacy.

At the death of Sixtus, Girolamo was only able to maintain himself in his usurped principality of Forli and Imola by the utmost exertions of his own, and by the aid of the House of Sforza. He was murdered in 1488. In the conclave (1484) which followed the death of Sixtus—that in which Innocent VIII. was elected—an incident occurred which seemed to furnish the Papacy with a new external guarantee. Two cardinals, who, at the same time, were princes of ruling houses, Giovanni

[1] Honorius II. wished, after the death of William I. (1127), to annex Apulia, as a feof reverted to St. Peter.

d'Aragona, son of King Ferrante, and Ascanio Sforza, brother of the Moor, sold their votes with the most shameless effrontery;[1] so that, at any rate, the ruling houses of Naples and Milan became interested, by their participation in the booty, in the continuance of the papal system. Once again, in the following Conclave, when all the cardinals but five sold themselves, Ascanio received enormous sums in bribes, not without cherishing the hope that at the next election he would himself be the favoured candidate.[2]

Lorenzo the Magnificent, on his part, was anxious that the House of Medici should not be sent away with empty hands. He married his daughter Maddalena to the son of the new Pope—the first who publicly acknowledged his children—Franceschetto Cybò, and expected not only favours of all kinds for his own son, Cardinal Giovanni, afterwards Leo X., but also the rapid promotion of his son-in-law.[3] But with respect to the latter, he demanded impossibilities. Under Innocent VIII. there was no opportunity for the audacious nepotism by which states had been founded, since Franceschetto himself was a poor creature who, like his father the Pope, sought power only for the lowest purpose of all—the acquisition and accumulation of money.[4] The manner, however, in which father and son practised this occupation must have led sooner or later to a final catastrophe—the dissolution of the state. If Sixtus had filled his treasury by the rule of spiritual dignities and favours, Innocent and his son, for their part, established an office for the sale of secular favours, in which pardons for murder and manslaughter were sold for large sums of money. Out of every fine 150

[1] Fabroni, *Laurentius Mag.* Adnot. 130. An informer, Vespucci, sends word of both, 'Hanno in ogni elezione a mettere a sacco questa corte, e sono i maggior ribaldi del mondo.'

[2] Corio, fol. 450. Details, partly from unpublished documents, of these acts of bribery in Gregorovius, vii. 310 sqq.

[3] A most characteristic letter of exhortation by Lorenzo in Fabroni, *Laurentius Magn.* Adnot. 217, and extracts in Ranke, *Popes*, i. p. 45, and in Reumont, *Lorenzo*, ii. pp. 482 sqq.

[4] And perhaps of certain Neapolitan feofs, for the sake of which Innocent called in the Angevins afresh against the immovable Ferrante. The conduct of the Pope in this affair and his participation in the second conspiracy of the barons, were equally foolish and dishonest. For his method of treating with foreign powers, see above p. 127, note 2.

ducats were paid into the papal exchequer, and what was over to Franceschetto. Rome, during the latter part of this pontificate, swarmed with licensed and unlicensed assassins; the factions, which Sixtus had begun to put down, were again as active as ever; the Pope, well guarded in the Vatican, was satisfied with now and then laying a trap, in which a wealthy misdoer was occasionally caught. For Franceschetto the chief point was to know by what means, when the Pope died, he could escape with well-filled coffers. He betrayed himself at last, on the occasion of a false report (1490) of his father's death; he endeavoured to carry off all the money in the papal treasury, and when this proved impossible, insisted that, at all events, the Turkish prince, Djem, should go with him, and serve as a living capital, to be advantageously disposed of, perhaps to Ferrante of Naples.[1] It is hard to estimate the political possibilities of remote periods, but we cannot help asking ourselves the question, if Rome could have survived two or three pontificates of this kind. Even with reference to the believing countries of Europe, it was imprudent to let matters go so far that not only travellers and pilgrims, but a whole embassy of Maximilian, King of the Romans, were stripped to their shirts in the neighbourhood of Rome, and that envoys had constantly to turn back without setting foot within the city.

Such a condition of things was incompatible with the conception of power and its pleasures which inspired the gifted Alexander VI. (1492–1503), and the first event that happened was the restoration, at least provisionally, of public order, and the punctual payment of every salary.

Strictly speaking, as we are now discussing phases of Italian civilization, this pontificate might be passed over, since the Borgias are no more Italian than the House of Naples. Alexander spoke Spanish in public with Cæsar; Lucretia, at her entrance to Ferrara, where she wore a Spanish costume, was sung to by Spanish buffoons; their confidential servants consisted of Spaniards, as did also the most ill-famed company of the troops of Cæsar in the war of 1500; and even his hang-

[1] Comp. in particular Infessura, in Eccard. *Scriptores*, ii. *passim*.

man, Don Micheletto, and his poisoner, Sebastian Pinzon,[1] seem to have been of the same nation. Among his other achievements, Cæsar, in true Spanish fashion, killed, according to the rules of the craft, six wild bulls in an enclosed court. But the Roman corruption, which seemed to culminate in this family, was already far advanced when they came to the city.

What they were and what they did has been often and fully described.[2] Their immediate purpose, which, in fact, they attained, was the complete subjugation of the pontifical state. All the petty despots,[3] who were mostly more or less refractory vassals of the Church, were expelled or destroyed; and in Rome itself the two great factions were annihilated, the so-called Guelph Orsini as well as the so-called Ghibelline Colonna. But the means employed were of so frightful a character, that they must certainly have ended in the ruin of the Papacy, had not the contemporaneous death of both father and son by poison suddenly intervened to alter the whole aspect of the situation. The moral indignation of Christendom was certainly no great source of danger to Alexander; at home he was strong enough to extort terror and obedience; foreign rulers were won over to his side, and Louis XII. even aided him to the utmost of his power. The mass of the people throughout Europe had hardly a conception of what was passing in Central Italy. The only moment which was really fraught with danger—when Charles VIII. was in Italy—went by with unexpected fortune, and even then it was not the Papacy as such that was in peril, but Alexander, who risked being supplanted by a more respectable Pope.[4] The great, permanent, and increasing danger for the

[1] According to the *Dispacci di Antonio Giustiniani*, i. p. 60, and iii. p. 309, Seb. Pinzon was a native of Cremona.

[2] Recently by Gregorovius, *Lucrezia Borgia*, 2 Bände 3 Aufl., Stuttgart, 1875.

[3] Except the Bentivoglio at Bologna, and the House of Este at Ferrara. The latter was compelled to form a family relationship, Lucrezia marrying Prince Alfonso.

[4] According to Corio (fol. 479) Charles had thoughts of a Council, of deposing the Pope, and even of carrying him away to France, this upon his return from Naples. According to Benedictus, *Carolus VIII.* (in Eccard, *Scriptores*, ii. col. 1584), Charles, while in Naples, when Pope and cardinals refused to recognise his new crown, had certainly entertained the thought 'de Italiæ imperio deque pontificis statu mutando,' but soon

Papacy lay in Alexander himself, and, above all, in his son Cæsar Borgia.

In the nature of the father, ambition, avarice, and sensuality were combined with strong and brilliant qualities. All the pleasures of power and luxury he granted himself from the first day of his pontificate in the fullest measure. In the choice of means to this end he was wholly without scruple; it was known at once that he would more than compensate himself for the sacrifices which his election had involved,[1] and that the simony of the seller would far exceed the simony of the buyer. It must be remembered that the vice-chancellorship and other offices which Alexander had formerly held had taught him to know better and turn to more practical account the various sources of revenue than any other member of the Curia. As early as 1494, a Carmelite, Adam of Genoa, who had preached at Rome against simony, was found murdered in his bed with twenty wounds. Hardly a single cardinal was appointed without the payment of enormous sums of money.

But when the Pope in course of time fell under the influence of his son Cæsar Borgia, his violent measures assumed that character of devilish wickedness which necessarily reacts upon the ends pursued. What was done in the struggle with the Roman nobles and with the tyrants of Romagna exceeded in faithlessness and barbarity even that measure to which the

after made up his mind to be satisfied with the personal humiliation of Alexander. The Pope, nevertheless, escaped him. Particulars in Pilorgerie, *Campagne et Bulletins de la Grande Armée d'Italie*, 1494, 1495 (Paris, 1866, 8vo.), where the degree of Alexander's danger at different moments is discussed (pp. 111, 117, &c.). In a letter, there printed, of the Archbishop of St. Malo to Queen Anne, it is expressly stated: 'Si nostre roy eust voulu obtemperer à la plupart des Messeigneurs les Cardinaulx, ilz eussent fait ung autre pappe en intention de refformer l'église ainsi qu'ilz disaient. Le roy désire bien la reformacion, mais il ne veult point entreprandre de sa depposicion.'

[1] Corio, fol. 450. Malipiero, *Ann. Veneti*, *Arch. Stor.* vii. i. p. 318. The rapacity of the whole family can be seen in Malipiero, among other authorities, l. c. p. 565. A 'nipote' was splendidly entertained in Venice as papal legate, and made an enormous sum of money by selling dispensations; his servants, when they went away, stole whatever they could lay their hands on, including a piece of embroidered cloth from the high altar of a church at Murano.

Aragonese rulers of Naples had already accustomed the world; and the genius for deception was also greater. The manner in which Cæsar isolated his father, murdering brother, brother-in-law, and other relations or courtiers, whenever their favour with the Pope or their position in any other respect became inconvenient to him, is literally appalling. Alexander was forced to acquiesce in the murder of his best-loved son, the Duke of Gandia, since he himself lived in hourly dread of Cæsar.[1]

What were the final aims of the latter? Even in the last months of his tyranny, when he had murdered the Condottieri at Sinigaglia, and was to all intents and purposes master of the ecclesiastical state (1503) those who stood near him gave the modest reply, that the Duke merely wished to put down the factions and the despots, and all for the good of the Church only; that for himself he desired nothing more than the lordship of the Romagna, and that he had earned the gratitude of

[1] This in Panvinio alone among contemporary historians (Contin. Platinæ, p. 339), 'insidiis Cæsaris fratris interfectus . . . connivente . . . ad scelus patre,' and to the same effect Jovius, *Elog. Vir. Ill.* p. 302. The profound emotion of Alexander looks like a sign of complicity. After the corpse was drawn out of the Tiber, Sannazaro wrote (*Opera Omnia Latine Scripta* 1535, fol. 41 *a*):

'Piscatorem hominum ne te non, Sixte, putemus
Piscaris natum retibus, ecce, tuum.'

Besides the epigram quoted there are others (fol. 36 *b*, 42 *b*, 47 *b*, 51 *a*, *b* —in the last passage 5) in Sannazaro on, i.e. against, Alexander. Among them is a famous one, referred to in Gregorovius i. 314, on Lucrezia Borgia:

Ergo te semper cupiet Lucretia Sextus?
O fatum diri nominis: hic pater est?

Others execrate his cruelty and celebrate his death as the beginning of an era of peace. On the Jubilee (see below, p. 108, note 1), there is another epigram, fol. 43 *b*. There are others no less severe (fol. 34 *b*, 35 *a*, *b*, 42 *b*, 43 *a*) against Cæsar Borgia, among which we find in one of the strongest:

Aut nihil aut Cæsar vult dici Borgia; quidni?
Cum simul et Cæsar possit, et esse nihil.

(made use of by Bandello, iv. nov. 11). On the murder of the Duke of Gandia, see especially the admirable collection of the most original sources of evidence in Gregorovius, vii. 399–407, according to which Cæsar's guilt is clear, but it seems very doubtful whether Alexander knew, or approved, of the intended assassination.

all the following Popes by ridding them of the Orsini and Colonna.[1] But no one will accept this as his ultimate design. The Pope Alexander himself, in his discussions with the Venetian ambassador, went farther than this, when committing his son to the protection of Venice: 'I will see to it,' he said, 'that one day the Papacy shall belong either to him or to you.'[2] Cæsar certainly added that no one could become Pope without the consent of Venice, and for this end the Venetian cardinals had only to keep well together. Whether he referred to himself or not we are unable to say; at all events, the declaration of his father is sufficient to prove his designs on the pontifical throne. We further obtain from Lucrezia Borgia a certain amount of indirect evidence, in so far as certain passages in the poems of Ercole Strozza may be the echo of expressions which she as Duchess of Ferrara may easily have permitted herself to use. Here too Cæsar's hopes of the Papacy are chiefly spoken of;[3] but now and then a supremacy over all Italy is hinted at,[4] and finally we are given to understand that as temporal ruler Cæsar's projects were of the greatest, and that for their sake he had formerly surrendered his cardinalate.[5] In fact, there can be no doubt whatever that Cæsar, whether chosen Pope or not after the death of Alexander, meant to keep possession of the pontifical state at any cost, and that this, after all the enormities he had committed, he could

[1] Macchiavelli, *Opere*, ed. Milan, vol. v. pp. 387, 393, 395, in the *Legazione al Duca Valentino*.

[2] Tommaso Gar, *Relazioni della Corte di Roma*, i. p. 12, in the *Rel. of P. Capello*. Literally: 'The Pope has more respect for Venice than for any other power in the world.' 'E però desidera, che ella (Signoria di Venezia) protegga il figliuolo, e dice voler fare tale ordine, che il papato o sia suo, ovvero della signoria nostra.' The word 'suo' can only refer to Cæsar. An instance of the uncertainty caused by this usage is found in the still lively controversy respecting the words used by Vasari in the *Vita di Raffaello*: 'A Bindo Altoviti fece il ritratto suo, &c.'

[3] *Strozzii Poetae*, p. 19, in the 'Venatio' of Ercole Strozza: '. . . cui triplicem fata invidere coronam.' And in the Elegy on Cæsar's death, p. 31 sqq.: 'Speraretque olim solii decora alta paterni.'

[4] *Ibid.* Jupiter had once promised

> 'Affore Alexandri sobolem, quæ poneret olim
> Italiæ leges, atque aurea sæcla referret,' etc.

[5] *Ibid.* 'Sacrumque decus majora parantem deposuisse.'

not as Pope have succeeded in doing permanently. He, if anybody, could have secularised the States of the Church, and he would have been forced to do so in order to keep them.[1] Unless we are much deceived, this is the real reason of the secret sympathy with which Macchiavelli treats the great criminal; from Cæsar, or from nobody, could it be hoped that he 'would draw the steel from the wound,' in other words, annihilate the Papacy—the source of all foreign intervention and of all the divisions of Italy. The intriguers who thought to divine Cæsar's aims, when holding out to him hopes of the kingdom of Tuscany, seem to have been dismissed with contempt.[2]

But all logical conclusions from his premisses are idle, not because of the unaccountable genius which in fact characterized him as little as it did the Duke of Friedland, but because the means which he employed were not compatible with any large and consistent course of action. Perhaps, indeed, in the very excess of his wickedness some prospect of salvation for the Papacy may have existed even without the accident which put an end to his rule.

Even if we assume that the destruction of the petty despots in the pontifical state had gained for him nothing but sympathy, even if we take as proof of his great projects the army, composed of the best soldiers and officers in Italy, with Lionardo da Vinci as chief engineer, which followed his fortunes in 1503, other facts nevertheless wear such a character of unreason that our judgment, like that of contemporary observers, is wholly at a loss to explain them. One fact of this kind is the devastation and maltreatment of the newly won state, which Cæsar still intended to keep and to rule over.[3] Another

[1] He was married, as is well known, to a French princess of the family of Albret, and had a daughter by her; in some way or other he would have attempted to found a dynasty. It is not known that he took steps to regain the cardinal's hat, although (acc. to Macchiavelli, l. c. p. 285) he must have counted on the speedy death of his father.

[2] Macchiavelli, l. c. p. 334. Designs on Siena and eventually on all Tuscany certainly existed, but were not yet ripe; the consent of France was indispensable.

[3] Macchiavelli, l. c. pp. 326, 351, 414; Matarazzo, *Cronaca di Perugia*, *Arch. Stor.* xvi. ii. pp. 157 and 221. He wished his soldiers to quarter themselves where they pleased, so that they gained more in time of peace

is the condition of Rome and of the Curia in the last decades of the pontificate. Whether it were that father and son had drawn up a formal list of proscribed persons,[1] or that the murders were resolved upon one by one, in either case the Borgias were bent on the secret destruction of all who stood in their way or whose inheritance they coveted. Of this money and movable goods formed the smallest part; it was a much greater source of profit for the Pope that the incomes of the clerical dignitaries in question were suspended by their death, and that he received the revenues of their offices while vacant, and the price of these offices when they were filled by the successors of the murdered men. The Venetian ambassador, Paolo Capello [2] announces in the year 1500: 'Every night four or five murdered men are discovered—bishops, prelates and others—so that all Rome is trembling for fear of being destroyed by the Duke (Cæsar).' He himself used to wander about Rome in the night time with his guards,[3] and there is every reason to believe that he did so not only because, like Tiberius, he shrank from showing his now repulsive features by daylight, but also to gratify his insane thirst for blood, perhaps even on the persons of those unknown to him.

As early as the year 1499 the despair was so great and so general that many of the Papal guards were waylaid and put to death.[4] But those whom the Borgias could not assail with

than of war. Petrus Alcyonius, *De Exilio* (1522), ed. Mencken, p. 19, says of the style of conducting war: 'Ea scelera et flagitia a nostris militibus patrata sunt quæ ne Scythæ quidem aut Turcæ, aut Pœni in Italia commisissent.' The same writer (p. 65) blames Alexander as a Spaniard: 'Hispani generis hominem, cujus proprium est, rationibus et commodis Hispanorum consultum velle, non Italorum.' See above, p. 109.

[1] To this effect Pierio Valeriano, *De Infelicitate Literat.* ed. Mencken, p. 282, in speaking of Giovanni Regio: 'In arcano proscriptorum albo positus.'

[2] Tommaso Gar, l. c. p. 11. From May 22, 1502, onwards the *Despatches of Giustiniani*, 3 vols. Florence, 1876, edited by Pasquale Villari, offer valuable information.

[3] Paulus Jovius, *Elogia*, Cæsar Borgia. In the *Commentarii Urbani* of Ralph. Volaterianus, lib. xxii. there is a description of Alexander VI., composed under Julius II., and still written very guardedly. We here read: 'Roma . . . nobilis jam carneficina facta erat.'

[4] *Diario Ferrarese*, in Muratori, xxiv. col. 362.

open violence, fell victims to their poison. For the cases in which a certain amount of discretion seemed requisite, a white powder [1] of an agreeable taste was made use of, which did not work on the spot, but slowly and gradually, and which could be mixed without notice in any dish or goblet. Prince Djem had taken some of it in a sweet draught, before Alexander surrendered him to Charles VIII. (1495), and at the end of their career father and son poisoned themselves with the same powder by accidentally tasting a sweetmeat intended for a wealthy cardinal, probably Adrian of Corneto.[2] The official epitomiser of the history of the Popes, Onufrio Panvinio,[3] mentions three cardinals, Orsini, Ferrerio, and Michiel, whom Alexander caused to be poisoned, and hints at a fourth, Giovanni Borgia, whom Cæsar took into his own charge—though probably wealthy prelates seldom died in Rome at that time without giving rise to suspicions of this sort. Even tranquil students who had withdrawn to some provincial town were not out of reach of the merciless poison. A secret horror seemed to hang about the Pope; storms and thunderbolts, crushing in walls and chambers, had in earlier times often visited and alarmed him; in the year 1500,[4] when these phenomena were repeated, they were held to be 'cosa diabolica.' The report of these events seems at last, through the well-attended jubilee [5]

[1] Paul. Jovius, *Histor.* ii. fol. 47.

[2] See the passages in Ranke, *Röm. Päpste*; Sämmtl. Werke, Bd. xxxvii. 35, and xxxix. Anh. Abschn. 1, Nro. 4, and Gregorovius, vii. 497, sqq. Giustiniani does not believe in the Pope's being poisoned. See his *Dispacci*, vol. ii. pp. 107 sqq.; Villari's Note, pp. 120 sqq., and App. pp. 458 sqq.

[3] Panvinius, *Epitome Pontificum*, p. 359. For the attempt to poison Alexander's successor, Julius II., see p. 363. According to Sismondi, xiii. p. 246, it was in this way that Lopez, Cardinal of Capua, for years the partner of all the Pope's secrets, came by his end; according to Sanuto (in Ranke, *Popes*, i. p. 52, note), the Cardinal of Verona also. When Cardinal Orsini died, the Pope obtained a certificate of natural death from a college of physicians.

[4] Prato, *Arch. Stor.* iii. p. 254; comp. Attilio Alessio, in Baluz. *Miscell.*, iv. p. 518 sqq.

[5] And turned to the most profitable account by the Pope. Comp. *Chron. Venetum*, in Murat. xxiv. col. 133, given only as a report: 'E si giudiceva, che il Pontefice dovesse cavare assai danari di questo Giubileo, che gli tornerà molto a proposito.

of 1500, to have been carried far and wide throughout the countries of Europe, and the infamous traffic in indulgences did what else was needed to draw all eyes upon Rome.[1] Besides the returning pilgrims, strange white-robed penitents came from Italy to the North, among them disguised fugitives from the Papal State, who are not likely to have been silent. Yet none can calculate how far the scandal and indignation of Christendom might have gone, before they became a source of pressing danger to Alexander. 'He would,' says Panvinio elsewhere,[2] 'have put all the other rich cardinals and prelates out of the way, to get their property, had he not, in the midst of his great plans for his son, been struck down by death.' And what might not Cæsar have achieved if, at the moment when his father died, he had not himself been laid upon a sick-bed! What a conclave would that have been, in which, armed with all his weapons, he had extorted his election from a college whose numbers he had judiciously reduced by poison—and this at a time when there was no French army at hand! In pursuing such a hypothesis the imagination loses itself in an abyss.

Instead of this followed the conclave in which Pius III. was elected, and, after his speedy death, that which chose Julius II.—both elections the fruits of a general reaction.

Whatever may have been the private morals of Julius II., in all essential respects he was the saviour of the Papacy. His familiarity with the course of events since the pontificate of his uncle Sixtus had given him a profound insight into the grounds and conditions of the Papal authority. On these he founded his own policy, and devoted to it the whole force and passion of his unshaken soul. He ascended the steps of St. Peter's chair without simony and amid general applause, and with him ceased, at all events, the undisguised traffic in the highest offices of the Church. Julius had favourites, and among them were some the reverse of worthy, but a special fortune put him above the temptation to nepotism. His brother, Giovanni della Rovere, was the husband of the heiress

[1] Anshelm, *Berner Chronik*, iii. pp. 146–156. Trithem. *Annales Hirsaug.* tom. ii. pp. 579, 584, 586.

[2] Panvin. *Contin. Platinae*, p. 341.

of Urbino, sister of the last Montefeltro Guidobaldo, and from this marriage was born, in 1491, a son, Francesco Maria della Rovere, who was at the same time Papal 'nipote' and lawful heir to the duchy of Urbino. What Julius elsewhere acquired, either on the field of battle or by diplomatic means, he proudly bestowed on the Church, not on his family; the ecclesiastical territory, which he found in a state of dissolution, he bequeathed to his successor completely subdued, and increased by Parma and Piacenza. It was not his fault that Ferrara too was not added to the dominions of the Church. The 700,000 ducats, which were stored up in the castle of St. Angelo, were to be delivered by the governor to none but the future Pope. He made himself heir of the cardinals, and, indeed, of all the clergy who died in Rome, and this by the most despotic means; but he murdered or poisoned none of them.[1] That he should himself lead his forces to battle was for him an unavoidable necessity, and certainly did him nothing but good at a time when a man in Italy was forced to be either hammer or anvil, and when personality was a greater power than the most indisputable right. If, despite all his high-sounding 'Away with the barbarians!' he nevertheless contributed more than any man to the firm settlement of the Spaniards in Italy, he may have thought it a matter of indifference to the Papacy, or even, as things stood, a relative advantage. And to whom, sooner than to Spain, could the Church look for a sincere and lasting respect,[2] in an age when the princes of Italy cherished none but sacrilegious projects against her? Be this as it may, the powerful, original nature, which could swallow no anger and conceal no genuine good-will, made on the whole the impression most desirable in his situation—that of the 'Pontefice terribile.' He could even, with a comparatively clear conscience, venture to summon a council to Rome, and so bid defiance to that outcry for a council which was

[1] Hence the splendour of the tombs of the prelates erected during their lifetime. A part of the plunder was in this way saved from the hands of the Popes.

[2] Whether Julius really hoped that Ferdinand the Catholic would be induced to restore to the throne of Naples the expelled Aragonese dynasty, remains, in spite of Giovio's declaration (*Vita Alfonsi Ducis*), very doubtful.

raised by the opposition all over Europe. A ruler of this stamp needed some great outward symbol of his conceptions; Julius found it in the reconstruction of St. Peter's. The plan of it, as Bramante wished to have it, is perhaps the grandest expression of power in unity which can be imagined. In other arts besides architecture the face and the memory of the Pope live on in their most ideal form, and it is not without significance that even the Latin poetry of those days gives proof of a wholly different enthusiasm for Julius than that shown for his predecessors. The entrance into Bologna, at the end of the 'Iter Julii Secundi,' by the Cardinal Adriano da Corneto, has a splendour of its own, and Giovan Antonio Flaminio,[1] in one of the finest elegies, appealed to the patriot in the Pope to grant his protection to Italy.

In a constitution of his Lateran Council, Julius had solemnly denounced the simony of the Papal elections.[2] After his death in 1513, the money-loving cardinals tried to evade the prohibition by proposing that the endowments and offices hitherto held by the chosen candidate should be equally divided among themselves, in which case they would have elected the best-endowed cardinal, the incompetent Rafael Riario.[3] But a reaction, chiefly arising from the younger members of the Sacred College, who, above all things, desired a liberal Pope, rendered the miserable combination futile; Giovanni Medici was elected —the famous Leo X.

We shall often meet with him in treating of the noonday of the Renaissance; here we wish only to point out that under him the Papacy was again exposed to great inward and out-

[1] Both poems in Roscoe, *Leone X.* ed. Bossi, iv. 257 and 297. Of his death the *Cronaca di Cremona* says: 'quale fu grande danno per la Italia, perchè era homo che non voleva tramontani in Italia, ed haveva cazato Francesi, e l'animo era de cazar le altri.' *Bibl. Hist. Ital.* (1876) i. 217. It is true that when Julius, in August, 1511, lay one day for hours in a fainting fit, and was thought to be dead, the more restless members of the noblest families—Pompeo Colonna and Antimo Savelli—ventured to call 'the people' to the Capitol, and to urge them to throw off the Papal yoke —'a vendicarsi in libertà . . . a publica ribellione,' as Guicciardini tells us in his tenth book. See, too, Paul. Jov. in the *Vita Pompeji Columnae*, and Gregorovius, viii. 71–75.

[2] *Septimo decretal.* l. i. tit. 3, cap. 1–3.

[3] Franc. Vettori, in the *Arch. Stor.* vi. 297.

ward dangers. Among these we do not reckon the conspiracy of the Cardinals Petrucci, De Saulis, Riario, and Corneto (1517) which at most could have occasioned a change of persons, and to which Leo found the true antidote in the unheard-of creation of thirty-nine new cardinals, a measure which had the additional advantage of rewarding, in some cases at least, real merit.[1]

But some of the paths which Leo allowed himself to tread during the first two years of his office were perilous to the last degree. He seriously endeavoured to secure, by negotiation, the kingdom of Naples for his brother Giuliano, and for his nephew Lorenzo a powerful North Italian state, to comprise Milan, Tuscany, Urbino, and Ferrara.[2] It is clear that the Pontifical State, thus hemmed in on all sides, would have become a mere Medicean appanage, and that, in fact, there would have been no further need to secularise it.

The plan found an insuperable obstacle in the political conditions of the time. Giuliano died early. To provide for Lorenzo, Leo undertook to expel the Duke Francesco Maria della Rovere from Urbino, but reaped from the war nothing but hatred and poverty, and was forced, when in 1519 Lorenzo followed his uncle to the grave, to hand over the hardly-won conquests to the Church.[3] He did on compulsion and without credit what, if it had been done voluntarily, would have been to his lasting honour. What, partly alone, and partly in alternate negotiations with Francis I. and Charles V., he attempted against Alfonso of Ferrara, and actually achieved against a few petty despots and Condottieri, was assuredly not of a kind to raise his reputation. And this was at a time when the monarchs of the West were yearly growing more and more accustomed to political gambling on a colossal scale,

[1] Besides which it is said (Paul. Lang. *Chronicon Cilicense*) to have produced not less than 500,000 gold florins; the order of the Franciscans alone, whose general was made a cardinal, paid 30,000. For a notice of the various sums paid, see Sanuto, xxiv. fol. 227; for the whole subject see Gregorovius, viii. 214 sqq.

[2] Franc. Vettori, l.c. p. 301. *Arch. Stor.* Append. i. p. 293 sqq. Roscoe, *Leone X.* ed. Bossi, vi. p. 232 sqq. Tommaso Gar, l. c. p. 42.

[3] Ariosto, Sat. vi. v. 106. 'Tutti morrete, ed è fatal che muoja Leone appresso.' Sat. 3 and 7 ridicule the hangers on at Leo's Court.

of which the stakes were this or that province of Italy.[1] Who could guarantee that, since the last decades had seen so great an increase of their power at home, their ambition could stop short of the States of the Church? Leo himself witnessed the prelude of what was fulfilled in the year 1527; a few bands of Spanish infantry appeared—of their own accord, it seems—at the end of 1520, on the borders of the Pontifical territory, with a view of laying the Pope under contribution,[2] but were driven back by the Papal forces. The public feeling, too, against the corruptions of the hierarchy had of late years been drawing rapidly to a head, and men with an eye for the future, like the younger Pico della Mirandola, called urgently for reform.[3] Meantime Luther had already appeared upon the scene.

Under Adrian VI. (1522–1523), the few and timid improvements, carried out in the face of the great German Reformation, came too late. He could do little more than proclaim his horror of the course which things had taken hitherto, of simony, nepotism, prodigality, brigandage, and profligacy. The danger from the side of the Lutherans was by no means the greatest; an acute observer from Venice, Girolamo Negro, uttered his fears that a speedy and terrible disaster would befall the city of Rome itself.[4]

[1] One of several instances of such combinations is given in the *Lettere dei Principi*, i. 65, in a despatch of the Cardinal Bibbiena from Paris of the year 1518.

[2] Franc. Vettori, l.c. p. 333.

[3] At the time of the Lateran Council, in 1512, Pico wrote an address: *J. E. P. Oratio ad Leonem X. et Concilium Lateranense de Reformandis Ecclesiæ Moribus* (ed. Hagenau, 1512, frequently printed in editions of his works). The address was dedicated to Pirckheimer and was again sent to him in 1517. Comp. *Vir. Doct. Epist. ad Pirck.*, ed. Freytag, Leipz. 1838, p. 8. Pico fears that under Leo evil may definitely triumph over good, 'et in te bellum a nostræ religionis hostibus ante audias geri quam pariri.'

[4] *Lettere dei Principi*, i. (Rome. 17th March, 1523): 'This city stands on a needle's point, and God grant that we are not soon driven to Avignon or to the end of the Ocean. I foresee the early fall of this spiritual monarchy . . . Unless God helps us we are lost.' Whether Adrian were really poisoned or not, cannot be gathered with certainty from Blas Ortiz, *Itinerar. Hadriani* (Baluz. *Miscell.* ed. Mansi, i. p. 383 sqq.); the worst of it was that everybody believed it.

Under Clement VII. the whole horizon of Rome was filled with vapours, like that leaden veil which the scirocco draws over the Campagna, and which makes the last months of summer so deadly. The Pope was no less detested at home than abroad. Thoughtful people were filled with anxiety,[1] hermits appeared upon the streets and squares of Rome, foretelling the fate of Italy and of the world, and calling the Pope by the name of Antichrist;[2] the faction of the Colonna raised its head defiantly; the indomitable Cardinal Pompeo Colonna, whose mere existence[3] was a permanent menace to the Papacy, ventured to surprise the city in 1526, hoping with the help of Charles V., to become Pope then and there, as soon as Clement was killed or captured. It was no piece of good fortune for Rome that the latter was able to escape to the Castle of St. Angelo, and the fate for which himself was reserved may well be called worse than death.

By a series of those falsehoods, which only the powerful can venture on, but which bring ruin upon the weak, Clement brought about the advance of the Germano-Spanish army under Bourbon and Frundsberg (1527). It is certain[4] that the Cabinet of Charles V. intended to inflict on him a severe castigation, and that it could not calculate beforehand how far the zeal of its unpaid hordes would carry them. It would have been vain to attempt to enlist men in Germany without paying any bounty, if it had not been well known that Rome was the object of the expedition. It may be that the written orders to Bourbon will be found some day or other, and it is not improbable that they will prove to be worded mildly. But historical criticism will not allow itself to be led astray. The Catholic King and Emperor owed it to his luck and nothing else, that Pope and cardinals were not murdered by his troops. Had this happened, no sophistry in the world could clear him of his share in the guilt. The massacre of

[1] Negro, l.c. on Oct. 24 (should be Sept.) and Nov. 9, 1526, April 11, 1527. It is true that he found admirers and flatterers. The dialogue of Petrus Alcyonus 'De Exilio' was written in his praise, shortly before he became Pope.

[2] Varchi, *Stor. Fiorent.* i. 43, 46 sqq.

[3] Paul. Jov., *Vita Pomp. Columnae.*

[4] Ranke, *Deutsche Geschichte* (4 Aufl.) ii. 262 sqq.

countless people of less consequence, the plunder of the rest, and all the horrors of torture and traffic in human life, show clearly enough what was possible in the 'Sacco di Roma.'

Charles seems to have wished to bring the Pope, who had fled a second time to the Castle of St. Angelo, to Naples, after extorting from him vast sums of money, and Clement's flight to Orvieto must have happened without any connivance on the part of Spain.[1] Whether the Emperor ever thought seriously of the secularisation of the States of the Church,[2] for which everybody was quite prepared, and whether he was really dissuaded from it by the representations of Henry VIII. of England, will probably never be made clear.

But if such projects really existed, they cannot have lasted long: from the devastated city arose a new spirit of reform both in Church and State. It made itself felt in a moment. Cardinal Sadoleto, one witness of many, thus writes: 'If through our suffering a satisfaction is made to the wrath and justice of God, if these fearful punishments again open the way to better laws and morals, then is our misfortune perhaps not of the greatest. . . . What belongs to God He will take care of; before us lies a life of reformation, which no violence can take from us. Let us so rule our deeds and thoughts as to seek in God only the true glory of the priesthood and our own true greatness and power.'[3]

In point of fact, this critical year, 1527, so far bore fruit. that the voices of serious men could again make themselves heard. Rome had suffered too much to return, even under a Paul III., to the gay corruption of Leo X.

The Papacy, too, when its sufferings became so great, began to excite a sympathy half religious and half political. The kings could not tolerate that one of their number should arrogate to himself the rights of Papal gaoler, and concluded (August 18, 1527) the Treaty of Amiens, one of the objects of which was the deliverance of Clement. They thus, at all

[1] Varchi, *Stor. Fiorent.* ii. 43 sqq.

[2] *Ibid.* and Ranke, *Deutsche Gesch.* ii. 278, note, and iii. 6 sqq. It was thought that Charles would transfer his seat of government to Rome.

[3] See his letter to the Pope, dated Carpentras, Sept. 1, 1527, in the *Anecdota litt.* iv. p. 335.

events, turned to their own account the unpopularity which the deeds of the Imperial troops had excited. At the same time the Emperor became seriously embarrassed, even in Spain, where the prelates and grandees never saw him without making the most urgent remonstrances. When a general deputation of the clergy and laity, all clothed in mourning, was projected, Charles, fearing that troubles might arise out of it, like those of the insurrection quelled a few years before, forbad the scheme.[1] Not only did he not dare to prolong the maltreatment of the Pope, but he was absolutely compelled, even apart from all considerations of foreign politics, to be reconciled with the Papacy which he had so grievously wounded. For the temper of the German people, which certainly pointed to a different course, seemed to him, like German affairs generally, to afford no foundation for a policy. It is possible, too, as a Venetian maintains,[2] that the memory of the sack of Rome lay heavy on his conscience, and tended to hasten that expiation which was sealed by the permanent subjection of the Florentines to the Medicean family of which the Pope was a member. The 'nipote' and new Duke, Alessandro Medici, was married to the natural daughter of the Emperor.

In the following years the plan of a Council enabled Charles to keep the Papacy in all essential points under his control, and at one and the same time to protect and to oppress it. The greatest danger of all—secularisation—the danger which came from within, from the Popes themselves and their 'nipoti,' was adjourned for centuries by the German Reformation. Just as this alone had made the expedition against Rome (1527) possible and successful, so did it compel the Papacy to become once more the expression of a world-wide spiritual power, to raise itself from the soulless debasement in which it lay, and to place itself at the head of all the enemies of this reformation. The institution thus developed during the latter years of Clement VII., and under Paul III., Paul IV., and their successors, in the face of the defection of half

[1] *Lettere dei Principi*, i. 72. Castiglione to the Pope, Burgos, Dec. 10, 1527.

[2] Tommaso Gar, *Relaz. della Corte di Roma*, i. 299.

Europe, was a new, regenerated hierarchy, which avoided all the great and dangerous scandals of former times, particularly nepotism, with its attempts at territorial aggrandisement,[1] and which, in alliance with the Catholic princes, and impelled by a new-born spiritual force, found its chief work in the recovery of what had been lost. It only existed and is only intelligible in opposition to the seceders. In this sense it can be said with perfect truth that, the moral salvation of the Papacy is due to its mortal enemies. And now its political position, too, though certainly under the permanent tutelage of Spain, became impregnable; almost without effort it inherited, on the extinction of its vasals, the legitimate line of Este and the house of Della Rovere, the duchies of Ferrara and Urbino. But without the Reformation—if, indeed, it is possible to think it away—the whole ecclesiastical State would long ago have passed into secular hands.

In conclusion, let us briefly consider the effect of these political circumstances on the spirit of the nation at large.

It is evident that the general political uncertainty in Italy during the fourteenth and fifteenth centuries, was of a kind to excite in the better spirits of the time a patriotic disgust and opposition. Dante and Petrarch,[2] in their day, proclaimed loudly a common Italy, the object of the highest efforts of all her children. It may be objected that this was only the enthusiasm of a few highly-instructed men, in which the mass of the people had no share; but it can hardly have been otherwise even in Germany, although in name at least that country was united, and recognised in the Emperor one supreme head. The first patriotic utterances of German Literature, if we except some verses of the 'Minnesänger,' belong to the huma-

[1] The Farnese succeeded in something of the kind, the Caraffa were ruined.

[2] Petrarca, *Epist. Fam.* i. 3. p. 574, when he thanks God that he was born an Italian. And again in the *Apologia contra cujusdam anonymi Galli Calumnias* of the year 1367 (*Opp.* ed. Bas. 1581) p. 1068 sqq. See L. Geiger, *Petrarca*, 129–145.

nists of the time of Maximilian I.[1] and after, and read like an echo of Italian declamations, or like a reply to Italian criticism on the intellectual immaturity of Germany. And yet, as a matter of fact, Germany had been long a nation in a truer sense than Italy ever was since the Roman days. France owes the consciousness of its national unity mainly to its conflicts with the English, and Spain has never permanently succeeded in absorbing Portugal, closely related as the two countries are. For Italy, the existence of the ecclesiastical State, and the conditions under which alone it could continue, were a permanent obstacle to national unity, an obstacle whose removal seemed hopeless. When, therefore, in the political intercourse of the fifteenth century, the common fatherland is sometimes emphatically named, it is done in most cases to annoy some other Italian State.[2] The first decades of the sixteenth century, the years when the Renaissance attained its fullest bloom, were not favourable to a revival of patriotism; the enjoyment of intellectual and artistic pleasures, the comforts and elegancies of life, and the supreme interests of self-development, destroyed or hampered the love of country. But those deeply serious and sorrowful appeals to national sentiment were not heard again till later, when the time for unity had gone by, when the country was inundated with Frenchmen and Spaniards, and when a German army had conquered Rome. The sense of local patriotism may be said in some measure to have taken the place of this feeling, though it was but a poor equivalent for it.

[1] Particularly those in vol. i. of Schardius, *Scriptores rerum Germanicarum*, Basel, 1574. For an earlier period, Felix Faber, *Historia Suevorum*, libri duo (in Goldast, *Script. rer. Suev.* 1605); for a later, Irenicus, *Exegesis Germaniæ*, Hagenau, 1518. On the latter work and the patriotic histories of that time, see various studies of A. Horawitz, *Hist. Zeitschrift*, bd. xxxiii. 118, anm. 1.

[2] One instance out of many: *The Answers of the Doge of Venice to a Florentine Agent respecting Pisa*, 1496, in Malipiero, *Ann. Veneti. Arch. Stor.* vii. i. p. 427.

PART II.

THE DEVELOPMENT OF THE INDIVIDUAL.

CHAPTER I.

THE ITALIAN STATE AND THE INDIVIDUAL.

In the character of these states, whether republics or despotisms, lies, not the only, but the chief reason for the early development of the Italian. To this it is due that he was the first-born among the sons of modern Europe.

In the Middle Ages both sides of human consciousness—that which was turned within as that which was turned without—lay dreaming or half awake beneath a common veil. The veil was woven of faith, illusion, and childish prepossession, through which the world and history were seen clad in strange hues. Man was conscious of himself only as member of a race, people, party, family, or corporation—only through some general category. In Italy this veil first melted into air; an *objective* treatment and consideration of the state and of all the things of this world became possible. The *subjective* side at the same time asserted itself with corresponding emphasis; man became a spiritual *individual*,[1] and recognised himself as such. In the same way the Greek had once distinguished himself from the barbarian, and the Arabian had felt himself an individual at a time when other Asiatics knew themselves only as members of a race. It will not be difficult to show that this result was owing above all to the political circumstances of Italy.

In far earlier times we can here and there detect a development of free personality which in Northern Europe either did not occur at all, or could not display itself in the same manner. The band of audacious wrongdoers in the sixteenth century described to us by Luidprand, some of the contemporaries of Gregory VII., and a few of the opponents of the first Hohenstaufen, show us characters of this kind. But at the close of the thirteenth century Italy began to swarm with individuality; the charm laid upon human personality was dissolved; and a

[1] Observe the expressions 'uomo singolare' and 'uomo unico' for the higher and highest stages of individual development.

thousand figures meet us each in its own special shape and dress. Dante's great poem would have been impossible in any other country of Europe, if only for the reason that they all still lay under the spell of race. For Italy the august poet, through the wealth of individuality which he set forth, was the most national herald of his time. But this unfolding of the treasures of human nature in literature and art—this many-sided representation and criticism—will be discussed in separate chapters; here we have to deal only with the psychological fact itself. This fact appears in the most decisive and unmistakeable form. The Italians of the fourteenth century knew little of false modesty or of hypocrisy in any shape; not one of them was afraid of singularity, of being and seeming[1] unlike his neighbours.[2]

Despotism, as we have already seen, fostered in the highest degree the individuality not only of the tyrant or Condottiere himself,[3] but also of the men whom he protected or used as his tools—the secretary, minister, poet, and companion. These people were forced to know all the inward resources of their own nature, passing or permanent; and their enjoyment of life was enhanced and concentrated by the desire to obtain the greatest satisfaction from a possibly very brief period of power and influence.

[1] By the year 1390 there was no longer any prevailing fashion of dress for men at Florence, each preferring to clothe himself in his own way. See the *Canzone* of Franco Sacchetti: 'Contro alle nuove foggie' in the *Rime*, publ. dal Poggiali, p. 52.

[2] At the close of the sixteenth century Montaigne draws the following parallel (*Essais*, l. iii. chap. 5, vol. iii. p. 367 of the Paris ed. 1816): 'Ils (les Italiens) ont plus communement des belles femmes et moins de laides que nous; mais des rares et excellentes beautés j'estime que nous allons à pair. Et j'en juge autant des esprits; de ceux de la commune façon, ils en ont beaucoup plus et evidemment; la brutalité y est sans comparaison plus rare; d'ames singulières et du plus hault estage, nous ne leur en debvons rien.'

[3] And also of their wives, as is seen in the family of Sforza and among other North Italian rulers. Comp. in the work of Jacobus Phil. Bergomensis, *De Plurimis Claris Selectisque Mulieribus*, Ferrara, 1497, the lives of Battista Malatesta, Paola Gonzaga, Bona Lombarda, Riccarda of Este, and the chief women of the House of Sforza, Beatrice and others. Among them are more than one genuine virago, and in several cases natural gifts are supplemented by great humanistic culture. (See below, chap. 3 and part v.)

But even the subjects whom they ruled over were not free from the same impulse. Leaving out of account those who wasted their lives in secret opposition and conspiracies, we speak of the majority who were content with a strictly private station, like most of the urban population of the Byzantine empire and the Mohammedan states. No doubt it was often hard for the subjects of a Visconti to maintain the dignity of their persons and families, and multitudes must have lost in moral character through the servitude they lived under. But this was not the case with regard to individuality; for political impotence does not hinder the different tendencies and manifestations of private life from thriving in the fullest vigour and variety. Wealth and culture, so far as display and rivalry were not forbidden to them, a municipal freedom which did not cease to be considerable, and a Church which, unlike that of the Byzantine or of the Mohammedan world, was not identical with the State—all these conditions undoubtedly favoured the growth of individual thought, for which the necessary leisure was furnished by the cessation of party conflicts. The private man, indifferent to politics, and busied partly with serious pursuits, partly with the interests of a *dilettante*, seems to have been first fully formed in these despotisms of the fourteenth century. Documentary evidence cannot, of course, be required on such a point. The novelists, from whom we might expect information, describe to us oddities in plenty, but only from one point of view and in so far as the needs of the story demand. Their scene, too, lies chiefly in the republican cities.

In the latter, circumstances were also, but in another way, favourable to the growth of individual character. The more frequently the governing party was changed, the more the individual was led to make the utmost of the exercise and enjoyment of power. The statesmen and popular leaders, especially in Florentine history,[1] acquired so marked a personal character, that we can scarcely find, even exceptionally, a parallel to them in contemporary history, hardly even in Jacob von Arteveldt.

[1] Franco Sacchetti, in his 'Capitolo' (*Rime*, publ. dal Poggiali, p. 56), enumerates about 1390 the names of over a hundred distinguished people

The members of the defeated parties, on the other hand, often came into a position like that of the subjects of the despotic States, with the difference that the freedom or power already enjoyed, and in some cases the hope of recovering them, gave a higher energy to their individuality. Among these men of involuntary leisure we find, for instance, an Agnolo Pandolfini (d. 1446), whose work on domestic economy [1] is the first complete programme of a developed private life. His estimate of the duties of the individual as against the dangers and thanklessness of public life [2] is in its way a true monument of the age.

Banishment, too, has this effect above all, that it either wears the exile out or develops whatever is greatest in him. 'In all our more populous cities,' says Giovanni Pontano,[3] 'we see a crowd of people who have left their homes of their own free-will; but a man takes his virtues with him wherever he goes.' And, in fact, they were by no means only men who had been actually exiled, but thousands left their native place voluntarily, because they found its political or economical condition intolerable. The Florentine emigrants at Ferrara and the Lucchese in Venice formed whole colonies by themselves.

The cosmopolitanism which grew up in the most gifted circles is in itself a high stage of individualism. Dante, as we have already said, finds a new home in the language and culture of Italy, but goes beyond even this in the words, 'My

in the ruling parties who had died within his memory. However many mediocrities there may have been among them, the list is still remarkable as evidence of the awakening of individuality. On the 'Vite' of Filippo Villani, see below.

[1] *Trattato del Governo della Famiglia* forms a part of the work: *La Cura della Famiglia* (*Opere Volg. di Leon Batt. Alberti*, publ. da Anicio Bonucci, Flor. 1844, vol. ii.). See there vol. i. pp. xxx.–xl., vol. ii. pp. xxxv. sqq. and vol. v. pp. 1–127. Formerly the work was generally, as in the text, attributed to Agnolo Pandolfini (d. 1446; see on him *Vesp. Fiorent.*, pp. 291 and 379); the recent investigations of Fr. Palermo (Florence 1871), have shown Alberti to be the author. The work is quoted from the ed. Torino, Pomba, 1828.

[2] Trattato, p. 65 sqq.

[3] Jov. Pontanus, *De Fortitudine*, l. ii. cap. 4, 'De tolerando Exilio,' Seventy years later, Cardanus (*De Vitâ Propriâ*, cap. 32) could ask bitterly: 'Quid est patria nisi consensus tyrannorum minutorum ad opprimendos imbelles timidos et qui plerumque sunt innoxii?

country is the whole world.'[1] And when his recall to Florence was offered him on unworthy conditions, he wrote back: 'Can I not everywhere behold the light of the sun and the stars; everywhere meditate on the noblest truths, without appearing ingloriously and shamefully before the city and the people. Even my bread will not fail me.'[2] The artists exult no less defiantly in their freedom from the constraints of fixed residence. 'Only he who has learned everything,' says Ghiberti,[3] 'is nowhere a stranger; robbed of his fortune and without friends, he is yet the citizen of every country, and can fearlessly despise the changes of fortune.' In the same strain an exiled humanist writes: 'Wherever a learned man fixes his seat, there is home.'[4]

[1] *De Vulgari Eloquio*, lib. i. cap. 6. On the ideal Italian language, cap. 17. The spiritual unity of cultivated men, cap. 18. On home-sickness, comp. the famous passages, *Purg.* viii. 1 sqq., and *Parad.* xxv. 1 sqq.

[2] *Dantis Alligherii Epistolae*, ed. Carolus Witte, p. 65.

[3] Ghiberti, *Secondo Commentario*, cap. xv. (Vasari ed Lemonnier, i. p. xxix.).

[4] *Codri Urcei Vita*, at the end of his works, first pub. Bologna 1502. This certainly comes near the old saying: 'ubi bene, ibi patria.' C. U. was not called after the place of his birth, but after Forli, where he lived long; see Malagola, *Codro Urceo*, Bologna, 1877, cap. v. and app. xi. The abundance of neutral intellectual pleasure, which is independent of local circumstances, and of which the educated Italians became more and more capable, rendered exile more tolerable to them. Cosmopolitanism is further a sign of an epoch in which new worlds are discovered, and men feel no longer at home in the old. We see it among the Greeks after the Peloponnesian war; Plato, as Niebuhr says, was not a good citizen, and Xenophon was a bad one; Diogenes went so far as to proclaim homelessness a pleasure, and calls himself, Laertius tells us, ἄπολις. Here another remarkable work may be mentioned. Petrus Alcyonius in his book: *Medices Legatus de Exilio lib. duo*, Ven. 1522 (printed in Mencken, *Analecta de Calam. Literatorum*, Leipzig, 1707, pp. 1–250) devotes to the subject of exile a long and prolix discussion. He tries logically and historically to refute the three reasons for which banishment is held to be an evil, viz. 1. Because the exile must live away from his fatherland. 2. Because he loses the honours given him at home. 3. Because he must do without his friends and relatives; and comes finally to the conclusion that banishment is not an evil. His dissertation culminates in the words, 'Sapientissimus quisque omnem orbem terrarum unam urbem esse ducit. Atque etiam illam veram sibi esse patriam arbitratur quæ se perigrinantem exciperit, quæ pudorem, probitatem, virtutem colit, quæ optima studia, liberales disciplinas amplectitur, quæ etiam facit ut peregrini omnes honesto otio teneant statum et famam dignitatis suæ.'

CHAPTER II.

THE PERFECTING OF THE INDIVIDUAL.

An acute and practised eye might be able to trace, step by step, the increase in the number of complete men during the fifteenth century. Whether they had before them as a conscious object the harmonious development of their spiritual and material existence, is hard to say; but several of them attained it, so far as is consistent with the imperfection of all that is earthly. It may be better to renounce the attempt at an estimate of the share which fortune, character, and talent had in the life of Lorenzo Magnifico. But look at a personality like that of Ariosto, especially as shown in his satires. In what harmony are there expressed the pride of the man and the poet, the irony with which he treats his own enjoyments, the most delicate satire, and the deepest goodwill!

When this impulse to the highest individual development[1] was combined with a powerful and varied nature, which had mastered all the elements of the culture of the age, then arose the 'all-sided man'—'l'uomo universale'—who belonged to Italy alone. Men there were of encyclopædic knowledge in many countries during the Middle Ages, for this knowledge was confined within narrow limits; and even in the twelfth century there were universal artists, but the problems of architecture were comparatively simple and uniform, and in sculpture and painting the matter was of more importance than the form. But in Italy at the time of the Renaissance, we find artists who in every branch created new and perfect works,

[1] This awakening of personality is also shown in the great stress laid on the independent growth of character, in the claim to shape the spiritual life for oneself, apart from parents and ancestors. Boccaccio (*De Cas. Vir. Ill.* Paris, s. a. fol. xxix. *b*) points out that Socrates came of uneducated, Euripides and Demosthenes of unknown, parents, and exclaims: 'Quasi animos a gignentibus habeamus!'

and who also made the greatest impression as men. Others, outside the arts they practised, were masters of a vast circle of spiritual interests.

Dante, who, even in his lifetime, was called by some a poet, by others a philosopher, by others a theologian,[1] pours forth in all his writings a stream of personal force by which the reader, apart from the interest of the subject, feels himself carried away. What power of will must the steady, unbroken elaboration of the 'Divine Comedy' have required! And if we look at the matter of the poem, we find that in the whole spiritual or physical world there is hardly an important subject which the poet has not fathomed, and on which his utterances —often only a few words—are not the most weighty of his time. For the plastic arts he is of the first importance, and this for better reasons than the few references to contemporary artists—he soon became himself the source of inspiration.[2]

The fifteenth century is, above all, that of the many-sided men. There is no biography which does not, besides the chief work of its hero, speak of other pursuits all passing beyond the limits of dilettantism. The Florentine merchant and statesman was often learned in both the classical languages; the most famous humanists read the ethics and politics of Aristotle to him and his sons;[3] even the daughters of the house were highly educated. It is in these circles that private education was first treated seriously. The humanist, on his side, was compelled to the most varied attainments, since his philological learning was not limited, as it now is, to the theoretical knowledge of classical antiquity, but had to serve the practical needs of daily life. While studying Pliny,[4] he made collections of

[1] Boccaccio, *Vita di Dante*, p. 16.

[2] The angels which he drew on tablets at the anniversary of the death of Beatrice (*Vita Nuova*, p. 61) may have been more than the work of a dilettante. Lion. Aretino says he drew 'egregiamente,' and was a great lover of music.

[3] For this and what follows, see esp. *Vespasiano Fiorentino*, an authority of the first order for Florentine culture in the fifteenth century Comp. pp. 359, 379, 401, etc. See, also, the charming and instructive *Vita Jannoctii Manetti* (b. 1396), by Naldus Naldius, in Murat. xx. pp. 529–608.

[4] What follows is taken, e.g., from Perticari's account of Pandolfo Collenuccio, in Roscoe, *Leone X.* ed Bossi iii. pp. 197 sqq., and from the *Opere del Conte Perticari*, Mil. 1823, vol. ii.

natural history; the geography of the ancients was his guide in treating of modern geography, their history was his pattern in writing contemporary chronicles, even when composed in Italian; he not only translated the comedies of Plautus, but acted as manager when they were put on the stage; every effective form of ancient literature down to the dialogues of Lucian he did his best to imitate; and besides all this, he acted as magistrate, secretary, and diplomatist—not always to his own advantage.

But among these many-sided men, some who may truly be called all-sided, tower above the rest. Before analysing the general phases of life and culture of this period, we may here, on the threshold of the fifteenth century, consider for a moment the figure of one of these giants—Leon Battista Alberti (b. 1404? d. 1472).[1] His biography,[2] which is only a fragment, speaks of him but little as an artist, and makes no mention at all of his great significance in the history of architecture. We shall now see what he was, apart from these special claims to distinction.

In all by which praise is won, Leon Battista was from his childhood the first. Of his various gymnastic feats and exercises we read with astonishment how, with his feet together, he could spring over a man's head; how, in the cathedral, he threw a coin in the air till it was heard to ring against the distant roof; how the wildest horses trembled under him. In three things he desired to appear faultless to others, in walking, in riding, and in speaking. He learned music without a master, and yet his compositions were admired by professional judges. Under the pressure of poverty, he studied both civil and canonical law for many years, till exhaustion brought on a

[1] For what follows compare Burckhardt, *Geschichte der Renaissance in Italien*, Stuttg. 1868, esp. p. 41 sqq., and A. Springer, *Abhandlungen zur neueren Kunstgeschichte*, Bonn, 1867, pp. 69–102. A new biography of Alberti is in course of preparation by Hub. Janitschek.

[2] In Murat. xxv. col. 295 sqq., with the Italian translation in the *Opere Volgari di L. B. Alberti*, vol. i. pp. lxxxix–cix, where the conjecture is made and shown to be probable that this 'Vita' is by Alberti himself. See, further, Vasari, iv. 52 sqq. Mariano Socini, if we can believe what we read of him in Æn. Sylvius (*Opera*, p. 622, *Epist.* 112) was a universal dilettante, and at the same time a master in several subjects.

severe illness. In his twenty-fourth year, finding his memory for words weakened, but his sense of facts unimpaired, he set to work at physics and mathematics. And all the while he acquired every sort of accomplishment and dexterity, cross-examining artists, scholars, and artisans of all descriptions, down to the cobblers, about the secrets and peculiarities of their craft. Painting and modelling he practised by the way, and especially excelled in admirable likenesses from memory. Great admiration was excited by his mysterious 'camera obscura,'[1] in which he showed at one time the stars and the moon rising over rocky hills, at another wide landscapes with mountains and gulfs receding into dim perspective, and with fleets advancing on the waters in shade or sunshine. And that which others created he welcomed joyfully, and held every human achievement which followed the laws of beauty for something almost divine.[2] To all this must be added his literary works, first of all those on art, which are landmarks and authorities of the first order for the Renaissance of Form, especially in architecture; then his Latin prose writings—novels and other works—of which some have been taken for productions of antiquity; his elegies, eclogues, and humorous dinner-speeches. He also wrote an Italian treatise on domestic life[3] in four books; various moral, philosophical, and historical works; and many speeches and poems, including a funeral oration on his dog. Notwithstanding his admiration for the Latin language, he wrote in Italian, and encouraged others to do the same; himself a disciple of Greek science, he maintained the doctrine, that without Christianity the world would wander in a labyrinth of error. His serious and witty sayings were thought worth collecting, and specimens of them, many columns long, are quoted in his biography. And all that he had and knew he

[1] Similar attempts, especially an attempt at a flying-machine, had been made about 880 by the Andalusian Abul Abbas Kasim ibn Firnas. Comp. Gyangos, *The History of the Muhammedan Dynasties in Spain* (London, 1840), i. 148 sqq. and 425–7; extracts in Hammer, *Literaturgesch. der Araber*, i. Introd. p. li.

[2] Quidquid ingenio esset hominum cum quadam effectum elegantia, id prope divinum ducebat.

[3] This is the book (comp. p. 185, note 2) of which one part, often printed alone, long passed for a work of Pandolfini.

imparted, as rich natures always do, without the least reserve, giving away his chief discoveries for nothing. But the deepest spring of his nature has yet to be spoken of—the sympathetic intensity with which he entered into the whole life around him. At the sight of noble trees and waving corn-fields he shed tears; handsome and dignified old men he honoured as 'a delight of nature,' and could never look at them enough. Perfectly-formed animals won his goodwill as being specially favoured by nature; and more than once, when he was ill, the sight of a beautiful landscape cured him.[1] No wonder that those who saw him in this close and mysterious communion with the world ascribed to him the gift of prophecy. He was said to have foretold a bloody catastrophe in the family of Este, the fate of Florence, and the death of the Popes years before they happened, and to be able to read into the countenances and the hearts of men. It need not be added that an iron will pervaded and sustained his whole personality; like all the great men of the Renaissance, he said, 'Men can do all things if they will.'

And Lionardo da Vinci was to Alberti as the finisher to the beginner, as the master to the *dilettante.* Would only that Vasari's work were here supplemented by a description like that of Alberti! The colossal outlines of Lionardo's nature can never be more than dimly and distantly conceived.

[1] In his work, *De Re Ædificatoria*, l. viii. cap. i., there is a definition of a beautiful road: 'Si modo mare, modo montes, modo lacum fluentem fontesve, modo aridam rupem aut planitiem, modo nemus vallemque exhibebit.'

CHAPTER III.

THE MODERN IDEA OF FAME.

To this inward development of the individual corresponds a new sort of outward distinction—the modern form of glory.[1]

In the other countries of Europe the different classes of society lived apart, each with its own mediæval caste sense of honour. The poetical fame of the Troubadours and Minnesänger was peculiar to the knightly order. But in Italy social equality had appeared before the time of the tyrannies or the democracies. We there find early traces of a general society, having, as will be shown more fully later on, a common ground in Latin and Italian literature; and such a ground was needed for this new element in life to grow in. To this must be added that the Roman authors, who were now zealously studied, and especially Cicero, the most read and admired of all, are filled and saturated with the conception of fame, and that their subject itself—the universal empire of Rome—stood as a permanent ideal before the minds of Italians. From henceforth all the aspirations and achievements of the people were governed by a moral postulate, which was still unknown elsewhere in Europe.

Here, again, as in all essential points, the first witness to be called is Dante. He strove for the poet's garland [2] with all the

[1] One writer among many: Blondus, *Roma Triumphans*, l. v. pp. 117 sqq., where the definitions of glory are collected from the ancients, and the desire of it is expressly allowed to the Christian. Cicero's work, *De Gloria*, which Petrarch claimed to own, was stolen from him by his teacher Convenevole, and has never since been seen. Alberti, in a youthful composition when he was only twenty years of age, praises the desire of fame. *Opere*, vol. i. pp. cxxvii–clxvi.

[2] *Paradiso*, xxv. at the beginning: 'Se mai continga,' &c. See above, p. 133, note 2. Comp. Boccaccio, *Vita di Dante*, p. 49. 'Vaghissimo fu e d' onore e di pompa, e per avventura più che alla sua inclita virtù non si sarebbe richiesto.'

power of his soul. As publicist and man of letters, he laid stress on the fact that what he did was new, and that he wished not only to be, but to be esteemed the first in his own walks.[1] But even in his prose writings he touches on the inconveniences of fame; he knows how often personal acquaintance with famous men is disappointing, and explains how this is due partly to the childish fancy of men, partly to envy, and partly to the imperfections of the hero himself.[2] And in his great poem he firmly maintains the emptiness of fame, although in a manner which betrays that his heart was not set free from the longing for it. In Paradise the sphere of Mercury is the seat of such blessed ones [3] as on earth strove after glory and thereby dimmed 'the beams of true love.' It is characteristic that the lost souls in hell beg of Dante to keep alive for them their memory and fame on earth,[4] while those in Purgatory only entreat his prayers and those of others for their deliverance.[5] And in a famous passage,[6] the passion for fame—'lo gran desio dell' eccellenza'—is reproved for the reason that intellectual glory is not absolute, but relative to the times, and may be surpassed and eclipsed by greater successors.

The new race of poet-scholars which arose soon after Dante quickly made themselves masters of this fresh tendency. They did so in a double sense, being themselves the most acknowledged celebrities of Italy, and at the same time, as poets and historians, consciously disposing of the reputation of others. An outward symbol of this sort of fame was the coronation of the poets, of which we shall speak later on.

A contemporary of Dante, Albertinus Musattus or Mussattus,

[1] *De Vulgari Eloquio*, l. i. cap. i. and esp. *De Monarchia*, l. i. cap. i., where he wishes to set forth the idea of monarchy not only in order to be useful to the world but also 'ut palmam tanti bravii primus in meam gloriam adipiscar.'

[2] *Convito*, ed. Venezia, 1529, fol. 5 and 6.

[3] *Paradiso*, vi. 112 sqq.

[4] E.g. *Inferno*, vi. 89; xiii. 53; xvi. 85; xxxi. 127.

[5] *Purgatorio*, v. 70, 87, 133; vi. 26; viii. 71; xi. 31; xiii. 147.

[6] *Purgatorio*, xi. 85–117. Besides 'gloria' we here find close together 'grido, fama, rumore, nominanza, onore' all different names for the same thing. Boccaccio wrote, as he admits in his letter to Joh. Pizinga (*Op. Volg.* xvi. 30 sqq.) 'perpetuandi nominis desiderio.'

crowned poet at Padua by the bishop and rector, enjoyed a fame which fell little short of deification. Every Christmas Day the doctors and students of both colleges at the University came in solemn procession before his house with trumpets and, as it seems, with burning tapers, to salute him [1] and bring him presents. His reputation lasted till, in 1318, he fell into disgrace with the ruling tyrant of the House of Carrara.

This new incense, which once was offered only to saints and heroes, was given in clouds to Petrarch, who persuaded himself in his later years that it was but a foolish and troublesome thing. His letter 'To Posterity' [2] is the confession of an old and famous man, who is forced to gratify the public curiosity. He admits that he wishes for fame in the times to come, but would rather be without it in his own day.[3] In his dialogue on fortune and misfortune,[4] the interlocutor, who maintains the futility of glory, has the best of the contest. But, at the same time, Petrarch is pleased that the autocrat of Byzantium [5] knows him as well by his writings as Charles IV.[6] knows him.

[1] Scardeonius, *De Urb. Patav. Antiqu.* (Græv. *Thesaur.* vi. iii. col. 260). Whether 'cereis' or 'certis muneribus' should be the reading, cannot be said. The somewhat solemn nature of Mussatus can be recognised in the tone of his history of Henry VII.

[2] Franc. Petrarca, *Posteritati*, or *Ad Posteros*, at the beginning of the editions of his works, or the only letter of Book xviii. of the *Epp. Seniles*; also in Fracassetti, *Petr. Epistolæ Familiares*, 1859, i. 1–11. Some modern critics of Petrarch's vanity would hardly have shown as much kindness and frankness had they been in his place.

[3] *Opera*, ed. 1581, p. 177: 'De celebritate nominis importuna.' Fame among the mass of people was specially offensive to him. *Epp. Fam.* i. 337, 340. In Petrarch, as in many humanists of the older generation, we can observe the conflict between the desire for glory and the claims of Christian humility.

[4] 'De Remediis Utriusque Fortunæ' in the editions of the works. Often printed separately, e.g. Bern, 1600. Compare Petrarch's famous dialogue, 'De Contemptu Mundi' or 'De Conflictu Curarum Suarum,' in which the interlocutor Augustinus blames the love of fame as a damnable fault.

[5] *Epp. Fam.* lib. xviii. (ed. Fracassetti) 2. A measure of Petrarch's fame is given a hundred years later by the assertion of Blondus (*Italia Illustrata*, p. 416) that hardly even a learned man would know anything of Robert the Good if Petrarch had not spoken of him so often and so kindly.

[6] It is to be noted that even Charles IV., perhaps influenced by Petrarch, speaks in a letter to the historian Marignola of fame as the object of every

And in fact, even in his lifetime, his fame extended far beyond Italy. And the emotion which he felt was natural when his friends, on the occasion of a visit to his native Arezzo (1350), took him to the house where he was born, and told him how the city had provided that no change should be made in it.[1] In former times the dwellings of certain great saints were preserved and revered in this way, like the cell of St. Thomas Aquinas in the Dominican convent at Naples, and the Portiuncula of St. Francis near Assisi; and one or two great jurists also enjoyed the half-mythical reputation which led to this honour. Towards the close of the fourteenth century the people at Bagnolo, near Florence, called an old building the 'Studio' of Accursius (b. about 1150), but, nevertheless, suffered it to be destroyed.[2] It is probable that the great incomes and the political influence which some jurists obtained as consulting lawyers made a lasting impression on the popular imagination.

To the cultus of the birthplaces of famous men must be added that of their graves,[3] and, in the case of Petrarch, of the spot where he died. In memory of him Arquà became a favourite resort of the Paduans, and was dotted with graceful little villas.[4] At this time there were no 'classic spots' in Northern Europe, and pilgrimages were only made to pictures and relics. It was a point of honour for the different cities to possess the bones of their own and foreign celebrities; and it is most remarkable how seriously the Florentines, even in the fourteenth century—long before the building of Santa Croce—laboured to make their cathedral a Pantheon. Accorso, Dante,

striving man. H. Friedjung, *Kaiser Karl IV. und sein Antheil am geistigen Leben seiner Zeit*, Vienna, 1876, p. 221.

[1] *Epist. Seniles*, xiii. 3, to Giovanni Aretino, Sept. 9, 1370.

[2] Filippo Villani, *Vite*, p. 19

[3] Both together in the epitaph on Boccaccio: 'Nacqui in Firenze al Pozzo Toscanelli; Di fuor sepolto a Certaldo giaccio,' &c. Comp. *Op. Volg. di Boccaccio*, xvi. 44.

[4] Mich. Savonarola, *De Laudibus Patavii*, in Murat. xxiv. col. 1157. Arquà remained from thenceforth the object of special veneration (comp. Ettore Conte Macola, *I Codici di Arquà*, Padua, 1874), and was the scene of great solemnities at the fifth centenary of Petrarch's death. His dwelling is said to have been lately given to the city of Padua by the last owner, Cardinal Silvestri.

Petrarch, Boccaccio, and the jurist Zanobi della Strada were to have had magnificent tombs there erected to them.[1] Late in the fifteenth century, Lorenzo Magnifico applied in person to the Spoletans, asking them to give up the corpse of the painter Fra Filippo Lippi for the cathedral, and received the answer that they had none too many ornaments to the city, especially in the shape of distinguished people, for which reason they begged him to spare them; and, in fact, he had to be contented with erecting a cenotaph.[2] And even Dante, in spite of all the applications to which Boccaccio urged the Florentines with bitter emphasis,[3] remained sleeping tranquilly by the side of San Francesco at Ravenna, 'among ancient tombs of emperors and vaults of saints, in more honourable company than thou, O Home, couldst offer him.' It even happened that a man once took away unpunished the lights from the altar on which the crucifix stood, and set them by the grave, with the words, 'Take them; thou art more worthy of them than He, the Crucified One!'[4]

And now the Italian cities began again to remember their ancient citizens and inhabitants. Naples, perhaps, had never forgotten its tomb of Virgil, since a kind of mythical halo had become attached to the name, and the memory of it had been revived by Petrarch and Boccaccio, who both stayed in the city.

The Paduans, even in the sixteenth century, firmly believed that they possessed not only the genuine bones of their founder Antenor, but also those of the historian Livy.[5] 'Sulmona,' says Boccaccio,[6] 'bewails that Ovid lies buried far away in exile; and Parma rejoices that Cassius sleeps within its walls.' The Mantuans coined a medal in 1257 with the bust of Virgil,

[1] The decree of 1396 and its grounds in Gaye, *Carteggio*, i. 123.

[2] Reumont, *Lorenzo de' Medici*, ii. 180.

[3] Boccaccio, *Vita di Dante*, p. 39.

[4] Franco Sacchetti, nov. 121.

[5] The former in the well-known sarcophagus near San Lorenzo, the latter over a door in the Palazzo della Ragione. For details as to their discovery in 1413, see Misson, *Voyage en Italie*, vol. i., and Michele Savonarola, col. 1157.

[6] *Vita di Dante*, l. c. How came the body of Cassius from Philippi back to Parma?

and raised a statue to represent him. In a fit of aristocratic insolence,[1] the guardian of the young Gonzaga, Carlo Malatesta, caused it to be pulled down in 1392, and was afterwards

[1] 'Nobilitatis fastu' and 'sub obtentu religionis, says Pius II. (*Comment.* x. p. 473). The new sort of fame must have been inconvenient to those who were accustomed to the old.

That Carlo Malatesta caused the statue of Virgil to be pulled down and thrown into the Mincio, and this, as he alleged, from anger at the veneration paid to it by the people of Mantua, is a well-authenticated fact, specially attested by an invective written in 1397 by P. P. Vergerio against C. M., *De dirutâ Statuâ Virgilii P. P. V. eloquentissimi Oratoris Epistola ex Tugurio Blondi sub Apolline*, ed. by Marco Mantova Benavides (publ. certainly before 1560 at Padua). From this work it is clear that till then the statue had not been set up again. Did this happen in consequence of the invective? Bartholomæus Facius (*De Vir. Ill.* p. 9 sqq. in the Life of P. P. V. 1456) says it did, 'Carolum Malatestam invectus Virgilii statua, quam ille Mantuæ in foro everterat, quoniam gentilis fuerat, ut ibidem restitueretur, effecit;' but his evidence stands alone. It is true that, so far as we know, there are no contemporary chronicles for the history of Mantua at that period (Platina, *Hist. Mant.* in Murat. xx. contains nothing about the matter), but later historians are agreed that the statue was not restored. See for evidence, Prendilacqua, *Vita di Vitt. da Feltre*, written soon after 1446 (ed. 1871, p. 78), where the destruction but not the restoration of the statue is spoken of, and the work of Ant. Possevini, jun. (*Gonzaga*, Mantua, 1628), where, p. 486, the pulling down of the statue, the murmurings and violent opposition of the people, and the promise given in consequence by the prince that he *would* restore it, are all mentioned, with the addition: 'Nec tamen restitutus est Virgilius.' Further, on March 17, 1499, Jacopo d'Hatry writes to Isabella of Este, that he has spoken with Pontano about a plan of the princess to raise a statue to Virgil at Mantua, and that Pontano cried out with delight that Vergerio, if he were alive, would be even more pleased 'che non se attristò quando el Conte Carola Malatesta persuase abuttare la statua di Virgilio nel fiume.' The writer then goes on to speak of the manner of setting it up, of the inscription 'P. Virgilius Mantuanus' and 'Isabella Marchionissa Mantuæ restituit,' and suggests that Andrea Mantegna would be the right man to be charged with the work. Mantegna did in fact make the drawings for it. (The drawing and the letter in question are given in Baschet, *Recherches de documents d'art et d'histoire dans les Archives de Mantoue; documents inédits concernant la personne et les œuvres d'Andrea Mantegna*, in the *Gazette des Beaux-Arts*, xx. (1866) 478–492, esp. 486 sqq.) It is clear from this letter that Carlo Malatesta did not have the statue restored. In Comparetti's work on Virgil in the Middle Ages, the story is told after Burckhardt, but without authorities. Dr. Geiger, on the authority of Professor Paul of Berlin, distinguishes between C. Cassius Longinus and Cassius Parmensis, the poet, both among the assassins of Cæsar.

forced, when he found the fame of the old poet too strong for him, to set it up again. Even then, perhaps, the grotto, a couple of miles from the town, where Virgil was said to have meditated,[1] was shown to strangers, like the 'Scuola di Virgilio' at Naples. Como claimed both the Plinys[2] for its own, and at the end of the fifteenth century erected statues in their honour, sitting under graceful baldachins on the façade of the cathedral.

History and the new topography were now careful to leave no local celebrity unnoticed. At the same period the northern chronicles only here and there, among the list of popes, emperors, earthquakes, and comets, put in the remark, that at such a time this or that famous man 'flourished.' We shall elsewhere have to show how, mainly under the influence of this idea of fame, an admirable biographical literature was developed. We must here limit ourselves to the local patriotism of the topographers who recorded the claims of their native cities to distinction.

In the Middle Ages, the cities were proud of their saints and of the bones and relics in their churches.[3] With these the panegyrist of Padua in 1440, Michele Savonarola,[4] begins his list; from them he passes to 'the famous men who were no saints, but who, by their great intellect and force (*virtus*) deserve to be added (*adnecti*) to the saints'—just as in classical antiquity the distinguished man came close upon the hero.[5] The further enumeration is most characteristic of the time. First comes Antenor, the brother of Priam, who founded Padua with a band of Trojan fugitives; King Dardanus, who defeated

[1] Comp. Keyssler's *Neueste Reisen*, p. 1016.

[2] The elder was notoriously a native of Verona.

[3] This is the tone of the remarkable work, *De Laudibus Papiæ*, in Murat. xx., dating from the fourteenth century—much municipal pride, but no idea of personal fame.

[4] *De Laudibus Patavii*, in Murat. xxiv. col. 1138 sqq. Only three cities, in his opinion—could be compared with Padua—Florence, Venice and Rome.

[5] 'Nam et veteres nostri tales aut divos aut æternâ memoriâ dignos non immerito prædicabant, quum virtus summa sanctitatis sit consocia et pari ematur pretio.' What follows is most characteristic: 'Hos itaque meo facili judicio æternos facio.'

Attila in the Euganean hills, followed him in pursuit, and struck him dead at Rimini with a chess-board; the Emperor Henry IV., who built the cathedral; a King Marcus, whose head was preserved in Monselice (*monte silicis arce*); then a couple of cardinals and prelates as founders of colleges, churches, and so forth; the famous Augustinian theologian, Fra Alberto; a string of philosophers beginning with Paolo Veneto and the celebrated Pietro of Albano; the jurist Paolo Padovano; then Livy and the poets Petrarch, Mussato, Lovato. If there is any want of military celebrities in the list, the poet consoles himself for it by the abundance of learned men whom he has to show, and by the more durable character of intellectual glory; while the fame of the soldier is buried with his body, or, if it lasts, owes its permanence only to the scholar.[1] It is nevertheless honourable to the city that foreign warriors lie buried here by their own wish, like Pietro de Rossi of Parma, Filippo Arcelli of Piacenza, and especially Gattamelata of Narni (d. 1642),[2] whose brazen equestrian statue, 'like a Cæsar in triumph,' already stood by the church of the Santo. The author then names a crowd of jurists and physicians, among the latter two friends of Petrarch, Johannes ab Horologio and Jacob de Dondis, nobles 'who had not only, like so many others, received, but deserved, the honour of knighthood.' Then follows a list of famous mechanicians, painters, and musicians, which is closed by the name of a fencing-master Michele Rosso, who, as the most distinguished man in his profession, was to be seen painted in many places.

By the side of these local temples of fame, which myth, legend, popular admiration, and literary tradition combined to create, the poet-scholars built up a great Pantheon of world-wide celebrity. They made collections of famous men and famous women, often in direct imitation of Cornelius Nepos, the pseudo-Suetonius, Valerius Maximus, Plutarch (*Mulierum*

[1] Similar ideas occur in many contemporary writers. Codrus Urceus, *Sermo* xiii. (*Opp.* 1506, fol. xxxviii. *b*), speaking of Galeazzo Bentivoglio, who was both a scholar and a warrior, 'Cognoscens artem militarem esse quidem excellentem, sed literas multo certe excellentiores.'

[2] What follows immediately is not, as the editor remarks (Murat. xxiv. col. 1059, note), from the pen of Mich. Savonarola.

virtutes), Hieronymus (*De Viris Illustribus*), and others: or they wrote of imaginary triumphal processions and Olympian assemblies, as was done by Petrarch in his 'Trionfo della Fama,' and Boccaccio in the 'Amorosa Visione,' with hundreds of names, of which three-fourths at least belong to antiquity and the rest to the Middle Ages.[1] By-and-by this new and comparatively modern element was treated with greater emphasis; the historians began to insert descriptions of character, and collections arose of the biographies of distinguished contemporaries, like those of Filippo Villani, Vespasiano Fiorentino, Bartolommeo Facio, Paolo Cortese,[2] and lastly of Paolo Giovio.[3]

[1] Petrarch, in the 'Triumph' here quoted, only dwells on characters of antiquity, and in his collection, *De Rebus Memorandis*, has little to say of contemporaries. In the *Casus Virorum Illustrium* of Boccaccio (among the men a number of women, besides Philippa Catinensis treated of at the end, are included, and even the goddess Juno is described), only the close of the eighth book and the last book—the ninth—deal with non-classical times. Boccaccio's remarkable work, *De Claris Mulieribus*, treats also almost exclusively of antiquity. It begins with Eve, speaks then of ninety-seven women of antiquity, and seven of the Middle ages, beginning with Pope Joan and ending with Queen Johanna of Naples. And so at a much later time in the *Commentarii Urbani* of Ralph. Volaterranus. In the work *De Claris Mulieribus* of the Augustinian Jacobus Bergomensis (printed 1497, but probably published earlier) antiquity and legend hold the chief place, but there are still some valuable biographies of Italian women. There are one or two lives of contemporary women by Vespasiano da Bisticci (*Arch. Stor. Ital.* iv. i. pp. 430 sqq.) In Scardeonius (*De Urb. Patav. Antiqu. Græv. Thesaur.* vi. iii. col. 405 sqq,) only famous Paduan women are mentioned. First comes a legend or tradition from the time of the fall of the empire, then tragical stories of the party struggles of the thirteenth and fourteenth centuries; then notices of several heroic women; then the foundress of nunneries, the political woman, the female doctor, the mother of many and distinguished sons, the learned woman, the peasant girl who dies defending her chastity; then the cultivated beauty of the sixteenth century, on whom everybody writes sonnets; and lastly, the female novelist and poet at Padua. A century later the woman-professor would have been added to these. For the famous woman of the House of Este, see Ariosto, *Orl.* xiii.

[2] Bartolommeo Facio and Paolo Cortese. B. F. *De Viris Illustribus Liber*, was first published by L. Mehus (Florence, 1745). The book was begun by the author (known by other historical works, and resident at the court of Alfonso of Naples) after he had finished the history of that king (1455), and ended, as references to the struggles of Hungary and the writer's ignorance of the elevation of Æneas Silvius to the cardinalate show, in 1456. (See, nevertheless, Wahlen, *Laurentii Vallæ Opuscula*

The North of Europe, until Italian influence began to tell upon its writers—for instance, on Trithemius, the first German who wrote the lives of famous men—possessed only either

Tria, Vienna, 1869, p. 67, note 1.) It is never quoted by contemporaries, and seldom by later writers. The author wishes in this book to describe the famous men, 'ætatis memoriæque nostræ,' and consequently only mentions such as were born in the last quarter of the fourteenth century, and were still living in, or had died shortly before, the middle of the fifteenth. He chiefly limits himself to Italians, except in the case of artists or princes, among the latter of whom he includes the Emperor Sigismund and Albrecht Achilles of Brandenburg; and in arranging the various biographies he neither follows chronological order nor the distinction which the subject of each attained, but puts them down 'ut quisque mihi occurrerit,' intending to treat in a second part of those whom he might have left out in the first. He divides the famous men into nine classes, nearly all of them prefaced by remarks on their distinctive qualities: 1. Poets; 2. Orators; 3. Jurists; 4. Physicians (with a few philosophers and theologians, as an appendix); 5. Painters; 6. Sculptors; 7. Eminent citizens; 8. Generals; 9. Princes and kings. Among the latter he treats with special fulness and care of Pope Nicholas V. and King Alfonso of Naples. In general he gives only short and mostly eulogistic biographies, confined in the case of princes and soldiers to the list of their deeds, and of artists and writers to the enumeration of their works. No attempt is made at a detailed description or criticism of these; only with regard to a few works of art which he had himself seen he writes more fully. Nor is any attempt made at an estimate of individuals; his heroes either receive a few general words of praise, or must be satisfied with the mere mention of their names. Of himself the author says next to nothing. He states only that Guarino was his teacher, that Manetti wrote a book on a subject which he himself had treated, that Bracellius was his countryman, and that the painter Pisano of Verona was known to him (pp. 17, 18, 19, 48; but says nothing in speaking of Laurentius Valla of his own violent quarrels with this scholar. On the other hand, he does not fail to express his piety and his hatred to the Turks (p. 64), to relieve his Italian patriotism by calling the Swiss barbarians (p. 60), and to say of P. P. Vergerius, 'dignus qui totam in Italia vitam scribens exegisset' (p. 9).

Of all celebrities he evidently sets most store by the scholars, and among these by the 'oratores,' to whom he devotes nearly a third of his book. He nevertheless has great respect for the jurists, and shows a special fondness for the physicians, among whom he well distinguishes the theoretical from the practical, relating the successful diagnoses and operations of the latter. That he treats of theologians and philosophers in connection with the physicians, is as curious as that he should put the painters immediately after the physicians, although, as he says, they are most allied to the poets. In spite of his reverence for learning, which shows itself in the praise given to the princes who patronised it, he is too

legends of the saints, or descriptions of princes and churchmen partaking largely of the character of legends and showing no traces of the idea of fame, that is, of distinction won by a man's

much of a courtier not to register the tokens of princely favour received by the scholars he speaks of, and to characterise the princes in the introduction to the chapters devoted to them as those who 'veluti corpus membra, ita omnia genera quæ supra memoravimus, regunt ac tuentur.'

The style of the book is simple and unadorned, and the matter of it full of instruction, notwithstanding its brevity. It is a pity that Facius did not enter more fully into the personal relations and circumstances of the men whom he described, and did not add to the list of their writings some notice of the contents and the value of them.

The work of Paolo Cortese (b. 1645, d. 1510), *De Hominibus Doctis Dialogus* (first ed. Florence, 1734), is much more limited in its character. This work, written about 1490, since it mentions Antonius Geraldinus as dead, who died in 1488, and was dedicated to Lorenzo de' Medici, who died in 1492, is distinguished from that of Facius, written a generation earlier, not only by the exclusion of all who are not learned men, but by various inward and outward characteristics. First by the form, which is that of a dialogue between the author and his two companions, Alexander Farnese and Antonius, and by the digressions and unequal treatment of the various characters caused thereby; and secondly by the manner of the treatment itself. While Facius only speaks of the men of his own time, Cortese treats only of the dead, and in part of those long dead, by which he enlarges his circle more than he narrows it by exclusion of the living; while Facius merely chronicles works and deeds, as if they were unknown, Cortese criticises the literary activity of his heroes as if the reader were already familiar with it. This criticism is shaped by the humanistic estimate of eloquence, according to which no man could be considered of importance unless he had achieved something remarkable in eloquence, *i.e.* in the classical, Ciceronian treatment of the Latin language. On this principle Dante and Petrarch are only moderately praised, and are blamed for having diverted so much of their powers from Latin to Italian; Guarino is described as one who had beheld perfect eloquence at least through a cloud; Lionardo Aretino as one who had offered his contemporaries 'aliquid splendidius;' and Enea Silvio as he 'in quo primum apparuit mutati sæculi signum.' This point of view prevailed over all others; never perhaps was it held so one-sidedly as by Cortese. To get a notion of his way of thinking we have only to hear his remarks on a predecessor, also the compiler of a great biographical collection, Sicco Polentone: 'Ejus sunt viginti ad filium libri scripti de claris scriptoribus, utiles admodum qui jam fere ab omnibus legi sent desiti. Est enim in judicando parum acer, nec servit aurium voluptati quum tractat res ab aliis ante tractatas; sed hoc ferendum. Illud certe molestum est, dum alienis verbis sententiisque scripta infarcit et explet sua; ex quo nascitur maxime vitiosum scribendi genus, quum modo lenis et candidus, modo durus et asper appareat, et sic in toto

personal efforts. Poetical glory was still confined to certain classes of society, and the names of northern artists are only known to us at this period in so far as they were members of certain guilds or corporations.

The poet-scholar in Italy had, as we have already said, the fullest consciousness that he was the giver of fame and im-

genere tanquam in unum agrum plura inter se inimicissima sparsa semina.'

All are not treated with so much detail; most are disposed of in a few brief sentences; some are merely named without a word being added. Much is nevertheless to be learned from his judgments, though we may not be able always to agree with them. We cannot here discuss him more fully, especially as many of his most characteristic remarks have been already made use of; on the whole, they give us a clear picture of the way in which a later time, outwardly more developed, looked down with critical scorn upon an earlier age, inwardly perhaps richer, but externally less perfect.

Facius, the author of the first-mentioned biographical work, is spoken of, but not his book. Like Facius, Cortese is the humble courtier, looking on Lorenzo de' Medici as Facius looked on Alfonso of Naples; like him, he is a patriot who only praises foreign excellence unwillingly and because he must; adding the assurance that he does not wish to oppose his own country (p. 48, speaking of Janus Pannonius).

Information as to Cortese has been collected by Bernardus Paperinius, the editor of his work; we may add that his Latin translation of the novel of L. B. Alberti, *Hippolytus and Dejanira*, is printed for the first time in the *Opere di L. B. A.* vol. iii. pp. 439–463.

[3] How great the fame of the humanists was is shown by the fact that impostors attempted to make capital out of the use of their names. There thus appeared at Verona a man strangely clad and using strange gestures, who, when brought before the mayor, recited with great energy passages of Latin verse and prose, taken from the works of Panormita, answered in reply to the questions put to him that he was himself Panormita, and was able to give so many small and commonly unknown details about the life of this scholar, that his statement obtained general credit. He was then treated with great honour by the authorities and the learned men of the city, and played his assumed part successfully for a considerable time, until Guarino and others who knew Panormita personally discovered the fraud. Comp. Rosmini, *Vita di Guarino*, ii. 44 sqq. 171 sqq. Few of the humanists were free from the habit of boasting. Codrus Urceus (*Vita*, at the end of the *Opera*, 1506, fol. lxx.), when asked for his opinion about this or that famous man, used to answer: 'Sibi scire videntur.' Barth. Facius, *De Vir. Ill.* p. 31, tells of the jurist Antonius Butriensis: 'Id unum in eo viro notandum est, quod neminem unquam, adeo excellere homines in eo studio volebat, ut doctoratu dignum in examine comprobavit.'

mortality, or, if he chose, of oblivion.[1] Petrarch, notwithstanding all the idealism of his love to Laura, gives utterance to the feeling, that his sonnets confer immortality on his beloved as well as on himself.[2] Boccaccio complains of a fair one to whom he had done homage, and who remained hard-hearted in order that he might go on praising her and making her famous, and he gives her a hint that he will try the effect of a little blame.[3] Sannazaro, in two magnificent sonnets, threatens Alfonso of Naples with eternal obscurity on account of his cowardly flight before Charles VIII.[4] Angelo Poliziano seriously exhorts (1491) King John of Portugal[5] to think betimes of his immortality in reference to the new discoveries in Africa, and to send him materials to Florence, there to be put into shape (*operosius excolenda*), otherwise it would befall him as it had befallen all the others whose deeds, unsupported by the help of the learned, 'lie hidden in the vast heap of human frailty.' The king, or his humanistic chancellor, agreed to this, and promised that at least the Portuguese chronicles of African affairs should be translated into Italian, and sent to Florence to be done into Latin. Whether the promise was kept is not known. These pretensions are by no means so groundless as they may appear at first sight; for the form in which events, even the greatest, are told to the living and to posterity is anything but a matter of indifference. The Italian humanists, with their mode of exposition and their Latin style, had long the complete control of the reading world of Europe, and till last century the Italian poets were more widely known and studied than those of any other nation. The baptismal name of the Florentine Amerigo Vespucci was given, on account of his book of travels—certainly at the proposal of its German translator into Latin, Martin Waldseemüller (Hylacomylus)[6]—to a new quarter of the globe, and if Paolo Giovio,

[1] A Latin poet of the twelfth century, one of the wandering scholars who barters his song for a coat, uses this as a threat. *Carmina Burana*, p. 76.

[2] Sonnet cli: Lasso ch' i ardo.

[3] Boccaccio, *Opere Volgari*, vol. xvi. in Sonnet 13: Pallido, vinto, etc.

[4] Elsewhere, and in Roscoe, *Leone X.* ed. Bossi, iv. 203.

[5] *Angeli Politiani Epp.* lib. x.

[6] Quatuor navigationes, etc. Deodatum (*St. Dié*), 1507. Comp. O. Peschel, *Geschichte des Zeitalters der Entdeckungen*, 1859, ed. 2, 1876.

with all his superficiality and graceful caprice, promised himself immortality,[1] his expectation has not altogether been disappointed.

Amid all these preparations outwardly to win and secure fame, the curtain is now and then drawn aside, and we see with frightful evidence a boundless ambition and thirst after greatness, independent of all means and consequences. Thus, in the preface to Macchiavelli's Florentine history, in which he blames his predecessors Lionardo Aretino and Poggio for their too considerate reticence with regard to the political parties in the city: 'They erred greatly and showed that they understood little the ambition of men and the desire to perpetuate a name. How many who could distinguish themselves by nothing praiseworthy, strove to do so by imfamous deeds! Those writers did not consider that actions which are great in themselves, as is the case with the actions of rulers and of states, always seem to bring more glory than blame, of whatever kind they are and whatever the result of them may be.'[2] In more than one remarkable and dreadful undertaking the motive assigned by serious writers is the burning desire to achieve something great and memorable. This motive is not a mere extreme case of ordinary vanity, but something demonic, involving a surrender of the will, the use of any means, however atrocious, and even an indifference to success itself. In this sense, for example, Macchiavelli conceives the character of Stefano Porcaro (p. 104);[3] of the murderers of Galeazzo Maria Sforza (p. 57), the documents tell us about the same; and the assassination of Duke Alessandro of Florence (1537) is ascribed by Varchi himself to the thirst for fame which tormented the murderer Lorenzino Medici (p. 60). Still more stress is laid on this motive by Paolo Giovio.[4] Lorenzino, according to him, pilloried by a pamphlet of Molza on account

[1] Paul. Jov. *De Romanis Piscibus*, Præfatio (1825). The first decade of his histories would soon be published, 'non sine aliqua spe immortalitatis.'

[2] Comp. *Discorsi*, i. 27. 'Tristizia' (crime) can have 'grandezza' and be 'in alcuna parte generosa'; 'grandezza' can take away 'infamia' from a deed; a man can be 'onorevolmente tristo' in contrast to one who is 'perfettamente buono.'

[3] *Storie Fiorentine*, l. vi.

[4] Paul. Jov. *Elog. Vir. Lit. Ill.* p. 192, speaking of Marius Molsa.

of the mutilation of some ancient statues at Rome, broods over a deed whose novelty shall make his disgrace forgotten, and ends by murdering his kinsman and prince. These are characteristic features of this age of overstrained and despairing passions and forces, and remind us of the burning of the temple of Diana at Ephesus in the time of Philip of Macedon.

CHAPTER IV.

MODERN WIT AND SATIRE.

THE corrective, not only of this modern desire for fame, but of all highly developed individuality, is found in ridicule, especially when expressed in the victorious form of wit.[1] We read in the Middle Ages how hostile armies, princes, and nobles, provoked one another with symbolical insult, and how the defeated party was loaded with symbolical outrage. Here and there, too, under the influence of classical literature, wit began to be used as a weapon in theological disputes, and the poetry of Provence produced a whole class of satirical compositions. Even the Minnesänger, as their political poems show, could adopt this tone when necessary.[2] But wit could not be an independent element in life till its appropriate victim, the developed individual with personal pretentions, had appeared. Its weapons were then by no means limited to the tongue and the pen, but included tricks and practical jokes—the so-called 'burle' and 'beffe'—which form a chief subject of many collections of novels.

The 'Hundred Old Novels,' which must have been composed about the end of the thirteenth century, have as yet neither wit, the fruit of contrast, nor the 'burla,' for their subject;[3]

[1] Mere railing is found very early, in Benzo of Alba, in the eleventh century (*Mon. Germ.* ss. xi. 591–681).

[2] The Middle Ages are further rich in so-called satirical poems; but the satire is not individual, but aimed at classes, categories, and whole populations, and easily passes into the didactic tone. The whole spirit of this literature is best represented by *Reineke Fuchs*, in all its forms among the different nations of the West. For this branch of French literature see a new and admirable work by Lenient, *La Satire en France au Moyen-âge*, Paris, 1860, and the equally excellent continuation, *La Satire en France, ou la littérature militante au XVIe Siècle*, Paris, 1866.

[3] See above, p. 7, note 2. Occasionally we find an insolent joke. nov. 37.

their aim is merely to give simple and elegant expression to wise sayings and pretty stories or fables. But if anything proves the great antiquity of the collection, it is precisely this absence of satire. For with the fourteenth century comes Dante, who, in the utterance of scorn, leaves all other poets in the world far behind, and who, if only on account of his great picture of the deceivers,[1] must be called the chief master of colossal comedy. With Petrarch[2] begin the collections of witty sayings after the pattern of Plutarch (Apophthegmata, etc.).

What stores of wit were concentrated in Florence during this century, is most characteristically shown in the novels of Franco Sacchetti. These are, for the most part, not stories but answers, given under certain circumstances—shocking pieces of *naïveté*, with which silly folks, court-jesters, rogues, and profligate women make their retort. The comedy of the tale lies in the startling contrast of this real or assumed *naïveté* with conventional morality and the ordinary relations of the world—things are made to stand on their heads. All means of picturesque representation are made use of, including the introduction of certain North Italian dialects. Often the place of wit is taken by mere insolence, clumsy trickery, blasphemy, and obscenity; one or two jokes told of Condottieri[3] are among the most brutal and malicious which are recorded. Many of the 'burle' are thoroughly comic, but many are only real or supposed evidence of personal superiority, of triumph over another. How much people were willing to put up with, how often the victim was satisfied with getting the laugh on his side by a retaliatory trick, cannot be said; there was much heartless and pointless malice mixed up with it all, and life in Florence was no doubt often made unpleasant enough from

[1] *Inferno*, xxi. xxii. The only possible parallel is with Aristophanes.

[2] A modest beginning *Opera*, p. 421, sqq., in *Rerum Memorandarum Libri IV*. Again, in *Epp. Seniles*, x. 2. Comp. *Epp. Fam.* ed. Fracass. i. 68 sqq., 70, 240, 245. The puns have a flavour of their mediæval home, the monasteries. Petrarch's invectives 'contra Gallum,' 'contra medicum objurgantem,' and his work, *De Sui Ipsius et Multorum Ignorantia;* perhaps also his *Epistolæ sine Titulo*,' may be quoted as early examples of satirical writing.

[3] Nov. 40, 41; Ridolfo da Camerino is the man.

this cause.[1] The inventors and retailers of jokes soon became inevitable figures,[2] and among them there must have been some who were classical—far superior to all the mere court-jesters, to whom competition, a changing public, and the quick apprehension of the audience, all advantages of life in Florence, were wanting. Some Florentine wits went starring among the despotic courts of Lombardy and Romagna,[3] and found themselves much better rewarded than at home, where their talent was cheap and plentiful. The better type of these people is the amusing man (l'uomo piacevole), the worse is the buffoon and the vulgar parasite who presents himself at weddings and banquets with the argument, 'If I am not invited, the fault is not mine.' Now and then the latter combine to pluck a young spendthrift,[4] but in general they are treated and despised as parasites, while wits of higher position bear themselves like princes, and consider their talent as something sovereign. Dolcibene, whom Charles IV., 'Imperator di Buem,' had pronounced to be the 'king of Italian jesters,' said to him at Ferrara: 'You will conquer the world, since you are my friend and the Pope's; you fight with the sword, the Pope with his bulls, and I with my tongue.'[5] This is no mere jest, but a foreshadowing of Pietro Aretino.

The two most famous jesters about the middle of the fifteenth century were a priest near Florence, Arlotto (1483), for more refined wit ('facezie'), and the court-fool of Ferrara,

[1] The well-known jest of Brunellesco and the fat wood-carver, Manetto Ammanatini, who is said to have fled into Hungary before the ridicule he encountered, is clever but cruel.

[2] The 'Araldo' of the Florentine Signoria. One instance among many, *Commissioni di Rinaldo degli Albizzi*, iii. 651, 669. The fool as necessary to enliven the company after dinner; Alcyonius, *De Exilio*, ed. Mencken, p. 129.

[3] Sacchetti, nov. 48. And yet, according to nov. 67, there was an impression that a Romagnole was superior to the worst Florentine.

[4] L. B. Alberti, *Del Governo della Famiglia*, *Opere*, ed. Bonucci, v. 171. Comp. above, p. 132, note 1.

[5] Franco Sacchetti, nov. 156; comp. 24 for Dolcibene and the Jews. (For Charles IV. and the fools, *Friedjung*, o.c. p. 109.) The *Facetiæ* of Poggio resemble Sacchetti's in substance—practical jokes, impertinences, refined indecency misunderstood by simple folk; the philologist is betrayed by the large number of verbal jokes. On L. A. Alberti, see pp. 136, sqq.

Gonnella, for buffoonery. We can hardly compare their stories with those of the Parson of Kalenberg and Till Eulenspiegel, since the latter arose in a different and half-mythical manner, as fruits of the imagination of a whole people, and touch rather on what is general and intelligible to all, while Arlotto and Gonnella were historical beings, coloured and shaped by local influences. But if the comparison be allowed, and extended to the jests of the non-Italian nations, we shall find in general that the joke in the French *fabliaux*,[1] as among the Germans, is chiefly directed to the attainment of some advantage or enjoyment; while the wit of Arlotto and the practical jokes of Gonnella are an end in themselves, and exist simply for the sake of the triumph of production. (Till Eulenspiegel again forms a class by himself, as the personified quiz, mostly pointless enough, of particular classes and professions). The court-fool of the Este saved himself more than once by his keen satire and refined modes of vengeance.[2]

The type of the 'uomo piacevole' and the 'buffone' long survived the freedom of Florence. Under Duke Cosimo flourished Barlacchia, and at the beginning of the seventeenth century Francesco Ruspoli and Curzio Marignolli. In Pope Leo X., the genuine Florentine love of jesters showed itself strikingly. This prince, whose taste for the most refined intellectual pleasures was insatiable, endured and desired at his table a number of witty buffoons and jack-puddings, among them two monks and a cripple;[3] at public feasts he treated them with deliberate scorn as parasites, setting before them monkeys and crows in the place of savoury meats. Leo, indeed, showed a peculiar fondness for the 'burla'; it belonged to his nature sometimes to treat his own favourite pursuits—music and poetry—ironically, parodying them with his factotum, Cardinal Bibbiena.[4] Neither of them found it beneath

[1] And consequently in those novels of the Italians whose subject is taken from them.

[2] According to Bandello, iv. nov. 2, Gonnella could twist his features into the likeness of other people, and mimic all the dialects of Italy.

[3] Paul. Jov. *Vita Leonis X.*

[4] 'Erat enim Bibiena mirus artifex hominibus ætate vel professione gravibus ad insaniam impellendis.' We are here reminded of the jests of Christine of Sweden with her philologists. Comp. the remarkable passage

him to fool an honest old secretary till he thought himself a master of the art of music. The Improvisatore, Baraballo of Gaeta, was brought so far by Leo's flattery, that he applied in all seriousness for the poet's coronation on the Capitol. On the anniversary of S. Cosmas and S. Damian, the patrons of the House of Medici, he was first compelled, adorned with laurel and purple, to amuse the papal guests with his recitations, and at last, when all were ready to split with laughter, to mount a gold-harnessed elephant in the court of the Vatican, sent as a present to Rome by Emanuel the Great of Portugal, while the Pope looked down from above through his eye-glass.[1] The brute, however, was so terrified by the noise of the trumpets and kettle-drums, and the cheers of the crowd, that there was no getting him over the bridge of S. Angelo.

The parody of what is solemn or sublime, which here meets us in the case of a procession, had already taken an important place in poetry.[2] It was naturally compelled to choose vic-

of Jovian. Pontanus, *De Sermone*, lib. ii. cap. 9: 'Ferdinandus Alfonsi filius, Neapolitanorum rex magnus et ipse fuit artifex et vultus componendi et orationes in quem ipse usus vellet. Nam ætatis nostri Pontifices maximi fingendis vultibus ac verbis vel histriones ipsos anteveniunt.'

[1] The eye-glass I not only infer from Rafael's portrait, where it can be explained as a magnifier for looking at the miniatures in the prayer-book, but from a statement of Pellicanus, according to which Leo views an advancing procession of monks through a 'specillum' (comp. *Züricher Taschenbuch* for 1858, p. 177), and from the 'cristallus concava,' which, according to Giovio, he used when hunting. (Comp. 'Leonis X. vita auctore anon. conscripta' in the Appendix to Roscoe.) In Attilius Alessius (Baluz. *Miscell.* iv. 518) we read, 'Oculari ex gemina (gemma?) utebatur quam manu gestans, signando aliquid videndum esset, oculis admovebat.' The shortsightedness in the family of the Medici was hereditary. Lorenzo was shortsighted, and replied to the Sienese Bartolommeo Soccini, who said that the air of Florence was bad for the eyes: 'E quella di Siena al cervello.' The bad sight of Leo X. was proverbial. After his election, the Roman wits explained the number MCCCCXL. engraved in the Vatican as follows: 'Multi cæci Cardinales creaverunt cæcum decimum Leonem.' Comp. Shepherd-Tonelli, *Vita del Poggio*, ii. 23, sqq., and the passages there quoted.

[2] We find it also in plastic art, e.g., in the famous plate parodying the group of the Laöcoon as three monkeys. But here parody seldom went beyond sketches and the like, though much, it is true, may have been destroyed. Caricature, again, is something different. Lionardo, in the grotesque faces in the Biblioteca Ambrosiana, represents what is hideous

tims of another kind than those of Aristophanes, who introduced the great tragedian into his plays. But the same maturity of culture which at a certain period produced parody among the Greeks, did the same in Italy. By the close of the fourteenth century, the love-lorn wailings of Petrarch's sonnets and others of the same kind were taken off by caricaturists; and the solemn air of this form of verse was parodied in lines of mystic twaddle. A constant invitation to parody was offered by the 'Divine Comedy,' and Lorenzo Magnifico wrote the most admirable travesty in the style of the 'Inferno' ('Simposio' or 'I Beoni'). Luigi Pulei obviously imitates the Improvisatori in his 'Morgante,' and both his poetry and Bojardo's are in part, at least, a half-conscious parody of the chivalrous poetry of the Middle Ages. Such a caricature was deliberately undertaken by the great parodist Teofilo Folengo (about 1520). Under the name of Limerno Pitocco, he composed the 'Orlandino,' in which chivalry appears only as a ludicrous setting for a crowd of modern figures and ideas. Under the name of Merlinus Coccajus he described the journeys and exploits of his phantastic vagabonds (also in the same spirit of parody) in half-Latin hexameters, with all the affected pomp of the learned Epos of the day. ('Opus Macaronicorum'). Since then caricature has been constantly, and often brilliantly, represented on the Italian Parnassus.

About the middle period of the Renaissance a theoretical analysis of wit was undertaken, and its practical application in good society was regulated more precisely. The theorist was Gioviano Pontano.[1] In his work on speaking, especially in the third and fourth books, he tries by means of the comparison of numerous jokes or 'facetiæ' to arrive at a general principle. How wit should be used among people of position is taught by Baldassar Castiglione in his 'Cortigiano.'[2] Its

when and because it is comical, and exaggerates the ludicrous element at pleasure.

[1] Jovian. Pontan. *De Sermone*, libri v. He attributes a special gift of wit to the Sienese and Peruginese, as well as to the Florentines, adding the Spanish court as a matter of politeness.

[2] *Il Cortigiano*, lib. ii. cap. 4 sqq., ed. Baude di Vesme, Florence, 1854, pp. 124 sqq. For the explanation of wit as the effect of contrast, though not clearly put, see *ibid.* cap. lxxiii. p. 136.

chief function is naturally to enliven those present by the repetition of comic or graceful stories and sayings; personal jokes, on the contrary, are discouraged on the ground that they wound unhappy people, show too much honour to wrong-doers, and make enemies of the powerful and the spoiled children of fortune;[1] and even in repetition, a wide reserve in the use of dramatic gestures is recommended to the gentleman. Then follows, not only for purposes of quotation, but as patterns for future jesters, a large collection of puns and witty sayings, methodically arranged according to their species, among them some that are admirable. The doctrine of Giovanni della Casa, some twenty years later, in his guide to good manners, is much stricter and more cautious;[2] with a view to the consequences, he wishes to see the desire of triumph banished altogether from jokes and 'burle.' He is the herald of a reaction, which was certain sooner or later to appear.

Italy had, in fact, become a school for scandal, the like of which the world cannot show, not even in France at the time of Voltaire. In him and his comrades there was assuredly no lack of the spirit of negation; but where, in the eighteenth century, was to be found the crowd of suitable victims, that countless assembly of highly and characteristically-developed human beings, celebrities of every kind, statesmen, churchmen, inventors, and discoverers, men of letters, poets and artists, all of whom then gave the fullest and freest play to their individuality? This host existed in the fifteenth and sixteenth centuries, and by its side the general culture of the time had educated a poisonous brood of impotent wits, of born critics and railers, whose envy called for hecatombs of victims; and to all this was added the envy of the famous men among themselves. In this the philologists notoriously led the way—Filelfo, Poggio, Lorenzo Valla, and others—while the artists of the fifteenth century lived in peaceful and friendly competition with one another. The history of art may take note of the fact.

Florence, the great market of fame, was in this point, as

[1] Pontanus, *De Sermone*, lib. iv. cap. 3, also advises people to abstain from using 'ridicula' either against the miserable or the strong.

[2] *Galateo del Casa*, ed. Venez. 1789, p. 26 sqq. 48.

we have said, in advance of other cities. 'Sharp eyes and bad tongues' is the description given of the inhabitants.[1] An easy-going contempt of everything and everybody was probably the prevailing tone of society. Macchiavelli, in the remarkable prologue to his 'Mandragola,' refers rightly or wrongly the visible decline of moral force to the general habit of evil speaking, and threatens his detractors with the news that he can say sharp things as well as they. Next to Florence comes the Papal court, which had long been a rendezvous of the bitterest and wittiest tongues. Poggio's 'Facetiæ' are dated from the Chamber of Lies (*bugiale*) of the apostolic notaries; and when we remember the number of disappointed place-hunters, of hopeless competitors and enemies of the favourites, of idle, profligate prelates there assembled, it is intelligible how Rome became the home of the savage pasquinade as well as of more philosophical satire. If we add to this the wide-spread hatred borne to the priests, and the well-known instinct of the mob to lay any horror to the charge of the great, there results an untold mass of infamy.[2] Those who were able protected themselves best by contempt both of the false and true accusations, and by brilliant and joyous display.[3] More sensitive natures sank into utter despair when they found themselves deeply involved in guilt, and still more deeply in slander.[4] In course of time calumny became uni-

[1] *Lettere Pittoriche*, i. p. 71, in a letter of Vinc. Borghini, 1577. Macchiavelli (*Stor. Fior.* vii. cap. 28) says of the young gentlemen in Florence soon after the middle of the fifteenth century: 'Gli studî loro erano apparire col vestire splendidi, e col parlare sagaci ed astuti, e quello che più destramente mordeva gli altri, era più savio e da più stimato.'

[2] Comp. Fedra Inghirami's funeral oration on Ludovico Podocataro (d. Aug. 25, 1504) in the *Anecd. Litt.* i. p. 319. The scandal-monger Massaino is mentioned in Paul. Jov. *Dialogues de Viris Litt. Illustr.* (Tiraboschi, tom. vii. parte iv. p. 1631).

[3] This was the plan followed by Leo X., and his calculations were not disappointed. Fearfully as his reputation was mangled after his death by the satirists, they were unable to modify the general estimate formed of him.

[4] This was probably the case with Cardinal Ardicino della Porta, who in 1491 wished to resign his dignity and take refuge in a monastery. See Infessura, in Eccard, ii. col. 2000.

versal, and the strictest virtue was most certain of all to challenge the attacks of malice. Of the great pulpit orator, Fra Egidio of Viterbo, whom Leo made a cardinal on account of his merits, and who showed himself a man of the people and a brave monk in the calamity of 1527,[1] Giovio gives us to understand that he preserved his ascetic pallor by the smoke of wet straw and other means of the same kind. Giovio is a genuine Curial in these matters.[2] He generally begins by telling his story, then adds that he does not believe it, and then hints at the end that perhaps after all there may be something in it. But the true scape-goat of Roman scorn was the pious and moral Adrian VI. A general agreement seemed to be made to take him only on the comic side. Adrian had contemptuously referred to the Laöcoon group as 'idola antiquorum,' had shut up the entrance to the Belvedere, had left the works of Raphael unfinished, and had banished the poets and players from the court; it was even feared that he would burn some ancient statues to lime for the new church of St. Peter. He fell out from the first with the formidable Francesco Berni, threatening to have thrown into the Tiber not, as people said,[3] the statue of Pasquino, but the writers of the satires themselves. The vengeance for this was the famous 'Capitolo' against Pope Adriano, inspired not exactly by hatred, but by contempt for the comical Dutch barbarian;[4] the more savage menaces were reserved for the cardinals who had elected him. The plague, which then was prevalent in Rome,

[1] See his funeral oration in the *Anecd. Litt.* iv. p. 315. He assembled an army of peasants in the March of Aneona, which was only hindered from acting by the treason of the Duke of Urbino. For his graceful and hopeless love-poems, see Trucchi, *Poesie Inedite*, iii. 123.

[2] How he used his tongue at the table of Clement VII. is told in Giraldi, *Hecatomithi*, vii. nov. 5.

[3] The charge of taking into consideration the proposal to drown Pasquino (in Paul. Jov. *Vita Hadriani*), is transferred from Sixtus IV. to Hadrian. Comp. *Lettere dei Principi*, i. 114 sqq., letter of Negro, dated April 7, 1523. On St. Mark's Day Pasquino had a special celebration, which the Pope forbade.

[4] In the passages collected in Gregorovius, viii. 380 note, 381 sqq. 393 sqq.

was ascribed to him;[1] Berni and others[2] sketch the environment of the Pope—the Germans by whom he was governed[3]—with the same sparkling untruthfulness with which the modern *feuilletoniste* turns black into white, and everything into anything. The biography which Paolo Giovio was commissioned to write by the Cardinal of Tortosa, and which was to have been a eulogy, is for any one who can read between the lines an unexampled piece of satire. It sounds ridiculous—at least for the Italians of that time—to hear how Adrian applied to the Chapter of Saragossa for the jaw-bone of St. Lambert; how the devout Spaniards decked him out till he looked 'like a right well-dressed Pope;' how he came in a confused and tasteless procession from Ostia to Rome, took counsel about burning or drowning Pasquino, would suddenly break off the most important business when dinner was announced; and lastly, at the end of an unhappy reign, how he died of drinking too much beer—whereupon the house of his physician was hung with garlands by midnight revellers, and adorned with the inscription, 'Liberatori Patriæ S. P. Q. R.' It is true that Giovio had lost his money in the general confiscation of public funds, and had only received a benefice by way of compensation because he was 'no poet,' that is to say, no pagan.[4] But it was decreed that Adrian should be the last

[1] Comp. Pier. Valer. *De Infel. Lit.* ed. Mencken, p. 178. 'Pestilentia quæ cum Adriano VI. invecta Romam invasit.'

[2] E.g. Firenzuola, *Opera* (Milano 1802), vol. i. p. 116, in the *Discorsi degli Animali.*

[3] Comp. the names in Höfler, *Sitzungsberichte der Wiener Academie* (1876), vol. 82, p. 435.

[4] The words of Pier. Valerian, *De Infel. Lit.* ed. Mencken, p. 382, are most characteristic of the public feeling at Rome: 'Ecce adest Musarum et eloquentiæ totiusque nitoris hostis acerrimis, qui literatis omnibus inimicitias minitaretur, quoniam, ut ipse dictitabat, Terentiani essent, quos quum odisse atque etiam persequi cœpisset voluntarium alii exilium, alias atque alias alii latebras quærentes tam diu latuere quoad Deo beneficio altero imperii anno decessit, qui si aliquanto diutius vixisset, Gothica illa tempora adversus bonas literas videbatur suscitaturus.' The general hatred of Adrian was also due partly to the fact that in the great pecuniary difficulties in which he found himself he adopted the expedient of a direct tax. Ranke, *Päpste*, i. 411. It may here be mentioned that there were, nevertheless, poets to be found who praised Adrian. Comp. various passages in the *Coryciana* (ed. Rome, 1524), esp. J. J. 2*b* sqq.

great victim. After the disaster which befell Rome in 1527, slander visibly declined along with the unrestrained wickedness of private life.

But while it was still flourishing was developed, chiefly in Rome, the greatest railer of modern times, Pietro Aretino. A glance at his life and character will save us the trouble of noticing many less distinguished members of his class.

We know him chiefly in the last thirty years of his life (1527–1557), which he passed in Venice, the only asylum possible for him. From hence he kept all that was famous in Italy in a kind of state of siege, and here were delivered the presents of the foreign princes who needed or dreaded his pen. Charles V. and Francis I. both pensioned him at the same time, each hoping that Aretino would do some mischief to the other. Aretino flattered both, but naturally attached himself more closely to Charles, because he remained master in Italy. After the Emperor's victory at Tunis in 1535, this tone of adulation passed into the most ludicrous worship, in observing which it must not be forgotten that Aretino constantly cherished the hope that Charles would help him to a cardinal's hat. It is probable that he enjoyed special protection as Spanish agent, as his speech or silence could have no small effect on the smaller Italian courts and on public opinion in Italy. He affected utterly to despise the Papal court because he knew it so well; the true reason was that Rome neither could nor would pay him any longer.[1] Venice, which sheltered him, he was wise enough to leave unassailed. The rest of his relations with the great is mere beggary and vulgar extortion.

Aretino affords the first great instance of the abuse of publicity to such ends. The polemical writings which a hundred years earlier Poggio and his opponents interchanged, are just as infamous in their tone and purpose, but they were not composed for the press, but for a sort of private circulation.

[1] To the Duke of Ferrara, January 1, 1536 (*Lettere*, ed. 1539, fol. 39): 'You will now journey from Rome to Naples,' 'ricreando la vista avvilita nel mirar le miserie pontificali con la contemplazione delle eccellenze imperiali.'

Aretino made all his profit out of a complete publicity, and in a certain sense may be considered the father of modern journalism. His letters and miscellaneous articles were printed periodically, after they had already been circulated among a tolerably extensive public.[1]

Compared with the sharp pens of the eighteenth century, Aretino had the advantage that he was not burdened with principles, neither with liberalism nor philanthropy nor any other virtue, nor even with science; his whole baggage consisted of the well-known motto, 'Veritas odium parit.' He never, consequently, found himself in the false position of Voltaire, who was forced to disown his 'Pucelle' and conceal all his life the authorship of other works. Aretino put his name to all he wrote, and openly gloried in his notorious 'Ragionamenti.' His literary talent, his clear and sparkling style, his varied observation of men and things, would have made him a considerable writer under any circumstances, destitute as he was of the power of conceiving a genuine work of art, such as a true dramatic comedy; and to the coarsest as well as the most refined malice he added a grotesque wit so brilliant that in some cases it does not fall short of that of Rabelais.[2]

In such circumstances, and with such objects and means, he set to work to attack or circumvent his prey. The tone in which he appealed to Clement VII. not to complain or to think of vengeance,[3] but to forgive, at the moment when the wailings of the devastated city were ascending to the Castle of St. Angelo, where the Pope himself was a prisoner, is the mockery of a devil or a monkey. Sometimes, when he is forced to give up all hope of presents, his fury breaks out into a savage howl, as in the 'Capitolo' to the Prince of Salerno, who after paying him for some time refused to do so any longer. On the other

[1] The fear which he caused to men of mark, especially artists, by these means, cannot be here described. The publicistic weapon of the German Reformation was chiefly the pamphlet dealing with events as they occurred; Aretino is a journalist in the sense that he has within himself a perpetual occasion for writing.

[2] E.g. in the *Capitolo* on Albicante, a bad poet; unfortunately the passages are unfit for quotation.

[3] *Lettere*, ed. Venez. 1539, fol. 12, dated May 31, 1527.

hand, it seems that the terrible Pierluigi Farnese, Duke of Parma, never took any notice of him at all. As this gentleman had probably renounced altogether the pleasures of a good reputation, it was not easy to cause him any annoyance; Aretino tried to do so by comparing his personal appearance to that of a constable, a miller, and a baker.[1] Aretino is most comical of all in the expression of whining mendicancy, as in the 'Capitolo' to Francis I.; but the letters and poems made up of menaces and flattery cannot, notwithstanding all that is ludicrous in them, be read without the deepest disgust. A letter like that one of his written to Michelangelo in November 1545[2] is alone of its kind; along with all the admiration he expresses for the 'Last Judgment' he charges him with irreligion, indecency, and theft from the heirs of Julius II., and adds in a conciliating postscript, 'I only want to show you that if you are "divino," I am not "d'acqua."' Aretino laid great stress upon it—whether from the insanity of conceit or by way of caricaturing famous men—that he himself should be called divine, as one of his flatterers had already begun to do; and he certainly attained so much personal celebrity that his house at Arezzo passed for one of the sights of the place.[3] There were indeed whole months during which he never ventured to cross his threshold at Venice, lest he should fall in with some incensed Florentine like the younger Strozzi. Nor did he escape the cudgels and the daggers of his enemies,[4] although they failed to have the effect which Berni prophesied him in a famous sonnet. Aretino died in his house, of apoplexy.

The differences he made in his modes of flattery are remarkable: in dealing with non-Italians he was grossly fulsome;[5]

[1] In the first *Capitolo* to Cosimo.

[2] Gaye, *Carteggio*, ii. 332.

[3] See the insolent letter of 1536 in the *Lettere Pittor.* i. Append. 34. See above, p. 142, for the house where Petrarch was born in Arezzo.

[4] L'Aretin, per Deo grazia, è vivo e sano,
Ma'l mostaccio ha fregiato nobilmente,
E più colpi ha, che dita in una mano.'
(Mauro, '*Capitolo in lode delle bugie.*')

[5] See e.g. the letter to the Cardinal of Lorraine, *Lettere*, ed. Venez. fol. 29, dated Nov. 21, 1534, and the letters to Charles V., in which he says that no man stands nearer to God than Charles.

people like Duke Cosimo of Florence he treated very differently. He praised the beauty of the then youthful prince, who in fact did share this quality with Augustus in no ordinary degree; he praised his moral conduct, with an oblique reference to the financial pursuits of Cosimo's mother Maria Salviati, and concluded with a mendicant whine about the bad times and so forth. When Cosimo pensioned him,[1] which he did liberally, considering his habitual parsimony—to the extent, at last, of 160 ducats a year—he had doubtless an eye to Aretino's dangerous character as Spanish agent. Aretino could ridicule and revile Cosimo, and in the same breath threaten the Florentine agent that he would obtain from the Duke his immediate recall; and if the Medicean prince felt himself at last to be seen through by Charles V. he would naturally not be anxious that Aretino's jokes and rhymes against him should circulate at the Imperial court. A curiously qualified piece of flattery was that addressed to the notorious Marquis of Marignano, who as Castellan of Musso (p. 27) had attempted to found an independent state. Thanking him for the gift of a hundred crowns, Aretino writes: 'All the qualities which a prince should have are present in you, and all men would think so, were it not that the acts of violence inevitable at the beginning of all undertakings cause you to appear a trifle rough (*aspro*).'[2]

It has often been noticed as something singular that Aretino only reviled the world, and not God also. The religious belief of a man who lived as he did is a matter of perfect indifference, as are also the edifying writings which he composed for reasons of his own.[3] It is in fact hard to say why he should have been a blasphemer. He was no professor, or theoretical thinker or writer; and he could extort no money from God by threats or flattery, and was consequently never goaded into blasphemy

[1] For what follows, see Gaye, *Carteggio*, ii. 336, 337, 345.

[2] *Lettere*, ed. Venez. 1539, fol. 15, dated June 16, 1529. Comp. another remarkable letter to M. A., dated April 15, 1528, fol. 212.

[3] He may have done so either in the hope of obtaining the red hat or from fear of the new activity of the Inquisition, which he had ventured to attack bitterly in 1535 (l. c. fol. 37), but which, after the reorganisation of the institution in 1542 suddenly took a fresh start, and soon silenced every opposing voice.

by a refusal. A man like him does not take trouble for nothing.

It is a good sign of the present spirit of Italy that such a character and such a career have become a thousand times impossible. But historical criticism will always find in Aretino an important study.

PART III.

THE REVIVAL OF ANTIQUITY.

CHAPTER I.

INTRODUCTORY REMARKS.

Now that this point in our historical view of Italian civilization has been reached, it is time to speak of the influence of antiquity, the 'new birth' of which has been one-sidedly chosen as the name to sum up the whole period. The conditions which have been hitherto described would have sufficed, apart from antiquity, to upturn and to mature the national mind; and most of the intellectual tendencies which yet remain to be noticed would be conceivable without it. But both what has gone before and what we have still to discuss are coloured in a thousand ways by the influence of the ancient world; and though the essence of the phenomena might still have been the same without the classical revival, it is only with and through this revival that they are actually manifested to us. The Renaissance would not have been the process of world-wide significance which it is, if its elements could be so easily separated from one another. We must insist upon it, as one of the chief propositions of this book, that it was not the revival of antiquity alone, but its union with the genius of the Italian people, which achieved the conquest of the western world. The amount of independence which the national spirit maintained in this union varied according to circumstances. In the modern Latin literature of the period, it is very small, while in plastic art, as well as in other spheres, it is remarkably great; and hence the alliance between two distant epochs in the civilisation of the same people, because concluded on equal terms, proved justifiable and fruitful. The rest of Europe was free either to repel or else partly or wholly to accept the mighty impulse which came forth from Italy. Where the latter was the case we may as well be spared the complaints over the early decay of mediæval faith and civilisation. Had these been strong enough to hold their ground, they would be alive to this day. If those elegiac natures which long to see them return could pass but one hour in the midst of them, they would gasp to be back in modern air. That in a great historical process of this kind flowers of exquisite beauty may perish, without being made immortal in poetry or tradition is undoubtedly true; nevertheless, we cannot wish the process undone. The general result of it consists in this—that by the side of the Church which had hitherto held the countries of the West together (though it was unable to do so much longer) there arose a new spiritual influence which, spreading itself abroad from Italy, became the breath of life for all the more instructed minds in Europe. The worst that can be said of the movement is, that it was anti-popular, that through it Europe became for the first time sharply divided into the cultivated and uncultivated classes. The reproach will appear groundless when we reflect that even now the fact, though clearly recognised, cannot be altered. The separation, too, is by no means so cruel and absolute in Italy as elsewhere. The most artistic of her poets, Tasso, is in the hands of even the poorest.

The civilisation of Greece and Rome, which, ever since the fourteenth century, obtained so powerful a hold on Italian life, as the source and basis of culture, as the object and ideal of existence, partly also as an avowed reaction against preceding tendencies—this civilisation had long been exerting a partial influence on mediæval Europe, even beyond the boundaries of Italy. The culture of which Charles the Great was a representative was, in face of the barbarism of the seventh and eighth centuries, essentially a Renaissance, and could appear under no other form. Just as in the Romanesque architecture of the North, beside the general outlines inherited from antiquity, remarkable direct imitations of the antique also occur, so too monastic scholarship had not only gradually absorbed an immense mass of materials from Roman writers, but the style of it, from the days of Eginhard onwards shows traces of conscious imitations.

But the resuscitation of antiquity took a different form in Italy from that which it assumed in the North. The wave of barbarism had scarcely gone by before the people, in whom the former life was but half effaced, showed a consciousness of its past and a wish to reproduce it. Elsewhere in Europe men deliberately and with reflection borrowed this or the other element of classical civilisation; in Italy the sympathies both of the learned and of the people were naturally engaged on the side of antiquity as a whole, which stood to them as a symbol of past greatness. The Latin language, too, was easy to an Italian, and the numerous monuments and documents in which the country abounded facilitated a return to the past. With this tendency other elements—the popular character which time had now greatly modified, the political institutions imported by the Lombards from Germany, chivalry and other northern forms of civilisation, and the influence of religion and the Church—combined to produce the modern Italian spirit, which was destined to serve as the model and ideal for the whole western world.

How antiquity began to work in plastic art, as soon as the flood of barbarism had subsided, is clearly shown in the Tuscan buildings of the twelfth and in the sculptures of the thirteenth centuries. In poetry, too, there will appear no want of similar analogies to those who hold that the greatest Latin poet of the twelfth century, the writer who struck the key-note of a whole class of Latin poems, was an Italian. We mean the author of the best pieces in the so-called 'Carmina Burana.' A frank enjoyment of life and its pleasures, as whose patrons the gods of heathendom are invoked, while Catos and Scipios hold the place of the saints and heroes of Christianity, flows in full current through the rhymed verses. Reading them through at a stretch, we can scarcely help coming to the conclusion that an Italian, probably a Lombard, is speaking; in fact, there are positive grounds for thinking so.[1] To a certain

[1] [Carmina Burana, in the *Bibliothek des literarischen Vereins in Stuttgart*, vol. xvi. (Stuttg. 1847). The stay in Pavia (p. 68 *bis*), the Italian local references in general, the scene with the 'pastorella' under the olive-tree (p. 146), the mention of the 'pinus' as a shady field tree (p. 156), the frequent use of the word 'bravium' (pp. 137, 144), and particularly the form Madii for Maji (p. 141), all speak in favour of our assumption.]

The conjecture of Dr. Burckhardt that the best pieces of the *Carmina*

degree these Latin poems of the 'Clerici vagantes' of the twelfth century, with all their remarkable frivolity, are, doubtless, a product in which the whole of Europe had a share; but the writer of the song 'De Phyllide et Flora'[1] and the 'Æstuans Interius' can have been a northerner as little as the polished Epicurean observer to whom we owe 'Dum Dianæ vitrea sero lampas oritur.' Here, in truth, is a reproduction of the whole ancient view of life, which is all the more striking from the mediæval form of the verse in which it is set forth. There are many works of this and the following centuries, in which a careful imitation of the antique appears both in the hexameter and pentameter of the metre in the classical, often

Burana were written by an Italian, is not tenable. The grounds brought forward in its support have little weight (e.g. the mention of Pavia: 'Quis Paviæ demorans castus habeatur?' which can be explained as a proverbial expression, or referred to a short stay of the writer at Pavia), cannot, further, hold their own against the reasons on the other side, and finally lose all their force in view of the probable identification of the author. The arguments of O. Hubatsch *Die lateinischen Vagantenlieder des Mittelalters*, Görlitz, 1870, p. 87) against the Italian origin of these poems are, among others, the attacks on the Italian and praise of the German clergy, the rebukes of the southerners as a 'gens proterva,' and the reference to the poet as 'transmontanus.' Who he actually was, however, is not clearly made out. That he bore the name of Walther throws no light upon his origin. He was formerly identified with Gualterus de Mapes, a canon of Salisbury and chaplain to the English kings at the end of the twelfth century; since, by Giesebrecht (*Die Vaganten oder Goliarden und ihre Lieder*, *Allgemeine Monatschrift*, 1855), with Walther of Lille or Chatillon, who passed from France into England and Germany, and thence possibly with the Archbishop Reinhold of Köln (1164 and 75) to Italy (Pavia, &c.). If this hypothesis, against which Hubatsch (l. c.) has brought forward certain objections, must be abandoned, it remains beyond a doubt that the origin of nearly all these songs is to be looked for in France, from whence they were diffused through the regular school which here existed for them over Germany, and there expanded and mixed with German phrases; while Italy, as Giesebrecht has shown, remained almost unaffected by this class of poetry. The Italian translator of Dr. Burckhardt's work, Prof. D. Valbusa, in a note to this passage (i. 235), also contests the Italian origin of the poem. [L. G.]

[1] *Carm. Bur.* p. 155, only a fragment: the whole in Wright, *Walter Mapes* (1841), p. 258. Comp. Hubatsch, p. 27 sqq., who points to the fact that a story often treated of in France is at the foundation. Æst. Inter. *Carm. Bur.* p. 67; Dum Dianæ, *Carm. Bur.* p. 124. Additional instances: 'Cor patet Jovi;' classical names for the loved one; once, when he calls her Blanciflor, he adds, as if to make up for it, the name of Helena.

mythological, character of the subject, and which yet have not anything like the same spirit of antiquity about them. In the hexameter chronicles and other works of Gulielmus Apuliensis and his successors (from about 1100), we find frequent traces of a diligent study of Virgil, Ovid, Lucan, Statius, and Claudian; but this classical form is after all here a mere matter of archæology, as is the classical subject in collectors like Vincent of Beauvais, or in the mythological and allegorical writer, Alanus ab Insulis. The Renaissance is not a mere fragmentary imitation or compilation, but a new birth; and the signs of this are visible in the poems of the unknown 'Clericus' of the twelfth century.

But the great and general enthusiasm of the Italians for classical antiquity did not display itself before the fourteenth century. For this a development of civic life was required, which took place only in Italy, and there not till then. It was needful that noble and burgher should first learn to dwell together on equal terms, and that a social world should arise (see p. 139) which felt the want of culture, and had the leisure and the means to obtain it. But culture, as soon as it freed itself from the fantastic bonds of the Middle Ages, could not at once and without help find its way to the understanding of the physical and intellectual world. It needed a guide, and found one in the ancient civilisation, with its wealth of truth and knowledge in every spiritual interest. Both the form and the substance of this civilisation were adopted with admiring gratitude; it became the chief part of the culture of the age.[1] The general condition of the country was favourable to this transformation. The mediæval empire, since the fall of the Hohenstaufen, had either renounced, or was unable to make good, its claims on Italy. The Popes had migrated to Avignon. Most of the political powers actually in existence owed their origin to violent and illegitimate means. The spirit of the people, now awakened to self-consciousness, sought for some new and stable ideal on which to rest. And thus the vision of the world-wide empire of Italy and Rome so possessed the

[1] In what way antiquity could serve as guide and teacher in all the higher regions of life, is briefly sketched by Æneas Sylvius (*Opera*, p. 603, in the *Epist.* 105, to the Archduke Sigismund).

popular mind, that Cola di Rienzi could actually attempt to put it in practice. The conception he formed of his task, particularly when tribune for the first time, could only end in some extravagant comedy; nevertheless, the memory of ancient Rome was no slight support to the national sentiment. Armed afresh with its culture, the Italian soon felt himself in truth citizen of the most advanced nation in the world.

It is now our task to sketch this spiritual movement, not indeed in all its fulness, but in its most salient features, and especially in its first beginnings.[1]

[1] For particulars we must refer the reader to Roscoe, *Lorenzo Mag.* and *Leo X.*, as well as to Voigt, *Enea Silvio* (Berlin, 1856–63); to the works of Reumont and to Gregorovius, *Geschichte der Stadt Rom im Mittelalter.*

To form a conception of the extent which studies at the beginning of the sixteenth century had reached, we cannot do better than turn to the *Commentarii Urbani* of Raphael Volatterranus (ed. Basil, 1544, fol. 16, &c.). Here we see how antiquity formed the introduction and the chief matter of study in every branch of knowledge, from geography and local history, the lives of great and famous men, popular philosophy, morals and the special sciences, down to the analysis of the whole of Aristotle, with which the work closes. To understand its significance as an authority for the history of culture, we must compare it with all the earlier encyclopædias. A complete and circumstantial account of the matter is given in Voigt's admirable work, *Die Wiederbelebung des classischen Alterthums* oder *Das erste Jahrhundert der Humanismus*, Berlin, 1859.

CHAPTER II.

ROME, THE CITY OF RUINS.

ROME itself, the city of ruins, now became the object of a wholly different sort of piety from that of the time when the 'Mirabilia Romæ' and the collection of William of Malmesbury were composed. The imaginations of the devout pilgrim, or of the seeker after marvels[1] and treasures, are supplanted in contemporary records by the interests of the patriot and the historian. In this sense we must understand Dante's words,[2] that the stones of the walls of Rome deserve reverence, and that the ground on which the city is built is more worthy than men say. The jubilees, incessant as they were, have scarcely left a single devout record in literature properly so called. The best thing that Giovanni Villani (p. 73) brought back from the jubilee of the year 1300 was the resolution to write his history which had been awakened in him by the sight of the ruins of Rome. Petrarch gives evidence of a taste divided between classical and Christian antiquity. He tells us how often with Giovanni Colonna he ascended the mighty vaults of the Baths of Diocletian,[3] and there in the transparent air, amid

[1] In William of Malmesbury, *Gesta Regum Anglor.* l. ii. § 169, 170, 205, 206 (ed. Lond. 1840, vol. i. p. 277 sqq. and p. 354 sqq.), we meet with the dreams of treasure-hunters, Venus as ghostly love, and the discovery of the gigantic body of Pallas, son of Evander, about the middle of the eleventh century. Comp. Jac. ab Aquis *Imago Mundi* (*Hist. Patr. Monum. Script.* t. iii. col. 1603), on the origin of the House of Colonna, with reference to the discovery of hidden treasure. Besides the tales of the treasure-seekers, William of Malmesbury mentions the elegy of Hildebert of Mans, Bishop of Tours, one of the most singular examples of humanistic enthusiasm in the first half of the twelfth century.

[2] Dante, *Convito*, tratt. iv. cap. v.

[3] *Epp. Familiares*, vi. 2; references to Rome before he had seen it, and expressions of his longing for the city, *Epp. Fam.* ed. Fracass. vol. i. pp. 125, 213; vol. ii. pp. 336 sqq. See also the collected references in L. Geiger,

the wide silence, with the broad panorama stretching far around them, they spoke, not of business, or political affairs, but of the history which the ruins beneath their feet suggested, Petrarch appearing in their dialogues as the partisan of classical, Giovanni of Christian antiquity; then they would discourse of philosophy and of the inventors of the arts. How often since that time, down to the days of Gibbon and Niebuhr, have the same ruins stirred men's minds to the same reflections!

This double current of feeling is also recognisable in the 'Dittamondo' of Fazio degli Uberti, composed about the year 1360—a description of visionary travels, in which the author is accompanied by the old geographer Solinus, as Dante was by Virgil. They visit Bari in memory of St. Nicholas, and Monte Gargano of the archangel Michael, and in Rome the legends of Araceli and of Santa Maria in Trastevere are mentioned. Still, the pagan splendour of ancient Rome unmistakably exercises a greater charm upon them. A venerable matron in torn garments—Rome herself is meant—tells them of the glorious past, and gives them a minute description of the old triumphs;[1] she then leads the strangers through the city, and points out to them the seven hills and many of the chief ruins—'che comprender potrai, quanto fui bella.'

Unfortunately this Rome of the schismatic and Avignonese popes was no longer, in respect of classical remains, what it had been some generations earlier. The destruction of 140 fortified houses of the Roman nobles by the senator Brancaleone in 1257 must have wholly altered the character of the most important buildings then standing; for the nobles had no doubt

Petrarca, p. 272, note 3. In Petrarch we already find complaints of the many ruined and neglected buildings, which he enumerates one by one (*De Rem. Utriusque Fort.* lib. i. dial. 118), adding the remark that many statues were left from antiquity, but no paintings (l. c. 41).

[1] *Dittamondo*, ii. cap. 3. The procession reminds one at times of the three kings and their suite in the old pictures. The description of the city (ii. cap. 31) is not without archæological value (Gregorovius, vi. 697, note 1). According to Polistoro (Murat. xxiv. col. 845), Niccolò and Ugo of Este journeyed in 1366 to Rome, 'per vedere quelle magnificenze antiche, che al presente sipossono vedere in Roma.'

ensconced themselves in the loftiest and best-preserved of the ruins.[1] Nevertheless, far more was left than we now find, and probably many of the remains had still their marble incrustation, their pillared entrances, and their other ornaments, where we now see nothing but the skeleton of brickwork. In this state of things, the first beginnings of a topographical study of the old city were made.

In Poggio's walks through Rome[2] the study of the remains themselves is for the first time more intimately combined with that of the ancient authors and inscriptions—the latter he sought out from among all the vegetation in which they were imbedded[3]—the writer's imagination is severely restrained, and the memories of Christian Rome carefully excluded. The only pity is that Poggio's work was not fuller and was not illustrated with sketches. Far more was left in his time than was found by Raphael eighty years later. He saw the tomb of Cæcilia Metella and the columns in front of one of the temples on the slope of the Capitol first in full preservation, and then afterwards half destroyed, owing to that unfortunate quality which marble possesses of being easily burnt into lime. A vast colonnade near the Minerva fell piecemeal a victim to the same fate. A witness in the year 1443 tells us that this manufacture of lime still went on; 'which is a shame, for the new buildings are pitiful, and the beauty of Rome is in its

[1] Gregorovius, v. 316 sqq. Parenthetically we may quote foreign evidence that Rome in the Middle Ages was looked upon as a quarry. The famous Abbot Sugerius, who about 1140 was in search of lofty pillars for the rebuilding of St. Denis, thought at first of nothing less then getting hold of the granite monoliths of the Baths of Diocletian, but afterwards changed his mind. See 'Sugerii Libellus Alter,' in Duchesne, *Hist. Franc. Scriptores*, iv. p. 352.

[2] *Poggii Opera*, fol. 50 sqq. 'Ruinarum Urbis Romæ Descriptio,' written about 1430, shortly before the death of Martin V. The Baths of Caracalla and Diocletian had then their pillars and coating of marble. See Gregorovius, vi. 700–705.

[3] Poggio appears as one of the earliest collectors of inscriptions, in his letter in the *Vita Poggii*, Muratori, xx. col. 177, and as collector of busts, (col. 183, and letter in Shepherd-Tonelli, i. 258). See also *Ambros. Traversarii Epistolæ*, xxv. 42. A little book which Poggio wrote on inscriptions seems to have been lost. Shepherd, *Life of Poggio*, trad. Tonelli, i. 154 sqq.

ruins.'[1] The inhabitants of that day, in their peasants' cloaks and boots, looked to foreigners like cowherds; and in fact the cattle were pastured in the city up to the Banchi. The only opportunities for social gatherings were the services at church, on which occasion it was possible to get a sight of the beautiful women.

In the last years of Eugenius IV. (d. 1447) Blondus of Forli wrote his 'Roma Instaurata,' making use of Frontinus and of the old 'Libri Regionali,' as well as, it seems, of Anastasius. His object is not only the description of what existed, but still more the recovery of what was lost. In accordance with the dedication to the Pope, he consoles himself for the general ruin by the thought of the precious relics of the saints in which Rome was so rich.[2]

With Nicholas V. (1447–1455) that new monumental spirit which was distinctive of the age of the Renaissance appeared on the papal throne. The new passion for embellishing the city brought with it on the one hand a fresh danger for the ruins, on the other a respect for them, as forming one of Rome's claims to distinction. Pius II. was wholly possessed by antiquarian enthusiasm, and if he speaks little of the antiquities of Rome,[3] he closely studied those of all other parts of Italy, and was the first to know and describe accurately the remains which abounded in the districts for miles around the capital.[4] It is true that, both as priest and cosmographer, he is interested alike in classical and Christian monuments and in the marvels of nature. Or was he doing violence to himself when he wrote

[1] Fabroni, *Cosmus*, Adnot. 86. From a letter of Alberto degli Alberti to Giovanni Medici. See also Gregorovius, vii. 557. For the condition of Rome under Martin V., see Platina, p. 227; and during the absence of Eugenius IV., see Vespasiano Fiorent., p. 21.

[2] *Roma Instaurata*, written in 1447, and dedicated to the Pope; first printed, Rome, 1474.

[3] See, nevertheless, his distichs in Voigt, *Wiederbelebung des Alterthums*, p. 275, note 2. He was the first Pope who published a Bull for the protection of old monuments (4 Kal. Maj. 1462), with penalties in case of disobedience. But these measures were ineffective. Comp. Gregorovius, vii. pp. 558 sqq.

[4] What follows is from Jo. Ant. Campanus, *Vita Pii II.*, in Muratori, iii. ii. col. 980 sqq. *Pii II. Commentarii*, pp. 48, 72 sqq., 206, 248 sqq., 501, and elsewhere.

that Nola was more highly honoured by the memory of St. Paulinus than by all its classical reminiscences and by the heroic struggle of Marcellus? Not, indeed, that his faith in relics was assumed; but his mind was evidently rather disposed to an inquiring interest in nature and antiquity, to a zeal for monumental works, to a keen and delicate observation of human life. In the last years of his Papacy, afflicted with the gout, and yet in the most cheerful mood, he was borne in his litter over hill and dale to Tusculum, Alba, Tibur, Ostia, Falerii, and Ocriculum, and whatever he saw he noted down. He followed the line of the Roman roads and aqueducts, and tried to fix the boundaries of the old tribes who dwelt round the city. On an excursion to Tivoli with the great Federigo of Urbino the time was happily spent in talk on the military system of the ancients, and particularly on the Trojan war. Even on his journey to the Congress of Mantua (1459) he searched, though unsuccessfully, for the labyrinth of Clusium mentioned by Pliny, and visited the so-called villa of Virgil on the Mincio. That such a Pope should demand a classical Latin style from his abbreviators, is no more than might be expected. It was he who, in the war with Naples, granted an amnesty to the men of Arpinum, as countrymen of Cicero and Marius, after whom many of them were named. It was to him alone, as both judge and patron, that Blondus could dedicate his 'Roma Triumphans,' the first great attempt at a complete exposition of Roman antiquity.[1]

Nor was the enthusiasm for the classical past of Italy confined at this period to the capital. Boccaccio[2] had already called the vast ruins of Baiæ 'old walls, yet new for modern spirits;' and since this time they were held to be the most interesting sight near Naples. Collections of antiquities of all sorts now became common. Ciriaco of Ancona (d. 1457), who explained (1433) the Roman monuments to the Emperor Sigismund, travelled, not only through Italy, but through other countries of the old world, Hellas, and the islands of the Archipelago, and even parts of Asia and Africa, and brought back with him countless inscriptions and sketches. When asked

[1] First dated edition, Brixen, 1482.

[2] Boccaccio, *Fiammetta*, cap. 5. *Opere*, ed. Montier, vi. 91.

why he took all this trouble, he replied, 'To wake the dead.'[1] The histories of the various cities of Italy had from the earliest times laid claim to some true or imagined connection with Rome, had alleged some settlement or colonisation which started from the capital;[2] and the obliging manufacturers of pedigrees seem constantly to have derived various families from the oldest and most famous blood of Rome. So highly was the distinction valued, that men clung to it even in the light of the dawning criticism of the fifteenth century. When Pius II. was at Viterbo[3] he said frankly to the Roman deputies who begged him to return, 'Rome is as much at home as Siena, for my House, the Piccolomini, came in early times from the capital to Siena, as is proved by the constant use of the names Æneas and Sylvius in my family.' He would probably have had no objection to be held a descendant of the Julii. Paul II., a Barbo of Venice, found his vanity flattered by deducing his House, notwithstanding an adverse pedigree, according to which it came from Germany, from the Roman Ahenobarbus, who led a colony to Parma, and whose successors were driven by party conflicts to migrate to Venice.[4] That the Massimi claimed descent from Q. Fabius Maximus, and the Cornaro from the Cornelii, cannot surprise us. On the other hand, it is a strikingly exceptional fact for the sixteenth century that the

[1] His work, *Cyriaci Anconitani Itinerarium*, ed. Mehus, Florence, 1742. Comp. Leandro Alberti, *Descriz. di tutta l'Italia*, fol. 285.

[2] Two instances out of many: the fabulous origin of Milan in Manipulus (Murat. xl. col. 552), and that of Florence in Gio. Villani (who here, as elsewhere, enlarges on the forged chroncle of Ricardo Malespini), according to which Florence, being loyally Roman in its sentiments, is always in the right against the anti-Roman rebellious Fiesole (i. 9, 38, 41; ii. 2). Dante, *Inf.* xv. 76.

[3] *Commentarii*, p. 206, in the fourth book.

Mich. Cannesius, *Vita Pauli II.*, in Murat. iii. ii. col. 993. Towards even Nero, son of Domitius Ahenobarbus, the author will not be impolite, on account of his connection with the Pope. He only says of him, 'De quo verum Scriptores multa ac diversa commemorant.' The family of Plato in Milan went still farther, and flattered itself on its descent from the great Athenian. Filelfo in a wedding speech, and in an encomium on the jurist Teodoro Plato, ventured to make this assertion; and a Giovanantonio Plato put the inscription on a portrait in relief carved by him in 1478 (in the court of the Pal. Magenta at Milan): 'Platonem suum, a quo originem et ingenium refert.'

novellist Bandello tried to connect his blood with a noble family of Ostrogoths (i. nov. 23).

To return to Rome. The inhabitants, 'who then called themselves Romans,' accepted greedily the homage which was offered them by the rest of Italy. Under Paul II., Sixtus IV., and Alexander VI. magnificent processions formed part of the Carnival, representing the scene most attractive to the imagination of the time—the triumph of the Roman Imperator. The sentiment of the people expressed itself naturally in this shape and others like it. In this mood of public feeling, a report arose, that on April 15, 1485, the corpse of a young Roman lady of the classical period—wonderfully beautiful and in perfect preservation—had been discovered.[1] Some Lombard masons digging out an ancient tomb on an estate of the convent of Santa Maria Novella, on the Appian Way beyond the Cæcilia Metella, were said to have found a marble sarcophagus with the inscription, 'Julia, daughter of Claudius.' On this basis the following story was built. The Lombards disappeared with the jewels and treasure which were found with the corpse in the sarcophagus. The body had been coated with an antiseptic essence, and was as fresh and flexible as that of a girl of fifteen the hour after death. It was said that she still kept the colours of life, with eyes and mouth half open. She was taken to the palace of the 'Conservatori' on the Capitol; and then a pilgrimage to see her began. Among the crowd were many who came to paint her; 'for she was more beautiful than can be said or written, and, were it said or written, it would not be believed by those who had not seen her.' By the order of Innocent VIII. she was secretly buried one night outside the Pincian Gate; the empty sarcophagus remained in the court of the 'Conservatori.' Probably a coloured mask of wax or some other material was modelled in the classical style on the face of the corpse, with which the gilded hair of which we read would harmonise admirably. The touching point in the story is not the fact

[1] See on this point, Nangiporto, in Murat. iii. ii. col. 1094; Infessura, in Eccard, *Scriptores*, ii. col. 1951; Matarazzo, in the *Arch. Stor.* xvi. ii. p. 180. Nangiporto, however, admits that it was no longer possible to decide whether the corpse was male or female.

itself, but the firm belief that an ancient body, which was now thought to be at last really before men's eyes, must of necessity be far more beautiful than anything of modern date.

Meanwhile the material knowledge of old Rome was increased by excavations. Under Alexander VI. the so-called 'Grotesques,' that is, the mural decorations of the ancients, were discovered, and the Apollo of the Belvedere was found at Porto d'Anzo. Under Julius II. followed the memorable discoveries of the Laöcoon, of the Venus of the Vatican, of the Torso, of the Cleopatra.[1] The palaces of the nobles and the cardinals began to be filled with ancient statues and fragments. Raphael undertook for Leo X. that ideal restoration of the whole ancient city which his celebrated letter (1518 or 1519) speaks of.[2] After a bitter complaint over the devastations which had not even then ceased, and which had been particularly frequent under Julius II., he beseeches the Pope to protect the few relics which were left to testify to the power and greatness of that divine soul of antiquity whose memory was inspiration to all who were capable of higher things. He then goes on with penetrating judgment to lay the foundations of a comparative history of art, and concludes by giving the definition of an architectural survey which has been accepted since his time; he requires the ground plan, section, and elevation separately of every building that remained. How archæology devoted itself after his day to the study of the venerated city and grew into a special science, and how the Vitruvian Academy at all events proposed to itself great aims,[3] cannot here be related. Let us rather pause at the days of Leo X., under whom the enjoyment of antiquity combined with all other pleasures to give to Roman life a unique stamp and consecra-

[1] As early as Julius II. excavations were made in the hope of finding statues. Vasari, xi. p. 302, *V. di Gio. da Udine.* Comp. Gregorovius, viii. 186.

[2] The letter was first attributed to Castiglione, *Lettere di Negozi del Conte Bald. Castiglione*, Padua, 1736 and 1769, but proved to be from the hand of Raphael by Daniele Francesconi in 1799. It is printed from a Munich MS. in Passavant, *Leben Raphael's*, iii. p. 44. Comp. Gruyer, *Raphael et l'Antiquité*, 1864, i. 435–457.

[3] *Lettere Pittoriche*, ii. 1, Tolomei to Landi, 14 Nov., 1542.

tion.[1] The Vatican resounded with song and music, and their echoes were heard through the city as a call to joy and gladness, though Leo did not succeed thereby in banishing care and pain from his own life, and his deliberate calculation to prolong his days by cheerfulness was frustrated by an early death.[2] The Rome of Leo, as described by Paolo Giovio, forms a picture too splendid to turn away from, unmistakable as are also its darker aspects—the slavery of those who were struggling to rise; the secret misery of the prelates, who, notwithstanding heavy debts, were forced to live in a style befitting their rank; the system of literary patronage, which drove men to be parasites or adventurers; and, lastly, the scandalous maladministration of the finances of the state.[3] Yet the same Ariosto who knew and ridiculed all this so well, gives in the sixth satire a longing picture of his expected intercourse with the accomplished poets who would conduct him through the city of ruins, of the learned counsel which he would there find for his own literary efforts, and of the treasures of the Vatican library. These, he says, and not the long-abandoned hope of Medicean protection, were the real baits which attracted him, when he was asked to go as Ferrarese ambassador to Rome.

But the ruins within and outside Rome awakened not only archæological zeal and patriotic enthusiasm, but an elegiac or sentimental melancholy. In Petrarch and Boccaccio we find touches of this feeling (pp. 177, 181). Poggio (p. 181) often visited the temple of Venus and Rome, in the belief that it was that of Castor and Pollux, where the senate used so often to meet, and would lose himself in memories of the great orators Crassus, Hortensius, Cicero. The language of Pius II., especially in describing Tivoli, has a thoroughly sentimental

[1] He tried 'curis animique doloribus quacunque ratione aditum intercludere;' music and lively conversation charmed him, and he hoped by their means to live longer. *Leonis X. Vita Anonyma*, in Roscoe, ed. Bossi, xii. p. 169.

[2] This point is referred to in the *Satires* of Ariosto. See the first ('Perc' ho molto,' &c.), and the fourth 'Poiche, Annibale').

[3] Ranke, *Päpste*, i. 408 sqq. '*Lettere dei Principi*, p. 107. Letter of Negri, September 1, 1522. . . . 'tutti questi cortigiani esausti da Papa Leone e falliti.' They avenged themselves after the death of Leo by satirical verses and inscriptions.

ring,[1] and soon afterwards (1467) appeared the first pictures of ruins, with a commentary by Polifilo.[2] Ruins of mighty arches and colonnades, half hid in plane-trees, laurels, cypresses, and brushwood, figure in his pages. In the sacred legends it became the custom, we can hardly say how, to lay the scene of the birth of Christ in the ruins of a magnificent palace.[3] That artificial ruins became afterwards a necessity of landscape gardening, is only a practical consequence of this feeling.

[1] *Pii II. Commentarii*, p. 251 in the 5th book. Comp. Sannazaro's elegy, 'Ad Ruinas Cumarum urbis vetustissimæ' (*Opera*, fol. 236 sqq.).

[2] Polifilo (i.e. Franciscus Columna) 'Hypnerotomachia, ubi humana omnia non nisi somnum esse docet atque obiter plurima scita sane quam digna commemorat,' Venice, Aldus Manutius, 1499. Comp. on this remarkable book and others, A. Didot, *Alde Manuce*, Paris, 1875, pp. 132–142; and Gruyer, *Raphael et l'Antiquité*, i. pp. 191 sqq.; J. Burckhardt, *Geschichte der Renaissance in Italien*, pp. 43 sqq., and the work of A. Ilg, Vienna, 1872.

[3] While all the Fathers of the Church and all the pilgrims speak only of a cave. The poets, too, do without the palace. Comp. Sannazaro, *De Partu Virginis*, l. ii.

CHAPTER III.

THE OLD AUTHORS.

But the literary bequests of antiquity, Greek as well as Latin, were of far more importance than the architectural, and indeed than all the artistic remains which it had left. They were held in the most absolute sense to be the springs of all knowledge. The literary conditions of that age of great discoveries have been often set forth; no more can be here attempted than to point out a few less-known features of the picture.[1]

Great as was the influence of the old writers on the Italian mind in the fourteenth century and before, yet that influence was due rather to the wide diffusion of what had long been known, than to the discovery of much that was new. The most popular Latin poets, historians, orators, and letter-writers, together with a number of Latin translations of single works of Aristotle, Plutarch, and a few other Greek authors, constituted the treasure from which a few favoured individuals in the time of Petrarch and Boccaccio drew their inspiration. The former, as is well known, owned and kept with religious care a Greek Homer, which he was unable to read. A complete Latin translation of the 'Iliad' and 'Odyssey,' though a very bad one, was made at Petrarch's suggestion and with Boccaccio's help by a Calabrian Greek, Leonzio Pilato.[2] But with the fifteenth century began the long list of new dis-

[1] Chiefly from Vespasiano Fiorentino, in the first vol. of the *Spicileg. Romanum*, by Mai, from which edition the quotations in this book are made. New edition by Bartoli, Florence, 1859. The author was a Florentine bookseller and copying agent, about and after the middle of the fifteenth century.

[2] Comp. Petr. *Epist. Fam.* ed. Fracass. l. xviii. 2, xxiv. 12, var. 25, with the notes of Fracassetti in the Italian translation, vol. iv. 92–101, v. 196 sqq., where the fragment of a translation of Homer before the time of Pilato is also given.

coveries, the systematic creation of libraries by means of copies, and the rapid multiplication of translations from the Greek.[1]

Had it not been for the enthusiasm of a few collectors of that age, who shrank from no effort or privation in their researches, we should certainly possess only a small part of the literature, especially that of the Greeks, which is now in our hands. Pope Nicholas V., when only a simple monk, ran deeply into debt through buying manuscripts or having them copied. Even then he made no secret of his passion for the two great interests of the Renaissance, books and buildings.[2] As Pope he kept his word. Copyists wrote and spies searched for him through half the world. Perotto received 500 ducats for the Latin translation of Polybius; Guarino, 1,000 gold florins for that of Strabo, and he would have been paid 500 more but for the death of the Pope. Filelfo was to have received 10,000 gold florins for a metrical translation of Homer, and was only prevented by the Pope's death from coming from Milan to Rome. Nicholas left a collection of 5,000, or, according to another way of calculating, of 9,000 volumes,[3] for the use of the members of the Curia, which became the foundation of the library of the Vatican. It was to be preserved in the palace itself, as its noblest ornament, like the library of Ptolemy Philadelphus at Alexandria. When the plague (1450) drove him and his court to Fabriano, whence then, as now, the best paper was procured, he took his translators and compilers with him, that he might run no risk of losing them.

The Florentine Niccolò Niccoli,[4] a member of that accom-

[1] Forgeries, by which the passion for antiquity was turned to the profit or amusement of rogues, are well known to have been not uncommon. See the articles in the literary histories on Annius of Viterbo.

[2] Vespas. Fiorent. p. 31. 'Tommaso da Serezana usava dire, che dua cosa farebbe, se egli potesse mai spendere, ch' era in libri e murare. E l'una e l'altra fece nel suo pontificato.' With respect to his translation, see Æen. Sylvius, *De Europa*, cap. 58, p. 459, and Papencordt, *Ges. der Stadt Rom.* p. 502. See esp. Voigt, op. cit. book v.

[3] Vespas. Fior. pp. 48 and 658, 665. Comp. J. Manetti, *Vita Nicolai V.*, in Murat. iii. ii. col. 925 sqq. On the question whether and how Calixtus III. partly dispersed the library again, see Vespas. Fiorent. p. 284, with Mai's note.

[4] Vespas. Fior. pp. 617 sqq.

plished circle of friends which surrounded the elder Cosimo de' Medici, spent his whole fortune in buying books. At last, when his money was all gone, the Medici put their purse at his disposal for any sum which his purpose might require. We owe to him the completion of Ammianus Marcellinus, of the 'De Oratore' of Cicero, the text of Lucretius which still has most authority, and other works; he persuaded Cosimo to buy the best manuscript of Pliny from a monastery at Lübeck. With noble confidence he lent his books to those who asked for them, allowed all comers to study them in his own house, and was ready to converse with the students on what they had read. His collection of 800 volumes, valued at 6,000 gold florins, passed after his death, through Cosimo's intervention, to the monastery of San Marco, on the condition that it should be accessible to the public, and is now one of the jewels of the Laurentian library.

Of the two great book-finders, Guarino and Poggio, the latter,[1] on the occasion of the Council of Constanz and acting partly as the agent of Niccoli, searched industriously among the abbeys of South Germany. He there discovered six orations of Cicero, and the first complete Quintilian, that of St. Gall, now at Zürich; in thirty-two days he is said to have copied the whole of it in a beautiful handwriting. He was able to make important additions to Silius Italicus, Manilius, Lucretius, Valerius, Flaccus, Asconius, Pedianus, Columella, Celsus, Aulus, Gellius, Statius, and others; and with the help of Lionardo Aretino he unearthed the last twelve comedies of Plautus, as well as the Verrine orations, the 'Brutus' and the 'De Oratore' of Cicero.

The famous Greek, Cardinal Bessarion,[2] in whom patriotism was mingled with a zeal for letters, collected, at a great sacrifice (30,000 gold florins), 600 manuscripts of pagan and Christian authors. He then looked round for some receptacle where they could safely lie until his unhappy country, if she ever regained her freedom, could reclaim her lost literature. The Venetian government declared itself ready to erect a suit-

[1] Vespas. Fior. pp. 457 sqq.

[2] Vespas. Fiorent. p. 193. Comp. Marin Sanudo, in Murat. xxii. col. 1185 sqq.

able building, and to this day the library of St. Mark retains a part of these treasures.[1]

The formation of the celebrated Medicean library has a history of its own, into which we cannot here enter. The chief collector for Lorenzo Magnifico was Johannes Lascaris. It is well known that the collection, after the plundering in the year 1494, had to be recovered piecemeal by the Cardinal Giovanni Medici, afterwards Leo X.

The library of Urbino,[2] now in the Vatican, was wholly the work of the great Frederick of Montefeltro (p. 44 sqq.). As a boy he had begun to collect; in after years he kept thirty or forty 'scrittori' employed in various places, and spent in the course of time no less than 30,000 ducats on the collection. It was systematically extended and completed, chiefly by the help of Vespasiano, and his account of it forms an ideal picture of a library of the Renaissance. At Urbino there were catalogues of the libraries of the Vatican, of St. Mark at Florence, of the Visconti at Pavia, and even of the library at Oxford. It was noted with pride that in richness and com-

[1] How the matter was provisionally treated is related in Malipiero, *Ann. Veneti*, *Arch. Stor.* vii. ii. pp. 653, 655.

[2] Vespas. Fior. pp. 124 sqq., and 'Inventario della Libreria Urbinata compilata nel Secolo XV. da Federigo Veterano, bibliotecario di Federigo I. da Montefeltro Duca d'Urbino,' given by C. Guasti in the *Giornale Storico degli Archivi Toscani*, vi. (1862), 127–147 and vii. (1863) 46–55, 130–154. For contemporary opinions on the library, see Favre, *Mélanges d'Hist. Lit.* i. 127, note 6. The following is the substance of Dr. Geiger's remarks on the subject of the old authors :—

For the Medicean Library comp. *Delle condicioni e delle vicende della libreria medicea privata dal* 1494 *al* 1508 *ricerche di Enea Piccolomini*, Arch. stor. ital., 265 sqq., 3 serie, vol. xix. pp. 101–129, 254–281, xx. 51–94, xxi. 102–112, 282–296. Dr. Geiger does not undertake an estimate of the relative values of the various rare and almost unknown works contained in the library, nor is he able to state where they are now to be found. He remarks that information as to Greece is much fuller than as to Italy, which is a characteristic mark of the time. The catalogue contains editions of the Bible, of single books of it, with text and annotations, also Greek and Roman works in their then most complete forms, together with some Hebrew books—*tractatus quidam rabbinorum hebr.*—with much modern work, chiefly in Latin, and with not a little in Italian.

Dr. Geiger doubts the absolute accuracy of Vespasiano Fiorentino's catalogue of the library at Urbino. See the German edition, i. 313, 314. [S.G.C.M.]

pleteness none could rival Urbino. Theology and the Middle Ages were perhaps most fully represented. There was a complete Thomas Aquinas, a complete Albertus Magnus, a complete Buonaventura. The collection, however, was a many-sided one, and included every work on medicine which was then to be had. Among the 'moderns' the great writers of the fourteenth century—Dante and Boccaccio, with their complete works—occupied the first place. Then followed twenty-five select humanists, invariably with both their Latin and Italian writings and with all their translations. Among the Greek manuscripts the Fathers of the Church far outnumbered the rest; yet in the list of the classics we find all the works of Sophocles, all of Pindar, and all of Menander. The last must have quickly disappeared from Urbino,[1] else the philologists would have soon edited it. There were men, however, in this book-collecting age who raised a warning voice against the vagaries of the passion. These were not the enemies of learning, but its friends, who feared that harm would come from a

[1] Perhaps at the capture of Urbino by the troops of Cæsar Borgia. The existence of the manuscript has been doubted; but I cannot believe that Vespasiano would have spoken of the gnomic extracts from Menander, which do not amount to more than a couple of hundred verses, as 'tutte le opere,' nor have mentioned them in the list of comprehensive manuscripts, even though he had before him only our present Pindar and Sophocles. It is not inconceivable that this Menander may some day come to light.

[The catalogue of the library at Urbino (see foregoing note), which dates back to the fifteenth century, is not perfectly in accordance with Vespasiano's report, and with the remarks of Dr. Burckhardt upon it. As an official document, it deserves greater credit than Vespasiano's description, which, like most of his descriptions, cannot be acquitted of a certain inaccuracy in detail and tendency to over-colouring. In this catalogue no mention is made of the manuscript of Menander. Mai's doubt as to its existence is therefore justified. Instead of 'all the works of Pindar,' we here find: 'Pindaris Olimpia et Pithia.' The catalogue makes no distinction between ancient and modern books, contains the works of Dante (among others, *Comœdiæ Thusco Carmine*), and Boccaccio, in a very imperfect form; those of Petrarch, however, in all completeness. It may be added that this catalogue mentions many humanistic writings which have hitherto remained unknown and unprinted, that it contains collections of the privileges of the princes of Montefeltro, and carefully enumerates the dedications offered by translators or original writers to Federigo of Urbino.—L. G.]

pursuit which had become a mania. Petrarch himself protested against the fashionable folly of a useless heaping up of books; and in the same century Giovanni Manzini ridiculed Andreolo de Ochis, a septuagenarian from Brescia, who was ready to sacrifice house and land, his wife and himself, to add to the stores of his library.

We have, further, a good deal of information as to the way in which manuscripts and libraries were multiplied.[1] The purchase of an ancient manuscript, which contained a rare, or the only complete, or the only existing text of an old writer, was naturally a lucky accident of which we need take no further account. Among the professional copyists those who understood Greek took the highest place, and it was they especially who bore the honourable name of 'scrittori.' Their number was always limited, and the pay they received very large.[2] The rest, simply called 'copisti,' were partly mere clerks who made their living by such work, partly schoolmasters and needy men of learning, who desired an addition to their income, partly monks, or even nuns, who regarded the pursuit as a work pleasing to God. In the early stages of the Renaissance the professional copyists were few and untrustworthy; their ignorant and dilatory ways were bitterly complained of by Petrarch. In the fifteenth century they were more numerous, and brought more knowledge to their calling, but in accuracy of work they never attained the conscientious precision of the old monks. They seem to have done their work in a sulky and perfunctory fashion, seldom putting their signatures at the foot of the codices, and showed no traces of that cheerful humour, or of that proud consciousness of a

[1] For what follows and in part for what has gone before, see W. Wattenbach, *Das Schriftwesen im Mittelalter*, 2nd. ed. Leipzig, 1875, pp. 392 sqq., 405 sqq., 505. Comp. also the poem, *De Officio Scribæ*, of Phil. Beroaldus, who, however, is rather speaking of the public scrivener.

[2] When Piero de' Medici, at the death of Matthias Corvinus, the book-loving King of Hungary, declared that the 'scrittori' must now lower their charges, since they would otherwise find no further employment (Scil. except in Italy), he can only have meant the Greek copyists, as the caligraphists, to whom one might be tempted to refer his words, continued to be numerous throughout all Italy. Fabroni, *Laurent. Magn.* Adnot. 156 Comp. Adnot. 154.

beneficent activity, which often surprises us in the French and German manuscripts of the same period. This is more curious, as the copyists at Rome in the time of Nicholas V. were mostly Germans or Frenchmen [1]—'barbarians' as the Italian humanists called them, probably men who were in search of favours at the papal court, and who kept themselves alive meanwhile by this means. When Cosimo de' Medici was in a hurry to form a library for his favourite foundation, the Badia below Fiesole, he sent for Vespasiano, and received from him the advice to give up all thoughts of purchasing books, since those which were worth getting could not be had easily, but rather to make use of the copyists; whereupon Cosimo bargained to pay him so much a day, and Vespasiano, with forty-five writers under him, delivered 200 volumes in twenty-two months.[2] The catalogue of the works to be copied was sent to Cosimo by Nicholas V.[3] who wrote it with his own hand. Ecclesiastical literature and the books needed for the choral services naturally held the chief place in the list.

The handwriting was that beautiful modern Italian which was already in use in the preceding century, and which makes the sight of one of the books of that time a pleasure. Pope Nicholas V., Poggio, Giannozzo Manetti, Niccolò Niccoli, and other distinguished scholars, themselves wrote a beautiful hand, and desired and tolerated none other. The decorative adjuncts, even when miniatures formed no part of them, were full of taste, as may be seen especially in the Laurentian manuscripts,

[1] Gaye, *Carteggio*, i. p. 164. A letter of the year 1455 under Calixtus III. The famous miniature Bible of Urbino is written by a Frenchman, a workman of Vespasiano's. See D'Agincourt, *La Peinture*, tab. 78. On German copyists in Italy, see further G. Campori, *Artisti Italiani e Stranieri negli Stati Estensi*, Modena, 1855, p. 277, and *Giornale di Erudizione Artistica*, vol. ii. pp. 360 sqq. Wattenbach, *Schriftwesen*, 411, note 5. For German printers, see below.

[2] Vespas. Fior. p. 335.

[3] Ambr. Trav. *Epist.* i. p. 63. The Pope was equally serviceable to the libraries of Urbino and Pesaro (that of Aless. Sforza, p. 38). Comp. Arch. Stor. ital. xxi. 103–106. The Bible and Commentaries on it; the Fathers of the Church; Aristotle, with his commentators, including Averroes and Avicenna; Moses Maimonides; Latin translations of Greek philosophers; the Latin prose writers; of the poets only Virgil, Statius, Ovid, and Lucan are mentioned.

with the light and graceful scrolls which begin and end the lines. The material used to write on, when the work was ordered by great or wealthy people, was always parchment; the binding, both in the Vatican and at Urbino, was a uniform crimson velvet with silver clasps. Where there was so much care to show honour to the contents of a book by the beauty of its outward form, it is intelligible that the sudden appearance of printed books was greeted at first with anything but favour. The envoys of Cardinal Bessarion, when they saw for the first time a printed book in the house of Constantine Lascaris, laughed at the discovery 'made among the barbarians in some German city,' and Frederick of Urbino 'would have been ashamed to own a printed book.' [1]

But the weary copyists—not those who lived by the trade, but the many who were forced to copy a book in order to have it—rejoiced at the German invention,[2] 'notwithstanding the praises and encouragements which the poets awarded to caligraphy.' It was soon applied in Italy to the multiplication first of the Latin and then of the Greek authors, and for a long period nowhere but in Italy, yet it spread with by no means the rapidity which might have been expected from the general enthusiasm for these works. After a while the modern relation between author and publisher began to develop itself,[3] and under Alexander VI., when it was no longer easy to destroy a book, as Cosimo could make Filelfo promise to do,[4] the prohibitive censorship made its appearance.

[1] Vespas. Fior. p. 129.

[2] 'Artes—Quis Labor est fessis demptus ab Articulis' in a poem by Robertus Ursus about 1470, *Rerum Ital. Script. ex Codd. Fiorent.* tom. ii. col. 693. He rejoices rather too hastily over the rapid spread of classical literature which was hoped for. Comp. Libri, *Hist. des Sciences Mathématiques*, ii. 278 sqq. (See also the eulogy of Lor. Valla, *Hist. Zeitschr.* xxxii. 62.) For the printers at Rome (the first were Germans: Hahn, Pannartz, Schweinheim), see Gaspar. Veron. *Vita Pauli II.* in Murat. iii. ii. col. 1046; and Laire, *Spec. Hist. Typographiæ Romanae, xv. sec.* Romæ, 1778; Gregorovius, vii. 525–33. For the first Privilegium in Venice, see Marin Sanudo, in Muratori, xxii. col. 1189.

[3] Something of the sort had already existed in the age of manuscripts. See Vespas. Fior. p. 656, on the *Cronaco del Mondo* of Zembino of Pistoia.

[4] Fabroni, *Laurent. Magn.* Adnot. 212. It happened in the case of the libel. *De Exilio.*

The growth of textual criticism which accompanied the advancing study of languages and antiquity, belongs as little to the subject of this book as the history of scholarship in general. We are here occupied, not with the learning of the Italians in itself, but with the reproduction of antiquity in literature and life. One word more on the studies themselves may still be permissible.

Greek scholarship was chiefly confined to Florence and to the fifteenth and the beginning of the sixteenth centuries. It was never so general as Latin scholarship, partly because of the far greater difficulties which it involved, partly and still more because of the consciousness of Roman supremacy and an instinctive hatred of the Greeks more than counterbalanced the attractions which Greek literature had for the Italians.[1]

The impulse which proceeded from Petrarch and Boccaccio, superficial as was their own acquaintance with Greek, was powerful, but did not tell immediately on their contemporaries;[2] on the other hand, the study of Greek literature died out about the year 1520[3] with the last of the colony of learned

[1] Even in Petrarch the consciousness of this superiority of Italians over Greeks is often to be noticed: *Epp. Fam.* lib. i. ep. 3; *Epp. Sen.* lib. xii. ep. 2; he praises the Greeks reluctantly: *Carmina*, lib. iii. 30 (ed. Rossetti, vol. ii. p. 342). A century later, Æneas Sylvius writes (Comm. to Panormita, 'De Dictis et Factis Alfonsi,' Append.): 'Alfonsus tanto est Socrate major quanto gravior Romanus homo quam Græcus putatur.' In accordance with this feeling the study of Greek was thought little of. From a document made use of below, written about 1460, it appears that Porcellio and Tomaso Seneca tried to resist the rising influence of Greek. Similarly, Paolo Cortese (1490) was averse to Greek, lest the hitherto exclusive authority of Latin should be impaired, *De Hominibus Doctis*, p. 20. For Greek studies in Italy, see esp. the learned work of Favre, *Mélanges d'Hist. Liter.* i. *passim.*

[2] See above p. 187, and comp. C. Voigt, *Wiederbelebung*, 323 sqq.

[3] The dying out of these Greeks is mentioned by Pierius Valerian, *De Infelicitate Literat.* in speaking of Lascaris. And Paulus Jovius, at the end of his *Elogia Literaria*, says of the Germans, 'Quum literæ non latinæ modo cum pudore nostro, sed græcæ et hebraicæ in eorum terras fatali commigratione transierint' (about 1450). Similarly, sixty years before (1482), Joh. Argyropulos had exclaimed, when he heard young Reuchlin translate Thucydides in his lecture-room at Rome, 'Græcia nostra exilio transvolavit Alpes.' Geiger, *Reuchlin* (Lpzg. 1871), pp. 26 sqq. Burchhardt, 273. A remarkable passage is to be found in Jov. Pontanus, *Anto-*

Greek exiles, and it was a singular piece of fortune that northerners like Agricola, Reuchlin, Erasmus, the Stephani, and Budæus had meanwhile made themselves masters of the language. That colony had begun with Manuel Chrysoloras and his relation John, and with George of Trebizond. Then followed, about and after the time of the conquest of Constantinople, John Argyropulos, Theodore Gaza, Demetrios Chalcondylas, who brought up his sons Theophilos and Basilios to be excellent Hellenists, Andronikos Kallistos, Marcos Musuros and the family of the Lascaris, not to mention others. But after the subjection of Greece by the Turks was completed, the succession of scholars was maintained only by the sons of the fugitives and perhaps here and there by some Candian or Cyprian refugee. That the decay of Hellenistic studies began about the time of the death of Leo X. was owing partly to a general change of intellectual attitude,[1] and to a certain satiety of classical influences which now made itself felt; but its coincidence with the death of the Greek fugitives was not wholly a matter of accident. The study of Greek among the Italians appears, if we take the year 1500 as our standard, to have been pursued with extraordinary zeal. The youths of that day learned to speak the language, and half a century later, like the Popes Paul III. and Paul IV., they could still do so in their old age.[2] But this sort of mastery of the study presupposes intercourse with native Greeks.

Besides Florence, Rome and Padua nearly always maintained paid teachers of Greek, and Verona, Ferrara, Venice, Perugia, Pavia and other cities occasional teachers.[3] Hellenistic studies

nius, opp. iv. p. 203: 'In Græcia magis nunc Turcaicum discas quam Græcum. Quicquid enim doctorum habent Græcæ disciplinæ, in Italia nobiscum victitat.

[1] Ranke, *Päpste*, i. 486 sqq. Comp. the end of this part of our work.

[2] Tommaso Gar, *Relazioni della Corte di Roma*, i. pp. 338, 379.

[3] George of Trebizond, teacher of rhetoric at Venice, with a salary of 150 ducats a year (see Malipiero, *Arch. Stor.* vii. ii. p. 653). For the Greek chair at Perugia, see *Arch. Stor.* xvi. ii. p. 19 of the Introduction. In the case of Rimini, there is some doubt whether Greek was taught or not. Comp. *Anecd. Litt.* ii. p. 300. At Bologna, the centre of juristic studies, Aurispa had but little success. Details on the subject in Malagola.

owed a priceless debt to the press of Aldo Manucci at Venice, where the most important and voluminous writers were for the first time printed in the original. Aldo ventured his all in the enterprise; he was an editor and publisher whose like the world has rarely seen.[1]

Along with this classical revival, Oriental studies now assumed considerable proportions.[2] Dante himself set a high value on Hebrew, though we cannot suppose that he understood it. From the fifteenth century onwards scholars were no longer content merely to speak of it with respect, but applied themselves to a thorough study of it. This scientific interest in the language was, however, from the beginning either furthered or hindered by religious considerations. Poggio, when resting from the labours of the Council of Constance, learnt Hebrew at that place and at Baden from a baptized Jew, whom he describes as 'stupid, peevish, and ignorant, like most converted Jews;' but he had to defend his conduct against Lionardo Bruni, who endeavoured to prove to him that Hebrew was useless or even injurious. The controversial writings of the great Florentine statesman and scholar, Giannozzo Manetti[3] (d. 1459) against the Jews afford an early instance of a complete mastery of their language and science. His son Agnolo was from his childhood instructed in Latin, Greek, and Hebrew. The father, at the bidding of Nicholas V., translated the Psalms, but had to defend the principles of his translation in a work addressed to Alfonso. Commissioned by the same Pope, who had offered a reward of 5,000 ducats for the discovery of the original Hebrew text of the Evangelist Matthew, he made a collection of Hebrew manuscripts, which is still preserved in the Vatican, and began a great apologetic work against the Jews.[4] The study of Hebrew was thus

[1] Exhaustive information on the subject in the admirable work of A. F. Didot, *Alde Manuce et l'Héllenisme à Venise*, Paris, 1875.

[2] For what follows see A. de Gubernatis, *Matériaux pour servir à l'Histoire des Études Orientales en Italie*, Paris, Florence, &c., 1876. Additions by Soave in the *Bolletino Italiano degli Studi Orientali*, i. 178 sqq. More precise details below.

[3] See below.

[4] See *Commentario della Vita di Messer Gianozzo Manetti, scritto da Vespasiano Bisticci*, Torino, 1862, esp. pp. 11, 44, 91 sqq.

enlisted in the service of the Church. The Camaldolese monk Ambrogio Traversari learnt the language,[1] and Pope Sixtus IV., who erected the building for the Vatican library, and added to the collection extensive purchases of his own, took into his service 'scrittori' (*librarios*) for Hebrew as well as for Greek and Latin.[2] The study of the language now became more general; Hebrew manuscripts were collected, and in some libraries, like that of Urbino, formed a specially valuable part of the rich treasure there stored up; the printing of Hebrew books began in Italy in 1475, and made the study easier both to the Italians themselves and to the other nations of Europe, who for many years drew their supply from Italy. Soon there was no good-sized town where there were not individuals who were masters of the language and many anxious to learn it, and in 1488 a chair for Hebrew was founded at Bologna, and another in 1514 at Rome. The study became so popular that it was even preferred to Greek.[3]

Among all those who busied themselves with Hebrew in the fifteenth century, no one was of more importance than Pico della Mirandola. He was not satisfied with a knowledge of the Hebrew grammar and Scriptures, but penetrated into the

[1] Vesp. Fior. p. 320. A. Trav. *Epist.* lib. xi. 16.

[2] Platina, *Vita Sixti IV.* p. 332.

[3] Benedictus Faleus, *De Origine Hebraicarum Græcarum Latinarumque Literarum*, Naples, 1520.

[4] For Dante, see Wegele, *Dante*, 2nd ed. p. 268, and Lasinio, *Dante e le Lingue semitiche* in the *Rivista Orientale* (Flor. 1867–8). On Poggio, *Opera*, p. 297; Lion. Bruni, *Epist.* lib. ix. 12, comp. Gregorovius, vii. 555, and Shepherd-Tonelli, *Vita di Poggio*, i. 65. The letter of Poggio to Niccoli, in which he treats of Hebrew, has been lately published in French and Latin under the title, *Les Bains de Bade par Pogge*, by Antony Méray, Paris, 1876. Poggio desired to know on what principles Jerome translated the Bible, while Bruni maintained that, now that Jerome's translation was in existence, distrust was shown to it by learning Hebrew. For Manetti as a collector of Hebrew MSS. see Steinschneider, in the work quoted below. In the library at Urbino there were in all sixty-one Hebrew manuscripts. Among them a Bible 'opus mirabile et integrum, cum glossis mirabiliter scriptus in modo avium, arborum et animalium in maximo volumine, ut vix a tribus hominibus feratur.' These, as appears from Assemanni's list, are now mostly in the Vatican. On the first printing in Hebrew, see Steinschneider and Cassel, *Jud. Typographie in Esch. u. Gruber, Realencyclop.* sect. ii. bd. 28, p. 34, and *Catal. Bodl.* by Steinschneider, 1852–60,

Jewish Cabbalah and even made himself familiar with the literature of the Talmud. That such pursuits, though they may not have gone very far, were at all possible to him, he owed to his Jewish teachers. Most of the instruction in Hebrew was in fact given by Jews, some of whom, though generally not till after conversion to Christianity, became distinguished University professors and much-esteemed writers. [1]

pp. 2821–2866. It is characteristic that of the two first printers one belonged to Mantua, the other to Reggio in Calabria, so that the printing of Hebrew books began almost contemporaneously at the two extremities of Italy. In Mantua the printer was a Jewish physician, who was helped by his wife. It may be mentioned as a curiosity that in the *Hypnerotomachia* of Polifilo, written 1467, printed 1499, fol. 68 *a*, there is a short passage in Hebrew; otherwise no Hebrew occurs in the Aldine editions before 1501. The Hebrew scholars in Italy are given by De Gubernatis (p. 80), but authorities are not quoted for them singly. (Marco Lippomanno is omitted; comp. Steinschneider in the book given below.) Paolo de Canale is mentioned as a learned Hebraist by Pier. Valerian. *De Infel. Literat.* ed. Mencken, p. 296; in 1488 Professor in Bologna, *Mag. Vicentius;* comp. *Costituzione, discipline e riforme dell' antico studio Bolognese. Memoria del Prof. Luciano Scarabelli*, Piacenza, 1876; in 1514 Professor in Rome, Agarius Guidacerius, acc. to Gregorovius, viii. 292, and the passages there quoted. On Guid. see Steinschneider, *Bibliogr. Handbuch*, Leipzig, 1859, pp. 56, 157–161.

[1] The literary activity of the Jews in Italy is too great and of too wide an influence to be passed over altogether in silence. The following paragraphs, which, not to overload the text, I have relegated to the notes, are wholly the substance of communications made me by Dr. M. Steinschneider, of Berlin, to whom I [Dr. Ludwig Geiger] here take the opportunity of expressing my thanks for his constant and friendly help. He has given exhaustive evidence on the subject in his profound and instructive treatise, 'Letteratura Italiana dei Giudei,' in the review *Il Buonarotti*, vols. vi. viii. xi. xii.; Rome, 1871–77 (also printed separately); to which, once for all, I refer the reader.

There were many Jews living in Rome at the time of the Second Temple. They had so thoroughly adopted the language and civilisation prevailing in Italy, that even on their tombs they used not Hebrew, but Latin and Greek inscriptions (communicated by Garucci, see Steinschneider, *Hebr. Bibliogr.* vi. p. 102, 1863). In Lower Italy, especially, Greek learning survived during the Middle Ages among the inhabitants generally, and particularly among the Jews, of whom some are said to have taught at the University of Salerno, and to have rivalled the Christians in literary productiveness (comp. Steinschneider, 'Donnolo,' in Virchow's *Archiv*, bd. 39, 40). This supremacy of Greek culture lasted till the Saracens conquered Lower Italy. But before this conquest the Jews

Among the Oriental languages, Arabic was studied as well as Hebrew. The science of medicine, no longer satisfied with the older Latin translations of the great Arabian physicians,

of Middle Italy had been striving to equal or surpass their bretheren of the South. Jewish learning centred in Rome, and from there spread, as early as the sixteenth century, to Cordova, Kairowan, and South Germany. By means of these emigrants, Italian Judaism became the teacher of the whole race. Through its works, especially through the work *Aruch* of Nathan ben Jechiel (1101), a great dictionary to the Talmud, the Midraschim, and the Thargum, 'which, though not informed by a genuine scientific spirit, offers so rich a store of matter and rests on such early authorities, that its treasures have even now not been wholly exhausted,' it exercised indirectly a great influence (Abraham Geiger, *Das Judenthum und seine Geschichte*, Breslau, bd. ii. 1865, p. 170; and the same author's *Nachgelassene Schriften*, bd. ii. Berlin, 1875, pp. 129 and 154). A little later, in the thirteenth century, the Jewish literature in Italy brought Jews and Christians into contact, and received through Frederick II., and still more perhaps through his son Manfred, a kind of official sanction. Of this contact we have evidence in the fact that an Italian, Niccolò di Giovinazzo, studied with a Jew, Moses ben Salomo, the Latin translation of the famous work of Maimonides, *More Nebuchim;* of this sanction, in the fact that the Emperor, who was distinguished for his freethinking as much as for his fondness for Oriental studies, probably was the cause of this Latin translation being made, and summoned the famous Anatoli from Provence into Italy, to translate works of Averroes into Hebrew (comp. Steinschneider, *Hebr. Bibliogr.* xv. 86, and Renan, *L'Averroes et l'Averroisme*, third edition, Paris, 1866, p. 290). These measures prove the acquaintance of early Jews with Latin, which rendered intercourse possible between them and Christians—an intercourse which bore sometimes a friendly and sometimes a polemical character. Still more than Anatoli, Hillel b. Samuel, in the latter half of the thirteenth century, devoted himself to Latin literature; he studied in Spain, returned to Italy, and here made many translations from Latin into Hebrew; among them of writings of Hippocrates in a Latin version. (This was printed 1647 by Gaiotius, and passed for his own.) In this translation he introduced a few Italian words by way of explanation, and thus perhaps, or by his whole literary procedure, laid himself open to the reproach of despising Jewish doctrines.

But the Jews went further than this. At the end of the thirteenth and in the fourteenth centuries, they drew so near to Christian science and to the representatives of the culture of the Renaissance, that one of them, Giuda Romano, in a series of hitherto unprinted writings, laboured zealously at the scholastic philosophy, and in one treatise used Italian words to explain Hebrew expressions. He is one of the first to do so (Steinschneider, *Giuda Romano*, Rome, 1870). Another, Giuda's cousin Manoello, a friend of Dante, wrote in imitation of him a sort of Divine Comedy in Hebrew, in which he extols Dante, whose death he also had constant recourse to the originals, to which an easy access was offered by the Venetian consulates in the East, where Italian doctors were regularly kept. But the Arabian scholarship of the Renaissance is only a feeble echo of the influence which Arabian civilisation in the Middle Ages exercised over Italy and the whole cultivated world—an influence which not only preceded that of the Renaissance, but in some respects was hostile to it, and which did not surrender without a struggle the place which it had long and vigorously asserted. Hieronimo Ramusio, a Venetian physician, translated a great part of Avicenna from the Arabic and died at Damascus in 1486. Andrea Mongajo of Belluno,[1] a disciple of the same Avicenna, lived long at Damascus, learnt Arabic, and improved on his master. The Venetian government afterwards appointed him as professor of this subject at Padua. The example set by

bewailed in an Italian sonnet (Abraham Geiger, *Jüd. Zeitsch.* v. 286–331, Breslau, 1867). A third, Mose Riete, born towards the end of the century, wrote works in Italian (a specimen in the Catalogue of Hebrew MSS., Leyden, 1858). In the fifteenth century we can clearly recognise the influence of the Renaissance in Messer Leon, a Jewish writer, who, in his *Rhetoric*, uses Quintilian and Cicero, as well as Jewish authorities. One of the most famous Jewish writers in Italy in the fifteenth century was Eliah del Medigo, a philosopher who taught publicly as a Jew in Padua and Florence, and was once chosen by the Venetian Senate as arbitrator in a philosophical dispute (Abr. Geiger, *Nachgelassene Schriften*, Berlin, 1876, bd. iii. 3). Eliah del Medigo was the teacher of Pico della Mirandola; besides him, Jochanan Alemanno (comp. Steinschneider, *Polem. u. Apolog. Lit.* Lpzg. 1877, anh. 7, § 25). The list of learned Jews in Italy may be closed by Kalonymos ben David and Abraham de Balmes (d. 1523), to whom the greater part of the translations of Averroes from Hebrew into Latin is due, which were still publicly read at Padua in the seventeenth century. To this scholar may be added the Jewish Aldus, Gerson Soncino, who not only made his press the centre of Jewish printing, but, by publishing Greek works, trespassed on the ground of the great Aldus himself (Steinschneider, *Gerson Soncino und Aldus Manutius*, Berlin, 1858).

[1] Pierius Valerian. *De Infelic. Lit.* ed. Mencken, 301, speaking of Mongajo. Gubernatis, p. 184, identifies him with Andrea Alpago, of Bellemo, said to have also studied Arabian literature, and to have travelled in the East. On Arabic studies generally, Gubernatis, pp. 173 sqq. For a translation made 1341 from Arabic into Italian, comp. Narducci, *Intorno ad una tradizione italiana di una composizione astronomica di Alfonso X. rè di Castiglia*, Roma 1865. On Ramusio, see Sansovino, *Venezia*, fol. 250.

Venice was followed by other governments. Princes and wealthy men rivalled one another in collecting Arabic manuscripts. The first Arabian printing-press was begun at Fano under Julius II. and consecrated in 1514 under Leo X. [1]

We must here linger for a moment over Pico della Mirandola, before passing on to the general effects of humanism. He was the only man who loudly and vigorously defended the truth and science of all ages against the one-sided worship of classical antiquity.[2] He knew how to value not only Averroes and the Jewish investigators, but also the scholastic writers of the Middle Ages, according to the matter of their writings. He seems to hear them say, 'We shall live for ever, not in the schools of word-catchers, but in the circle of the wise, where they talk not of the mother of Andromache or of the sons of Niobe, but of the deeper causes of things human and divine; he who looks closely will see that even the barbarians had intelligence (*mercurium*), not on the tongue but in the breast.' Himself writing a vigorous and not inelegant Latin, and a master of clear exposition, he despised the purism of pedants and the current over-estimate of borrowed forms, especially when joined, as they often are, with one-sidedness, and involving indifference to the wider truth of the things themselves. Looking at Pico, we can guess at the lofty flight which Italian philosophy would have taken had not the counter-reformation annihilated the higher spiritual life of the people.

[1] Gubernatis, p. 188. The first book contains Christian prayers in Arabic; the first Italian translations of the Koran appeared in 1547. In 1499 we meet with a few not very successful Arabic types in the work of Polifilo, b. 7 *a*. For the beginnings of Egyptian studies, see Gregorovius, viii. p. 304.

[2] Especially in the important letter of the year 1485 to Ermolao Barbaro, in *Ang. Politian. Epistolæ*, l. ix. Comp. Jo. Pici, *Oratio de Hominis Dignitate*. For this discourse, see the end of part iv.; on Pico himself more will be given in part vi. chap. 4.

CHAPTER IV.

HUMANISM IN THE FOURTEENTH CENTURY.

WHO now were those who acted as mediators between their own age and a venerated antiquity, and made the latter a chief element in the culture of the former?

They were a crowd of the most miscellaneous sort, wearing one face to-day and another to-morrow; but they clearly felt themselves, and it was fully recognised by their time, that they formed a wholly new element in society. The 'clerici vagantes' of the twelfth century, whose poetry we have already referred to (p. 174), may perhaps be taken as their forerunners—the same unstable existence, the same free and more than free views of life, and the germs at all events of the same pagan tendencies in their poetry. But now, as competitor with the whole culture of the Middle Ages, which was essentially clerical and was fostered by the Church, there appeared a new civilisation, founding itself on that which lay on the other side of the Middle Ages. Its active representatives became influential[1] because they knew what the ancients knew, because they tried to write as the ancients wrote, because they began to think, and soon to feel, as the ancients thought and felt. The tradition to which they devoted themselves passed at a thousand points into genuine reproduction.

Some modern writers deplore the fact that the germs of a far more independent and essentially national culture, such as appeared in Florence about the year 1300, were afterwards so completely swamped by the humanists.[2] There was then, we are told, nobody in Florence who could not read; even the

[1] Their estimate of themselves is indicated by Poggio (*De Avaritia*, fol. 2), according to whom only such persons could say that they had lived (*se vixisse*) who had written learned and eloquent books in Latin or translated Greek into Latin.

[2] Esp. Libri, *Histoires des Sciences Mathém.* ii. 159 sqq., 258 sqq.

donkey-men sang the verses of Dante; the best Italian manuscripts which we possess belonged orginally to Florentine artisans; the publication of a popular encyclopædia, like the 'Tesoro' of Brunetto Latini, was then possible; and all this was founded on a strength and soundness of character due to the universal participation in public affairs, to commerce and travel, and to the systematic reprobation of idleness. The Florentines, it is urged, were at that time respected and influential throughout the whole world, and were called in that year, not without reason, by Pope Boniface VIII., 'the fifth element.' The rapid progress of humanism after the year 1400 paralysed native impulses. Henceforth men looked to antiquity only for the solution of every problem, and consequently allowed literature to sink into mere quotation. Nay, the very fall of civil freedom is partly to be ascribed to all this, since the new learning rested on obedience to authority, sacrificed municipal rights to Roman law, and thereby both sought and found the favour of the despots.

These charges will occupy us now and then at a later stage of our inquiry, when we shall attempt to reduce them to their true value, and to weigh the losses against the gains of this movement. For the present we must confine ourselves to showing how the civilisation even of the vigorous fourteenth century necessarily prepared the way for the complete victory of humanism, and how precisely the greatest representatives of the national Italian spirit were themselves the men who opened wide the gate for the measureless devotion to antiquity in the fifteenth century.

To begin with Dante. If a succession of men of equal genius had presided over Italian culture, whatever elements their natures might have absorbed from the antique, they still could not fail to retain a characteristic and strongly-marked national stamp. But neither Italy nor Western Europe produced another Dante, and he was and remained the man who first thrust antiquity into the foreground of national culture. In the 'Divine Comedy' he treats the ancient and the Christian worlds, not indeed as of equal authority, but as parallel to one another. Just as, at an earlier period of the Middle Ages types and antitypes were sought in the history of the Old and New

Testaments, so does Dante constantly bring together a Christian and a pagan illustration of the same fact.[1] It must be remembered that the Christian cycle of history and legend was familiar, while the ancient was relatively unknown, was full of promise and of interest, and must necessarily have gained the upper hand in the competition for public sympathy when there was no longer a Dante to hold the balance between the two.

Petrarch, who lives in the memory of most people nowadays chiefly as a great Italian poet, owed his fame among his contemporaries far rather to the fact that he was a kind of living representative of antiquity, that he imitated all styles of Latin poetry, endeavoured by his voluminous historical and philosophical writings not to supplant but to make known the works of the ancients, and wrote letters that, as treatises on matters of antiquarian interest, obtained a reputation which to us is unintelligible, but which was natural enough in an age without handbooks. Petrarch himself trusted and hoped that his Latin writings would bring him fame with his contemporaries and with posterity, and thought so little of his Italian poems that, as he often tell us, he would gladly have destroyed them if he could have succeeded thereby in blotting them out from the memory of men.

It was the same with Boccaccio. For two centuries, when but little was known of the 'Decameron'[2] north of the Alps, he was famous all over Europe simply on account of his Latin compilations on mythology, geography, and biography.[3] One of these, 'De Genealogia Deorum,' contains in the fourteenth and fifteenth books a remarkable appendix, in which he dis-

[1] *Purgatorio*, xviii. contains striking instances. Mary hastens over the mountains, Cæsar to Spain; Mary is poor and Fabricius disinterested. We may here remark on the chronological introduction of the Sibyls into the profane history of antiquity as attempted by Uberti in his *Dittamondo* (i. cap. 14, 15), about 1360.

[2] The first German translation of the *Decameron*, by H. Steinhovel, was printed in 1472, and soon became popular. The translations of the whole *Decameron* were almost everywhere preceded by those of the story of Griselda, written in Latin by Petrarch.

[3] These Latin writings of Boccaccio have been admirably discussed recently by Schück, *Zur Characteristik des ital. Hum. im* 14 *und* 15 *Jahrh.* Breslau, 1865; and in an article in Fleckeisen and Masius, *Jahrbücher fur Phil. und Pädag.* bd. xx. (1874).

cusses the position of the then youthful humanism with regard to the age. We must not be misled by his exclusive references to 'poesia,' as closer observation shows that he means thereby the whole mental activity of the poet-scholars.[1] This it is whose enemies he so vigorously combats—the frivolous ignoramuses who have no soul for anything but debauchery; the sophistical theologian, to whom Helicon, the Castalian fountain, and the grove of Apollo were foolishness; the greedy lawyers, to whom poetry was a superfluity, since no money was to be made by it; finally the mendicant friars, described periphrastically, but clearly enough, who made free with their charges of paganism and immorality.[2] Then follows the defence of poetry, the proof that the poetry of the ancients and of their modern followers contains nothing mendacious, the praise of it, and especially of the deeper and allegorical meanings which we must always attribute to it, and of that calculated obscurity which is intended to repel the dull minds of the ignorant.

And finally, with a clear reference to his own scholarly work,[3] the writer justifies the new relation in which his age stood to paganism. The case was wholly different, he pleads, when the Early Church had to fight its way amongt he heathen. Now—praised be Jesus Christ!—true religion was strengthened, paganism destroyed, and the victorious Church in possession of the hostile camp. It was now possible to touch and study paganism almost (*fere*) without danger. Boccaccio, however, did not hold this liberal view consistently. The ground of his

[1] 'Poeta,' even in Dante (*Vita Nuova*, p. 47), means only the writer of Latin verses, while for Italian the expressions 'Rimatore, Dicitore per rima,' are used. It is true that the names and ideas became mixed in course of time.

[2] Petrarch, too, at the height of his fame complained in moments of melancholy that his evil star decreed him to pass his last years among scoundrels (*extremi fures*). In the imaginary letter to Livy, *Epp. Fam.* ed. Fracass. lib. xxiv. ep. 8. That Petrarch defended poetry, and how, is well known (comp. Geiger, *Petr.* 113–117). Besides the enemies who beset him in common with Boccaccio, he had to face the doctors (comp. *Invectivæ in Medicum Objurgantem*, lib. i. and ii.).

[3] Boccaccio, in a later letter to Jacobus Pizinga (*Opere Volgari*, vol. xvi.), confines himself more strictly to poetry properly so called. And yet he only recognises as poetry that which treated of antiquity, and ignores the Troubadours.

apostasy lay partly in the mobility of his character, partly in the still powerful and widespread prejudice that classical pursuits were unbecoming in a theologian. To these reasons must be added the warning given him in the name of the dead Pietro Petroni by the monk Gioacchino Ciani to give up his pagan studies under pain of early death. He accordingly determined to abandon them, and was only brought back from this cowardly resolve by the earnest exhortations of Petrarch, and by the latter's able demonstration that humanism was reconcileable with religion.[1]

There was thus a new cause in the world and a new class of men to maintain it. It is idle to ask if this cause ought not to have stopped short in its career of victory, to have restrained itself deliberately, and conceded the first place to purely national elements of culture. No conviction was more firmly rooted in the popular mind, than that antiquity was the highest title to glory which Italy possessed.

There was a symbolical ceremony familiar to this generation of poet-scholars which lasted on into the fifteenth and sixteenth centuries, though losing the higher sentiment which inspired it—the coronation of the poets with the laurel wreath. The origin of this system in the Middle Ages is obscure, and the ritual of the ceremony never became fixed. It was a public demonstration, an outward and visible expression of literary enthusiasm,[2] and naturally its form was variable. Dante, for instance, seems to have understood it in the sense of a half-religious consecration; he desired to assume the wreath in the baptistery of San Giovanni, where, like thousands of other Florentine children, he had received baptism.[3] He could, says his biographer, have anywhere received the crown in virtue of his fame, but desired it nowhere but in his native city, and therefore died uncrowned. From the same source we learn that the usage was till then uncommon, and was held to be inherited by the ancient Romans from the Greeks. The most

[1] Petr. *Epp. Senil.* lib. i. ep. 5.

[2] Boccaccio (*Vita di Dante*, p. 50): 'La quale (laurea) non scienza accresce ma è dell' acquistata certissimo testimonio e ornamento.'

[3] *Paradiso*, xxv. 1 sqq. Boccaccio, *Vita di Dante*, p. 50. 'Sopra le fonti di San Giovanni si era disporto di coronare.' Comp. *Paradiso*, i. 25.

recent source to which the practices could be referred is to be found in the Capitoline contests of musicians, poets, and other artists, founded by Domitian in imitation of the Greeks and celebrated every five years, which may possibly have survived for a time the fall of the Roman Empire; but as few other men would venture to crown themselves, as Dante desired to do, the question arises, to whom did this office belong? Albertino Mussato (p. 140) was crowned at Padua in 1310 by the bishop and the rector of the University. The University of Paris, the rector of which was then a Florentine (1341), and the municipal authorities of Rome, competed for the honour of crowning Petrarch. His self-elected examiner, King Robert of Anjou, would gladly have performed the ceremony at Naples, but Petrarch preferred to be crowned on the Capitol by the senator of Rome. This honour was long the highest object of ambition, and so it seemed to Jacobus Pizinga, an illustrious Sicilian magistrate.[1] Then came the Italian journey of Charles IV., whom it amused to flatter the vanity of ambitious men, and impress the ignorant multitude by means of gorgeous ceremonies. Starting from the fiction that the coronation of poets was a prerogative of the old Roman emperors, and consequently was no less his own, he crowned (May 15, 1355) the Florentine scholar, Zanobi della Strada, at Pisa, to the annoyance of to Petrarch, who complained that 'the barbarian laurel had dared adorn the man loved by the Ausonian Muses,' and to the great disgust of Boccaccio, who declined to recognise this 'laurea Pisana' as legitimate.[2] Indeed it might be fairly asked with what right this stranger, half Slavonic by birth, came to sit in judgment on the merits of Italian poets. But from henceforth the emperors crowned poets wherever they went on their travels; and in the fifteenth century the popes and other princes assumed the same right, till at last no regard whatever was

[1] See Boccaccio's letter to him in the *Opere Volgari*, vol. xvi. p. 36: 'Si præstet Deus, concedente senatu Romuleo.' . . . .

[2] Matt. Villani, v. 26. There was a solemn procession on horseback round the city, when the followers of the Emperor, his 'baroni,' accompanied the poet. Boccaccio, l. c. Petrarch: *Invectivæ contra Med. Præf.* See also *Epp. Fam. Volgarizzate da Fracassetti*, iii. 128. For the speech of Zanobi at the coronation, Friedjung, l. c. 308 sqq. Fazio degli Uberti was also crowned, but it is not known where or by whom.

paid to place or circumstances. In Rome, under Sixtus IV., the academy[1] of Pomponius Lætus gave the wreath on its own authority. The Florentines had the good taste not to crown their famous humanists till after death. Carlo Aretino and Lionardo Aretino were thus crowned; the eulogy of the first was pronounced by Matteo Palmieri, of the latter by Giannozzo Manetti, before the members of the council and the whole people, the orator standing at the head of the bier, on which the corpse lay clad in a silken robe.[2] Carlo Aretino was further honoured by a tomb in Santa Croce, which is among the most beautiful in the whole course of the Renaissance.

[1] Jac. Volaterran. in Murat. xxiii. col. 185.

[2] Vespas. Fiorent. pp. 575, 589. *Vita Jan. Manetti*, in Murat. xx. col. 543, The celebrity of Lionardo Aretino was in his lifetime sc great that people came from all parts merely to see him; a Spaniard fell on his knees before him.—Vesp. p. 568. For the monument of Guarino, the magistrate of Ferrara allowed, in 1461, the then considerable sum of 100 ducats. On the coronation of poets in Italy there is a good summary of notices in Favre, *Mélanges d'Hist. Lit.* (1856) i. 65 sqq.

CHAPTER V.

THE UNIVERSITIES AND SCHOOLS.

THE influence of antiquity on culture, of which we have now to speak, presupposes that the new learning had gained possession of the universities. This was so, but by no means to the extent and with the results which might have been expected.

Few of the Italian universities[1] show themselves in their full vigour till the thirteenth and fourteenth centuries, when the increase of wealth rendered a more systematic care for education possible. At first there were generally three sorts of professorships—one for civil law, another for canonical law, the third for medicine; in course of time professorships of rhetoric, of philosophy, and of astronomy were added, the last commonly, though not always, identical with astrology. The salaries varied greatly in different cases. Sometimes a capital sum was paid down. With the spread of culture competition became so active that the different universities tried to entice away distinguished teachers from one another, under which circumstances Bologna is said to have sometimes devoted the half of its public income (20,000 ducats) to the university. The appointments were as a rule made only for a certain time,[2]

[1] Comp. Libri, *Histoire des Sciences Mathém.* ii. p. 92 sqq. Bologna, as is well known, was older. Pisa flourished in the fourteenth century, fell through the wars with Florence, and was afterwards restored by Lorenzo Magnifico, 'ad solatium veteris amissæ libertatis,' as Giovio says, *Vita Leonis X.* l. i. The university of Florence (comp. Gaye, *Carteggio*, i. p. 461 to 560 *passim; Matteo Villani*, i. 8; vii. 90), which existed as early as 1321, with compulsory attendance for the natives of the city, was founded afresh after the Black Death in 1348, and endowed with an income of 2,500 gold florins, fell again into decay, and was refounded in 1357. The chair for the explanation of Dante, established in 1373 at the request of many citizens, was afterwards commonly united with the professorship of philology and rhetoric, as when Filelfo held it.

[2] This should be noticed in the lists of professors, as in that of the University of Pavia in 1400 (Corio, *Storia di Milano*, fol. 290), where among others) no less than twenty jurists appear.

sometimes for only half a year, so that the teachers were forced to lead a wandering life, like actors. Appointments for life were, however, not unknown. Sometimes the promise was exacted not to teach elsewhere what had already been taught at one place. There were also voluntary, unpaid professors.

Of the chairs which have been mentioned, that of rhetoric was especially sought by the humanist; yet it depended only on his familiarity with the matter of ancient learning whether or no he could aspire to those of law, medicine, philosophy, or astronomy. The inward conditions of the science of the day were as variable as the outward conditions of the teacher. Certain jurists and physicians received by far the largest salaries of all, the former chiefly as consulting lawyers for the suits and claims of the state which employed them. In Padua a lawyer of the fifteenth century received a salary of 1,000 ducats,[1] and it was proposed to appoint a celebrated physician with a yearly payment of 2,000 ducats, and the right of private practice,[2] the same man having previously received 700 gold florins at Pisa. When the jurist Bartolommeo Socini, professor at Pisa, accepted a Venetian appointment at Padua, and was on the point of starting on his journey, he was arrested by the Florentine government and only released on payment of bail to the amount of 18,000 gold florins.[3] The high estimation in which these branches of science were held makes it intelligible why distinguished philologists turned their attention to law and medicine, while on the other hand specialists were more and more compelled to acquire something of a wide literary culture. We shall presently have occasion to speak of the work of the humanists in other departments of practical life.

Nevertheless, the position of the philologists, as such, even where the salary was large,[4] and did not exclude other sources of income, was on the whole uncertain and temporary, so that one and the same teacher could be connected with a great

[1] Marin Sanudo, in Murat. xxii. col. 990.

[2] Fabroni, *Laurent. Magn.* Adnot. 52, in the year 1491.

[3] Allegretto, *Diari Sanesi*, in Murat. xiii. col. 824.

[4] Filelfo, when called to the newly founded University of Pisa, demanded at least 500 gold florins. Comp. Fabroni, *Laur. Magn.* ii. 75 sqq. The negotiations were broken off, not only on account of the high salary asked for.

variety of institutions. It is evident that change was desired for its own sake, and something fresh expected from each new comer, as was natural at a time when science was in the making, and consequently depended to no small degree on the personal influence of the teacher. Nor was it always the case that a lecturer on classical authors really belonged to the university of the town where he taught. Communication was so easy, and the supply of suitable accommodation, in monasteries and elsewhere, was so abundant, that a private undertaking was often practicable. In the first decades of the fifteenth century,[1] when the University of Florence was at its greatest brilliance, when the courtiers of Eugenius IV., and perhaps even of Martin V. thronged to the lecture-rooms, when Carlo Aretino and Filelfo were competing for the largest audience, there existed, not only an almost complete university among the Augustinians of Santo Spirito, not only an association of scholars among the Camaldolesi of the Angeli, but individuals of mark, either singly or in common, arranged to provide philosophical and philological teaching for themselves and others. Linguistic and antiquarian studies in Rome had next to no connection with the university (Sapienza), and depended almost exclusively either on the favour of individual popes and prelates, or on the appointments made in the Papal chancery. It was not till Leo X. (1513) that the great reorganisation of the Sapienza took place, with its eighty-eight lecturers, among whom there were able men, though none of the first rank, at the head of the archæological department. But this new brilliancy was of short duration. We have already spoken briefly of the Greek and Hebrew professorships in Italy (pp. 195 sqq.).

To form an accurate picture of the method of scientific instruction then pursued, we must turn away our eyes as far as possible from our present academic system. Personal intercourse between the teachers and the taught, public disputations, the constant use of Latin and often of Greek, the frequent changes of lecturers and the scarcity of books, gave the studies

[1] Comp. Vespasian. Fiorent. pp. 271, 572, 582, 625. *Vita. Jan. Manetti*, in Murat. xx. col. 531 sqq.

of that time a colour which we cannot represent to ourselves without effort.

There were Latin schools in every town of the least importance, not by any means merely as preparatory to higher education, but because, next to reading, writing, and arithmetic, the knowledge of Latin was a necessity; and after Latin came logic. It is to be noted particularly that these schools did not depend on the Church, but on the municipality; some of them, too, were merely private enterprises.

This school system, directed by a few distinguished humanists, not only attained a remarkable perfection of organisation, but became an instrument of higher education in the modern sense of the phrase. With the education of the children of two princely houses in North Italy institutions were connected which may be called unique of their kind.

At the court of Giovan Francesco Gonzaga at Mantua (reg. 1407 to 1444) appeared the illustrious Vittorino da Feltre[1] (b. 1397, d. 1446), otherwise Vittore dai Rambaldoni—he preferred to be called a Mantuan rather than a Feltrese—one of those men who devote their whole life to an object for which their natural gifts constitute a special vocation. He wrote almost nothing, and finally destroyed the few poems of his youth which he had long kept by him. He studied with unwearied industry; he never sought after titles, which, like all outward distinctions, he scorned; and he lived on terms of the closest friendship with teachers, companions, and pupils, whose goodwill he knew how to preserve. He excelled in bodily no less than in mental exercises, was an admirable rider, dancer, and fencer, wore the same clothes in winter as in summer, walked in nothing but sandals even during the severest frost, and lived so that till his old age he was never ill. He so restrained his passions, his natural inclination to sensuality and anger, that he remained chaste his whole life through, and hardly ever hurt any one by a hard word.

[1] Vespas. Fiorent. p. 1460. Prendilacqua (a pupil of Vitt.), *Intorno alla Vita di V. da F.*, first ed. by Natale dalle Laste, 1774, translated by Giuseppe Brambilla, Como, 1871. C. Rosmini, *Idea dell' ottimo Precettore nella Vita e Disciplina di Vittorino da Feltre e de' suoi Discepoli*, Bassano, 1801. Later works by Racheli (Milan, 1832), and Venoit (Paris, 1853).

He directed the education of the sons and daughters of the princely house, and one of the latter became under his care a woman of learning. When his reputation extended far and wide over Italy, and members of great and wealthy families came from long distances, even from Germany, in search of his instructions, Gonzaga was not only willing that they should be received, but seems to have held it an honour for Mantua to be the chosen school of the aristocratic world. Here for the first time gymnastics and all noble bodily exercises were treated along with scientific instruction as indispensable to a liberal education. Besides these pupils came others, whose instruction Vittorino probably held to be his highest earthly aim, the gifted poor, often as many as seventy together, whom he supported in his house and educated, 'per l' amore di Dio,' along with the high-born youths who here learned to live under the same roof with untitled genius. The greater the crowd of pupils who flocked to Mantua, the more teachers were needed to impart the instruction which Vittorino only directed—an instruction which aimed at giving each pupil that sort of learning which he was most fitted to receive. Gonzaga paid him a yearly salary of 240 gold florins, built him besides a splendid house, 'La Giocosa,' in which the master lived with his scholars, and contributed to the expenses caused by the poorer pupils. What was still further needed Vittorino begged from princes and wealthy people, who did not always, it is true, give a ready ear to his entreaties, and forced him by their hardheartedness to run into debt. Yet in the end he found himself in comfortable circumstances, owned a small property in town and an estate in the country, where he stayed with his pupils during the holidays, and possessed a famous collection of books which he gladly lent or gave away, though he was not a little angry when they were taken without leave. In the early morning he read religious books, then scourged himself and went to church; his pupils were also compelled to go to church, like him, to confess once a month, and to observe fast days most strictly. His pupils respected him, but trembled before his glance. When they did anything wrong, they were punished immediately after the offence. He was honoured by all contemporaries no less than by his pupils, and people took the journey to Mantua merely to see him.

More stress was laid on pure scholarship by Guarino of Verona[1] (1370–1460), who in the year 1429 was called to Ferrara by Niccolò d' Este to educate his son Lionello, and who, when his pupil was nearly grown up in 1436, began to teach at the university as professor of eloquence and of the ancient languages. While still acting as tutor to Lionello, he had many other pupils from various parts of the country, and in his own house a select class of poor scholars, whom he partly or wholly supported. His evening hours till far into the night were devoted to hearing lessons or to instructive conversation. His house, too, was the home of a strict religion and morality. Guarino was a student of the Bible, and lived in friendly intercourse with pious contemporaries, though he did not hesitate to write a defence of pagan literature against them. It signified little to him or to Vittorino that most of the humanists of their day deserved small praise in the matter of morals or religion. It is inconceivable how Guarino, with all the daily work which fell upon him, still found time to write translations from the Greek and voluminous original works.[2] He was wanting in that wise self-restraint and kindly sweetness which graced the character of Vittorino, and was easily betrayed into a violence of temper which led to frequent quarrels with his learned contemporaries.

[1] Vespas. Fior. p. 646, of which, however, C. Rosmini, *Vita e Disciplina di Guarino Veronese e de' suoi Discepoli*, Brescia, 1856 (3 vols.), says that it is (ii. 56), 'formicolante di errori di fatto.'

[2] For these and for Guarino generally, see Facius, *De Vir. Illustribus*, p. 17 sqq.; and Cortesius, *De Hom. Doctis*, p. 13. Both agree that the scholars of the following generation prided themselves on having been pupils of Guarino; but while Fazio praises his works, Cortese thinks that he would have cared better for his fame if he had written nothing, Guarino and Vittorino were friends and helped one another in their studies. Their contemporaries were fond of comparing them, and in this comparison Guarino commonly held the first place (Sabellico, *Dial. de Lingu. Lat. Reparata*, in Rosmini, ii. 112). Guarino's attitude with regard to the 'Ermafrodito' is remarkable; see Rosmini, ii. 46 sqq. In both these teachers an unusual moderation in food and drink was observed; they never drank undiluted wine: in both the principles of education were alike; they neither used corporal punishment; the hardest penalty which Vittorino inflicted was to make the boy kneel and lie upon the ground in the presence of his fellow-pupils.

Not only in these two courts, but generally throughout Italy, the education of the princely families was in part and for certain years in the hands of the humanists, who thereby mounted a step higher in the aristocratic world. The writing of treatises on the education of princes, formerly the business of theologians, fell now within their province.

From the time of Pier Paolo Vergerio the Italian princes were well taken care of in this respect, and the custom was transplanted into Germany by Æneas Sylvius, who addressed detailed exhortations to two young German princes of the House of Habsburg [1] on the subject of their further education, in which they are both urged, as might be expected, to cultivate and nurture humanism, but are chiefly bidden to make themselves able rulers and vigorous, hardy warriors. Perhaps Æneas was aware that in addressing these youths he was talking in the air, and therefore took measures to put his treatise into public circulation. But the relations of the humanists to the rulers will be discussed separately.

[1] To the Archduke Sigismond, *Epist.* 105, p. 600, and to King Ladislaus Postumus, p. 695; the latter as *Tractatus de Liberorum Educatione* (1450).

CHAPTER VI.

THE FURTHERERS OF HUMANISM.

We have here first to speak of those citizens, mostly Florentines, who made antiquarian interests one of the chief objects of their lives, and who were themselves either distinguished scholars, or else distinguished *dilettanti* who maintained the scholars. (Comp. pp. 193 sqq.) They were of peculiar significance during the period of transition at the beginning of the fifteenth century, since it was in them that humanism first showed itself practically as an indispensable element in daily life. It was not till after this time that the popes and princes began seriously to occupy themselves with it.

Niccolò Niccoli and Giannozzo Manetti have been already spoken of more than once. Niccoli is described to us by Vespasiano [1] as a man who would tolerate nothing around him out of harmony with his own classical spirit. His handsome long-robed figure, his kindly speech, his house adorned with the noblest remains of antiquity, made a singular impression. He was scrupulously cleanly in everything, most of all at table, where ancient vases and crystal goblets stood before him on the whitest linen.[2] The way in which he won over a pleasure-loving young Florentine to intellectual interests is too charming not to be here described.[3] Piero de' Pazzi, son of a distinguished merchant, and himself destined to the same calling, fair to behold, and much given to the pleasures of the world, thought about anything rather than literature. One day, as he was passing the Palazzo del Podestà,[4] Niccolò called the young man

[1] P. 625. On Niccoli, see further a speech of Poggio, *Opera*, ed. 1513, fol. 102 sqq.; and a life by Manetti in his book, *De Illustribus Longaevis*.

[2] The following words of Vespasiano are untranslatable: 'A vederlo in tavola cosi antico come era, era una gentilezza.'

[3] *Ibid.* p. 495.

[4] According to Vespas. p. 271, learned men were in the habit of meeting here for discussion.

to him, and although they had never before exchanged a word, the youth obeyed the call of one so respected. Niccolò asked him who his father was. He answered, 'Messer Andrea de' Pazzi.' When he was further asked what his pursuit was, Piero replied, as young people are wont to do, 'I enjoy myself' ('attendo a darmi buon tempo'). Niccolò said to him, 'As son of such a father, and so fair to look upon, it is a shame that thou knowest nothing of the Latin language, which would be so great an ornament to thee. If thou learnest it not, thou wilt be good for nothing, and as soon as the flower of youth is over, wilt be a man of no consequence' (*virtù*). When Piero heard this, he straightway perceived that it was true, and said that he would gladly take pains to learn, if only he had a teacher. Whereupon Niccolò answered that he would see to that. And he found him a learned man for Latin and Greek, named Pontano, whom Piero treated as one of his own house, and to whom he paid 100 gold florins a year. Quitting all the pleasures in which he had hitherto lived, he studied day and night, and became a friend of all learned men and a noble-minded statesman. He learned by heart the whole 'Æneid' and many speeches of Livy, chiefly on the way between Florence and his country house at Trebbio.[1] Antiquity was represented in another and higher sense by Giannozzo Manetti (1393–1459).[2] Precocious from his first years, he was hardly

[1] Of Niccoli it may be further remarked that, like Vittorino, he wrote nothing, being convinced that he could not treat of anything in as perfect a form as he desired; that his senses were so delicately poised that he 'neque rudentem asinum, neque secantem serram, neque muscipulam vagientem sentire audireve poterat.' But the less favourable sides of Niccoli's character must not be forgotten. He robbed his brother of his sweetheart Benvenuta, roused the indignation of Lionardo Aretino by this act, and was embittered by the girl against many of his friends. He took ill the refusal to lend him books, and had a violent quarrel with Guarino on this account. He was not free from a petty jealousy, under the influence of which he tried to drive Chrysoloras, Poggio, and Filelfo away from Florence.

[2] See his *Vita*, by Naldus Naldi, in Murat. xx. col. 532 sqq. See further Vespasiano Bisticci, *Commentario della Vita di Messer Giannozzo Manetti*, first published by P. Fanfani in *Collezione di Opere inedite o rare*, vol. ii. Torino, 1862. This 'Commentario' must be distinguished from the short 'Vita' of Manetti by the same author, in which frequent reference is made to the former. Vespasiano was on intimate terms with Giannozzo

more than a child when he had finished his apprenticeship in commerce, and became book-keeper in a bank. But soon the life he led seemed to him empty and perishable, and he began to yearn after science, through which alone man can secure immortality. He then busied himself with books as few laymen had done before him, and became, as has been said (p. 209), one of the most profound scholars of his time. When appointed by the government as its representative magistrate and tax-collector at Pescia and Pistoja, he fulfilled his duties in accordance with the lofty ideal with which his religious feeling and humanistic studies combined to inspire him. He succeeded in collecting the most unpopular taxes which the Florentine state imposed, and declined payment for his services. As provincial governor he refused all presents, abhorred all bribes, checked gambling, kept the country well supplied with corn, required from his subordinates strict obedience and thorough disinterestedness, was indefatigable in settling law-suits amicably, and did wonders in calming inflamed passions by his goodness. The Pistojese loved and reverenced him as a saint, and were never able to discover to which of the two political parties he leaned; when his term of office was over, both sent ambassadors to Florence to beg that it might be prolonged. As if to symbolise the common rights and interests of all, he spent his leisure hours in writing the history of the city, which was preserved, bound in a purple cover, as a sacred relic in the town-hall.[1] When he took his leave the city presented him with a banner bearing the municipal arms and a splendid silver helmet. On diplomatic missions to Venice, Rome, and King Alfonso, Manetti represented, as at Pistoja, the interests of his native city, watching vigilantly over its honour, but declining the distinctions which were offered to him, obtained great glory by his speeches and nego-

Manetti, and in the biography tried to draw an ideal picture of a statesman for the degenerate Florence. Vesp. is Naldi's authority. Comp. also the fragment in Galetti, *Phil. Vill. Liber Flor.* 1847, pp. 129–138. Half a century after his death Manetti was nearly forgotten. Comp. Paolo Cortese, p. 21.

[1] The title of the work, in Latin and Italian, is given in Bisticci, *Commentario*, pp. 109, 112.

tiations, and acquired by his prudence and foresight the name of a prophet.

For further information as to the learned citizens of Florence at this period the reader must all the more be referred to Vespasiano, who knew them all personally, because the tone and atmosphere in which he writes, and the terms and conditions on which he mixed in their society, are of even more importance than the facts which he records. Even in a translation, and still more in the brief indications to which we are here compelled to limit ourselves, this chief merit of his book is lost. Without being a great writer, he was thoroughly familiar with the subject he wrote on, and had a deep sense of its intellectual significance.

If we seek to analyse the charm which the Medici of the fifteenth century, especially Cosimo the Elder (d. 1464) and Lorenzo the Magnificent (d. 1492) exercised over Florence and over all their contemporaries, we shall find that it lay less in their political capacity than in their leadership in the culture of the age. A man in Cosimo's position—a great merchant and party leader, who also had on his side all the thinkers, writers, and investigators, a man who was the first of the Florentines by birth and the first of the Italians by culture—such a man was to all intents and purposes already a prince. To Cosimo belongs the special glory of recognising in the Platonic philosophy the fairest flower of the ancient world of thought,[1] of inspiring his friends with the same belief, and thus of fostering within humanistic circles themselves another and a higher resuscitation of antiquity. The story is known to us minutely.[2] It all hangs on the calling of the learned

[1] What was known of Plato before can only have been fragmentary. A strange discussion on the antagonism of Plato and Aristotle took place at Ferrara in 1438, between Ugo of Siena and the Greeks who came to the Council. Comp. Æneas Sylvius, *De Europa*, cap. 52 (*Opera*, p. 450).

[2] In Niccolò Valori, *Life of Lorenzo the Magnificent.* Comp. Vespas. Fiorent. p. 426. The first supporters of Argyropulos were the Acciajuoli. *Ib.* 192: Cardinal Bessarion and his parallels between Plato and Aristotle. *Ib.* 223: Cusanus as Platonist. *Ib.* 308: The Catalonian Narciso and his disputes with Argyropulos. *Ib.* 571: Single Dialogues of Plato, translated by Lionardo Aretino. *Ib.* 298: The rising influence of Neoplatonism. On Marsilio Ficino, see Reumont, *Lorenzo de' Medici*, ii. 27 sqq.

Johannes Argyropulos, and on the personal enthusiasm of Cosimo himself in his last years, which was such, that the great Marsilio Ficino could style himself, as far as Platonism was concerned, the spiritual son of Cosimo. Under Pietro Medici, Ficino was already at the head of a school; to him Pietro's son and Cosimo's grandson, the illustrious Lorenzo, came over from the Peripatetics. Among his most distinguished fellow-scholars were Bartolommeo Valori, Donato Acciajuoli, and Pierfilippo Pandolfini. The enthusiastic teacher declares in several passages of his writings that Lorenzo had sounded all the depths of the Platonic philosophy, and had uttered his conviction that without Plato it would be hard to be a good Christian or a good citizen. The famous band of scholars which surrounded Lorenzo was united together, and distinguished from all other circles of the kind, by this passion for a higher and idealistic philosophy. Only in such a world could a man like Pico della Mirandola feel happy. But perhaps the best thing of all that can be said about it is, that, with all this worship of antiquity, Italian poetry found here a sacred refuge, and that of all the rays of light which streamed from the circle of which Lorenzo was the centre, none was more powerful than this. As a statesman, let each man judge him as he pleases; a foreigner will hesitate to pronounce what was due to human guilt and what to circumstances in the fate of Florence, but no more unjust charge was ever made than that in the field of culture Lorenzo was the protector of Mediocrity, that through his fault Lionardo da Vinci and the mathematician Fra Luca Pacciolo lived abroad, and that Toscanella, Vespucci, and others at least remained unsupported. He was not, indeed, a man of universal mind; but of all the great men who have striven to favour and promote spiritual interests, few certainly have been so many-sided, and in none probably was the inward need to do so equally deep.

The age in which we live is loud enough in proclaiming the worth of culture, and especially of the culture of antiquity. But the enthusiastic devotion to it, the recognition that the need of it is the first and greatest of all needs, is nowhere to be found but among the Florentines of the fifteenth and the early part of the sixteenth centuries. On this point we have indirect proof which precludes all doubt. It would not have been so common to give the daughters of the house a share in the same studies, had they not been held to be the noblest of earthly pursuits; exile would not have been turned into a happy retreat, as was done by Palla Strozzi; nor would men who indulged in every conceivable excess have retained the strength and the spirit to write critical treatises on the 'Natural History' of Pliny like Filippo Strozzi.[1] Our business here is not to deal out either praise or blame, but to understand the spirit of the age in all its vigorous individuality.

Besides Florence, there were many cities of Italy where individuals and social circles devoted all their energies to the support of humanism and the protection of the scholars who lived among them. The correspondence of that period is full of references to personal relations of this kind.[2] The feeling of the instructed classes set strongly and almost exclusively in this direction.

But it is now time to speak of humanism at the Italian courts. The natural alliance between the despot and the scholar, each relying solely on his personal talent, has already been touched upon (p. 9); that the latter should avowedly prefer the princely courts to the free cities, was only to be expected from the higher pay which they there received. At a time when the great Alfonso of Aragon seemed likely to become master of all Italy, Æneas Sylvius wrote to another citizen of Siena:[3] 'I had rather that Italy attained peace under his rule than under that of the free cities, for kingly generosity rewards excellence of every kind.[4] Too much stress has latterly been laid on the unworthy

[1] Varchi, *Stor. Fior.* p. 321. An admirable sketch of character.

[2] The lives of Guarino and Vittorino by Rosmini mentioned above (p. 213, note 1; and 215, note 1), as well as the life of Poggio by Shepherd, especially in the enlarged Italian translation of Tonelli (2 vols. Florence, 1825); the Correspondence of Poggio, edited by the same writer (2 vols. Flor. 1832); and the letters of Poggio in Mai's *Spicilegium*, tom. x. Rome, 1844, pp. 221–272, all contain much on this subject.

[3] *Epist.* 39; *Opera*, p. 526, to Mariano Socino.

[4] We must not be misled by the fact that along with all this complaints were frequently heard of the inadequacy of princely patronage and of the indifference of many princes to their fame. See e.g. Bapt. Mantan, Eclog. v. as early as the fifteenth century; and Ambrogio Traversari, *De Infelicitate Principum.* It was impossible to satisfy all.

side of this relation, and the mercenary flattery to which it gave rise, just as formerly the eulogies of the humanists led to a too favourable judgment on their patrons. Taking all things together, it is greatly to the honour of the latter that they felt bound to place themselves at the head of the culture of their age and country, one-sided though this culture was. In some of the popes,[1] the fearlessness of the consequences to which the new learning might lead strikes us as something truly, but unconsciously, imposing. Nicholas V. was confident of the future of the Church, since thousands of learned men supported her. Pius II. was far from making such splendid sacrifices for humanism as were made by Nicholas, and the poets who frequented his court were few in number; but he himself was much more the personal head of the republic of letters than his predecessor, and enjoyed his position without the least misgiving. Paul II. was the first to dread and mistrust the culture of his secretaries, and his three successors, Sixtus, Innocent, and Alexander, accepted dedications and allowed themselves to be sung to the hearts' content of the poets—there even existed a 'Borgiad,' probably in hexameters[2]—but were too busy elsewhere, and too occupied in seeking other foundations for their power, to trouble themselves much about the poet-scholars. Julius II. found poets to eulogise him, because he himself was no mean subject for poetry (p. 117), but he does not seem to have troubled himself much about them. He was followed by Leo X., 'as Romulus by Numa'—in other words after the warlike turmoil of the first pontificate, a new one was hoped for wholly given to the muses. The enjoyment of elegant Latin prose and melodious verse was part of the programme of Leo's

[1] For the literary and scientific patronage of the popes down to the end of the fifteenth century, see Gregorovius, vols. vii. and viii. For Pius II., see Voigt, *En. Silvio als Papst Pius II.* bd. iii. (Berlin, 1863), pp. 406–440.

[2] Lil. Greg. Gyraldus, *De Poetis Nostri Temporis.* speaking of the *Sphaerulus* of Camerino. The worthy man did not finish it in time, and his work lay for forty years in his desk. For the scanty payments made by Sixtus IV., comp. Pierio Valer. *De Infelic. Lit.* on Theodorus Gaza. He received for a translation and commentary of a work of Aristotle fifty gold florins, 'ab eo a quo se totum inauratum iri speraverat.' On the deliberate exclusion of the humanists from the cardinalate by the popes before Leo, comp. Lor. Grana's funeral oration on Cardinal Egidio, *Anecdot. Litt.* iv. p. 307.

life, and his patronage certainly had the result that his Latin poets have left us a living picture of that joyous and brilliant spirit of the Leonine days, with which the biography of Jovius is filled, in countless epigrams, elegies, odes, and orations.[1] Probably in all European history there is no prince who, in proportion to the few striking events of his life, has received such manifold homage. The poets had access to him chiefly about noon, when the musicians had ceased playing;[2] but one of the best among them[3] tells us how they also pursued him when he walked in his garden or withdrew to the privacy of his chamber, and if they failed to catch him there, would try to win him with a mendicant ode or elegy, filled, as usual, with the whole population of Olympus.[4] For Leo, prodigal of his money, and disliking to be surrounded by any but cheerful faces, displayed a generosity in his gifts which was fabulously exaggerated in the hard times that followed.[5] His reorganisation of the Sapienza (p. 212) has been already spoken of. In order not to underrate Leo's influence on humanism we must guard against being misled by the toy-work that was mixed up with it, and must not allow ourselves to be deceived by the apparent irony with which he himself sometimes treated these matters (p. 157). Our judgment must rather dwell on the countless spiritual possibilities which are included in the word 'stimulus,' and which, though they cannot be measured as a whole, can still, on closer study, be actually followed out in particular cases. Whatever influence in Europe the Italian humanists have had since 1520 depends in some way or other on the impulse which was given by Leo. He was the Pope who in granting per-

[1] The best are to be found in the *Deliciae Poetarum Italorum*, and in the Appendices to the various editions of Roscoe, *Leo X.* Several poets and writers, like Alcyonius, *De Exilio*, ed. Menken, p. 10, say frankly that they praise Leo in order themselves to become immortal.

[2] Paul. Jov. *Elogia* speaking of Guido Posthumus.

[3] Pierio Valeriano in his *Simia*.

[4] See the elegy of Joh. Aurelius Mutius in the *Deliciae Poetarum Italorum*.

[5] The well-known story of the purple velvet purse filled with packets of gold of various sizes, in which Leo used to thrust his hand blindly, is in Giraldi *Hecatommithi*, vi. nov. 8. On the other hand, the Latin 'improvisatori,' when their verses were too faulty, were whipped. Lil. Greg. Gyraldus, *De Poetis Nostri Temp. Opp.* ii. 398 (Basil, 1580).

mission to print the newly found Tacitus,[1] could say that the great writers were a rule of life and a consolation in misfortune; that helping learned men and obtaining excellent books had ever been one of his highest aims; and that he now thanked heaven that he could benefit the human race by furthering the publication of this book.

The sack of Rome in the year 1527 scattered the scholars no less than the artists in every direction, and spread the fame of the great departed Mæcenas to the furthest boundaries of Italy.

Among the secular princes of the fifteenth century, none displayed such enthusiasm for antiquity as Alfonso the Great of Aragon, King of Naples (see p. 35). It appears that his zeal was thoroughly unaffected, and that the monuments and writings of the ancient world made upon him, from the time of his arrival in Italy, an impression deep and powerful enough to reshape his life. Possibly he was influenced by the example of his ancestor Robert, Petrarch's great patron, whom he may have wished to rival or surpass. With strange readiness he surrendered the stubborn Aragon to his brother, and devoted himself wholly to his new possessions. He had in his service,[2] either successively or together, George of Trebizond, the younger Chrysoloras, Lorenzo Valla, Bartolommeo Facio and Antonio Panormita, of whom the two latter were his historians; Panormita daily instructed the King and his court in Livy, even during military expeditions. These men cost him yearly 20,000 gold florins. He gave Panormita 1,000 for his work: Facio received for the 'Historia Alfonsi,' besides a yearly income of 500 ducats, a present of 1,500 more when it was finished, with the words, 'It is not given to pay you, for your work would not be paid for if I gave you the fairest of my cities; but in time I hope to satisfy you.'[3] When he took Giannozzo Manetti as his

[1] Roscoe, *Leone X.* ed. Bossi, iv. 181.

[2] Vespas. Fior. p. 68 sqq. For the translations from Greek made by Alfonso's orders, see p. 93; *Vita Jan. Manetti*, in Murat. xx. col. 541 sqq., 450 sqq., 495. Panormita, *Dicta et Facta Alfonsi*, with the notes by Æneas Sylvius, ed. by Jacob Spiegel, Basel, 1538.

[3] Even Alfonso was not able to please everybody—Poggio, for example. See Shepherd-Tonelli, *Poggio*, ii. 108 sqq. and Poggio's letter to Facius in

secretary on the most brilliant conditions, he said to him, 'My last crust I will share with you.' When Giannozzo first came to bring the congratulations of the Florentine government on the marriage of Prince Ferrante, the impression he made was so great, that the King sat motionless on the throne, 'like a brazen statue, and did not even brush away a fly, which had settled on his nose at the beginning of the oration.' In restoring the castle, he took Vitruvius as his guide; wherever he went, he had the ancient classics with him; he looked on a day as lost in which he had read nothing; when he was reading, he suffered no disturbance, not even the sound of music; and he despised all contemporary princes who were not either scholars or the patrons of learning. His favourite haunt seems to have been the library of the castle at Naples, which he opened himself if the librarian was absent, and where he would sit at a window overlooking the bay, and listen to learned debates on the Trinity. For he was profoundly religious, and had the Bible, as well as Livy and Seneca, read to him, till after fourteen perusals he knew it almost by heart. He gave to those who wished to be nuns the money for their entrance to the monastery, was a zealous churchgoer, and listened with great attention to the sermon. Who can fully understand the feeling with which he regarded the supposititious remains (p. 143) of Livy at Padua? When, by dint of great entreaties, he obtained an arm-bone of the skeleton from the Venetians, and received it with solemn pomp at Naples, how strangely Christian and pagan sentiment must have been blended in his heart! During a campaign in the Abruzzi, when the distant Sulmona, the birthplace of Ovid, was pointed out to him, he saluted the spot and returned thanks to its tutelary genius. It gladdened him to make good the prophecy of the great poet as to his future fame.[1] Once indeed, at his famous entry into the conquered city of Naples (1443), he himself chose to appear before the world in ancient style. Not far from the market a breach forty ells wide was made in the wall, and through this he drove

Fac. de Vir. Ill. ed. Mehus, p. 88, where he writes of Alfonso: 'Ad ostentationem quædam facit quibus videatur doctis viris favere;' and Poggio's letter in Mai, *Spicil.* tom. x. p. 241.

[1] Ovid. *Amores*, iii. 11, vs. ii.; Jovian. Pontan. *De Principe.*

in a gilded chariot like a Roman Triumphator.[1] The memory of the scene is preserved by a noble triumphal arch of marble in the Castello Nuovo. His Neapolitan successors (p. 37) inherited as little of this passion for antiquity as of his other good qualities.

Alfonso was far surpassed in learning by Frederick of Urbino[2] —the great pupil of the great teacher Vittorino da Feltre— who had but few courtiers around him, squandered nothing, and in his appropriation of antiquity, as in all other things, went to work considerately. It was for him and for Nicholas V. that most of the translations from the Greek, and a number of the best commentaries and other such works, were written. He spent much on the scholars whose services he used, but spent it to good purpose. There were no traces of the official poet at Urbino, where the Duke himself was the most learned in the whole court. Classical antiquity, indeed, only formed a part of his culture. An accomplished ruler, captain, and gentleman, he had mastered the greater part of the science of the day, and this with a view to its practical application. As a theologian, he was able to compare Scotus with Aquinas, and was familar with the writings of the old fathers of the Eastern and Western Churches, the former in Latin translations. In philosophy, he seems to have left Plato altogether to his contemporary Cosimo, but he knew thoroughly not only the 'Ethics' and 'Politics' of Aristotle but the 'Physics' and some other works. The rest of his reading lay chiefly among the ancient historians, all of whom he possessed; these, and not the poets, 'he was always reading and having read to him.'

The Sforza,[3] too, were all of them men of more or less learning and patrons of literature; they have been already referred to in passing (pp. 38 sqq.). Duke Francesco probably looked on humanistic culture as a matter of course in the education of his

[1] *Giorn. Napolet.* in Murat. xxi. col. 1127

[2] Vespas. Fior. pp. 3, 119 sqq. 'Volle aver piena notizia d' ogni cosa, cosi sacra come gentile.'

[3] The last Visconti divided his interest between Livy, the French chivalrous romances, Dante, and Petrarch. The humanists who presented themselves to him with the promise 'to make him famous,' were generally sent away after a few days. Comp. *Decembrio*, in Murat. xx. col. 1114.

children, if only for political reasons. It was felt universally to be an advantage if the Prince could mix with the most instructed men of his time on an equal footing. Ludovico Moro, himself an excellent Latin scholar, showed an interest in intellectual matters which extended far beyond classical antiquity (p. 41 sqq.).

Even the petty despots strove after similar distinctions, and we do them injustice by thinking that they only supported the scholars at their courts as a means of diffusing their own fame. A ruler like Borso of Ferrara (p. 49), with all his vanity, seems by no means to have looked for immortality from the poets, eager as they were to propitiate him with a 'Borseid' and the like. He had far too proud a sense of his own position as a ruler for that. But intercourse with learned men, interest in antiquarian matters, and the passion for elegant Latin correspondence were a necessity for the princes of that age. What bitter complaints are those of Duke Alfonso, competent as he was in practical matters, that his weakliness in youth had forced him to seek recreation in manual pursuits only![1] or was this merely an excuse to keep the humanists at a distance? A nature like his was not intelligible even to contemporaries.

Even the most insignificant despots of Romagna found it hard to do without one or two men of letters about them. The tutor and secretary were often one and the same person, who sometimes, indeed, acted as a kind of court factotum.[2] We are apt to treat the small scale of these courts as a reason for dismissing them with a too ready contempt, forgetting that the highest spiritual things are not precisely matters of measurement.

Life and manners at the court of Rimini must have been a singular spectacle under the bold pagan Condottiere Sigismondo

[1] Paul. Jov. *Vita Alfonsi Ducis.*

[2] On Collenuccio at the court of Giovanni Sforza of Pesaro (son of Alessandro, p. 28), who finally, in 1508, put him to death, see p. 135, note 4. At the time of the last Ordelaffi at Forli, the place was occupied by Codrus Urceus (1477–80); death-bed complaint of C. U. *Opp.* Ven. 1506, fol. liv.; for his stay in Forli, *Sermo*, vi. Comp. Carlo Malagola, *Della Vita di C. U.* Bologna, 1877, Ap. iv. Among the instructed despots, we may mention Galeotto Manfreddi of Faenza, murdered in 1488 by his wife, and some of the Bentivoglio family at Bologna.

Malatesta. He had a number of scholars around him, some of whom he provided for liberally, even giving them landed estates, while others earned at least a livelihood as officers in his army.[1] In his citadel—'arx Sismundea'—they used to hold discussions, often of a very venomous kind, in the presence of the 'rex,' as they termed him. In their Latin poems they sing his praises and celebrate his amour with the fair Isotta, in whose honour and as whose monument the famous rebuilding of San Francesco at Rimini took place—'Divæ Isottæ Sacrum.' When the humanists themselves came to die, they were laid in or under the sarcophagi with which the niches of the outside walls of the church were adorned, with an inscription testifying that they were laid here at the time when Sigismundus, the son of Pandulfus, ruled.[2] It is hard for us nowadays to believe that a monster like this prince felt learning and the friendship of cultivated people to be a necessity of life; and yet the man who excommunicated him, made war upon him, and burnt him in effigy, Pope Pius II., says: 'Sigismund knew history and had a great store of philosophy; he seemed born to all that he undertook.[3]

[1] *Anecdota Literar.* ii. pp. 305 sqq., 405. Basinius of Parma ridicules Porcellio and Tommaso Seneca; they are needy parasites, and must play the soldier in their old age, while he himself was enjoying an 'ager' and a 'villa.'

[2] For details respecting these graves, see Keyssler, *Neueste Reisen*, s. 924.

[3] *Pii II. Comment.* l. ii. p. 92. By history he means all that has to do with antiquity. Cortesius also praises him highly, p. 34 sqq.

CHAPTER VII.

THE REPRODUCTION OF ANTIQUITY: LATIN CORRESPONDENCE AND ORATIONS.

There were two purposes, however, for which the humanist was as indispensable to the republics as to princes or popes, namely, the official correspondence of the state, and the making of speeches on public and solemn occasions.

Not only was the secretary required to be a competent Latinist, but conversely, only a humanist was credited with the knowledge and ability necessary for the post of secretary. And thus the greatest men in the sphere of science during the fifteenth century mostly devoted a considerable part of their lives to serve the state in this capacity. No importance was attached to a man's home or origin. Of the four great Florentine secretaries who filled the office between 1427 and 1465,[1] three belonged to the subject city of Arezzo, namely, Lionardo (Bruni), Carlo (Marsuppini), and Benedetto Accolti; Poggio was from Terra Nuova, also in Florentine territory. For a long period, indeed, many of the highest officers of state were on principle given to foreigners. Lionardo, Poggio, and Giannozzo Manetti were at one time or another private secretaries to the popes, and Carlo Aretino was to have been so. Blondus of Forli, and, in spite of everything, at last even Lorenzo Valla, filled the same office. From the time of Nicholas V. and Pius II. onwards,[2] the Papal chancery continued more and more to attract the ablest men, and this was still the case even under

[1] Fabroni, *Cosmus*, Adnot. 118. Vespasian. Fior. *passim*. An important passage respecting the demands made by the Florentines on their secretaries ('quod honor apud Florentinos magnus habetur,' says B. Facius, speaking of Poggio's appointment to the secretaryship, *De Vir. Ill.* p. 17), is to be found in Æneas Sylvius, *De Europâ*, cap. 54 (*Opera*, p. 454).

[2] See Voigt, *En. Silvio als Papst Pius II.* bd. iii. 488 sqq., for the often-discussed and often-misunderstood change which Pius II. made with respect to the Abbreviators.

the last popes of the fifteenth century, little as they cared for letters. In Platina's 'History of the Popes," the life of Paul II. is a charming piece of vengeance taken by a humanist on the one Pope who did not know how to behave to his chancery —to that circle 'of poets and orators who bestowed on the Papal court as much glory as they received from it.' It is delightful to see the indignation of these haughty and wealthy gentlemen, who knew as well as the Pope himself how to use their position to plunder foreigners,[1] when some squabble about precedence happened, when, for instance, the 'Advocati consistoriales' claimed equal or superior rank to theirs.[2] The Apostle John, to whom the 'Secreta cœlestia' were revealed; the secretary of Porsenna, whom Mucius Scævola mistook for the king; Mæcenas, who was private secretary to Augustus; the archbishops, who in Germany were called chancellors, are all appealed to in turn.[3] 'The apostolic secretaries have the most weighty business of the world in their hands. For who but they decide on matters of the Catholic faith, who else combat heresy, re-establish peace, and mediate between great monarchs? who but they write the statistical accounts of Christendom? It is they who astonish kings, princes, and nations by what comes forth from the Pope. They write commands and instructions for the legates, and receive their orders only from the Pope, on whom they wait day and night.' But the highest summit of glory was only attained by the two famous secretaries and stylists of Leo X.: Pietro Bembo and Jacopo Sadoleto.[4]

[1] Comp. the statement of Jacob Spiegel (1521) given in the reports of the Vienna Academy, lxxviii. 333.

[2] *Anecdota Lit.* i. p. 119 sqq. A plea ('Actio ad Cardinales Deputatos') of Jacobus Volaterranus in the name of the Secretaries, no doubt of the time of Sixtus IV. (Voigt, l. c. 552, note). The humanistic claims of the 'advocati consistoriales' rested on their oratory, as that of the Secretaries on their correspondence.

[3] The Imperial chancery under Frederick III. was best known to Æneas Sylvius. Comp. *Epp.* 23 and 105; *Opera*, pp. 516 and 607.

[4] The letters of Bembo and Sadoleto have been often printed; those of the former, e.g. in the *Opera*, Basel, 1556, vol. ii., where the letters written in the name of Leo X. are distinguished from private letters; those of the latter most fully, 5 vols. Rome, 1760. Some additions to both have been given by Carlo Malagola in the review *Il Baretti*, Turin, 1875.

All the chanceries did not turn out equally elegant documents. A leathern official style, in the impurest of Latin, was very common. In the Milanese documents preserved by Corio there is a remarkable contrast between this sort of composition and the few letters written by members of the princely house, which must have been written, too, in moments of critical importance.[1] They are models of pure Latinity. To maintain a faultless style under all circumstances was a rule of good breeding, and a result of habit. Besides these officials, private scholars of all kinds naturally had correspondence of their own. The object of letter-writing was seldom what it is nowadays, to give information as to the circumstances of the writer, or news of other people; it was rather treated as a literary work done to give evidence of scholarship and to win the consideration of those to whom it was addressed. These letters began early to serve the purpose of learned disquisition; and Petrarch, who introduced this form of letter-writing, revived the forms of the old epistolary style, putting the classical 'thou' in place of the 'you' of mediæval Latin. At a later period letters became collections of neatly-turned phrases, by which subjects were encouraged or humiliated, colleagues flattered or insulted, and patrons eulogised or begged from.[2]

The letters of Cicero, Pliny, and others, were at this time

Bembo's *Asolani* will be spoken of below; Sadoleto's significance for Latin style has been judged as follows by a contemporary, Petrus Alcyonius, *De Exilio*, ed. Menken, p. 119: 'Solus autem nostrorum temporum aut certe cum paucis animadvertit elocutionem emendatam et latinam esse fundamentum oratoris; ad eamque obtinendam necesse esse latinam linguam expurgare quam inquinarunt nonnulli exquisitarum literarum omnino rudes et nullius judicii homines, qui partim a circumpadanis municipiis, partim ex transalpinis provinciis, in hanc urbem confluxerunt. Emendavit igitur eruditissimus hic vir corruptam et vitiosam linguæ latinæ consuetudinem, pura ac integra loquendi ratione.'

[1] Corio, *Storia di Milano*, fol. 449, for the letter of Isabella of Aragon to her father, Alfonso of Naples; fols. 451, 464, two letters of the Moor to Charles VIII. Compare the story in the *Lettere Pittoriche*, iii. 86 (Sebastiano del Piombo to Aretino), how Clement VII., during the sack of Rome, called his learned men round him, and made each of them separately write a letter to Charles V.

[2] For the correspondence of the period in general, see Voigt, *Wiederbelebung*, 414–427.

diligently studied as models. As early as the fifteenth century a mass of forms and instructions for Latin correspondence had appeared, as accessory to the great grammatical and lexicographic works, the mass of which is astounding to us even now when we look at them in the libraries. But just as the existence of these helps tempted many to undertake a task to which they had no vocation, so were the really capable men stimulated to a more faultless excellence, till at length the letters of Politian, and at the beginning of the sixteenth century those of Pietro Bembo, appeared, and took their place as unrivalled masterpieces, not only of Latin style in general, but also of the more special art of letter-writing.

Together with these there appeared in the sixteenth century the classical style of Italian correspondence, at the head of which stands Bembo again.[1] Its form is wholly modern, and deliberately kept free from Latin influence, and yet its spirit is thoroughly penetrated and possessed by the ideas of antiquity. These letters, though partly of a confidential nature, are mostly written with a view to possible publication in the future, and always on the supposition that they might be worth showing on account of their elegance. After the year 1530, printed collections began to appear, either the letters of miscellaneous correspondents in irregular succession, or of single writers; and the same Bembo whose fame was so great as a Latin correspondent won as high a position in his own language.[2]

But, at a time and among a people where 'listening' was among the chief pleasures of life, and where every imagination was filled with the memory of the Roman senate and its great speakers, the orator occupied a far more brilliant place than the letter-writer.[3] Eloquence had shaken off the influence of the Church, in which it had found a refuge during the Middle Ages, and now became an indispensable element and ornament

[1] Bembo thought it necessary to excuse himself for writing in Italian: 'Ad Sempronium,' *Bembi Opera*, Bas. 1556, vol. iii. 156 sqq.

[2] On the collection of the letters of Aretino, see above, pp. 164 sqq., and the note. Collections of Latin letters had been printed even in the fifteenth century.

[3] Comp. the speeches in the *Opera* of Philelphus, Sabellicus, Beroaldus, &c.; and the writings and lives of Giann. Manetti, Æneas Sylvius, and others.

of all elevated lives. Many of the social hours which are now filled with music were then given to Latin or Italian oratory; and yet Bartolommeo Fazio complained that the orators of his time were at a disadvantage compared with those of antiquity; of three kinds of oratory which were open to the latter, one only was left to the former, since forensic oratory was abandoned to the jurists, and the speeches in the councils of the government had to be delivered in Italian.[1]

The social position of the speaker was a matter of perfect indifference; what was desired was simply the most cultivated humanistic talent. At the court of Borso of Ferrara, the Duke's physician, Jeronimo da Castello, was chosen to deliver the congratulatory address on the visits of Frederick III. and of Pius II.[2] Married laymen ascended the pulpits of the churches at any scene of festivity or mourning, and even on the feast-days of the saints. It struck the non-Italian members of the Council of Basel as something strange, that the Archbishop of Milan should summon Æneas Sylvius, who was then unordained, to deliver a public discourse at the feast of Saint Ambrogius; but they suffered it in spite of the murmurs of the theologians, and listened to the speaker with the greatest curiosity.[3]

Let us glance for a moment at the most frequent and important occasions of public speaking.

It was not for nothing, in the first place, that the ambassadors from one state to another received the title of orators. Whatever else might be done in the way of secret negotiation, the envoy never failed to make a public appearance and deliver a public speech, under circumstances of the greatest possible pomp and ceremony.[4] As a rule, however numerous the

[1] B. F. *De Viris Illustribus*, ed. Mehus, p. 7. Manetti, as Vesp. Bisticci, *Commentario*, p. 51, states, delivered many speeches in Italian, and then afterwards wrote them out in Latin. The scholars of the fifteenth century, e.g. Paolo Cortese, judge the achievements of the past solely from the point of view of 'Eloquentia.'

[2] *Diario Ferrarese*, in Murat. xxiv. col. 198, 205.

[3] *Pii II. Comment.* l. i. p. 10.

[4] The success of the fortunate orator was great, and the humiliation of the speaker who broke down before distinguished audiences no less great. Examples of the latter in Petrus Crinitus, *De Honestâ Disciplinâ*, v. cap. 3. Comp. Vespas. Fior. pp. 319, 430.

embassy might be, one individual spake for all; but it happened to Pius II., a critic before whom all were glad to be heard, to be forced to sit and listen to a whole deputation, one after another.[1] Learned princes who had the gift of speech were themselves fond of discoursing in Latin or Italian. The children of the House of Sforza were trained to this exercise. The boy Galeazzo Maria delivered in 1455 a fluent speech before the Great Council at Venice,[2] and his sister Ippolita saluted Pope Pius II. with a graceful address at the Congress of Mantua.[3] Pius himself through all his life did much by his oratory to prepare the way for his final elevation to the Papal chair. Great as he was both as scholar and diplomatist, he would probably never have become Pope without the fame and the charm of his eloquence. 'For nothing was more lofty than the dignity of his oratory.'[4] Without doubt this was a reason why multitudes held him to be the fittest man for the office, even before his election.

Princes were also commonly received on public occasions with speeches, which sometimes lasted for hours. This happened of course only when the prince was known as a lover of eloquence,[5] or wished to pass for such, and when a competent

[1] *Pii II. Comment.* l. iv. p. 205. There were some Romans, too, who awaited him at Viterbo. 'Singuli per se verba facere, ne alius alio melior videretur, cum essent eloquentiâ ferme pares.' The fact that the Bishop of Arezzo was not allowed to speak in the name of the general embassy of the Italian states to the newly chosen Alexander VI., is seriously placed by Guicciardini (at the beginning of book i.) among the causes which helped to produce the disaster of 1494.

[2] Told by Marin Sanudo, in Murat. xxii. col. 1160.

[3] *Pii II. Comment.* l. ii. p. 107. Comp. p. 87. Another oratorical princess, Madonna Battista Montefeltro, married to a Malatesta, harangued Sigismund and Martin. Comp. *Arch. Stor.* iv. i. p. 442, note.

[4] *De Expeditione in Turcas*, in Murat. xxiii. col. 68. 'Nihil enim Pii concionantis majestate sublimius.' Not to speak of the naïve pleasure with which Pius describes his own triumphs, see Campanus, *Vita Pii II.*, in Murat. iii. ii. *passim*. At a later period these speeches were judged less admiringly. Comp. Voigt, *Enea Silvio*, ii. 275 sqq.

[5] Charles V., when unable on one occasion to follow the flourishes of a Latin orator at Genoa, replied in the ear of Giovio: 'Ah, my tutor Adrian was right, when he told me I should be chastened for my childish idleness in learning Latin.' Paul. Jov. *Vita Hadriani VI.* Princes

speaker was present, whether university professor, official, ecclesiastic, physician, or court-scholar.

Every other political opportunity was seized with the same eagerness, and according to the reputation of the speaker, the concourse of the lovers of culture was great or small. At the yearly change of public officers, and even at the consecration of new bishops, a humanist was sure to come forward, and sometimes addressed his audience in hexameters or Sapphic verses.[1] Often a newly appointed official was himself forced to deliver a speech more or less relevant to his department, as for instance, on justice; and lucky for him if he were well up in his part! At Florence even the Condottieri, whatever their origin or education might be, were compelled to accommodate themselves to the popular sentiment, and on receiving the insignia of their office, were harangued before the assembled people by the most learned secretary of state.[2] It seems that beneath or close to the Loggia dei Lanzi—the porch where the government was wont to appear solemnly before the people—a tribune or platform (*rostra ringhiera*) was erected for such purposes.

Anniversaries, especially those of the death of princes, were commonly celebrated by memorial speeches. Even the funeral oration strictly so-called was generally entrusted to a humanist, who delivered it in church, clothed in a secular dress; nor was it only princes, but officials, or persons otherwise distinguished, to whom this honour was paid.[3] This was also the case with the speeches delivered at weddings or betrothals, with the difference that they seem to have been made in the palace, instead of in church, like that of Filelfo at the betrothal of Anna Sforza with Alfonso of Este in the castle of Milan. It is still possible that the ceremony may have taken place in the

replied to these speeches through their official orators; Frederick III. through Enea Silvio, in answer to Giannozzo Manetti. Vesp. Bist. *Comment.* p. 64.

[1] Lil. Greg. Gyraldus, *De poetis Nostri Temp.* speaking of Collenuccio. Filelfo, a married layman, delivered an introductory speech in the Cathedral at Como for the Bishop Scarampi, in 1460. Rosmini, *Filelfo*, ii. 122, iii. 147.

[2] Fabroni, *Cosmus*, Adnot. 52.

[3] Which, nevertheless, gave some offence to Jac. Volaterranus (in Murat. xxiii. col. 171) at the service in memory of Platina.

chapel of the castle. Private families of distinction no doubt also employed such wedding orators as one of the luxuries of high life. At Ferrara, Guarino was requested on these occasions to send some one or other of his pupils.[1] The church simply took charge of the religious ceremonies at weddings and funerals.

The academical speeches, both those made at the installation of a new teacher and at the opening of a new course of lectures,[2] were delivered by the professor himself, and treated as occasions of great rhetorical display. The ordinary university lectures also usually had an oratorical character.[3]

With regard to forensic eloquence, the quality of the audience determined the form of speech. In case of need it was enriched with all sorts of philosophical and antiquarian learning.

As a special class of speeches we may mention the addresses made in Italian on the battle-field, either before or after the combat. Frederick of Urbino[4] was esteemed a classic in this style; he used to pass round among his squadrons as they

[1] *Anecdota Lit.* i. p. 299, in Fedra's funeral oration on Lod. Podacataro, whom Guarino commonly employed on these occasions. Guarino himself delivered over fifty speeches at festivals and funerals, which are enumerated in Rosmini, *Guarino*, ii. 139–146. Burckhardt, 332. Dr. Geiger here remarks that Venice also had its professional orators. Comp. G. Voigt, ii. 425.

[2] Many of these opening lectures have been preserved in the works of Sabellicus, Beroaldus Major, Codrus Urceus, &c. In the works of the latter there are also some poems which he recited 'in principio studii.'

[3] The fame of Pomponazzo's delivery is preserved in Paul. Jov. *Elogia Vir. Doct.* p. 134. In general, it seems that the speeches, the form of which was required to be perfect, were learnt by heart. In the case of Giannozzo Manetti we know positively that it was so on one occasion (*Commentario*, 39). See, however, the account p. 64, with the concluding statement that Manetti spoke better *impromptu* than Aretino with preparation. We are told of Codrus Urceus, whose memory was weak, that he read his orations (*Vita*, at the end of his works, Ven. 1506, fol. lxx.). The following passage will illustrate the exaggerated value set on oratory: 'Ausim affirmare perfectum oratorem (si quisquam modo sit perfectus orator) ita facile posse nitorem, lætitiam, lumina et umbras rebus dare quas oratione exponendas suscipit, ut pictorem suis coloribus et pigmentis facere videmus.' (Petr. Alcyonius, *De Exilio*, ed. Menken, p. 136.)

[4] Vespas. Fior. p. 103. Comp. p. 598, where he describes how Giannozzo Manetti came to him in the camp.

stood drawn up in order of battle, inspiring them in turn with pride and enthusiasm. Many of the speeches in the military historians of the fifteenth century, as for instance in Porcellius (p. 99), may be, in fact at least, imaginary, but may be also in part faithful representations of words actually spoken. The addresses again which were delivered to the Florentine Militia,[1] organised in 1506 chiefly through the influence of Macchiavelli, and which were spoken first at reviews, and afterwards at special annual festivals, were of another kind. They were simply general appeals to the patriotism of the hearers, and were addressed to the assembled troops in the church of each quarter of the city by a citizen in armour, sword in hand.

Finally, the oratory of the pulpit began in the fifteenth century to lose its distinctive peculiarities. Many of the clergy had entered into the circle of classical culture, and were ambitious of success in it. The street-preacher Bernardino da Siena, who even in his lifetime passed for a saint and who was worshipped by the populace, was not above taking lessons in rhetoric from the famous Guarino, although he had only to preach in Italian. Never indeed was more expected from preachers than at that time—especially from the Lenten preachers; and there were not a few audiences which could not only tolerate, but which demanded a strong dose of philosophy from the pulpit.[2] But we have here especially to speak of the distinguished occasional preachers in Latin. Many of their opportunities had been taken away from them, as has been observed, by learned laymen. Speeches on particular saints' days, at weddings and funerals, or at the installation of a bishop, and even the introductory speech at the first mass of a clerical friend, or the address at the festival of some religious order, were all left to laymen.[3] But at all events at the Papal

[1] *Archiv. Stor.* xv. pp. 113, 121. Canestrini's Introduction, p. 32 sqq. Reports of two such speeches to soldiers; the first, by Alamanni, is wonderfully fine and worthy of the occasion (1528).

[2] On this point see Faustinus Terdoceus, in his satire *De Triumpho Stultitiae*, lib. ii.

[3] Both of these extraordinary cases occur in Sabellicus, *Opera*, fol. 61–82. *De Origine et Auctu Religionis*, delivered at Verona from the pulpit before the barefoot friars; and *De Sacerdotii Laudibus*, delivered at Venice.

court in the fifteenth century, whatever the occasion might be, the preachers were generally monks. Under Sixtus IV., Giacomo da Volterra regularly enumerates these preachers, and criticises them according to the rules of the art.[1] Fedra Inghirami, famous as an orator under Julius II., had at least received holy orders and was canon at St. John Lateran; and besides him, elegant Latinists were now common enough among the prelates. In this matter, as in others, the exaggerated privileges of the profane humanists appear lessened in the sixteenth century—on which point we shall presently speak more fully.

What now was the subject and general character of these speeches? The national gift of eloquence was not wanting to the Italians of the Middle Ages, and a so-called 'rhetoric' belonged from the first to the seven liberal arts; but so far as the revival of the ancient methods is concerned, this merit must be ascribed, according to Filippo Villani,[2] to the Florentine Bruno Casini, who died of the plague in 1348. With the practical purpose of fitting his countrymen to speak with ease and effect in public, he treated, after the pattern of the ancients, invention, declamation, bearing, and gesticulation, each in its proper connection. Elsewhere too we read of an oratorical training directed solely to practical application. No accomplishment was more highly esteemed than the power of elegant improvisation in Latin.[3] The growing study of Cicero's speeches and theoretical writings, of Quintilian and of the imperial panegyrists, the appearance of new and original treatises,[4] the general progress of antiquarian learning, and the

[1] Jac. Volaterrani, *Diar. Roman.* in Murat. xxiii. *passim.* In col. 173 a remarkable sermon before the court, though in the absence of Sixtus IV., is mentioned. Pater Paolo Toscanella thundered against the Pope, his family, and the cardinals. When Sixtus heard of it, he smiled.

[2] Fil. Villani, *Vitae*, ed. Galetti, p. 30.

[3] See above, p. 237, note 3.

[4] Georg. Trapezunt, *Rhetorica*, the first complete system of instruction. Æn. Sylvius, *Artis Rhetoricae Praecepta*, in the *Opera*, p. 992, treats purposely only of the construction of sentences and the position of words. It is characteristic as an instance of the routine which was followed. He names several other theoretical writers who are some of them no longer known. Comp. C. Voigt, ii. 262 sqq.

stores of ancient matter and thought which now could and must be drawn from—all combined to shape the character of the new eloquence.

This character nevertheless differed widely according to the individual. Many speeches breathe a spirit of true eloquence, especially those which keep to the matter treated of; of this kind is the mass of what is left to us of Pius II. The miraculous effects produced by Giannozzo Manetti [1] point to an orator the like of whom has not been often seen. His great audiences as envoy before Nicholas V. and before the Doge and Council of Venice were events not to be soon forgotten. Many orators, on the contrary, would seize the opportunity, not only to flatter the vanity of distinguished hearers, but to load their speeches with an enormous mass of antiquarian rubbish. How it was possible to endure this infliction for two and even three hours, can only be understood when we take into account the intense interest then felt in everything connected with antiquity, and the rarity and defectiveness of treatises on the subject at a time when printing was but little diffused. Such orations had at least the value which we have claimed (p. 232) for many of Petrarch's letters. But some speakers went too far. Most of Filelfo's speeches are an atrocious patchwork of classical and biblical quotations, tacked on to a string of commonplaces, among which the great people he wishes to flatter are arranged under the head of the cardinal virtues, or some such category, and it is only with the greatest trouble, in his case and in that of many others, that we can extricate the few historical notices of value which they really contain. The speech, for instance, of a scholar and professor of Piacenza at the reception of the Duke Galeazzo Maria, in 1467, begins with Julius Cæsar, then proceeds to mix up a mass of classical quotations with a number from an allegorical work by the

[1] His life in Murat. xx. is full of the triumphs of his eloquence. Comp. Vespas. Fior. 592 sqq., and *Commentario*, p. 30. On us these speeches make no great impression, e.g. that at the coronation of Frederick III. in Freher-Struve, *Script. Rer. Germ.* iii. 4–19. Of Manetti's oration at the burial of Lion. Aretino, Shepherd-Tonelli says (*Poggio*, ii. 67 sqq.): 'L' orazione ch' ei compose, è ben la cosa la più meschina che potesse udirsi, piena di puerilità volgare nello stile, irrelevante negli argomenti e d' una prolissità insopportabile.'

speaker himself, and concludes with some exceedingly indiscreet advice to the ruler.[1] Fortunately it was late at night, and the orator had to be satisfied with handing his written panegyric to the prince. Filelfo begins a speech at a betrothal with the words: 'Aristotle, the peripatetic.' Others start with P. Cornelius Scipio, and the like, as though neither they nor their hearers could wait a moment for a quotation. At the end of the fifteenth century public taste suddenly improved, chiefly through Florentine influence, and the practice of quotation was restricted within due limits. Many works of reference were now in existence, in which the first comer could find as much as he wanted of what had hitherto been the admiration of princes and people.

As most of the speeches were written out beforehand in the study, the manuscripts served as a means of further publicity afterwards. The great extemporaneous speakers, on the other hand, were attended by shorthand writers.[2] We must further remember, that all the orations which have come down to us were not intended to be actually delivered. The panegyric, for example, of the elder Beroaldus on Ludovico Moro was presented to him in manuscript.[3] In fact, just as letters were written addressed to all conceivable persons and parts of the world as exercises, as formularies, or even to serve a controversial end, so there were speeches for imaginary occasions[4] to be used as models for the reception of princes, bishops, and other dignitaries.

For oratory, as for the other arts, the death of Leo X. (1521) and the sack of Rome (1527) mark the epoch of decadence.

[1] *Annales Placentini*, in Murat. xx. col. 918.

[2] *E.g.* Manetti. Comp. Vesp. *Commentario*, p. 30; so, too, Savonarola Comp. Perrens, *Vie de Savonarole*, i. p. 163. The shorthand writers, however, could not always follow him, or, indeed, any rapid 'Improvisatori.' Savonarola preached in Italian. See Pasq. Villari: *Vita di Savonarola.*

[3] It was by no means one of the best (*Opuscula Beroaldi*, Basel, 1509, fol. xviii.–xxi). The most remarkable thing in it is the flourish at the end: 'Esto tibi ipsi archetypon et exemplar, teipsum imitare,' etc.

[4] Letters and speeches of this kind were written by Alberto di Ripalta; comp. the *Annales Placentini*, written by his father Antonius and continued by himself, in Murat. xx. col. 914 sqq., where the pedant gives an instructive account of his own literary career.

Giovio,[1] but just escaped from the desolation of the eternal city, describes, not exhaustively, but on the whole truly, the causes of this decline.

'The plays of Platus and Terence, once a school of Latin style for the educated Romans, are banished to make room for Italian comedies. Graceful speakers no longer find the recognition and reward which they once did. The Consistorial advocates no longer prepare anything but the introductions to their speeches, and deliver the rest—a confused muddle—on the inspiration of the moment. Sermons and occasional speeches have sunk to the same level. If a funeral oration is wanted for a cardinal or other great personage, the executors do not apply to the best orators in the city, to whom they would have to pay a hundred pieces of gold, but they hire for a trifle the first impudent pedant whom they come across, and who only wants to be talked of whether for good or ill. The dead, they say, is none the wiser if an ape stands in a black dress in the pulpit, and beginning with a hoarse, whimpering mumble, passes little by little into a loud howling. Even the sermons preached at great papal ceremonies are no longer profitable, as they used to be. Monks of all orders have again got them into their hands, and preach as if they were speaking to the mob. Only a few years ago a sermon at mass before the Pope, might easily lead the way to a bishopric.'

[1] *Pauli Jovii Dialogus de Viris Litteris Illustribus*, in Tiraboschi, tom. vii. parte iv. Yet he says some ten years later, at the close of the *Elogia Litteraria:* 'Tenemus adhuc (after the leadership in philology had passed to the Germans) sincerae et constantis eloquentiae munitam arcem,' etc. The whole passage, given in German in Gregorovius, viii. 217 sqq. is important, as showing the view taken of Germany by an Italian, and is again quoted below in this connection.

CHAPTER VIII.

LATIN TREATISES AND HISTORY.

From the oratory and the epistolary writings of the humanists, we shall here pass on to their other creations, which were all, to a greater or less extent, reproductions of antiquity.

Among these must be placed the treatise, which often took the shape of a dialogue.[1] In this case it was borrowed directly from Cicero. In order to do anything like justice to this class of literature—in order not to throw it aside at first sight as a bore—two things must be taken into consideration. The century which escaped from the influence of the Middle Ages felt the need of something to mediate between itself and antiquity in many questions of morals and philosophy; and this need was met by the writer of treatises and dialogues. Much which appears to us as mere commonplace in their writings, was for them and their contemporaries a new and hardly-won view of things upon which mankind had been silent since the days of antiquity. The language too, in this form of writing, whether Italian or Latin, moved more freely and flexibly than in historical narrative, in letters, or in oratory, and thus became in itself the source of a special pleasure. Several Italian compositions of this kind still hold their place as patterns of style. Many of these works have been, or will be mentioned on account of their contents; we here refer to them as a class. From the time of Petrarch's letters and treatises down to near the end of the fifteenth century, the heaping up of learned quotations, as in the case of the orators, is the main business of most of these writers. The whole style, especially in Italian, was then suddenly clarified, till, in the 'Asolani,' of Bembo,

[1] A special class is formed by the semi-satirical dialogues, which Collenuccio, and still more Pontano, copied from Lucian. Their example stimulated Erasmus and Hutten. For the treatises properly so-called, parts of the ethical writings of Plutarch may have served as models.

and the 'Vita Sobria,' of Luigi Cornaro,[1] a classical perfection was reached. Here too the decisive fact was, that antiquarian matter of every kind had meantime begun to be deposited in encyclopædic works (now printed), and no longer stood in the way of the essayist.

It was inevitable too that the humanistic spirit should control the writing of history. A superficial comparison of the histories of this period with the earlier chronicles, especially with works so full of life, colour, and brilliancy as those of the Villani, will lead us loudly to deplore the change. How insipid and conventional appear by their side the best of the humanists, and particularly their immediate and most famous successors among the historians of Florence, Lionardo Aretino and Poggio![2] The enjoyment of the reader is incessantly marred by the sense that, in the classical phrases of Facius, Sabellicus, Folieta, Senarega, Platina in the chronicles of Mantua, Bembo in the annals of Venice, and even of Giovio in his histories, the best local and individual colouring and the full sincerity of interest in the truth of events have been lost. Our mistrust is increased when we hear that Livy, the pattern of this school of writers, was copied just where he is least worthy of imitation—on the ground, namely,[3] 'that he turned a dry and naked tradition into grace and richness.' In the same place we meet with the suspicious declaration, that it is the function of the historian—just as if he were one with the poet—to excite, charm, or overwhelm the reader. We must further remember that many humanistic historians knew but little of what happened outside their own sphere, and this little they were often compelled to adapt to the taste of their patrons and employers. We ask ourselves finally, whether the contempt for modern things, which these same humanists sometimes avowed openly[4] must not necessarily have had an

[1] See below, part iv. chap. 5.

[2] Comp. the epigram of Sannazaro:

> 'Dum patriam laudat, damnat dum Poggius hostem,
> Nec malus est civis, nec bonus historicus.'

[3] Benedictus: *Caroli VIII. Hist.* in Eccard, Scriptt. vi. col. 1577.

[4] Petrus Crinitus deplores this contempt, *De honesta disciplina*, l. xviii. cap. 9. The humanists here resemble the writers in the decline of antiquity, who also severed themselves from their own age. Comp. Burck-

unfortunate influence on their treatment of them. Unconsciously the reader finds himself looking with more interest and confidence on the unpretending Latin and Italian annalists, like those of Bologna and Ferrara, who remained true to the old style, and still more grateful does he feel to the best of the genuine chroniclers who wrote in Italian—to Marin Sanudo, Corio, and Infessura—who were followed at the beginning of the sixteenth century by that new and illustrious band of great national historians who wrote in their mother tongue.

Contemporary history, no doubt, was written far better in the language of the day than when forced into Latin. Whether Italian was also more suitable for the narrative of events long past, or for historical research, is a question which admits, for that period, of more answers than one. Latin was, at that time, the 'Lingua franca' of instructed people, not only in an international sense, as a means of intercourse between Englishmen, Frenchmen, and Italians, but also in an interprovincial sense. The Lombard, the Venetian, and the Neapolitan modes of writing, though long modelled on the Tuscan, and bearing but slight traces of the dialect, were still not recognised by the Florentines. This was of less consequence in local contemporary histories, which were sure of readers at the place where they were written, than in the narratives of the past, for which a larger public was desired. In these the local interests of the people had to be sacrificed to the general interests of the learned. How far would the influence of a man like Blondus of Forli have reached if he had written his great monuments of learning in the dialect of the Romagna? They would have assuredly sunk into neglect, if only through the contempt of the Florentines, while written in Latin they exercised the profoundest influence on the whole European world of learning. And even the Florentines in the fifteenth century wrote Latin, not only because their minds were imbued with humanism, but in order to be more widely read.

Finally, there exist certain Latin essays in contemporary history, which stand on a level with the best Italian works of the kind. When the continuous narrative after the manner

hardt, *Die Zeit Constantin's des Grossen.* See for the other side several declarations of Poggio in Voigt, *Wiederbelebung*, p. 443 sqq.

of Livy—that Procrustean bed of so many writers—is abandoned, the change is marvellous. The same Platina and Giovio, whose great histories we only read because and so far as we must, suddenly come forward as masters in the biographical style. We have already spoken of Tristan Caracciolo, of the biographical works of Facius and of the Venetian topography of Sabellico, and others will be mentioned in the sequel. Historical composition, like letters and oratory, soon had its theory. Following the example of Cicero, it proclaims with pride the worth and dignity of history, boldly claims Moses and the Evangelists as simple historians, and concludes with earnest exhortations to strict impartiality and love of truth.[1]

The Latin treatises on past history were naturally concerned, for the most part, with classical antiquity. What we are more surprised to find among these humanists are some considerable works on the history of the Middle Ages. The first of this kind was the chronicle of Matteo Palmieri (449–1449), beginning where Prosper Aquitanus ceases, the style of which was certainly an offence to later critics like Paolo Cortese. On opening the 'Decades' of Blondus of Forli, we are surprised to find a universal history, 'ab inclinatione Romanorum imperii,' as in Gibbon, full of original studies on the authors of each century, and occupied, through the first 300 folio pages, with early mediæval history down to the death of Frederick II. And this when in Northern countries nothing more was wanted than chronicles of the popes and emperors, and the 'Fasciculus temporum.' We cannot here stay to show what writings Blondus made use of, and where he found his materials, though this justice will some day be done to him by the historians of literature. This book alone would entitle us to say that it was the study of antiquity which made the study of the Middle Ages possible, by first training the mind to habits of impartial historical criticism. To this must be added, that the Middle Ages were now over for Italy, and that the Italian mind could the better appreciate them, because it stood outside them. It

[1] Lorenzo Valla, in the preface to the *Historia Ferdinandi Regis Arag.*; in opposition to him, Giacomo Zeno in the *Vita Caroli Zeni*, Murat. xix. p. 204. See, too, Guarino, in Rosmini, ii. 62 sqq. 177 sqq.

cannot, nevertheless, be said that it at once judged them fairly, and still less that it judged them with piety. In art a fixed prejudice showed itself against all that those centuries had created, and the humanists date the new era from the time of their own appearance. 'I begin,' says Boccaccio,[1] 'to hope and believe that God has had mercy on the Italian name, since I see that His infinite goodness puts souls into the breasts of the Italians like those of the ancients—souls which seek fame by other means than robbery and violence, but rather, on the path of poetry, which makes men immortal.' But this narrow and unjust temper did not preclude investigation in the minds of the more gifted men, at a time, too, when elsewhere in Europe any such investigation would have been out of the question. A historical criticism[2] of the Middle Ages was practicable, just because the rational treatment of all subjects by the humanists had trained the historical spirit. In the fifteenth century this spirit had so far penetrated the history even of the individual cities of Italy, that the stupid fairy tales about the origin of Florence, Venice, and Milan vanished, while at the same time, and long after, the chronicles of the North were stuffed with this fantastic rubbish, destitute for the most part of all poetical value, and invented as late as the fourteenth century.

The close connection between local history and the sentiment of glory has already been touched on in reference to Florence (part i. chap. vii.). Venice would not be behindhand. Just as a great rhetorical triumph of the Florentines[3] would cause a Venetian embassy to write home post-haste for an orator to be sent after them, so too the Venetians felt the need of a history which would bear comparison with those of

[1] In the letter to Pizinga, *Opere Volgari*, vol. xvi. p. 38. With Raph. Volaterranus, l. xxi. the intellectual world begins in the fourteenth century. He is the same writer whose early books contain so many notices —excellent for his time—of the history of all countries.

[2] Here, too, Petrarch cleared the way. See especially his critical investigation of the Austrian Charter, claiming to descend from Cæsar. *Epp. Sen.* xvi. 1.

[3] Like that of Giannozzo Manetti in the presence of Nicholas V., of the whole Papal court, and of a great concourse of strangers from all parts. Comp. Vespas. Fior. p. 591, and more fully in the *Commentario*, pp. 37–40.

Lionardo Aretino and Poggio. And it was to satisfy this feeling that, in the fifteenth century, after negotiations with Giovanni Maria Filelfo and others had failed, the 'Decades' of Sabellico appeared, and in the sixteenth the 'Historia rerum Venetarum' of Pietro Bembo, both written at the express charge of the republic, the latter a continuation of the former.

The great Florentine historians at the beginning of the sixteenth century (pp. 81 sqq.) were men of a wholly different kind from the Latinists Bembo and Giovio. They wrote Italian, not only because they could not vie with the Ciceronian elegance of the philologists, but because, like Macchiavelli, they could only record in a living tongue the living results of their own immediate observations—and we may add in the case of Macchiavelli, of his observation of the past—and because, as in the case of Guicciardini, Varchi, and many others, what they most desired was, that their view of the course of events should have as wide and deep a practical effect as possible. Even when they only write for a few friends, like Francesco Vettori, they feel an inward need to utter their testimony on men and events, and to explain and justify their share in the latter.

And yet, with all that is characteristic in their language and style, they were powerfully affected by antiquity, and, without its influence, would be inconceivable. They were not humanists, but they had passed through the school of humanism, and they have in them more of the spirit of the ancient historians than most of the imitators of Livy. Like the ancients, they were citizens who wrote for citizens.

CHAPTER IX.

GENERAL LATINISATION OF CULTURE.

We cannot attempt to trace the influence of humanism in the special sciences. Each has its own history, in which the Italian investigators of this period, chiefly through their rediscovery of the results attained by antiquity,[1] mark a new epoch, with which the modern period of the science in question begins with more or less distinctness. With regard to philosophy, too, we must refer the reader to the special historical works on the subject. The influence of the old philosophers on Italian culture will appear at times immense, at times inconsiderable; the former, when we consider how the doctrines of Aristotle, chiefly drawn from the Ethics[2] and Politics—both widely diffused at an early period—became the common property of educated Italians, and how the whole method of abstract thought was governed by him;[3] the latter, when we

[1] In fact, it was already said that Homer alone contained the whole of the arts and sciences—that he was an encyclopædia. Comp. *Codri Urcei Opera*, Sermo xiii. at the end. It is true that we met with a similar opinion in several ancient writers. The words of C. U. (Sermo xiii., habitus in laudem liberalium artium; *Opera*, ed. Ven. 1506, fol. xxxviii. *b*) are as follows: 'Eia ergo bono animo esto; ego graecas litteras tibi exponam; et praecipue divinum Homerum, a quo ceu fonte perenni, ut scribit Naso, vatum Pieriis ora rigantur aquis. Ab Homero grammaticum dicere poteris, ab Homero rhetoricam, ab Homero medicinam, ab Homero astrologiam, ab Homero fabulas, ab Homero historias, ab Homero mores, ab Homero philosophorum dogmata, ab Homero artem militarem, ab Homero coquinariam, ab Homero architecturam, ab Homero regendarum urbium modum percipies; et in summa, quidquid boni quidquid honesti animus hominis discendi cupidus optare potest, in Homero facile poteris invenire.' To the same effect 'Sermo' vii. and viii. *Opera*, fol. xxvi. sqq., which treat of Homer only.

[2] A cardinal under Paul II. had his cooks instructed in the Ethics of Aristotle. Comp. Gaspar. Veron. *Vita Pauli II.* in Muratori, iii. ii. col. 1034.

[3] For the study of Aristotle in general, a speech of Hermolaus Barbarus is specially instructive.

remember how slight was the dogmatic influence of the old philosophies, and even of the enthusiastic Florentine Platonists, on the spirit of the people at large. What looks like such an influence is generally no more than a consequence of the new culture in general, and of the special growth and development of the Italian mind. When we come to speak of religion, we shall have more to say on this head. But in by far the greater number of cases, we have to do, not with the general culture of the people, but with the utterances of individuals or of learned circles; and here, too, a distinction must be drawn between the true assimilation of ancient doctrines and fashionable make-believe. For with many antiquity was only a fashion, even among very learned people.

Nevertheless, all that looks like affectation to our age, need not then have been actually so. The giving of Greek and Latin names to children, for example, is better and more respectable than the present practice of taking them, especially the female names, from novels. When the enthusiasm for the ancient world was greater than for the saints, it was simple and natural enough that noble families called their sons Agamemnon, Tydeus, and Achilles,[1] and that a painter named his son Apelles and his daughter Minerva.[2] Nor will it appear

[1] Bursellis, *Ann. Bonon.* in Murat. xxiii. col. 898.

[2] Vasari, xi. pp. 189, 257. *Vite di Sodoma e di Garofalo.* It is not surprising that the profligate women at Rome took the most harmonious ancient names—Julia, Lucretia, Cassandra, Portia, Virginia, Penthesilea, under which they appear in Aretino. It was, perhaps, then that the Jews took the names of the great Semitic enemies of the Romans—Hannibal, Hamilcar, Hasdrubal, which even now they commonly bear in Rome. [This last assertion cannot be maintained. Neither Zunz, *Namen der Juden*, Leipzig, 1837, reprinted in Zunz *Gesammelte Schriften*, Berlin, 1876, nor Steinschneider in his collection in *Il Buonarotti*, ser. ii. vol. vi. 1871, pp. 196–199, speaks of any Jew of that period who bore these names, and even now, according to the enquiries of Prince Buoncompagni from Signor Tagliacapo, in charge of the Jewish archives in Rome, there are only a few who are named Asdrubale, and none Amilcare or Annibale. L. G.] Burckhardt, 352. A careful choice of names is recommended by L. B. Alberti, *Della familia*, opp. ii. p. 171. Maffeo Vegio (*De educatione liberorum.* lib. i. c. x.) warns his readers against the use of *nomina indecora barbara aut nova, aut quae gentilium deorum sunt.* Names like 'Nero' disgrace the bearer; while others such as Cicero, Brutus, Naso, Maro, can be used *qualiter per se parum venusta propter tamen eximiam illorum virtutem.*

unreasonable that, instead of a family name, which people were often glad to get rid of, a well-sounding ancient name was chosen. A local name, shared by all residents in the place, and not yet transformed into a family name, was willingly given up, especially when its religious associations made it inconvenient; Filippo da San Gemignano called himself Callimachus. The man, misunderstood and insulted by his family, who made his fortune as a scholar in foreign cities, could afford, even if he were a Sanseverino, to change his name to Julius Pomponius Laetus. Even the simple translation of a name into Latin or Greek, as was almost uniformly the custom in Germany, may be excused to a generation which spoke and wrote Latin, and which needed names that could be not only declined, but used with facility in verse and prose. What was blameworthy and ridiculous was, the change of half a name, baptismal or family, to give it a classical sound and a new sense. Thus Giovanni was turned into Jovianus or Janus, Pietro to Petreius or Pierius, Antonio to Aonius, Sannazzaro to Syncerus, Luca Grasso to Lucius Crassus. Ariosto, who speaks with such derision of all this,[1] lived to see children called after his own heroes and heroines.[2]

Nor must we judge too severely the Latinisation of many usages of social life, such as the titles of officials, of ceremonies, and the like, in the writers of the period. As long as people were satisfied with a simple, fluent Latin style, as was the case with most writers from Petrarch to Æneas Sylvius, this practice was not so frequent and striking; it became inevitable when a faultless, Ciceronian Latin was demanded. Modern names and things no longer harmonised with the style, unless they were first artificially changed. Pedants found a pleasure in addressing municipal counsellors as 'Patres Conscripti,' nuns as 'Virgines Vestales,' and entitling every saint 'Divus' or 'Deus;' but men of better taste, such as Paolo Giovio, only

[1] 'Quasi che 'l nome i buon giudici inganni,
E che quel meglio t' abbia a far poeta,
Che non farà lo studio di molt' anni!'

So jests Ariosto, to whom fortune had certainly given a harmonious name, in the *Seventh Satire*, vs. 64.

[2] Or after those of Bojardo, which are in part the same as his.

did so when and because they could not help it. But as Giovio does it naturally, and lays no special stress upon it, we are not offended if, in his melodious language, the cardinals appear as 'Senatores,' their dean as 'Princeps Senatus,' excommunication as 'Dirae,'[1] and the carnival as 'Lupercalia.' This example of this author alone is enough to warn us against drawing a hasty inference from these peculiarities of style as to the writer's whole mode of thinking.

The history of Latin composition cannot here be traced in detail. For fully two centuries the humanists acted as if Latin were, and must remain, the only language worthy to be written. Poggio[2] deplores that Dante wrote his great poem in Italian; and Dante, as is well known, actually made the attempt in Latin, and wrote the beginning of the 'Inferno' first in hexameters. The whole future of Italian poetry hung on his not continuing in the same style,[3] but even Petrarch relied more on his Latin poetry than on the Sonnets and 'Canzoni,' and Ariosto himself was desired by some to write his poem in Latin. A stronger coercion never existed in literature;[4] but

[1] The soldiers of the French army in 1512 were 'omnibus diris ad inferos devocati!' The honest canon, Tizio, who, in all seriousness, pronounced a curse from Macrobius against foreign troops, will be spoken of further on.

[2] *De infelicitate principum*, in Poggii *Opera*, fol. 152: 'Cujus (Dantis) exstat poema praeclarum, neque, si literis Latinis constaret, ullâ ex parte poetis superioribus (the ancients) postponendum.' According to Boccaccio, *Vita di Dante*, p. 74, 'Many wise men' even then discussed the question why Dante had not written in Latin. Cortesius (*De hominibus doctis*, p. 7) complains: 'Utinam tam bene cogitationes suas Latinus litteris mandare potuisset, quam bene patrium sermonem illustravit!' He makes the same complaint in speaking of Petrarch and Boccaccio.

[3] His work *De vulgari eloquio* was for long almost unknown, and, valuable as it is to us, could never have exercised the influence of the *Divina Commedia*.

[4] To know how far this fanaticism went, we have only to refer to Lil. Greg. Gyraldus, *De poetis nostri temporis*, *passim*. Vespasiano Bisticci is one of the few Latin writers of that time who openly confessed that they knew little of Latin (*Commentario della vita di G. Manetti*, p. 2), but he knew enough to introduce Latin sentences here and there in his writings, and to read Latin letters (*ibid.* 96, 165). In reference to this exclusive regard for Latin, the following passage may be quoted from Petr. Alcyonius, *De exilio*, ed. Menken, p. 213. He says that if Cicero could rise up and behold Rome, 'Omnium maxime illum credo pertur-

poetry shook it off for the most part, and it may be said, without the risk of too great optimism, that it was well for Italian poetry to have had both means of expressing itself. In both something great and characteristic was achieved, and in each we can see the reason why Latin or Italian was chosen. Perhaps the same may be said of prose. The position and influence of Italian culture throughout the world depended on the fact that certain subjects were treated in Latin[1]—'urbi et orbi'—while Italian prose was written best of all by those to whom it cost an inward struggle not to write in Latin.

From the fourteenth century Cicero was recognised universally as the purest model of prose. This was by no means due solely to a dispassionate opinion in favour of his choice of language, of the structure of his sentences, and of his style of composition, but rather to the fact that the Italian spirit responded fully and instinctively to the amiability of the letter-writer, to the brilliancy of the orator, and to the lucid exposition of the philosophical thinker. Even Petrarch recognised clearly the weakness of Cicero as a man and a statesman,[2] though he respected him too much to rejoice over them. After Petrarch's time, the epistolary style was formed entirely on the pattern of Cicero; and the rest, with the exception of the narrative style, followed the same influence. Yet the true Ciceronianism, which rejected every phrase which could not be justified out of the great authority, did not appear till the end of the fifteenth century, when the grammatical writings of Lorenzo Valla had begun to tell on all Italy, and when the opinions of the Roman historians of literature had been sifted

barent ineptiae quorumdam qui, amisso studio veteris linguae quae eadem hujus urbis et universae Italiae propria erat, dies noctesque incumbunt in linguam Geticam aut Dacicam discendam eandemque omni ratione ampliendam, cum Goti, Visigothi et Vandali (qui erant olim Getae et Daci) eam in Italos invexerant, ut artes et linguam et nomen Romanum delerent.'

[1] There were regular stylistic exercises, as in the *Orationes* of the elder Beroaldus, where there are two tales of Boccaccio, and even a 'Canzone' of Petrarch translated into Latin.

[2] Comp. Petrarch's letter from the earth to illustrious shades below. *Opera*, p. 704 sqq. See also p. 372 in the work *De rep. optime administranda:* 'Sic esse doleo, sed sic est.'

and compared.[1] Then every shade of difference in the style of the ancients was studied with closer and closer attention, till the consoling conclusion was at last reached, that in Cicero alone was the perfect model to be found, or, if all forms of literature were to be embraced, in 'that immortal and almost heavenly age of Cicero.'[2] Men like Pietro Bembo and Pierio Valeriano now turned all their energies to this one object. Even those who had long resisted the tendency, and had formed for themselves an archaic style from the earlier authors,[3] yielded at last, and joined in the worship of Cicero. Longolius, at Bembo's advice, determined to read nothing but Cicero for five years long, and finally took an oath to use no word which did not occur in this author. It was this temper which broke out at last in the great war among the scholars, in which Erasmus and the elder Scaliger led the battle.

For all the admirers of Cicero were by no means so one-sided as to consider him the only source of language. In the fifteenth century, Politian and Ermolao Barbaro made a conscious and deliberate effort to form a style of their own,[4] naturally on the basis of their 'overflowing' learning, though they failed to inspire their pupils with a similar desire for independence; and our informant of this fact, Paolo Giovio, pursued the same end. He first attempted, not always successfully, but

[1] A burlesque picture of the fanatical purism prevalent in Rome is given by Jovian. Pontanus in his *Antonius*.

[2] *Hadriani* (*Cornetani*) *Card. S. Chrysogoni de sermone latino liber*, especially the introduction. He finds in Cicero and his contemporaries Latinity in its absolute form (*an sich*). The same Codrus Urceus, who found in Homer the sum of all science (see above, p. 249, note 1) says (*Opp.* ed. 1506, fol. lxv.): 'Quidquid temporibus meis aut vidi aut studui libens omne illud Cicero mihi felici dedit omine,' and goes so far as to say in another poem (*ibid.*): 'Non habet huic similem doctrinae Graecia mater.'

[3] Paul. Jov. *Elogia doct. vir.* p. 187 sqq., speaking of Bapt. Pius.

[4] Paul Jov. *Elogia*, on Naugerius. Their ideal, he says, was: 'Aliquid in stylo proprium, quod peculiarem ex certâ notâ mentis effigiem referret, ex naturae genio effinxisse.' Politian, when in a hurry, objected to write his letters in Latin. Comp. Raph. Volat. *Comment. urban.* l. xxi. Politian to Cortesius (*Epist.* lib. viii. ep. 16): 'Mihi vero longe honestior tauri facies, aut item leonis, quam simiae videtur;' to which Cortesius replied: 'Ego malo esse assecla et simia Ciceronis quam alumnus.' For Pico's opinion on the Latin language, see the letter quoted above, p. 202.

often with remarkable power and elegance, and at no small cost of effort, to reproduce in Latin a number of modern, particularly of æsthetic, ideas. His Latin characteristics of the great painters and sculptors of his time contain a mixture of the most intelligent and of the most blundering interpretation.[1] Even Leo X., who placed his glory in the fact, 'ut lingua latina nostra pontificatu dicatur factu auctior,'[2] was inclined to a liberal and not too exclusive Latinity, which, indeed, was in harmony with his pleasure-loving nature. He was satisfied when the Latin which he had to read and hear was lively, elegant, and idiomatic. Then, too, Cicero offered no model for Latin conversation, so that here other gods had to be worshipped beside him. The want was supplied by representations of the comedies of Plautus and Terence, frequent both in and out of Rome, which for the actors were an incomparable exercise in Latin as the language of daily life. The impulse to the study of the old Latin comedies and to modern imitations of them was given by the discovery of plays by Plautus in the 'Cod. Ursinianus,' which was brought to Rome in 1428 or 1429. A few years later, in the pontificate of Paul II., the learned Cardinal of Teano[3] (probably Niccolò Forteguerra of Pistoja) became famous for his critical labours in this branch of scholarship. He set to work upon the most defective plays of Plautus, which were destitute even of the list of the characters, and went carefully through the whole remains of this author, chiefly with an eye to the language. Possibly it was he who gave the first impulse for the public representations of these plays. Afterwards Pomponius Laetus took up the same subject, and acted as manager when Plautus was put on the stage in the houses of great churchmen.[4] That these representations

[1] Paul. Jov. *Dialogus de viris literis illustribus*, in Tiraboschi, ed. Venez. 1766, tom. vii. p. iv. It is well known that Giovio was long anxious to undertake the great work which Vasari accomplished. In the dialogue mentioned above it is foreseen and deplored that Latin would now altogether lose it supremacy.

[2] In the 'Breve' of 1517 to Franc. de' Rosi, composed by Sadoleto, in Roscoe, *Leone X.* ed. Bossi, vi. p. 172.

[3] Gasp. Veronens. *Vita Pauli II.* in Murat. iii. ii. col. 1031. The plays of Seneca and Latin translations of Greek dramas were also performed.

[4] At Ferrara, Plautus was played chiefly in the Italian adaptations of

became less common after 1520, is mentioned by Giovio, as we have seen (p. 242), among the causes of the decline of eloquence.

We may mention, in conclusion, the analogy between Ciceronianism in literature and the revival of Vitruvius by the architects in the sphere of art.[1] And here, too, the law holds good which prevails elsewhere in the history of the Renaissance, that each artistic movement is preceded by a corresponding movement in the general culture of the age. In this case, the interval is not more than about twenty years, if we reckon from Cardinal Hadrian of Corneto (1505?) to the first avowed Vitruvians.

Collenuccio, the younger Guarino, and others, and principally for the sake of the plots. Isabella Gonzaga took the liberty of finding him dull. For Latin comedy in general, see R. Peiper in Fleckeisen and Masius, *Neue Jahrb. für Phil. u. Pädag.*, Lpzg. 1874, xx. 131–138, and *Archiv für Literaturgesch.* v. 541 sqq. On Pomp. Laetus, see *Sabellici Opera*, Epist. l. xi. fol. 56 sqq., and below, at the close of Part III.

[1] Comp. Burckhardt. *Gesch. der Renaissance in Italien*, 38–41.

CHAPTER X.

MODERN LATIN POETRY.

THE chief pride of the humanists is, however, their modern Latin poetry. It lies within the limits of our task to treat of it, at least in so far as it serves to characterise the humanistic movement.

How favourable public opinion was to that form of poetry, and how nearly it supplanted all others, has been already shown (p. 252). We may be very sure that the most gifted and highly developed nation then existing in the world did not renounce the use of a language such as the Italian out of mere folly and without knowing what they were doing. It must have been a weighty reason which led them to do so.

This cause was the devotion to antiquity. Like all ardent and genuine devotion it necessarily prompted men to imitation. At other times and among other nations we find many isolated attempts of the same kind. But only in Italy were the two chief conditions present which were needful for the continuance and development of neo-Latin poetry: a general interest in the subject among the instructed classes, and a partial reawakening of the old Italian genius among the poets themselves—the wondrous echo of a far-off strain. The best of what is produced under these conditions is not imitation, but free production. If we decline to tolerate any borrowed forms in art, if we either set no value on antiquity at all, or attribute to it some magical and unapproachable virtue, or if we will pardon no slips in poets who were forced, for instance, to guess or to discover a multitude of syllabic quantities, then we had better let this class of literature alone. Its best works were not created in order to defy criticism, but to give pleasure to the poet and to thousands of his contemporaries.[1]

[1] For what follows see *Deliciae poetarum Italorum;* Paul. Jov. *Elogia;* Lil. Greg. Gyraldus, *De poetis nostri temporis;* and the Appendices to Roscoe, *Leone X.* ed. Bossi.

The least success of all was attained by the epic narratives drawn from the history or legends of antiquity. The essential conditions of a living epic poetry were denied, not only to the Romans who now served as models, but even to the Greeks after Homer. They could not be looked for among the Latins of the Renaissance. And yet the 'Africa' of Petrarch[1] probably found as many and as enthusiastic readers and hearers as any epos of modern times. The purpose and origin of the poem are not without interest. The fourteenth century recognised with sound historical tact the time of the second Punic war as the noon-day of Roman greatness; and Petrarch could not resist writing of this time. Had Silius Italicus been then discovered, Petrarch would probably have chosen another subject; but, as it was, the glorification of Scipio Africanus the Elder was so much in accordance with the spirit of the fourteenth century, that another poet, Zanobi di Strada, also proposed to himself the same task, and only from respect for Petrarch withdrew the poem with which he had already made great progress.[2] If any justification were needed for the 'Africa,' it lies in the fact that in Petrarch's time and afterwards Scipio was as much an object of public interest as if he were then alive, and that he was held by many to be a greater man than Alexander, Pompey, and Cæsar.[3] How many modern epics treat of a subject at once so popular, so historical in its basis, and so striking to the imagination? For us, it is true, the poem is unreadable. For other themes of the same kind the reader may be referred to the histories of literature.

A richer and more fruitful vein was discovered in expanding and completing the Greco-Roman mythology. In this too

[1] There are two new editions of the poem, that of Pingaud (Paris, 1872), and that of Corradini (Padua, 1874). In 1874 two Italian translations also appeared by G. B. Gaudo and A. Palesa. On the *Africa*, compare L. Geiger: *Petrarca*, pp. 122 sqq., and p. 270, note 7.

[2] Filippo Villani, *Vite*, ed. Galetti, p. 16.

[3] *Franc. Aleardi Oratio in laudem Franc. Sfortiae*, in Marat. xxv. col. 384. In comparing Scipio with Caesar, Guarino and Cyriacus Anconitanus held the latter, Poggio (*Opera*, epp. fol. 125, 134 sqq.) the former, to be the greater. For Scipio and Hannibal in the miniatures of Attavante, see Vasari, iv. 41. *Vita di Fiesole.* The names of both used for Picinino and Sforza. See p. 99. There were great disputes as to the relative greatness of the two. Shepherd-Tonelli, i. 262 sqq. and Rosmini: Guarino, ii. 97–111.

Italian poetry began early to take a part, beginning with the 'Teseide' of Boccaccio, which passes for his best poetical work. Under Martin V. Maffeo Vegio wrote in Latin a thirteenth book to the Æneid; besides which we meet with many less considerable attempts, especially in the style of Claudian—a 'Meleagris,' a 'Hesperis,' and so forth. Still more curious were the newly-invented myths, which peopled the fairest regions of Italy with a primæval race of gods, nymphs, genii, and even shepherds, the epic and bucolic styles here passing into one another. In the narrative or conversational eclogue after the time of Petrarch, pastoral life was treated in a purely conventional manner,[1] as a vehicle of all possible feelings and fancies; and this point will be touched on again in the sequel. For the moment, we have only to do with the new myths. In them, more clearly than anywhere else, we see the double significance of the old gods to the men of the Renaissance. On the one hand, they replace abstract terms in poetry, and render allegorical figures superfluous; and, on the other, they serve as free and independent elements in art, as forms of beauty which can be turned to some account in any and every poem. The example was boldly set by Boccaccio, with his fanciful world of gods and shepherds who people the country round Florence in his 'Ninfale d' Ameto' and 'Ninfale Fiesolano.' Both these poems were written in Italian. But the masterpiece in this style was the 'Sarca' of Pietro Bembo,[2] which tells how the rivergod of that name wooed the nymph Garda; of the brilliant marriage feast in a cave of Monte Baldo; of the prophecies of Manto, daughter of Tiresias; of the birth of the child Mincius; of the founding of Mantua, and of the future glory of Virgil, son of Mincius and of Maia, nymph of Andes. This humanistic rococo is set forth by Bembo in verses of great beauty, concluding with an address to Virgil, which any poet might envy him. Such works are often slighted as mere

[1] The brilliant exceptions, where rural life is treated realistically, will also be mentioned below.

[2] Printed in Mai, *Spicilegium Romanum*, vol. viii. pp. 488–504; about 500 hexameter verses. Pierio Valeriano followed out the myth in his poetry. See his *Carpio*, in the *Deliciae poetarum Italorum*. The frescoes of Brusasorci in the Pal. Murari at Verona represent the subject of the *Sarca*.

declamation. This is a matter of taste on which we are all free to form our own opinion.

Further, we find long epic poems in hexameters on biblical or ecclesiastical subjects. The authors were by no means always in search of preferment or of papal favour. With the best of them, and even with less gifted writers, like Battista Mantovano, the author of the 'Parthenice,' there was probably an honest desire to serve religion by their Latin verses—a desire with which their half-pagan conception of Catholicism harmonised well enough. Gyraldus goes through a list of these poets, among whom Vida, with his 'Christiad' and Sannazaro, with his three books, 'De partu Virginis,'[1] hold the first place. Sannazaro (b. 1458, d. 1530) is impressive by the steady and powerful flow of his verse, in which Christian and pagan elements are mingled without scruple, by the plastic vigour of his description, and by the perfection of his workmanship. He could venture to introduce Virgil's fourth eclogue into his song of the shepherds at the manger (III. 200 sqq.) without fearing a comparison. In treating of the unseen world, he sometimes gives proofs of a boldness worthy of Dante, as when King David in the Limbo of the Patriarchs rises up to sing and prophesy (I. 236 sqq.), or when the Eternal, sitting on the throne clad in a mantle shining with pictures of all the elements, addresses the heavenly host (III. 17 sqq). At other times he does not hesitate to weave the whole classical mythology into his subject, yet without spoiling the harmony of the whole, since the pagan deities are only accessory figures, and play no important part in the story. To appreciate the artistic genius of that age in all its bearings, we must not refuse to notice such works as these. The merit of Sannazaro will appear the greater, when we consider that the mixture of Christian and pagan elements is apt to disturb us much more in poetry than in the plastic arts. The latter can still satisfy the eye by beauty of form and colour, and in general are much more independent of the significance of the subject than poetry. With them, the imagination is interested chiefly in the form,

[1] Newly edited and translated by Th. A. Fassnacht in *Drei Perlen der neulateinischen Poesie.* Leutkirch and Leipzig, 1875. See further, Goethe's *Werke* (Hempel'sche Ausgabe), vol. xxxii. pp. 157 and 411.

with poetry, in the matter. Honest Battista Mantovano in his calendar of the festivals,[1] tried another expedient. Instead of making the gods and demigods serve the purposes of sacred history, he put them, as the Fathers of the Church did, in active opposition to it. When the angel Gabriel salutes the Virgin at Nazareth, Mercury flies after him from Carmel, and listens at the door. He then announces the result of his eavesdropping to the assembled gods, and stimulates them thereby to desperate resolutions. Elsewhere,[2] it is true, in his writings, Thetis, Ceres, Æolus, and other pagan deities pay willing homage to the glory of the Madonna.

The fame of Sannazaro, the number of his imitators, the enthusiastic homage which was paid to him by the greatest men—by Bembo, who wrote his epitaph, and by Titian, who painted his portrait—all show how dear and necessary he was to his age. On the threshold of the Reformation he solved for the Church the problem, whether it were possible for a poet to be a Christian as well as a classic; and both Leo and Clement were loud in their thanks for his achievements.

And, finally, contemporary history was now treated in hexameters or distichs, sometimes in a narrative and sometimes in a panegyrical style, but most commonly to the honour of some prince or princely family. We thus meet with a Sforziad,[3] a Borseid, a Laurentiad, a Borgiad (see p. 223), a Triulziad, and the like. The object sought after was certainly not attained; for those who became famous and are now immortal owe it to anything rather than to this sort of poems, to which the world has always had an ineradicable dislike, even when they happen to be written by good poets. A wholly different effect is produced by smaller, simpler and more unpretentious scenes from the lives of distinguished men, such as the beautiful poem on Leo X.'s 'Hunt at Palo,'[4] or the 'Journey of Julius II.' by

[1] *De sacris diebus.*

[2] E.g. in his eighth eclogue.

[3] There are two unfinished and unprinted Sforziads, one by the elder, the other by the younger Filelfo. On the latter, see Favre, *Mélanges d'Hist. Lit.* i. 156; on the former, see Rosmini, *Filelfo*, ii. 157–175. It is said to be 12,800 lines long, and contains the passage: 'The sun falls in love with Bianca.

[4] Roscoe, *Leone X.* ed. Bossi, viii. 184. A poem in a similar style, xii.

Hadrian of Corneto (p. 119). Brilliant descriptions of hunting-parties are found in Ercole Strozza, in the above-mentioned Hadrian, and in others; and it is a pity that the modern reader should allow himself to be irritated or repelled by the adulation with which they are doubtless filled. The masterly treatment and the considerable historical value of many of these most graceful poems, guarantee to them a longer existence than many popular works of our own day are likely to attain.

In general, these poems are good in proportion to the sparing use of the sentimental and the general. Some of the smaller epic poems, even of recognised masters, unintentionally produce, by the ill-timed introduction of mythological elements, an impression that is indescribably ludicrous. Such, for instance, is the lament of Ercole Strozza [1] on Cæsar Borgia. We there listen to the complaint of Rome, who had set all her hopes on the Spanish Popes Calixtus III. and Alexander VI., and who saw her promised deliverer in Cæsar. His history is related down to the catastrophe of 1503. The poet then asks the Muse what were the counsels of the gods at that moment,[2] and Crato tells how, upon Olympus, Pallas took the part of the Spaniards, Venus of the Italians, how both then embrace the knees of Jupiter, how thereupon he kisses them, soothes them, and explains to them that he can do nothing against the fate woven by the Parcæ, but that the divine promises will be fulfilled by the child of the House of Este-Borgia.[3] After relating the fabulous origin of both families, he declares that he can confer immortality on Cæsar as little as he could once, in spite of all entreaties, on Memnon or Achilles; and concludes with the consoling assurance that Cæsar, before his own death, will destroy many people in war. Mars then hastens to Naples to stir up war and confusion, while Pallas goes to Nepi, and there appears to the dying Cæsar under the form of Alexander

130. The poem of Angilbert on the Court of Charles the Great curiously reminds us of the Renaissance. Comp. Pertz. *Monum.* ii.

[1] Strozzi, *Poetae*, p. 31 sqq. 'Caesaris Borgiae ducis epicedium.'

[2] 'Pontificem addiderat, flammis lustralibus omneis
Corporis ablutum labes, Dis Juppiter ipsis,' etc.

[3] This was Ercole II. of Ferrara, b. April 4, 1508, probably either shortly before or shortly after the composition of this poem. 'Nascere, magne puer, matri expectate patrique,' is said near the end.

VI. After giving him the good advice to submit to his fate and be satisfied with the glory of his name, the papal goddess vanishes 'like a bird.'

Yet we should needlessly deprive ourselves of an enjoyment, which is sometimes very great, if we threw aside everything in which classical mythology plays a more or less appropriate part. Here, as in painting and sculpture, art has often ennobled what is in itself purely conventional. The beginnings of parody are also to be found by lovers of that class of literature (pp. 159 sqq.) *e.g.* in the Macaroneid—to which the comic Feast of the Gods, by Giovanni Bellini, forms an early parallel.

Many, too, of the narrative poems in hexameters are merely exercises, or adaptations of histories in prose, which latter the reader will prefer, where he can find them. At last, everything—every quarrel and every ceremony—came to be put into verse, and this even by the German humanists of the Reformation.[1] And yet it would be unfair to attribute this to mere want of occupation, or to an excessive facility in stringing verses together. In Italy, at all events, it was rather due to an abundant sense of style, as is further proved by the mass of contemporary reports, histories, and even pamphlets, in the 'terza rima.' Just as Niccolò da Uzzano published his scheme for a new constitution, Macchiavelli his view of the history of his own time, a third, the life of Savonarola, and a fourth, the siege of Piombino by Alfonso the Great,[2] in this difficult metre, in order to produce a stronger effect, so did many others feel the need of hexameters, in order to win their special public. What was then tolerated and demanded, in this shape, is best shown by the didactic poetry of the time. Its popularity in the fifteenth century is something astounding. The most distinguished humanists were ready to celebrate in

[1] Comp. the collections of the *Scriptores* by Schardius, Freher, &c., and see above p. 126, note 1.

[2] Uzzano, see *Archiv.* iv. i. 296. Macchiavelli, *i Decennali.* The life of Savonarola, under the title *Cedrus Libani*, by Fra Benedetto. *Assedio di Piombino*, Murat. xxv. We may quote as a parallel the *Teuerdank* and other northern works in rhyme (new ed. of that by Haltaus, Quedlinb. and Leipzig, 1836). The popular historical songs of the Germans, which were produced in great abundance in the fifteenth and sixteenth centuries, may be compared with these Italian poems.

Latin hexameters the most commonplace, ridiculous, or disgusting themes, such as the making of gold, the game of chess, the management of silkworms, astrology, and venereal diseases (*morbus gallicus*), to say nothing of many long Italian poems of the same kind. Nowadays this class of poems is condemned unread, and how far, as a matter of fact, they are really worth the reading, we are unable to say.[1] One thing is certain, that epochs far above our own in the sense of beauty—the Renaissance and the Greco-Roman world—could not dispense with this form of poetry. It may be urged in reply, that it is not the lack of a sense of beauty, but the greater seriousness and the altered method of scientific treatment which renders the poetical form inappropriate, on which point it is unnecessary to enter.

One of these didactic works has of late years been occasionally republished[2]—the 'Zodiac of Life,' by Marcellus Palingenius (Pier Angello Manzolli), a secret adherent of Protestantism at Ferrara, written about 1528. With the loftiest speculations on God, virtue, and immortality, the writer connects the discussion of many questions of practical life, and is, on this account, an authority of some weight in the history of morals. On the whole, however, his work must be considered as lying outside the boundaries of the Renaissance, as is further indicated by the fact that, in harmony with the serious didactic purpose of the poem, allegory tends to supplant mythology.

But it was in lyric, and more particularly in elegiac poetry, that the poet-scholar came nearest to antiquity; and next to this, in epigram.

In the lighter style, Catullus exercised a perfect fascination over the Italians. Not a few elegant Latin madrigals, not a

[1] We may remark of the *Coltivazione* of L. Alamanni, written in Italian 'versi sciolti,' that all the really poetical and enjoyable passages are directly or indirectly borrowed from the ancients (an old ed., Paris, 1540; new ed. of the works of A., 2 vols., Florence, 1867).

[2] E.g. by C. G. Weise, Leipzig, 1832. The work, divided into twelve books, named after the twelve constellations, is dedicated to Hercules II. of Ferrara. In the dedication occur the remarkable words: 'Nam quem alium patronum in totâ Italiâ invenire possum, cui musae cordisunt, qui carmen sibi oblatum aut intelligat, aut examine recto expendere sciat?' Palingenius uses 'Juppiter' and 'Deus' indiscriminately.

few little satires and malicious epistles, are mere adaptations from him; and the death of parrots and lapdogs is bewailed, even where there is no verbal imitation, in precisely the tone and style of the verses on Lesbia's Sparrow. There are short poems of this sort, the date of which even a critic would be unable to fix,[1] in the absence of positive evidence that they are works of the fifteenth and sixteenth centuries.

On the other hand, we can find scarcely an ode in the Sapphic or Alcaic metre, which does not clearly betray its modern origin. This is shown mostly by a rhetorical verbosity, rare in antiquity before the time of Statius, and by a singular want of the lyrical concentration which is indispensable to this style of poetry. Single passages in an ode, sometimes two or three strophes together, may look like an ancient fragment; but a longer extract will seldom keep this character throughout. And where it does so, as, for instance, in the fine Ode to Venus, by Andrea Navagero, it is easy to detect a simple paraphrase of ancient masterpieces.[2] Some of the ode-writers take the saints for their subject, and invoke them in verses tastefully modelled after the pattern of analogous odes of Horace and Catullus. This is the manner of Navagero, in the Ode to the Archangel Gabriel, and particularly of Sannazaro (p. 260), who goes still further in his appropriation of pagan sentiment. He celebrates above all his patron saint,[3] whose chapel was attached to his lovely villa on the shores of Posilippo, 'there where the waves of the sea drink up the stream from the rocks, and surge against the walls of the little sanctuary.' His delight is in the annual feast of S. Nazzaro, and the branches and garlands with which the chapel is hung on this day, seem to him like sacrificial gifts. Full of sorrow, and far off in exile, at St. Nazaire, on the banks of the Loire, with the banished Frederick of Aragon, he brings wreaths of box and

[1] L. B. Alberti's first comic poem, which purported to be by an author Lepidus, was long considered as a work of antiquity.

[2] In this case (see below, p. 266, note 2) of the introduction to Lucretius, and of Horace, *Od.* iv. 1.

[3] The invocation of a patron saint is an essentially pagan undertaking, as has been noticed at p. 57. On a more serious occasion, comp. Sannazaro's Elegy: 'In festo die divi Nazarii martyris.' Sann. *Elegiae*, 1535, fol. 166 sqq.

oak leaves to his patron saint on the same anniversary, thinking of former years, when all the youth of Posilippo used to come forth to greet him on flower-hung boats, and praying that he may return home.[1]

Perhaps the most deceptive likeness to the classical style is borne by a class of poems in elegiacs or hexameters, whose subject ranges from elegy, strictly so-called, to epigram. As the humanists dealt most freely of all with the text of the Roman elegiac poets, so they felt themselves most at home in imitating them. The elegy of Navagero addressed to the night, like other poems of the same age and kind, is full of points which remind us of his models; but it has the finest antique ring about it. Indeed Navagero[2] always begins by choosing a truly poetical subject, which he then treats, not with servile imitation, but with masterly freedom, in the style of the Anthology, of Ovid, of Catullus, or of the Virgilian eclogues. He makes a sparing use of mythology, only, for instance, to introduce a sketch of country life, in a prayer to Ceres and other rural divinities. An address to his country, on his return from an embassy to Spain, though left unfinished, might have been worthy of a place beside the 'Bella Italia, amate sponde' of Vincenzo Monti, if the rest had been equal to this beginning:

> 'Salve, cura Deûm, mundi felicior ora,
> Formosae Veneris dulces salvete recessus;
> Ut vos post tantos animi mentisque labores
> Aspicio lustroque libens, ut munere vestro
> Sollicitas toto depello e pectore curas!'[3]

The elegiac or hexametral form was that in which all higher sentiment found expression, both the noblest patriotic enthusiasm (see p. 119, the elegy on Julius II.) and the most

[1] Si satis ventos tolerasse et imbres
Ac minas fatorum hominumque fraudes
Da Pater tecto salientem avito
Cernere fumum!

[2] *Andr. Naugerii, Orationes duae carminaque aliquot*, Venet. 1530, 4º. The few 'Carmina' are to be found partly or wholly in the *Deliciae*. On N. and his death, see Pier. Val. *De inf. lit.* ed. Menken, 326 sqq.

[3] Compare Petrarch's greeting to Italy, written more than a century earlier (1353) in *Petr. Carmina Minora*, ed. Rossetti, ii. pp. 266 sqq.

elaborate eulogies on the ruling houses,[1] as well as the tender melancholy of a Tibullus. Francesco Mario Molza, who rivals Statius and Martial in his flattery of Clement VII. and the Farnesi, gives us in his elegy to his 'comrades,' written from a sick-bed, thoughts on death as beautiful and genuinely antique as can be found in any of the poets of antiquity, and this without borrowing anything worth speaking of from them.[2] The spirit and range of the Roman elegy were best understood and reproduced by Sannazaro, and no other writer of his time offers us so varied a choice of good poems in this style as he. We shall have occasion now and then to speak of some of these elegies in reference to the matter they treat of.

The Latin epigram finally became in those days an affair of serious importance, since a few clever lines, engraved on a monument or quoted with laughter in society, could lay the foundation of a scholar's celebrity. This tendency showed itself early in Italy. When it was known that Guido della Polenta wished to erect a monument at Dante's grave, epitaphs poured in from all directions,[3] 'written by such as wished to *show themselves*, or to honour the dead poet, or to win the favour of Polenta.' On the tomb of the Archbishop Giovanni Visconti (d. 1354), in the Cathedral at Milan, we read at the foot of 36 hexameters: 'Master Gabrius de Zamoreis of Parma, Doctor of Laws, wrote these verses.' In course of time, chiefly under the influence of Martial, and partly of Catullus, an extensive literature of this sort was formed. It was held the greatest of all triumphs, when an epigram was mistaken for a genuine copy from some old marble,[4] or when it was so good that all Italy learned it by heart, as happened in the case of some of Bembo's. When the Venetian government paid San-

[1] To form a notion of what Leo X. could swallow, see the prayer of Guido Postumo Silvestri to Christ, the Virgin, and all the Saints, that they would long spare this 'numen' to earth, since heaven had enough of such already. Printed in Roscoe, *Leone X.* ed. Bossi, v. 337.

[2] Molza's *Poesie volgari e Latine*, ed. by Pierantonio Serassi, Bergamo 1747.

[3] Boccaccio, *Vita di Dante*, p. 36.

[4] Sannazaro ridicules a man who importuned him with such forgeries: 'Sint vetera haec aliis, mî nova semper erunt.' (Ad Rufum, *Opera*, 1535, fol. 41 *a*.)

nazaro 600 ducats for a eulogy in three distichs,[1] no one thought it an act of generous prodigality. The epigram was prized for what it was, in truth, to all the educated classes of that age—the concentrated essence of fame. Nor, on the other hand, was any man then so powerful as to be above the reach of a satirical epigram, and even the most powerful needed, for every inscription which they set before the public eye, the aid of careful and learned scholars, lest some blunder or other should qualify it for a place in the collections of ludicrous epitaphs.[2] The epigraph and the epigram were branches of the same pursuit; the reproduction of the former was based on a diligent study of ancient monuments.

The city of epigrams and inscriptions was, above all others, Rome. In this state without hereditary honours, each man had to look after his own immortality, and at the same time found the epigram an effective weapon against his competitors. Pius II. counts with satisfaction the distichs which his chief poet Campanus wrote on any event of his government which could be turned to poetical account. Under the following popes satirical epigrams came into fashion, and reached, in the opposition to Alexander VI. and his family, the highest pitch of defiant invective. Sannazaro, it is true, wrote his verses in a place of comparative safety, but others in the immediate neighbourhood of the court ventured on the most reckless attacks (p. 112). On one occasion when eight threatening distichs were found fastened to the door of the library,[3] Alexander strengthened his guard by 800 men; we can imagine what he would have done to the poet if he had caught him.

1 'De mirabili urbe Venetiis' (*Opera*, fol. 38 *b*):

Viderat Adriacis Venetam Neptunus in undis
  Stare urbem et toto ponere jura mari:
Nunc mihi Tarpejas quantum vis Juppiter arceis
  Objice et illa tui mœnia Martis ait,
Si pelago Tybrim praefers, urbem aspice utramque
  Illam homines dices, hanc posuisse deos.

2 *Lettere de' principi*, i. 88, 98.

3 Malipiero, *Ann. Veneti*, *Arch. Stor.* vii. i. p. 508. At the end we read, in reference to the bull as the arms of the Borgia:

'Merge, Tyber, vitulos animosas ultor in undas;
  Bos cadat inferno victima magna Jovi!'

Under Leo X., Latin epigrams were like daily bread. For complimenting or for reviling the pope, for punishing enemies and victims, named or unnamed, for real or imaginary subjects of wit, malice, grief, or contemplation, no form was held more suitable. On the famous group of the Virgin with Saint Anna and the Child, which Andrea Sansovino carved for S. Agostino, no less than 120 persons wrote Latin verses, not so much, it is true, from devotion, as from regard for the patron who ordered the work.[1] This man, Johann Goritz of Luxemburg, papal referendary of petitions, not only held a religious service on the feast of Saint Anna, but gave a great literary dinner in his garden on the slopes of the Capitol. It was then worth while to pass in review, in a long poem 'De poetis urbanis,' the whole crowd of singers who sought their fortune at the court of Leo. This was done by Franciscus Arsillus[2]—a man who needed the patronage neither of pope nor prince, and who dared to speak his mind, even against his colleagues. The epigram survived the pontificate of Paul III. only in a few rare echoes, while the epigraph continued to flourish till the seventeenth century, when it perished finally of bombast.

In Venice, also, this form of poetry had a history of its own,

[1] On the whole affair, see Roscoe, *Leone X.*, ed. Bossi, vii. 211, viii. 214 sqq. The printed collection, now rare, of these *Coryciana* of the year 1524 contains only the Latin poems; Vasari saw another book in the possession of the Augustinians in which were sonnets. So contagious was the habit of affixing poems, that the group had to be protected by a railing, and even hidden altogether. The change of Goritz into 'Corycius senex' is suggested by Virgil, *Georg.* iv. 127. For the miserable end of the man at the sack of Rome, see Pierio Valeriano, *De infelic. literat.* ed. Menken, p. 369.

[2] The work appeared first in the *Coryciana*, with introductions by Silvanus and Corycius himself; also reprinted in the Appendices to Roscoe, *Leone X.* ed. Bossi, and in the *Deliciae.* Comp Paul. Jov. *Elogia*, speaking of Arsillus. Further, for the great number of the epigrammatists, see Lil. Greg. Gyraldus, l. c. One of the most biting pens was Marcantonio Casanova. Among the less known, Jo. Thomas Muscanius (see *Deliciae*) deserves mention. On Casanova, see Pier. Valer. *De infel. lit.* ed. Menken, p. 376 sqq.; and Paul. Jov. *Elogia*, p. 142 sqq., who says of him: 'Nemo autem eo simplicitate ac innocentiâ vitae melior;' Arsillus (l. c.) speaks of his 'placidos sales.' Some few of his poems in the *Coryciana*, J. 3 *a* sqq. L. 1 *a*, L. 4 *b*.

which we are able to trace with the help of the 'Venezia' of Francesco Sansovino. A standing task for the epigram-writers was offered by the mottos (Brievi) on the pictures of the Doges in the great hall of the ducal palace—two or four hexameters, setting forth the most noteworthy facts in the government of each.[1] In addition to this, the tombs of the Doges in the fourteenth century bore short inscriptions in prose, recording merely facts, and beside them turgid hexameters or leonine verses. In the fifteenth century more care was taken with the style; in the sixteenth century it is seen at its best; and then soon after came pointless antithesis, prosopopœia, false pathos, praise of abstract qualities—in a word, affectation and bombast. A good many traces of satire can be detected, and veiled criticism of the living is implied in open praise of the dead. At a much later period we find a few instances of a deliberate recurrence to the old, simple style.

Architectural works and decorative works in general were constructed with a view to receiving inscriptions, often in frequent repetition; while the Northern Gothic seldom, and with difficulty, offered a suitable place for them, and in sepulchral monuments, for example, left free only the most exposed parts—namely the edges.

By what has been said hitherto we have, perhaps, failed to convince the reader of the characteristic value of this Latin poetry of the Italians. Our task was rather to indicate its position and necessity in the history of civilisation. In its own day, a caricature of it appeared[2]—the so-called maccaronic poetry. The masterpiece of this style, the 'opus maccaronicorum,' was written by Merlinus Coccaius (Teofilo Folengo of Mantua). We shall now and then have occasion to refer to the matter of this poem. As to the form—hexameter and other verses, made up of Latin words and Italian words with Latin endings—its comic effect lies chiefly in the fact that

[1] Marin Sanudo, in the *Vite de' duchi di Venezia*, Murat. xii. quotes them regularly.

[2] Scardeonius, *De urb. Patav. antiq.* (Graev. thes. vi. 11, col. 270), names as the inventor a certain Odaxius of Padua, living about the middle of the fifteenth century. Mixed verses of Latin and the language of the country are found much earlier in many parts of Europe.

these combinations sound like so many slips of the tongue, or the effusions of an over-hasty Latin 'improvisatore.' The German imitations do not give the smallest notion of this effect.

CHAPTER XI.

FALL OF THE HUMANISTS IN THE SIXTEENTH CENTURY.

After a brilliant succession of poet-scholars had, since the beginning of the fourteenth century, filled Italy and the world with the worship of antiquity, had determined the forms of education and culture, had often taken the lead in political affairs and had, to no small extent, reproduced ancient literature—at length in the sixteenth century, before their doctrines and scholarship had lost hold of the public mind, the whole class fell into deep and general disgrace. Though they still served as models to the poets, historians, and orators, personally no one would consent to be reckoned of their number. To the two chief accusations against them—that of malicious self-conceit, and that of abominable profligacy—a third charge of irreligion was now loudly added by the rising powers of the Counter-reformation.

Why, it may be asked, were not these reproaches, whether true or false, heard sooner? As a matter of fact, they were heard at a very early period, but the effect they produced was insignificant, for the plain reason that men were far too dependent on the scholars for their knowledge of antiquity—that the scholars were personally the possessors and diffusers of ancient culture. But the spread of printed editions of the classics,[1] and of large and well-arranged hand-books and dictionaries, went far to free the people from the necessity of personal intercourse with the humanists, and, as soon as they could be but partly dispensed with, the change in popular feeling became manifest. It was a change under which the good and bad suffered indiscriminately.

The first to make these charges were certainly the humanists

[1] It must not be forgotten that they were very soon printed with both the old Scholia and modern commentaries.

themselves. Of all men who ever formed a class, they had the least sense of their common interests, and least respected what there was of this sense. All means were held lawful, if one of them saw a chance of supplanting another. From literary discussion they passed with astonishing suddenness to the fiercest and the most groundless vituperation. Not satisfied with refuting, they sought to annihilate an opponent. Something of this must be put to the account of their position and circumstances; we have seen how fiercely the age, whose loudest spokesmen they were, was borne to and fro by the passion for glory and the passion for satire. Their position, too, in practical life was one that they had continually to fight for. In such a temper they wrote and spoke and described one another. Poggio's works alone contain dirt enough to create a prejudice against the whole class—and these 'Opera Poggii' were just those most often printed, on the north, as well as on the south, side of the Alps. We must take care not to rejoice too soon, when we meet among these men a figure which seems immaculate; on further inquiry there is always a danger of meeting with some foul charge, which, even when it is incredible, still discolours the picture. The mass of indecent Latin poems in circulation, and such things as the ribaldry on the subject of his own family, in Pontano's dialogue, 'Antonius,' did the rest to discredit the class. The sixteenth century was not only familiar with all these ugly symptoms, but had also grown tired of the type of the humanist. These men had to pay both for the misdeeds they had done, and for the excess of honour which had hitherto fallen to their lot. Their evil fate willed it that the greatest poet of the nation wrote of them in a tone of calm and sovereign contempt.[1]

Of the reproaches which combined to excite so much hatred, many were only too well founded. Yet a clear and unmistakable tendency to strictness in matters of religion and morality was alive in many of the philologists, and it is a proof of small knowledge of the period, if the whole class is condemned. Yet many, and among them the loudest speakers, were guilty.

Three facts explain, and perhaps diminish their guilt: the overflowing excess of favour and fortune, when the luck was

[1] Ariosto, *Satira*, vii. Date 1531.

on their side: the uncertainty of the future, in which luxury or misery depended on the caprice of a patron or the malice of an enemy; and finally, the misleading influence of antiquity. This undermined their morality, without giving them its own instead; and in religious matters, since they could never think of accepting the positive belief in the old gods, it affected them only on the negative and sceptical side. Just because they conceived of antiquity dogmatically—that is, took it as the model for all thought and action—its influence was here pernicious. But that an age existed, which idolised the ancient world and its products with an exclusive devotion, was not the fault of individuals. It was the work of a historical providence, and all the culture of the ages which have followed, and of the ages to come, rests upon the fact that it was so, and that all the ends of life but this one were then deliberately put aside.

The career of the humanists was, as a rule, of such a kind that only the strongest characters could pass through it unscathed. The first danger came, in some cases, from the parents, who sought to turn a precocious child into a miracle of learning,[1] with an eye to his future position in that class which then was supreme. Youthful prodigies, however, seldom rise above a certain level; or, if they do, are forced to achieve their further progress and development at the cost of the bitterest trials. For an ambitious youth, the fame and the brilliant position of the humanists were a perilous temptation; it seemed to him that he too 'through inborn pride could no longer regard the low and common things of life.' He was thus led to plunge into a life of excitement and vicissitude, in which exhausting studies, tutorships, secretaryships, professor-

[1] Of such children we meet with several, yet I cannot give an instance in which they were demonstrably so treated. The youthful prodigy Giulio Campagnola was not one of those who were forced with an ambitious object. Comp. Scardeonius, *De urb. Patav. antiq.* in Graev. thes. vi. 3, col. 276. For the similar case of Cecchino Bracci, d. 1445 in his fifteenth year, comp. Trucchi, *Poesie Ital. inedite*, iii. p. 229. The father of Cardano tried 'memoriam artificialem instillare,' and taught him, when still a child, the astrology of the Arabians. See Cardanus, *De propria vita*, cap. 34. Manoello may be added to the list, unless we are to take his expression, 'At the age of six years I am as good as at eighty,' as a meaningless phrase. Comp. *Litbl. des Orients*, 1843, p. 21.

ships, offices in princely households, mortal enmities and perils, luxury and beggary, boundless admiration and boundless contempt, followed confusedly one upon the other, and in which the most solid worth and learning were often pushed aside by superficial impudence. But the worst of all was, that the position of the humanist was almost incompatible with a fixed home, since it either made frequent changes of dwelling necessary for a livelihood, or so affected the mind of the individual that he could never be happy for long in one place. He grew tired of the people, and had no peace among the enmities which he excited, while the people themselves in their turn demanded something new (p. 211). Much as this life reminds us of the Greek sophists of the Empire, as described to us by Philostratus, yet the position of the sophists was more favourable. They often had money, or could more easily do without it than the humanists, and as professional teachers of rhetoric, rather than men of learning, their life was freer and simpler. But the scholar of the Renaissance was forced to combine great learning with the power of resisting the influence of ever-changing pursuits and situations. Add to this the deadening effect of licentious excess, and—since do what he might, the worst was believed of him—a total indifference to the moral laws recognised by others. Such men can hardly be conceived to exist without an inordinate pride. They needed it, if only to keep their heads above water, and were confirmed in it by the admiration which alternated with hatred in the treatment they received from the world. They are the most striking examples and victims of an unbridled subjectivity.

The attacks and the satirical pictures began, as we have said, at an early period. For all strongly marked individuality, for every kind of distinction, a corrective was at hand in the national taste for ridicule. And in this case the men themselves offered abundant and terrible materials which satire had but to make use of. In the fifteenth century, Battista Mantovano, in discoursing of the seven monsters,[1] includes the humanists, with many others, under the head 'Superbia.' He describes how, fancying themselves children of Apollo, they walk along with affected solemnity and with sullen, malicious

[1] Bapt. Mantuan. *De calamitatibus temporum*, l. i.

looks, now gazing at their own shadow, now brooding over the popular praise they hunted after, like cranes in search of food. But in the sixteenth century the indictment was presented in full. Besides Ariosto, their own historian Gyraldus[1] gives evidence of this, whose treatise, written under Leo X., was probably revised about the year 1540. Warning examples from ancient and modern times of the moral disorder and the wretched existence of the scholars meet us in astonishing abundance, and along with these accusations of the most serious nature are brought formally against them. Among these are anger, vanity, obstinacy, self-adoration, a dissolute private life, immorality of all descriptions, heresy, atheism; further, the habit of speaking without conviction, a sinister influence on government, pedantry of speech, thanklessness towards teachers. and abject flattery of the great, who first give the scholar a taste of their favours and then leave him to starve. The description is closed by a reference to the golden age, when no such thing as science existed on the earth. Of these charges, that of heresy soon became the most dangerous, and Gyraldus himself, when he afterwards republished a perfectly harmless youthful work,[2] was compelled to take refuge beneath the mantle of Duke Hercules II. of Ferrara,[3] since men now had the upper hand who held that people had better spend their time on Christian themes than on mythological researches. He justifies himself on the ground that the latter, on the contrary, were at such a time almost the only harmless branches of study, as they deal with subjects of a perfectly neutral character.

But if it is the duty of the historian to seek for evidence in which moral judgment is tempered by human sympathy, he will find no authority comparable in value to the work so often quoted of Pierio Valeriano,[4] 'On the Infelicity of the Scholar.'

[1] Lil. Greg. Gyraldus, *Progymnasma adversus literas et literatos. Opp.* ed. Basil. 1580, ii. 422–445. Dedications 1540–1541; the work itself addressed to Giov. Franc. Pico, and therefore finished before 1533.

[2] Lil. Greg. Gyraldus, *Hercules.* The dedication is a striking evidence of the first threatening movements of the Inquisition.

[3] He passed, as we have seen, for the last protector of the scholars.

[4] *De infelicitate literatorum.* On the editions, see above, p. 86, note 4. Pier. Val., after leaving Rome, lived long in a good position as professor

It was written under the gloomy impressions left by the sack of Rome, which seems to the writer, not only the direct cause of untold misery to the men of learning, but, as it were, the fulfilment of an evil destiny which had long pursued them. Pierio is here led by a simple and, on the whole, just feeling. He does not introduce a special power, which plagued the men of genius on account of their genius, but he states facts, in which an unlucky chance often wears the aspect of fatality. Not wishing to write a tragedy or to refer events to the conflict of higher powers, he is content to lay before us the scenes of every-day life. We are introduced to men, who in times of trouble lose, first their incomes, and then their places; to others, who in trying to get two appointments, miss both; to unsociable misers, who carry about their money sewn into their clothes, and die mad when they are robbed of it; to others, who accept well-paid offices, and then sicken with a melancholy longing for their lost freedom. We read how some died young of a plague or fever, and how the writings which had cost them so much toil were burnt with their bed and clothes; how others lived in terror of the murderous threats of their colleagues; how one was slain by a covetous servant, and another caught by highwaymen on a journey, and left to pine in a dungeon, because unable to pay his ransom. Many died of unspoken grief for the insults they received and the prizes of which they were defrauded. We are told of the death of a Venetian, because his son, a youthful prodigy, was dead; and the mother and brothers followed, as if the lost child drew them all after him. Many, especially Florentines, ended their lives by suicide;[1] others through the secret justice of a tyrant. Who, after all, is happy?—and by what means? By blunting all feeling for such misery? One of the speakers in the dialogue in which Pierio clothed his argument, can give an answer to these questions—the illustrious Gasparo Contarini, at the mention of whose name we turn with the expectation to hear at least something of the

at Padua. At the end of his work he expresses the hope that Charles V. and Clement VII. would bring about a better time for the scholars.

[1] Comp. Dante, *Inferno*, xiii. 58 sqq., especially 93 sqq., where Petrus de Vineis speaks of his own suicide.

truest and deepest which was then thought on such matters. As a type of the happy scholar, he mentions Fra Urbano Valeriano of Belluno,[1] who was for years teacher of Greek at Venice, who visited Greece and the East, and towards the close of his life travelled, now through this country, now through that, without ever mounting a horse; who never had a penny of his own, rejected all honours and distinctions, and after a gay old age, died in his eighty-fourth year, without, if we except a fall from a ladder, having ever known an hour of sickness. And what was the difference between such a man and the humanists? The latter had more free will, more subjectivity, than they could turn to purposes of happiness. The mendicant friar, who had lived from his boyhood in the monastery, and never eaten or slept except by rule, ceased to feel the compulsion under which he lived. Through the power of this habit he led, amid all outward hardships, a life of inward peace, by which he impressed his hearers far more than by his teaching. Looking at him, they could believe that it depends on ourselves whether we bear up against misfortune or surrender to it. 'Amid want and toil he was happy, because he willed to be so, because he had contracted no evil habits, was not capricious, inconstant, immoderate; but was always contented with little or nothing.' If we heard Contarini himself, religious motives would no doubt play a part in the argument—but the practical philosopher in sandals speaks plainly enough. An allied character, but placed in other circumstances, is that of Fabio Calvi of Ravenna, the commentator of Hippocrates.[2] He lived to a great age in Rome, eating only pulse 'like the Pythagoreans,' and dwelt in a hovel little better than the tub of Diogenes. Of the pension, which Pope Leo gave him, he spent enough to keep body and soul together, and gave the rest away. He was not a healthy man, like Fra Urbano, nor is it likely that, like him, he died with a smile on his lips. At the age of ninety, in the sack of Rome, he was dragged away by the Spaniards, who hoped for a ransom, and died of hunger in a

[1] Pier. Valer. pp. 397 sqq., 402. He was the uncle of the writer.

[2] Cœlii Calcagnini, *Opera*, ed. Basil. 1544, p. 101, in the Seventh Book of the Epistles, No. 27, letter to Jacob Ziegler. Comp. Pierio Val. *De inf. lit.* ed. Menken, p. 369 sqq.

hospital. But his name has passed into the kingdom of the immortals, for Raphael loved the old man like a father, and honoured him as a teacher, and came to him for advice in all things. Perhaps they discoursed chiefly of the projected restoration of ancient Rome (p. 184), perhaps of still higher matters. Who can tell what a share Fabio may have had in the conception of the School of Athens, and in other great works of the master?

We would gladly close this part of our essay with the picture of some pleasing and winning character. Pomponius Laetus, of whom we shall briefly speak, is known to us principally through the letter of his pupil Sabellicus,[1] in which an antique colouring is purposely given to his character. Yet many of its features are clearly recognisable. He was (p. 251) a bastard of the House of the Neapolitan Sanseverini, princes of Salerno, whom he nevertheless refused to recognise, writing, in reply to an invitation to live with them, the famous letter: 'Pomponius Laetus cognatis et propinquis suis, salutem. Quod petitis fieri non potest. Valete.' An insignificant little figure, with small, quick eyes, and quaint dress, he lived during the last decades of the fifteenth century, as professor in the University of Rome, either in his cottage in a garden on the Esquiline hill, or in his vineyard on the Quirinal. In the one he bred his ducks and fowls; the other he cultivated according to the strictest precepts of Cato, Varro, and Columella. He spent his holidays in fishing or bird-catching in the Campagna, or in feasting by some shady spring or on the banks of the Tiber. Wealth and luxury he despised. Free himself from envy and uncharitable speech, he would not suffer them in others. It was only against the hierarchy that he gave his tongue free play, and passed, till his latter years, for a scorner of religion altogether. He was involved in the persecution of the humanists begun by Pope Paul II., and surrendered to this pontiff by the Venetians; but no means could be found to wring unworthy confessions from him. He was afterwards befriended and supported by popes and prelates, and when his

[1] *M. Ant. Sabellici Opera*, Epist. l. xi. fol. 56. See, too, the biography in the *Elogia* of Paolo Giovio, p. 76 sqq. The former appeared separately at Strasburg in 1510, under the title Sabellicus: *Vita Pomponii Laeti.*

house was plundered in the disturbances under Sixtus IV., more was collected for him than he had lost. No teacher was more conscientious. Before daybreak he was to be seen descending the Esquiline with his lantern, and on reaching his lecture-room found it always filled to overflowing with pupils who had come at midnight to secure a place. A stutter compelled him to speak with care, but his delivery was even and effective. His few works give evidence of careful writing. No scholar treated the text of ancient authors more soberly and accurately. The remains of antiquity which surrounded him in Rome touched him so deeply, that he would stand before them as if entranced, or would suddenly burst into tears at the sight of them. As he was ready to lay aside his own studies in order to help others, he was much loved and had many friends; and at his death, even Alexander VI. sent his courtiers to follow the corpse, which was carried by the most distinguished of his pupils. The funeral service in the Araceli was attended by forty bishops and by all the foreign ambassadors.

It was Laetus who introduced and conducted the representations of ancient, chiefly Plautine, plays in Rome (p. 255). Every year, he celebrated the anniversary of the foundation of the city by a festival, at which his friends and pupils recited speeches and poems. Such meetings were the origin of what acquired, and long retained, the name of the Roman Academy. It was simply a free union of individuals, and was connected with no fixed institution. Besides the occasions mentioned, it met [1] at the invitation of a patron, or to celebrate the memory of a deceased member, as of Platina. At such times, a prelate belonging to the academy would first say mass; Pomponio would then ascend the pulpit and deliver a speech; some one else would then follow him and recite an elegy. The customary banquet, with declamations and recitations, concluded the festival, whether joyous or serious, and the academicians, notably Platina himself, early acquired the reputation of epicures.[2] At other times, the guests performed farces in the old Atellan style. As a free association of very varied elements,

[1] Jac. Volaterran. *Diar. Rom.* in Muratori. xxiii. col. 161, 171, 185. *Anecdota literaria*, ii. pp. 168 sqq.

[2] Paul. Jov. *De Romanis piscibus*, cap. 17 and 34.

the academy lasted in its original form down to the sack of Rome, and included among its guests Angelus Coloccius, Joh. Corycius (p. 269) and others. Its precise value as an element in the intellectual life of the people is as hard to estimate as that of any other social union of the same kind; yet a man like Sadoleto[1] reckoned it among the most precious memories of his youth. A large number of other academies appeared and passed away in many Italian cities, according to the number and significance of the humanists living in them, and to the patronage bestowed by the great and wealthy. Of these we may mention the Academy of Naples, of which Jovianus Pontanus was the centre, and which sent out a colony to Lecce,[2] and that of Pordenone, which formed the court of the Condottiere Alviano. The circle of Ludovico Moro, and its peculiar importance for that prince, has been already spoken of (p. 42).

About the middle of the sixteenth century, these associations seem to have undergone a complete change. The humanists, driven in other spheres from their commanding position, and viewed askance by the men of the Counter-reformation, lost the control of the academies: and here, as elsewhere, Latin poetry was replaced by Italian. Before long every town of the least importance had its academy, with some strange, fantastic name,[3] and its own endowment and subscriptions. Besides the recitation of verses, the new institutions inherited from their predecessors the regular banquets and the representation of plays, sometimes acted by the members themselves, sometimes under their direction by young amateurs, and sometimes by paid players. The fate of the Italian stage, and afterwards of the opera, was long in the hands of these associations.

[1] Sadoleti, Epist. 106, of the year 1529.

[2] Anton. Galatei, Epist. 10 and 12, in Mai, *Spicileg. Rom.* vol. viii.

[3] This was the case even before the middle of the century. Comp. Lil. Greg. Gyraldus, *De poetis nostri temp.* ii.

PART IV.

THE DISCOVERY OF THE WORLD AND OF MAN.

CHAPTER I.

JOURNEYS OF THE ITALIANS.

Freed from the countless bonds which elsewhere in Europe checked progress, having reached a high degree of individual development and been schooled by the teachings of antiquity, the Italian mind now turned to the discovery of the outward universe, and to the representation of it in speech and in form.

On the journeys of the Italians to distant parts of the world, we can here make but a few general observations. The crusades had opened unknown distances to the European mind, and awakened in all the passion for travel and adventure. It may be hard to indicate precisely the point where this passion allied itself with, or became the servant of, the thirst for knowledge; but it was in Italy that this was first and most completely the case. Even in the crusades the interest of the Italians was wider than that of other nations, since they already were a naval power and had commercial relations with the East. From time immemorial the Mediterranean sea had given to the nations that dwelt on its shores mental impulses different from those which governed the peoples of the North; and never, from the very structure of their character, could the Italians be adventurers in the sense which the word bore among the Teutons. After they were once at home in all the eastern harbours of the Mediterranean, it was natural that the most enterprising among them should be led to join that vast international movement of the Mohammedans which there found its outlet. A new half of the world lay, as it were, freshly discovered before them. Or, like Polo of Venice, they were caught in the current of the Mongolian peoples, and carried on to the steps of the throne of the Great Khan. At an early period, we find Italians sharing in the discoveries made in the Atlantic ocean; it was the Genoese who, in the 13th century, found the

Canary Islands.[1] In the same year, 1291, when Ptolemais, the last remnant of the Christian East, was lost, it was again the Genoese who made the first known attempt to find a sea-passage to the East Indies.[2] Columbus himself is but the greatest of a long list of Italians who, in the service of the western nations, sailed into distant seas. The true discoverer, however, is not the man who first chances to stumble upon anything, but the man who finds what he has sought. Such a one alone stands in a link with the thoughts and interests of his predecessors, and this relationship will also determine the account he gives of his search. For which reason the Italians, although their claim to be the first comers on this or that shore may be disputed, will yet retain their title to be pre-eminently the nation of discoverers for the whole latter part of the Middle Ages. The fuller proof of this assertion belongs to the special history of discoveries.[3] Yet ever and again we turn with admiration to the august figure of the great Genoese, by whom a new continent beyond the ocean was demanded, sought and found; and who was the first to be able to say: 'il mondo è poco'—the world is not so large as men have thought. At the time when Spain gave Alexander VI. to the Italians, Italy gave Columbus to the Spaniards. Only a few weeks before the death of that pope (July 7th, 1503), Columbus wrote from Jamaica his noble letter to the thankless Catholic kings, which the ages to come can never read without profound emotion. In a codicil to his will, dated Valladolid, May 4th, 1506, he bequeathed to 'his beloved home, the Republic of Genoa, the prayer-book which Pope Alexander had given him, and which in prison, in conflict, and in every kind of adversity had been to him the greatest of comforts.' It seems as if these words cast upon the abhorred name of Borgia one last gleam of grace and mercy.

[1] Luigi Bossi, *Vita di Cristoforo Colombo*, in which there is a sketch of earlier Italian journeys and discoveries, p. 91 sqq.

[2] See on this subject a treatise by Pertz. An inadequate account is to be found in Æneas Sylvius, *Europae status sub Frederico III. Imp.* cap. 44 (in Freher's *Scriptores*, ed. 1624, vol. ii. p. 87). On Æn. S. see Peschel o.c. 217 sqq.

[3] Comp. O. Peschel, *Geschichte der Erdkunde*, 2nd edit., by Sophus Ruge, Munich, 1877, p. 209 sqq. *et passim.*

The development of geographical and the allied sciences among the Italians must, like the history of their voyages, be touched upon but very briefly. A superficial comparison of their achievements with those of other nations shows an early and striking superiority on their part. Where, in the middle of the fifteenth century, could be found, anywhere but in Italy, such an union of geographical, statistical, and historical knowledge as was found in Æneas Sylvius? Not only in his great geographical work, but in his letters and commentaries, he describes with equal mastery landscapes, cities, manners, industries and products, political conditions and constitutions, wherever he can use his own observation or the evidence of eye-witnesses. What he takes from books is naturally of less moment. Even the short sketch[1] of that valley in the Tyrolese Alps, where Frederick III. had given him a benefice, and still more his description of Scotland, leaves untouched none of the relations of human life, and displays a power and method of unbiassed observation and comparison impossible in any but a countryman of Columbus, trained in the school of the ancients. Thousands saw and, in part, knew what he did, but they felt no impulse to draw a picture of it, and were unconscious that the world desired such pictures.

In geography[2] as in other matters, it is vain to attempt to

[1] *Pii II. Comment.* l. i. p. 14. That he did not always observe correctly, and sometimes filled up the picture from his fancy, is clearly shown, e.g., by his description of Basel. Yet his merit on the whole is nevertheless great. On the description of Basel see G. Voigt; Enea Silvio, i. 228; on E. S. as Geographer, ii. 302–309. Comp. i. 91 sqq.

[2] In the sixteenth century, Italy continued to be the home of geographical literature, at a time when the discoverers themselves belonged almost exclusively to the countries on the shores of the Atlantic. Native geography produced in the middle of the century the great and remarkable work of Leandro Alberti, *Descrizione di tutta l' Italia*, 1582. In the first half of the sixteenth century, the maps in Italy were in advance of those of other countries. See Wieser: *Der Portulan des Infanten Philipp II. von Spanien* in *Sitzungsberichte der Wien. Acad. Phil. Hist. Kl.* Bd. 82 (1876), pp. 541 sqq. For the different Italian maps and voyages of discovery, see the excellent work of Oscar Peschel: *Abhandl. zur Erd- und Völkerkunde* (Leipzig, 1878). Comp. also, *inter alia:* Berchet, *Il planisfero di Giovanni Leandro del' anno* 1452 *fa-simil nella grandezza del' original Nota illustrativa*, 16 S. 4°. Venezia, 1879. Comp. Voigt, ii. 516; and G. B. de Rossi, *Piante iconogrofiche di Roma anteriori al secolo*

distinguish how much is to be attributed to the study of the ancients, and how much to the special genius of the Italians. They saw and treated the things of this world from an objective point of view, even before they were familiar with ancient literature, partly because they were themselves a half-ancient people, and partly because their political circumstances predisposed them to it; but they would not so rapidly have attained to such perfection had not the old geographers showed them the way. The influence of the existing Italian geographies on the spirit and tendencies of the travellers and discoverers was also inestimable. Even the simple 'dilettante' of a science—if in the present case we should assign to Æneas Sylvius so low a rank—can diffuse just that sort of general interest in the subject which prepares for new pioneers the indispensable groundwork of a favourable predisposition in the public mind. True discoverers in any science know well what they owe to such mediation.

XVI. Rome, 1879. For Petrarch's attempt to draw out a map of Italy, comp. Flavio Biondo: *Italia illustrata* (ed. Basil.), p. 352 sqq.; also *Petr. Epist. var. LXI.* ed. Fracass. iii. 476. A remarkable attempt at a map of Europe, Asia and Africa is to be found on the obverse of a medal of Charles IV. of Anjou, executed by Francesco da Laurana in 1462.

CHAPTER II.

NATURAL SCIENCE IN ITALY.

For the position of the Italians in the sphere of the natural sciences, we must refer the reader to the special treatises on the subject, of which the only one with which we are familiar is the superficial and depreciatory work of Libri.[1] The dispute as to the priority of particular discoveries concerns us all the less, since we hold that, at any time, and among any civilised people, a man may appear who, starting with very scanty preparation, is driven by an irresistible impulse into the path of scientific investigation, and through his native gifts achieves the most astonishing success. Such men were Gerbert of Rheims and Roger Bacon. That they were masters of the whole knowledge of the age in their several departments, was a natural consequence of the spirit in which they worked. When once the veil of illusion was torn asunder, when once the dread of nature and the slavery to books and tradition were overcome, countless problems lay before them for solution. It is another matter when a whole people takes a natural delight in the study and investigation of nature, at a time when other nations are indifferent, that is to say, when the discoverer is not threatened or wholly ignored, but can count on the friendly support of congenial spirits. That this was the case in Italy, is unquestionable.[2] The Italian students of nature trace with pride in the 'Divine Comedy' the hints and proofs

[1] Libri, *Histoire des Sciences Mathématiques en Italie.* 4 vols. Paris, 1838.

[2] To pronounce a conclusive judgment on this point, the growth of the habit of collecting observations, in other than the mathematical sciences, would need to be illustrated in detail. But this lies outside the limits of our task.

of Dante's scientific interest in nature.[1] On his claim to priority in this or that discovery or reference, we must leave the men of science to decide; but every layman must be struck by the wealth of his observations on the external world, shown merely in his pictures and comparisons. He, more than any other modern poet, takes them from reality, whether in nature or human life, and uses them, never as mere ornament, but in order to give the reader the fullest and most adequate sense of his meaning. It is in astronomy that he appears chiefly as a scientific specialist, though it must not be forgotten that many astronomical allusions in his great poem, which now appear to us learned, must then have been intelligible to the general reader. Dante, learning apart, appeals to a popular knowledge of the heavens, which the Italians of his day, from the mere fact that they were a nautical people, had in common with the ancients. This knowledge of the rising and setting of the constellations has been rendered superfluous to the modern world by calendars and clocks, and with it has gone whatever interest in astronomy the people may once have had. Nowadays, with our schools and hand-books, every child knows—what Dante did not know—that the earth moves round the sun; but the interest once taken in the subject itself has given place, except in the case of astronomical specialists, to the most absolute indifference.

The pseudo-science, which also dealt with the stars, proves nothing against the inductive spirit of the Italians of that day. That spirit was but crossed, and at times overcome, by the passionate desire to penetrate the future. We shall recur to the subject of astrology when we come to speak of the moral and religious character of the people.

The Church treated this and other pseudo-sciences nearly always with toleration; and showed itself actually hostile even to genuine science only when a charge of heresy or necromancy

[1] Libri, op. cit. ii. p. 174 sqq. See also Dante's treatise, *De aqua et terra;* and W. Schmidt, *Dante's Stellung in der Geschichte der Cosmographie*, Graz, 1876. The passages bearing on geography and natural science from the *Tesoro* of Brunetto Latini are published separately: *Il trattato della Sfera di S. Br. L.*, by Bart. Sorio (Milan, 1858), who has added B. L.'s system of historical chronology.

was also in question—which certainly was often the case. A point which it would be interesting to decide is this: whether, and in what cases, the Dominican (and also the Franciscan) Inquisitors in Italy, were conscious of the falsehood of the charges, and yet condemned the accused, either to oblige some enemy of the prisoner or from hatred to natural science, and particularly to experiments. The latter doubtless occurred, but it is not easy to prove the fact. What helped to cause such persecutions in the North, namely, the opposition made to the innovators by the upholders of the received official, scholastic system of nature, was of little or no weight in Italy. Pietro of Albano, at the beginning of the fourteenth century, is well known to have fallen a victim to the envy of another physician, who accused him before the Inquisition of heresy and magic;[1] and something of the same kind may have happened in the case of his Paduan contemporary, Giovannino Sanguinnacci, who was known as an innovator in medical practice. He escaped, however, with banishment. Nor must it be forgotten that the inquisitorial power of the Dominicans was exercised less uniformly in Italy than in the North. Tyrants and free cities in the fourteenth century treated the clergy at times with such sovereign contempt, that very different matters from natural science went unpunished.[2] But when, with the fifteenth century, antiquity became the leading power in Italy, the breach it made in the old system was turned to account by every branch of secular science. Humanism, nevertheless, attracted to itself the best strength of the nation, and thereby, no doubt, did injury to the inductive investigation of nature.[3] Here and there the Inquisition suddenly started into life, and punished or burned physicians as blasphemers or magicians.

[1] Scardeonius, *De urb. Patav. antiq.* in *Graevii Thesaur. ant. Ital.* tom. vi. pars iii. col. 227. A. died in 1312 during the investigation; his statue was burnt. On Giov. Sang. see op. cit. col. 228 sqq. Comp. on him, Fabricius, *Bibl. Lat.* s. v. Petrus de Apono. Sprenger in *Esch. u. Gruber*, i. 33. He translated (a. 1292–1293) astrological works of Abraham ibn Esra, printed 1506.

[2] See below, part vi. chapter 2.

[3] See the exaggerated complaints of Libri, op. cit. ii. p. 258 sqq. Regrettable as it may be that a people so highly gifted did not devote more of its strength to the natural sciences, we nevertheless believe that it pursued, and in part attained, still more important ends.

In such cases it is hard to discover what was the true motive underlying the condemnation. And after all, Italy, at the close of the fifteenth century, with Paolo Toscanelli, Luca Paccioli and Lionardo da Vinci, held incomparably the highest place among European nations in mathematics and the natural sciences, and the learned men of every country, even Regiomontanus and Copernicus, confessed themselves its pupils.[1]

A significant proof of the wide-spread interest in natural history is found in the zeal which showed itself at an early period for the collection and comparative study of plants and animals. Italy claims to be the first creator of botanical gardens, though possibly they may have served a chiefly practical end, and the claim to priority may be itself disputed.[2] It is of far greater importance that princes and wealthy men in laying out their pleasure-gardens, instinctively made a point of collecting the greatest possible number of different plants in all their species and varieties. Thus in the fifteenth century the noble grounds of the Medicean Villa Careggi appear from the descriptions we have of them to have been almost a botanical garden,[3] with countless specimens of different trees and shrubs. Of the same kind was a villa of the Cardinal Triulzio, at the beginning of the sixteenth century, in the Roman Campagna towards Tivoli,[4] with hedges made up of various species of roses, with trees of every description—the fruit-trees especially showing an astonishing variety—with twenty different sorts of vines and a large kitchen-garden. This is evidently something very different from the score or two of familiar medicinal plants, which were to be found in the garden of any castle or monastery in Western Europe. Along with a careful cultivation of fruit for the purposes of the table, we find

[1] On the studies of the latter in Italy, comp. the thorough investigation by C. Malagola in his work on Codro Urceo (Bologna, 1878, cap. vii. 360–366).

[2] Italians also laid out botanical gardens in foreign countries, e.g. Angelo, of Florence, a contemporary of Petrarch, in Prag. Friedjung: *Carl IV*. p. 311, note 4.

[3] *Alexandri Braccii descriptio horti Laurentii Med.*, printed as Appendix No. 58 to Roscoe's *Life of Lorenzo*. Also to be found in the Appendices to Fabroni's *Laurentius*.

[4] *Mondanarii Villa*, printed in the *Poemata aliquot insignia illustr. poetar. recent.*

an interest in the plant for its own sake, on account of the pleasure it gives to the eye. We learn from the history of art at how late a period this passion for botanical collections was laid aside, and gave place to what was considered the picturesque style of landscape-gardening.

The collections, too, of foreign animals not only gratified curiosity, but served also the higher purposes of observation. The facility of transport from the southern and eastern harbours of the Mediterranean and the mildness of the Italian climate, made it practicable to buy the largest animals of the south, or to accept them as presents from the Sultans.[1] The cities and princes were especially anxious to keep live lions, even when the lion was not, as in Florence, the emblem of the state.[2] The lions' den was generally in or near the government palace, as in Perugia and Florence; in Rome, it lay on the slope of the Capitol. The beasts sometimes served as executioners of political judgments,[3] and no doubt, apart from this, they kept alive a certain terror in the popular mind. Their condition was also held to be ominous of good or evil. Their fertility,

[1] On the zoological garden at Palermo under Henry VI., see Otto de S. Blasio ad a. 1194. That of Henry I. of England in the park of Woodstock (Guliel. Malmes. p. 638) contained lions, leopards, camels, and a porcupine, all gifts of foreign princes.

[2] As such he was called, whether painted or carved in stone, 'Marzocco.' At Pisa eagles were kept. See the commentators on Dante, *Inf.* xxxiii. 22. The falcon in Boccaccio, *Decam.* v. 9. See for the whole subject: *Due trattati del governo e delle infermità degli uccelli, testi di lingua inediti.* Rome, 1864. They are works of the fourteenth century, possibly translated from the Persian.

[3] See the extract from Ægid. Viterb. in Papencordt, *Gesch. der Stadt Rom im Mittelalter*, p. 367, note, with an incident of the year 1328. Combats of wild animals among themselves and with dogs served to amuse the people on great occasions. At the reception of Pius II. and of Galeazzo Maria Sforza at Florence, in 1459, in an enclosed space on the Piazza della Signoria, bulls, horses, boars, dogs, lions, and a giraffe were turned out together, but the lions lay down and refused to attack the other animals. Comp. *Ricordi di Firenze*, *Rer. Ital. script. ex Florent. codd.* tom. ii. col. 741. A different account in *Vita Pii II.* Murat. iii. ii. col. 976. A second giraffe was presented to Lorenzo the Magnificent by the Mameluke Sultan Kaytbey. Comp. Paul. Jov. *Vita Leonis X.* l. i. In Lorenzo's menagerie one magnificent lion was especially famous, and his destruction by the other lions was reckoned a presage of the death of his owner.

especially, was considered a sign of public prosperity, and no less a man than Giovanni Villani thought it worth recording that he was present at the delivery of a lioness.[1] The cubs were often given to allied states and princes, or to Condottieri, as a reward of valour.[2] In addition to the lions, the Florentines began very early to keep leopards, for which a special keeper was appointed.[3] Borso[4] of Ferrara used to set his lions to fight with bulls, bears, and wild boars.

By the end of the fifteenth century, however, true menageries (serragli), now reckoned part of the suitable appointments of a court, were kept by many of the princes. 'It belongs to the

[1] Gio. Villani, x. 185, xi. 66. Matteo Villani, iii. 90, v. 68. It was a bad omen if the lions fought, and worse still if they killed one another. Com. Varchi, *Stor. fiorent.* iii. p. 143. Matt. V. devotes the first of the two chapters quoted to prove (1) that lions were born in Italy, and (2) that they came into the world alive.

[2] *Cron. di Perugia, Arch. Stor.* xvi. ii. p. 77, year 1497. A pair of lions once escaped from Perugia; *ibid.* xvi. i. p. 382, year 1434. Florence, for example, sent to King Wladislaw of Poland (May, 1406), a pair of lions, *ut utriusque sexus animalia ad procreandos catulos haberetis.* The accompanying statement is amusing in a diplomatic document: 'Sunt equidem hi leones Florentini, et satis quantum natura promittere potuit mansueti, depositâ feritate, quam insitam habent, hique in Gætulorum regionibus nascuntur et Indorum, in quibus multitudo dictorum animalium evalescit, sicuti prohibent naturales. Et cum leonum complexio sit frigoribus inimica, quod natura sagax ostendit, natura in regionibus aestu ferventibus generantur, necessarium est, quod vostra serenitas, si dictorum animalium vitam et sobolis propagationem, ut remur, desiderat, faciat provideri, quod in locis calidis educentur et maneant. Conveniunt nempe cum regia majestate leones quoniam leo græce latine rex dicitur. Sicut enim rex dignitate potentia, magnanimitate ceteros homines antecellit, sic leonis generositas et vigor imperterritus animalia cuncta praesit. Et sicut rex, sic leo adversus imbecilles et timidos clementissimum se ostendit, et adversus inquietos et tumidos terribilem se offert animadversione justissima.' (*Cod. epistolaris sæculi. Mon. med. ævi hist. res gestas Poloniæ illustr.* Krakau, 1876, p. 25.)

[3] Gage, *Carteggio*, i. p. 422, year 1291. The Visconti used trained leopards for hunting hares, which were started by little dogs. See v. Kobel, *Wildanger*, p. 247, where later instances of hunting with leopards are mentioned.

[4] *Strozzii poetae*, p. 146: *De leone Borsii Ducis.* The lion spares the hare and the small dog, imitating (so says the poet) his master. Comp. the words fol. 188, 'et inclusis condita septa feris,' and fol. 193, an epigram of fourteen lines, 'in leporarii ingressu quam maximi;' see *ibid.* for the hunting-park.

position of the great,' says Matarazzo,[1] 'to keep horses, dogs, mules, falcons, and other birds, court-jesters, singers, and foreign animals.' The menagerie at Naples, in the time of Ferrante and others, contained a giraffe and a zebra, presented, it seems, by the ruler of Bagdad.[2] Filippo Maria Visconti possessed not only horses which cost him each 500 or 1,000 pieces of gold, and valuable English dogs, but a number of leopards brought from all parts of the East; the expense of his hunting-birds which were collected from the countries of Northern Europe, amounted to 3,000 pieces of gold a month.[3] 'The Cremonese say that the Emperor Frederick II. brought an elephant into their city, sent him from India by Prester John,' we read in Brunetto Latini; Petrarch records the dying out of the elephants in Italy.[4] King Emanuel the Great of Portugal knew well what he was about when he presented Leo X. with an elephant and a rhinoceros.[5] It was under such circumstances that the foundations of a scientific zoology and botany were laid.

A practical fruit of these zoological studies was the establishment of studs, of which the Mantuan, under Francesco Gonzaga, was esteemed the first in Europe.[6] All interest in, and knowledge of the different breeds of horses is as old, no doubt, as

[1] *Cron. di Perugia*, l. c. xvi. ii. p. 199. Something of the same kind is to be found in Petrarch, *De remed. utriusque fortunae*, but less clearly expressed. Here Gaudium, in the conversation with Ratio, boasts of owning monkeys and 'ludicra animalia,'

[2] Jovian. Pontan. *De magnificentia.* In the zoological garden of the Cardinal of Aquileja, at Albano, there were, in 1463, peacocks and Indian fowls and Syrian goats with long ears. *Pii II. Comment.* l. xi. p. 562 sqq.

[3] *Decembrio*, ap. Muratori, xx. col. 1012.

[4] Brunetti Latini, *Tesor.* (ed. Chabaille, Paris, 1863), lib. i. In Petrarch's time there were no elephants in Italy. 'Itaque et in Italia avorum memoria unum Frederico Romanorum principi fuisse et nunc Egyptio tyranno nonnisi unicum esse fama est.' *De rem. utr. fort.* i. 60.

[5] The details which are most amusing, in Paul. Jov. *Elogia*, on Tristanus Acunius. On the porcupines and ostriches in the Pal. Strozzi, see Rabelais, *Pantagruel*, iv. chap. 11. Lorenzo the Magnificent received a giraffe from Egypt through some merchants, Baluz. *Miscell.* iv. 416. The elephant sent to Leo was greatly bewailed by the people when it died, its portrait was painted, and verses on it were written by the younger Beroaldus.

[6] Comp Paul. Jov. *Elogia*, p. 234, speaking of Francesco Gonzaga. For the luxury at Milan in this respect, see Bandello, Parte II. Nov. 3 and 8. In the narrative poems we also sometimes hear the opinion of a judge of horses. Comp. Pulci, *Morgante*, xv. 105 sqq.

riding itself, and the crossing of the European with the Asiatic must have been common from the time of the crusades. In Italy, a special inducement to perfect the breed was offered by the prizes at the horse-races held in every considerable town in the peninsula. In the Mantuan stables were found the infallible winners in these contests, as well as the best military chargers, and the horses best suited by their stately appearance for presents to great people. Gonzaga kept stallions and mares from Spain, Ireland, Africa, Thrace, and Cilicia, and for the sake of the last he cultivated the friendship of the Sultan. All possible experiments were here tried, in order to produce the most perfect animals.

Even human menageries were not wanting. The famous Cardinal Ippolito Medici,[1] bastard of Giuliano, Duke of Nemours, kept at his strange court a troop of barbarians who talked no less than twenty different languages, and who were all of them perfect specimens of their races. Among them were incomparable *voltigeurs* of the best blood of the North African Moors, Tartar bowmen, Negro wrestlers, Indian divers, and Turks, who generally accompanied the Cardinal on his hunting expeditions. When he was overtaken by an early death (1535), this motley band carried the corpse on their shoulders from Itri to Rome, and minged with the general mourning for the open-handed Cardinal their medley of tongues and violent gesticulations.[2]

[1] Paul Jov. *Elogia*, speaking of Hipp. Medices.

[2] At this point a few notices on slavery in Italy at the time of the Renaissance will not be out of place. A short, but important, passage in Jovian. Pontan. *De obedientia*, l. iii. cap. i.: ‘An homo, cum liber natura sit, domino parere debeat?’ In North Italy there were no slaves. Elsewhere, even Christians, as well as Circassians and Bulgarians, were bought from the Turks, and made to serve till they had earned their ransom. The negroes, on the contrary, remained slaves; but it was not permitted, at least in the kingdom of Naples, to emasculate them. The word ‘moro’ signifies any dark-skinned man; the negro was called ‘moro nero.’—Fabroni, *Cosmos*, Adn. 110: Document on the sale of a female Circassian slave (1427); Adn. 141: List of the female slaves of Cosimo.—Nantiporto. Murat. iii. ii. col. 1106. Innocent VIII. received 100 Moors as a present from Ferdinand the Catholic, and gave them to cardinals and other great men (1488).—Marsuccio, *Novelle*, 14: sale of slaves; do. 24 and 25, negro slaves who also (for the benefit of their owner?) work as ‘facchini,’ and gain the love of the women; do. 48 Moors from Tunis caught by Catalans and sold at Pisa.—Gaye, *Carteggio*, i. 360: manumission and reward of a negro

These scattered notices of the relations of the Italians to natural science, and their interest in the wealth and variety of the products of nature, are only fragments of a great subject. No one is more conscious than the author of the defects in his knowledge on this point. Of the multitude of special works in which the subject is adequately treated, even the names are but imperfectly known to him.

slave in a Florentine will (1490).—Paul. Jov. *Elogia*, sub Franc. Sfortia; Porzio, *Congiura*, iii. 195; and Comines, *Charles VIII.* chap. 18: negroes as gaolers and executioners of the House of Aragon in Naples.—Paul. Jov. *Elogia*, sub Galeatio: negroes as followers of the prince on his excursions. —Æneæ Sylvii, *Opera*, p. 456: a negro slave as a musician.—Paul Jov. *De piscibus*, cap 3: a (free?) negro as diver and swimming-master at Genoa. —Alex. Benedictus, *De Carolo VIII.* in Eccard, *Scriptores*, ii. col. 1608: a negro (Æthiops) as superior officer at Venice, according to which we are justified in thinking of Othello as a negro.—Bandello, Parte III. Nov. 21: when a slave at Genoa deserved punishment he was sold away to Iviza, one of the Balearic isles, to carry salt.

The foregoing remarks, although they make no claim to completeness, may be allowed to stand as they are in the new edition, on account of the excellent selection of instances they contain, and because they have not met with sufficient notice in the works upon the subject. Latterly a good deal has been written on the slave-trade in Italy. The very curious book of Filippo Zamboni: *Gli Ezzelini, Dante e gli Schiavi, ossia Roma e la Schiavitù personale domestica. Con documenti inediti. Seconda edizione aumentata* (Vienna, 1870), does not contain what the title promises, but gives, p. 241 sqq., valuable information on the slave-trade; p. 270, a remarkable document on the buying and selling of a female slave; p. 282, a list of various slaves (with the place were they were bought and sold, their home, age, and price) in the thirteenth and three following centuries. A treatise by Wattenbach: *Sklavenhandel im Mittelalter* (*Anzeiger für Kunde der deutschen Vorzeit*, 1874, pp. 37–40) refers only in part to Italy: Clement V. decides in 1309 that the Venetian prisoners should be made slaves of; in 1501, after the capture of Capua, many Capuan women were sold at Rome for a low price. In the *Monum. historica Slavorum meridionalium*, ed. Vinc. Macusceo, tom. i. Warsaw, 1874, we read at p. 199 a decision (Ancona, 1458) that the 'Greci, Turci, Tartari, Sarraceni, Bossinenses, Burgari vel Albanenses,' should be and always remain slaves, unless their masters freed them by a legal document. Egnatius, *Exempl. ill. vir.* Ven. fol. 246 *a*, praises Venice on the ground that 'servorum Venetis ipsis nullum unquam usum extitisse;' but, on the other hand, comp. Zamboni, p. 223, and especially Vincenzo Lazari: 'Del traffico e delle condizioni degli schiavi, in Venezia nel tempo di mezzo,' in *Miscellanea di Stor. Ital.* Torino, 1862, vol. i. 463–501.

CHAPTER III.

THE DISCOVERY OF NATURAL BEAUTY.

But, outside the sphere of scientific investigation, there is another way to draw near to nature. The Italians are the first among modern peoples by whom the outward world was seen and felt as something beautiful.[1]

The power to do so is always the result of a long and complicated development, and its origin is not easily detected, since a dim feeling of this kind may exist long before it shows itself in poetry and painting, and thereby becomes conscious of itself. Among the ancients, for example, art and poetry had gone through the whole circle of human interests, before they turned to the representation of nature, and even then the latter filled always a limited and subordinate place. And yet, from the time of Homer downwards, the powerful impression made by nature upon man is shown by countless verses and chance expressions. The Germanic races, which founded their states on the ruins of the Roman Empire, were thoroughly and specially fitted to understand the spirit of natural scenery; and though Christianity compelled them for awhile to see in the springs and mountains, in the lakes and woods, which they had till then revered, the working of evil demons, yet this transitional conception was soon outgrown. By the year 1200, at the height of the Middle Ages, a genuine, hearty enjoyment of the external world was again in existence, and found lively expression in the minstrelsy of different nations,[2] which gives evidence of the sympathy felt with all the simple phenomena of nature—spring with its flowers, the green fields and the

[1] It is hardly necessary to refer the reader to the famous chapters on this subject in Humboldt's *Kosmos*.

[2] See on this subject the observations of Wilhelm Grimm, quoted by Humboldt in the work referred to.

woods. But these pictures are all foreground without perspective. Even the crusaders, who travelled so far and saw so much, are not recognisable as such in these poems. The epic poetry, which describes armour and costumes so fully, does not attempt more than a sketch of outward nature; and even the great Wolfram von Eschenbach scarcely anywhere gives us an adequate picture of the scene on which his heroes move. From these poems it would never be guessed that their noble authors in all countries inhabited or visited lofty castles, commanding distant prospects. Even in the Latin poems of the wandering clerks (p. 174), we find no traces of a distant view—of landscape properly so called—but what lies near is sometimes described with a glow and splendour which none of the knightly minstrels can surpass. What picture of the Grove of Love can equal that of the Italian poet—for such we take him to be—of the twelfth century?

'Immortalis fieret
Ibi manens homo;
Arbor ibi quaelibet
Suo gaudet pomo;
Viae myrrha, cinnamo
Fragrant, et amomo—
Conjectari poterat
Dominus ex domo,'[1] etc.

To the Italian mind, at all events, nature had by this time lost its taint of sin, and had shaken off all trace of demoniacal powers. Saint Francis of Assisi, in his Hymn to the Sun, frankly praises the Lord for creating the heavenly bodies and the four elements.

But the unmistakable proofs of a deepening effect of nature on the human spirit begin with Dante. Not only does he awaken in us by a few vigorous lines the sense of the morning airs and the trembling light on the distant ocean, or of the grandeur of the storm-beaten forest, but he makes the ascent of lofty peaks, with the only possible object of enjoying the view[2]—the first man, perhaps, since the days of antiquity who

[1] Carmina Burana, p. 162, *De Phyllide et Flora*, str. 66.

[2] It would be hard to say what else he had to do at the top of the Bismantova in the province of Reggio, *Purgat.* iv. 26. The precision with which he brings before us all the parts of his supernatural world

did so. In Boccaccio we can do little more than infer how country scenery affected him;[1] yet his pastoral romances show his imagination to have been filled with it. But the significance of nature for a receptive spirit is fully and clearly displayed by Petrarch—one of the first truly modern men. That clear soul—who first collected from the literature of all countries evidence of the origin and progress of the sense of natural beauty, and himself, in his 'Ansichten der Natur,' achieved the noblest masterpiece of description—Alexander von Humboldt, has not done full justice to Petrarch; and, following in the steps of the great reaper, we may still hope to glean a few ears of interest and value.

Petrarch was not only a distinguished geographer—the first map of Italy is said to have been drawn by his direction[2]—and not only a reproducer of the sayings of the ancients,[3] but felt himself the influence of natural beauty. The enjoyment of nature is, for him, the favourite accompaniment of intellectual pursuits; it was to combine the two that he lived in learned retirement at Vaucluse and elsewhere, that he from time to time fled from the world and from his age.[4] We

shows a remarkable sense of form and space. That there was a belief in the existence of hidden treasures on the tops of mountains, and that such spots were regarded with superstitious terror, may be clearly inferred from the *Chron. Novaliciense*, ii. 5, in Pertz, *Script.* vii., and *Monum. hist. patriae*, *Script.* iii.

[1] Besides the description of Baiæ in the *Fiammetta*, of the grove in the Ameto, etc., a passage in the *De genealogia deorum*, xiv. 11, is of importance, where he enumerates a number of rural beauties—trees, meadows, brooks, flocks and herds, cottages, etc.—and adds that these things 'animum mulcent;' their effect is 'mentem in se colligere.'

[2] Flavio Biondo, *Italia Illustrata* (ed. Basil), p. 352 sqq. Comp. *Epist. Var.* ed. Fracass. (lat.) iii. 476. On Petrarch's plan of writing a great geographical work, see the proofs given by Attilio Hortis, *Accenni alle Scienze Naturali nelle Opere di G. Boccacci*, Trieste, 1877, p. 45 sqq.

[3] Although he is fond of referring to them: e.g. *De vita solitaria* (*Opera*, ed. Basil, 1581), esp. p. 241, where he quotes the description of a vine-arbour from St. Augustine.

[4] *Epist. famil.* vii. 4. 'Interea utinam scire posses, quanta, cum voluptate solivagus et liber, inter montes et nemora, inter fontes et flumina, inter libros et maximorum hominum ingenia respiro, quamque me in ea, quae ante sunt, cum Apostolo extendens et praeterita oblivisci nitor et praesentia non videre.' Comp. vi. 3, o. c. 316 sqq. esp. 334 sqq. Comp. L. Geiger: *Petrarca*, p. 75, note 5, and p. 269.

should do him wrong by inferring from his weak and undeveloped power of describing natural scenery that he did not feel it deeply. His picture, for instance, of the lovely Gulf of Spezzia and Porto Venere, which he inserts at the end of the sixth book of the 'Africa,' for the reason that none of the ancients or moderns had sung of it,[1] is no more than a simple enumeration, but the descriptions in letters to his friends of Rome, Naples, and other Italian cities in which he willingly lingered, are picturesque and worthy of the subject. Petrarch is also conscious of the beauty of rock scenery, and is perfectly able to distinguish the picturesqueness from the utility of nature.[2] During his stay among the woods of Reggio, the sudden sight of an impressive landscape so affected him that he resumed a poem which he had long laid aside.[3] But the deepest impression of all was made upon him by the ascent of Mont Ventoux, near Avignon.[4] An indefinable longing for a distant panorama grew stronger and stronger in him, till at length the accidental sight of a passage in Livy, where King Philip, the enemy of Rome, ascends the Hæmus, decided him. He thought that what was not blamed in a grey-headed monarch, might be well *excused* in a young man of private station. The ascent of a mountain for its own sake was unheard of, and there could be no thought of the companionship of friends or acquaintances. Petrarch took with him only his younger brother and two country people from the last place where he halted. At the foot of the mountain an old herdsman besought him to turn back, saying that he himself had attempted to climb it fifty years before, and had brought home nothing but repentance, broken bones, and torn clothes, and that neither before nor after had anyone ventured to do the same. Nevertheless, they struggled forward and upward, till

[1] 'Jacuit sine carmine sacro.' Comp. *Itinerar. Syriacum*, *Opp.* p. 558.

[2] He distinguishes in the *Itinerar. Syr.* p. 357, on the Riviera di Levante: 'colles asperitate gratissima et mira fertilitate conspicuos.' On the port of Gaeta, see his *De remediis utriusque fortunae*, i. 54.

[3] *Letter to Posterity:* 'Subito loco specie percussus.' Descriptions of great natural events: A Storm at Naples, 1343: *Epp. fam.* i. 263 sqq.; An Earthquake at Basel, 1355, *Epp. seniles*, lib. x. 2, and *De rem. utr. fort.* ii. 91.

[4] *Epist. fam.* ed. Fracassetti, i. 193 sqq.

the clouds lay beneath their feet, and at last they reached the top. A description of the view from the summit would be looked for in vain, not because the poet was insensible to it, but, on the contrary, because the impression was too overwhelming. His whole past life, with all its follies, rose before his mind; he remembered that ten years ago that day he had quitted Bologna a young man, and turned a longing gaze towards his native country; he opened a book which then was his constant companion, the 'Confessions of St. Augustine,' and his eye fell on the passage in the tenth chapter, 'and men go forth, and admire lofty mountains and broad seas, and roaring torrents, and the ocean, and the course of the stars, and forget their own selves while doing so.' His brother, to whom he read these words, could not understand why he closed the book and said no more.

Some decades later, about 1360, Fazio degli Uberti describes in his rhyming geography[1] (p. 178), the wide panorama from the mountains of Auvergne, with the interest, it is true, of the geographer and antiquarian only, but still showing clearly that he himself had seen it. He must, however, have ascended far higher peaks, since he is familiar with facts which only occur at a height of 10,000 feet or more above the sea—mountain-sickness and its accompaniments—of which his imaginary comrade Solinus tries to cure him with a sponge dipped in an essence. The ascents of Parnassus and Olympus,[2] of which he speaks, are perhaps only fictions.

In the fifteenth century, the great masters of the Flemish school, Hubert and Johann van Eyck, suddenly lifted the veil from nature. Their landscapes are not merely the fruit of an endeavour to reflect the real world in art, but have, even if expressed conventionally, a certain poetical meaning—in short, a soul. Their influence on the whole art of the West is un-

[1] *Il Dittamondo*, iii. cap. 9.

[2] *Dittamondo*, iii. cap. 21, iv. cap. 4. Papencordt, *Gesch. der Stadt Rom*, says that the Emperor Charles IV. had a strong taste for beautiful scenery, and quotes on this point Pelzel, *Carl IV.* p. 456. (The two other passages, which he quotes, do not say the same.) It is possible that the Emperor took this fancy from intercourse with the humanists (see above, pp. 141–2). For the interest taken by Charles in natural science see H. Friedjung, op. cit. p. 224, note 1.

deniable, and extended to the landscape-painting of the Italians, but without preventing the characteristic interest of the Italian eye for nature from finding its own expression.

On this point, as in the scientific description of nature, Æneas Sylvius is again one of the most weighty voices of his time. Even if we grant the justice of all that has been said against his character, we must nevertheless admit that in few other men was the picture of the age and its culture so fully reflected, and that few came nearer to the normal type of the men of the early Renaissance. It may be added parenthetically, that even in respect to his moral character he will not be fairly judged, if we listen solely to the complaints of the German Church, which his fickleness helped to baulk of the Council it so ardently desired.[1]

He here claims our attention as the first who not only enjoyed the magnificence of the Italian landscape, but described it with enthusiasm down to its minutest details. The ecclesiastical State and the south of Tuscany—his native home—he knew thoroughly, and after he became pope he spent his leisure during the favourable season chiefly in excursions to the country. Then at last the gouty man was rich enough to have himself carried in a litter through the mountains and valleys; and when we compare his enjoyments with those of the popes who succeeded him, Pius, whose chief delight was in nature, antiquity, and simple, but noble, architecture, appears almost a saint. In the elegant and flowing Latin of his 'Commentaries' he freely tells us of his happiness.[2]

[1] We may also compare Platina, *Vitae Pontiff.* p. 310: 'Homo fuit (Pius II.) verus, integer, apertus; nil habuit ficti, nil simulati'—an enemy of hypocrisy and superstition, courageous and consistent. See Voigt, ii. 261 sqq. and iii. 724. He does not, however, give an analysis of the character of Pius.

[2] The most important passages are the following: *Pii II. P. M. Commentarii*, l. iv. p. 183; spring in his native country; l. v. p. 251: summer residence at Tivoli; l. vi. p. 306: the meal at the spring of Vicovaro; l. viii. p. 378: the neighbourhood of Viterbo; p. 387: the mountain monastery of St. Martin; p. 388: the Lake of Bolsena; l. ix. p. 396: a splendid description of Monte Amiata; l. x. p. 483: the situation of Monte Oliveto; p. 497: the view from Todi; l. xi. p. 554: Ostia and Porto; p. 562: description of the Alban Hills; l. xii. p. 609: Frascati and Grottaferrata; comp. 568–571.

His eye seems as keen and practised as that of any modern observer. He enjoys with rapture the panoramic splendour of the view from the summit of the Alban Hills—from the Monte Cavo—whence he could see the shores of St. Peter from Terracina and the promontory of Circe as far as Monte Argentaro, and the wide expanse of country round about, with the ruined cities of the past, and with the mountain-chains of central Italy beyond; and then his eye would turn to the green woods in the hollows beneath and the mountain-lakes among them. He feels the beauty of the position of Todi, crowning the vineyards and olive-clad slopes, looking down upon distant woods and upon the valley of the Tiber, where towns and castles rise above the winding river. The lovely hills about Siena, with villas and monasteries on every height, are his own home, and his descriptions of them are touched with a peculiar feeling. Single picturesque glimpses charm him too, like the little promontory of Capo di Monte that stretches out into the Lake of Bolsena. 'Rocky steps,' we read, 'shaded by vines, descend to the water's edge, where the evergreen oaks stand between the cliffs, alive with the song of thrushes.' On the path round the Lake of Nemi, beneath the chestnuts and fruit-trees, he feels that here, if anywhere, a poet's soul must awake—here in the hiding-place of Diana! He often held consistories or received ambassadors under huge old chestnut-trees, or beneath the olives on the green sward by some gurgling spring. A view like that of a narrowing gorge, with a bridge arched boldly over it, awakens at once his artistic sense. Even the smallest details give him delight through something beautiful, or perfect, or characteristic in them—the blue fields of waving flax, the yellow gorse which covers the hills, even tangled thickets, or single trees, or springs, which seem to him like wonders of nature.

The height of his enthusiasm for natural beauty was reached during his stay on Monte Amiata, in the summer of 1462, when plague and heat made the lowlands uninhabitable. Half-way up the mountain, in the old Lombard monastery of San Salvatore, he and his court took up their quarters. There, between the chestnuts which clothe the steep declivity, the eye may wander over all southern Tuscany, with the towers of Siena in the distance. The ascent of the highest peak he left to his companions, who were joined by the Venetian envoy; they found at the top two vast blocks of stone one upon the other —perhaps the sacrificial altar of a pre-historical people—and fancied that in the far distance they saw Corsica and Sardinia [1] rising above the sea. In the cool air of the hills, among the old oaks and chestnuts, on the green meadows where there were no thorns to wound the feet, and no snakes or insects to hurt or to annoy, the pope passed days of unclouded happiness. For the 'Segnatura,' which took place on certain days of the week, he selected on each occasion some new shady retreat [2] 'novas in convallibus fontes et novas inveniens umbras, quæ dubiam facerent electionem.' At such times the dogs would perhaps start a great stag from his lair, who, after defending himself a while with hoofs and antlers, would fly at last up the mountain. In the evening the pope was accustomed to sit before the monastery on the spot from which the whole valley of the Paglia was visible, holding lively conversations with the cardinals. The courtiers, who ventured down from the heights on their hunting expeditions, found the heat below intolerable, and the scorched plains like a very hell, while the monastery, with its cool, shady woods, seemed like an abode of the blessed.

All this is genuine modern enjoyment, not a reflection of antiquity. As surely as the ancients themselves felt in the same manner, so surely, nevertheless, were the scanty expressions of the writers whom Pius knew insufficient to awaken in him such enthusiasm.[3]

The second great age of Italian poetry, which now followed at the end of the fifteenth and the beginning of the sixteenth centuries, as well as the Latin poetry of the same period, is rich in proofs of the powerful effect of nature on the human mind.

[1] So we must suppose it to have been written, not Sicily.

[2] He calls himself, with an allusion to his name: 'Silvarum amator et varia videndi cupidus.'

[3] On Leonbattista Alberti's feeling for landscapes see above, p. 136 sqq. Alberti, a younger contemporary of Æneas Silvius (*Trattato del Governo della Famiglia*, p. 90; see above, p. 132, note 1), is delighted when in the country with 'the bushy hills,' 'the fair plains and rushing waters.' Mention may here be made of a little work *Ætna*, by P. Bembus, first published at Venice, 1495, and often printed since, in which, among much that is rambling and prolix, there are remarkable geographical descriptions and notices of landscapes.

The first glance at the lyric poets of that time will suffice to convince us. Elaborate descriptions, it is true, of natural scenery, are very rare, for the reason that, in this energetic age, the novels and the lyric or epic poetry had something else to deal with. Bojardo and Ariosto paint nature vigorously, but as briefly as possible, and with no effort to appeal by their descriptions to the feelings of the reader,[1] which they endeavour to reach solely by their narrative and characters. Letter-writers and the authors of philosophical dialogues are, in fact, better evidence of the growing love of nature than the poets. The novelist Bandello, for example, observes rigorously the rules of his department of literature; he gives us in his novels themselves not a word more than is necessary on the natural scenery amid which the action of his tales takes place,[2] but in the dedications which always precede them we meet with charming descriptions of nature as the setting for his dialogues and social pictures. Among letter-writers, Aretino[3] unfortunately must be named as the first who has fully painted in words the splendid effect of light and shadow in an Italian sunset.

We sometimes find the feeling of the poets, also, attaching itself with tenderness to graceful scenes of country life. Tito Strozza, about the year 1480, describes in a Latin elegy[4] the dwelling of his mistress. We are shown an old ivy-clad house, half hidden in trees, and adorned with weather-stained frescoes of the saints, and near it a chapel, much damaged by the violence of the river Po, which flowed hard by; not far off, the priest ploughs his few barren roods with borrowed cattle. This is no reminiscence of the Roman elegists, but true modern sentiment; and the parallel to it—a sincere, unartificial description of country life in general—will be found at the end of this part of our work.

It may be objected that the German painters at the begin-

[1] A most elaborate picture of this kind in Ariosto; his sixth canto is all foreground.

[2] He deals differently with his architectural framework, and in this modern decorative art can learn something from him even now.

[3] *Lettere Pittoriche*, iii. 36, to Titian, May, 1544.

[4] *Strozzii Poetae*, in the *Erotica*, l. vi. fol. 183; in the poem: 'Hortatur se ipse, ut ad amicam properet.'

ning of the sixteenth century succeed in representing with perfect mastery these scenes of country life, as, for instance, Albrecht Dürer, in his engraving of the Prodigal Son.[1] But it is one thing if a painter, brought up in a school of realism, introduces such scenes, and quite another thing if a poet, accustomed to an ideal or mythological framework, is driven by inward impulse into realism. Besides which, priority in point of time is here, as in the descriptions of country life, on the side of the Italian poets.

[1] Comp. Thausing: *Dürer*, Leipzig, 1876, p. 166.

CHAPTER IV.

THE DISCOVERY OF MAN. SPIRITUAL DESCRIPTION IN POETRY.

To the discovery of the outward world the Renaissance added a still greater achievement, by first discerning and bringing to light the full, whole nature of man.[1]

This period, as we have seen, first gave the highest development to individuality, and then led the individual to the most zealous and thorough study of himself in all forms and under all conditions. Indeed, the development of personality is essentially involved in the recognition of it in oneself and in others. Between these two great processes our narrative has placed the influence of ancient literature, because the mode of conceiving and representing both the individual and human nature in general was defined and coloured by that influence. But the power of conception and representation lay in the age and in the people.

The facts which we shall quote in evidence of our thesis will be few in number. Here, if anywhere in the course of this discussion, the author is conscious that he is treading on the perilous ground of conjecture, and that what seems to him a clear, if delicate and gradual, transition in the intellectual movement of the fourteenth and fifteenth centuries, may not be equally plain to others. The gradual awakening of the soul of a people is a phenomenon which may produce a different impression on each spectator. Time will judge which impression is the most faithful.

Happily the study of the intellectual side of human nature began, not with the search after a theoretical psychology—for that, Aristotle still sufficed—but with the endeavour to observe and to describe. The indispensable ballast of theory was

[1] These striking expressions are taken from the seventh volume of Michelet's *Histoire de France* (Introd.).

limited to the popular doctrine of the four temperaments, in its then habitual union with the belief in the influence of the planets. Such conceptions may remain ineradicable in the minds of individuals, without hindering the general progress of the age. It certainly makes on us a singular impression, when we meet them at a time when human nature in its deepest essence and in all its characteristic expressions was not only known by exact observation, but represented by an immortal poetry and art. It sounds almost ludicrous when an otherwise competent observer considers Clement VII. to be of a melancholy temperament, but defers his judgment to that of the physicians, who declare the pope of a sanguine-choleric nature;[1] or when we read that the same Gaston de Foix, the victor of Ravenna, whom Giorgione painted and Bambaja carved, and whom all the historians describe, had the saturnine temperament.[2] No doubt those who use these expressions mean something by them; but the terms in which they tell us their meaning are strangely out of date in the Italy of the sixteenth century.

As examples of the free delineation of the human spirit, we shall first speak of the great poets of the fourteenth century.

If we were to collect the pearls from the courtly and knightly poetry of all the countries of the West during the two preceding centuries, we should have a mass of wonderful divinations and single pictures of the inward life, which at first sight would seem to rival the poetry of the Italians. Leaving lyrical poetry out of account, Godfrey of Strasburg gives us, in 'Tristram and Isolt,' a representation of human passion, some features of which are immortal. But these pearls lie scattered in the ocean of artificial convention, and they are altogether something very different from a complete objective picture of the inward man and his spiritual wealth.

Italy, too, in the thirteenth century had, through the 'Trova-

[1] Tomm. Gar, *Relaz. della Corte di Roma*, i. pp. 278 and 279. In the Rel. of Soriano, year 1533.

[2] Prato, *Arch. Stor.* iii. p. 295 sqq. The word 'saturnico' means 'unhappy' as well as 'bringing misfortune.' For the influence of the planets on human character in general, see Corn. Agrippa, *De occulta philosophia*, c. 52.

tori,' its share in the poetry of the courts and of chivalry. To them is mainly due the 'Canzone,' whose construction is as difficult and artificial as that of the songs of any northern minstrel. Their subject and mode of thought represents simply the conventional tone of the courts, be the poet a burgher or a scholar.

But two new paths at length showed themselves, along which Italian poetry could advance to another and a characteristic future. They are not the less important for being concerned only with the formal and external side of the art.

To the same Brunetto Latini—the teacher of Dante—who, in his 'Canzoni,' adopts the customary manner of the 'Trovatori,' we owe the first-known 'Versi Sciolti,' or blank hendecasyllabic verses,[1] and in his apparent absence of form, a true and genuine passion suddenly showed itself. The same voluntary renunciation of outward effect, through confidence in the power of the inward conception, can be observed some years later in fresco-painting, and later still in painting of all kinds, which began to cease to rely on colour for its effect, using simply a lighter or darker shade. For an age which laid so much stress on artificial form in poetry, these verses of Brunetto mark the beginning of a new epoch.[2]

About the same time, or even in the first half of the thirteenth century, one of the many strictly-balanced forms of metre, in which Europe was then so fruitful, became a normal and recognised form in Italy—the sonnet. The order of rhymes and even the number of the lines varied for a whole century,[3] till Petrarch fixed them permanently. In this form all higher lyrical or meditative subjects, and at a later time subjects of every possible description, were treated, and the madrigals, the sestine, and even the 'Canzoni' were reduced to a subordinate

[1] See Trucchi, *Poesie Italiane inedite*, i. p. 165 sqq.

[2] Blank verse became at a later time the usual form for dramatic compositions. Trissino, in the dedication of his *Sofonisba* to Leo X., expressed the hope that the Pope would recognise this style for what it was—as better, nobler, and *less easy* than it looked. Roscoe, *Leone X.*, ed. Bossi, viii. 174.

[3] Comp. e.g. the striking forms adopted by Dante, *Vita Nuova*, ed. Witte, p. 13 sqq., 16 sqq. Each has twenty irregular lines; in the first, one rhyme occurs eight times.

place. Later Italian writers complain, half jestingly, half resentfully, of this inevitable mould, this Procrustean bed, to which they were compelled to make their thoughts and feelings fit. Others were, and still are, quite satisfied with this particular form of verse, which they freely use to express any personal reminiscence or idle sing-song without necessity or serious purpose. For which reason there are many more bad or insignificant sonnets than good ones.

Nevertheless, the sonnet must be held to have been an unspeakable blessing for Italian poetry. The clearness and beauty of its structure, the invitation it gave to elevate the thought in the second and more rapidly moving half, and the ease with which it could be learned by heart, made it valued even by the greatest masters. In fact, they would not have kept it in use down to our own century, had they not been penetrated with a sense of its singular worth. These masters could have given us the same thoughts in other and wholly different forms. But when once they had made the sonnet the normal type of lyrical poetry, many other writers of great, if not the highest, gifts, who otherwise would have lost themselves in a sea of diffusiveness, were forced to concentrate their feelings. The sonnet became for Italian literature a condenser of thoughts and emotions such as was possessed by the poetry of no other modern people.

Thus the world of Italian sentiment comes before us in a series of pictures, clear, concise, and most effective in their brevity. Had other nations possessed a form of expression of the same kind, we should perhaps have known more of their inward life; we might have had a number of pictures of inward and outward situations—reflexions of the national character and temper—and should not be dependent for such knowledge on the so-called lyrical poets of the fourteenth and fifteenth centuries, who can hardly ever be read with any serious enjoyment. In Italy we can trace an undoubted progress from the time when the sonnet came into existence. In the second half of the thirteenth century the 'Trovatori della transizione,' as they have been recently named,[1] mark the passage from the Troubadours to the poets—that is, to those who wrote under the influence of antiquity. The simplicity and strength of their feeling, the vigorous

[1] Trucchi, op. cit. i. 181 sqq.

delineation of fact, the precise expression and rounding off of their sonnets and other poems, herald the coming of a Dante. Some political sonnets of the Guelphs and Ghibellines (1260–1270) have about them the ring of his passion, and others remind us of his sweetest lyrical notes.

Of his own theoretical view of the sonnet, we are unfortunately ignorant, since the last books of his work, 'De vulgari eloquio,' in which he proposed to treat of ballads and sonnets, either remained unwritten or have been lost. But, as a matter of fact, he has left us in his Sonnets and 'Canzoni,' a treasure of inward experience. And in what a framework he has set them! The prose of the 'Vita Nuova,' in which he gives an account of the origin of each poem, is as wonderful as the verses themselves, and forms with them a uniform whole, inspired with the deepest glow of passion. With unflinching frankness and sincerity he lays bare every shade of his joy and his sorrow, and moulds it resolutely into the strictest forms of art. Reading attentively these Sonnets and 'Canzoni,' and the marvellous fragments of the diary of his youth which lie between them, we fancy that throughout the Middle Ages the poets have been purposely fleeing from themselves, and that he was the first to seek his own soul. Before his time we meet with many an artistic verse; but he is the first artist in the full sense of the word—the first who consciously cast immortal matter into an immortal form. Subjective feeling has here a full objective truth and greatness, and most of it is so set forth that all ages and peoples can make it their own.[1] Where he writes in a thoroughly objective spirit, and lets the force of his sentiment be guessed at only by some outward fact, as in the magnificent sonnets 'Tanto gentile,' etc., and 'Vedi perfettamente,' etc., he seems to feel the need of excusing himself.[2] The most beautiful of these poems really belongs to this class—the 'Deh peregrini che pensosi andate.'

Even apart from the 'Divine Comedy,' Dante would have marked by these youthful poems the boundary between mediæ-

[1] These were the 'Canzoni' and Sonnets which every blacksmith and donkey-driver sang and parodied—which made Dante not a little angry. (Comp. Franco Sachetti, Nov. 114, 115.) So quickly did these poems find their way among the people.

[2] *Vita Nuova*, ed. Witte, pp. 81, 82 sqq. 'Deh peregrini,' *ibid.* 116.

valism and modern times. The human spirit had taken a mighty step towards the consciousness of its own secret life.

The revelations in this matter which are contained in the 'Divine Comedy' itself are simply immeasurable; and it would be necessary to go through the whole poem, one canto after another, in order to do justice to its value from this point of view. Happily we have no need to do this, as it has long been a daily food of all the countries of the West. Its plan, and the ideas on which it is based, belong to the Middle Ages, and appeal to our interest only historically; but it is nevertheless the beginning of all modern poetry, through the power and richness shown in the description of human nature in every shape and attitude.[1]

From this time forwards poetry may have experienced unequal fortunes, and may show, for half a century together, a so-called relapse. But its nobler and more vital principle was saved for ever; and whenever in the fourteenth, fifteenth, and in the beginning of the sixteenth centuries, an original mind devotes himself to it, he represents a more advanced stage than any poet out of Italy, given—what is certainly not always easy to settle satisfactorily—an equality of natural gifts to start with.

Here, as in other things, in Italy, culture—to which poetry belongs—precedes the plastic arts and, in fact, gives them their chief impulse. More than a century elapsed before the spiritual element in painting and sculpture attained a power of expression in any way analogous to that of the 'Divine Comedy.' How far the same rule holds good for the artistic development of other nations,[2] and of what importance the whole question may be, does not concern us here. For Italian civilisation it is of decisive weight.

The position to be assigned to Petrarch in this respect must be settled by the many readers of the poet. Those who come to him in the spirit of a cross-examiner, and busy themselves in

[1] For Dante's psychology, the beginning of *Purg.* iv. is one of the most important passages. See also the parts of the *Convito* bearing on the subject.

[2] The portraits of the school of Van Eyck would prove the contrary for the North. They remained for a long period far in advance of all descriptions in words.

detecting the contradictions between the poet and the man, his infidelities in love, and the other weak sides of his character, may perhaps, after sufficient effort, end by losing all taste for his poetry. In place, then, of artistic enjoyment, we may acquire a knowledge of the man in his 'totality.' What a pity that Petrarch's letters from Avignon contain so little gossip to take hold of, and that the letters of his acquaintances and of the friends of these acquaintances have either been lost or never existed! Instead of Heaven being thanked when we are not forced to enquire how and through what struggles a poet has rescued something immortal from his own poor life and lot, a biography has been stitched together for Petrarch out of these so-called 'remains,' which reads like an indictment. But the poet may take comfort. If the printing and editing of the correspondence of celebrated people goes on for another half-century as it has begun in England and Germany, he will have illustrious company enough sitting with him on the stool of repentance.

Without shutting our eyes to much that is forced and artificial in his poetry, where the writer is merely imitating himself and singing on in the old strain, we cannot fail to admire the marvellous abundance of pictures of the inmost soul—descriptions of moments of joy and sorrow which must have been thoroughly his own, since no one before him gives us anything of the kind, and on which his significance rests for his country and for the world. His verse is not in all places equally transparent; by the side of his most beautiful thoughts, stand at times some allegorical conceit, or some sophistical trick of logic, altogether foreign to our present taste. But the balance is on the side of excellence.

Boccaccio, too, in his imperfectly-known Sonnets,[1] succeeds sometimes in giving a most powerful and effective picture of his feeling. The return to a spot consecrated by love (Son. 22), the melancholy of spring (Son. 33), the sadness of the poet who feels himself growing old (Son. 65), are admirably treated by him. And in the 'Ameto' he has described the ennobling and trans-

[1] Printed in the sixteenth volume of his *Opere Volgari*. See M. Landau, *Giov. Boccaccio* (Stuttg. 1877), pp. 36–40; he lays special stress on B.'s dependence on Dante and Petrarch.

figuring power of love in a manner which would hardly be expected from the author of the 'Decamerone.'[1] In the 'Fiammetta' we have another great and minutely-painted picture of the human soul, full of the keenest observation, though executed with anything but uniform power, and in parts marred by the passion for high-sounding language and by an unlucky mixture of mythological allusions and learned quotations. The 'Fiammetta,' if we are not mistaken, is a sort of feminine counterpart to the 'Vita Nuova' of Dante, or at any rate owes its origin to it.

That the ancient poets, particularly the elegists, and Virgil, in the fourth book of the Æneid, were not without influence[2] on the Italians of this and the following generation is beyond a doubt; but the spring of sentiment within the latter was nevertheless powerful and original. If we compare them in this respect with their contemporaries in other countries, we shall find in them the earliest complete expression of modern European feeling. The question, be it remembered, is not to know whether eminent men of other nations did not feel as deeply and as nobly, but who first gave documentary proof of the widest knowledge of the movements of the human heart.

Why did the Italians of the Renaissance do nothing above the second rank in tragedy? That was the field on which to display human character, intellect, and passion, in the thousand forms of their growth, their struggles, and their decline. In other words: why did Italy produce no Shakespeare? For with the stage of other northern countries besides England the Italians of the sixteenth and seventeenth centuries had no reason to fear a comparison; and with the Spaniards they could not enter into competition, since Italy had long lost all traces of

[1] In the song of the shepherd Teogape, after the feast of Venus, *Opp.* ed. Montier, vol. xv. 2, p. 67 sqq. Comp. Landau, 58-64; on the *Fiammetta*, see Landau, 96–105.

[2] The famous Lionardo Aretino, the leader of the humanists at the beginning of the fifteenth century, admits, 'Che gli antichi Greci d' umanita e di gentilezza di cuore abbino avanzanto di gran lunga i nostri Italiani;' but he says it at the beginning of a novel which contains the sentimental story of the invalid Prince Antiochus and his step-mother Stratonice—a document of an ambiguous and half-Asiatic character. (Printed as an Appendix to the *Cento Novelle Antiche*.)

religious fanaticism, treated the chivalrous code of honour only as a form, and was both too proud and too intelligent to bow down before its tyrannical and illegitimate masters.[1] We have therefore only to consider the English stage in the period of its brief splendour.

It is an obvious reply that all Europe produced but one Shakespeare, and that such a mind is the rarest of Heaven's gifts. It is further possible that the Italian stage was on the way to something great when the Counter-reformation broke in upon it, and, aided by the Spanish rule over Naples and Milan, and indirectly over the whole peninsula, withered the best flowers of the Italian spirit. It would be hard to conceive of Shakespeare himself under a Spanish viceroy, or in the neighbourhood of the Holy Inquisition at Rome, or even in his own country a few decades later, at the time of the English Revolution. The stage, which in its perfection is a late product of every civilisation, must wait for its own time and fortune.

We must not, however, quit this subject without mentioning certain circumstances, which were of a character to hinder or retard a high development of the drama in Italy, till the time for it had gone by.

As the most weighty of these causes we must mention without doubt that the scenic tastes of the people were occupied elsewhere, and chiefly in the mysteries and religious processions. Throughout all Europe dramatic representations of sacred history and legend form the origin of the secular drama; but Italy, as it will be shown more fully in the sequel, had spent on the mysteries such a wealth of decorative splendour as could not but be unfavourable to the dramatic element. Out of all the countless and costly representations, there sprang not even a branch of poetry like the 'Autos Sagramentales' of Calderon and other Spanish poets, much less any advantage or foundation for the legitimate drama.[2]

And when the latter did at length appear, it at once gave itself up to magnificence of scenic effects, to which the mysteries had already accustomed the public taste to far too

[1] No doubt the court and prince received flattery enough from their occasional poets and dramatists.

[2] Comp. the contrary view taken by Gregorovius, *Gesch. Roms*, vii. 619.

great an extent. We learn with astonishment how rich and splendid the scenes in Italy were, at a time when in the North the simplest indication of the place was thought sufficient. This alone might have had no such unfavourable effect on the drama, if the attention of the audience had not been drawn away from the poetical conception of the play partly by the splendour of the costumes, partly and chiefly by fantastic interludes (Intermezzi).

That in many places, particularly in Rome and Ferrara, Plautus and Terence, as well as pieces by the old tragedians, were given in Latin or in Italian (pp. 242. 255), that the academies (p. 280) of which we have already spoken, made this one of their chief objects, and that the poets of the Renaissance followed these models too servilely, were all untoward conditions for the Italian stage at the period in question. Yet I hold them to be of secondary importance. Had not the Counter-reformation and the rule of foreigners intervened, these very disadvantages might have been turned into useful means of transition. At all events, by the year 1520 the victory of the mother-tongue in tragedy and comedy was, to the great disgust of the humanists, as good as won.[1] On this side, then, no obstacle stood in the way of the most developed people in Europe, to hinder them from raising the drama, in its noblest forms, to be a true reflexion of human life and destiny. It was the Inquisitors and Spaniards who cowed the Italian spirit, and rendered impossible the representation of the greatest and most sublime themes, most of all when they were associated with patriotic memories. At the same time, there is no doubt that the distracting 'Intermezzi' did serious harm to the drama. We must now consider them a little more closely.

When the marriage of Alfonso of Ferrara with Lucrezia Borgia was celebrated, Duke Hercules in person showed his illustrious guests the 110 costumes which were to serve at the representation of five comedies of Plautus, in order that all might see that not one of them was used twice.[2] But all this

[1] Paul. Jovius, *Dialog. de viris lit. illustr.*, in Tiraboschi, tom. vii. iv. Lil. Greg. Gyraldus, *De poetis nostri temp.*

[2] Isabella Gonzaga to her husband, Feb. 3, 1502, *Arch. Stor.* Append. ii. p. 306 sqq. Comp. Gregorovius, *Lucrezia Borgia*, i. 255–266, ed. 3. In

display of silk and camlet was nothing to the ballets and pantomimes which served as interludes between the acts of the Plautine dramas. That in comparison, Plautus himself seemed mortally dull to a lively young lady like Isabella Gonzaga, and that while the play was going on everybody was longing for the interludes, is quite intelligible, when we think of the picturesque brilliancy with which they were put on the stage. There were to be seen combats of Roman warriors, who brandished their weapons to the sound of music, torch-dances executed by Moors, a dance of savages with horns of plenty, out of which streamed waves of fire—all as the ballet of a pantomime in which a maiden was delivered from a dragon. Then came a dance of fools, got up as punches, beating one another with pigs' bladders, with more of the same kind. At the Court of Ferrara they never gave a comedy without 'its' ballet (Moresca).[1] In what style the 'Amphitryo' of Plautus was there represented (1491, at the first marriage of Alfonso with Anna Sforza), is doubtful. Possibly it was given rather as a pantomime with music, than as a drama.[2] In any case, the accessories were more considerable than the play itself. There was a choral dance of ivy-clad youths, moving in intricate figures, done to the music of a ringing orchestra; then came

the French *Mystères* the actors themselves first marched before the audience in procession, which was called the 'montre.'

[1] *Diario Ferrarese*, in Murat. xxiv. col. 404. Other passages referring to the stage in that city, cols. 278, 279, 282 to 285, 361, 380, 381, 393, 397, from which it appears that Plautus was the dramatist most popular on these occasions, that the performances sometimes lasted till three o'clock in the morning, and were even given in the open air. The ballets were without any meaning or reference to the persons present and the occasion solemnized. Isabella Gonzaga, who was certainly at the time longing for her husband and child, and was dissatisfied with the union of her brother with Lucrezia, spoke of the 'coldness and frostiness' of the marriage and the festivities which attended it.

[2] *Strozzii Poetæ*, fol. 232, in the fourth book of the *Æolosticha* of Tito Strozza. The lines run:

'Ecce superveniens rerum argumenta retexit
Mimus, et ad populum verba diserta refert.
Tum similes habitu formaque et voce Menæchmi
Dulcibus oblectant lumina nostra modis.'

The *Menæchmi* was also given at Ferrara in 1486, at the cost of more than 1,000 ducats. Murat. xxiv. 278.

Apollo, striking the lyre with the plectrum, and singing an ode to the praise of the House of Este; then followed, as an interlude within an interlude, a kind of rustic farce, after which the stage was again occupied by classical mythology—Venus, Bacchus and their followers—and by a pantomime representing the judgment of Paris. Not till then was the second half of the fable of Amphitryo performed, with unmistakable references to the future birth of a Hercules of the House of Este. At a former representation of the same piece in the courtyard of the palace (1487), 'a paradise with stars and other wheels,' was constantly burning, by which is probably meant an illumination with fireworks, that, no doubt, absorbed most of the attention of the spectators. It was certainly better when such performances were given separately, as was the case at other courts. We shall have to speak of the entertainments given by the Cardinal Pietro Riario, by the Bentivogli at Bologna, and by others, when we come to treat of the festivals in general.

This scenic magnificence, now become universal, had a disastrous effect on Italian tragedy. 'In Venice formerly,' writes Francesco Sansovino,[1] 'besides comedies, tragedies by ancient and modern writers were put on the stage with great pomp. The fame of the scenic arrangements (*apparati*) brought spectators from far and near. Nowadays, performances are given by private individuals in their own houses, and the custom has long been fixed of passing the carnival in comedies and other cheerful entertainments.' In other words, scenic display had helped to kill tragedy.

The various starts or attempts of these modern tragedians, among which the 'Sofonisba' of Trissino was the most celebrated, belong to the history of literature. The same may be said of genteel comedy, modelled on Plautus and Terence.

[1] Franc. Sansovino, *Venezia*, fol. 169. The passage in the original is as follows: 'Si sono anco spesso recitate delle tragedie con grandi apparecchi, comporte da poeti antichi o da moderni. Alle quali per la fama degli apparati concorrevano le genti estere e circonvicine per vederle e udirle. Ma hoggi le feste da particolari si fanno fra i parenti et essendosi la città regolata per se medesima da certi anni in quà, si passano i tempi del Carnovale in comedie e in altri più lieti e honorati diletti.' The passage is not thoroughly clear.

Even Ariosto could do nothing of the first order in this style. On the other hand, popular prose-comedy, as treated by Macchiavelli, Bibiena, and Aretino, might have had a future, if its matter had not condemned it to destruction. This was, on the one hand, licentious to the last degree, and on the other, aimed at certain classes in society, which, after the middle of the sixteenth century, ceased to afford a ground for public attacks. If in the 'Sofonisba' the portrayal of character gave place to brilliant declamation, the latter, with its half-sister caricature, was used far too freely in comedy also. Nevertheless, these Italian comedies, if we are not mistaken, were the first written in prose and copied from real life, and for this reason deserve mention in the history of European literature.

The writing of tragedies and comedies, and the practice of putting both ancient and modern plays on the stage, continued without intermission; but they served only as occasions for display. The national genius turned elsewhere for living interest. When the opera and the pastoral fable came up, these attempts were at length wholly abandoned.

One form of comedy only was and remained national—the unwritten, improvised 'Commedia dell' Arte.' It was of no great service in the delineation of character, since the masks used were few in number and familiar to everybody. But the talent of the nation had such an affinity for this style, that often in the middle of written comedies the actors would throw themselves on their own inspiration,[1] so that a new mixed form of comedy came into existence in some places. The plays given in Venice by Burchiello, and afterwards by the company of Armonio, Val. Zuccato, Lod. Dolce, and others, were perhaps of this character.[2] Of Burchiello we know expressly that he used to heighten the comic effect by mixing Greek and Sclavonic words with the Venetian dialect. A complete 'Commedia dell' Arte,' or very nearly so, was represented by Angelo Beolco, known as 'Il Ruzzante' (1502–1542), who enjoyed the highest reputation as poet and actor, was compared as poet to

[1] This must be the meaning of Sansovino, *Venezia*, fol. 168, when he complains that the 'recitanti' ruined the comedies 'con invenzioni o personaggi troppo ridicoli.'

[2] Sansovino, l. c.

Plautus, and as actor to Roscius, and who formed a company with several of his friends, who appeared in his pieces as Paduan peasants, with the names Menato, Vezzo, Billora, &c. He studied their dialect when spending the summer at the villa of his patron Luigi Cornaro (Aloysius Cornelius) at Codevico.[1] Gradually all the famous local masks made their appearance, whose remains still delight the Italian populace at our day: Pantalone, the Doctor, Brighella, Pulcinella, Arlecchino, and the rest. Most of them are of great antiquity, and possibly are historically connected with the masks in the old Roman farces; but it was not till the sixteenth century that several of them were combined in one piece. At the present time this is less often the case; but every great city still keeps to its local mask—Naples to the Pulcinella, Florence to the Stentorello, Milan to its often so admirable Meneghino.[2]

This is indeed scanty compensation for a people which possessed the power, perhaps to a greater degree than any other, to reflect and contemplate its own highest qualities in the mirror of the drama. But this power was destined to be marred for centuries by hostile forces, for whose predominance the Italians were only in part responsible. The universal talent for dramatic representation could not indeed be uprooted, and in music Italy long made good its claim to supremacy in Europe. Those who can find in this world of sound a compensation for the drama, to which all future was denied, have, at all events, no meagre source of consolation.

But perhaps we can find in epic poetry what the stage fails to offer us. Yet the chief reproach made against the heroic

[1] Scardeonius, *De urb. Patav. antiq.*, in Graevius, Thes. vi. iii. col. 288 sqq. An important passage for the literature of the dialects generally. One of the passages is as follows: 'Hinc ad recitandas comœdias socii scenici et gregales et æmuli fuere nobiles juvenes Patavini, Marcus Aurelius Alvarotus quem in comœdiis suis Menatum appellitabat, et Hieronymus Zanetus quem Vezzam, et Castegnola quem Billoram vocitabat, et alii quidam qui sermonem agrestium imitando præ ceteris callebant.'

[2] That the latter existed as early as the fifteenth century may be inferred from the *Diario Ferrerese*, Feb. 2nd, 1501: 'Il duca Hercole fece una festa di Menechino secondo il suo uso.' Murat. xxiv. col. 393. There cannot be a confusion with the Menæchmi of Plautus, which is correctly written, l. c. col. 278. See above, p. 318, note 2.

poetry of Italy is precisely on the score of the insignificance and imperfect representation of its characters.

Other merits are allowed to belong to it, among the rest, that for three centuries it has been actually read and constantly reprinted, while nearly the whole of the epic poetry of other nations has become a mere matter of literary or historical curiosity. Does this perhaps lie in the taste of the readers, who demand something different from what would satisfy a northern public? Certainly, without the power of entering to some degree into Italian sentiment, it is impossible to appreciate the characteristic excellence of these poems, and many distinguished men declare that they can make nothing of them. And in truth, if we criticise Pulci, Bojardo, Ariosto, and Berni solely with an eye to their thought and matter, we shall fail to do them justice. They are artists of a peculiar kind, who write for a people which is distinctly and eminently artistic.

The mediæval legends had lived on after the gradual extinction of the poetry of chivalry, partly in the form of rhyming adaptations and collections, and partly of novels in prose. The latter was the case in Italy during the fourteenth century; but the newly-awakened memories of antiquity were rapidly growing up to a gigantic size, and soon cast into the shade all the fantastic creations of the Middle Ages. Boccaccio, for example, in his 'Visione Amorosa,' names among the heroes in his enchanted palace Tristram, Arthur, Galeotto, and others, but briefly, as if he were ashamed to speak of them (p. 206); and following writers either do not name them at all, or name them only for purposes of ridicule. But the people kept them in its memory, and from the people they passed into the hands of the poets of the fifteenth century. These were now able to conceive and represent their subject in a wholly new manner. But they did more. They introduced into it a multitude of fresh elements, and in fact recast it from beginning to end. It must not be expected of them that they should treat such subjects with the respect once felt for them. All other countries must envy them the advantage of having a popular interest of this kind to appeal to; but they could not without hypocrisy treat these myths with any respect.[1]

[1] Pulci mischievously invents a solemn old-world legend for his story

Instead of this, they moved with victorious freedom in the new field which poetry had won. What they chiefly aimed at seems to have been that their poems, when recited, should produce the most harmonious and exhilarating effect. These works indeed gain immensely when they are repeated, not as a whole, but piecemeal, and with a slight touch of comedy in voice and gesture. A deeper and more detailed portrayal of character would do little to enhance this effect; though the reader may desire it, the hearer, who sees the rhapsodist standing before him, and who hears only one piece at a time, does not think about it at all. With respect to the figures which the poet found ready made for him, his feeling was of a double kind; his humanistic culture protested against their mediæval character, and their combats as counterparts of the battles and tournaments of the poet's own age exercised all his knowledge and artistic power, while at the same time they called forth all the highest qualities in the reciter. Even in Pulci,[1] accordingly, we find no parody, strictly speaking, of chivalry, nearly as the rough humour of his paladins at times approaches it. By their side stands the ideal of pugnacity—the droll and jovial Morgante—who masters whole armies with his bell-clapper, and who is himself thrown into relief by contrast with the grotesque and most interesting monster Margutte. Yet Pulci lays no special stress on these two rough and vigorous characters, and his story, long after they had disappeared from it, maintains its singular course. Bojardo[2] treats his characters with the same mastery, using them for serious or comic purposes as he pleases; he has his fun even out of supernatural beings, whom he sometimes intentionally depicts as louts. But there is one artistic aim which he pursues as earnestly as Pulci, namely, the lively and exact description of all that goes forward. Pulci recited his poem, as one book after another

of the giant Margutte (*Morgante*, canto xix. str. 153 sqq.). The critical introduction of Limerno Pitocco is still droller (*Orlandino*, cap. i. str. 12–22).

[1] The *Morgante* was written in 1460 and the following years, and first printed at Venice in 1481. Last ed. by P. Sermolli, Florence, 1872. For the tournaments, see part v. chap. i. See, for what follows, Ranke: *Zur Geschichte der italienischen Poesie*, Berlin, 1837.

[2] The *Orlando inamorato* was first printed in 1496.

was finished, before the society of Lorenzo Magnifico, and in the same way Bojardo recited his at the court of Hercules of Ferrara. It may be easily imagined what sort of excellence such an audience demanded, and how little thanks a profound exposition of character would have earned for the poet. Under these circumstances the poems naturally formed no complete whole, and might just as well be half or twice as long as they now are. Their composition is not that of a great historical picture, but rather that of a frieze, or of some rich festoon entwined among groups of picturesque figures. And precisely as in the figures or tendrils of a frieze we do not look for minuteness of execution in the individual forms, or for distant perspectives and different planes, so we must as little expect anything of the kind from these poems.

The varied richness of invention which continually astonishes us, most of all in the case of Bojardo, turns to ridicule all our school definitions as to the essence of epic poetry. For that age, this form of literature was the most agreeable diversion from archæological studies, and, indeed, the only possible means of re-establishing an independent class of narrative poetry. For the versification of ancient history could only lead to the false tracks which were trodden by Petrarch in his 'Africa,' written in Latin hexameters, and a hundred and fifty years later by Trissino in his 'Italy delivered from the Goths,' composed in 'versi sciolti'—a never-ending poem of faultless language and versification, which only makes us doubt whether an unlucky alliance has been most disastrous to history or to poetry.[1]

And whither did the example of Dante beguile those who imitated him? The visionary 'Trionfi' of Petrarch were the last of the works written under this influence which satisfy our taste. The 'Amorosa Visione' of Boccaccio is at bottom no more than an enumeration of historical or fabulous characters, arranged under allegorical categories.[2] Others preface

[1] *L' Italia liberata da Goti*, Rome, 1547.

[2] See above, p. 319, and Landau's *Boccaccio*, 64–69. It must, nevertheless, be observed that the work of Boccaccio here mentioned was written before 1344, while that of Petrarch was written after Laura's death, that is, after 1348.

what they have to tell with a baroque imitation of Dante's first canto, and provide themselves with some allegorical comparison, to take the place of Virgil. Uberti, for example, chose Solinus for his geographical poem—the 'Dittamondo'—and Giovanni Santi, Plutarch for his encomium on Frederick of Urbino.[1] The only salvation of the time from these false tendencies lay in the new epic poetry which was represented by Pulci and Bojardo. The admiration and curiosity with which it was received, and the like of which will perhaps never fall again to the lot of epic poetry to the end of time, is a brilliant proof how great was the need of it. It is idle to ask whether that epic ideal which our own day has formed from Homer and the 'Nibelungenlied' is or is not realised in these works; an ideal of their own age certainly was. By their endless descriptions of combats, which to us are the most fatiguing part of these poems, they satisfied, as we have already said, a practical interest of which it is hard for us to form a just conception[2]—as hard, indeed, as of the esteem in which a lively and faithful reflection of the passing moment was then held.

Nor can a more inappropriate test be applied to Ariosto than the degree in which his 'Orlando Furioso'[3] serves for the representation of character. Characters, indeed, there are, and drawn with an affectionate care; but the poem does not depend on these for its effect, and would lose, rather than gain, if more stress were laid upon them. But the demand for them is part of a wider and more general desire which Ariosto fails to satisfy as our day would wish it satisfied. From a poet of such fame and such mighty gifts we would gladly receive something better than the adventures of Orlando. From him we might have hoped for a work expressing the deepest conflicts of the human soul, the highest thoughts of his time on human and divine things—in a word, one of those supreme syntheses like the 'Divine Comedy' or 'Faust.' Instead of which he goes to work like the plastic artists of his own day, not caring for originality in our sense of the word, simply reproducing a

[1] Vasari, viii. 71, in the Commentary to the *Vita di Rafaelle.*

[2] Much of this kind our present taste could dispense with in the *Iliad.*

[3] First edition, 1516.

familiar circle of figures, and even, when it suits his purpose, making use of the details left him by his predecessors. The excellence which, in spite of all this, can nevertheless be attained, will be the more incomprehensible to people born without the artistic sense, the more learned and intelligent in other respects they are. The artistic aim of Ariosto is brilliant, living action, which he distributes equally through the whole of his great poem. For this end he needs to be excused, not only from all deeper expression of character, but also from maintaining any strict connection in his narrative. He must be allowed to take up lost and forgotten threads when and where he pleases; his heroes must come and go, not because their character, but because the story requires it. Yet in this apparently irrational and arbitrary style of composition he displays a harmonious beauty, never losing himself in description, but giving only such a sketch of scenes and persons as does not hinder the flowing movement of the narrative. Still less does he lose himself in conversation and monologue,[1] but maintains the lofty privilege of the true epos, by transforming all into living narrative. His pathos does not lie in the words,[2] not even in the famous twenty-third and following cantos, where Roland's madness is described. That the love-stories in the heroic poem are without all lyrical tenderness, must be reckoned a merit, though from a moral point of view they cannot be always approved. Yet at times they are of such truth and reality, notwithstanding all the magic and romance which surrounds them, that we might think them personal affairs of the poet himself. In the full consciousness of his own genius, he does not scruple to interweave the events of his own day into the poem, and to celebrate the fame of the house of Este in visions and prophecies. The wonderful stream of his octaves bears it all forwards in even and dignified movement.

With Teofilo Folengo, or, as he here calls himself, Limerno Pitocco, the parody of the whole system of chivalry attained the end it had so long desired.[3] But here comedy, with its realism, demanded of necessity a stricter delineation of char-

[1] The speeches inserted are themselves narratives.

[2] As was the case with Pulci, *Morgante*, canto xix. str. 20 sqq.

[3] The *Orlandino*, first edition, 1526.

acter. Exposed to all the rough usage of the half-savage street-lads in a Roman country town, Sutri, the little Orlando grows up before our eyes into the hero, the priest-hater, and the disputant. The conventional world which had been recognised since the time of Pulci and had served as framework for the epos, falls here to pieces. The origin and position of the paladins is openly ridiculed, as in the tournament of donkeys in the second book, where the knights appear with the most ludicrous armament. The poet utters his ironical regrets over the inexplicable faithlessness which seems implanted in the house of Gano of Mainz, over the toilsome acquisition of the sword Durindana, and so forth. Tradition, in fact, serves him only as a substratum for episodes, ludicrous fancies, allusions to events of the time (among which some, like the close of cap. vi. are exceedingly fine), and indecent jokes. Mixed with all this, a certain derision of Ariosto is unmistakable, and it was fortunate for the 'Orlando Furioso' that the 'Orlandino,' with its Lutheran heresies, was soon put out of the way by the Inquisition. The parody is evident when (cap. v. str. 28) the house of Gonzaga is deduced from the paladin Guidone, since the Colonna claimed Orlando, the Orsini Rinaldo, and the house of Este—according to Ariosto—Ruggiero as their ancestors. Perhaps Ferrante Gonzaga, the patron of the poet, was a party to this sarcasm on the house of Este.

That in the 'Jerusalem Delivered' of Torquato Tasso the delineation of character is one of the chief tasks of the poet, proves only how far his mode of thought differed from that prevalent half a century before. His admirable work is a true monument of the Counter-reformation which had been meanwhile accomplished, and of the spirit and tendency of that movement.

CHAPTER V.

BIOGRAPHY.

OUTSIDE the sphere of poetry also, the Italians were the first of all European nations who displayed any remarkable power and inclination accurately to describe man as shown in history, according to his inward and outward characteristics.

It is true that in the Middle Ages considerable attempts were made in the same direction; and the legends of the Church, as a kind of standing biographical task, must, to some extent, have kept alive the interest and the gift for such descriptions. In the annals of the monasteries and cathedrals, many of the churchmen, such as Meinwerk of Paderborn, Godehard of Kildesheim, and others, are brought vividly before our eyes; and descriptions exist of several of the German emperors, modelled after old authors—particularly Suetonius—which contain admirable features. Indeed these and other profane 'vitae' came in time to form a continuous counterpart to the sacred legends. Yet neither Einhard nor Radevicus [1] can be named by the side of Joinville's picture of St. Louis, which certainly stands almost alone as the first complete spiritual portrait of a modern European nature. Characters like St. Louis are rare at all times, and his was favoured by the rare good fortune that a sincere and naïve observer caught the spirit of all the events and actions of his life, and represented it admirably. From what scanty sources are we left to guess at the inward nature of Frederick II. or of Philip the Fair. Much of what, till the close of the Middle Ages, passed for biography, is properly speaking nothing but contemporary narrative, written without any sense of what is individual in the subject of the memoir.

[1] Radevicus, *De gestis Friderici imp.*, especially ii. 76. The admirable *Vita Henrici IV.* contains very little personal description, as is also the case with the *Vita Chuonradi imp.* by Wipo.

Among the Italians, on the contrary, the search for the characteristic features of remarkable men was a prevailing tendency; and this it is which separates them from the other western peoples, among whom the same thing happens but seldom, and in exceptional cases. This keen eye for individuality belongs only to those who have emerged from the half-conscious life of the race and become themselves individuals.

Under the influence of the prevailing conception of fame (p. 139, sqq.), an art of comparative biography arose which no longer found it necessary, like Anastasius,[1] Agnellus,[2] and their successors, or like the biographers of the Venetian doges, to adhere to a dynastic or ecclesiastical succession. It felt itself free to describe a man if and because he was remarkable. It took as models Suetonius, Nepos (the 'viri illustres'), and Plutarch, so far as he was known and translated; for sketches of literary history, the lives of the grammarians, rhetoricians, and poets, known to us as the 'Appendices' to Suetonius,[3] seem to have served as patterns, as well as the widely-read life of Virgil by Donatus.

It has been already mentioned that biographical collections —lives of famous men and famous women—began to appear in the fourteenth century (p. 146). Where they do not describe contemporaries, they are naturally dependent on earlier narratives. The first great original effort is the life of Dante by Boccaccio. Lightly and rhetorically written, and full, as it is, of arbitrary fancies, this work nevertheless gives us a lively sense of the extraordinary features in Dante's nature.[4] Then follow, at the end of the fourteenth century, the 'vite' of

[1] The librarian Anastasius (middle of ninth century) is here meant. The whole collection of the lives of the Popes (*Liber Pontificalis*) was formerly ascribed to him, but erroneously. Comp. Wattenbach, *Deutschland's Geschichtsquellen*, i. 223 sqq. 3rd ed.

[2] Lived about the same time as Anastasius; author of a history of the bishopric of Ravenna. Wattenbach, l. c. 227.

[3] How early Philostratus was used in the same way, I am unable to say. Suetonius was no doubt taken as a model in times still earlier. Besides the life of Charles the Great, written by Eginhard, examples from the twelfth century are offered by William of Malmesbury in his descriptions of William the Conqueror (p. 446 sqq., 452 sqq.), of William II. (pp. 494, 504), and of Henry I. (p. 640).

[4] See the admirable criticism in Landau, *Boccaccio*, 180–182.

illustrious Florentines, by Filippo Villani. They are men of every calling: poets, jurists, physicians, scholars, artists, statesmen, and soldiers, some of them then still living. Florence is here treated like a gifted family, in which all the members are noticed in whom the spirit of the house expresses itself vigorously. The descriptions are brief, but show a remarkable eye for what is characteristic, and are noteworthy for including the inward and outward physiognomy in the same sketch.[1] From that time forward,[2] the Tuscans never ceased to consider the description of man as lying within their special competence, and to them we owe the most valuable portraits of the Italians of the fifteenth and sixteenth centuries. Giovanni Cavalcanti, in the appendices to his Florentine history, written before the year 1450,[3] collects instances of civil virtue and abnegation, of political discernment and of military valour, all shown by Florentines. Pius II. gives us in his 'Commentaries' valuable portraits of famous contemporaries; and not long ago a separate work of his earlier years,[4] which seems preparatory to these portraits, but which has colours and features that are very singular, was reprinted. To Jacob of Volterra we owe piquant sketches of members of the Curia[5] in the time of Sixtus IV. Vespasiano Fiorentino has been often referred to already, and as a historical authority a high place must be assigned to him; but his gift as a painter of character is not to be compared with that of Macchiavelli, Niccolò Valori, Guicciardini, Varchi,

[1] See above, p. 131. The original (Latin) was first published in 1847 at Florence, by Galletti, with the title, *Philippi Villani Liber de civitatis Florentiae famosis civibus*; an old Italian translation has been often printed since 1747, last at Trieste, 1858. The first book, which treats of the earliest history of Florence and Rome, has never been printed. The chapter in Villani, *De semipoetis*, i.e. those who wrote in prose as well as in verse, or those who wrote poems besides following some other profession, is specially interesting.

[2] Here we refer the reader to the biography of L. B. Alberti, from which extracts are given above (p. 136), and to the numerous Florentine biographies in Muratori, in the *Archivio Storico*, and elsewhere. The life of Alberti is probably an autobiography, l. c. note 2.

[3] *Storia Fiorentina*, ed. F. L. Polidori, Florence, 1838.

[4] *De viris illustribus*, in the publications of the *Stuttgarter liter. Vereins*, No. i. Stuttg. 1839. Comp. C. Voigt, ii. 324. Of the sixty-five biographies, twenty-one are lost.

[5] His *Diarium Romanum* from 1472 to 1484, in Murat. xiii. 81–202.

Francesco Vettori, and others, by whom European history has been probably as much influenced in this direction as by the ancients. It must not be forgotten that some of these authors soon found their way into northern countries by means of Latin translations. And without Giorgio Vasari of Arezzo and his all-important work, we should perhaps to this day have no history of northern art, or of the art of modern Europe, at all.[1]

Among the biographers of North Italy in the fifteenth century, Bartolommeo Facio of Spezzia holds a high rank (p. 147). Platina, born in the territory of Cremona, gives us, in his 'Life of Paul II.' (p. 231), examples of biographical caricatures. The description of the last Visconti,[2] written by Piercandido Decembrio—an enlarged imitation of Suetonius—is of special importance. Sismondi regrets that so much trouble has been spent on so unworthy an object, but the author would hardly have been equal to deal with a greater man, while he was thoroughly competent to describe the mixed nature of Filippo Maria, and in and through it to represent with accuracy the conditions, the forms, and the consequences of this particular kind of despotism. The picture of the fifteenth century would be incomplete without this unique biography, which is characteristic down to its minutest details. Milan afterwards possessed, in the historian Corio, an excellent portrait-painter; and after him came Paolo Giovio of Como, whose larger biographies and shorter 'Elogia' have achieved a world-wide reputation, and become models for future writers in all countries. It is easy to prove by a hundred passages how superficial and even dishonest he was; nor from a man like him can any high and serious purpose be expected. But the breath of the age moves in his pages, and his Leo, his Alfonso, his Pompeo Colonna, live and act before us with such perfect truth and reality, that we seem admitted to the deepest recesses of their nature.

[1] *Ugolini Verini poetae Florentini* (a contemporary of Lorenzo, a pupil of Landinus, fol. 13, and teacher of Petrus Crinitus, fol. 14), *De illustratione urbis Florentinae libri tres*, Paris, 1583, deserves mention, esp. lib. 2. Dante, Petrarch, Boccaccio are spoken of and characterised without a word of blame. For several women, see fol. 11.

[2] *Petri Candidi Decembrii Vita Philippi Mariae Vicecomitis*, in Murat. xx. Comp. above, p. 38.

Among Neapolitan writers, Tristano Caracciolo (p. 36), so far as we are able to judge, holds indisputably the first place in this respect, although his purpose was not strictly biographical. In the figures which he brings before us, guilt and destiny are wondrously mingled. He is a kind of unconscious tragedian. That genuine tragedy which then found no place on the stage, 'swept by' in the palace, the street, and the public square. The 'Words and Deeds of Alfonso the Great,' written by Antonio Panormita [1] during the lifetime of the king, and consequently showing more of the spirit of flattery than is consistent with historical truth, are remarkable as one of the first of such collections of anecdotes and of wise and witty sayings.

The rest of Europe followed the example of Italy in this respect but slowly,[2] although great political and religious movements had broken so many bands, and had awakened so many thousands to new spiritual life. Italians, whether scholars or diplomatists, still remained, on the whole, the best source of information for the characters of the leading men all over Europe. It is well known how speedily and unanimously in recent times the reports of the Venetian embassies in the sixteenth and seventeenth centuries have been recognised as authorities of the first order for personal description.[3] Even autobiography takes here and there in Italy a bold and vigorous flight, and puts before us, together with the most varied incidents of external life, striking revelations of the inner man. Among other nations, even in Germany at the time of the Reformation, it deals only with outward experiences, and leaves us to guess at the spirit within from the style of the

[1] See above, p. 225.

[2] On Comines, see above, p. 96, note 1. While Comines, as is there indicated, partly owes his power of objective criticism to intercourse with Italians, the German humanists and statesmen, notwithstanding the prolonged residence of some of them in Italy, and their diligent and often most successful study of the classical world, acquired little or nothing of the gift of biographical representation or of the analysis of character. The travels, biographies, and historical sketches of the German humanists in the fifteenth, and often in the early part of the sixteenth centuries, are mostly either dry catalogues or empty, rhetorical declamations.

[3] See above, p. 96.

narrative.[1] It seems as though Dante's 'Vita Nuova,' with the inexorable truthfulness which runs through it, had shown his people the way.

The beginnings of autobiography are to be traced in the family histories of the fourteenth and fifteenth centuries, which are said to be not uncommon as manuscripts in the Florentine libraries—unaffected narratives written for the sake of the individual or of his family, like that of Buonaccorso Pitti.

A profound self-analysis is not to be looked for in the 'Commentaries' of Pius II. What we here learn of him as a man seems at first sight to be chiefly confined to the account which he gives of the different steps in his career. But further reflexion will lead us to a different conclusion with regard to this remarkable book. There are men who are by nature mirrors of what surrounds them. It would be irrelevant to ask incessantly after their convictions, their spiritual struggles, their inmost victories and achievements. Æneas Sylvius lived wholly in the interest which lay near, without troubling himself about the problems and contradictions of life. His Catholic orthodoxy gave him all the help of this kind which he needed. And at all events, after taking part in every intellectual movement which interested his age, and notably furthering some of them, he still at the close of his earthly course retained character enough to preach a crusade against the Turks, and to die of grief when it came to nothing.

Nor is the autobiography of Benvenuto Cellini, any more than that of Pius II., founded on introspection. And yet it describes the whole man—not always willingly—with marvellous truth and completeness. It is no small matter that Benvenuto, whose most important works have perished half finished, and who, as an artist, is perfect only in his little decorative specialty, but in other respects, if judged by the works of him which remain, is surpassed by so many of his

[1] Here and there we find exceptions. Letters of Hutten, containing autobiographical notices, bits of the chronicle of Barth. Sastrow, and the *Sabbata* of Joh. Kessler, introduce us to the inward conflicts of the writers, mostly, however, bearing the specifically religious character of the Reformation.

greater contemporaries—that Benvenuto as a man will interest mankind to the end of time. It does not spoil the impression when the reader often detects him bragging or lying; the stamp of a mighty, energetic, and thoroughly developed nature remains. By his side our northern autobiographers, though their tendency and moral character may stand much higher, appear incomplete beings. He is a man who can do all and dares do all, and who carries his measure in himself.[1] Whether we like him or not, he lives, such as he was, as a significant type of the modern spirit.

Another man deserves a brief mention in connection with this subject—a man who, like Benvenuto, was not a model of veracity: Girolamo Cardano of Milan (b. 1500). His little book, 'De propria vita'[2] will outlive and eclipse his fame in philosophy and natural science, just as Benvenuto's life, though its value is of another kind, has thrown his works into the shade. Cardano is a physician who feels his own pulse, and describes his own physical, moral, and intellectual nature, together with all the conditions under which it had developed, and this, to the best of his ability, honestly and sincerely. The work which he avowedly took as his model—the 'Confessions' of Marcus Aurelius—he was able, hampered as he was by no stoical maxims, to surpass in this particular. He desires to spare neither himself nor others, and begins the narrative of his career with the statement that his mother tried, and failed, to procure abortion. It is worth remark that he attributes to the stars which presided over his birth only the events of his life and his intellectual gifts, but not his moral qualities; he confesses (cap. 10) that the astrological prediction that he would not live to the age of forty or fifty years did him much harm in his youth. But there is no need to quote from so well-known and accessible a book; whoever opens it will not lay it down till the last page. Cardano admits that he cheated at play, that he was vindictive, incapable of all compunction,

[1] Among northern autobiographies we might, perhaps, select for comparison that of Agrippa d'Aubigné (though belonging to a later period) as a living and speaking picture of human individuality.

[2] Written in his old age, about 1576. On Cardano as an investigator and discoverer, see Libri, *Hist. des Sciences Mathém.* iii. p. 167 sqq.

purposely cruel in his speech. He confesses it without impudence and without feigned contrition, without even wishing to make himself an object of interest, but with the same simple and sincere love of fact which guided him in his scientific researches. And, what is to us the most repulsive of all, the old man, after the most shocking experiences [1] and with his confidence in his fellow-men gone, finds himself after all tolerably happy and comfortable. He has still left him a grandson, immense learning, the fame of his works, money, rank and credit, powerful friends, the knowledge of many secrets, and, best of all, belief in God. After this, he counts the teeth in his head, and finds that he has fifteen.

Yet when Cardano wrote, Inquisitors and Spaniards were already busy in Italy, either hindering the production of such natures, or, where they existed, by some means or other putting them out of the way. There lies a gulf between this book and the memoirs of Alfieri.

Yet it would be unjust to close this list of autobiographers without listening to a word from one man who was both worthy and happy. This is the well-known philosopher of practical life, Luigi Cornaro, whose dwelling at Padua, classical as an architectural work, was at the same time the home of all the muses. In his famous treatise 'On the Sober Life,' [2] he describes the strict regimen by which he succeeded, after a sickly youth, in reaching an advanced and healthy age, then of eighty-three years. He goes on to answer those who despise life after the age of sixty-five as a living death, showing them that his own life had nothing deadly about it. 'Let them come and see, and wonder at my good health, how I mount on horseback without help, how I run upstairs and up hills, how cheerful, amusing, and contented I am, how free from care and disagreeable thoughts. Peace and joy never quit me. . . . My friends are wise, learned, and distinguished people of good position, and when they are not with me I read and write, and

[1] E.g. the execution of his eldest son, who had taken vengeance for his wife's infidelity by poisoning her (cap. 27, 50).

[2] *Discorsi della Vita Sobria*, consisting of the 'trattato,' of a 'compendio,' of an 'esortazione,' and of a 'lettera' to Daniel Barbaro. The book has been often reprinted.

try thereby, as by all other means, to be useful to others. Each of these things I do at the proper time, and at my ease, in my dwelling, which is beautiful and lies in the best part of Padua, and is arranged both for summer and winter with all the resources of architecture, and provided with a garden by the running water. In the spring and autumn, I go for awhile to my hill in the most beautiful part of the Euganean mountains, where I have fountains and gardens, and a comfortable dwelling; and there I amuse myself with some easy and pleasant chase, which is suitable to my years. At other times I go to my villa on the plain;[1] there all the paths lead to an open space, in the middle of which stands a pretty church; an arm of the Brenta flows through the plantations—fruitful, well-cultivated fields, now fully peopled, which the marshes and the foul air once made fitter for snakes than for men. It was I who drained the country; then the air became good, and people settled there and multiplied, and the land became cultivated as it now is, so that I can truly say: "On this spot I gave to God an altar and a temple, and souls to worship Him." This is my consolation and my happiness whenever I come here. In the spring and autumn, I also visit the neighbouring towns, to see and converse with my friends, through whom I make the acquaintance of other distinguished men, architects, painters, sculptors, musicians, and cultivators of the soil. I see what new things they have done, I look again at what I know already, and learn much that is of use to me. I see palaces, gardens, antiquities, public grounds, churches, and fortifications. But what most of all delights me when I travel, is the beauty of the country and the cities, lying now on the plain, now on the slopes of the hills, or on the banks of rivers and streams, surrounded by gardens and villas. And these enjoyments are not diminished through weakness of the eyes or the ears; all my senses (thank God!) are in the best condition, including the sense of taste; for I enjoy more the simple food which I now take in moderation, than all the delicacies which I ate in my years of disorder.'

After mentioning the works he had undertaken on behalf of

[1] Was this the villa of Codevico mentioned above, p. 321?

the republic for draining the marshes, and the projects which he had constantly advocated for preserving the lagunes, he thus concludes:—

'These are the true recreations of an old age which God has permitted to be healthy, and which is free from those mental and bodily sufferings to which so many young people and so many sickly older people succumb. And if it be allowable to add the little to the great, to add jest to earnest, it may be mentioned as a result of my moderate life, that in my eighty-third year I have written a most amusing comedy, full of blameless wit. Such works are generally the business of youth, as tragedy is the business of old age. If it is reckoned to the credit of the famous Greek that he wrote a tragedy in his seventy-third year, must I not, with my ten years more, be more cheerful and healthy than he ever was? And that no consolation may be wanting in the overflowing cup of my old age, I see before my eyes a sort of bodily immortality in the persons of my descendants. When I come home I see before me, not one or two, but eleven grandchildren, between the ages of two and eighteen, all from the same father and mother, all healthy, and, so far as can already be judged, all gifted with the talent and disposition for learning and a good life. One of the younger I have as my playmate (buffoncello), since children from the third to the fifth year are born to tricks; the elder ones I treat as my companions, and, as they have admirable voices, I take delight in hearing them sing and play on different instruments. And I sing myself, and find my voice better, clearer, and louder than ever. These are the pleasures of my last years. My life, therefore, is alive, and not dead; nor would I exchange my age for the youth of such as live in the service of their passions.

In the 'Exhortation' which Cornaro added at a much later time, in his ninety-fifth year, he reckons it among the elements of his happiness that his 'Treatise' had made many converts. He died at Padua in 1565, at the age of over a hundred years.

CHAPTER VI.

THE DESCRIPTION OF NATIONS AND CITIES.

THIS national gift did not, however, confine itself to the criticism and description of individuals, but felt itself competent to deal with the qualities and characteristics of whole peoples. Throughout the Middle Ages the cities, families, and nations of all Europe were in the habit of making insulting and derisive attacks on one another, which, with much caricature, contained commonly a kernel of truth. But from the first the Italians surpassed all others in their quick apprehension of the mental differences among cities and populations. Their local patriotism, stronger probably than in any other mediæval people, soon found expression in literature, and allied itself with the current conception of 'Fame.' Topography became the counterpart of biography (p. 145); while all the more important cities began to celebrate their own praises in prose and verse,[1] writers appeared who made the chief towns and districts the subject partly of a serious comparative description, partly of satire, and sometimes of notices in which jest and earnest are not easy to be distinguished. Brunetto Latini must first be mentioned. Besides his own country, he knew France from a residence of seven years, and gives a long list of the characteristic differences in costume and modes of life between Frenchmen and Italians, noticing the distinction between the monarchical government of France and the republican constitution of the Italian cities.[2]

[1] In some cases very early; in the Lombard cities as early as the twelfth century. Comp. Landulfus senior, *Ricobaldus*, and (in Murat. x.) the remarkable anonymous work, *De laudibus Papiae*, of the fourteenth century. Also (in Murat. i.) *Liber de Situ urbis Mediol.* Some notices on Italian local history in O. Lorenzo, *Deutschland's Geschichtsquellen im Mittelalter seit dem 13ten Jahr.* Berlin, 1877; but the author expressly refrains from an original treatment of the subject.

[2] *Li Tresors*, ed. Chabaille, Paris, 1863, pp. 179–180. Comp. *ibid.* p. 577 (lib. iii. p. ii. c. 1).

After this, next to some famous passages in the 'Divine Comedy,' comes the 'Dittamondo' of Uberti (about 1360). As a rule, only single remarkable facts and characteristics are here mentioned: the Feast of the Crows at Sant' Apollinare in Ravenna, the springs at Treviso, the great cellar near Vicenza, the high duties at Mantua, the forest of towers at Lucca. Yet mixed up with all this, we find laudatory and satirical criticisms of every kind. Arezzo figures with the crafty disposition of its citizens, Genoa with the artificially blackened eyes and teeth (?) of its women, Bologna with its prodigality, Bergamo with its coarse dialect and hard-headed people.[1] In the fifteenth century the fashion was to belaud one's own city even at the expense of others. Michele Savonarola allows that, in comparison with his native Padua, only Rome and Venice are more splendid, and Florence perhaps more joyous[2]—by which our knowledge is naturally not much extended. At the end of the century, Jovianus Pontanus, in his 'Antonius,' writes an imaginary journey through Italy, simply as a vehicle for malicious observations. But in the sixteenth century we meet with a series of exact and profound studies of national characteristics, such as no other people of that time could rival.[3] Macchiavelli sets forth in some of his valuable essays the character and the political condition of the Germans and French in such a way, that the born northerner, familiar with the history of his own country, is grateful to the Florentine thinker for his flashes of insight. The Florentines (p. 71 sqq.) begin to take pleasure in describing themselves;[4] and basking in the well-earned sunshine of their intellectual

[1] On Paris, which was a much more important place to the mediæval Italian than to his successor a hundred years later, see *Dittamondo*, iv. cap. 18. The contrast between France and Italy is accentuated by Petrarch in his *Invectivae contra Gallum*.

[2] Savonarola, in Murat. xxiv. col. 1186 (above, p. 145). On Venice, see above, p. 62 sqq. The oldest description of Rome, by Signorili (MS.), was written in the pontificate of Martin V. (1417); see Gregorovius, vii. 569; the oldest by a German is that of H. Muffel (middle of fifteenth century), ed. by Voigt, Tübingen, 1876.

[3] The character of the restless and energetic Bergamasque, full of curiosity and suspicion, is charmingly described in Bandello, parte i. nov. 34.

[4] E.g. Varchi, in the ninth book of the *Storie Fiorentine* (vol. iii. p. 56 sqq.).

glory, their pride seems to attain its height when they derive the artistic pre-eminence of Tuscany among Italians, not from any special gifts of nature, but from hard patient work.[1] The homage of famous men from other parts of Italy, of which the sixteenth Capitolo of Ariosto is a splendid example, they accepted as a merited tribute to their excellence.

An admirable description of the Italians, with their various pursuits and characteristics, though in few words and with special stress laid on the Lucchese, to whom the work was dedicated, was given by Ortensio Landi, who, however, is so fond of playing hide-and-seek with his own name, and fast-and-loose with historical facts, that even when he seems to be most in earnest, he must be accepted with caution and only after close examination.[2] The same Landi published an anonymous 'Commentario'

[1] Vasari, xii. p. 158. *V. di Michelangelo*, at the beginning. At other times mother nature is praised loudly enough, as in the sonnet of Alfons de' Pazzi to the non-Tuscan Annibal Caro (in Trucchi, l. c. iii. p. 187):

> 'Misero il Varchi! e più infelici noi,
> Se a vostri virtudi accidentali
> Aggiunto fosse 'l natural, ch' è in noi!'

[2] *Forcianae Quaestiones, in quibus varia Italorum ingenia explicantur, multaque alia scitu non indigna.* Autore Philalette Polytopiensi cive. Among them, *Mauritii Scaevae Carmen.*

> 'Quos hominum mores varios quas denique mentes
> Diverso profert Itala terra solo,
> Quisve vinis animus, mulierum et strenua virtus
> Pulchre hoc exili codice lector habes.'

Neapoli excudebat Martinus de Ragusia, Anno MDXXXVI. This little work, made use of by Ranke, *Päpste*, i. 385, passes as being from the hand of Ortensio Landi (comp. Tiraboschi, vii. 800 to 812), although in the work itself no hint is given of the author. The title is explained by the circumstance that conversations are reported which were held at Forcium, a bath near Lucca, by a large company of men and women, on the question whence it comes that there are such great differences among mankind. The question receives no answer, but many of the differences among the Italians of that day are noticed—in studies, trade, warlike skill (the point quoted by Ranke), the manufacture of warlike implements, modes of life, distinctions in costume, in language, in intellect, in loving and hating, in the way of winning affection, in the manner of receiving guests, and in eating. At the close, come some reflections on the differences among philosophical systems. A large part of the work is devoted to women—their differences in general, the power of their beauty, and especially the question whether women are equal or inferior to men. The work has been made use of in

some ten years later,[1] which contains among many follies not a few valuable hints on the unhappy ruined condition of Italy in

various passages below. The following extract may serve as an example (fol. 7 *b* sqq.):—'Aperiam nunc quæ sint in consilio aut dando aut accipiendo dissimilitudo. Præstant consilio Mediolanenses, sed aliorum gratia potius quam sua. Sunt nullo consilio Genuenses. Rumor est Venetos abundare. Sunt perutili consilio Lucenses, idque aperte indicarunt, cum in tanto totius Italiæ ardore, tot hostibus circumsepti suam libertatem, ad quam nati videntur semper tutati sint, nulla, quidem, aut capitis aut fortunarum ratione habita. Quis porro non vehementer admiretur? Quis callida consilia non stupeat? Equidem quotiescunque cogito, quanta prudentia ingruentes procellas evitarint, quanta solertia impendentia pericula effugerint, adducor in stuporem. Lucanis vero summum est studium, eos deludere qui consilii captandi gratia adeunt, ipsi vero omnia inconsulte ac temere faciunt. Brutii optimo sunt consilio, sed ut incommodent, aut perniciem afferant, in rebus quæ magnæ deliberationis dictu mirum quam stupidi sint, eisdem plane dotibus instructi sunt Volsci quod ad cædes et furta paulo propensiores sint. Pisani bono quidem sunt consilio, sed parum constanti, si quis diversum ab eis senserit, mox acquiescunt, rursus si aliter suadeas, mutabunt consilium, illud in caussa fuit quod tam duram ac diutinam obsidionem ad extremum usque non pertulerint. Placentini utrisque abundant consiliis, scilicet salutaribus ac pernitiosis, non facile tamen ab iis impetres pestilens consilium, apud Regienses neque consilii copiam invenies. Si sequare Mutinensium consilia, raro cedet infeliciter, sunt enim peracutissimo consilio, et voluntate plane bona. Providi sunt Florentini (si unumquemque seorsum accipias) si vero simul conjuncti sint, non admodum mihi consilia eorum probabuntur; feliciter cedunt Senensium consilia, subita sunt Perusinorum; salutaria Ferrariensium, fideli sunt consilio Veronenses, semper ambigui sunt in consiliis aut dandis aut accipiendis Patavini. Sunt pertinaces in eo quod cœperint consilio Bergomates, respuunt omnium consilia Neapolitani, sunt consultissimi Bononienses.'

[1] *Commentario delle più notabili e mostruose cose d'Italia et altri luoghi, di Lingua Aramea in Italiana tradotta. Con un breve Catalogo degli inventori delle cose che si mangiano et beveno, novamente ritrovato.* In Venetia 1553 (first printed 1548, based on a journey taken by Ortensio Landi through Italy in 1543 and 1544). That Landi was really the author of this *Commentario* is clear from the concluding remarks of Nicolo Morra (fol. 46 *a*): 'Il presente commentario nato del constantissimo cervello di M. O. L.;' and from the signature of the whole (fol. 70 *a*): SVISNETROH SVDNAL, ROTUA TSE, 'Hortensius Landus autor est.' After a declaration as to Italy from the mouth of a mysterious grey-haired sage, a journey is described from Sicily through Italy to the East. All the cities of Italy are more or less fully discussed: that Lucca should receive special praise is intelligible from the writer's way of thinking. Venice, where he claims to have been much with Pietro Aretino (p. 166), and Milan are described in detail, and in connexion with the latter the maddest stories are told (fol. 25 sqq.). There is no want of such elsewhere—of roses which flower all the

the middle of the century.[1] Leandro Alberti[2] is not so fruitful as might be expected in his description of the character of the different cities.

To what extent this comparative study of national and local characteristics may, by means of Italian humanism, have influenced the rest of Europe, we cannot say with precision. To Italy, at all events, belongs the priority in this respect, as in the description of the world in general.

year round, stars which shine at midday, birds which are changed into men, and men with bulls' heads on their shoulders, mermen, and men who spit fire from their mouths. Among all these there are often authentic bits of information, some of which will be used in the proper place; short mention is made of the Lutherans (fol. 32 *a*, 38 *a*), and frequent complaints are heard of the wretched times and unhappy state of Italy. We there read (fol. 22 *a*); 'Son questi quelli Italiani li quali in un fatto d' armi uccisero ducento mila Francesi? sono finalmente quelli che di tutto il mondo s' impadronirono? Hai quanto (per quel che io vego) degenerati sono. Hai quanto dissimili mi paiono dalli antichi padri loro, liquali et singolar virtu di cuore e disciplina militare ugualmente monstrarno havere.' On the catalogue of eatables which is added, see below.

[1] *Descrizione di tutta l' Italia.*

[2] Satirical lists of cities are frequently met with later, e.g. Macaroneide, *Phantas.* ii. For France, Rabelais, who knew the Macaroneide, is the chief source of all the jests and malicious allusions of this local sort.

CHAPTER VII.

DESCRIPTION OF THE OUTWARD MAN.

But the discoveries made with regard to man were not confined to the spiritual characteristics of individuals and nations; his outward appearance was in Italy the subject of an entirely different interest from that shown in it by northern peoples.[1]

Of the position held by the great Italian physicians with respect to the progress of physiology, we cannot venture to speak; and the artistic study of the human figure belongs, not to a work like the present, but to the history of art. But something must here be said of that universal education of the eye, which rendered the judgment of the Italians as to bodily beauty or ugliness perfect and final.

On reading the Italian authors of that period attentively, we are astounded at the keenness and accuracy with which outward features are seized, and at the completeness with which personal appearance in general is described.[2] Even to-day the Italians, and especially the Romans, have the art of sketching a man's picture in a couple of words. This rapid apprehension of what is characteristic is an essential condition for detecting and representing the beautiful. In poetry, it is true, circumstantial description may be a fault, not a merit, since a single feature, suggested by deep passion or insight, will often awaken in the reader a far more powerful impression of the figure described. Dante gives us nowhere a more splendid idea of his Beatrice than where he only describes the influence which goes forth from her upon all around. But here we have not to treat

[1] It is true that many decaying literatures are full of painfully minute descriptions. See e.g. in Sidonius Apollinaris the descriptions of a Visigoth king (*Epist.* i. 2), of a personal enemy (*Epist.* iii. 13), and in his poems the types of the different German tribes.

[2] On Filippo Villani, see p. 330.

particularly of poetry, which follows its own laws and pursues its own ends, but rather of the general capacity to paint in words real or imaginary forms.

In this Boccaccio is a master—not in the 'Decameron,' where the character of the tales forbids lengthy description, but in the romances, where he is free to take his time. In his 'Ameto'[1] he describes a blonde and a brunette much as an artist a hundred years later would have painted them—for here, too, culture long precedes art. In the account of the brunette—or, strictly speaking, of the less blonde of the two—there are touches which deserve to be called classical. In the words 'la spaziosa testa e distesa' lies the feeling for grander forms, which go beyond a graceful prettiness; the eyebrows with him no longer resemble two bows, as in the Byzantine ideal, but a single wavy line; the nose seems to have been meant to be aquiline;[2] the broad, full breast, the arms of moderate length, the effect of the beautiful hand, as it lies on the purple mantle—all both foretells the sense of beauty of a coming time, and unconsciously approaches to that of classical antiquity. In other descriptions Boccaccio mentions a flat (not mediævally rounded) brow, a long, earnest, brown eye, and round, not hollowed neck, as well as—in a very modern tone—the 'little feet' and the 'two roguish eyes' of a black-haired nymph.[3]

Whether the fifteenth century has left any written account of its ideal of beauty, I am not able to say. The works of the painters and sculptors do not render such an account as unnecessary as might appear at first sight, since possibly, as opposed to their realism, a more ideal type might have been favoured and preserved by the writers.[4] In the sixteenth cen-

[1] *Parnasso teatrale*, Lipsia, 1829. Introd. p. vii.

[2] The reading is here evidently corrupt. The passage is as follows (*Ameto*, Venezia, 1856, p. 54): 'Del mezo de' quali non camuso naso in linea diretta discende, quanto ad aquilineo non essere dimanda il dovere.'

[3] 'Due occhi ladri nel loro movimento.' The whole work is rich in such descriptions.

[4] The charming book of songs by Giusto dei Conti, *La bella Mano* (best ed. Florence, 1715), does not tell us as many details of this famous hand of his beloved as Boccaccio in a dozen passages of the *Ameto* of the hands of his nymphs.

tury Firenzuola came forward with his remarkable work on female beauty.[1] We must clearly distinguish in it what he had learned from old authors or from artists, such as the fixing of proportions according to the length of the head, and certain abstract conceptions. What remains, is his own genuine observation, illustrated with examples of women and girls from Prato. As his little work is a kind of lecture, delivered before the women of this city—that is to say, before very severe critics—he must have kept pretty closely to the truth. His principle is avowedly that of Zeuxis and of Lucian—to piece together an ideal beauty out of a number of beautiful parts. He defines the shades of colour which occur in the hair and skin, and gives to the 'biondo' the preference, as the most beautiful colour for the hair,[2] understanding by it a soft yellow, inclining to brown. He requires that the hair should be thick, long, and locky; the forehead serene, and twice as broad as high; the skin bright and clear (candida), but not of a dead white (bianchezza); the eyebrows dark, silky, most strongly marked in the middle, and shading off towards the ears and the nose; the white of the eye faintly touched with blue, the iris not actually black, though all the poets praise 'occhi neri' as a gift of Venus, despite that even goddesses were known for their eyes of heavenly blue, and that soft, joyous, brown eyes were admired by everybody. The eye itself should be large and full, and brought well forward; the lids white, and marked with almost invisible tiny red veins; the lashes neither too long, nor too thick, nor too dark. The hollow round the eye should have the same colour as the cheek.[3] The ear, neither too large

[1] 'Della bellezza delle donne,' in the first vol. of the *Opere di Firenzuola*, Milano, 1802. For his view of bodily beauty as a sign of beauty of soul, comp. vol. ii. pp. 48 to 52, in the 'ragionamenti' prefixed to his novels. Among the many who maintain this doctrine, partly in the style of the ancients, we may quote one, Castiglione, *Il Cortigiana*, l. iv. fol. 176.

[2] This was a universal opinion, not only the professional opinion of painters. See below.

[3] This may be an opportunity for a word on the eyes of Lucrezia Borgia, taken from the distichs of a Ferrarese court-poet, Ercole Strozza (*Strozzii Poetae*, fol. 85–88). The power of her glance is described in a manner only explicable in an artistic age, and which would not now be permitted. Sometimes it turns the beholder to fire, sometimes to stone.

nor too small, firmly and neatly fitted on, should show a stronger colour in the winding than in the even parts, with an edge of the transparent ruddiness of the pomegranate. The temples must be white and even, and for the most perfect beauty ought not to be too narrow.[1] The red should grow deeper as the cheek gets rounder. The nose, which chiefly determines the value of the profile, must recede gently and uniformly in the direction of the eyes; where the cartilage ceases, there may be a slight elevation, but not so marked as to make the nose aquiline, which is not pleasing in women; the lower part must be less strongly coloured than the ears, but not of a chilly whiteness, and the middle partition above the lips lightly tinted with red. The mouth, our author would have rather small, and neither projecting to a point, nor quite flat, with the lips not too thin, and fitting neatly together; an accidental opening, that is, when the woman is neither speaking nor laughing, should not display more than six upper teeth. As delicacies of detail, he mentions a dimple in the upper lip, a certain fulness of the under lip, and a tempting smile in the left corner of the mouth—and so on. The teeth should not be too small, regular, well marked off from one another, and of the colour of ivory; and the gums must not be too dark or even like red velvet. The chin is to be round, neither pointed nor curved outwards, and growing slightly red as it rises; its glory is the dimple. The neck should be white and round and rather

He who looks long at the sun, becomes blind; he who beheld Medusa, became a stone; but he who looks at the countenance of Lucrezia

'Fit primo intuitu cæcus et inde lapis.'

Even the marble Cupid sleeping in her halls is said to have been petrified by her gaze:

'Lumine Borgiado saxificatur Amor.'

Critics may dispute, if they please, whether the so-called Eros of Praxiteles or that of Michelangelo is meant, since she was the possessor of both.

And the same glance appeared to another poet, Marcello Filosseno, only mild and lofty, 'mansueto e altero' (Roscoe, *Leone X.* ed. Bossi, vii. p. 306).

Comparisons with ideal figures of antiquity occur (p. 30). Of a boy ten years old we read in the *Orlandino* (ii. str. 47), 'ed ha capo romano.'

[1] Referring to the fact that the appearance of the temples can be altogether changed by the arrangement of the hair, Firenzuola makes a comical attack on the overcrowding of the hair with flowers, which causes the head to 'look like a pot of pinks or a quarter of goat on the spit.' He is, as a rule, thoroughly at home in caricature.

long than short, with the hollow and the Adam's apple but faintly marked; and the skin at every movement must show pleasing lines. The shoulders he desires broad, and in the breadth of the bosom sees the first condition of its beauty. No bone may be visible upon it, its fall and swell must be gentle and gradual, its colour 'candidissimo.' The leg should be long and not too hard in the lower parts, but still not without flesh on the shin, which must be provided with white, full calves. He likes the foot small, but not bony, the instep (it seems) high, and the colour white as alabaster. The arms are to be white, and in the upper parts tinted with red; in their consistence fleshy and muscular, but still soft as those of Pallas, when she stood before the shepherd on Mount Ida—in a word, ripe, fresh, and firm. The hand should be white, especially towards the wrist, but large and plump, feeling soft as silk, the rosy palm marked with a few, but distinct and not intricate lines; the elevations in it should be not too great, the space between thumb and forefinger brightly coloured and without wrinkles, the fingers long, delicate, and scarcely at all thinner towards the tips, with nails clear, even, not too long nor too square, and cut so as to show a white margin about the breadth of a knife's back.

Æsthetic principles of a general character occupy a very subordinate place to these particulars. The ultimate principles of beauty, according to which the eye judges 'senza appello,' are for Firenzuola a secret, as he frankly confesses; and his definitions of 'Leggiadria,' 'Grazia,' 'Vaghezza,' 'Venustà,' 'Aria,' 'Maestà,' are partly, as has been remarked, philological, and partly vain attempts to utter the unutterable. Laughter he prettily defines, probably following some old author, as a radiance of the soul.

The literature of all countries can, at the close of the Middle Ages, show single attempts to lay down theoretic principles of beauty;[1] but no other work can be compared to that of Firenzuola. Brantome, who came a good half-century later, is a bungling critic by his side, because governed by lasciviousness and not by a sense of beauty.

[1] For the ideal of the 'Minnesänger,' see Falke, *Die deutsche Trachten- und Modenwelt*, i. pp. 85 sqq.

CHAPTER VIII.

DESCRIPTIONS OF LIFE IN MOVEMENT.

Among the new discoveries made with regard to man, we must reckon, in conclusion, the interest taken in descriptions of the daily course of human life.

The comical and satirical literature of the Middle Ages could not dispense with pictures of every-day events. But it is another thing, when the Italians of the Renaissance dwelt on this picture for its own sake—for its inherent interest—and because it forms part of that great, universal life of the world whose magic breath they felt everywhere around them. Instead of and together with the satirical comedy, which wanders through houses, villages, and streets, seeking food for its derision in parson, peasant, and burgher, we now see in literature the beginnings of a true *genre*, long before it found any expression in painting. That *genre* and satire are often met with in union, does not prevent them from being wholly different things.

How much of earthly business must Dante have watched with attentive interest, before he was able to make us see with our own eyes all that happened in his spiritual world.[1] The famous pictures of the busy movement in the arsenal at Venice, of the blind men laid side by side before the church door,[2] and the like, are by no means the only instances of this kind: for the art, in which he is a master, of expressing the inmost soul by the outward gesture, cannot exist without a close and incessant study of human life.

The poets who followed rarely came near him in this respect, and the novelists were forbidden by the first laws of their literary style to linger over details. Their prefaces and narratives might be as long as they pleased, but what we under-

[1] On the accuracy of his sense of form, p. 290.

[2] *Inferno*, xxi. 7; *Purgat.* xiii. 61.

stand by *genre* was outside their province. The taste for this class of description was not fully awakened till the time of the revival of antiquity.

And here we are again met by the man who had a heart for everything—Æneas Sylvius. Not only natural beauty, not only that which has an antiquarian or a geographical interest, finds a place in his descriptions (p. 248; ii. p. 28), but any living scene of daily life.[1] Among the numerous passages in his memoirs in which scenes are described which hardly one of his contemporaries would have thought worth a line of notice, we will here only mention the boat-race on the Lake of Bolsena.[2] We are not able to detect from what old letter-writer or story-teller the impulse was derived to which we owe such life-like pictures. Indeed, the whole spiritual communion between antiquity and the Renaissance is full of delicacy and of mystery.

To this class belong those descriptive Latin poems of which we have already spoken (p. 262)—hunting-scenes, journeys, ceremonies, and so forth. In Italian we also find something of the same kind, as, for example, the descriptions of the famous Medicean tournament by Politian and Luca Pulci.[3] The true epic poets, Luigi Pulci, Bojardo, and Ariosto, are carried on more rapidly by the stream of their narrative; yet in all of them we must recognise the lightness and precision of their descriptive touch, as one of the chief elements of their great-

[1] We must not take it too seriously, if we read (in Platina, *Vitae Pontiff.* p. 310) that he kept at his court a sort of buffoon, the Florentine Greco, 'hominem certe cujusvis mores, naturam, linguam cum maximo omnium qui audiebant risu facile exprimentem.'

[2] *Pii. II. Comment.* viii. p. 391.

[3] Two tournaments must be distinguished, Lorenzo's in 1468 and Guiliano's in 1475 (a third in 1481?). See Reumont, *L. M.* i. 264 sqq. 361, 267, note 1; ii. 55, 67, and the works there quoted, which settle the old dispute on these points. The first tournament is treated in the poem of Luca Pulci, ed. *Ciriffo Calvaneo di Luca Pulci Gentilhuomo Fiorentino, con la Giostra del Magnifico Lorenzo de' Medici*, Florence, 1572, pp. 75, 91; the second in an unfinished poem of Ang. Poliziano, best ed. Carducci, *Le Stanze, l' Orfeo e le Rime di M. A. P.* Florence, 1863. The description of Politian breaks off at the setting out of Guiliano for the tournament. Pulci gives a detailed account of the combatants and the manner of fighting. The description of Lorenzo is particularly good (p. 82).

ness. Franco Sacchetti amuses himself with repeating the short speeches of a troop of pretty women caught in the woods by a shower of rain.[1]

Other scenes of moving life are to be looked for in the military historians (p. 99). In a lengthy poem,[2] dating from an earlier period, we find a faithful picture of a combat of mercenary soldiers in the fourteenth century, chiefly in the shape of the orders, cries of battle, and dialogue with which it is accompanied.

But the most remarkable productions of this kind are the realistic descriptions of country life, which are found most abundantly in Lorenzo Magnifico and the poets of his circle.

Since the time of Petrarch,[3] an unreal and conventional style of bucolic poetry had been in vogue, which, whether written in Latin or Italian, was essentially a copy of Virgil. Parallel to this, we find the pastoral novel of Boccaccio (p. 259) and other works of the same kind down to the 'Arcadia' of Sannazaro, and later still, the pastoral comedy of Tasso and Guarini. They are works whose style, whether poetry or prose, is admirably finished and perfect, but in which pastoral life is only an ideal dress for sentiments which belong to a wholly different sphere of culture.[4]

[1] This so-called 'Caccia' is printed in the Commentary to Castiglione's *Eclogue* from a Roman MS. (*Lettere del conte B. Castiglione*, ed. Pierantonio Lerassi (Padua, 1771), ii. p. 269.

[2] See the *Serventese* of Giannozzo of Florence, in Trucchi, *Poesie italiane inedite*, ii. p. 99. The words are many of them quite unintelligible, borrowed really or apparently from the languages of the foreign mercenaries. Macchiavelli's description of Florence during the plague of 1527 belongs, to certain extent, to this class of works. It is a series of living, speaking pictures of a frightful calamity.

[3] According to Boccaccio (*Vita di Dante*, p. 77), Dante was the author of two eclogues, probably written in Latin. They are addressed to Joh. de Virgiliis. Comp. Fraticelli, *Opp. min. di Dante*, i. 417. Petrarch's bucolic poem in *P. Carmina minora*, ed. Rossetti, i. Comp. L. Geiger, *Petr.* 120–122 and 270, note 6, especially A. Hortis, *Scritti inediti di F. P.* Triest, 1874.

[4] Boccaccio gives in his *Ameto* (above, p. 344) a kind of mythical Decameron, and sometimes fails ludicrously to keep up the character. One of his nymphs is a good Catholic, and prelates shoot glances of unholy love at her in Rome. Another marries. In the *Ninfale fiesolano*, the nymph Mensola, who finds herself pregnant, takes counsel of an 'old and wise nymph.'

But by the side of all this there appeared in Italian poetry, towards the close of the fifteenth century, signs of a more realistic treatment of rustic life. This was not possible out of Italy; for here only did the peasant, whether labourer or proprietor, possess human dignity, personal freedom, and the right of settlement, hard as his lot might sometimes be in other respects.[1] The difference between town and country is far from being so marked here as in northern countries. Many of the smaller towns are peopled almost exclusively by peasants who, on coming home at nightfall from their work, are transformed into townsfolk. The masons of Como wandered over nearly all Italy; the child Giotto was free to leave his sheep and join a guild at Florence; everywhere there was a human stream flowing from the country into the cities, and some mountain populations seemed born to supply this current.[2] It is true that the pride and local conceit supplied poets and novelists with abundant motives for making game of the 'villano,'[3] and what they left undone was taken charge of by the comic improvisers (p. 320 sqq). But nowhere do we find a trace of that brutal and contemptuous class-hatred against the 'vilains' which inspired the aristocratic poets of Provence, and often, too, the French chroniclers. On the contrary,[4] Italian

[1] In general the prosperity of the Italian peasants was greater then than that of the peasantry anywhere else in Europe. Comp. Sacchetti, nov. 88 and 222; L. Pulci in the *Beca da Dicamano* (Villari, *Macchiavelli*, i. 198, note 2).

[2] 'Nullum est hominum genus aptius urbi,' says Battista Mantovano (*Ecl.* viii.) of the inhabitants of the Monte Baldo and the Val. Cassina, who could turn their hands to anything. Some country populations, as is well known, have even now privileges with regard to certain occupations in the great cities.

[3] Perhaps one of the strongest passages, *Orlandino*, cap. v. str. 54–58. The tranquil and unlearned Vesp. Bisticci says (*Comm. sulla vita di Giov. Manetti*, p. 96): 'Sono due ispezie di uomini difficili a supportare per la loro ignoranza; l' una sono i servi, la seconda i contadini.'

[4] In Lombardy, at the beginning of the sixteenth century, the nobles did not shrink from dancing, wrestling, leaping, and racing with the peasants. *Il Cortigiano*, l. ii. fol. 54. A. Pandolfini (L. B. Alberti) in the *Trattato del governo della famiglia*, p. 86, is an instance of a land-owner who consoles himself for the greed and fraud of his peasant tenantry with the reflection that he is thereby taught to bear and deal with his fellow-creatures.

authors of every sort gladly recognise and accentuate what is great or remarkable in the life of the peasant. Gioviano Pontano mentions with admiration instances of the fortitude of the savage inhabitants of the Abruzzi;[1] in the biographical collections and in the novelists we meet with the figure of the heroic peasant-maiden[2] who hazards her life to defend her family and her honour.[3]

Such conditions made the poetical treatment of country-life possible. The first instance we shall mention is that of Battista Mantovano, whose eclogues, once much read and still worth reading, appeared among his earliest works about 1480. They are a mixture of real and conventional rusticity, but the former tends to prevail. They represent the mode of thought of a well-meaning village clergyman, not without a certain leaning to liberal ideas. As Carmelite monk, the writer may have had occasion to mix freely with the peasantry.[4]

But it is with a power of a wholly different kind that

[1] Jovian. Pontan. *De fortitudine*, lib. ii.

[2] The famous peasant-woman of the Valtellina—Bona Lombarda, wife of the Condottiere Pietro Brunoro—is known to us from Jacobus Bergomensis and from Porcellius, in Murat. xxv. col. 43.

[3] On the condition of the Italian peasantry in general, and especially of the details of that condition in several provinces, we are unable to particularise more fully. The proportions between freehold and leasehold property, and the burdens laid on each in comparison with those borne at the present time, must be gathered from special works which we have not had the opportunity of consulting. In stormy times the country people were apt to have appalling relapses into savagery (*Arch. Stor.* xvi. i. pp. 451 sqq., ad. a. 1440; Corio, fol. 259; *Annales Foroliv.* in Murat. xxii. col. 227, though nothing in the shape of a general peasants' war occurred. The rising near Piacenza in 1462 was of some importance and interest. Comp. Corio, *Storia di Milano*, fol. 409; *Annales Placent.* in Murat. xx. col. 907; Sismondi, x. p. 138. See below, part vi. cap. 1.

[4] *F. Bapt. Mantuani Bucolica seu Adolescentia in decem Eclogas divisa*; often printed, e.g. Strasburg, 1504, The date of composition is indicated by the preface, written in 1498, from which it also appears that the ninth and tenth eclogues were added later. In the heading to the tenth are the words, 'post religionis ingressum;' in that of the seventh, 'cum jam autor ad religionem aspiraret.' The eclogues by no means deal exclusively with peasant life; in fact, only two of them do so—the sixth, 'disceptatione rusticorum et civium,' in which the writer sides with the rustics; and the eighth, 'de rusticorum religione.' The others speak of love, of the relations between poets and wealthy men, of conversion to religion, and of the manners of the Roman court.

Lorenzo Magnifico transports himself into the peasant's world. His 'Nencia di Barberino'[1] reads like a crowd of genuine extracts from the popular songs of the Florentine country, fused into a great stream of octaves. The objectivity of the writer is such that we are in doubt whether the speaker—the young peasant Vallera, who declares his love to Nencia—awakens his sympathy or ridicule. The deliberate contrast to the conventional eclogue is unmistakable. Lorenzo surrenders himself purposely to the realism of simple, rough country-life, and yet his work makes upon us the impression of true poetry.

The 'Beca da Dicomano' of Luigi Pulci[2] is an admitted counterpart to the 'Nencia' of Lorenzo. But the deeper purpose is wanting. The 'Beca' is written not so much from the inward need to give a picture of popular life, as from the desire to win the approbation of the educated Florentine world by a successful poem. Hence the greater and more deliberate coarseness of the scenes, and the indecent jokes. Nevertheless, the point of view of the rustic lover is admirably maintained.

Third in this company of poets comes Angelo Poliziano, with his 'Rusticus'[3] in Latin hexameters. Keeping clear of all imitation of Virgil's Georgics, he describes the year of the Tuscan peasant, beginning with the late autumn, when the countryman gets ready his new plough and prepares the seed for the winter. The picture of the meadows in spring is full and beautiful, and the 'Summer' has fine passages; but the vintage-feast in autumn is one of the gems of modern Latin poetry. Politian wrote poems in Italian as well as Latin, from which we may infer that in Lorenzo's circle it was possible to give a realistic picture of the passionate life of the lower

[1] *Poesie di Lorenzo Magnifico*, i. p. 37 sqq. The remarkable poems belonging to the period of the German 'Minnesänger,' which bear the name of Neithard von Reuenthal, only depict peasant life in so far as the knight chooses to mix with it for his amusement. The peasants reply to the ridicule of Reuenthal in songs of their own. Comp. Karl Schroder, *Die höfische Dorfpoesie des deutschen Mittelalters* in Rich. Gosche, *Jahrb. für Literaturgesch.* 1 vol. Berlin, 1875, pp. 45–98, esp. 75 sqq.

[2] *Poesie di Lor. Magn.* ii. 149.

[3] In the *Deliciae poetar. ital.*, and in the works of Politian. First separate ed. Florence, 1493. The didactic poem of Rucellai, *Le Api*, first printed 1519, and *La coltivazione*, Paris, 1546, contain something of the same kind.

classes. His gipsy's love-song [1] is one of the earliest products of that wholly modern tendency to put oneself with poetic consciousness into the position of another class. This had probably been attempted for ages with a view to satire,[2] and the opportunity for it was offered in Florence at every carnival by the songs of the maskers. But the sympathetic understanding of the feelings of another class was new; and with it the 'Nencia' and this 'Canzone zingaresca' mark a new starting-point in the history of poetry.

Here, too, we must briefly indicate how culture prepared the way for artistic development. From the time of the 'Nencia,' a period of eighty years elapses to the rustic genre-painting of Jacopo Bassano and his school.

In the next part of this work we shall show how differences of birth had lost their significance in Italy. Much of this was doubtless owing to the fact that men and man were here first thoroughly and profoundly understood. This one single result of the Renaissance is enough to fill us with everlasting thankfulness. The logical notion of humanity was old enough—but here the notion became a fact.

The loftiest conceptions on this subject were uttered by Pico della Mirandola in his speech on the dignity of man,[3] which

[1] *Poesie di Lor. Magnifico*, ii. 75.

[2] The imitation of different dialects and of the manners of different districts spring from the same tendency. Comp. p. 155.

[3] *Jo. Pici oratio de hominis dignatate.* The passage is as follows: 'Statuit tandem optimus opifex ut cui dari nihil proprium poterat commune esset quidquid privatum singulis fuerat. Igitur hominem accepit indiscretae opus imaginis atque in mundi posito meditullio sic est allocutus; Nec certam sedem, nec propriam faciem, nec munus ullum peculiare tibi dedimus, O Adam, ut quam sedem, quam faciem, quae munera tute optaveris, ea pro voto pro tua sententia habeas et possideas. Definita caeteris natura inter praescriptas a nobis leges coercetur, tu nullis augustiis coercitus pro tuo arbitrio, in cujus manus te posui, tibi illam praefinies. Medium te mundi posui ut circumspiceres inde commodius quidquid est in mundo. Nec te caelestem neque terrenum, neque mortalem neque immortalem fecimus, ut tui ipsius quasi arbitrarius honorariusque plastes et fictor in quam malueris tute formam effingas. Poteris in inferiora quae sunt bruta degenerare, poteris in superiora quae sunt divina ex tui animi sententia regenerari. O summam dei patris liberalitatem, summam et admirandam hominis felicitatem. Cui datum id habere quod optat, id esse quod velit. Bruta simulatque nascuntur id

may justly be called one of the noblest bequests of that great age. God, he tells us, made man at the close of the creation, to know the laws of the universe, to love its beauty, to admire its greatness. He bound him to no fixed place, to no prescribed form of work, and by no iron necessity, but gave him freedom to will and to move. 'I have set thee,' says the Creator to Adam, 'in the midst of the world, that thou mayst the more easily behold and see all that is therein. I created thee a being neither heavenly nor earthly, neither mortal nor immortal only, that thou mightest be free to shape and to overcome thyself. Thou mayst sink into a beast, and be born anew to the divine likeness. The brutes bring from their mother's body what they will carry with them as long as they live; the higher spirits are from the beginning, or soon after,[1] what they will be for ever. To thee alone is given a growth and a development depending on thine own free will. Thou bearest in thee the germs of a universal life.'

secum afferunt, ut ait Lucilius, e bulga matris quod possessura sunt; supremi spiritus aut ab initio aut paulo mox id fuerunt quod sunt futuri in perpetuas aeternitates. Nascenti homini omnifaria semina et omnigenae vitæ germina indidit pater; quæ quisque excoluerit illa adolescent et fructus suos ferent in illo. Si vegetalia, planta fiet, si sensualia, obbrutescet, si rationalia, coeleste evadet animal, si intellectualia, angelus erit et dei filius, et si nulla creaturarum sorte contentus in unitatis centrum suae se receperit, unus cum deo spiritus factus in solitaria patris caligine qui est super omnia constitutus omnibus antestabit.'

The speech first appears in the *commentationes* of Jo. Picus without any special title; the heading 'de hominis dignitate' was added later. It is not altogether suitable, since a great part of the discourse is devoted to the defence of the peculiar philosophy of Pico, and the praise of the Jewish Cabbalah. On Pico, see above, p. 202 sqq.; and below, part. vi. chap. 4. More than two hundred years before, Brunetto Latini (*Tesoro*, lib. i. cap. 13, ed. Chabaille, p. 20) had said: 'Toutes choses dou ciel en aval sont faites pour l'ome; mais li hom at faiz pour lui meisme.' The words seemed to a contemporary to have too much human pride in them, and he added: 'e por Dieu amer et servir et por avoir la joie pardurable.'

[1] An allusion to the fall of Lucifer and his followers.

PART V.

SOCIETY AND FESTIVALS.

CHAPTER I.

THE EQUALISATION OF CLASSES.

Every period of civilisation, which forms a complete and consistent whole, manifests itself not only in political life, in religion, art, and science, but also sets its characteristic stamp on social life. Thus the Middle Ages had their courtly and aristocratic manners and etiquette, differing but little in the various countries of Europe, as well as their peculiar forms of middle-class life.

Italian customs at the time of the Renaissance offer in these respects the sharpest contrast to mediævalism. The foundation on which they rest is wholly different. Social intercourse in its highest and most perfect form now ignored all distinctions of caste, and was based simply on the existence of an educated class as we now understand the word. Birth and origin were without influence, unless combined with leisure and inherited wealth. Yet this assertion must not be taken in an absolute and unqualified sense, since mediæval distinctions still sometimes made themselves felt to a greater or less degree, if only as a means of maintaining equality with the aristocratic pretensions of the less advanced countries of Europe. But the main current of the time went steadily towards the fusion of classes in the modern sense of the phrase.

The fact was of vital importance that, from certainly the twelfth century onwards, the nobles and the burghers dwelt together within the walls of the cities.[1] The interests and pleasures of both classes were thus identified, and the feudal lord learned to look at society from another point of view than

[1] The habit among the Piedmontese nobility of living in their castles in the country struck the other Italians as exceptional. Bandello, parte ii. nov. 7 (?).

that of his mountain-castle. The Church, too, in Italy never suffered itself, as in northern countries, to be used as a means of providing for the younger sons of noble families. Bishoprics, abbacies, and canonries were often given from the most unworthy motives, but still not according to the pedigrees of the applicants; and if the bishops in Italy were more numerous, poorer, and, as a rule, destitute of all sovereign rights, they still lived in the cities where their cathedrals stood, and formed, together with their chapters, an important element in the cultivated society of the place. In the age of despots and absolute princes which followed, the nobility in most of the cities had the motives and the leisure to give themselves up to a private life (p. 131) free from political danger and adorned with all that was elegant and enjoyable, but at the same time hardly distinguishable from that of the wealthy burgher. And after the time of Dante, when the new poetry and literature were in the hands of all Italy,[1] when to this was added the revival of ancient culture and the new interest in man as such, when the successful Condottiere became a prince, and not only good birth, but legitimate birth, ceased to be indispensable for a throne (p. 21), it might well seem that the age of equality had dawned, and the belief in nobility vanished for ever.

From a theoretical point of view, when the appeal was made to antiquity, the conception of nobility could be both justified and condemned from Aristotle alone. Dante, for example,[2] adapts from the Aristotelian definition, 'Nobility rests on excellence and inherited wealth,' his own saying, 'Nobility rests on personal excellence or on that of predecessors.' But elsewhere he is not satisfied with this conclusion. He blames himself,[3] because even in Paradise, while talking with his ancestor Cacciaguida, he made mention of his noble origin, which is but as a mantle from which time is ever cutting something away, unless we ourselves add daily fresh worth to it. And in the

[1] This was the case long before printing. A large number of manuscripts, and among them the best, belonged to Florentine artisans. If it had not been for Savonarola's great bonfire, many more of them would be left.

[2] Dante, *De monarchia*, l. ii. cap. 3.

[3] *Paradiso*, xvi. at the beginning.

'Convito'[1] he disconnects 'nobile' and 'nobiltà' from every condition of birth, and identifies the idea with the capacity for moral and intellectual eminence, laying a special stress on high culture by calling 'nobiltà' the sister of 'filosofia.'

And as time went on, the greater the influence of humanism on the Italian mind, the firmer and more widespread became the conviction that birth decides nothing as to the goodness or badness of a man. In the fifteenth century this was the prevailing opinion. Poggio, in his dialogue 'On nobility,'[2] agrees with his interlocutors—Niccolò Niccoli, and Lorenzo Medici, brother of the great Cosimo—that there is no other nobility than that of personal merit. The keenest shafts of his ridicule are directed against much of what vulgar prejudice thinks indispensable to an aristocratic life. 'A man is all the farther removed from true nobility, the longer his forefathers have plied the trade of brigands. The taste for hawking and hunting savours no more of nobility than the nests and lairs of the hunted creatures of spikenard. The cultivation of the soil, as practised by the ancients, would be much nobler than this senseless wandering through the hills and woods, by which men make themselves liker to the brutes than to the reasonable creatures. It may serve well enough as a recreation, but not as the business of a lifetime.' The life of the English and French chivalry in the country or in the woody fastnesses seems to him thoroughly ignoble, and worst of all the doings of the robber-knights of Germany. Lorenzo here begins to take the part of the nobility, but not—which is characteristic—appealing to any natural sentiment in its favour, but because Aristotle in the fifth book of the 'Politics' recognises the nobility as existent, and defines it as resting on excellence and inherited wealth. To this Niccoli retorts that Aristotle gives this not as his own conviction, but as the popular impression; in his 'Ethics,' where

[1] Dante, *Convito*, nearly the whole *Trattato*, iv., and elsewhere. Brunetto Latini says (*Il tesoro*, lib. i. p. ii. cap. 50, ed. Chabaille, p. 343): 'De ce (la vertu) nasqui premierement la nobleté de gentil gent, non pas de ses ancêtres;' and he warns men (lib. ii. p. ii. cap. 196, p. 440) that they may lose true nobility by bad actions. Similarly Petrarch, *de rem. utr. fort.* lib. i. dial. xvii.: 'Verus nobilis non nascitur, sed fit.'

[2] *Poggi Opera*, *Dial. de nobilitate.* Aristotle's view is expressly combatted by B. Platina, *De vera nobilitate.*

he speaks as he thinks, he calls him noble who strives after that which is truly good. Lorenzo urges upon him vainly that the Greek word for nobility means good birth; Niccoli thinks the Roman word 'nobilis' (*i.e.* remarkable) a better one, since it makes nobility depend on a man's deeds.[1] Together with these discussions, we find a sketch of the condition of the nobles in various parts of Italy. In Naples they will not work, and busy themselves neither with their own estates nor with trade and commerce, which they hold to be discreditable; they either loiter at home or ride about on horseback.[2] The Roman nobility also despise trade, but farm their own property; the cultivation of the land even opens the way to a title;[3] 'it is a respectable but boorish nobility.' In Lombardy the nobles live upon the rent of their inherited estates; descent and the abstinence from any regular calling constitute nobility.[4] In Venice, the 'nobili,' the ruling caste, were all merchants. Similarly in Genoa the nobles and non-nobles were alike merchants and sailors, and only separated by their birth; some few of the former, it is true, still lurked as brigands in their mountain-castles. In Florence a part of the old nobility had devoted themselves to trade; another, and certainly by far the smaller part, enjoyed the satisfaction of their titles, and spent their time, either in nothing at all, or else in hunting and hawking.[5]

[1] This contempt of noble birth is common among the humanists. See the severe passages in Æn. Sylvius, *Opera*, pp. 84 (*Hist. bohem.* cap. 2) and 640. (*Stories of Lucretia and Euryalus.*)

[2] This is the case in the capital itself. See Bandello, parte ii. nov. 7; *Joviani Pontani Antonius*, where the decline of energy in the nobility is dated from the coming of the Aragonese dynasty.

[3] Throughout Italy it was universal that the owner of large landed property stood on an equality with the nobles. It is only flattery when J. A. Campanus adds to the statement of Pius II. (*Commentarii*, p. 1), that as a boy he had helped his poor parents in their rustic labours, the further assertion that he only did so for his amusement, and that this was the custom of the young nobles (Voigt, ii. 339).

[4] For an estimate of the nobility in North Italy, Bandello, with his repeated rebukes of *mésalliances*, is of importance (parte i. nov. 4, 26; parte iii. nov. 60). For the participation of the nobles in the games of the peasants, see above.

[5] The severe judgment of Macchiavelli, *Discorsi*, i. 55, refers only to those of the nobility who still retained feudal rights, and who were thoroughly idle and politically mischievous. Agrippa of Nettesheim, who

The decisive fact was, that nearly everywhere in Italy, even those who might be disposed to pride themselves on their birth could not make good the claims against the power of culture and of wealth, and that their privileges in politics and at court were not sufficient to encourage any strong feeling of caste. Venice offers only an apparent exception to this rule, for there the 'nobili' led the same life as their fellow-citizens, and were distinguished by few honorary privileges. The case was certainly different at Naples, which the strict isolation and the ostentatious vanity of its nobility excluded, above all other causes, from the spiritual movement of the Renaissance. The traditions of mediæval Lombardy and Normandy, and the French aristocratic influences which followed, all tended in this direction; and the Aragonese government, which was established by the middle of the fifteenth century, completed the work, and accomplished in Naples what followed a hundred years later in the rest of Italy—a social transformation in obedience to Spanish ideas, of which the chief features were the contempt for work and the passion for titles. The effect of this new influence was evident, even in the smaller towns, before the year 1500. We hear complaints from La Cava that the place had been proverbially rich, as long at it was filled with masons and weavers; whilst now, since instead of looms and trowels nothing but spurs, stirrups and gilded belts was to be seen, since everybody was trying to become Doctor of Laws or of Medicine, Notary, Officer or Knight, the most intolerable poverty prevailed.[1] In Florence an analogous change appears to have taken place by the time of Cosimo, the first Grand

owes his most remarkable ideas chiefly to his life in Italy, has a chapter on the nobility and princes (*De Incert. et Vanit. Scient.* cap, 80), the bitterness of which exceeds anything to be met with elsewhere, and is due to the social ferment then prevailing in the North. A passage at p. 213 is as follows: 'Si . . . . nobilitatis primordia requiramus, comperiemus hanc nefaria perfidia et crudelitate partam, si ingressum spectemus, reperiemus hanc mercenaria militia et latrociniis auctam. Nobilitas revera nihil aliud est quam robusta improbitas atque dignitas non nisi scelere quaesita benedictio et hereditas pessimorum quorumcunque filiorum.' In giving the history of the nobility he makes a passing reference to Italy (p. 227).

[1] Massuccio, nov. 19 (ed. Settembrini, Nap. 1874, p. 220). The first ed. of the novels appeared in 1476.

Duke; he is thanked for adopting the young people, who now despise trade and commerce, as knights of his order of St. Stephen.[1] This goes straight in the teeth of the good old Florentine custom,[2] by which fathers left property to their children on the condition that they should have some occupation (p. 79). But a mania for title of a curious and ludicrous sort sometimes crossed and thwarted, especially among the Florentines, the levelling influence of art and culture. This was the passion for knighthood, which became one of the most striking follies of the day, at a time when the dignity itself had lost every shadow of significance.

'A few years ago,' writes Franco Sacchetti,[3] towards the end of the fourteenth century, 'everybody saw how all the work-people down to the bakers, how all the wool-carders, usurers, money-changers and blackguards of all descriptions, became knights. Why should an official need knighthood when he goes to preside over some little provincial town? What has this title to do with any ordinary bread-winning pursuit? How art thou sunken, unhappy dignity! Of all the long list of knightly duties, what single one do these knights of ours discharge? I wished to speak of these things that the reader might see that knighthood is dead.[4] And as we have gone so far as to confer the honour upon dead men, why not upon figures of wood and stone, and why not upon an ox?' The stories which Sacchetti tells by way of illustration speak plainly enough. There we read how Bernabò Visconti knighted the victor in a drunken brawl, and then did the same derisively to the vanquished; how German knights with their decorated helmets and devices were ridiculed—and more of the same kind. At a later period Poggio[5] makes merry over

[1] Jacopo Pitti to Cosimo I., *Archiv. Stor.* iv. ii. p. 99. In North Italy the Spanish rule brought about the same results. Bandello, parte ii. nov. 40, dates from this period.

[2] When, in the fifteenth century, Vespasiano Fiorentino (pp. 518, 632) implies that the rich should not try to increase their inherited fortune, but should spend their whole annual income, this can only, in the mouth of a Florentine, refer to the great landowners.

[3] Franco Sacchetti, nov. 153. Comp. nov. 82 and 150.

[4] 'Che la cavalleria è morta.'

[5] Poggius, *De Nobilitate*, fol. 27. See above, p. 19. Æenea Silvio

the many knights of his day without a horse and without military training. Those who wished to assert the privilege of the order, and ride out with lance and colours, found in Florence that they might have to face the government as well as the jokers.[1]

On considering the matter more closely, we shall find that this belated chivalry, independent of all nobility of birth, though partly the fruit of an insane passion for title, had nevertheless another and a better side. Tournaments had not yet ceased to be practised, and no one could take part in them who was not a knight. But the combat in the lists, and especially the difficult and perilous tilting with the lance, offered a favourable opportunity for the display of strength, skill, and courage, which no one, whatever might be his origin, would willingly neglect in an age which laid such stress on personal merit.[2]

It was in vain that from the time of Petrarch downwards the tournament was denounced as a dangerous folly. No one was converted by the pathetic appeal of the poet: 'In what book do we read that Scipio and Cæsar were skilled at the joust?'[3] The practice became more and more popular in

(*Hist. Fried. III.* ed. Kollar, p. 294) finds fault with the readiness with which Frederick conferred knighthood in Italy.

[1] Vasari, iii. 49, and note. *Vita di Dello.* The city of Florence claimed the right of conferring knighthood. On the ceremonies of this kind in 1378 and 1389, see Reumont, *Lorenzo*, ii. 444 sqq.

[2] Senarega, *De Reb. Gen.* in Murat. xxiv. col. 525. At a wedding of Joh. Adurnus with Leonora di Sanseverino, 'certamina equestria in Sarzano edita sunt . . . . proposita et data victoribus praemia. Ludi multiformes in palatio celebrati a quibus tanquam a re nova pendebat plebs et integros dies illis spectantibus impendebat.' Politian writes to Joh. Picus of the cavalry exercise of his pupils (*Aug. Pol. Epist.* lib. xii. ep. 6): 'Tu tamen a me solos fieri poetas aut oratores putas, at ego non minus facio bellatores.' Ortensio Landi in the *Commentario*, fol. 180, tells of a duel between two soldiers at Correggio with a fatal result, reminding one of the old gladiatorial combats. The writer, whose imagination is generally active, gives us here the impression of truthfulness. The passages quoted show that knighthood was not absolutely necessary for these public contests.

[3] Petrarch, *Epist. Senil.* xi. 13, to Ugo of Este. Another passage in the *Epist. Famil.* lib. v. ep. 6, Dec. 1st, 1343, describes the disgust he felt at seeing a knight fall at a tournament in Naples. For legal pre-

Florence. Every honest citizen came to consider his tournament—now, no doubt, less dangerous than formerly—as a fashionable sport. Franco Sacchetti [1] has left us a ludicrous picture of one of these holiday cavaliers—a notary seventy years old. He rides out on horseback to Peretola, where the tournament was cheap, on a jade hired from a dyer. A thistle is stuck by some wag under the tail of the steed, who takes fright, runs away, and carries the helmeted rider, bruised and shaken, back into the city. The inevitable conclusion of the story is a severe curtain-lecture from the wife, who is not a little enraged at these break-neck follies of her husband.[2]

It may be mentioned in conclusion that a passionate interest in this sport was displayed by the Medici, as if they wished to show—private citizens as they were, without noble blood in their veins—that the society which surrounded them was in no respects inferior to a Court.[3] Even under Cosimo (1459), and

scriptions as to the tournament at Naples, see Fracassetti's Italian translation of Petrarch's letters, Florence, 1864, ii. p. 34. L. B. Alberti also points out the danger, uselessness, and expense of tournaments. *Della Famiglia*, *Op. Volg.* ii. 229.

[1] Nov. 64. With reference to this practice, it is said expressly in the *Orlandino* (ii. str. 7), of a tournament under Charlemagne: 'Here they were no cooks and scullions, but kings, dukes, and marquises, who fought.'

[2] This is one of the oldest parodies of the tournament. Sixty years passed before Jacques Cœur, the burgher-minister of finance under Charles VII., gave a tournament of donkeys in the courtyard of his palace at Bourges (about 1450). The most brilliant of all these parodies—the second canto of the *Orlandino* just quoted—was not published till 1526.

[3] Comp. the poetry, already quoted, of Politian and Luca Pulci (p. 349, note 3). Further, Paul. Jov., *Vita Leonis X.* l. i.; Macchiavelli, *Storie Fiorent.*, l. vii.; Paul. Jov. *Elog*, speaking of Pietro de' Medici, who neglected his public duties for these amusements, and of Franc. Borbonius, who lost his life in them; Vasari, ix. 219, *Vita di Granacci.* In the *Morgante* of Pulci, written under the eyes of Lorenzo, the knights are comical in their language and actions, but their blows are sturdy and scientific. Bojardo, too, writes for those who understand the tournament and the art of war. Comp. p. 323. In earlier Florentine history we read of a tournament in honour of the king of France, c. 1380, in Leon. Aret., *Hist. Flor.* lib. xi. ed. Argent. p. 222. The tournaments at Ferrara in 1464 are mentioned in the *Diario Ferrar.* in Murat. xxiv. col. 208; at Venice, see Sansovino, *Venezia*, fol. 153 sqq.; at Bologna in 1470 and after, see Bursellis, *Annal. Bonon.* Muratori xxiii. col. 898, 903, 906, 908, 911, where it is curious to note the odd mixture of sentimentalism attaching to the celebration of Roman triumphs; 'ut antiquitas Romana reno-

afterwards under the elder Pietro, brilliant tournaments were held at Florence. The younger Pietro neglected the duties of government for these amusements, and would never suffer himself to be painted except clad in armour. The same practice prevailed at the Court of Alexander VI., and when the Cardinal Ascanio Sforza asked the Turkish Prince Djem (pp. 109, 115) how he liked the spectacle, the barbarian replied with much discretion that such combats in his country only took place among slaves, since then, in the case of accident, nobody was the worse for it. The oriental was unconsciously in accord with the old Romans in condemning the manners of the Middle Ages.

Apart, however, from this particular prop of knighthood, we find here and there in Italy, for example at Ferrara (p. 46 sqq.), orders of court service, whose members had a right to the title.

But, great as were individual ambitions and the vanities of nobles and knights, it remains a fact that the Italian nobility took its place in the centre of social life, and not at the extremity. We find it habitually mixing with other classes on a footing of perfect equality, and seeking its natural allies in culture and intelligence. It is true that for the courtier a certain rank of nobility was required,[1] but this exigence is expressly declared to be caused by a prejudice rooted in the public mind —'per l' oppenion universale'—and never was held to imply the belief that the personal worth of one who was not of noble blood was in any degree lessened thereby, nor did it follow from this rule that the prince was limited to the nobility for his society. It was meant simply that the perfect man—the true courtier—should not be wanting in any conceivable advantage, and therefore not in this. If in all the relations of life he was

vata videretur,' we read in one place. Frederick of Urbino (p. 44 sqq.) lost his right eye at a tournament 'ab ictu lanceae.' On the tournament as held at that time in northern countries, see Olivier de la Marche, *Mémoires*, *passim*, and especially cap. 8, 9, 14, 16, 18, 19, 21, &c.

[1] Bald. Castiglione, *Il Cortigiano*, l. i. fol. 18.

specially bound to maintain a dignified and reserved demeanour, the reason was not found in the blood which flowed in his veins, but in the perfection of manner which was demanded from him. We are here in the presence of a modern distinction, based on culture and on wealth, but on the latter solely because it enables men to devote their life to the former, and effectually to promote its interests and advancement.

CHAPTER II.

THE OUTWARD REFINEMENT OF LIFE.

But in proportion as distinctions of birth ceased to confer any special privilege, was the individual himself compelled to make the most of his personal qualities, and society to find its worth and charm in itself. The demeanour of individuals, and all the higher forms of social intercourse, became ends pursued with a deliberate and artistic purpose.

Even the outward appearance of men and women and the habits of daily life were more perfect, more beautiful, and more polished than among the other nations of Europe. The dwellings of the upper classes fall rather within the province of the history of art; but we may note how far the castle and the city mansion in Italy surpassed in comfort, order, and harmony the dwellings of the northern noble. The style of dress varied so continually that it is impossible to make any complete comparison with the fashions of other countries, all the more because since the close of the fifteenth century imitations of the latter were frequent. The costumes of the time, as given us by the Italian painters, are the most convenient and the most pleasing to the eye which were then to be found in Europe; but we cannot be sure if they represent the prevalent fashion, or if they are faithfully reproduced by the artist. It is nevertheless beyond a doubt that nowhere was so much importance attached to dress as in Italy. The people was, and is, vain; and even serious men among it looked on a handsome and becoming costume as an element in the perfection of the individual. At Florence, indeed, there was a brief period, when dress was a purely personal matter, and every man set the fashion for himself (p. 130, note 1), and till far into the sixteenth century there were exceptional people who still had the courage to do so;[1] and the majority at all events showed themselves capable of varying the fashion according to their individual tastes. It is a symptom of decline when Giovanni della Casa warns his readers not to be singular or to depart from existing fashions.[2] Our own age, which, in men's dress at any rate, treats uniformity as the supreme law, gives up by so doing far more than it is itself aware of. But it saves itself much time, and this, according to our notions of business, outweighs all other disadvantages.

In Venice[3] and Florence at the time of the Renaissance there were rules and regulations prescribing the dress of the men and restraining the luxury of the women. Where the fashions were less free, as in Naples, the moralists confess with regret that no difference can be observed between noble and burgher.[4] They further deplore the rapid changes of fashion, and—if we rightly understand their words—the senseless idolatry of whatever comes from France, though in many cases the fashions which were received back from the French were originally Italian. It does not further concern us, how far these frequent changes, and the adoption of French and Spanish ways,[5] con-

[1] Paul. Jovii, *Elogia*, sub tit. Petrus Gravina, Alex. Achillinus, Balth. Castellio, &c. pp. 138 sqq. 112 sqq. 143 sqq.

[2] Casa, *Il Galateo*, p. 78.

[3] See on this point the Venetian books of fashions, and Sansovino, *Venezia*, fol. 150 sqq. The bridal dress at the betrothal—white, with the hair falling freely on the shoulders—is that of Titian's Flora. The 'Proveditori alle pompe' at Venice established 1514. Extracts from their decisions in Armand Baschet, *Souvenirs d'une Mission*, Paris, 1857. Prohibition of gold-embroidered garments in Venice, 1481, which had formerly been worn even by the bakers' wives; they were now to be decorated 'gemmis unionibus,' so that 'frugalissimus ornatus' cost 4,000 gold florins. M. Ant. Sabellici, *Epist.* lib. iii. (to M. Anto. Barbavarus).

[4] Jovian. Pontan. *De Principe:* 'Utinam autem non eo impudentiae perventum esset, ut inter mercatorem et patricium nullum sit in vestitu ceteroque ornatu discrimen. Sed haec tanta licentia reprehendi potest, coerceri non potest, quanquam mutari vestes sic quotidie videamus, ut quas quarto ante mense in deliciis habebamus, nunc repudiemus et tanquam veteramenta abjiciamus. Quodque tolerari vix potest, nullum fere vestimenti genus probatur, quod e Galliis non fuerit adductum, in quibus levia pleraque in pretio sunt, tametsi nostri persaepe homines modum illis et quasi formulam quandam praescribant.'

[5] See e.g. the *Diario Ferrarese*, in Murat. xxiv. col. 297, 320, 376, sqq.,

tributed to the national passion for external display; but we find in them additional evidence of the rapid movement of life in Italy in the decades before and after the year 1500. The occupation of different parts of Italy by foreigners caused the inhabitants not only to adopt foreign fashions, but sometimes to abandon all luxury in matters of dress. Such a change in public feeling at Milan is recorded by Landi. But the differences, he tells us, in costume continued to exist, Naples distinguishing itself by splendour, and Florence, to the eye of the writer, by absurdity.[1]

We may note in particular the efforts of the women to alter their appearance by all the means which the toilette could afford. In no country of Europe since the fall of the Roman empire was so much trouble taken to modify the face, the

in which the last German fashions are spoken of; the chronicler says, 'Che pareno buffoni tali portatori.'

[1] This interesting passage from a very rare work may be here quoted. See above, p. 83 note 1. The historical event referred to is the conquest of Milan by Antonio Leiva, the general of Charles V., in 1522. 'Olim splendidissime vestiebant Mediolanenses. Sed postquam Carolus Cæsar in eam urbem tetram et monstruosam Bestiam immisit, ita consumpti et exhausti sunt, ut vestimentorum splendorem omnium maxime oderint, et quemadmodum ante illa durissima Antoniana tempora nihil aliud fere cogitabant quam de mutandis vestibus, nunc alia cogitant ac in mente versant. Non potuit tamen illa Leviana rabies tantum perdere, neque illa in exhausta depraedandi libidine tantum expilare, quin a re familiari adhuc belle parati fiant atque ita vestiant quemadmodum decere existimant. Et certe nisi illa Antonii Levae studia egregios quosdam imitatores invenisset, meo quidem judicio, nulli cederent. Neapolitani nimium exercent in vestitu sumptus. Genuensium vestitum perelegantem judico, neque sagati sunt neque togati. Ferme oblitus eram Venetorum. Ii togati omnes. Decet quidem ille habitus adulta aetate homines, juvenes vero (si quid ego judico) minime utuntur panno quem ipsi vulgo Venetum appellant, ita probe confecto ut perpetuo durare existimes, saepissime vero eas vestes gestant nepotes, quas olim tritavi gestarunt. Noctu autem dum scortantur ac potant, Hispanicis palliolis utuntur. Ferrarienses ac Mantuani nihil tam diligenter curant, quam ut pileos habeant aureis quibusdam frustillis adornatos, atque nutanti capite incedunt seque quovis honore dignos existimant, Lucenses neque superbo, neque abjecto vestitu. Florentinorum habitus mihi quidem ridiculus videtur. Reliquos omitto, ne nimius sim.' Ugolinus Verinus, 'de illustratione urbis Florentiae,' says of the simplicity of the good old time:

'Non externis advecta Britannis
Lana erat in pretio, non concha aut coccus in usu.'

colour of skin and the growth of the hair, as in Italy at this time.[1] All tended to the formation of a conventional type, at the cost of the most striking and transparent deceptions. Leaving out of account costume in general, which in the fourteenth century[2] was in the highest degree varied in colour and loaded with ornament, and at a later period assumed a character of more harmonious richness, we here limit ourselves more particularly to the toilette in the narrower sense.

No sort of ornament was more in use than false hair, often made of white or yellow silk.[3] The law denounced and forbade it in vain, till some preacher of repentance touched the worldly minds of the wearers. Then was seen, in the middle of the public square, a lofty pyre (talamo), on which, beside lutes, dice-boxes, masks, magical charms, song-books, and other vanities, lay masses of false hair,[4] which the purging fires soon turned into a heap of ashes. The ideal colour sought for both in natural and artificial hair, was blond. And as the sun was supposed to have the power of making the hair of this colour,[5] many ladies would pass their whole time in the open air on sunshiny days.[6] Dyes and other mixtures were also used freely

[1] Comp. the passages on the same subject in Falke, *Die deutsche Trachten- und Modenwelt*, Leipzig, 1858.

[2] On the Florentine women, see the chief references in Giov. Villani, x. 10 and 150 (Regulations as to dress and their repeal); Matteo Villani, i. 4 (Extravagant living in consequence of the plague). In the celebrated edict on fashions of the year 1330, embroidered figures only were allowed on the dresses of women, to the exclusion of those which were painted (dipinto). What was the nature of these decorations appears doubtful. There is a list of the arts of the toilette practised by women in Boccaccio, *De Cas. Vir. Ill.* lib. i. cap. 18, 'in mulieres.'

[3] Those of real hair were called 'capelli morti.' Wigs were also worn by men, as by Giannozzo Manetti, *Vesp. Bist. Commentario*, p. 103; so at least we explain this somewhat obscure passage. For an instance of false teeth made of ivory, and worn, though only for the sake of clear articulation, by an Italian prelate, see Anshelm, *Berner Chronik*, iv. p. 30 (1508). Ivory teeth in Boccaccio, l. c.: 'Dentes casu sublatos reformare ebore fuscatos pigmentis gemmisque in albedinem revocare pristinam.'

[4] Infessura, in Eccard, *Scriptores*, ii. col. 1874: Allegretto, in Murat. xxiii. col. 823. For the writers on Savonarola, see below.

[5] Sansovino, *Venezia*, fol. 152: 'Capelli biondissimi per forza di sole.' Comp. p. 89, and the rare works quoted by Yriarte, '*Vie d'un Patricien de Venise*' (1874), p. 56.

[6] As was the case in Germany too. *Poesie satiriche*, p. 119. From the

for the same purpose. Besides all these, we meet with an endless list of beautifying waters, plasters, and paints for every single part of the face—even for the teeth and eyelids—of which in our day we can form no conception. The ridicule of the poets,[1] the invectives of the preachers, and the experience of the baneful effects of these cosmetics on the skin, were powerless to hinder women from giving their faces an unnatural form and colour. It is possible that the frequent and splendid representations of Mysteries,[2] at which hundreds of people appeared painted and masked, helped to further this practice in daily life. It is certain that it was widely spread, and that the countrywomen vied in this respect with their sisters in the towns.[3] It was vain to preach that such decorations were the mark of the courtesan; the most honourable matrons, who all the year round never touched paint, used it nevertheless on holidays when they showed themselves in public.[4] But whether we look on this bad habit as a remnant of barbarism, to which the painting of savages is a parallel, or as a consequence of the desire for perfect youthful beauty in features and in colour, as the art and complexity of the toilette would lead us to think—in either case there was no lack of good advice on the part of the men.

The use of perfumes, too, went beyond all reasonable limits. They were applied to everything with which human beings

satire of Bern. Giambullari, 'Per prendere moglie' (pp. 107–126), we can form a conception of the chemistry of the toilette, which was founded largely on superstition and magic.

[1] The poets spared no pains to show the ugliness, danger, and absurdity of these practices. Comp. Ariosto, *Sat.* iii. 202 sqq.; Aretino, *Il Marescalco*, atto ii. scena 5; and several passages in the *Ragionamenti;* Giambullari, l. c. Phil. Beroald. sen. *Carmina.* Also Filelfo in his Satires (Venice, 1502, iv. 2–5 sqq.).

[2] Cennino Cennini, *Trattato della Pittura*, gives in cap. 161 a recipe for painting the face, evidently for the purpose of mysteries or masquerades, since, in cap. 162, he solemnly warns his readers against the general use of cosmetics and the like, which was peculiarly common, as he tells us (p. 146 sqq.), in Tuscany.

[3] Comp. *La Nencia di Barberino*, str. 20 and 40. The lover promises to bring his beloved cosmetics from the town (see on this poem of Lorenzo dei Medici, above, p. 101).

[4] Agnolo Pandolfini, *Trattato della Governo della Famiglia*, p. 118. He condemns this practice most energetically.

came into contact. At festivals even the mules were treated with scents and ointments,[1] Pietro Aretino thanks Cosimo I. for a perfumed roll of money.[2]

The Italians of that day lived in the belief that they were more cleanly than other nations. There are in fact general reasons which speak rather for than against this claim. Cleanliness is indispensable to our modern notion of social perfection, which was developed in Italy earlier than elsewhere. That the Italians were one of the richest of existing peoples, is another presumption in their favour. Proof, either for or against these pretensions, can of course never be forthcoming, and if the question were one of priority in establishing rules of cleanliness, the chivalrous poetry of the Middle Ages is perhaps in advance of anything that Italy can produce. It is nevertheless certain that the singular neatness and cleanliness of some distinguished representatives of the Renaissance, especially in their behaviour at meals, was noticed expressly,[3] and that 'German' was the synonym in Italy for all that is filthy.[4]

[1] Tristan. Caracciolo, in Murat. xxii. col. 87. Bandello, parte ii. nov. 47.

[2] Cap. i. to Cosimo: 'Quei cento scudi nuovi e profumati che l' altro di mi mandaste a donare." Some objects which date from that period have not yet lost their odour.

[3] Vespasiano Fiorent. p. 453, in the life of Donato Acciajuoli, and p. 625, in the life of Niccoli. See above, vol. i. p. 303 sqq.

[4] Giraldi, *Hecatommithi*, Introduz. nov. 6. A few notices on the Germans in Italy may not here be out of place. On the fear of German invasion, see p. 91, note 2; on Germans as copyists and printers, p. 193 sqq. and the notes; on the ridicule of Hadrian VI. as a German, p. 227 and notes. The Italians were in general ill-disposed to the Germans, and showed their ill-will by ridicule. Boccaccio (*Decam.* viii. 1) says: 'Un Tedesco in soldo prò della persona è assai leale a coloro ne' cui servigi si mattea; il che rade volte suole de' Tedeschi avenire.' The tale is given as an instance of German cunning. The Italian humanists are full of attacks on the German barbarians, and especially those who, like Poggio, had seen Germany. Comp. Voigt, *Wiederbelebung*, 374 sqq.; Geiger, *Beziehungen zwischen Deutschland und Italien Zeit des Humanismus* in *Zeitschrift für deutsche Culturgeschichte*, 1875, pp. 104–124; see also Janssen, *Gesch. der deutschen Volkes*, i. 262. One of the chief opponents of the Germans was Joh. Ant. Campanus. See his works, ed. Mencken, who delivered a discourse 'De Campani odio in Germanos.' The hatred of the Germans was strengthened by the conduct of Hadrian VI., and still more by the conduct of the troops at the sack of Rome

The dirty habits which Massimiliano Sforza picked up in the course of his German education, and the notice they attracted on his return to Italy, are recorded by Giovio.[1] It is at the same time very curious that, at least in the fifteenth century, the inns and hotels were left chiefly in the hands of Germans,[2] who probably, however, made their profit mostly out of the pilgrims journeying to Rome. Yet the statements on this point may refer rather to the country districts, since it is notorious that in the great cities Italian hotels held the first place.[3] The want of decent inns in the country may also be explained by the general insecurity of life and property.

To the first half of the sixteenth century belongs the manual of politeness which Giovanni della Casa, a Florentine by birth, published under the title 'Il Galateo.' Not only cleanliness in the strict sense of the word, but the dropping of all the tricks and habits which we consider unbecoming, is here prescribed

(Gregorovius, viii. 548, note). Bandello III. nov. 30, chooses the German as the type of the dirty and foolish man (see iii. 51, for another German). When an Italian wishes to praise a German he says, as Petrus Alcyonius in the dedication to his dialogue *De Exilio*, to Nicolaus Schomberg, p. 9: 'Itaque etsi in Misnensi clarissima Germaniæ provincia illustribus natalibus ortus es, tamen in Italiae luce cognosceris.' Unqualified praise is rare, e.g. of German women at the time of Marius, *Cortigiano*, iii. cap. 33.

It must be added that the Italians of the Renaissance, like the Greeks of antiquity, were filled with aversion for all barbarians. Boccaccio, *De claris Mulieribus*, in the article 'Carmenta,' speaks of 'German barbarism, French savagery, English craft, and Spanish coarseness.'

[1] Paul. Jov. *Elogia*, p. 289, who, however, makes no mention of the German education. Maximilian could not be induced, even by celebrated women, to change his underclothing.

[2] Æneas Sylvius (*Vitae Paparum*, ap. Murat. iii. ii. col. 880) says, in speaking of Baccano: 'Pauca sunt mapalia, eaque hospitia faciunt Theutonici; hoc hominum genus totam fere Italiam hospitalem facit; ubi non repereris hos, neque diversorium quaeras.'

[3] Franco Sacchetti, Nov. 21. Padua, about the year 1450, boasted of a great inn—the 'Ox'—like a palace, containing stabling for two hundred horses. Michele Savonarola, in Mur. xxiv. col. 1175. At Florence, outside the Porta San Gallo, there was one of the largest and most splendid inns then known, but which served, it seems, only as a place of amusement for the people of the city. Varchi, *Stor. Fior.* iii. p. 86. At the time of Alexander VI. the best inn at Rome was kept by a German. See the remarkable notices taken from the MS. of Burcardus in Gregorovius, vii. 361, note 2. Comp. *ibid.* p. 93, notes 2 and 3.

with the same unfailing tact with which the moralist discerns the highest ethical truths. In the literature of other countries the same lessons are taught, though less systematically, by the indirect influence of repulsive descriptions.[1]

In other respects also, the 'Galateo' is a graceful and intelligent guide to good manners—a school of tact and delicacy. Even now it may be read with no small profit by people of all classes, and the politeness of European nations is not likely to outgrow its precepts. So far as tact is an affair of the heart, it has been inborn in some men from the dawn of civilization, and acquired through force of will by others; but the Italian first recognised it as a universal social duty and a mark of culture and education. And Italy itself had altered much in the course of two centuries. We feel at their close that the time for practical jokes between friends and acquaintances—for 'burle' and 'beffe' (p. 155 sqq.)—was over in good society,[2] that the people had emerged from the walls of the cities and had learned a cosmopolitan politeness and consideration. We shall speak later on of the intercourse of society in the narrower sense.

Outward life, indeed, in the fifteenth and the early part of the sixteenth centuries was polished and ennobled as among no other people in the world. A countless number of those small things and great things which combine to make up what we mean by comfort, we know to have first appeared in Italy. In the well-paved streets of the Italian cities,[3] driving was universal, while elsewhere in Europe walking or riding was the customs, and at all events no one drove for amusement. We

[1] Comp. e.g. the passages in Sebastian Brant's *Narrenschiff*, in the Colloquies of Erasmus, in the Latin poem of Grobianus, &c., and poems on behaviour at table, where, besides descriptions of bad habits, rules are given for good behaviour. For one of these, see C. Weller, *Deutsche Gedichte der Jahrhunderts*, Tübingen, 1875.

[2] The diminution of the 'burla' is evident from the instances in the *Cortigiano*, l. ii. fol. 96. The Florence practical jokes kept their ground tenaciously. See, for evidence, the tales of Lasca (Ant. Franc. Grazini, b. 1503, d. 1582), which appeared at Florence in 1750.

[3] For Milan, see Bandello, parte i. nov. 9. There were more than sixty carriages with four, and numberless others with two, horses, many of them carved and richly gilt and with silken tops. Comp. *ibid.* nov. 4. Ariosto, *Sat.* iii. 127.

read in the novelists of soft, elastic beds, of costly carpets and bedroom furniture, of which we hear nothing in other countries.[1] We often hear especially of the abundance and beauty of the linen. Much of all this is drawn within the sphere of art. We note with admiration the thousand ways in which art ennobles luxury, not only adorning the massive sideboard or the light brackets with noble vases and clothing the walls with the moving splendour of tapestry, and covering the toilet-table with numberless graceful trifles, but absorbing whole branches of mechanical work—especially carpentering—into its province. All western Europe, as soon as its wealth enabled it to do so, set to work in the same way at the close of the Middle Ages. But its efforts produced either childish and fantastic toy-work, or were bound by the chains of a narrow and purely Gothic art, while the Renaissance moved freely, entering into the spirit of every task it undertook and working for a far larger circle of patrons and admirers than the northern artist. The rapid victory of Italian decorative art over northern in the course of the sixteenth century is due partly to this fact, though partly the result of wider and more general causes.

[1] Bandello, parte i. nov. 3, iii. 42, iv. 25.

CHAPTER III.

LANGUAGE AS THE BASIS OF SOCIAL INTERCOURSE.

The higher forms of social intercourse, which here meet us as a work of art—as a conscious product and one of the highest products of national life—have no more important foundation and condition than language.

In the most flourishing period of the Middle Ages, the nobility of Western Europe had sought to establish a 'courtly' speech for social intercourse as well as for poetry. In Italy, too, where the dialects differed so greatly from one another, we find in the thirteenth century a so-called 'Curiale,' which was common to the courts and to the poets. It is of decisive importance for Italy that the attempt was there seriously and deliberately made to turn this into the language of literature and society. The introduction to the 'Cento Novelle Antiche,' which were put into their present shape before 1300, avow this object openly. Language is here considered apart from its uses in poetry; its highest function is clear, simple, intelligent utterance in short speeches, epigrams, and answers. This faculty was admired in Italy, as nowhere else but among the Greeks and Arabians: 'how many in the course of a long life have scarcely produced a single "bel parlare."'

But the matter was rendered more difficult by the diversity of the aspects under which it was considered. The writings of Dante transport us into the midst of the struggle. His work on 'the Italian language'[1] is not only of the utmost importance for the subject itself, but is also the first complete treatise on any modern language. His method and results belong to the history of linguistic science, in which they will always hold a

[1] *De Vulgari Eloquio*, ed. Corbinelli, Parisiis, 1577. According to Boccaccio, *Vita di Dante*, p. 77, it was written shortly before his death. He mentions in the *Convito* the rapid and striking changes which took place during his lifetime in the Italian language.

high place. We must here content ourselves with the remark that long before the appearance of this book the subject must have been one of daily and pressing importance, that the various dialects of Italy had long been the objects of eager study and dispute, and that the birth of the one classical language was not accomplished without many throes.[1]

Nothing certainly contributed so much to this end as the great poem of Dante. The Tuscan dialect became the basis of the new national speech.[2] If this assertion may seem to some to go too far, as foreigners we may be excused, in a matter on which much difference of opinion prevails, for following the general belief.

Literature and poetry probably lost more than they gained by the contentious purism which was long prevalent in Italy, and which marred the freshness and vigour of many an able writer. Others, again, who felt themselves masters of this magnificent language, were tempted to rely upon its harmony and flow, apart from the thought which it expressed. A very insignificant melody, played upon such an instrument, can produce a very great effect. But however this may be, it is certain that socially the language had great value. It was, as

[1] See on this subject the investigations of Lionardo Aretino (*Epist.* ed. Mehus. ii. 62 sqq. lib. vi. 10) and Poggio (*Historiae disceptativae convivales tres*, in the *Opp.* fol. 14 sqq.), whether in earlier times the language of the people and of scholars was the same. Lionardo maintains the negative; Poggio expressly maintains the affirmative against his predecessor. See also the detailed argument of L. B. Alberti in the introduction to *Della Famiglia*, book iii., on the necessity of Italian for social intercourse.

[2] The gradual progress which this dialect made in literature and social intercourse could be tabulated without difficulty by a native scholar. It could be shown to what extent in the fourteenth and fifteenth centuries the various dialects kept their places, wholly or partly, in correspondence, in official documents, in historical works, and in literature generally. The relations between the dialects and a more or less impure Latin, which served as the official language, would also be discussed. The modes of speech and pronunciation in the different cities of Italy are noticed in Landi, *Forcianae Quaestiones*, fol. 7 *a*. Of the former he says: 'Hetrusci vero quanquam caeteris excellant, effugere tamen non possunt, quin et ipsi ridiculi sint, aut saltem quin se mutuo lacerent;' as regards pronunciation, the Sienese, Lucchese, and Florentines are specially praised; but of the Florentines it is said: 'Plus (jucunditatis) haberet si voces non ingurgitaret aut non ita palato lingua jungeretur.'

it were, the crown of a noble and dignified behaviour, and compelled the gentleman, both in his ordinary bearing and in exceptional moments to observe external propriety. No doubt this classical garment, like the language of Attic society, served to drape much that was foul and malicious; but it was also the adequate expression of all that is noblest and most refined. But politically and nationally it was of supreme importance, serving as an ideal home for the educated classes in all the states of the divided peninsula.[1] Nor was it the special property of the nobles or of any one class, but the poorest and humblest might learn it if they would. Even now—and perhaps more than ever—in those parts of Italy where, as a rule, the most unintelligible dialect prevails, the stranger is often astonished at hearing pure and well-spoken Italian from the mouths of peasants or artisans, and looks in vain for anything analogous in France or in Germany, where even the educated classes retain traces of a provincial speech. There are certainly a larger number of people able to read in Italy than we should be led to expect from the condition of many parts of the country—as for instance, the States of the Church—in other respects; but what is of more importance is the general and undisputed respect for pure language and pronunciation as something precious and sacred. One part of the country after another came to adopt the classical dialect officially. Venice, Milan, and Naples did so at the noontime of Italian literature, and partly through its influences. It was not till the present century that Piedmont became of its own free will a genuine Italian province by sharing in this chief treasure of the people—pure speech.[2] The dialects were from the beginning of the sixteenth century purposely left to deal with a certain class of subjects, serious as well as comic,[3] and

[1] It is so felt to be by Dante, *De Vulgari Eloquio.*

[2] Tuscan, it is true, was read and written long before this in Piedmont —but very little reading and writing was done at all.

[3] The place, too, of the dialect in the usage of daily life was clearly understood. Gioviano Pontano ventured especially to warn the prince of Naples against the use of it (Jov. Pontan. *De Principe*). The last Bourbons were notoriously less scrupulous in this respect. For the way in which a Milanese Cardinal, who wished to retain his native dialect in Rome was ridiculed, see Bandello, parte ii. nov. 31.

the style which was thus developed proved equal to all its tasks. Among other nations a conscious separation of this kind did not occur till a much later period.

The opinion of educated people as to the social value of language, is fully set forth in the 'Cortigiano.'[1] There were then persons, at the beginning of the sixteenth century, who purposely kept to the antiquated expressions of Dante and the other Tuscan writers of his time, simply because they were old. Our author forbids the use of them altogether in speech, and is unwilling to permit them even in writing, which he considers a form of speech. Upon this follows the admission that the best style of speech is that which most resembles good writing. We can clearly recognise the author's feeling that people who have anything of importance to say must shape their own speech, and that language is something flexible and changing because it is something living. It is allowable to make use of any expression, however ornate, as long as it is used by the people; nor are non-Tuscan words, or even French and Spanish words forbidden, if custom has once applied them to definite purposes.[2] Thus care and intelligence will produce a language, which, if not the pure old Tuscan, is still Italian, rich in flowers and fruit like a well-kept garden. It belongs to the completeness of the 'Cortigiano' that his wit, his polished manners, and his poetry, must be clothed in this perfect dress.

[1] Bald. Castiglione, *Il Cortigiano*, l. i. fol. 27 sqq. Throughout the dialogue we are able to gather the personal opinion of the writer. The opposition to Petrarch and Boccaccio is very curious (Dante is not once mentioned). We read that Politian, Lorenzo de' Medici, and others were also Tuscans, and as worthy of imitation as they, 'e forse di non minor dottrina e guidizio.'

[2] There was a limit, however, to this. The satirists introduce bits of Spanish, and Folengo (under the pseudonym Limerno Pitocco, in his *Orlandino*) of French, but only by way of ridicule. It is an exceptional fact that a street in Milan, which at the time of the French (1500 to 1512, 1515 to 1522) was called Rue Belle, now bears the name Rugabella. The long Spanish rule has left almost no traces on the language, and but rarely the name of some governor in streets and public buildings. It was not till the eighteenth century that, together with French modes of thought, many French words and phrases found their way into Italian. The purism of our century is still busy in removing them.

When style and language had once become the property of a living society, all the efforts of purists and archaists failed to secure their end. Tuscany itself was rich in writers and talkers of the first order, who ignored and ridiculed these endeavours. Ridicule in abundance awaited the foreign scholar who explained to the Tuscans how little they understood their own language.[1] The life and influence of a writer like Macchiavelli was enough to sweep away all these cobwebs. His vigorous thoughts, his clear and simple mode of expression wore a form which had any merit but that of the 'Trecentisti.' And on the other hand there were too many North Italians, Romans, and Neapolitans, who were thankful if the demand for purity of style in literature and conversation was not pressed too far. They repudiated, indeed, the forms and idioms of their dialect; and Bandello, with what a foreigner might suspect to be false modesty, is never tired of declaring: 'I have no style; I do not write like a Florentine, but like a barbarian; I am not ambitious of giving new graces to my language; I am a Lombard, and from the Ligurian border into the bargain.'[2] But the claims of the purists were most successfully met by the express renunciation of the higher qualities of style, and the adoption of a vigorous, popular language in their stead. Few could hope to rival Pietro Bembo who, though born in Venice, nevertheless wrote the purest Tuscan, which to him was a foreign language, or the Neapolitan Sannazaro, who did the same. But the essential point was that language, whether spoken or written, was held to be an object of respect. As long as this feeling was prevalent, the fanaticism of the purists—their linguistic congresses and the rest of it[3]—did little harm. Their bad influence was

[1] Firenzuola, *Opera*, i. in the preface to the discourse on female beauty, and ii. in the *Ragionamenti* which precede the novels.

[2] Bandello, parte i. *Proemio*, and nov. 1 and 2. Another Lombard, the before-mentioned Teofilo Folengo in his *Orlandino*, treats the whole matter with ridicule.

[3] Such a congress appears to have been held at Bologna at the end of 1531 under the presidency of Bembo. See the letter of Claud. Tolomai, in Firenzuola, *Opere*, vol. ii. append. p. 231 sqq. But this was not so much a matter of purism, but rather the old quarrel between Lombards and Tuscans.

not felt till much later, when the original power of Italian literature relaxed, and yielded to other and far worse influences. At last it became possible for the Accademia della Crusca to treat Italian like a dead language. But this association proved so helpless that it could not even hinder the invasion of Gallicism in the eighteenth century.

This language—loved, tended, and trained to every use—now served as the basis of social intercourse. In northern countries, the nobles and the princes passed their leisure either in solitude, or in hunting, fighting, drinking, and the like; the burghers in games and bodily exercises, with a mixture of literary or festive amusement. In Italy there existed a neutral ground, where people of every origin, if they had the needful talent and culture, spent their time in conversation and the polished interchange of jest and earnest. As eating and drinking formed a small part of such entertainments,[1] it was not difficult to keep at a distance those who sought society for these objects. If we are to take the writers of dialogues literally, the loftiest problems of human existence were not excluded from the conversation of thinking men, and the production of noble thoughts was not, as was commonly the case in the North, the work of solitude, but of society. But we must here limit ourselves to the less serious side of social intercourse—to the side which existed only for the sake of amusement.

[1] Luigi Cornaro complains about 1550 (at the beginning of his *Trattato della Vita Sobria*) that latterly Spanish ceremonies and compliments, Lutheranism and gluttony had been gaining ground in Italy. With moderation in respect to the entertainment offered to guests, the freedom and ease of social intercourse disappeared.

CHAPTER IV.

THE HIGHER FORMS OF SOCIETY.

This society, at all events at the beginning of the sixteenth century, was a matter of art; and had, and rested on, tacit or avowed rules of good sense and propriety, which are the exact reverse of all mere etiquette. In less polished circles, where society took the form of a permanent corporation, we meet with a system of formal rules and a prescribed mode of entrance, as was the case with those wild sets of Florentine artists of whom Vasari tells us that they were capable of giving representations of the best comedies of the day.[1] In the easier intercourse of society it was not unusual to select some distinguished lady as president, whose word was law for the evening. Everybody knows the introduction to Boccaccio's 'Decameron,' and looks on the presidency of Pampinea as a graceful fiction. That it was so in this particular case is a matter of course; but the fiction was nevertheless based on a practice which often occurred in reality. Firenzuola, who nearly two centuries later (1523) prefaces his collection of tales in a similar manner, with express reference to Boccaccio, comes assuredly nearer to the truth when he puts into the mouth of the queen of the society a formal speech on the mode of spending the hours during the stay which the company proposed to make in the country. The day was to begin with a stroll among the hills passed in philosophical talk; then followed breakfast,[2] with music and singing, after which came the reci-

[1] Vasari, xii. p. 9 and 11, *Vita di Rustici*. For the School for Scandal of needy artists, see xi. 216 sqq. *Vita d' Aristotile*. Macchiavelli's *Capitoli* for a circle of pleasure-seekers (*Opere minori*, p. 407) are a ludicrous caricature of these social statutes. The well-known description of the evening meeting of artists in Rome in Benvenuto Cellini, i. cap. 30 is incomparable.

[2] Which must have been taken about 10 or 11 o'clock. See Bandello, parte ii. nov. 10.

tation, in some cool, shady spot, of a new poem, the subject of which had been given the night before; in the evening the whole party walked to a spring of water where they all sat down and each one told a tale; last of all came supper and lively conversation 'of such a kind that the women might listen to it without shame and the men might not seem to be speaking under the influence of wine.' Bandello, in the introductions and dedications to single novels, does not give us, it is true, such inaugural discourses as this, since the circles before which the stories are told are represented as already formed; but he gives us to understand in other ways how rich, how manifold, and how charming the conditions of society must have been. Some readers may be of opinion that no good was to be got from a world which was willing to be amused by such immoral literature. It would be juster to wonder at the secure foundations of a society which, notwithstanding these tales, still observed the rules of order and decency, and which knew how to vary such pastimes with serious and solid discussion. The need of noble forms of social intercourse was felt to be stronger than all others. To convince ourselves of it, we are not obliged to take as our standard the idealised society which Castiglione depicts as discussing the loftiest sentiments and aims of human life at the court of Guidobaldo of Urbino, and Pietro Bembo at the castle of Asolo. The society described by Bandello, with all the frivolities which may be laid to its charge, enables us to form the best notion of the easy and polished dignity, of the urbane kindliness, of the intellectual freedom, of the wit and the graceful dilettantism which distinguished these circles. A significant proof of the value of such circles lies in the fact that the women who were the centres of them could become famous and illustrious without in any way compromising their reputation. Among the patronesses of Bandello, for example, Isabella Gonzaga (born an Este, p. 44) was talked of unfavourably not through any fault of her own, but on account of the too free-lived young ladies who filled her court.[1] Giulia Gonzaga Colonna, Ippolita Sforza married to a Bentivoglio, Bianca Ran-

[1] Prato, *Arch. Stor.* iii. p. 309, calls the ladies 'alquante ministre di Venere.'

gona, Cecilia Gallerana, Camilla Scarampa, and others were either altogether irreproachable, or their social fame threw into the shade whatever they may have done amiss. The most famous woman of Italia, Vittoria Colonna[1] (b. 1490, d. 1547), the friend of Castiglione and Michelangelo, enjoyed the reputation of a saint. It is hard to give such a picture of the unconstrained intercourse of these circles in the city, at the baths, or in the country, as will furnish literal proof of the superiority of Italy in this respect over the rest of Europe. But let us read Bandello,[2] and then ask ourselves if anything of the same kind would have been then possible, say, in France, before this kind of society was there introduced by people like himself. No doubt the supreme achievements of the human mind were then produced independently of the helps of the drawing-room. Yet it would be unjust to rate the influence of the latter on art and poetry too low, if only for the reason that society helped to shape that which existed in no other country—a widespread interest in artistic production and an intelligent and critical public opinion. And apart from this, society of the kind we have described was in itself a natural flower of that life and culture which then was purely Italian, and which since then has extended to the rest of Europe.

In Florence society was powerfully affected by literature and politics. Lorenzo the Magnificent was supreme over his circle, not, as we might be led to believe, through the princely position which he occupied, but rather through the wonderful tact he displayed in giving perfect freedom of action to the many and varied natures which surrounded him.[3] We see how gently he dealt with his great tutor Politian, and how the sovereignty of the poet and scholar was reconciled, though not without difficulty, with the inevitable reserve prescribed by the approaching change in the position of the house of Medici and by consideration for the sensitiveness of the wife. In re-

[1] Biographical imformation and some of her letters in A. v. Reumont's *Briefe heiliger und gottesfürchtiger Italiener.* Freiburg (1877) p. 22 sqq.

[2] Important passages: parte i. nov. 1, 3, 21, 30, 44; ii. 10, 34, 55; iii. 17, &c.

[3] Comp. *Lorenzo Magn. dei Med., Poesie,* i. 204 (the Symposium); 291 (the Hawking-Party). Roscoe, *Vita di Lorenzo,* iii. p. 140, and append. 17 to 19.

turn for the treatment he received, Politian became the herald and the living symbol of Medicean glory. Lorenzo, after the fashion of a true Medici, delighted in giving an outward and artistic expression to his social amusements. In his brilliant improvisation—the Hawking Party—he gives us a humorous description of his comrades, and in the Symposium a burlesque of them, but in both cases in such a manner that we clearly feel his capacity for more serious companionship.[1] Of this intercourse his correspondence and the records of his literary and philosophical conversation give ample proof. Some of the social unions which were afterwards formed in Florence were in part political clubs, though not without a certain poetical and philosophical character also. Of this kind was the so-called Platonic Academy which met after Lorenzo's death in the gardens of the Ruccellai.[2]

At the courts of the princes, society naturally depended on the character of the ruler. After the beginning of the sixteenth century they became few in number, and these few soon lost their importance. Rome, however, possessed in the unique court of Leo X. a society to which the history of the world offers no parallel.

[1] The title 'Simposio' is inaccurate; it should be called, 'The return from the Vintage.' Lorenzo, in a parody of Dante's Hell, gives an amusing account of his meeting in the Via Faenza all his good friends coming back from the country more or less tipsy. There is a most comical picture in the eighth chapter of Piovanno Arlotto, who sets out in search of his lost thirst, armed with dry meat, a herring, a piece of cheese, a sausage, and four sardines, 'e tutte si cocevan nel sudore.'

[2] On Cosimo Ruccellai as centre of this circle at the beginning of the sixteenth century, see Macchiavelli, *Arte della Guerra*, l. i.

CHAPTER V.

THE PERFECT MAN OF SOCIETY.

It was for this society—or rather for his own sake—that the 'Cortigiano,' as described to us by Castiglione, educated himself. He was the ideal man of society, and was regarded by the civilisation of that age as its choicest flower; and the court existed for him far rather than he for the court. Indeed, such a man would have been out of place at any court, since he himself possessed all the gifts and the bearing of an accomplished ruler, and because his calm supremacy in all things, both outward and spiritual, implied a too independent nature. The inner impulse which inspired him was directed, though our author does not acknowledge the fact, not to the service of the prince, but to his own perfection. One instance will make this clear.[1] In time of war the courtier refuses even useful and perilous tasks, if they are not beautiful and dignified in themselves, such as for instance the capture of a herd of cattle; what urges him to take part in war is not duty, but 'l' onore.' The moral relation to the prince, as prescribed in the fourth book, is singularly free and independent. The theory of well-bred love-making, set forth in the third book, is full of delicate psychological observation, which perhaps would be more in place in a treatise on human nature generally; and the magnificent praise of ideal love, which occurs at the end of the fourth book, and which rises to a lyrical elevation of feeling, has no connection whatever with the special object of the work. Yet here, as in the 'Asolani' of Bembo, the culture of the time shows itself in the delicacy with which this sentiment is represented and analysed. It is true that these writers are not in all cases to be taken literally; but that the discourses they give us were actually frequent in good society, cannot be

[1] *Il Cortigiano*, l. ii. fol. 53. See above pp. 121, 139.

doubted, and that it was no affectation, but genuine passion, which appeared in this dress, we shall see further on.

Among outward accomplishments, the so-called knightly exercises were expected in thorough perfection from the courtier, and besides these much that could only exist at courts highly organised and based on personal emulation, such as were not to be found out of Italy. Other points obviously rest on an abstract notion of individual perfection. The courtier must be at home in all noble sports, among them running, leaping, swimming, and wrestling; he must, above all things, be a good dancer and, as a matter of course, an accomplished rider. He must be master of several languages; at all events of Latin and Italian; he must be familiar with literature and have some knowledge of the fine arts. In music a certain practical skill was expected of him, which he was bound, nevertheless, to keep as secret as possible. All this is not to be taken too seriously, except what relates to the use of arms. The mutual interaction of these gifts and accomplishments results in the perfect man, in whom no one quality usurps the place of the rest.

So much is certain, that in the sixteenth century the Italians had all Europe for their pupils both theoretically and practically in every noble bodily exercise and in the habits and manners of good society. Their instructions and their illustrated books on riding, fencing, and dancing served as the model to other countries. Gymnastics as an art, apart both from military training and from mere amusement, was probably first taught by Vittorino da Feltre (p. 213) and after his time became essential to a complete education.[1] The important fact

[1] Caelius Calcagninus (*Opere*, p. 514) describes the education of a young Italian of position about the year 1506, in the funeral speech on Antonio Costabili: first, 'artes liberales et ingenuae disciplinae; tum adolescentia in iis exercitationibus acta, quæ ad rem militarem corpus et animum praemuniunt. Nunc gymnastae (i.e. the teachers of gymnastics) operam dare, luctari, excurrere, natare, equitare, venari, aucupari, ad palum et apud lanistam ictus inferre aut declinare, caesim punctimve hostem ferire, hastam vibrare, sub armis hyemen juxta et aestatem traducere, lanceis occursare, veri ac communis Martis simulacra imitari.' Cardanus (*De prop. Vita*, c. 7) names among his gymnastic exercises the springing on to a wooden horse. Comp. Rabelais, *Gargantua*, i. 23, 24, for education in general, and 35 for gymnastic art. Even for the philo-

is that they were taught systematically, though what exercises were most in favour, and whether they resembled those now in use, we are unable to say. But we may infer, not only from the general character of the people, but from positive evidence which has been left for us, that not only strength and skill, but grace of movement was one of the main objects of physical training. It is enough to remind the reader of the great Frederick of Urbino (p. 44) directing the evening games of the young people committed to his care.

The games and contests of the popular classes did not differ essentially from those which prevailed elsewhere in Europe. In the maritime cities boat-racing was among the number, and the Venetian regattas were famous at an early period.[1] The classical game of Italy was and is the ball; and this was probably played at the time of the Renaissance with more zeal and brilliancy than elsewhere. But on this point no distinct evidence is forthcoming.

A few words on music will not be out of place in this part of our work.[2] Musical composition down to the year 1500 was

logists, Marsilius Ficinus (*Epist.* iv. 171 Galeotto) requires gymnastics, and Maffeo Vegio (*De Puerorum Educatione*, lib. iii. c. 5) for boys.

[1] Sansovino, *Venezia*, fol. 172 sqq. They are said to have arisen through the rowing out to the Lido, where the practice with the crossbow took place. The great regatta on the feast of St. Paul was prescribed by law from 1315 onwards. In early times there was much riding in Venice, before the streets were paved and the level wooden bridges turned into arched stone ones. Petrarch (*Epist. Seniles*, iv. 4) describes a brilliant tournament held in 1364 on the square of St. Mark, and the Doge Steno, about the year 1400, had as fine a stable as any prince in Italy. But riding in the neighbourhood of the square was prohibited as a rule after the year 1291. At a later time the Venetians naturally had the name of bad riders. See Ariosto, *Sat.* v. 208.

[2] See on this subject: *Ueber den Einfluss der Renaissance auf die Entwickelung der Musik*, by Bernhard Loos, Basel, 1875, which, however, hardly offers for this period more than is given here. On Dante's position with regard to music, and on the music to Petrarch's and Boccaccio's poems, see Trucchi, *Poesie Ital. inedite*, ii. p. 139. See also *Poesie Musicali dei Secoli XIV., XV. e XVI. tratte da vari codici per cura di Antonio Cappelli*, Bologna, 1868. For the theorists of the fourteenth century, Filippo Villani, *Vite*, p. 46, and Scardeonius, *De urb. Pativ. antiq.* in Graev. Thesaur, vi. iii. col. 297. A full account of the music at the court of Frederick of Urbino, is to be found in *Vespes. Fior.* p. 122. For the

chiefly in the hands of the Flemish school, whose originality and artistic dexterity were greatly admired. Side by side with this, there nevertheless existed an Italian school, which probably stood nearer to our present taste. Half a century later came Palestrina, whose genius still works powerfully among us. We learn among other facts that he was a great innovator; but whether he or others took the decisive part in shaping the musical language of the modern world lies beyond the judgment of the unprofessional critic. Leaving on one side the history of musical composition, we shall confine ourselves to the position which music held in the social life of the day.

A fact most characteristic of the Renaissance and of Italy is the specialisation of the orchestra, the search for new instru-

children's chapel (ten children 6 to 8 years old whom F. had educated in his house, and who were taught singing), at the court of Hercules I., see *Diario Ferrarese*, in Murat. xxiv. col. 359. Out of Italy it was still hardly allowable for persons of consequence to be musicians; at the Flemish court of the young Charles V. a serious dispute took place on the subject. See Hubert. Leod. *De Vita Frid. II. Palat.* l. iii. Henry VIII. of England is an exception, and also the German Emperor Maximilian, who favoured music as well as all other arts. Joh. Cuspinian, in his life of the Emperor, calls him 'Musices singularis amator' and adds, 'Quod vel hinc maxime patet, quod nostra aetate musicorum principes omnes, in omni genere musices omnibusque instrumentis in ejus curia, veluti in fertilissimo agro succreverant. Scriberem catalogum musicorum quos novi, nisi magnitudinem operis vererer.' In consequence of this, music was much cultivated at the University of Vienna. The presence of the musical young Duke Francesco Sforza of Milan contributed to this result. See Aschbach, *Gesch. der Wiener Universität* (1877), vol. ii. 79 sqq.

A remarkable and comprehensive passage on music is to be found, where we should not expect it, in the Maccaroneide, Phant. xx. It is a comic description of a quartette, from which we see that Spanish and French songs were often sung, that music already had its enemies (1520), and that the chapel of Leo X. and the still earlier composer, Josquin des Près, whose principal works are mentioned, were the chief subjects of enthusiasm in the musical world of that time. The same writer (Folengo) displays in his *Orlandino* (iii. 23 &c.), published under the name Limerno Pitocco, a musical fanaticism of a thoroughly modern sort.

Barth. Facius, *De Vir. Ill.* p. 12, praises Leonardus Justinianus as a composer, who produced love-songs in his youth, and religious pieces in his old age. J. A. Campanus (*Epist.* i. 4, ed. Mencken) extols the musician Zacarus at Teramo and says of him, 'Inventa pro oraculis habentur.' Thomas of Forli 'musicien du pape' in *Burchardi Diarium*, ed. Leibnitz, pp. 62 sqq.

ments and modes of sound, and, in close connection with this tendency, the formation of a class of 'virtuosi,' who devoted their whole attention to particular instruments or particular branches of music.

Of the more complex instruments, which were perfected and widely diffused at a very early period, we find not only the organ, but a corresponding string-instrument, the 'gravicembalo' or 'clavicembalo.' Fragments of these, dating from the beginning of the fourteenth century, have come down to our own days, adorned with paintings from the hands of the greatest masters. Among other instruments the first place was held by the violin, which even then conferred great celebrity on the successful player. At the court of Leo X., who, when cardinal, had filled his house with singers and musicians, and who enjoyed the reputation of a critic and performer, the Jew Giovan Maria and Jacopo Sansecondo were among the most famous. The former received from Leo the title of count and a small town;[1] the latter has been taken to be the Apollo in the Parnassus of Raphael. In the course of the sixteenth century, celebrities in every branch of music appeared in abundance, and Lomazzo (about the year 1580) names the then most distinguished masters of the art of singing, of the organ, the lute, the lyre, the 'viola da gamba,' the harp, the cithern, the horn, and the trumpet, and wishes that their portraits might be painted on the instruments themselves.[2] Such many-

[1] *Leonis Vita anonyma*, in Roscoe, ed. Bossi, xii. p. 171. May he not be the violinist in the Palazzo Sciarra? A certain Giovan Maria da Corneto is praised in the *Orlandino* (Milan, 1584, iii. 27).

[2] Lomazzo, *Trattato dell' Arte della Pittura*, &c. p. 347. The text, however, does not bear out the last statement, which perhaps rests on a misunderstanding of the final sentence, 'Et insieme vi si possono gratiosamente rappresentar convitti et simili abbellimenti, che il pittore leggendo i poeti e gli historici può trovare copiosamente et anco essendo ingenioso et ricco d' invenzione può per se stesso imaginare?' Speaking of the lyre, he mentions Lionardo da Vinci and Alfonso (Duke?) of Ferrara. The author includes in his work all the celebrities of the age, among them several Jews. The most complete list of the famous musicians of the sixteenth century, divided into an earlier and a later generation, is to be found in Rabelais, in the 'New Prologue' to the fourth book. A virtuoso, the blind Francesco of Florence (d. 1390), was crowned at Venice with a wreath of laurel by the King of Cyprus.

sided comparative criticism would have been impossible anywhere but in Italy, although the same instruments were to be found in other countries.

The number and variety of these instruments is shown by the fact that collections of them were now made from curiosity. In Venice, which was one of the most musical cities of Italy,[1] there were several such collections, and when a sufficient number of performers happened to be on the spot, a concert was at once improvised. In one of these museums there were a large number of instruments, made after ancient pictures and descriptions, but we are not told if anybody could play them, or how they sounded. It must not be forgotten that such instruments were often beautifully decorated, and could be arranged in a manner pleasing to the eye. We thus meet with them in collections of other rarities and works of art.

The players, apart from the professional performers, were either single amateurs, or whole orchestras of them, organised into a corporate Academy.[2] Many artists in other branches were at home in music, and often masters of the art. People of position were averse to wind-instruments, for the same reason[3] which made them distasteful to Alcibiades and Pallas Athene. In good society singing, either alone or accompanied with the violin, was usual; but quartettes of string-instruments were also common,[4] and the 'clavicembalo' was liked on account of its varied effects. In singing the solo only was permitted, 'for a single voice is heard, enjoyed, and judged far

[1] Sansovino, *Venezia*, fol. 138. The same people naturally collected books of music. Sansovino's words are, 'è vera cosa che la musica ha la sua propria sede in questa città.'

[2] The 'Academia de' Filarmonici' at Verona is mentioned by Vasari, xi. 133, in the life of Sanmichele. Lorenzo Magnifico was in 1480 already the centre of a School of Harmony consisting of fifteen members, among them the famous organist and organ-builder Squarcialupi. See Delecluze, *Florence et ses Vicissitudes*, vol. ii. p. 256, and Reumont, *L. d. M.* i. 177 sqq., ii. 471–473. Marsilio Ficino took part in these exercises and gives in his letters (*Epist.* i. 73, iii. 52, v. 15) remarkable rules as to music. Lorenzo seems to have transmitted his passion for music to his son Leo X. His eldest son Pietro was also musical.

[3] *Il Cortigiano*, fol. 56, comp. fol. 41.

[4] Quatro viole da arco'—a high and, except in Italy, rare achievement for amateurs.

better.' In other words, as singing, notwithstanding all conventional modesty, is an exhibition of the individual man of society, it is better that each should be seen and heard separately. The tender feelings produced in the fair listeners are taken for granted, and elderly people are therefore recommended to abstain from such forms of art, even though they excel in them. It was held important that the effect of the song should be enhanced by the impression made on the sight. We hear nothing however of the treatment in these circles of musical composition as an independent branch of art. On the other hand it happened sometimes that the subject of the song was some terrible event which had befallen the singer himself.[1]

This dilettantism, which pervaded the middle as well as the upper classes, was in Italy both more widely spread and more genuinely artistic than in any other country of Europe. Wherever we meet with a description of social intercourse, there music and singing are always and expressly mentioned. Hundreds of portraits show us men and women, often several together, playing or holding some musical instrument, and the angelic concerts represented in the ecclesiastical pictures prove how familiar the painters were with the living effects of music. We read of the lute-player Antonio Rota, at Padua (d. 1549), who became a rich man by his lessons, and published a handbook to the practice of the lute.[2]

At a time when there was no opera to concentrate and monopolise musical talent, this general cultivation of the art must have been something wonderfully varied, intelligent, and original. It is another question how much we should find to satisfy us in these forms of music, could they now be reproduced for us.

[1] Bandello, parte i. nov. 26. The song of Antonio Bologna in the House of Ippolita Bentivoglio. Comp. iii. 26. In these delicate days, this would be called a profanation of the holiest feelings. (Comp. the last song of Britannicus, Tacit. *Annal.* xiii. 15.) Recitations accompanied by the lute or 'viola' are not easy to distinguish, in the accounts left us, from singing properly so-called.

[2] Scardeonius, l. c.

CHAPTER VI.

THE POSITION OF WOMEN.

To understand the higher forms of social intercourse at this period, we must keep before our minds the fact that women stood on a footing of perfect equality with men.[1] We must not suffer ourselves to be misled by the sophistical and often malicious talk about the assumed inferiority of the female sex, which we meet with now and then in the dialogues of this time,[2] nor by such satires as the third of Ariosto,[3] who treats woman as a dangerous grown-up child, whom a man must learn how to manage, in spite of the great gulf between them.

[1] For biographies of women, see above, p. 147 and note 1. Comp. the excellent work of Attilio Hortis: *Le Donne Famose, descritte da Giovanni Boccacci.* Trieste, 1877.

[2] E.g. in Castiglione, *Il Cortigiano.* In the same strain Francesco Barbaro, *De Re Uxoria;* Poggio, *An Seni sit Uxor ducenda*, in which much evil is said of women; the ridicule of Codro Urceo, especially his remarkable discourse, *An Uxor sit ducenda* (*Opera*, 1506, fol. xviii.–xxi.), and the sarcasms of many of the epigrammatists. Marcellus Palingenius, (vol. i. 304) recommends celibacy in various passages, lib. iv. 275 sqq., v. 466–585; as a means of subduing disobedient wives he recommends to married people,

'Tu verbera misce
Tergaque nunc duro resonent pulsata bacillo.'

Italian writers on the woman's side are Benedetto da Cesena, *De Honore Mulierum*, Venice, 1500, Dardano, *La defesa della Donna*, Ven. 1554, *Per Donne Romane*, ed. Manfredi, Bol. 1575. The defence of, or attack on, women, supported by instances of famous or infamous women down to the time of the writer, was also treated by the Jews, partly in Italian and partly in Hebrew; and in connection with an earlier Jewish literature dating from the thirteenth century, we may mention Abr. Sarteano and Eliah Gennazzano, the latter of whom defended the former against the attacks of Abigdor (for their MS. poems about year 1500, comp. Steinschneider, *Hebr. Bibliogr.* vi. 48).

[3] Addressed to Annibale Maleguccio, sometimes numbered as the 5th or the 6th.

There is, indeed, a certain amount of truth in what he says. Just because the educated woman was on a level with the man, that communion of mind and heart which comes from the sense of mutual dependence and completion, could not be developed in marriage at this time, as it has been developed later in the cultivated society of the North.

The education given to women in the upper classes was essentially the same as that given to men. The Italian, at the time of the Renaissance, felt no scruple in putting sons and daughters alike under the same course of literary and even philological instruction (p. 222). Indeed, looking at this ancient culture as the chief treasure of life, he was glad that his girls should have a share in it. We have seen what perfection was attained by the daughters of princely houses in writing and speaking Latin (p. 234).[1] Many others must at least have been able to read it, in order to follow the conversation of the day, which turned largely on classical subjects. An active interest was taken by many in Italian poetry, in which, whether prepared or improvised, a large number of Italian women, from the time of the Venetian Cassandra Fedele onwards (about the close of the fifteenth century), made themselves famous.[2] One, indeed, Vittoria Colonna, may be called immortal. If any proof were needed of the assertion made above, it would be found in the manly tone of this poetry. Even the love-sonnets and religious poems are so precise and definite in their character, and so far removed from the tender twilight of sentiment, and from all the dilettantism which we commonly find in the poetry of women, that we should not hesitate to attribute them to male authors, if we had not clear external evidence to prove the contrary.

For, with education, the individuality of women in the

[1] When the Hungarian Queen Beatrice, a Neapolitan princess, came to Vienna in 1485, she was addressed in Latin, and 'arrexit diligentissime aures domina regina saepe, cum placide audierat, subridendo.' Aschbach, o. c. vol. ii. 10 note.

[2] The share taken by women in the plastic arts was insignificant. The learned Isotta Nogarola deserves a word of mention. On her intercourse with Guarino, see Rosmini, ii. 67 sqq.; with Pius II. see Voigt, iii. 515 sqq.

upper classes was developed in the same way as that of men. Till the time of the Reformation, the personality of women out of Italy, even of the highest rank, comes forward but little. Exceptions like Isabella of Bavaria, Margaret of Anjou, and Isabella of Castille, are the forced result of very unusual circumstances. In Italy, throughout the whole of the fifteenth century, the wives of the rulers, and still more those of the Condottieri, have nearly all a distinct, recognisable personality, and take their share of notoriety and glory. To these came gradually to be added a crowd of famous women of the most varied kind (i. p. 147, note 1); among them those whose distinction consisted in the fact that their beauty, disposition, education, virtue, and piety, combined to render them harmonious human beings.[1] There was no question of 'woman's rights' or female emancipation, simply because the thing itself was a matter of course. The educated woman, no less than the man, strove naturally after a characteristic and complete individuality. The same intellectual and emotional development which perfected the man, was demanded for the perfection of the woman. Active literary work, nevertheless, was not expected from her, and if she were a poet, some powerful utterance of feeling, rather than the confidences of the novel

[1] It is from this point of view that we must judge of the life of Allessandra de' Bardi in Vespasiano Fiorentino (Mai, *Spicileg.* rom. i. p. 593 sqq.) The author, by the way, is a great 'laudator temporis acti,' and it must not be forgotten that nearly a hundred years before what he calls the good old time, Boccaccio wrote the *Decameron.* On the culture and education of the Italian women of that day, comp. the numerous facts quoted in Gregorovius, *Lucrezia Borgia.* There is a catalogue of the books possessed by Lucrezia in 1502 and 3 (Gregorovius, ed. 3, i. 310, ii. 167), which may be considered characteristic of the Italian women of the period. We there find a Breviary; a little book with the seven psalms and some prayers; a parchment book with gold miniature, called *De Coppelle alla Spagnola;* the printed letters of Catherine of Siena; the printed epistles and gospels in Italian; a religious book in Spanish; a MS. collection of Spanish odes, with the proverbs of Domenico Lopez; a printed book, called *Aquila Volante;* the *Mirror of Faith* printed in Italian; an Italian printed book called *The Supplement of Chronicles;* a printed Dante, with commentary; an Italian book on philosophy; the legends of the saints in Italian; an old book *De Ventura;* a Donatus; a Life of Christ in Spanish; a MS. Petrarch, on duodecimo parchment. A second catalogue of the year 1516 contains no secular books whatever.

or the diary, was looked for. These women had no thought of the public;[1] their function was to influence distinguished men, and to moderate male impulse and caprice.

The highest praise which could then be given to the great Italian women was that they had the mind and the courage of men. We have only to observe the thoroughly manly bearing of most of the women in the heroic poems, especially those of Bojardo and Ariosto, to convince ourselves that we have before us the ideal of the time. The title 'virago,' which is an equivocal compliment in the present day, then implied nothing but praise. It was borne in all its glory by Caterina Sforza, wife and afterwards widow of Giroloma Riario, whose hereditary possession, Forli, she gallantly defended first against his murderers, and then against Cæsar Borgia. Though finally vanquished, she retained the admiration of her countrymen and the title 'prima donna d' Italia.'[2] This heroic vein can be detected in many of the women of the Renaissance, though none found the same opportunity of showing their heroism to the world. In Isabella Gonzaga this type is clearly recognisable, and not less in Clarice, of the House of Medici, the wife of Filippo Strozzi.[3]

Women of this stamp could listen to novels like those of Bandello, without social intercourse suffering from it. The ruling genius of society was not, as now, womanhood, or the respect for certain presuppositions, mysteries, and susceptibilities, but the consciousness of energy, of beauty, and of a social state full of danger and opportunity. And for this reason we find, side by side with the most measured and polished social

[1] Ant. Galateo, *Epist.* 3, to the young Bona Sforza, the future wife of Sigismund of Poland: 'Incipe aliquid de viro sapere, quoniam ad imperandum viris nata es . . . Ita fac, ut sapientibus viris placeas, ut te prudentes et graves viri admirentur, et vulgi et muliercularum studia et judicia despicias,' &c. A remarkable letter in other respects also (Mai. *Spicileg. Rom.* viii. p. 532).

[2] She is so called in the *Chron. Venetum*, in Muratori, xxiv. col. 121 sqq. (in the account of her heroic defence, *ibid.* col. 121 she is called a virago). Comp. Infessura in Eccard, *Scriptt.* ii. col. 1981, and *Arch. Stor.* append. ii. p. 250, and Gregorovius, vii. 437 note 1.

[3] Contemporary historians speak of her more than womanly intellect and eloquence. Comp. Ranke's *Filippo Strozzi*, in *Historisch-biographische Studien*, p. 371 note 2.

forms, something our age would call immodesty,[1] forgetting that by which it was corrected and counterbalanced—the powerful characters of the women who were exposed to it.

That in all the dialogues and treatises together we can find no absolute evidence on these points is only natural, however freely the nature of love and the position and capacities of women were discussed.

What seems to have been wanting in this society were the young girls,[2] who, even when not brought up in the monasteries, were still carefully kept away from it. It is not easy to say whether their absence was the cause of the greater freedom of conversation, or whether they were removed on account of it.

Even the intercourse with courtesans seems to have assumed a more elevated character, reminding us of the position of the Hetairae in Classical Athens. The famous Roman courtesan Imperia was a woman of intelligence and culture, had learned from a certain Domenico Campana the art of making sonnets, and was not without musical accomplishments.[3] The beautiful Isabella de Luna, of Spanish extraction, who was reckoned amusing company, seems to have been an odd compound of a

[1] And rightly so, sometimes. How ladies should behave while such tales are telling, we learn from *Cortigiano*, l. iii. fol. 107. That the ladies who were present at his dialogues must have known how to conduct themselves in case of need, is shown by the strong passage, l. ii. fol. 100. What is said of the 'Donna di Palazzo'—the counterpart of the Cortigiano—that she should neither avoid frivolous company nor use unbecoming language, is not decisive, since she was far more the servant of the princess than the Cortigiano of the prince. See Bandello, i. nov. 44. Bianca d'Este tells the terrible love-story of her ancestor, Niccolò of Ferrara, and Parisina. The tales put into the mouths of the women in the *Decameron* may also serve as instances of this indelicacy. For Bandello, see above, p. 145; and Landau, *Beitr. z. Gesch. der Ital. Nov.* Vienna, 1875, p. 102, note 32.

[2] Sansovino, *Venezia*, fol. 152 sqq. How highly the travelled Italians valued the freer intercourse with girls in England and the Netherlands is shown by Bandello, ii. nov. 44, and iv. nov. 27. For the Venetian women and the Italian women generally, see the work of Yriarte, pp. 50 sqq.

[3] Paul. Jov. *De Rom. Piscibus*, cap. 5; Bandello, parte iii. nov. 42. Aretino, in the *Ragionamento del Zoppino*, p. 327, says of a courtesan: 'She knows by heart all Petrarch and Boccaccio, and many beautiful verses of Virgil, Horace, Ovid, and a thousand other authors.'

kind heart with a shockingly foul tongue, which latter sometimes brought her into trouble.[1] At Milan, Bandello knew the majestic Caterina di San Celso,[2] who played and sang and recited superbly. It is clear from all we read on the subject that the distinguished people who visited these women, and from time to time lived with them, demanded from them a considerable degree of intelligence and instruction, and that the famous courtesans were treated with no slight respect and consideration. Even when relations with them were broken off, their good opinion was still desired,[3] which shows that departed passion had left permanent traces behind. But on the whole this intellectual intercourse is not worth mentioning by the side of that sanctioned by the recognised forms of social life, and the traces which it has left in poetry and literature are for the most part of a scandalous nature. We may well be astonished that among the 6,800 persons of this class, who were to be found in Rome in 1490[4]—that is, before the appear-

[1] Bandello, ii. 51, iv. 16.

[2] Bandello, iv. 8.

[3] For a characteristic instance of this, see Giraldi, *Hecatomithi*, vi. nov. 7.

[4] Infessura, in Eccard, *Scriptores*, ii. col. 1997. The public women only, not the kept women, are meant. The number, compared with the population of Rome, is certainly enormous, perhaps owing to some clerical error. According to Giraldi, vi. 7, Venice was exceptionally rich 'di quella sorte di donne che cortigiane son dette;' see also the epigram of Pasquinus (Gregor. viii. 279, note 2); but Rome did not stand behind Venice (Giraldi, *Introduz.* nov. 2). Comp. the notice of the 'meretrices' in Rome (1480) who met in a church and were robbed of their jewels and ornaments, Murat. xxii. 342 sqq., and the account in *Burchardi*, *Diarium*, ed. Leibnitz, pp. 75–77, &c. Landi (*Commentario*, fol. 76) mentions Rome, Naples, and Venice as the chief seats of the 'cortigiane;' *ibid.* 286, the fame of the women of Chiavenna is to be understood ironically. The *Quaestiones Forcianae*, fol. 9, of the same author give most interesting information on love and love's delights, and the style and position of women in the different cities of Italy. On the other hand, Egnatius (*De Exemp. III. Vir.* Ven. fol. 212 *b* sqq.) praises the chastity of the Venetian women, and says that the prostitutes come every year from Germany. Corn. Agr. *de van. Scientiae*, cap. 63 (*Opp.* ed. Lugd. ii. 158) says: 'Vidi ego nuper atque legi sub titulo "Cortosanæ" Italica lingua editum et Venetiis typis excusum de arte meretricia dialogum, utriusque Veneris omnium flagitiosissimum et dignissimum, qui ipse cum autore suo ardeat.' Ambr. Traversari (*Epist.* viii. 2 sqq.) calls the beloved of Niccolò Niccoli

ance of syphilis—scarcely a single woman seems to have been remarkable for any higher gifts. These whom we have mentioned all belong to the period which immediately followed. The mode of life, the morals and the philosophy of the public women, who with all their sensuality and greed were not always incapable of deeper passions, as well as the hypocrisy and devilish malice shown by some in their later years, are best set forth by Giraldi, in the novels which form the introduction to the 'Hecatommithi.' Pietro Aretino, in his 'Ragionamenti,' gives us rather a picture of his own depraved character than of this unhappy class of women as they really were.

The mistresses of the princes, as has already been pointed out (p. 53), were sung by poets and painted by artists, and in consequence have been personally familiar to their contemporaries and to posterity. We hardly know more than the name of Alice Perrers and of Clara Dettin, the mistress of Frederick the Victorious, and of Agnes Sorel have only a half-legendary story. With the monarchs of the age of the Renaissance—Francis I. and Henry II.—the case is different.

'foemina fidelissima.' In the *Lettere dei Principi*, i. 108 (report of Negro, Sept. 1, 1522) the 'donne Greche' are described as 'fonte di ogni cortesia et amorevolezza.' A great authority, esp. for Siena, is the *Hermaphroditus* of Panormitanus. The enumeration of the 'lenae lupaeque' in Florence (ii. 37) is hardly fictitious; the line there occurs:

'Annaque *Theutonico* tibi si dabit obvia cantu.'

CHAPTER VII.

DOMESTIC ECONOMY.

AFTER treating of the intercourse of society, let us glance for a moment at the domestic life of this period. We are commonly disposed to look on the family life of the Italians at this time as hopelessly ruined by the national immorality, and this side of the question will be more fully discussed in the sequel. For the moment we must content ourselves with pointing out that conjugal infidelity has by no means so disastrous an influence on family life in Italy as in the North, so long at least as certain limits are not overstepped.

The domestic life of the Middle Ages was a product of popular morals, or if we prefer to put it otherwise, a result of the inborn tendencies of national life, modified by the varied circumstances which affected them. Chivalry at the time of its splendour left domestic economy untouched. The knight wandered from court to court, and from one battle-field to another. His homage was given systematically to some other woman than his own wife, and things went how they might at home in the castle.[1] The spirit of the Renaissance first brought order into domestic life, treating it as a work of deliberate contrivance. Intelligent economical views (p. 77), and a rational style of domestic architecture served to promote this end. But the chief cause of the change was the thoughtful study of all questions relating to social intercourse, to education, to domestic service and organisation.

The most precious document on this subject is the treatise on the management of the home by Agnolo Pandolfini (L. B. Alberti).[2] He represents a father speaking to his grown-up

[1] Were these wandering knights really married?

[2] *Trattato del Governo della Famiglia.* See above, p. 132, note 1. Pandolfini died in 1446, L. B. Alberti, by whom the work was really written, in 1472.

sons, and initiating them into his method of administration. We are introduced into a large and wealthy household, which if governed with moderation and reasonable economy, promises happiness and prosperity for generations to come. A considerable landed estate, whose produce furnishes the table of the house, and serves as the basis of the family fortune, is combined with some industrial pursuit, such as the weaving of wool or silk. The dwelling is solid and the food good. All that has to do with the plan and arrangement of the house is great, durable and costly, but the daily life within it is as simple as possible. All other expenses, from the largest in which the family honour is at stake, down to the pocket-money of the younger sons, stand to one another in a rational, not a conventional relation. Nothing is considered of so much importance as education, which the head of the house gives not only to the children, but to the whole household. He first develops his wife from a shy girl, brought up in careful seclusion, to the true woman of the house, capable of commanding and guiding the servants. The sons are brought up without any undue severity,[1] carefully watched and counselled, and controlled 'rather by authority than by force.' And finally the servants

[1] A thorough history of 'flogging' among the Germanic and Latin races treated with some psychological power, would be worth volumes of dispatches and negotiations. (A modest beginning has been made by Lichtenberg, *Vermischte Schriften*, v. 276–283.) When, and through what influence, did flogging become a daily practice in the German household? Not till after Walther sang: 'Nieman kan mit gerten kindes zuht beherten.'

In Italy beating ceased early; Maffeo Vegio (d. 1458) recommends (*De Educ. Liber.* lib. i. c. 19) moderation in flogging, but adds: 'Caedendos magis esse filios quam pestilentissmis blanditiis laetandos.' At a later time a child of seven was no longer beaten. The little Roland (*Orlandino*, cap. vii. str. 42) lays down the principle:

'Sol gli asini si ponno bastonare,
Se una tal bestia fussi, patirei.'

The German humanists of the Renaissance, like Rudolf Agricola and Erasmus, speak decisively against flogging, which the elder schoolmasters regarded as an indispensable means of education. In the biographies of the *Fahrenden Schüler* at the close of the fifteenth century (*Platter's Lebensbeschriebung*, ed. Fechter, Basel, 1840; *Butzbach's Wanderbuch*, ed. Becher, Regensburg, 1869) there are gross examples of the corporal punishment of the time.

are chosen and treated on such principles that they gladly and faithfully hold by the family.

One feature of this book must be referred to, which is by no means peculiar to it, but which it treats with special warmth—the love of the educated Italian for country life.[1] In northern countries the nobles lived in the country in their castles, and the monks of the higher orders in their well-guarded monasteries, while the wealthiest burghers dwelt from one year's end to another in the cities. But in Italy, so far as the neighbourhood of certain towns at all events was concerned,[2] the security of life and property was so great, and the passion for a country residence was so strong, that men were willing to risk a loss in time of war. Thus arose the villa, the country-house of the well-to-do citizen. This precious inheritance of the old Roman world was thus revived, as soon as the wealth and culture of the people were sufficiently advanced.

One author finds at his villa a peace and happiness, for an account of which the reader must hear him speak himself: 'While every other possession causes work and danger, fear and disappointment, the villa brings a great and honourable advantage; the villa is always true and kind; if you dwell in it at the right time and with love, it will not only satisfy you, but add reward to reward. In spring the green trees and the song of the birds will make you joyful and hopeful; in autumn a moderate exertion will bring forth fruit a hundredfold; all through the year melancholy will be banished from you. The villa is the spot where good and honest men love to congregate. Nothing secret, nothing treacherous, is done here; all see all; here is no need of judges or witnesses, for all are kindly and peaceably disposed one to another. Hasten hither, and fly away from the pride of the rich, and the dishonour of the bad. O blessed life in the villa, O unknown fortune!' The econ-

[1] But the taste was not universal. J. A. Campanus (*Epist.* iv. 4) writes vigorously against country life. He admits: 'Ego si rusticus natus non essem, facile tangerer voluptate;' but since he was born a peasant, 'quod tibi deliciae, mihi satietas est.'

[2] Giovanni Villani, xi. 93, our principal authority for the building of villas before the middle of the fourteenth century. The villas were more beautiful than the town houses, and great exertions were made by the Florentines to have them so, 'onde erano tenuti matti.'

omical side of the matter is that one and the same property must, if possible, contain everything—corn, wine, oil, pasture-land and woods, and that in such cases the property was paid for well, since nothing needed then to be got from the market. But the higher enjoyment derived from the villa is shown by some words of the introduction: 'Round about Florence lie many villas in a transparent atmosphere, amid cheerful scenery, and with a splendid view; there is little fog, and no injurious winds; all is good, and the water pure and healthy. Of the numerous buildings many are like palaces, many like castles, costly and beautiful to behold.' He is speaking of those unrivalled villas, of which the greater number were sacrificed, though vainly, by the Florentines themselves in the defence of their city in the year 1529.[1]

In these villas, as in those on the Brenta, on the Lombard hills, at Posilippo and on the Vomero, social life assumed a freer and more rural character than in the palaces within the city. We meet with charming descriptions of the intercourse of the guests, the hunting-parties, and all the open-air pursuits and amusements.[2] But the noblest achievements of poetry and thought are sometimes also dated from these scenes of rural peace.

[1] *Trattato del Governo della Famiglia* (Torino, 1829), pp. 84, 88.

[2] See above, part iv. chap. 2. Petrarch was called 'Silvanus,' on the ground of his dislike of the town and love of the country. *Epp. Fam.* ed. Fracass. ii. 87 sqq. Guarino's description of a villa to Gianbattista Candrata, in Rosmini, ii. 13 sqq., 157 sqq. Poggio, in a letter to Facius (*De Vir. Ill.* p. 106): 'Sum enim deditior senectutis gratia rei rusticæ quam antea.' See also Poggio, *Opp.* (1513), p. 112 sqq.; and Shepherd-Tonelli, i. 255 and 261. Similarly Maffeo Vegio (*De Lib. Educ.* vi. 4), and B. Platina at the beginning of his dialogue, 'De Vera Nobilitate.' Politian's descriptions of the country-houses of the Medici in Reumont, *Lorenzo*, ii. 73, 87. For the Farnesina, see Gregorovius, viii. 114.

CHAPTER VIII.

THE FESTIVALS.

It is by no arbitrary choice that in discussing the social life of this period, we are led to treat of the processions and shows which formed part of the popular festivals.[1] The artistic power of which the Italians of the Renaissance gave proof on such occasions,[2] was attained only by means of that free intercourse of all classes which formed the basis of Italian society. In Northern Europe the monasteries, the courts, and the burghers had their special feasts and shows as in Italy; but in the one case the form and substance of these displays differed according to the class which took part in them, in the other an art and culture common to the whole nation stamped them with both a higher and a more popular character. The decorative architecture, which served to aid in these festivals, deserves a chapter to itself in the history of art, although our imagination can only form a picture of it from the descriptions which have been left to us. We are here more especially concerned with the festival as a higher phase in the life of the people, in which its religious, moral, and poetical ideas took visible shape. The Italian festivals in their best form mark the point of transition from real life into the world of art.

The two chief forms of festal display were originally here, as elsewhere in the West, the Mystery, or the dramatisation of sacred history and legend, and the Procession, the motive and character of which was also purely ecclesiastical.

The performances of the Mysteries in Italy were from the first more frequent and splendid than elsewhere, and were most favourably affected by the progress of poetry and of the other

[1] Comp. J. Burckhardt, *Geschichte der Renaissance in Italien* (Stuttg 1868), pp. 320–332.

[2] Compare pp. 47 sqq., where the magnificence of the festivals is shown to have been a hindrance to the higher development of the drama.

arts. In the course of time not only did the farce and the secular drama branch off from the Mystery, as in other countries of Europe, but the pantomime also, with its accompaniments of singing and dancing, the effect of which depended on the richness and beauty of the spectacle.

The Procession, in the broad, level, and well-paved streets of the Italian cities,[1] was soon developed into the 'Trionfo,' or train of masked figures on foot and in chariots, the ecclesiastical character of which gradually gave way to the secular. The processions at the Carnival and at the feast of Corpus Christi[2] were alike in the pomp and brilliancy with which they were conducted, and set the pattern afterwards followed by the royal or princely progresses. Other nations were willing to spend vast sums of money on these shows, but in Italy alone do we find an artistic method of treatment which arranged the procession as a harmonious and significative whole.

What is left of these festivals is but a poor remnant of what once existed. Both religious and secular displays of this kind have abandoned the dramatic element—the costumes—partly from dread of ridicule, and partly because the cultivated classes, who formerly gave their whole energies to these things, have for several reasons lost their interest in them. Even at the Carnival, the great processions of masks are out of fashion. What still remains, such as the costumes adopted in imitation of certain religious confraternities, or even the brilliant festival of Santa Rosalia at Palermo, shows clearly how far the higher culture of the country has withdrawn from such interests.

The festivals did not reach their full development till after the decisive victory of the modern spirit in the fifteenth century,[3] unless perhaps Florence was here, as in other things, in

[1] In comparison with the cities of the North.

[2] The procession at the feast of Corpus Christi was not established at Venice until 1407; Cecchetti, *Venezia e la Corte di Roma*, i. 108.

[3] The festivities which took place when Visconti was made Duke of Milan, 1395 (Corio, fol. 274), had, with all their splendour, something of mediæval coarseness about them, and the dramatic element was wholly wanting. Notice, too, the relative insignificance of the processions in

advance of the rest of Italy. In Florence, the several quarters of the city were, in early times, organized with a view to such exhibitions, which demanded no small expenditure of artistic effort. Of this kind was the representation of Hell, with a scaffold and boats in the Arno, on the 1st of May, 1304, when the Ponte alla Carraja broke down under the weight of the spectators.[1] That at a later time Florentines used to travel through Italy as directors of festivals (festaiuoli), shows that the art was early perfected at home.[2]

In setting forth the chief points of superiority in the Italian festivals over those of other countries, the first that we shall have to remark is the developed sense of individual characteristics, in other words, the capacity to invent a given mask, and to act the part with dramatic propriety. Painters and sculptors not merely did their part towards the decoration of the place where the festival was held, but helped in getting up the characters themselves, and prescribed the dress, the paints (p. 373), and the other ornaments to be used. The second fact to be pointed out is the universal familiarity of the people with the poetical basis of the show. The Mysteries, indeed, were equally well understood all over Europe, since the biblical story and the legends of the saints were the common property of Christendom; but in all other respects the advantage was on the side of Italy. For the recitations, whether of religious or secular heroes, she possessed a lyrical poetry so rich and harmonious that none could resist its charm.[3] The majority, too, of the spectators—at least in the cities—understood the meaning of mythological figures, and could guess without much difficulty at the allegorical and historical, which were drawn from sources familiar to the mass of Italians.

This point needs to be more fully discussed. The Middle Ages were essentially the ages of allegory. Theology and

Pavia during the fourteenth century (*Anonymus de Laudibus Papiae*, in Murat. xi. col. 34 sqq).

[1] Gio. Villani, viii. 70.

[2] See e.g. Infessura, in Eccard, *Scrippt.* ii. col. 1896; Corio, fols. 417, 421.

[3] The dialogue in the Mysteries was chiefly in octaves, the monologue in 'terzine.' For the Mysteries, see J. L. Klein, *Geschichte der Ital. Dramas*, i. 153 sqq.

philosophy treated their categories as independent beings,[1] and poetry and art had but little to add, in order to give them personality. Here all the countries of the West were on the same level. Their world of ideas was rich enough in types and figures, but when these were put into concrete shape, the costume and attributes were likely to be unintelligible and unsuited to the popular taste. This, even in Italy, was often the case, and not only so during the whole period of the Renaissance, but down to a still later time. To produce the confusion, it was enough if a predicate of the allegorical figures was wrongly translated by an attribute. Even Dante is not wholly free from such errors,[2] and, indeed, he prides himself on the obscurity of his allegories in general.[3] Petrarch, in his 'Trionfi,' attempts to give clear, if short, descriptions of at all events the figures of Love, of Chastity, of Death, and of Fame. Others again load their allegories with inappropriate attributes. In the Satires of Vinciguerra,[4] for example, Envy is depicted with rough, iron teeth, Gluttony as biting its own lips, and with a shock of tangled hair, the latter probably to show its indifference to all that is not meat and drink. We cannot here discuss the bad influence of these misunderstandings on the plastic arts. They, like poetry, might think themselves fortunate if allegory could be expressed by a mythological figure—by a figure which antiquity saved from absurdity—if Mars might stand for war, and Diana [5] for the love of the chase.

[1] We have no need to refer to the realism of the schoolmen for proof of this. About the year 970 Bishop Wibold of Cambray recommended to his clergy, instead of dice, a sort of spiritual bézique, with fifty-six abstract names represented by as many combinations of cards. 'Gesta Episcopori Cameracens.' in *Mon. Germ.* SS. vii. p. 433.

[2] E.g. when he found pictures on metaphors. At the gate of Purgatory the central broken step signifies contrition of heart (*Purg.* ix. 97), though the slab through being broken loses its value as a step. And again (*Purg.* xviii. 94), the idle in this world have to show their penitence by running in the other, though running could be a symbol of flight.

[3] *Inferno*, ix. 61; *Purgat.* viii. 19.

[4] *Poesie Satiriche*, ed. Milan. p. 70 sqq. Dating from the end of the fourteenth century.

[5] The latter e.g. in the *Venatio* of the Cardinal Adriano da Corneto (Strasburg, 1512; often printed). Ascanio Sforza is there supposed to find consolation for the fall of his house in the pleasures of the chase. See above, p. 261.

Nevertheless art and poetry had better allegories than these to offer, and we may assume with regard to such figures of this kind as appeared in the Italian festivals, that the public required them to be clearly and vividly characteristic, since its previous training had fitted it to be a competent critic. Elsewhere, particularly at the Burgundian court, the most inexpressive figures, and even mere symbols, were allowed to pass, since to understand, or to seem to understand them, was a part of aristocratic breeding. On the occasion of the famous 'Oath of the Pheasant' in the year 1453,[1] the beautiful young horsewoman, who appears as 'Queen of Pleasure,' is the only pleasing allegory. The huge dishes, with automatic or even living figures within them, are either mere curiosities or are intended to convey some clumsy moral lesson. A naked female statue guarding a live lion was supposed to represent Constantinople and its future saviour, the Duke of Burgundy. The rest, with the exception of a Pantomime—Jason in Colchis—seems either too recondite to be understood or to have no sense at all. Olivier himself, to whom we owe the description of the scene, appeared costumed as 'The Church,' in a tower on the back of an elephant, and sang a long elegy on the victory of the unbelievers.[2]

But although the allegorical element in the poetry, the art, and the festivals of Italy is superior both in good taste and in unity of conception to what we find in other countries, yet it is not in these qualities that it is most characteristic and unique. The decisive point of superiority[3] lay rather in the fact, that besides the personifications of abstract qualities, historical representatives of them were introduced in great number—that

[1] More properly 1454. See Olivier de la Marche, *Mémoires*, chap. 29.

[2] For other French festivals. see e.g. Juvénal des Ursins (Paris, 1614) ad. a. 1389 (entrance of Queen Isabella); John de Troyes, ad. a. 1461) (often printed) (entrance of Louis XI.). Here, too, we meet with living statues, machines for raising bodies, and so forth; but the whole is confused and disconnected, and the allegories are mostly unintelligible. The festivals at Lisbon in 1452, held at the departure of the Infanta Eleonora, the bride of the Emperor Frederick III., lasted several days and were remarkable for their magnificence. See Freher-Struve, *Rer. German. Script.* ii. fol. 51—the report of Nic. Lauckmann.

[3] A great advantage for those poets and artists who knew how to use it.

both poetry and plastic art were accustomed to represent famous men and women. The 'Divine Comedy,' the 'Trionfi' of Petrarch, the 'Amorosa Visione' of Boccaccio—all of them works constructed on this principle—and the great diffusion of culture which took place under the influence of antiquity, had made the nation familiar with this historical element. These figures now appeared at festivals, either individualised, as definite masks, or in groups, as characteristic attendants on some leading allegorical figure. The art of grouping and composition was thus learnt in Italy at a time when the most splendid exhibitions in other countries were made up of unintelligible symbolism or unmeaning puerilities.

Let us begin with that kind of festival which is perhaps the oldest of all—the Mysteries.[1] They resembled in their main features those performed in the rest of Europe. In the public squares, in the churches, and in the cloisters extensive scaffolds were constructed, the upper story of which served as a Paradise to open and shut at will, and the ground-floor often as a Hell, while between the two lay the stage properly so called, representing the scene of all the earthly events of the drama. In Italy, as elsewhere, the biblical or legendary play often began with an introductory dialogue between Apostles, Prophets, Sibyls, Virtues, and Fathers of the Church, and sometimes ended with a dance. As a matter of course the half-comic 'Intermezzi' of secondary characters were not wanting in Italy, yet this feature was hardly so broadly marked as in northern countries.[2] The artificial means by which figures were made to rise and float in the air—one of the chief delights of these representations—were probably much better understood in Italy than elsewhere; and at Florence in the fourteenth century the

[1] Comp. Bartol. Gambia, *Notizie intorno alle Opere di Feo Belcari*, Milano, 1808; and especially the introduction to the work, *Le Rappresentazioni di Feo Belcari ed altre di lui Poesie*, Firenze, 1833. As a parallel, see the introduction of the bibliophile Jacob to his edition of Pathelin (Paris, 1859).

[2] It is true that a Mystery at Siena on the subject of the Massacre of the Innocents closed with a scene in which the disconsolate mothers seized one another by the hair. Della Valle, *Lettere Sanesi*, iii. p. 53. It was one of the chief aims of Feo Belcari (d. 1484), of whom we have spoken, to free the Mysteries from these monstrosities.

hitches in these performances were a stock subject of ridicule.[1] Soon after Brunellesco invented for the Feast of the Annunciation in the Piazza San Felice a marvellous apparatus consisting of a heavenly globe surrounded by two circles of angels, out of which Gabriel flew down in a machine shaped like an almond. Cecca, too, devised the mechanism for such displays.[2] The spiritual corporations or the quarters of the city which undertook the charge and in part the performance of these plays spared, at all events in the larger towns, no trouble and expense to render them as perfect and artistic as possible. The same was no doubt the case at the great court festivals, when Mysteries were acted as well as pantomimes and secular dramas. The court of Pietro Riario (p. 106), and that of Ferrara were assuredly not wanting in all that human invention could produce.[3] When we picture to ourselves the theatrical talent and the splendid costumes of the actors, the scenes constructed in the style of the architecture of the period, and hung with garlands and tapestry, and in the background the noble buildings of an Italian piazza, or the slender columns of some great courtyard or cloister, the effect is one of great brilliance. But just as the secular drama suffered from this passion for display, so the higher poetical development of the Mystery was arrested by the same cause. In the texts which are left we find for the most part the poorest dramatic groundwork, relieved now and then by a fine lyrical or rhetorical passage, but no trace of the grand symbolic enthusiasm which distinguishes the 'Autos Sagramentales' of Calderon.

In the smaller towns, where the scenic display was less, the effect of these spiritual plays on the character of the spectators

[1] Franco Sacchetti, nov. 72.

[2] Vasari, iii. 232 sqq.: *Vita di Brunellesco;* v. 36 sqq.: *Vita del Cecca.* Comp. v. 32, *Vita di Don Bartolommeo.*

[3] *Arch. Stor.* append. ii. p. 310. The Mystery of the Annunciation at Ferrara, on the occasion of the wedding of Alfonso, with fireworks and flying apparatus. For an account of the representation of Susanna, John the Baptist, and of a legend, at the house of the Cardinal Riario, see Corio, fol. 417. For the Mystery of Constantine the Great in the Papal Palace at the Carnival, 1484, see Jac. Volaterran. (Murat. xxiii. col. 194). The chief actor was a Genoese born and educated at Constantinople.

may have been greater. We read[1] that one of the great preachers of repentance of whom more will be said later on, Roberto da Lecce, closed his Lenten sermons during the plague of 1448, at Perugia, with a representation of the Passion. The piece followed the New Testament closely. The actors were few, but the whole people wept aloud. It is true that on such occasions emotional stimulants were resorted to which were borrowed from the crudest realism. We are reminded of the pictures of Matteo da Siena, or of the groups of clay-figures by Guido Mazzoni, when we read that the actor who took the part of Christ appeared covered with wales and apparently sweating blood, and even bleeding from a wound in the side.[2]

The special occasions on which these mysteries were performed, apart from the great festivals of the Church, from princely weddings, and the like, were of various kinds. When, for example, S. Bernardino of Siena was canonised by the Pope (1450), a sort of dramatic imitation of the ceremony took place (rappresentazione), probably on the great square of his native city, and for two days there was feasting with meat and drink for all comers.[3] We are told that a learned monk celebrated his promotion to the degree of Doctor of Theology, by giving a representation of the legend about the patron saint of the city.[4] Charles VIII. had scarcely entered Italy before he was welcomed at Turin by the widowed Duchess Bianca of Savoy with a sort of half-religious pantomime,[5] in which a pastoral scene first symbolised the Law of Nature, and then a

[1] Graziani, *Cronaco di Perugia*, *Arch. Stor.* xvi. 1. p. 598. At the Crucifixion, a figure was kept ready and put in the place of the actor.

[2] For this, see Graziani, l. c. and *Pii II. Comment.* l. viii. pp. 383, 386. The poetry of the fifteenth century sometimes shows the same coarseness. A 'canzone' of Andrea da Basso traces in detail the corruption of the corpse of a hard-hearted fair one. In a monkish drama of the twelfth century King Herod was put on the stage with the worms eating him (*Carmina Burana*, pp. 80 sqq.). Many of the German dramas of the seventeenth century offer parallel instances.

[3] Allegretto, *Diarii Sanesi*, in Murat. xxiii. col. 767.

[4] Matarazzo, *Arch. Stor.* xvi. ii. p. 36. The monk had previously undertaken a voyage to Rome to make the necessary studies for the festival.

[5] Extracts from the 'Vergier d'honneur,' in Roscoe, *Leone X.*, ed. Bossi, i. p. 220, and iii. p. 263.

procession of patriarchs the Law of Grace. Afterwards followed the story of Lancelot of the Lake, and that 'of Athens.' And no sooner had the King reached Chieri, than he was received with another pantomime, in which a woman in childbed was shown, surrounded by distinguished visitors.

If any church festival was held by universal consent to call for exceptional efforts, it was the feast of Corpus Christi, which in Spain (p. 413) gave rise to a special class of poetry. We possess a splendid description of the manner in which that feast was celebrated at Viterbo by Pius II. in 1482.[1] The procession itself, which advanced from a vast and gorgeous tent in front of S. Francesco along the main street to the Cathedral, was the least part of the ceremony. The cardinals and wealthy prelates had divided the whole distance into parts, over which they severally presided, and which they decorated with curtains, tapestry, and garlands.[2] Each of them had also erected a stage of his own, on which, as the procession passed by, short historical and allegorical scenes were represented. It is not clear from the account whether all the characters were living beings or some merely draped figures; [3] the expense was certainly very great. There was a suffering Christ amid singing cherubs, the Last Supper with a figure of St. Thomas Aquinas, the combat between the Archangel Michael and the devils, fountains of wine and orchestras of angels, the grave of Christ with all the scene of the Resurrection, and finally, on the square before the Cathedral, the tomb of the Virgin. It opened after High Mass and the benediction, and the Mother of God ascended singing to Paradise, where she was crowned by her Son, and led into the presence of the Eternal Father.

Among these representations in the public street, that given by the Cardinal Vice-Chancellor Roderigo Borgia, afterwards Pope Alexander VI., was remarkable for its splendour and

[1] *Pii II. Comment.* l. viii. pp. 382 sqq. Another gorgeous celebration of the 'Corpus Domini' is mentioned by Bursellis, *Annal. Bonon.* in Murat. xxiii. col. 911, for the year 1492. The representations were from the Old and New Testaments.

[2] On such occasions we read, 'Nulla di muro si potea vedere.'

[3] The same is true of many such descriptions.

obscure symbolism.[1] It offers an early instance of the fondness for salvos of artillery[2] which was characteristic of the house of Borgia.

The account is briefer which Pius II. gives us of the procession held the same year in Rome on the arrival of the skull of St. Andrew from Greece. There, too, Roderigo Borgia distinguished himself by his magnificence; but this festival had a more secular character than the other, as, besides the customary choirs of angels, other masks were exhibited, as well as 'strong men,' who seemed to have performed various feats of muscular prowess.

Such representations as were wholly or chiefly secular in their character were arranged, especially at the more important princely courts, mainly with a view to splendid and striking scenic effects. The subjects were mythological or allegorical, and the interpretation commonly lay on the surface. Extravagancies, indeed, were not wanting—gigantic animals from which a crowd of masked figures suddenly emerged, as at Siena[3] in the year 1465, when at a public reception a ballet of twelve persons came out of a golden wolf; living table ornaments, not always, however, showing the tasteless exaggeration of the Burgundian Court (p. 182)—and the like. Most of them showed some artistic or poetical feeling. The mixture of

[1] Five kings with an armed retinue, and a savage who fought with a (tamed?) lion; the latter, perhaps, with an allusion to the name of the Pope—Sylvius.

[2] Instances under Sixtus IV., Jac. Volaterr. in Murat. xxiii. col. 135 (bombardorum et sclopulorum crepitus), 139. At the accession of Alexander VI. there were great salvos of artillery. Fireworks, a beautiful invention due to Italy, belong, like festive decorations generally, rather to the history of art than to our present work. So, too, the brilliant illuminations we read of in connexion with many festivals, and the hunting-trophies and table-ornaments. (See p. 319. The elevation of Julius II. to the Papal throne was celebrated at Venice by three days' illumination. Brosch, *Julius II.* p. 325, note 17.)

[3] Allegretto, in Murat. xxiii. col. 772. See, besides, col. 770, for the reception of Pius II. in 1459. A paradise, or choir of angels, was represented, out of which came an angel and sang to the Pope, 'in modo che il Papa si commosse a lagrime per gran tenerezza da si dolci parole.'

pantomime and the drama at the Court of Ferrara has been already referred to in the treating of poetry (p. 318). The entertainments given in 1473 by the Cardinal Pietro Riario at Rome when Leonora of Aragon, the destined bride of Prince Hercules of Ferrara, was passing through the city, were famous far beyond the limits of Italy.[1] The plays acted were mysteries on some ecclesiastical subject, the pantomimes on the contrary, were mythological. There were represented Orpheus with the beasts, Perseus and Andromeda, Ceres drawn by dragons, Bacchus and Ariadne by panthers, and finally the education of Achilles. Then followed a ballet of the famous lovers of ancient times, with a troop of nymphs, which was interrupted by an attack of predatory centaurs, who in their turn were vanquished and put to flight by Hercules. The fact, in itself a trifle, may be mentioned, as characteristic of the taste of the time, that the human beings who at all the festivals appeared as statues in niches or on pillars and triumphal arches, and then showed themselves to be alive by singing or speaking, wore their natural complexion and a natural costume, and thus the sense of incongruity was removed; while in the house of

[1] See the authorities quoted in Favre, *Mélanges d'Hist. Lit.* i. 138; Corio, fol. 417 sqq. The *menu* fills almost two closely printed pages. 'Among other dishes a mountain was brought in, out of which stepped a living man, with signs of astonishment to find himself amid this festive splendour; he repeated some verses and then disappeared' (Gregorovius, vii. 241). Infessura, in Eccard, *Scriptt.* ii. col. 1896; *Strozzii Poetae,* fol. 193 sqq. A word or two may here be added on eating and drinking. Leon. Aretino (*Epist.* lib. iii. ep. 18) complains that he had to spend so much for his wedding feast, garments, and so forth, that on the same day he had concluded a 'matrimonium' and squandered a 'patrimonium.' Ermolao Barbaro describes, in a letter to Pietro Cara, the bill of fare at a wedding-feast at Trivulzio's (*Angeli Politiani Epist.* lib. iii.). The list of meats and drinks in the Appendix to Landi's *Commentario* (above) is of special interest. Landi speaks of the great trouble he had taken over it, collecting it from five hundred writers. The passage is too long to be quoted (we there read: 'Li antropofagi furono i primi che mangiassero carne humana'). Poggio (*Opera,* 1513, fol. 14 sqq.) discusses the question' 'Uter alteri gratias debeat pro convivio impenso, isne qui vocatus est ad convivium an qui vocavit?' Platina wrote a treatise 'De Arte Coquinaria,' said to have been printed several times, and quoted under various titles, but which, according to his own account (*Dissert. Vossiane,* i. 253 sqq.), contains more warnings against excess than instructions on the art in question.

Riario there was exhibited a living child, gilt from head to foot, who showered water round him from a spring.[1]

Brilliant pantomimes of the same kind were given at Bologna, at the marriage of Annibale Bentivoglio with Lucrezia of Este.[2] Instead of the orchestra, choral songs were sung, while the fairest of Diana's nymphs flew over to the Juno Pronuba, and while Venus walked with a lion—which in this case was a disguised man—among a troop of savages. The decorations were a faithful representation of a forest. At Venice, in 1491, the princesses of the house of Este[3] were met and welcomed by the Bucentaur, and entertained by boat-races and a splendid pantomime, called 'Meleager,' in the court of the ducal palace. At Milan Lionardo da Vinci[4] directed the festivals of the Duke and of some leading citizens. One of his machines, which must have rivalled that of Brunellesco (p. 411), represented the heavenly bodies with all their movements on a colossal scale. Whenever a planet approached Isabella, the bride of the young Duke, the divinity whose name it bore stepped forth from the globe,[5] and sang some verses written by the court-poet Bellincioni (1489). At another festival (1493) the model of the equestrian statue of Francesco Sforza appeared with other objects under a triumphal arch on the square before the castle. We read in Vasari of the ingenious automata which Lionardo invented to welcome the French kings as masters of Milan. Even in the smaller cities great efforts were sometimes made on these occasions. When Duke Borso came in 1453 to Reggio[6]

[1] Vasari, ix. p. 37, *Vita di Puntormo*, tells how a child, during such a festival at Florence in the year 1513, died from the effects of the exertion —or shall we say, of the gilding? The poor boy had to represent the 'golden age'!

[2] Phil. Beroaldi, *Nuptiae Bentivolorum*, in the *Orationes Ph. B.* Paris. 1492, c. 3 sqq. The description of the other festivities at this wedding is very remarkable.

[3] M. Anton. Sabellici, *Epist.* l. iii. fol. 17.

[4] Amoretti, *Memorie, &c. su. Lionardo da Vinci*, pp. 38 sqq.

[5] To what extent astrology influenced even the festivals of this century is shown by the introduction of the planets (not described with sufficient clearness) at the reception of the ducal brides at Ferrara. *Diario Ferrarese*, in Muratori, xxiv. col. 248, ad. a. 1473; col. 282, ad. a. 1491. So, too, at Mantua, *Arch. Stor.* append. ii. p. 233.

[6] *Annal. Estens.* in Murat. xx. col. 468 sqq. The description is unclear and printed from an incorrect transcript.

to receive the homage of the city, he was met at the door by a great machine, on which S. Prospero, the patron saint of the town, appeared to float, shaded by a baldachino held by angels, while below him was a revolving disc with eight singing cherubs, two of whom received from the saint the sceptre and keys of the city, which they then delivered to the Duke, while saints and angels held forth in his praise. A chariot drawn by concealed horses now advanced, bearing an empty throne, behind which stood a figure of Justice attended by a genius. At the corners of the chariot sat four grey-headed lawgivers, encircled by angels with banners; by its side rode standard-bearers in complete armour. It need hardly be added that the goddess and the genius did not suffer the Duke to pass by without an address. A second car, drawn by an unicorn, bore a Caritas with a burning torch; between the two came the classical spectacle of a car in the form of a ship, moved by men concealed within it. The whole procession now advanced before the Duke. In front of the Church of S. Pietro, a halt was again made. The saint, attended by two angels, descended in an aureole from the façade, placed a wreath of laurel on the head of the Duke, and then floated back to his former position.[1] The clergy provided another allegory of a purely religious kind. Idolatry and Faith stood on two lofty pillars, and after Faith, represented by a beautiful girl, had uttered her welcome, the other column fell to pieces with the lay figure upon it. Further on, Borso was met by Cæsar with seven beautiful women, who were presented to him as the seven Virtues which he was exhorted to pursue. At last the Cathedral was reached, but after the service the Duke again took his seat on a lofty golden throne, and a second time received the homage of some of the masks already mentioned. To conclude all, three angels flew down from an adjacent building, and, amid songs of joy, delivered to him branches of palm, as symbols of peace.

Let us now give a glance at those festivals the chief feature of which was the procession itself.

[1] We read that the ropes of the machine used for this purpose were made to imitate garlands.

There is no doubt that from an early period of the Middle Ages the religious processions gave rise to the use of masks. Little angels accompanied the sacrament or the sacred pictures and reliques on their way through the streets; or characters in the Passion—such as Christ with the cross, the thieves and the soldiers, or the faithful women—were represented for public edification. But the great feasts of the Church were from an early time accompanied by a civic procession, and the naïveté of the Middle Ages found nothing unfitting in the many secular elements which it contained. We may mention especially the naval car (*carrus navalis*), which had been inherited from pagan times,[1] and which, as an instance already quoted shows, was admissible at festivals of very various kinds, and has permanently left its name on one of them in particular—the Carnival. Such ships, decorated with all possible splendour, delighted the eyes of spectators long after the original meaning of them was forgotten. When Isabella of England met her bridegroom, the Emperor Frederick II., at Cologne, she was met by a number of such chariots, drawn by invisible horses, and filled with a crowd of priests who welcomed her with music and singing.

But the religious processions were not only mingled with secular accessories of all kinds, but were often replaced by processions of clerical masks. Their origin is perhaps to be found in the parties of actors who wound their way through the streets of the city to the place where they were about to act the mystery; but it is possible that at an early period the clerical procession may have constituted itself as a distinct species. Dante[2] describes the 'Trionfo' of Beatrice, with the twenty-four Elders of the Apocalypse, with the four mystical Beasts, with the three Christian and four Cardinal Virtues, and with Saint Luke, Saint Paul, and other Apostles, in a way which almost forces us to conclude that such processions

[1] Strictly the ship of Isis, which entered the water on the 5th of March, as a symbol that navigation was reopened. For analogies in the German religion, see Jac. Grimm, *Deutsche Mythologie*.

[2] *Purgatorio*, xxix. 43 to the end, and xxx. at the beginning. According to v. 115, the chariot is more splendid than the triumphal chariot of Scipio, of Augustus, and even of the Sun-God.

actually occurred before his time. We are chiefly led to this conclusion by the chariot in which Beatrice drives, and which in the miraculous forest of the vision would have been unnecessary or rather out of place. It is possible, on the other hand, that Dante looked on the chariot as a symbol of victory and triumph, and that his poem rather served to give rise to these processions, the form of which was borrowed from the triumph of the Roman Emperors. However this may be, poetry and theology continued to make free use of the symbol. Savonarola[1] in his 'Triumph of the Cross' represents Christ on a Chariot of Victory, above his head the shining sphere of the Trinity, in his left hand the Cross, in his right the Old and New Testaments; below him the Virgin Mary; on both sides the Martyrs and Doctors of the Church with open books; behind him all the multitude of the saved; and in the distance the countless host of his enemies—emperors, princes, philosophers, heretics—all vanquished, their idols broken, and their books burned. A great picture of Titian, which is known only as a woodcut, has a good deal in common with this description. The ninth and tenth of Sabellico's (p. 62) thirteen Elegies on the Mother of God contain a minute account of her triumph, richly adorned with allegories, and especially interesting from that matter-of-fact air which also characterises the realistic painting of the fifteenth century.

Nevertheless, the secular 'Trionfi' were far more frequent than the religious. They were modelled on the procession of the Roman Imperator, as it was known from the old reliefs and from the writings of ancient authors.[2] The historical conceptions then prevalent in Italy, with which these shows were closely connected, have been already discussed (p. 139).

We now and then read of the actual triumphal entrance of a victorious general, which was organised as far as possible on the ancient pattern, even against the will of the hero himself. Francesco Sforza had the courage (1450) to refuse the triumphal

[1] Ranke, *Gesch. der Roman. und German. Völker*, ed. 2, p. 95. P. Villari, *Savonarola.*

[2] Fazio degli Uberti, *Dittamondo* (lib. ii. cap. 3), treats specially 'del modo del triumphare.'

chariot which had been prepared for his return to Milan, on the ground that such things were monarchical superstitions.[1] Alfonso the Great, on his entrance into Naples (1443), declined the wreath of laurel,[2] which Napoleon did not disdain to wear at his coronation in Notre-Dame. For the rest, Alfonso's procession, which passed by a breach in the wall through the city to the cathedral, was a strange mixture of antique, allegorical, and purely comic elements. The car, drawn by four white horses, on which he sat enthroned, was lofty and covered with gilding; twenty patricians carried the poles of the canopy of cloth of gold which shaded his head. The part of the procession which the Florentines then present in Naples had undertaken was composed of elegant young cavaliers, skilfully brandishing their lances, of a chariot with the figure of Fortune, and of seven Virtues on horseback. The goddess herself,[3] in accordance with the inexorable logic of allegory to which even the painters at that time conformed, wore hair only on the front part of her head, while the back part was bald, and the genius who sat on the lower steps of the car, and who symbolised the fugitive character of fortune, had his feet immersed (?) in a basin of water. Then followed, equipped by the same Florentines, a troop of horsemen in the costumes of various nations, dressed as foreign princes and nobles, and then, crowned with laurel and standing above a revolving globe, a Julius Cæsar,[4] who explained to the king in Italian verse the

[1] Corio, fol. 401: 'dicendo tali cose essere superstitioni de' Re.' Comp. Cagnola, *Arch. Stor.* iii. p. 127, who says that the duke declined from modesty.

[2] See above, vol. i. p. 315 sqq.; comp. i. p. 15, note 1. 'Triumphus Alfonsi,' as appendix to the *Dicta et Facta* of Panormita, ed. 1538, pp. 129–139, 256 sqq. A dislike to excessive display on such occasions was shown by the gallant Comneni. Comp. Cinnamus, i. 5, vi. 1.

[3] The position assigned to Fortune is characteristic of the naïveté of the Renaissance. At the entrance of Massimiliano Sforza into Milan (1512), she stood as the chief figure of a triumphal arch *above* Fama, Speranza, Audacia, and Penitenza, all represented by living persons. Comp. Prato, *Arch. Stor.* iii. p. 305.

[4] The entrance of Borso of Este into Reggio, described above (p. 417), shows the impression which Alfonso's triumph had made in all Italy, On the entrance of Cæsar Borgia into Rome in 1500, see Gregorovius vii. 439.

meaning of the allegories, and then took his place in the procession. Sixty Florentines, all in purple and scarlet, closed this splendid display of what their home could achieve. Then a band of Catalans advanced on foot, with lay figures of horses fastened on to them before and behind, and engaged in a mock combat with a body of Turks, as though in derision of the Florentine sentimentalism. Last of all came a gigantic tower, the door of which was guarded by an angel with a drawn sword; on it stood four Virtues, who each addressed the king with a song. The rest of the show had nothing specially characteristic about it.

At the entrance of Louis XII. into Milan in the year 1507 [1] we find, besides the inevitable chariot with Virtues, a living group representing Jupiter, Mars, and a figure of Italy caught in a net. After which came a car laden with trophies, and so forth.

And when there were in reality no triumphs to celebrate, the poets found a compensation for themselves and their patrons. Petrarch and Boccaccio had described the representation of every sort of fame as attendants each of an allegorical figure (p. 409); the celebrities of past ages were now made attendants of the prince. The poetess Cleofe Gabrielli of Gubbio paid this honour to Borso of Ferrara.[2] She gave him seven queens—the seven liberal arts—as his handmaids, with whom he mounted a chariot; further, a crowd of heroes, distinguished by names written on their foreheads; then followed all the famous poets; and after them the gods driving in their chariots. There is, in fact, at this time simply no end to the mythological and allegorical charioteering, and the most important work of art of Borso's time—the frescoes in the Palazzo Schifanoja—shows us a whole frieze filled with these motives.[3] Raphael, when he had to paint the Camera della

[1] Prato, *Arch. Stor.* iii. 260 sqq. The author says expressly, 'le quali cose da li triumfanti Romani se soliano anticamente usare.'

[2] Her three 'capitoli' in terzines, *Anecd. Litt.* iv. 461 sqq.

[3] Old paintings of similar scenes are by no means rare, and no doubt often represent masquerades actually performed. The wealthy classes soon became accustomed to drive in chariots at every public solemnity. We read that Annibale Bentivoglio, eldest son of the ruler of Bologna, returned to the palace after presiding as umpire at the regular military

Segnatura, found this mode of artistic thought completely vulgarised and worn out. The new and final consecration which he gave to it will remain a wonder to all ages.

The triumphal processions, strictly speaking, of victorious generals, formed the exception. But all the festive processions, whether they celebrated any special event or were mainly held for their own sakes, assumed more or less the character and nearly always the name of a 'Trionfo.' It is a wonder that funerals were not also treated in the same way.[1]

It was the practice, both at the Carnival and on other occasions, to represent the triumphs of ancient Roman commanders, such as that of Paulus Æmilius under Lorenzo the Magnificent at Florence, and that of Camillus on the visit of Leo X. Both were conducted by the painter Francesco Gronacci.[2] In Rome, the first complete exhibition of this kind was the triumph of Augustus after the victory over Cleopatra,[3] under Paul II., where, besides the comic and mythological masks, which, as a matter of fact, were not wanting in the ancient triumphs, all the other requisites were to be found—kings in chains, tablets with decrees of the senate and people, a senate clothed in the ancient costume, praetors, aediles, and quaestors, four chariots filled with singing masks, and, doubtless, cars laden with trophies. Other processions rather aimed at setting forth, in a general way, the universal empire of ancient Rome; and in answer to the very real danger which threatened Europe from the side of the Turks, a cavalcade of camels bearing masks representing Ottoman prisoners, appeared before the people. Later, at the Carnival of the year 1500, Cæsar Borgia, with a bold allusion to himself, celebrated the triumph of Julius Cæsar,

exercises, 'cum triumpho more romano.' Bursellis, l. c. col. 909. ad. a. 1490.

[1] The remarkable funeral of Malatesta Baglione, poisoned at Bologna in 1437 (Graziani, *Arch. Stor.* xvi. i. p. 413), reminds us of the splendour of an Etruscan funeral. The knights in mourning, however, and other features of the ceremony, were in accordance with the customs of the nobility throughout Europe. See e.g. the funeral of Bertrand Duguesclin, in Juvénal des Ursins, ad. a. 1389. See also Graziani, l. c. p. 360.

[2] Vasari, ix. p. 218, *Vita di Granacci.* On the triumphs and processions in Florence, see Reumont, *Lorenzo*, ii. 433.

[3] Mich. Cannesius, *Vita Pauli II.* in Murat. iii. ii. col. 118 sqq.

with a procession of eleven magnificent chariots,[1] doubtless to the scandal of the pilgrims who had come for the Jubilee (vol. i. p. 116). Two 'Trionfi,' famous for their taste and beauty, were given by rival companies in Florence, on the election of Leo X. to the Papacy.[2] One of them represented the three Ages of Man, the other the four Ages of the World, ingeniously set forth in five scenes of Roman history, and in two allegories of the golden age of Saturn and of its final return. The imagination displayed in the adornment of the chariots, when the great Florentine artists undertook the work, made the scene so impressive that such representations became in time a permanent element in the popular life. Hitherto the subject cities had been satisfied merely to present their symbolical gifts—costly stuffs and wax-candles—on the day when they annually did homage. The guild of merchants now built ten chariots, to which others were afterwards to be added, not so much to carry as to symbolise the tribute, and Andrea del Sarto, who painted some of them, no doubt did his work to perfection.[3] These cars, whether used to hold tribute or trophies, now formed a part of all such celebrations, even when there was not much money to be laid out. The Sienese announced, in 1477, the alliance between Ferrante and Sixtus IV., with which they themselves were associated, by driving a chariot round the city, with 'one clad as the goddess of peace standing on a hauberk and other arms.' [4]

At the Venetian festivals the processions, not on land but on water, were marvellous in their fantastic splendour. The sailing of the Bucentaur to meet the Princess of Ferrara in the year 1491 (p. 136) seems to have been something belonging to fairyland.[5] Countless vessels with garlands and hangings, filled with the richly-dressed youth of the city, moved in front;

[1] Tommasi, *Vita di Caesare Borgia*, p. 251.

[2] Vasari ix. p. 34 sqq. *Vita di Puntormo.* A most important passage of its kind.

[3] Vasari, viii. p. 264, *Vita di Andrea del Sarto.*

[4] Allegretto, in Murat. xxiii. col. 783. It was reckoned a bad omen that one of the wheels broke.

[5] *M. Anton. Sabellici Epist.* l. iii. letter to M. Anton. Barbavarus. He says: 'Vetus est mos civitatis in illustrium hospitum adventu eam navim auro et purpura insternere.'

genii with attributes symbolising the various gods, floated on machines hung in the air; below stood others grouped as tritons and nymphs; the air was filled with music, sweet odours, and the fluttering of embroidered banners. The Bucentaur was followed by such a crowd of boats of every sort that for a mile all round (*octo stadia*) the water could not be seen. With regard to the rest of the festivities, besides the pantomime mentioned above, we may notice as something new, a boat-race of fifty powerful girls. In the sixteenth century,[1] the nobility were divided into corporations with a view to these festivals, whose most noteworthy feature was some extraordinary machine placed on a ship. So, for instance, in the year 1541, at the festival of the 'Sempiterni,' a round 'universe' floated along the Grand Canal, and a splendid ball was given inside it. The Carnival, too, in this city was famous for its dances, processions, and exhibitions of every kind. The Square of St. Mark was found to give space enough not only for tournaments (p. 390), but for 'Trionfi,' similar to those common on the mainland. At a festival held on the conclusion of peace,[2] the pious brotherhoods ('scuole') took each its part in the procession. There, among golden chandeliers with red candles, among crowds of musicians and winged boys with golden bowls and horns of plenty, was seen a car on which Noah and David sat together enthroned; then came Abigail, leading a camel laden with treasures, and a second car with a group of political figures—Italy sitting between Venice and Liguria, the two last with their coats of arms, the former with a stork, the symbol of unity—and on a raised step three female symbolical figures with the arms of the allied princes. This was followed by a great globe with the constellations, as it seems, round it. The princes themselves, or rather their bodily representatives, appeared on other chariots with their servants and their coats of arms, if we have rightly interpreted our author.[3]

[1] Sansovino, *Venezia*, fol. 151 sqq. The names of these corporations were: Pavoni, Accessi, Eterni, Reali, Sempiterni. The academies probably had their origin in these guilds.

[2] Probably in 1495. Comp. *M. Anton. Sabellici Epist.* l. v. fol. 28; last letter to M. Ant. Barbavarus.

[3] 'Terræ globum socialibus signis circunquaque figuratum,' and

There was also music at these and all other similar processions.

The Carnival, properly so called, apart from these great triumphal marches, had nowhere, perhaps, in the fifteenth century, so varied a character as in Rome.[1] There were races of every kind—of horses, asses, buffalos, old men, young men, Jews, and so on. Paul II. entertained the people in crowds before the Palazzo di Venezia, in which he lived. The games in the Piazza Navona, which had probably never altogether ceased since the classical times, were remarkable for their warlike splendour. We read of a sham fight of cavalry, and a review of all the citizens in arms. The greatest freedom existed with regard to the use of masks, which were sometimes allowed for several months together.[2] Sixtus IV. ventured, in the most populous part of the city—at the Campofiore and near the Banchi—to make his way through crowds of masks, though he declined to receive them as visitors in the Vatican. Under Innocent VIII., a discreditable usage, which had already appeared among the Cardinals, attained its height. In the Carnival of 1491, they sent one another chariots full of splendid masks, of singers, and of buffoons, chanting scandalous verses. They were accompanied by men on horseback.[3] Apart from the Carnival, the Romans seem to have been the first to discover the effect of a great procession by torchlight. When Pius II. came back from the Congress of Mantua in 1459,[4] the people waited on him with a squadron of horsemen bearing torches, who rode in shining circles before his palace. Sixtus IV. however, thought it better to decline a nocturnal visit of

'quinis pegmatibus, quorum singula foederatorum regum, principumque suas habuere effigies et cum his ministros signaque in auro affabre caelata.'

[1] Infessura, in Eccard, *Scriptt.* ii. col. 1093, 2000; Mich. Cannesius, *Vita Pauli II.* in Murat. iii. ii. col. 1012; Platina. *Vitae Pontiff.* p. 318; Jac. Volaterran. in Murat. xiii. col. 163, 194; Paul. Jov. *Elogia*, sub Juliano Cæsarino. Elsewhere, too, there were races for women, *Diario Ferrarese*, in Murat. xxiv. col. 384: comp. Gregorovius, vi. 690 sqq., vii. 219, 616 sqq.

[2] Once under Alexander VI. from October till Lent. See Tommasi, l. c. p. 322.

[3] Baluz. *Miscell.* iv. 517 (comp. Gregorovius, vii. 288 sqq).

[4] *Pii II. Comment.* l. iv. p. 211.

the people, who proposed to wait on him with torches and olive-branches.[1]

But the Florentine Carnival surpassed the Roman in a certain class of processions, which have left their mark even in literature.[2] Among a crowd of masks on foot and on horseback appeared some huge, fantastic chariot, and upon it an allegorical figure or group of figures with the proper accompaniments, such as Jealousy with four spectacled faces on one head; the four temperaments (p. 309) with the planets belonging to them; the three Fates; Prudence enthroned above Hope and Fear, which lay bound before her; the four Elements, Ages, Winds, Seasons, and so on; as well as the famous chariot of Death with the coffins, which presently opened. Sometimes we meet with a splendid scene from classical mythology—Bacchus and Ariadne, Paris and Helen, and others. Or else a chorus of figures forming some single class or category, as the beggars, the hunters and nymphs, the lost souls, who in their lifetime were hard-hearted women, the hermits, the astrologers, the vagabonds, the devils, the sellers of various kinds of wares, and even on one occasion 'il popolo,' the people as such, who all reviled one another in their songs. The songs, which still remain and have been collected, give the explanation of the masquerade sometimes in a pathetic, sometimes in a humorous, and sometimes in an excessively indecent tone. Some of the worst in this respect are attributed to Lorenzo the Magnificent, probably because the real author did not venture to declare himself. However this may be, we must certainly ascribe to him the beautiful song which accompanied the masque of Bacchus and Ariadne, whose refrain still echoes to us from the fifteenth century, like a regret-

[1] Nantiporto, in Murat. iii. ii. col. 1080. They wished to thank him for a peace which he had concluded, but found the gates of the palace closed and troops posted in all the open places.

[2] 'Tutti i trionfi, carri, mascherate, o canti carnascialeschi.' Cosmopoli, 1750. Macchiavelli, *Opere Minori*, p. 505; Vasari, vii. p. 115 sqq. *Vita di Piero di Cosimo*, to whom a chief part in the development of these festivities is ascribed. Comp. B. Loos (above, p. 154, note 1) p. 12 sqq. and Reumont, *Lorenzo*, ii. 443 sqq., where the authorities are collected which show that the Carnival was soon restrained. Comp. ibid. ii. p. 24.

ful presentiment of the brief splendour of the Renaissance itself:—

> 'Quanto è bella giovinezza,
> Che si fugge tuttavia!
> Chi vuol esser lieto, sia:
> Di doman non c' è certezza.

PART VI.

MORALITY AND RELIGION.

CHAPTER I.

MORALITY.

The relation of the various peoples of the earth to the supreme interests of life, to God, virtue, and immortality, may be investigated up to a certain point, but can never be compared to one another with absolute strictness and certainty. The more plainly in these matters our evidence seems to speak, the more carefully must we refrain from unqualified assumptions and rash generalisations.

This remark is especially true with regard to our judgment on questions of morality. It may be possible to indicate many contrasts and shades of difference among different nations, but to strike the balance of the whole is not given to human insight. The ultimate truth with respect to the character, the conscience, and the guilt of a people remains for ever a secret; if only for the reason that its defects have another side, where they reappear as peculiarities or even as virtues. We must leave those who find a pleasure in passing sweeping censures on whole nations, to do so as they like. The peoples of Europe can maltreat, but happily not judge one another. A great nation, interwoven by its civilisation, its achievements, and its fortunes with the whole life of the modern world, can afford to ignore both its advocates and its accusers. It lives on with or without the approval of theorists.

Accordingly, what here follows is no judgment, but rather a string of marginal notes, suggested by a study of the Italian Renaissance extending over some years. The value to be attached to them is all the more qualified as they mostly touch on the life of the upper classes, with respect to which we are far better informed in Italy than in any other country in Europe at that period. But though both fame and infamy sound louder here than elsewhere, we are not helped thereby in forming an adequate moral estimate of the people.

What eye can pierce the depths in which the character and fate of nations are determined?—in which that which is inborn and that which has been experienced combine to form a new whole and a fresh nature?—in which even those intellectual capacities, which at first sight we should take to be most original, are in fact evolved late and slowly? Who can tell if the Italian before the thirteenth century possessed that flexible activity and certainty in his whole being—that play of power in shaping whatever subject he dealt with in word or in form, which was peculiar to him later? And if no answer can be found to these questions, how can we possibly judge of the infinite and infinitely intricate channels through which character and intellect are incessantly pouring their influence one upon the other. A tribunal there is for each one of us, whose voice is our conscience; but let us have done with these generalities about nations. For the people that seems to be most sick the cure may be at hand; and one that appears to be healthy may bear within it the ripening germs of death, which the hour of danger will bring forth from their hiding-place.

At the beginning of the sixteenth century, when the civilisation of the Renaissance had reached its highest pitch, and at the same time the political ruin of the nation seemed inevitable, there were not wanting serious thinkers who saw a connexion between this ruin and the prevalent immorality. It was not one of those methodistical moralists who in every age think themselves called to declaim against the wickedness of the time, but it was Macchiavelli, who, in one of his most well-considered works,[1] said openly: 'We Italians are irreligious and corrupt above others.' Another man had perhaps said, 'We are individually highly developed; we have outgrown the limits of morality and religion which were natural to us in our undeveloped state, and we despise outward law, because our rulers are illegitimate, and their judges and officers wicked

[1] *Discorsi*, l. i. c. 12. Also c. 55: Italy is more corrupt than all other countries; then come the French and Spaniards.

men.' Macchiavelli adds, 'because the Church and her representatives set us the worst example.'

Shall we add also, 'because the influence exercised by antiquity was in this respect unfavourable'? The statement can only be received with many qualifications. It may possibly be true of the humanists (p. 272 sqq.), especially as regards the profligacy of their lives. Of the rest it may perhaps be said with some approach to accuracy, that, after they became familiar with antiquity, they substituted for holiness—the Christian ideal of life—the cultus of historical greatness (see Part II. chap. iii.). We can understand, therefore, how easily they would be tempted to consider those faults and vices to be matters of indifference, in spite of which their heroes were great. They were probably scarcely conscious of this themselves, for if we are summoned to quote any statement of doctrine on this subject, we are again forced to appeal to humanists like Paolo Giovio, who excuses the perjury of Giangaleazzo Visconti, through which he was enabled to found an empire, by the example of Julius Cæsar.[1] The great Florentine historians and statesmen never stoop to these slavish quotations, and what seems antique in their deeds and their judgments is so because the nature of their political life necessarily fostered in them a mode of thought which has some analogy with that of antiquity.

Nevertheless, it cannot be denied that Italy at the beginning of the sixteenth century found itself in the midst of a grave moral crisis, out of which the best men saw hardly any escape.

Let us begin by saying a few words about that moral force which was then the strongest bulwark against evil. The highly gifted men of that day thought to find it in the sentiment of honour. This is that enigmatic mixture of conscience and egoism which often survives in the modern man after he has lost, whether by his own fault or not, faith, love, and hope. This sense of honour is compatible with much selfishness and great vices, and may be the victim of astonishing illusions; yet, nevertheless, all the noble elements that are left

[1] Paul. Jov. *Viri Illustres:* Jo. Gal. Vicecomes. Comp. p. 12 sqq. and notes.

in the wreck of a character may gather around it, and from this fountain may draw new strength. It has become, in a far wider sense than is commonly believed, a decisive test of conduct in the minds of the cultivated Europeans of our own day, and many of those who yet hold faithfully by religion and morality are unconsciously guided by this feeling in the gravest decisions of their lives.[1]

It lies without the limits of our task to show how the men of antiquity also experienced this feeling in a peculiar form, and how, afterwards, in the Middle Ages, a special sense of honour became the mark of a particular class. Nor can we here dispute with those who hold that conscience, rather than honour, is the motive power. It would indeed be better and nobler if it were so; but since it must be granted that even our worthier resolutions result from 'a conscience more or less dimmed by selfishness,' it is better to call the mixture by its right name.[2] It is certainly not always easy, in treating of the Italian of this period, to distinguish this sense of honour from the passion for fame, into which, indeed, it easily passes. Yet the two sentiments are essentially different.

There is no lack of witnesses on this subject. One who speaks plainly may here be quoted as a representative of the rest. We read in the recently-published 'Aphorisms' of Guicciardini:[3] 'He who esteems honour highly, succeeds in all that he undertakes, since he fears neither trouble, danger, nor expense; I have found it so in my own case, and may say it and write it; vain and dead are the deeds of men which have not this as their motive.' It is necessary to add that, from what is known of the life of the writer, he can here be only speaking of honour, and not of fame. Rabelais has put the matter more clearly than perhaps any Italian. We quote him, indeed, unwillingly in these pages. What the great, baroque Frenchman gives us, is a picture of what the Renaissance

[1] On the part filled by the sense of honour in the modern world, see Prévost-Paradol, *La France Nouvelle*, liv. iii. chap. 2.

[2] Compare what Mr. Darwin says of blushing in the 'Expression of the Emotions,' and of the relations between shame and conscience.

[3] Franc. Guicciardini, *Ricordi Politici e Civili*, n. 118 (*Opere inedite*, vol. i.).

would be without form and without beauty.[1] But his description of an ideal state of things in the Thelemite monastery is decisive as historical evidence. In speaking of his gentlemen and ladies of the Order of Free Will,[2] he tells us as follows :—

'En leur reigle n'estoit que ceste clause : Fay ce que vouldras. Parce que gens liberes, bien nayz,[3] bien instruictz, conversans en compaignies honnestes, ont par nature ung instinct et aguillon qui toujours les poulse à faitz vertueux, et retire de vice ; lequel ilz nommoyent honneur.'

This is that same faith in the goodness of human nature which inspired the men of the second half of the eighteenth century, and helped to prepare the way for the French Revolution. Among the Italians, too, each man appeals to this noble instinct within him, and though with regard to the people as a whole—chiefly in consequence of the national disasters—judgments of a more pessimistic sort became prevalent, the importance of this sense of honour must still be rated highly. If the boundless development of individuality, stronger than the will of the individual, be the work of a historical providence, not less so is the opposing force which then manifested itself in Italy. How often, and against what passionate attacks of selfishness it won the day, we cannot tell, and therefore no human judgment can estimate with certainty the absolute moral value of the nation.

A force which we must constantly take into account in judging of the morality of the more highly-developed Italian

[1] His closest counterpart is Merlinus Coccajus (Teofilo Folengo), whose *Opus Maccaronicorum* Rabelais certainly knew, and quotes more than once (*Pantagruel*, l. ii. ch. 1. and ch. 7, at the end). It is possible that Merlinus Coccajus may have given the impulse which resulted in Pantagruel and Gargantua.

[2] *Gargantua*, l. i. cap. 57.

[3] That is, well-born in the higher sense of the word, since Rabelais, son of the innkeeper of Chinon, has here no motive for assigning any special privilege to the nobility. The preaching of the Gospel, which is spoken of in the inscription at the entrance to the monastery, would fit in badly with the rest of the life of the inmates ; it must be understood in a negative sense, as implying defiance of the Roman Church.

of this period, is that of the imagination. It gives to his virtues and vices a peculiar colour, and under its influence his unbridled egoism shows itself in its most terrible shape.

The force of his imagination explains, for example, the fact that he was the first gambler on a large scale in modern times. Pictures of future wealth and enjoyment rose in such life-like colours before his eyes, that he was ready to hazard everything to reach them. The Mohammedan nations would doubtless have anticipated him in this respect, had not the Koran, from the beginning, set up the prohibition against gambling as a chief safeguard of public morals, and directed the imagination of its followers to the search after buried treasures. In Italy, the passion for play reached an intensity which often threatened or altogether broke up the existence of the gambler. Florence had already, at the end of the fourteenth century, its Casanova —a certain Buonaccorso Pitti,[1] who, in the course of his incessant journeys as merchant, political agent, diplomatist and professional gambler, won and lost sums so enormous that none but princes like the Dukes of Brabant, Bavaria, and Savoy, were able to compete with him. That great lottery-bank, which was called the Court of Rome, accustomed people to a need of excitement, which found its satisfaction in games of hazard during the intervals between one intrigue and another. We read, for example, how Franceschetto Cybò, in two games with the Cardinal Raffaello Riario, lost no less than 14,000 ducats, and afterwards complained to the Pope that his opponent had cheated him.[2] Italy has since that time been the home of the lottery.

It was to the imagination of the Italians that the peculiar character of their vengeance was due. The sense of justice was, indeed, one and the same throughout Europe, and any violation of it, so long as no punishment was inflicted, must have been felt in the same manner. But other nations, though they found it no easier to forgive, nevertheless forgot more easily, while the Italian imagination kept the picture of the

[1] See extracts from his diary in Delécluze, *Florence et ses Vicissitudes*, vol. 2.

[2] Infessura, ap. Eccard, *Scriptt.* ii. col. 1992. On F. C. see above, p. 108.

wrong alive with frightful vividness.[1] The fact that, according to the popular morality, the avenging of blood is a duty—a duty often performed in a way to make us shudder—gives to this passion a peculiar and still firmer basis. The government and the tribunals recognise its existence and justification, and only attempt to keep it within certain limits. Even among the peasantry, we read of Thyestean banquets and mutual assassination on the widest scale. Let us look at an instance.[2]

In the district of Aquapendente three boys were watching cattle, and one of them said: 'Let us find out the way how people are hung.' While one was sitting on the shoulders of the other, and the third, after fastening the rope round the neck of the first, was tying it to an oak, a wolf came, and the two who were free ran away and left the other hanging. Afterwards they found him dead, and buried him. On the Sunday his father came to bring him bread, and one of the two confessed what had happened, and showed him the grave. The old man then killed him with a knife, cut him up, brought away the liver, and entertained the boy's father with it at home. After dinner, he told him whose liver it was. Hereupon began a series of reciprocal murders between the two families, and within a month thirty-six persons were killed, women as well as men.

And such 'vendette,' handed down from father to son, and extending to friends and distant relations, were not limited to the lower classes, but reached to the highest. The chronicles and novels of the period are full of such instances, especially of vengeance taken for the violation of women. The classic land for these feuds was Romagna, where the 'vendetta' was interwoven with intrigues and party divisions of every conceivable sort. The popular legends present an awful picture of the savagery into which this brave and energetic people had relapsed. We are told, for instance, of a nobleman at Ravenna, who had got all his enemies together in a tower, and might have burned them; instead of which he let them out, embraced

[1] This opinion of Stendhal (*La Chartreuse de Parme*, ed. Delahays, p. 335) seems to me to rest on profound psychological observation.

[2] Graziani, *Cronaca di Perugia*, for the year 1437 (*Arch. Stor.* xvi. i. p. 415).

them, and entertained them sumptuously; whereupon shame drove them mad, and they conspired against him.[1] Pious and saintly monks exhorted unceasingly to reconciliation, but they can scarcely have done more than restrain to a certain extent the feuds already established; their influence hardly prevented the growth of new ones. The novelists sometimes describe to us this effect of religion—how sentiments of generosity and forgiveness were suddenly awakened, and then again paralysed by the force of what had once been done and could never be undone. The Pope himself was not always lucky as a peace-maker. 'Pope Paul II. desired that the quarrel between Antonio Caffarello and the family of Alberino should cease, and ordered Giovanni Alberino and Antonio Caffarello to come before him, and bade them kiss one another, and promised them a fine of 2,000 ducats in case they renewed this strife, and two days after Antonio was stabbed by the same Giacomo Alberino, son of Giovanni, who had wounded him once before; and the Pope was full of anger, and confiscated the goods of Alberino, and destroyed his houses, and banished father and son from Rome.'[2] The oaths and ceremonies by which reconciled enemies attempted to guard themselves against a relapse, are sometimes utterly horrible. When the parties of the 'Nove' and the 'Popolari' met and kissed one another by twos in the cathedral at Siena on Christmas Eve, 1494,[3] an oath was read by which all salvation in time and eternity was denied to the future violator of the treaty—'an oath more astonishing and dreadful than had ever yet been heard.' The last consolations of religion in the hour of death were to turn to the damnation of the man who should break it. It is clear, however, that such a ceremony rather represents the despairing mood of the mediators than offers any real guarantee of peace, inasmuch as the truest reconciliation is just that one which has least need of it.

This personal need of vengeance felt by the cultivated and highly placed Italian, resting on the solid basis of an analogous

[1] Giraldi, *Hecatommithi*, i. nov. 7.

[2] Infessura, in Eccard, *Scriptt.* ii. col. 1892, for the year 1464.

[3] Allegretto, *Diari Sanisi*, in Murat. xxiii. col. 837. Allegretto was himself present when the oath was taken, and had no doubt of its efficacy.

popular custom, naturally displays itself under a thousand different aspects, and receives the unqualified approval of public opinion, as reflected in the works of the novelists.[1] All are at one on the point, that, in the case of those injuries and insults for which Italian justice offered no redress, and all the more in the case of those against which no human law can ever adequately provide, each man is free to take the law into his own hands. Only there must be art in the vengeance, and the satisfaction must be compounded of the material injury and moral humiliation of the offender. A mere brutal, clumsy triumph of force was held by public opinion to be no satisfaction. The whole man with his sense of fame and of scorn, not only his fist, must be victorious.

The Italian of that time shrank, it is true, from no dissimulation in order to attain his ends, but was wholly free from hypocrisy in matters of principle. In these he attempted to deceive neither himself nor others. Accordingly, revenge was declared with perfect frankness to be a necessity of human nature. Cool-headed people declared that it was then most worthy of praise, when it was disengaged from passion, and worked simply from motives of expedience, 'in order that other men may learn to leave us unharmed.'[2] Yet such instances must have formed only a small minority in comparison with those in which passion sought an outlet. This sort of revenge differs clearly from the avenging of blood, which has been already spoken of; while the latter keeps more or less within the limits of retaliation—the 'jus talionis'—the former necessarily goes much farther, not only requiring the sanction of the sense of justice, but craving admiration, and even striving to get the laugh on its own side.

Here lies the reason why men were willing to wait so long for their revenge. A 'bella vendetta' demanded as a rule a combination of circumstances for which it was necessary to wait patiently. The gradual ripening of such opportunities is described by the novelists with heartfelt delight.

There is no need to discuss the morality of actions in which

[1] Those who leave vengeance to God are ridiculed by Pulci, *Morgante*, canto xxi. str. 83 sqq. 104 sqq.

[2] Guicciardini, *Ricordi*, l. c. n. 74.

plaintiff and judge are one and the same person. If this Italian thirst for vengeance is to be palliated at all, it must be by proving the existence of a corresponding national virtue, namely gratitude. The same force of imagination which retains and magnifies wrong once suffered, might be expected also to keep alive the memory of kindness received.[1] It is not possible, however, to prove this with regard to the nation as a whole, though traces of it may be seen in the Italian character of to-day. The gratitude shown by the inferior classes for kind treatment, and the good memory of the upper for politeness in social life, are instances of this.

This connexion between the imagination and the moral qualities of the Italian repeats itself continually. If, nevertheless, we find more cold calculation in cases where the Northerner rather follows his impulses, the reason is that individual development in Italy was not only more marked and earlier in point of time, but also far more frequent. Where this is the case in other countries, the results are also analogous. We find, for example, that the early emancipation of the young from domestic and paternal authority is common to North America with Italy. Later on, in the more generous natures, a tie of freer affection grows up between parents and children.

It is in fact a matter of extreme difficulty to judge fairly of other nations in the sphere of character and feeling. In these respects a people may be developed highly, and yet in a manner so strange that a foreigner is utterly unable to understand it. Perhaps all the nations of the West are in this point equally favoured.

But where the imagination has exercised the most powerful and despotic influence on morals is in the illicit intercourse of the two sexes. It is well known that prostitution was freely practised in the Middle Ages, before the appearance of syphilis. A discussion, however, on these questions does not belong to our present work. What seems characteristic of Italy at this

[1] Thus Cardanus (*De Propria Vita*, cap. 13) describes himself as very revengeful, but also as 'verax, memor beneficiorum, amans justitiæ.'

time, is that here marriage and its rights were more often and more deliberately trampled under foot than anywhere else. The girls of the higher classes were carefully secluded, and of them we do not speak. All passion was directed to the married women.

Under these circumstances it is remarkable that, so far as we know, there was no diminution in the number of marriages, and that family life by no means underwent that disorganisation which a similar state of things would have produced in the North. Men wished to live as they pleased, but by no means to renounce the family, even when they were not sure that it was all their own. Nor did the race sink, either physically or mentally, on this account; for that apparent intellectual decline which showed itself towards the middle of the sixteenth century may be certainly accounted for by political and ecclesiastical causes, even if we are not to assume that the circle of achievements possible to the Renaissance had been completed. Notwithstanding their profligacy, the Italians continued to be, physically and mentally, one of the healthiest and best-born populations in Europe,[1] and have retained this position, with improved morals, down to our own time.

When we come to look more closely at the ethics of love at the time of the Renaissance, we are struck by a remarkable contrast. The novelists and comic poets give us to understand that love consists only in sensual enjoyment, and that to win this, all means, tragic or comic, are not only permitted, but are interesting in proportion to their audacity and unscrupulousness. But if we turn to the best of the lyric poets and writers of dialogues, we find in them a deep and spiritual passion of the noblest kind, whose last and highest expression is a revival of the ancient belief in an original unity of souls in the Divine Being. And both modes of feeling were then genuine, and could co-exist in the same individual. It is not exactly a matter of glory, but it is a fact, that in the cultivated man of modern times, this sentiment can be not merely unconsciously present in both its highest and lowest stages, but may thus

[1] It is true that when the Spanish rule was fully established the population fell off to a certain extent. Had this fact been due to the demoralisation of the people, it would have appeared much earlier.

manifest itself openly, and even artistically. The modern man, like the man of antiquity, is in this respect too a microcosm, which the mediæval man was not and could not be.

To begin with the morality of the novelists. They treat chiefly, as we have said, of married women, and consequently of adultery.

The opinion mentioned above (p. 395) of the equality of the two sexes is of great importance in relation to this subject. The highly developed and cultivated woman disposes of herself with a freedom unknown in Northern countries; and her unfaithfulness does not break up her life in the same terrible manner, so long as no outward consequence follow from it. The husband's claim on her fidelity has not that firm foundation which it acquires in the North through the poetry and passion of courtship and betrothal. After the briefest acquaintance with her future husband, the young wife quits the convent or the paternal roof to enter upon a world in which her character begins rapidly to develop. The rights of the husband are for this reason conditional, and even the man who regards them in the light of a 'jus quaesitum' thinks only of the outward conditions of the contract, not of the affections. The beautiful young wife of an old man sends back the presents and letters of a youthful lover, in the firm resolve to keep her honour (honesta). 'But she rejoices in the love of the youth for the sake of his great excellence; and she perceives that a noble woman may love a man of merit without loss to her honour.'[1] But the way is short from such a distinction to a complete surrender.

The latter seems indeed as good as justified, when there is unfaithfulness on the part of the husband. The woman, conscious of her own dignity, feels this not only as a pain, but also as a humiliation and deceit, and sets to work, often with the calmest consciousness of what she is about, to devise the vengeance which the husband deserves. Her tact must decide as to the measure of punishment which is suited to the particular case. The deepest wound, for example, may prepare the way for a reconciliation and a peaceful life in the future, if

[1] Giraldi, *Hecatommithi*, iii. nov. 2. In the same strain, *Cortigiano*, l. iv. fol. 180.

only it remain secret. The novelists, who themselves undergo such experiences or invent them according to the spirit of the age, are full of admiration when the vengeance is skilfully adapted to the particular case, in fact, when it is a work of art. As a matter of course, the husband never at bottom recognises this right of retaliation, and only submits to it from fear or prudence. Where these motives are absent, where his wife's unfaithfulness exposes him or may expose him to the derision of outsiders, the affair becomes tragical, and not seldom ends in murder or other vengeance of a violent sort. It is characteristic of the real motive from which these deeds arise, that not only the husbands, but the brothers[1] and the father of the woman feel themselves not only justified in taking vengeance, but bound to take it. Jealousy, therefore, has nothing to do with the matter, moral reprobation but little; the real reason is the wish to spoil the triumph of others. 'Nowadays,' says Bandello,[2] 'we see a woman poison her husband to gratify her lusts, thinking that a widow may do whatever she desires. Another, fearing the discovery of an illicit amour, has her husband murdered by her lover. And though fathers, brothers, and husbands arise to extirpate the shame with poison, with the sword, and by every other means, women still continue to follow their passions, careless of their honour and their lives.' Another time, in a milder strain, he exclaims: 'Would that we were not daily forced to hear that one man has murdered his wife because he suspected her of infidelity; that another has killed his daughter, on account of a secret marriage; that a third has caused his sister to be murdered, because she would not marry as he wished! It is great cruelty that we claim the right to do whatever we list, and will not suffer women to do the same. If they do anything which does not please us, there we are at once with cords

[1] A shocking instance of vengeance taken by a brother at Perugia in the year 1455, is to be found in the chronicle of Graziani (*Arch. Stor.* xvi. p. 629). The brother forces the gallant to tear out the sister's eyes, and then beats him from the place. It is true that the family was a branch of the Oddi, and the lover only a cordwainer.

[2] Bandello, parte i. nov. 9 and 26. Sometimes the wife's confessor is bribed by the husband and betrays the adultery.

and daggers and poison. What folly it is of men to suppose their own and their house's honour depends on the appetite of a woman!' The tragedy in which such affairs commonly ended was so well known that the novelist looked on the threatened gallant as a dead man, even while he went about alive and merry. The physician and lute-player Antonio Bologna[1] had made a secret marriage with the widowed Duchess of Amalfi, of the house of Aragon. Soon afterwards her brother succeeded in securing both her and her children, and murdered them in a castle. Antonio, ignorant of their fate, and still cherishing the hope of seeing them again, was staying at Milan, closely watched by hired assassins, and one day in the society of Ippolita Sforza sang to the lute the story of his misfortunes. A friend of the house, Delio, 'told the story up to this point to Scipione Attelano, and added that he would make it the subject of a novel, as he was sure that Antonio would be murdered.' The manner in which this took place, almost under the eyes of Delio and Atellano, is thrillingly described by Bandello (i. 26).

Nevertheless, the novelists habitually show a sympathy for all the ingenious, comic, and cunning features which may happen to attend adultery. They describe with delight how the lover manages to hide himself in the house, all the means and devices by which he communicates with his mistress, the boxes with cushions and sweetmeats in which he can be hidden and carried out of danger. The deceived husband is described sometimes as a fool to be laughed at, sometimes as a bloodthirsty avenger of his honour; there is no third situation except when the woman is painted as wicked and cruel, and the husband or lover is the innocent victim. It may be remarked, however, that narratives of the latter kind are not strictly speaking novels, but rather warning examples taken from real life.[2]

When in the course of the sixteenth century Italian life fell more and more under Spanish influence, the violence of the means to which jealousy had recourse perhaps increased. But this new phase must be distinguished from the punish-

[1] See above p. 394, and note 1.

[2] As instance, Bandello, part i. nov. 4.

ment of infidelity which existed before, and which was founded in the spirit of the Renaissance itself. As the influence of Spain declined, these excesses of jealousy declined also, till towards the close of the seventeenth century they had wholly disappeared, and their place was taken by that indifference which regarded the 'Cicisbeo' as an indispensable figure in every household, and took no offence at one or two supernumerary lovers ('Patiti').

But who can undertake to compare the vast sum of wickedness which all these facts imply, with what happened in other countries? Was the marriage-tie, for instance, really more sacred in France during the fifteenth century than in Italy? The 'fabliaux' and farces would lead us to doubt it, and rather incline us to think that unfaithfulness was equally common, though its tragic consequences were less frequent, because the individual was less developed and his claims were less consciously felt than in Italy. More evidence, however, in favour of the Germanic peoples lies in the fact of the social freedom enjoyed among them by girls and women, which impressed Italian travellers so pleasantly in England and in the Netherlands (p. 399, note 2). And yet we must not attach too much importance to this fact. Unfaithfulness was doubtless very frequent, and in certain cases led to a sanguinary vengeance. We have only to remember how the northern princes of that time dealt with their wives on the first suspicion of infidelity.

But it was not merely the sensual desire, not merely the vulgar appetite of the ordinary man, which trespassed upon forbidden ground among the Italians of that day, but also the passion of the best and noblest; and this, not only because the unmarried girl did not appear in society, but also because the man, in proportion to the completeness of his own nature, felt himself most strongly attracted by the woman whom marriage had developed. These are the men who struck the loftiest notes of lyrical poetry, and who have attempted in their treatises and dialogues to give us an idealised image of the devouring passion—'l' amor divino.' When they complain of the cruelty of the winged god, they are not only thinking of the coyness or hard-heartedness of the beloved one, but also of the unlawfulness of the passion itself. They seek to raise themselves above this painful consciousness by that spiritualisation of love which found a support in the Platonic doctrine of the soul, and of which Pietro Bembo is the most famous representative. His thoughts on this subject are set forth by himself in the third book of the 'Asolani,' and indirectly by Castiglione, who puts in his mouth the splendid speech with which the fourth book of the 'Cortigiano' concludes; neither of these writers was a stoic in his conduct, but at that time it meant something to be at once a famous and a good man, and this praise must be accorded to both of them; their contemporaries took what these men said to be a true expression of their feeling, and we have not the right to despise it as affectation. Those who take the trouble to study the speech in the 'Cortigiano' will see how poor an idea of it can be given by an extract. There were then living in Italy several distinguished women, who owed their celebrity chiefly to relations of this kind, such as Giulia Gonzaga, Veronica da Coreggio, and, above all, Vittoria Colonna. The land of profligates and scoffers respected these women and this sort of love—and what more can be said in their favour? We cannot tell how far vanity had to do with the matter, how far Vittoria was flattered to hear around her the sublimated utterances of hopeless love from the most famous men in Italy. If the thing was here and there a fashion, it was still no trifling praise for Vittoria that she, at least, never went out of fashion, and in her latest years produced the most profound impressions. It was long before other countries had anything similar to show.

In the imagination then, which governed this people more than any other, lies one general reason why the course of every passion was violent, and why the means used for the gratification of passion were often criminal. There is a violence which cannot control itself because it is born of weakness; but in Italy what we find is the corruption of powerful natures. Sometimes this corruption assumes a colossal shape, and crime seems to acquire almost a personal existence of its own.

The restraints of which men were conscious were but few. Each individual, even among the lowest of the people, felt himself inwardly emancipated from the control of the State and its police, whose title to respect was illegitimate, and itself founded on violence; and no man believed any longer in the justice of the law. When a murder was committed, the sympathies of the people, before the circumstances of the case were known, ranged themselves instinctively on the side of the murderer.[1] A proud, manly bearing before and at the execution excited such admiration that the narrator often forgets to tell us for what offence the criminal was put to death.[2] But when we add to this inward contempt of law and to the countless grudges and enmities which called for satisfaction, the impunity which crime enjoyed during times of political disturbance, we can only wonder that the state and society were not utterly dissolved. Crises of this kind occurred at Naples during the transition from the Aragonese to the French and Spanish rule, and at Milan, on the repeated expulsions and returns of the Sforzas; at such times those men who have never in their hearts recognised the bonds of law and society, come forward and give free play to their instincts of murder and rapine. Let us take, by way of example, a picture drawn from a humbler sphere.

When the Duchy of Milan was suffering from the disorders which followed the death of Giangaleazzo Sforza, about the year 1480 (pp. 40, 126), all safety came to an end in the provincial cities. This was the case in Parma,[3] where the Milanese Governor, terrified by threats of murder, and after vainly offering rewards for the discovery of the offenders,

[1] 'Piaccia al Signore Iddio che non si ritrovi,' say the women in Giraldi (iii. nov. 10), when they are told that the deed may cost the murderer his head.

[2] This is the case, for example, with Gioviano Pontano (*De Fortitudine*, l. ii.). His heroic Ascolans, who spend their last night in singing and dancing, the Abruzzian mother, who cheers up her son on his way to the gallows, &c., belong probably to brigand families, but he forgets to say so.

[3] *Diarium Parmense*, in Murat. xxii. col. 330 to 349 *passim*. The sonnet, col. 340.

consented to throw open the gaols and let loose the most abandoned criminals. Burglary, the demolition of houses, shameless offences against decency, public assassination and murders, especially of Jews, were events of everyday occurrence. At first the authors of these deeds prowled about singly, and masked; soon large gangs of armed men went to work every night without disguise. Threatening letters, satires, and scandalous jests circulated freely; and a sonnet in ridicule of the Government seems to have roused its indignation far more than the frightful condition of the city. In many churches the sacred vessels with the host were stolen, and this fact is characteristic of the temper which prompted these outrages. It is impossible to say what would happen now in any country of the world, if the government and police ceased to act, and yet hindered by their presence the establishment of a provisional authority; but what then occurred in Italy wears a character of its own, through the great share which personal hatred and revenge had in it. The impression, indeed, which Italy at this period makes on us is, that even in quiet times great crimes were commoner than in other countries. We may, it is true, be misled by the fact that we have far fuller details on such matters here than elsewhere, and that the same force of imagination, which gives a special character to crimes actually committed, causes much to be invented which never really happened. The amount of violence was perhaps as great elsewhere. It is hard to say for certain, whether in the year 1500 men were any safer, whether human life was after all better protected, in powerful, wealthy Germany, with its robber knights, extortionate beggars, and daring highwaymen. But one thing is certain, that premeditated crimes, committed professionally and for hire by third parties, occurred in Italy with great and appalling frequency.

So far as regards brigandage, Italy, especially in the more fortunate provinces, such as Tuscany, was certainly not more, and probably less, troubled than the countries of the North. But the figures which do meet us are characteristic of the country. It would be hard, for instance, to find elsewhere the case of a priest, gradually driven by passion from one excess to another, till at last he came to head a band of robbers. That age offers us this example among others.[1] On August 12, 1495, the priest Don Niccolò de' Pelegati of Figarolo was shut up in an iron cage outside the tower of San Giuliano at Ferrara. He had twice celebrated his first mass; the first time he had the same day committed murder, but afterwards received absolution at Rome; he then killed four people and married two wives, with whom he travelled about. He afterwards took part in many assassinations, violated women, carried others away by force, plundered far and wide, and infested the territory of Ferrara with a band of followers in uniform, extorting food and shelter by every sort of violence. When we think of what all this implies, the mass of guilt on the head of this one man is something tremendous. The clergy and monks had many privileges and little supervision, and among them were doubtless plenty of murderers and other malefactors—but hardly a second Pelegati. It is another matter, though by no means creditable, when ruined characters sheltered themselves in the cowl in order to escape the arm of the law, like the corsair whom Massuccio knew in a convent at Naples.[2] What the real truth was with regard to Pope John XXIII. in this respect, is not known with certainty.[3]

The age of the famous brigand chief did not begin till later, in the seventeenth century, when the political strife of Guelph and Ghibelline, of Frenchman and Spaniard, no longer agitated the country. The robber then took the place of the partisan.

In certain districts of Italy, where civilization had made little progress, the country people were disposed to murder any stranger who fell into their hands. This was especially the case in the more remote parts of the Kingdom of Naples, where

[1] *Diario Ferrarese*, in Murat. xxiv. col. 312. We are reminded of the gang led by a priest, which for some time before the year 1837 infested western Lombardy.

[2] Massuccio, nov. 29. As a matter of course, the man has luck in his amours.

[3] If he appeared as a corsair in the war between the two lines of Anjou for the possession of Naples, he may have done so as a political partisan, and this, according to the notions of the time, implied no dishonour. The Archbishop Paolo Fregoso of Genoa, in the second half of the fifteenth century probably allowed himself quite as much freedom, or more. Contemporaries and later writers, e.g. Aretino and Poggio, record much worse things of John. Gregorovius, vi. p. 600.

the barbarism dated probably from the days of the Roman 'latifundia,' and when the stranger and the enemy ('hospes' and 'hostis') were in all good faith held to be one and the same. These people were far from being irreligious. A herdsman once appeared in great trouble at the confessional, avowing that, while making cheese during Lent, a few drops of milk had found their way into his mouth. The confessor, skilled in the customs of the country, discovered in the course of his examination that the penitent and his friends were in the practice of robbing and murdering travellers, but that, through the force of habit, this usage gave rise to no twinges of conscience within them.[1] We have already mentioned (p. 352, note 3) to what a degree of barbarism the peasants elsewhere could sink in times of political confusion.

A worse symptom than brigandage of the morality of that time was the frequency of paid assassination. In that respect Naples was admitted to stand at the head of all the cities of Italy. 'Nothing,' says Pontano,[2] 'is cheaper here than human life.' But other districts could also show a terrible list of these crimes. It is hard, of course, to classify them according to the motives by which they were prompted, since political expediency, personal hatred, party hostility, fear, and revenge, all play into one another. It is no small honour to the Florentines, the most highly-developed people of Italy, that offences of this kind occurred more rarely among them than anywhere else,[3] perhaps because there was a justice at hand for legitimate grievances which was recognised by all, or because the higher culture of the individual gave him different views as to the right of men to interfere with the decrees of fate. In Florence, if anywhere, men were able to feel the incalculable con-

[1] Poggio, *Facetiae*, fol. 164. Anyone familiar with Naples at the present time, may have heard things as comical, though bearing on other sides of human life.

[2] *Jovian. Pontani Antonius:* 'Nec est quod Neapoli quam hominis vita minoris vendatur.' It is true he thinks it was not so under the House of Anjou, 'sicam ab iis (the Aragonese) accepimus.' The state of things about the year 1534 is described by Benvenuto Cellini, i. 70.

[3] Absolute proof of this cannot be given, but few murders are recorded, and the imagination of the Florentine writers at the best period is not filled with the suspicion of them.

sequences of a deed of blood, and to understand how insecure the author of a so-called profitable crime is of any true and lasting gain. After the fall of Florentine liberty, assassination, especially by hired agents, seems to have rapidly increased, and continued till the government of Cosimo I. had attained such strength that the police[1] was at last able to repress it.

Elsewhere in Italy paid crimes were probably more or less frequent in proportion to the number of powerful and solvent buyers. Impossible as it is to make any statistical estimate of their amount, yet if only a fraction of the deaths which public report attributed to violence were really murders, the crime must have been terribly frequent. The worst example of all was set by princes and governments, who without the faintest scruple reckoned murder as one of the instruments of their power. And this, without being in the same category with Cæsar Borgia. The Sforzas, the Aragonese monarchs, the Republic of Venice,[2] and later on, the agents of Charles V. resorted to it whenever it suited their purpose. The imagination of the people at last became so accustomed to facts of this kind, that the death of any powerful man was seldom or never attributed to natural causes.[3] There were certainly absurd notions current with regard to the effect of various poisons. There may be some truth in the story of that terrible white powder used by the Borgias, which did its work at the end of a definite period (p. 116), and it is possible that it was really a 'velenum atterminatum' which the Prince of Salerno handed to the Cardinal of Aragon, with the words: 'In a few days you will die, because your father, King Ferrante, wished to

[1] See on this point the report of Fedeli, in Alberi, *Relazioni Serie* ii. vol. i. pp. 353 sqq.

[2] M. Brosch (*Hist. Zeitschr.* bd. 27, p. 295 sqq.) has collected from the Venetian archives five proposals, approved by the council, to poison the Sultan (1471–1504), as well as evidence of the plan to murder Charles VIII. (1495) and of the order given to the Proveditor at Faenza to have Cæsar Borgia put to death (1504).

[3] Dr. Geiger adds several conjectural statements and references on this subject. It may be remarked that the suspicion of poisoning, which I believe to be now generally unfounded, is often expressed in certain parts of Italy with regard to any death not at once to be accounted for.—[The Translator.]

trample upon us all.'[1] But the poisoned letter which Caterina Riario sent to Pope Alexander VI.[2] would hardly have caused his death even if he had read it; and when Alfonso the Great was warned by his physicians not to read in the 'Livy' which Cosimo de' Medici had presented to him, he told them with justice not to talk like fools.[3] Nor can that poison with which the secretary of Piccinino wished to anoint the sedan-chair of Pius II.,[4] have affected any other organ than the imagination. The proportion which mineral and vegetable poisons bore to one another, cannot be ascertained precisely. The poison with which the painter Rosso Fiorentino destroyed himself (1541) was evidently a powerful acid,[5] which it would have been impossible to administer to another person without his knowledge. The secret use of weapons, especially of the dagger, in the service of powerful individuals, was habitual in Milan, Naples, and other cities. Indeed, among the crowds of armed retainers who were necessary for the personal safety of the great, and who lived in idleness, it was natural that outbreaks of this mania for blood should from time to time occur. Many

[1] Infessura, in Eccard, *Scriptor.* ii. col. 1956.

[2] *Chron. Venetum*, in Murat. xxiv. col. 131. In northern countries still more wonderful things were believed as to the art of poisoning in Italy. See *Juvénal des Ursins*, ad. ann. 1382 (ed. Buchon, p. 336), for the lancet of the poisoner, whom Charles of Durazzo took into his service; whoever looked at it steadily, died.

[3] Petr. Crinitus, *De Honesta Disciplina*, l. xviii. cap. 9.

[4] *Pii II. Comment.* l. xi. p. 562. Joh. Ant. Campanus, *Vita Pii II.* in Murat. iii. ii. col. 988.

[5] Vasari, ix. 82, *Vita di Rosso.* In the case of unhappy marriages it is hard to say whether there were more real or imaginary instances of poisoning. Comp. Bandello ii. nov. 5 and 54: ii. nov. 40 is more serious. In one and the same city of Western Lombardy, the name of which is not given, lived two poisoners. A husband, wishing to convince himself of the genuineness of his wife's despair, made her drink what she believed to be poison, but which was really coloured water, whereupon they were reconciled. In the family of Cardanus alone four cases of poisoning occurred (*De Propria Vita*, cap. 30, 50). Even at a banquet given at the coronation of a pope each cardinal brought his own cupbearer with him, and his own wine, 'probably because they knew from experience that otherwise they would run the risk of being poisoned.' And this usage was general at Rome, and practised 'sine injuria invitantis!' Blas Ortiz, *Itinerar. Hadriani VI.* ap. Baluz. Miscell. ed. Mansi, i. 380.

a deed of horror would never have been committed, had not the master known that he needed but to give a sign to one or other of his followers.

Among the means used for the secret destruction of others—so far, that is, as the intention goes—we find magic,[1] practised, however, sparingly. Where 'maleficii,' 'malie,' and so forth, are mentioned, they appear rather as a means of heaping up additional terror on the head of some hated enemy. At the courts of France and England in the fourteenth and fifteenth centuries, magic, practised with a view to the death of an opponent, plays a far more important part in Italy.

In this country, finally, where individuality of every sort attained its highest development, we find instances of that ideal and absolute wickedness which delights in crimes for their own sake, and not as means to an end, or at any rate as means to ends for which our psychology has no measure.

Among these appalling figures we may first notice certain of the 'Condottieri,'[2] such as Braccio di Montone, Tiberto Brandolino, and that Werner von Urslingen whose silver hauberk bore the inscription: 'The enemy of God, of pity and of mercy.' This class of men offers us some of the earliest instances of criminals deliberately repudiating every moral restraint. Yet we shall be more reserved in our judgment of them when we remember that the worst part of their guilt—in the estimate of those who record it—lay in their defiance of spiritual threats and penalties, and that to this fact is due that air of horror with which they are represented as surrounded. In the case of Braccio, the hatred of the Church went so far that he was infuriated at the sight of monks at their psalms,

[1] For the magic arts used against Leonello of Ferrara, see *Diario Ferrarese*, in Murat. xxiv. col. 194, ad a. 1445. When the sentence was read in the public square to the author of them, a certain Benato, a man in other respects of bad character, a noise was heard in the air and the earth shook, so that many people fled away or fell to the ground; this happened because Benato 'havea chiamato e scongiurato il diavolo.' What Guicciardini (l. i.) says of the wicked arts practised by Ludovico Moro against his nephew Giangaleazzo, rests on his own responsibility. On magic, see below, cap. 4.

[2] Ezzelino da Romano might be put first, were it not that he rather acted under the influence of ambitious motives and astrological delusions.

and had thrown them down from the top of a tower; [1] but at the same time 'he was loyal to his soldiers and a great general.' As a rule, the crimes of the 'Condottieri' were committed for the sake of some definite advantage, and must be attributed to a position in which men could not fail to be demoralised. Even their apparently gratuitous cruelty had commonly a purpose, if it were only to strike terror. The barbarities of the House of Aragon, as we have seen, were mainly due to fear and to the desire for vengeance. The thirst for blood on its own account, the devilish delight in destruction, is most clearly exemplified in the case of the Spaniard Cæsar Borgia, whose cruelties were certainly out of all proportion to the end which he had in view (p. 114 sqq.). In Sigismondo Malatesta, tyrant of Rimini (pp. 32, 228), the same disinterested love of evil may also be detected. It is not only the Court of Rome,[2] but the verdict of history, which convicts him of murder, rape, adultery, incest, sacrilege, perjury and treason, committed not once but often. The most shocking crime of all—the unnatural attempt on his own son Roberto, who frustrated it with his drawn dagger,[3]—may have been the result, not merely of moral corruption, but perhaps of some magical or astrological superstition. The same conjecture has been made to account for the rape of the Bishop of Fano [4] by Pierluigi Farnese of Parma, son of Paul III.

If we now attempt to sum up the principal features in the Italian character of that time, as we know it from a study of the life of the upper classes, we shall obtain something like the following result. The fundamental vice of this character was at the same time a condition of its greatness, namely, excessive individualism. The individual first inwardly casts off the

[1] *Giornali Napoletani*, in Murat. xxi. col. 1092 ad a. 1425. According to the narrative this deed seems to have been committed out of mere pleasure in cruelty. Br., it is true, believed neither in God nor in the saints, and despised and neglected all the precepts and ceremonies of the Church.

[2] *Pii II. Comment.* l. vii. p. 338.

[3] Jovian. Pontan. *De Immanitate*, cap. 17, where he relates how Malatesta got his own daughter with child—and so forth.

[4] Varchi, *Storie Fiorentine*, at the end. (When the work is published without expurgations, as in the Milanese edition.)

authority of a state which, as a fact, is in most cases tyrannical and illegitimate, and what he thinks and does is, rightly or wrongly, now called treason. The sight of victorious egoism in others drives him to defend his own right by his own arm. And, while thinking to restore his inward equilibrium, he falls, through the vengeance which he executes, into the hands of the powers of darkness. His love, too, turns mostly for satisfaction to another individuality equally developed, namely, to his neighbour's wife. In face of all objective facts, of laws and restraints of whatever kind, he retains the feeling of his own sovereignty, and in each single instance forms his decision independently, according as honour or interest, passion or calculation, revenge or renunciation, gain the upper hand in his own mind.

If therefore egoism in its wider as well as narrower sense is the root and fountain of all evil, the more highly developed Italian was for this reason more inclined to wickedness than the member of other nations of that time.

But this individual development did not come upon him through any fault of his own, but rather through an historical necessity. It did not come upon him alone, but also, and chiefly by means of Italian culture, upon the other nations of Europe, and has constituted since then the higher atmosphere which they breathe. In itself it is neither good nor bad, but necessary; within it has grown up a modern standard of good and evil—a sense of moral responsibility—which is essentially different from that which was familiar to the Middle Ages.

But the Italian of the Renaissance had to bear the first mighty surging of a new age. Through his gifts and his passions, he has become the most characteristic representative of all the heights and all the depths of his time. By the side of profound corruption appeared human personalities of the noblest harmony, and an artistic splendour which shed upon the life of man a lustre which neither antiquity nor mediævalism either could or would bestow upon it.

CHAPTER II.

RELIGION IN DAILY LIFE.

THE morality of a people stands in the closest connection with its consciousness of God, that is to say, with its firmer or weaker faith in the divine government of the world, whether this faith looks on the world as destined to happiness or to misery and speedy destruction.[1] The infidelity then prevalent in Italy is notorious, and whoever takes the trouble to look about for proofs, will find them by the hundred. Our present task, here as elsewhere, is to separate and discriminate; refraining from an absolute and final verdict.

The belief in God at earlier times had its source and chief support in Christianity and the outward symbol of Christianity, the Church. When the Church became corrupt, men ought to have drawn a distinction, and kept their religion in spite of all. But this is more easily said than done. It is not every people which is calm enough, or dull enough, to tolerate a lasting contradiction between a principle and its outward expression. But history does not record a heavier responsibility than that which rests upon the decaying Church. She set up as absolute truth and by the most violent means, a doctrine which she had distorted to serve her own aggrandisement. Safe in the sense of her inviolability, she abandoned herself to the most scandalous profligacy, and, in order to maintain herself in this state, she levelled mortal blows against the conscience and the intellect of nations, and drove multitudes of the noblest spirits, whom she had inwardly estranged, into the arms of unbelief and despair.

[1] On which point feeling differs according to the place and the people. The Renaissance prevailed in times and cities where the tendency was to enjoy life heartily. The general darkening of the spirits of thoughtful men did not begin to show itself till the time of the foreign supremacy in the sixteenth century.

Here we are met by the question: Why did not Italy, intellectually so great, react more energetically against the hierarchy; why did she not accomplish a reformation like that which occurred in Germany, and accomplish it at an earlier date?

A plausible answer has been given to this question. The Italian mind, we are told, never went further than the denial of the hierarchy, while the origin and the vigour of the German Reformation was due to its positive religious doctrines, most of all to the doctrines of justification by faith and of the inefficacy of good works.

It is certain that these doctrines only worked upon Italy through Germany, and this not till the power of Spain was sufficiently great to root them out without difficulty, partly by itself and partly by means of the Papacy, and its instruments.[1] Nevertheless, in the earlier religious movements of Italy, from the Mystics of the thirteenth century down to Savonarola, there was a large amount of positive religious doctrine which, like the very definite Christianity of the Huguenots, failed to achieve success only because circumstances were against it. Mighty events like the Reformation elude, as respects their details, their outbreak and their development, the deductions of the philosophers, however clearly the necessity of them as a whole may be demonstrated. The movements of the human spirit, its sudden flashes, its expansions and its pauses, must for ever remain a mystery to our eyes, since we can but know this or that of the forces at work in it, never all of them together.

The feeling of the upper and middle classes in Italy with regard to the Church at the time when the Renaissance culminated, was compounded of deep and contemptuous aver-

[1] What is termed the spirit of the Counter-Reformation was developed in Spain some time before the Reformation itself, chiefly through the sharp surveillance and partial reorganisation of the Church under Ferdinand and Isabella. The principal authority on this subject is Gomez, *Life of Cardinal Ximenes*, in Rob. Belus, *Rer. Hispan. Scriptores*, 3 vols. 1581.

sion, of acquiescence in the outward ecclesiastical customs which entered into daily life, and of a sense of dependence on sacraments and ceremonies. The great personal influence of religious preachers may be added as a fact characteristic of Italy.

That hostility to the hierarchy, which displays itself more especially from the time of Dante onwards in Italian literature and history, has been fully treated by several writers. We have already (p. 223) said something of the attitude of public opinion with regard to the Papacy. Those who wish for the strongest evidence which the best authorities offer us, can find it in the famous passages of Macchiavelli's 'Discorsi,' and in the unmutilated edition of Guicciardini. Outside the Roman Curia, some respect seems to have been felt for the best men among the bishops,[1] and for many of the parochial clergy. On the other hand, the mere holders of benefices, the canons, and the monks were held in almost universal suspicion, and were often the objects of the most scandalous aspersions, extending to the whole of their order.

It has been said that the monks were made the scapegoats for the whole clergy, for the reason that none but they could be ridiculed without danger.[2] But this is certainly incorrect. They are introduced so frequently in the novels and comedies, because these forms of literature need fixed and well-known types where the imagination of the reader can easily fill up an outline. Besides which, the novelists do not as a fact spare the secular clergy.[3] In the third place, we have abundant

[1] It is to be noticed that the novelists and satirists scarcely ever mention the bishops, although they might, under altered names, have attacked them like the rest. They do so, however, e.g. in Bandello ii. nov. 45; yet in ii. 40, he describes a virtuous bishop. Gioviano Pontano in the *Charon* introduces the ghost of a luxurious bishop with a 'duck's walk.'

[2] Foscolo, *Discorso sul testo del Decamerone*, 'Ma dei preti in dignità niuno poteva far motto senza pericolo; onde ogni frate fu l' irco delle iniquita d' Israele,' &c. Timotheus Maffeus dedicates a book against the monks to Pope Nicholas V.; Facius, *De Vir. Ill.* p. 24. There are specially strong passages against the monks and clergy in the work of Palingenius already mentioned iv. 289, v. 184 sqq. 586 sqq.

[3] Bandello prefaces ii. nov. i. with the statement that the vice of avarice was more discreditable to priests than to any other class of men, since they had no families to provide for. On this ground he justifies

proof in the rest of Italian literature that men could speak boldly enough about the Papacy and the Court of Rome. In works of imagination we cannot expect to find criticism of this kind. Fourthly, the monks, when attacked, were sometimes able to take a terrible vengeance.

It is nevertheless true that the monks were the most unpopular class of all, and that they were reckoned a living proof of the worthlessness of conventual life, of the whole ecclesiastical organisation, of the system of dogma, and of religion altogether, according as men pleased, rightly or wrongly, to draw their conclusions. We may also assume that Italy retained a clearer recollection of the origin of the two great mendicant orders than other countries, and had not forgotten that they were the chief agents in the reaction[1] against what is called the heresy of the thirteenth century, that is to say, against an early and vigorous movement of the modern Italian spirit. And that spiritual police which was permanently entrusted to the Dominicans certainly never excited any other feeling than secret hatred and contempt.

After reading the 'Decameron' and the novels of Franco Sacchetti, we might imagine that the vocabulary of abuse directed at the monks and nuns was exhausted. But towards the time of the Reformation this abuse became still fiercer. To say nothing of Aretino, who in the 'Ragionamenti' uses conventual life merely as a pretext for giving free play to his own poisonous nature, we may quote one author as typical of the rest—Massuccio, in the first ten of his fifty novels. They are written in a tone of the deepest indignation, and with this purpose to make the indignation general; and are dedicated to men in the highest position, such as King Ferrante and Prince Alfonso of Naples. The stories are many of them old, and some of them familiar to readers of Boccaccio. But others reflect, with a frightful realism, the actual state of things at

the disgraceful attack made on a parsonage by two soldiers or brigands at the orders of a young gentleman, on which occasion a sheep was stolen from the stingy and gouty old priest. A single story of this kind illustrates the ideas in which men lived and acted better than all the dissertations in the world.

[1] Giov. Villani, iii. 29, says this clearly a century later.

Naples. The way in which the priests befool and plunder the people by means of spurious miracles, added to their own scandalous lives, is enough to drive any thoughtful observer to despair. We read of the Minorite friars who travelled to collect alms: 'They cheat, steal, and fornicate, and when they are at the end of their resources, they set up as saints and work miracles, one displaying the cloak of St. Vincent, another the handwriting[1] of St. Bernadino, a third the bridle of Capistrano's donkey.' Others 'bring with them confederates who pretend to be blind or afflicted with some mortal disease, and after touching the hem of the monk's cowl, or the reliques which he carried, are healed before the eyes of the multitude. All then shout "Misericordia," the bells are rung, and the miracle is recorded in a solemn protocol.' Or else a monk in the pulpit is denounced as a liar by another who stands below among the audience; the accuser is immediately possessed by the devil, and then healed by the preacher. The whole thing was a pre-arranged comedy, in which, however, the principal with his assistant made so much money that he was able to buy a bishopric from a Cardinal, on which the two confederates lived comfortably to the end of their days. Massuccio makes no great distinction between Franciscans and Dominicans, finding the one worth as much as the other. 'And yet the foolish people lets itself be drawn into their hatreds and divisions, and quarrels about them in public places,[2] and calls itself "franceschino" or "domenichino."' The nuns are the exclusive property of the monks. Those of the former who have anything to do with the laity, are prosecuted and put in prison, while others are wedded in due form to the monks, with the accompaniments of mass, a marriage-contract, and a liberal indulgence in food and wine. 'I myself,' says the author, 'have been there not once, but several times, and seen it all with my own eyes. The nuns afterwards bring forth pretty little monks or else use means to hinder that result. And if any one charges me with falsehood, let him search the

[1] *L' Ordine.* Probably the tablet with the inscription I. H. S. is meant.

[2] He adds, 'and in the *seggi*,' i.e. the clubs into which the Neapolitan nobility was divided. The rivalry of the two orders is often ridiculed, e.g. Bandello, iii. nov. 14.

nunneries well, and he will find there as many little bones as in Bethlehem at Herod's time.'[1] These things, and the like, are among the secrets of monastic life. The monks are by no means too strict with one another in the confessional, and impose a Paternoster in cases where they would refuse all absolution to a layman as if he were a heretic. 'Therefore may the earth open and swallow up the wretches alive, with those who protect them!' In another place Massuccio, speaking of the fact that the influence of the monks depends chiefly on the dread of another world, utters the following remarkable wish: 'The best punishment for them would be for God to abolish Purgatory; they would then receive no more alms, and would be forced to go back to their spades.'

If men were free to write, in the time of Ferrante, and to him, in this strain, the reason is perhaps to be found in the fact that the king himself had been incensed by a false miracle which had been palmed off on him.[2] An attempt had been made to urge him to a persecution of the Jews, like that carried out in Spain and imitated by the Popes,[3] by producing a tablet with an inscription bearing the name of St. Cataldus, said to have been buried at Tarentum, and afterwards dug up again. When he discovered the fraud, the monks defied him. He had also managed to detect and expose a pretended instance of fasting, as his father Alfonso had done before him.[4] The Court, certainly, was no accomplice in maintaining these blind superstitions.[5]

[1] Nov. 6, ed. Settembrini, p. 83, where it is remarked that in the Index of 1564 a book is mentioned, *Matrimonio delli Preti e delle Monache.*

[2] For what follows, see Jovian. Pontan. *De Sermone*, l. ii. cap. 17, and Bandello, parte i. nov. 32. The fury of brother Franciscus, who attempted to work upon the king by a vision of St. Cataldus, was so great at his failure, and the talk on the subject so universal, 'ut Italia ferme omnis ipse in primis Romanus pontifex de tabulæ hujus fuerit inventione sollicitus atque anxius.'

[3] Alexander VI. and Julius II., whose cruel measures, however, did not appear to the Venetian ambassadors Giustiniani and Soderini as anything but a means of extorting money. Comp. M. Brosch, *Hist. Zeitscher.* bd. 37.

[4] Panormita, *De Dictis et Factis Alphonsi*, lib. ii. Æneas Sylvius in his commentary to it (*Opp.* ed. 1651, p. 79) tells of the detection of a pretended faster, who was said to have eaten nothing for four years.

[5] For which reason they could be openly denounced in the neighbour-

We have been quoting from an author who wrote in earnest, and who by no means stands alone in his judgment. All the Italian literature of that time is full of ridicule and invective aimed at the begging friars.[1] It can hardly have been doubted that the Renaissance would soon have destroyed these two Orders, had it not been for the German Reformation, and the Counter-Reformation which that provoked. Their saints and popular preachers could hardly have saved them. It would only have been necessary to come to an understanding at a favourable moment with a Pope like Leo X., who despised the Mendicant Orders. If the spirit of the age found them ridiculous or repulsive, they could no longer be anything but an embarrassment to the Church. And who can say what fate was in store for the Papacy itself, if the Reformation had not saved it?

The influence which the Father Inquisitor of a Dominican monastery was able habitually to exercise in the city where it was situated, was in the latter part of the fifteenth century just considerable enough to hamper and irritate cultivated people, but not strong enough to extort any lasting fear or obedience.[2] It was no longer possible to punish men for their thoughts, as it once was (p. 290 sqq.), and those whose tongues wagged most impudently against the clergy could easily keep clear of heretical doctrine. Except when some powerful party had an end to serve, as in the case of Savonarola, or when there was a question of the use of magical arts, as was often the case in the cities of North Italy, we seldom read at this time of men being burnt at the stake. The Inquisitors were in some instances satisfied with the most superficial retractation, in others it even happened that the victim was saved out of their hands on the way to the place of execution. In Bologna (1452) the priest Niccolò da Verona had been publicly

hood of the court. See Jovian. Pontan. *Antonius* and *Charon.* One of the stories is the same as in Massuccio, nov. ii.

[1] See for one example the eighth canto of the *Macaroneide.*

[2] The story in Vasari, v. p. 120, *Vita di Sandro Botticelli* shows that the Inquisition was sometimes treated jocularly. It is true that the 'Vicario' here mentioned may have been the archbishop's deputy instead of the inquisitor's.

degraded on a wooden scaffold in front of San Domenico as a wizard and profaner of the sacraments, and was about to be led away to the stake, when he was set free by a gang of armed men, sent by Achille Malvezzi, a noted friend of heretics and violater of nuns. The legate, Cardinal Bessarion, was only able to catch and hang one of the party; Malvezzi lived on in peace.[1]

It deserves to be noticed that the higher monastic orders—the Benedictines, with their many branches—were, notwithstanding their great wealth and easy lives, far less disliked than the mendicant friars. For ten novels which treat of 'frati,' hardly one can be found in which a 'monaco' is the subject and the victim. It was no small advantage to this order that it was founded earlier, and not as an instrument of police, and that it did not interfere with private life. It contained men of learning, wit, and piety, but the average has been described by a member of it, Firenzuola,[2] who says: 'These well-fed gentlemen with the capacious cowls do not pass their time in barefooted journeys and in sermons, but sit in elegant slippers with their hands crossed over their paunches, in charming cells wainscotted with cyprus-wood. And when they are obliged to quit the house, they ride comfortably, as if for their amusement, on mules and sleek, quiet horses. They do not overstrain their minds with the study of many books, for fear lest knowledge might put the pride of Lucifer in the place of monkish simplicity.'

Those who are familiar with the literature of the time, will see that we have only brought forward what is absolutely necessary for the understanding of the subject.[3] That the reputation attaching to the monks and the secular clergy must

[1] Bursellis, *Ann. Bonon.* ap. Murat. xxiii. col. 886, cf. 896. Malv. died 1468; his 'beneficium' passed to his nephew.

[2] See p. 88 sqq. He was abbot at Vallombrosa. The passage, of which we give a free translation, is to be found *Opere*, vol. ii. p. 209, in the tenth novel. See an inviting description of the comfortable life of the Carthusians in the *Commentario d'Italia*, fol. 32 sqq. quoted at p. 84.

[3] Pius II. was on principle in favour of the abolition of the celibacy of the clergy. One of his favourite sentences was, 'Sacerdotibus magna ratione sublatus nuptias majori restituendas videri.' Platina, *Vitae Pontiff.* p. 311.

have shattered the faith of multitudes in all that is sacred, is of course obvious.

And some of the judgments which we read are terrible; we will quote one of them in conclusion, which has been published only lately and is but little known. The historian Guicciardini, who was for many years in the service of the Medicean Popes says (1529) in his 'Aphorisms'[1]: 'No man is more disgusted than I am with the ambition, the avarice, and the profligacy of the priests, not only because each of these vices is hateful in itself, but because each and all of them are most unbecoming in those who declare themselves to be men in special relations with God, and also because they are vices so opposed to one another, that they can only co-exist in very singular natures. Nevertheless, my position at the Court of several Popes forced me to desire their greatness for the sake of my own interest. But, had it been for this, I should have loved Martin Luther as myself, not in order to free myself from the laws which Christianity, as generally understood and explained, lays upon us, but in order to see this swarm of scoundrels ('questa caterva di scellerati') put back into their proper place, so that they may be forced to live either without vices or without power.'[2]

The same Guicciardini is of opinion that we are in the dark as to all that is supernatural, that philosophers and theologians have nothing but nonsense to tell us about it, that miracles occur in every religion and prove the truth of none in particular, and that all of them may be explained as unknown phenomena of nature. The faith which moves mountains, then common among the followers of Savonarola, is mentioned by Guicciardini as a curious fact, but without any bitter remark.

Notwithstanding this hostile public opinion, the clergy and the monks had the great advantage that the people was used to them, and that their existence was interwoven with the everyday existence of all. This is the advantage which every old and powerful institution possesses. Everybody had some

[1] Ricordi, n. 28, in the *Opere inedite*, vol. i.

[2] Ricordi, n. i. 123, 125.

cowled or frocked relative, some prospect of assistance or future gain from the treasure of the Church; and in the centre of Italy stood the Court of Rome, where men sometimes became rich in a moment. Yet it must never be forgotten that all this did not hinder people from writing and speaking freely. The authors of the most scandalous satires were themselves mostly monks or beneficed priests. Poggio, who wrote the 'Facetiae,' was a clergyman; Francesco Berni, the satirist, held a canonry; Teofilo Folengo, the author of the 'Orlandino,' was a Benedictine, certainly by no means a faithful one; Matteo Bandello, who held up his own order to ridicule, was a Dominican, and nephew of a general of this order. Were they encouraged to write by the sense that they ran no risk? Or did they feel an inward need to clear themselves personally from the infamy which attached to their order? Or were they moved by that selfish pessimism which takes for its maxim, 'it will last our time'? Perhaps all of these motives were more or less at work. In the case of Folengo, the unmistakable influence of Lutheranism must be added.[1]

The sense of dependence on rites and sacraments, which we have already touched upon in speaking of the Papacy (p. 103), is not surprising among that part of the people which still believed in the Church. Among those who were more emancipated, it testifies to the strength of youthful impressions, and to the magical force of traditional symbols. The universal desire of dying men for priestly absolution shows that the last remnants of the dread of hell had not, even in the case of one like Vitellozzo, been altogether extinguished. It would hardly be possible to find a more instructive instance than this. The doctrine taught by the Church of the 'character indelibilis' of the priesthood, independently of the personality of the priest, had so far borne fruit that it was possible to loathe the individual and still desire his spiritual gifts. It is true, nevertheless, that there were defiant natures like Galeotto of Mirandola,[2] who died unabsolved in 1499, after living for sixteen years under the ban of the Church. All this time the city lay under

[1] See the *Orlandino*, cap. vi. str. 40 sqq.; cap. vii. str. 57; cap. viii. str. 3 sqq., especially 75.

[2] *Diaria Ferrarese*, in Murat. xxiv. col. 362.

an interdict on his account, so that no mass was celebrated and no Christian burial took place.

A splendid contrast to all this is offered by the power exercised over the nation by its great Preachers of Repentance. Other countries of Europe were from time to time moved by the words of saintly monks, but only superficially, in comparison with the periodical upheaval of the Italian conscience. The only man, in fact, who produced a similar effect in Germany during the fifteenth century,[1] was an Italian, born in the Abruzzi, named Giovanni Capistrano. Those natures which bear within them this religious vocation and this commanding earnestness, wore then in Northern countries an intuitive and mystical aspect. In the South they were practical and expansive, and shared in the national gift of language and oratorical skill. The North produced an 'Imitation of Christ,' which worked silently, at first only within the walls of the monastery, but worked for the ages; the South produced men who made on their fellows a mighty but passing impression.

This impression consisted chiefly in the awakening of the conscience. The sermons were moral exhortations, free from abstract notions and full of practical application, rendered more impressive by the saintly and ascetic character of the preacher, and by the miracles which, even against his will, the inflamed imagination of the people attributed to him.[2] The most powerful argument used was not the threat of Hell and Purgatory, but rather the living results of the 'maledizione,' the temporal ruin wrought on the individual by the curse which clings to wrong-doing. The grieving of Christ and the Saints has its consequences in this life. And only thus could men,

[1] He had with him a German and a Slavonian interpreter. St. Bernard had to use the same means when he preached in the Rhineland.

[2] Capistrano, for instance, contented himself with making the sign of the cross over the thousands of sick persons brought to him, and with blessing them in the name of the Trinity and of his master San Bernadino, after which some of them not unnaturally got well. The Brescian chronicle puts it in this way, 'He worked fine miracles, yet not so many as were told of him' (Murat. xxi.).

sunk in passion and guilt, be brought to repentance and amendment—which was the chief object of these sermons.

Among these preachers were Bernadino da Siena, and his two pupils, Alberto da Sarteano and Jacopo della Marca, Giovanni Capistrano, Roberto da Lecce (p. 413), and finally, Girolamo Savonarola. No prejudice of the day was stronger than that against the mendicant friar, and this they overcame. They were criticised and ridiculed by a scornful humanism; [1] but when they raised their voices, no one gave heed to the humanists. The thing was no novelty, and the scoffing Florentines had already in the fourteenth century learned to caricature it whenever it appeared in the pulpit.[2] But no sooner did Savonarola come forward than he carried the people so triumphantly with him, that soon all their beloved art and culture melted away in the furnace which he lighted. Even the grossest profanation done to the cause by hypocritical monks, who got up an effect in the audience by means of confederates (p. 460), could not bring the thing itself into discredit. Men kept on laughing at the ordinary monkish sermons, with their spurious miracles and manufactured reliques; [3] but did not cease to honour the great and genuine prophets. These are a true Italian specialty of the fifteenth century.

The Order—generally that of St. Francis, and more particularly the so-called Observantines—sent them out according as they were wanted. This was commonly the case when there was some important public or private feud in a city, or some alarming outbreak of violence, immorality, or disease. When

[1] So e.g. Poggio, *De Avaritia*, in the *Opera*, fol. 2. He says they had an easy matter of it, since they said the same thing in every city, and sent the people away more stupid than they came. Poggio elsewhere (*Epist.* ed. Tonelli i. 281) speaks of Albert of Sarteano as 'doctus' and 'perhumanus.' Filelfo defended Bernadino of Siena and a certain Nicolaus, probably out of opposition to Poggio (*Sat.* ii. 3, vi. 5) rather than from liking for the preachers. Filelfo was a correspondent of A. of Sarteano. He also praises Roberto da Lecce in some respects, but blames him for not using suitable gestures and expressions, for looking miserable when he ought to look cheerful, and for weeping too much and thus offending the ears and tastes of his audience. Fil. *Epist.* Venet. 1502, fol. 96 *b*.

[2] Franco Sacchetti, nov. 72. Preachers who fail are a constant subject of ridicule in all the novels.

[3] Compare the well-known story in the *Decamerone* vi. nov. 10.

once the reputation of a preacher was made, the cities were all anxious to hear him even without any special occasion. He went wherever his superiors sent him. A special form of this work was the preaching of a Crusade against the Turks;[1] but here we have to speak more particularly of the exhortations to repentance.

The order of these, when they were treated methodically, seems to have followed the customary list of the deadly sins. The more pressing, however, the occasion is, the more directly does the preacher make for his main point. He begins perhaps in one of the great churches of the Order, or in the cathedral. Soon the largest piazza is too small for the crowds which throng from every side to hear him, and he himself can hardly move without risking his life.[2] The sermon is commonly followed by a great procession; but the first magistrates of the city, who take him in their midst, can hardly save him from the multitude of women who throng to kiss his hands and feet, and cut off fragments from his cowl.[3]

The most immediate consequences which follow from the preacher's denunciations of usury, luxury, and scandalous fashions, are the opening of the gaols—which meant no more than the discharge of the poorer creditors—and the burning of various instruments of luxury and amusement, whether innocent or not. Among these are dice, cards, games of all kinds, written incantations,[4] masks, musical instruments, song-books,

[1] In which case the sermons took a special colour. See Malipiero, *Ann. Venet. Archiv. Stor.* vii. i. p. 18. *Chron. Venet.* in Murat. xxiv. col. 114. *Storia Bresciana*, in Murat. xxi. col. 898. Absolution was freely promised to those who took part in, or contributed money for the crusade.

[2] *Storia Bresciana*, in Murat. xxiii. col. 865 sqq. On the first day 10,000 persons were present, 2,000 of them strangers.

[3] Allegretto, *Diari Sanesi*, in Murat. xxiii. col. 819 sqq. (July 13 to 18, 1486); the preacher was Pietro dell' Osservanza di S. Francesco.

[4] Infessura (in Eccard, *Scriptores* il. col. 1874) says: 'Canti, brevi, sorti.' The first may refer to song-books, which actually were burnt by Savonarola. But Graziani (*Cron. di Perugia*, *Arch. Stor.* xvi. i., p. 314) says on a similar occasion, 'brieve incanti,' when we must without doubt read 'brevi e incanti,' and perhaps the same emendation is desirable in Infessura, whose 'sorti' point to some instrument of superstition, perhaps a pack of cards for fortune-telling. Similarly after the introduction of printing, collections were made of all the attainable copies of Martial, which then were burnt. Bandello, iii. 10.

false hair, and so forth. All these would then be gracefully arranged on a scaffold ('talamo'), a figure of the devil fastened to the top, and then the whole set on fire (comp. p. 372).

Then came the turn of the more hardened consciences. Men who had long never been near the confessional, now acknowledged their sins. Ill-gotten gains were restored, and insults which might have borne fruit in blood retracted. Orators like Bernadino of Siena[1] entered diligently into all the details of the daily life of men, and the moral laws which are involved in it. Few theologians nowadays would feel tempted to give a morning sermon 'on contracts, restitutions, the public debt ("monte"), and the portioning of daughters,' like that which he once delivered in the Cathedral at Florence. Imprudent speakers easily fell into the mistake of attacking particular classes, professions, or offices, with such energy that the enraged hearers proceeded to violence against those whom the preacher had denounced.[2] A sermon which Bernadino once preached in Rome (1424) had another consequence besides a bonfire of vanities on the Capitol: 'after this,'[3] we read, 'the witch Finicella was burnt, because by her diabolical arts she had killed many children and bewitched many other persons; and all Rome went to see the sight.'

But the most important aim of the preacher was, as has been already said, to reconcile enemies and persuade them to give up thoughts of vengeance. Probably this end was seldom attained till towards the close of a course of sermons, when the

[1] See his remarkable biography in *Vespasiano Fiorent.* p. 244 sqq., and that by Æneas Sylvius, *De Viris Illustr.* p. 24. In the latter we read: 'Is quoque in tabella pictum nomen Jesus deferebat, hominibusque adorandum ostendebat multumque suadebat ante ostia domorum hoc nomen depingi.'

[2] Allegretto, l. c. col. 823. A preacher excited the people against the judges (if instead of 'giudici' we are not to read 'giudei),' upon which they narrowly escaped being burnt in their houses. The opposite party threatened the life of the preacher in return.

[3] Infessura, l. c. In the date of the witch's death there seems to be a clerical error. How the same saint caused an ill-famed wood near Arezzo to be cut down, is told in Vasari, iii. 148, *Vita di Parri Spinelli.* Often, no doubt, the penitential zeal of the hearers went no further than such outward sacrifices.

tide of penitence flooded the city, and when the air resounded[1] with the cry of the whole people: 'Misericordia!' Then followed those solemn embracings and treaties of peace, which even previous bloodshed on both sides could not hinder. Banished men were recalled to the city to take part in these sacred transactions. It appears that these 'Paci' were on the whole faithfully observed, even after the mood which prompted them was over; and then the memory of the monk was blessed from generation to generation. But there were sometimes terrible crises like those in the families Della Valle and Croce in Rome (1482), where even the great Roberto da Lecce raised his voice in vain.[2] Shortly before Holy Week he had preached to immense crowds in the square before the Minerva. But on the night before Maunday Thursday a terrible combat took place in front of the Palazzo della Valle, near the Ghetto. In the morning Pope Sixtus gave orders for its destruction, and then performed the customary ceremonies of the day. On Good Friday Roberto preached again with a crucifix in his hand; but he and his hearers could do nothing but weep.

Violent natures, which had fallen into contradiction with themselves, often resolved to enter a convent, under the impression made by these men. Among such were not only brigands and criminals of every sort, but soldiers without employment.[3] This resolve was stimulated by their admiration of the holy man, and by the desire to copy at least his outward position.

[1] 'Pareva che l'aria si fendesse,' we read somewhere.

[2] Jac. Volaterran. in Murat. xxiii. col. 166 sqq. It is not expressly said that he interfered with this feud, but it can hardly be doubted that he did so. Once (1445), when Jacopo della Marca had but just quitted Perugia after an extraordinary success, a frightful *vendetta* broke out in the family of the Ranieri. Comp. Graziani, l. c. p. 565 sqq. We may here remark that Perugia was visited by these preachers remarkably often, comp. pp. 597, 626, 631, 637, 647.

[3] Capistrano admitted fifty soldiers after one sermon, *Stor. Bresciana* l. c. Graziani, l. c. p. 565 sqq. Æn. Sylvius (*De Viris Illustr.* p. 25), when a young man, was once so affected by a sermon of San Bernadino as to be on the point of joining his Order. We read in Graziani of a convert quitting the order; he married, 'e fu magiore ribaldo, che non era prima.'

The concluding sermon is a general benediction, summed up in the words: 'la pace sia con voi!' Throngs of hearers accompany the preacher to the next city, and there listen for a second time to the whole course of sermons.

The enormous influence exercised by these preachers made it important, both for the clergy and for the government, at least not to have them as opponents; one means to this end was to permit only monks[1] or priests who had received at all events the lesser consecration, to enter the pulpit, so that the Order or Corporation to which they belonged was, to some extent, responsible for them. But it was not easy to make the rule absolute, since the Church and pulpit had long been used as a means of publicity in many ways, judicial, educational, and others, and since even sermons were sometimes delivered by humanists and other laymen (p. 234 sqq.). There existed, too, in Italy a dubious class of persons,[2] who were neither monks nor priests, and who yet had renounced the world—that is to say, the numerous class of hermits who appeared from time to time in the pulpit on their own authority, and often carried the people with them. A case of this kind occurred at Milan in 1516, after the second French conquest, certainly at a time when public order was much disturbed. A Tuscan hermit Hieronymus of Siena, possibly an adherent

[1] That there was no want of disputes between the famous Observantine preachers and their Dominican rivals is shown by the quarrel about the blood of Christ which was said to have fallen from the cross to the earth (1462). See Voigt. *Enea Silvio* iii. 591 sqq. Fra Jacopo della Marca, who would not yield to the Dominican Inquisitor, is criticised by Pius II. in his detailed account (*Comment.* l. xi. p. 511), with delicate irony: 'Pauperiem pati, et famam et sitim et corporis cruciatum et mortem pro Christi nomine nonnulli possunt; jacturam nominis vel minimam ferre recusant tanquam sua deficiente fama Dei quoque gloria pereat.'

[2] Their reputation oscillated even then between two extremes. They must be distinguished from the hermit-monks. The line was not always clearly drawn in this respect. The Spoletans, who travelled about working miracles, took St. Anthony and St. Paul as their patrons, the latter on account of the snakes which they carried with them. We read of the money they got from the peasantry even in the thirteenth century by a sort of clerical conjuring. Their horses were trained to kneel down at the name of St. Anthony. They pretended to collect for hospitals (Massuccio, nov. 18; Bandello iii., nov. 17). Firenzuola in his *Asino d'Oro* makes them play the part of the begging priests in Apulejus.

of Savonarola, maintained his place for months together in the pulpit of the Cathedral, denounced the hierarchy with great violence, caused a new chandelier and a new altar to be set up in the church, worked miracles, and only abandoned the field after a long and desperate struggle.[1] During the decades in which the fate of Italy was decided, the spirit of prophecy was unusually active, and nowhere where it displayed itself was it confined to any one particular class. We know with what a tone of true prophetic defiance the hermits came forward before the sack of Rome (p. 122). In default of any eloquence of their own, these men made use of messengers with symbols of one kind or another, like the ascetic near Siena (1429), who sent a 'little hermit,' that is a pupil, into the terrified city with a skull upon a pole, to which was attached a paper with a threatening text from the Bible.[2]

Nor did the monks themselves scruple to attack princes, governments, the clergy, or even their own order. A direct exhortation to overthrow a despotic house, like that uttered by Jacopo Bussolaro at Pavia in the fourteenth century,[3] hardly occurs again in the following period; but there is no want of courageous reproofs, addressed even to the Pope in his own chapel (p. 239, note 1), and of naïve political advice given in the presence of rulers who by no means held themselves in need of it.[4] In the Piazza del Castello at Milan, a blind preacher from the Incoronata—consequently an Augustinian—ventured in 1494 to exhort Ludovico Moro from the pulpit:

[1] Prato, *Arch. Stor.* iii. p. 357. Burigozzo, *ibid.* p. 431 sqq.

[2] Allegretto, in Murat. xxiii. col. 856 sqq. The quotation was: 'Ecce venio cito et velociter. Estote parati.'

[3] Matteo Villani, viii. cap. 2 sqq. He first preached against tyranny in general, and then, when the ruling house of the Beccaria tried to have him murdered, he began to preach a change of government and constitution, and forced the Beccaria to fly from Pavia (1357). See Petrarch, *Epp. Fam.* xix. 18, and A. Hortis, *Scritti Inediti di F. P.* 174–181.

[4] Sometimes at critical moments the ruling house itself used the services of monks to exhort the people to loyalty. For an instance of this kind at Ferrara, see Sanudo (Murat. xxii. col. 1218). A preacher from Bologna reminded the people of the benefits they had received from the House of Este, and of the fate that awaited them at the hands of the victorious Venetians.

'My lord, beware of showing the French the way, else you will repent it.'[1] There were further prophetic monks, who, without exactly preaching political sermons, drew such appalling pictures of the future that the hearers almost lost their senses. After the election of Leo X. in the year 1513, a whole association of these men, twelve Franciscan monks in all, journeyed through the various districts of Italy, of which one or other was assigned to each preacher. The one who appeared in Florence,[2] Fra Francesco di Montepulciano, struck terror into the whole people. The alarm was not diminished by the exaggerated reports of his prophecies which reached those who were too far off to hear him. After one of his sermons he suddenly died 'of pain in the chest.' The people thronged in such numbers to kiss the feet of the corpse that it had to be secretly buried in the night. But the newly awakened spirit of prophecy, which seized upon even women and peasants, could not be controlled without great difficulty. 'In order to restore to the people their cheerful humour, the Medici—Giuliano, Leo's brother, and Lorenzo—gave on St. John's Day, 1514, those splendid festivals, tournaments, processions, and hunting-parties, which were attended by many distinguished persons from Rome, and among them, though disguised, by no less than six cardinals.'

But the greatest of the prophets and apostles had been already burnt in Florence in the year 1498—Fra Giorolamo Savonarola of Ferrara. We must content ourselves with saying a few words respecting him.[3]

The instrument by means of which he transformed and ruled the city of Florence (1494–8) was his eloquence. Of this the

[1] Prato, *Arch. Stor.* iii. p. 251. Other fanatical anti-French preachers, who appeared after the expulsion of the French, are mentioned by Burigozzo, *ibid.* pp. 443, 449, 485; ad a. 1523, 1526, 1529.

[2] Jac. Pitti, *Storia Fior.* l. ii. p. 112.

[3] Perrens, *Jérôme Savonarole*, two vols. Perhaps the most systematic and sober of all the many works on the subject. P. Villari, *La Storia di Girol. Savonarola* (two vols. 8vo. Firenze, Lemonnier). The view taken by the latter writer differs considerably from that maintained in the text. Comp. also Ranke in *Historisch-biographische Studien*, Lpzg. 1878, pp. 181–358. On Genaz. see Vill. i. 57 sqq. ii. 343 sqq. Reumont, *Lorenzo*, ii. 522–526, 533 sqq.

meagre reports that are left to us, which were taken down mostly on the spot, give us evidently a very imperfect notion. It was not that he possessed any striking outward advantages, for voice, accent, and rhetorical skill constituted precisely his weakest side; and those who required the preacher to be a stylist, went to his rival Fra Mariano da Genazzano. The eloquence of Savonarola was the expression of a lofty and commanding personality, the like of which was not seen again till the time of Luther. He himself held his own influence to be the result of a divine illumination, and could therefore, without presumption, assign a very high place to the office of the preacher, who, in the great hierarchy of spirits, occupies the next place below the angels.

This man, whose nature seemed made of fire, worked another and greater miracle than any of his oratorical triumphs. His own Dominican monastery of San Marco, and then all the Dominican monasteries of Tuscany, became like-minded with himself, and undertook voluntarily the work of inward reform. When we reflect what the monasteries then were, and what measureless difficulty attends the least change where monks are concerned, we are doubly astonished at so complete a revolution. While the reform was still in progress large numbers of Savonarola's followers entered the Order, and thereby greatly facilitated his plans. Sons of the first houses in Florence entered San Marco as novices.

This reform of the Order in a particular province was the first step to a national Church, in which, had the reformer himself lived longer, it must infallibly have ended. Savonarola, indeed, desired the regeneration of the whole Church, and near the end of his career sent pressing exhortations to the great powers urging them to call together a Council. But in Tuscany his Order and party were the only organs of his spirit—the salt of the earth—while the neighbouring provinces remained in their old condition. Fancy and asceticism tended more and more to produce in him a state of mind to which Florence appeared as the scene of the kingdom of God upon earth.

The prophecies, whose partial fulfilment conferred on Savonarola a supernatural credit, were the means by which the ever-active Italian imagination seized control of the soundest and most cautious natures. At first the Franciscans of the Osservanza, trusting in the reputation which had been bequeathed to them by San Bernadino of Siena, fancied that they could compete with the great Dominican. They put one of their own men into the Cathedral pulpit, and outbid the Jeremiads of Savonarola by still more terrible warnings, till Pietro de' Medici, who then still ruled over Florence, forced them both to be silent. Soon after, when Charles VIII. came into Italy and the Medici were expelled, as Savonarola had clearly foretold, he alone was believed in.

It must be frankly confessed that he never judged his own premonitions and visions critically, as he did those of others. In the funeral oration on Pico della Mirandola, he deals somewhat harshly with his dead friend. Since Pico, notwithstanding an inner voice which came from God, would not enter the Order, he had himself prayed to God to chasten him for his disobedience. He certainly had not desired his death, and alms and prayers had obtained the favour that Pico's soul was safe in Purgatory. With regard to a comforting vision which Pico had upon his sick-bed, in which the Virgin appeared and promised him that he should not die, Savonarola confessed that he had long regarded it as a deceit of the Devil, till it was revealed to him that the Madonna meant the second and eternal death.[1] If these things and the like are proofs of presumption, it must be admitted that this great soul at all events paid a bitter penalty for his fault. In his last days Savonarola seems to have recognised the vanity of his visions and prophecies. And yet enough inward peace was left him to enable him to meet death like a Christian. His partisans held to his doctrine and predictions for thirty years longer.

He only undertook the reorganisation of the state for the reason that otherwise his enemies would have got the government into their own hands. It is unfair to judge him by the semi-democratic constitution (p. 83, note 1) of the beginning of the year 1495. Nor is it either better or worse than other Florentine constitutions.[2]

[1] Sermons on Haggai; close of sermon 6.

[2] Savonarola was perhaps the only man who could have made the sub-

He was at bottom the most unsuitable man who could be found for such a work. His ideal was a theocracy, in which all men were to bow in blessed humility before the Unseen, and all conflicts of passion were not even to be able to arise. His whole mind is written in that inscription on the Palazzo della Signoria, the substance of which was his maxim [1] as early as 1495, and which was solemnly renewed by his partisans in 1527: 'Jesus Christus Rex populi Florentini S. P. Q. decreto creatus.' He stood in no more relation to mundane affairs and their actual conditions than any other inhabitant of a monastery. Man, according to him, has only to attend to those things which make directly for his salvation.

This temper comes out clearly in his opinions on ancient literature: 'The only good thing which we owe to Plato and Aristotle, is that they brought forward many arguments which we can use against the heretics. Yet they and other philosophers are now in Hell. An old woman knows more about the Faith than Plato. It would be good for religion if many books that seem useful were destroyed. When there were not so many books and not so many arguments ("ragioni naturali") and disputes, religion grew more quickly than it has done since.' He wished to limit the classical instruction of the schools to Homer, Virgil, and Cicero, and to supply the rest from Jerome and Augustine. Not only Ovid and Catullus, but Terence and Tibullus, were to be banished. This may be no more than the expression of a nervous morality, but elsewhere in a special work he admits that science as a whole is harmful. He holds that only a few people should have to do with it, in order that the tradition of human knowledge may not perish, and particularly that there may be no want of intellectual athletes to confute the sophisms of the heretics. For all others, grammar, morals, and religious teaching ('litterae sacrae') suffice. Culture and education would thus return wholly into the charge of the monks, and as, in his opinion, the 'most learned and the most pious' are to rule over the states and empires, these rulers

ject cities free and yet kept Tuscany together. But he never seems to have thought of doing so. Pisa he hated like a genuine Florentine.

[1] A remarkable contrast to the Sienese who in 1483 solemnly dedicated their distracted city to the Madonna. Allegretto, in Murat. xxiii. col. 815.

would also be monks. Whether he really foresaw this conclusion, we need not inquire.

A more childish method of reasoning cannot be imagined. The simple reflection that the new-born antiquity and the boundless enlargement of human thought and knowledge which was due to it, might give splendid confirmation to a religion able to adapt itself thereto, seems never even to have occurred to the good man. He wanted to forbid what he could not deal with by any other means. In fact, he was anything but liberal, and was ready, for example, to send the astrologers to the same stake at which he afterwards himself died.[1]

How mighty must have been the soul which dwelt side by side with this narrow intellect! And what a flame must have glowed within him before he could constrain the Florentines, possessed as they were by the passion for culture, to surrender themselves to a man who could thus reason!

How much of their heart and their worldliness they were ready to sacrifice for his sake is shown by those famous bonfires by the side of which all the 'talami' of Bernadino da Siena and others were certainly of small account.

All this could not, however, be effected without the agency of a tyrannical police. He did not shrink from the most vexatious interferences with the much-prized freedom of Italian private life, using the espionage of servants on their masters as a means of carrying out his moral reforms. That transformation of public and private life which the iron Calvin was but just able to effect at Geneva with the aid of a permanent state of siege necessarily proved impossible at Florence, and the attempt only served to drive the enemies of Savonarola to a more implacable hostility. Among his most unpopular measures may be mentioned those organised parties of boys, who forced their way into the houses and laid violent hands on any objects which seemed suitable for the bonfire. As it happened that they were sometimes sent away with a beating, they were afterwards attended, in order to keep up the figment of a pious 'rising generation,' by a body-guard of grown-up persons.

[1] He says of the 'impii astrologi': 'non è dar disputar (con loro) altrimenti che col fuoco.'

On the last day of the Carnival in the year 1497, and on the same day the year after, the great 'Auto da Fé' took place on the Piazza della Signoria. In the centre of it rose a great pyramidal flight of stairs like the 'rogus' on which the Roman Emperors were commonly burned. On the lowest tier were arranged false beards, masks, and carnival disguises; above came volumes of the Latin and Italian poets, among others Boccaccio, the 'Morgante' of Pulci, and Petrarch, partly in the form of valuable printed parchments and illuminated manuscripts; then women's ornaments and toilette articles, scents, mirrors, veils, and false hair; higher up, lutes, harps, chess-boards, playing-cards; and finally, on the two uppermost tiers, paintings only, especially of female beauties, partly fancy-pictures, bearing the classical names of Lucretia, Cleopatra, or Faustina, partly portraits of the beautiful Bencina, Lena Morella, Bina, and Maria de' Lenzi; all the pictures of Bartolommeo della Porta, who brought them of his own accord; and, as it seems, some female heads—masterpieces of ancient sculptors. On the first occasion a Venetian merchant who happened to be present offered the Signoria 22,000 gold florins for the objects on the pyramid; but the only answer he received was that his portrait, too, was taken, and burned along with the rest. When the pile was lighted, the Signoria appeared on the balcony, and the air echoed with song, the sound of trumpets, and the pealing of bells. The people then adjourned to the Piazza di San Marco, where they danced round in three concentric circles. The innermost was composed of monks of the monastery, alternating with boys, dressed as angels; then came young laymen and ecclesiastics; and on the outside old men, citizens, and priests, the latter crowned with wreaths of olive.[1]

All the ridicule of his victorious enemies, who in truth had no lack of justification or of talent for ridicule, was unable to discredit the memory of Savonarola. The more tragic the fortunes of Italy became, the brighter grew the halo which in the recollection of the survivors surrounded the figure of the great monk and prophet. Though his predictions may not

[1] See Villari on this point.

have been confirmed in detail, the great and general calamity which he foretold was fulfilled with appalling truth.

Great, however, as the influence of all these preachers may have been, and brilliantly as Savonarola justified the claim of the monks to this office,[1] nevertheless the order as a whole could not escape the contempt and condemnation of the people. Italy showed that she could give her enthusiasm only to individuals.

If, apart from all that concerns the priests and the monks, we attempt to measure the strength of the old faith, it will be found great or small according to the light in which it is considered. We have spoken already of the need felt for the Sacraments as something indispensable (pp. 103, 464). Let us now glance for a moment at the position of faith and worship in daily life. Both were determined partly by the habits of the people and partly by the policy and example of the rulers.

All that has to do with penitence and the attainment of salvation by means of good works was in much the same stage of development or corruption as in the North of Europe, both among the peasantry and among the poorer inhabitants of the cities. The instructed classes were here and there influenced by the same motives. Those sides of popular Catholicism which had their origin in the old pagan ways of addressing, rewarding, and reconciling the gods have fixed themselves ineradicably in the consciousness of the people. The eighth eclogue of Battista Mantovano,[2] which has been already quoted elsewhere, contains the prayer of a peasant to the Madonna, in which she is called upon as the special patroness of all rustic and agricultural interests. And what conceptions they were which the people formed of their protectress in heaven! What was in the mind of the Florentine woman[3] who gave 'ex voto'

[1] See the passage in the fourteenth sermon on Ezechiel, in Perrens, o. c. vol. i. 30 note.

[2] With the title, *De Rusticorum Religione.* See above p. 352.

[3] Franco Sacchetti, nov. 109, where there is more of the same kind.

a keg of wax to the Annunziata, because her lover, a monk, had gradually emptied a barrel of wine without her absent husband finding it out! Then, too, as still in our own days, different departments of human life were presided over by their respective patrons. The attempt has often been made to explain a number of the commonest rites of the Catholic Church as remnants of pagan ceremonies, and no one doubts that many local and popular usages, which are associated with religious festivals, are forgotten fragments of the old pre-christian faiths of Europe. In Italy, on the contrary, we find instances in which the affiliation of the new faith on the old seems consciously recognised. So, for example, the custom of setting out food for the dead four days before the feast of the Chair of St. Peter, that is to say, on February 18, the date of the ancient Feralia.[1] Many other practices of this kind may then have prevailed and have since then been extirpated. Perhaps the paradox is only apparent if we say that the popular faith in Italy had a solid foundation just in proportion as it was pagan.

The extent to which this form of belief prevailed in the upper classes can to a certain point be shown in detail. It had, as we have said in speaking of the influence of the clergy, the power of custom and early impressions on its side. The love for ecclesiastical pomp and display helped to confirm it, and now and then there came one of those epidemics of revivalism,

[1] Bapt. Mantuan. *De Sacris Diebus*, l. ii. exclaims :—

> Ista superstitio, ducens a Manibus ortum
> Tartareis, sancta de religione facessat
> Christigenûm! vivis epulas date, sacra sepultis.

A century earlier, when the army of John XXII. entered the Marches to attack the Ghibellines, the pretext was avowedly 'eresia' and 'idolatria.' Recanti, which surrendered voluntarily, was nevertheless burnt, 'because idols had been worshipped there,' in reality, as a revenge for those whom the citizens had killed. Giov. Villani, ix. 139, 141. Under Pius II. we read of an obstinate sun-worshipper, born at Urbino. Æn. Sylv. *Opera*, p. 289. *Hist. Rer. ubique Gestar.* c. 12. More wonderful still was what happened in the Forum in Rome under Leo X. (more properly in the interregnum between Hadrian and Leo. June 1522, Gregorovius viii. 388). To stay the plague, a bull was solemnly offered up with pagan rites. Paul. Jov. *Hist.* xxi. 8.

which few even among the scoffers and the sceptics were able to withstand.

But in questions of this kind it is perilous to grasp too hastily at absolute results. We might fancy, for example, that the feeling of educated men towards the reliques of the saints would be a key by which some chambers of their religious consciousness might be opened. And in fact, some difference of degree may be demonstrable, though by no means as clearly as might be wished. The Government of Venice in the fifteenth century seems to have fully shared in the reverence felt throughout the rest of Europe for the remains of the bodies of the saints (p. 72). Even strangers who lived in Venice found it well to adapt themselves to this superstition.[1] If we can judge of scholarly Padua from the testimony of its topographer Michele Savonarola (p. 145), things must have been much the same there. With a mixture of pride and pious awe, Michele tells us how in times of great danger the saints were heard to sigh at night along the streets of the city, how the hair and nails on the corpse of a holy nun in Santa Chiara kept on continually growing, and how the same corpse, when any disaster was impending, used to make a noise and lift up the arms.[2] When he sets to work to describe the chapel of St. Anthony in the Santo, the writer loses himself in ejaculations and fantastic dreams. In Milan the people at least showed a fanatical devotion to relics; and when once, in the year 1517, the monks of San Simpliciano were careless enough to expose six holy corpses during certain alterations of the high altar, which event was followed by heavy floods of rain, the people[3] attributed the visitation to this sacrilege, and gave the monks a sound beating whenever they met them in the street. In other parts of Italy, and even in the case of the Popes themselves, the sincerity of this feeling is much more dubious, though here, too, a positive conclusion is hardly at-

[1] See Sabellico, *De Situ Venetae Urbis.* He mentions the names of the saints, after the manner of many philologists, without the addition of 'sanctus' or 'divus,' but speaks frequently of different relics, and in the most respectful tone, and even boasts that he kissed several of them.

[2] *De Laudibus Patavii*, in Murat. xxiv. col. 1149 to 1151.

[3] Prato, *Arch. Stor.* iii. pp. 408 sqq. Though he is by no means a freethinker, he still protests against the causal nexus.

tainable. It is well known amid what general enthusiasm Pius II. solemnly deposited the head of the Apostle Andrew, which had been brought from Greece, and then from Santa Maura, in the Church of St. Peter (1462); but we gather from his own narrative that he only did it from a kind of shame, as so many princes were competing for the relic. It was not till afterwards that the idea struck him of making Rome the common refuge for all the remains of the saints which had been driven from their own churches.[1] Under Sixtus IV. the population of the city was still more zealous in this cause than the Pope himself, and the magistracy (1483) complained bitterly that Sixtus had sent to Louis XI., the dying king of France, some specimens of the Lateran relics.[2] A courageous voice was raised about this time at Bologna, advising the sale of the skull of St. Dominic to the king of Spain, and the application of the money to some useful public object.[3] But those who had the least reverence of all for the relics were the Florentines. Between the decision to honour their saint S. Zanobi with a new sarcophagus and the final execution of the project by Ghiberti nineteen years elapsed (1409–28), and then it only happened by chance, because the master had executed a smaller order of the same kind with great skill.[4]

Perhaps through being tricked by a cunning Neapolitan abbess (1352), who sent them a spurious arm of the patroness of the Cathedral, Santa Reparata, made of wood and plaster, they began to get tired of relics.[5] Or perhaps it would be truer to say that their æsthetic sense turned them away in disgust from dismembered corpses and mouldy clothes. Or

[1] *Pii II. Comment.* l. viii. pp. 352 sqq. 'Verebatur Pontifex, ne in honore tanti apostoli diminute agere videretur,' &c.

[2] Jac. Volaterran. in Murat. xxiii. col. 187. The Pope excused himself on the ground of Louis' great services to the Church, and by the example of other Popes, e.g. St. Gregory, who had done the like. Louis was able to pay his devotion to the relic, but died after all. The Catacombs were at that time forgotten, yet even Savonarola (l. c. col. 1150) says of Rome: 'Velut ager Aceldama Sanctorum habita est.'

[3] Bursellis, *Annal. Bonon.* in Murat. xxiii. col. 905. It was one of the sixteen patricians, Bartol. della Volta, d. 1485 or 1486.

[4] Vasari, iii. 111 sqq. note. *Vita di Ghiberti.*

[5] Matteo Villani, iii. 15 and 16.

perhaps their feeling was rather due to that sense for glory which thought Dante and Petrarch worthier of a splendid grave than all the twelve apostles put together. It is probable that throughout Italy, apart from Venice and from Rome, the condition of which latter city was exceptional, the worship of relics had been long giving way to the adoration of the Madonna,[1] at all events to a greater extent than elsewhere in Europe; and in this fact lies indirect evidence of an early development of the æsthetic sense.

It may be questioned whether in the North, where the vastest cathedrals are nearly all dedicated to Our Lady, and where an extensive branch of Latin and indigenous poetry sang the praises of the Mother of God, a greater devotion to her was possible. In Italy, however, the number of miraculous pictures of the Virgin was far greater, and the part they played in the daily life of the people much more important. Every town of any size contained a quantity of them, from the ancient, or ostensibly ancient, paintings by St. Luke, down to the works of contemporaries, who not seldom lived to see the miracles wrought by their own handiwork. The work of art was in these cases by no means as harmless as Battista Mantovano[2] thinks; sometimes it suddenly acquired a magical virtue. The popular craving for the miraculous, especially strong in

[1] We must make a further distinction between the Italian cultus of the bodies of historical saints of recent date, and the northern practice of collecting bones and relics of a sacred antiquity. Such remains were preserved in great abundance in the Lateran, which, for that reason, was of special importance for pilgrims. But on the tombs of St. Dominic and St. Anthony of Padua rested, not only the halo of sanctity, but the splendour of historical fame.

[2] The remarkable judgment in his *De Sacris Diebus*, the work of his later years, refers both to sacred and profane art (l. i.). Among the Jews, he says, there was a good reason for prohibiting all graven images, else they would have relapsed into the idolatry or devil-worship of the nations around them :

Nunc autem, postquam penitus natura Satanum
Cognita, et antiqua sine majestate relicta est,
Nulla ferunt nobis statuae discrimina, nullos
Fert pictura dolos ; jam sunt innoxia signa ;
Sunt modo virtutum testes monimentaque laudum
Marmora, et aeternae decora immortalia famae.

women, may have been fully satisfied by these pictures, and for this reason the relics been less regarded. It cannot be said with certainty how far the respect for genuine relics suffered from the ridicule which the novelists aimed at the spurious.[1]

The attitude of the educated classes towards Mariolatry is more clearly recognisable than towards the worship of images. One cannot but be struck with the fact that in Italian literature Dante's 'Paradise'[2] is the last poem in honour of the Virgin, while among the people hymns in her praise have been constantly produced down to our own day. The names of Sannazaro and Sabellico[3] and other writers of Latin poems prove little on the other side, since the object with which they wrote was chiefly literary. The poems written in Italian in the fifteenth[4] and at the beginning of the sixteenth centuries, in which we meet with genuine religious feeling, such as the hymns of Lorenzo the Magnificent, and the sonnets of Vittoria Colonna and of Michelangelo, might have been just as well composed by Protestants. Besides the lyrical expression of faith in God, we chiefly notice in them the sense of sin, the consciousness of deliverance through the death of Christ, the longing for a better world. The intercession of the Mother of God is only mentioned by the way.[5] The same phenomenon is repeated in the classical literature of the French at the time of Louis XIV. Not till the time of the Counter-Reformation

[1] Battista Mantovano complains of certain 'nebulones' (*De Sacris Diebus*, l. v.) who would not believe in the genuineness of the Sacred Blood at Mantua. The same criticism which called in question the Donation of Constantine was also, though indirectly, hostile to the belief in relics.

[2] Especially the famous prayer of St. Bernard, *Paradiso* xxxiii. 1, 'Vergine madre, figlia del tuo figlio.'

[3] Perhaps we may add Pius II., whose elegy on the Virgin is printed in the *Opera*, p. 964, and who from his youth believed himself to be under her special protection. Jac. Card. Papiens. 'De Morte Pii,' *Opp.* p. 656.

[4] That is, at the time when Sixtus IV. was so zealous for the Immaculate Conception. *Extravag. Commun.* l. iii. tit. xii. He founded, too, the Feast of the Presentation of the Virgin in the Temple, and the Feasts of St. Anne and St. Joseph. See Trithem. *Ann. Hirsaug.* ii. p. 518.

[5] The few frigid sonnets of Vittoria on the Madonna are most instructive in this respect (n. 85 sqq. ed. P. Visconti, Rome, 1840).

did Mariolatry reappear in the higher Italian poetry. Meanwhile the plastic arts had certainly done their utmost to glorify the Madonna. It may be added that the worship of the saints among the educated classes often took an essentially pagan form (p. 260).

We might thus critically examine the various sides of Italian Catholicism at this period, and so establish with a certain degree of probability the attitude of the instructed classes toward popular faith. Yet an absolute and positive result cannot be reached. We meet with contrasts hard to explain. While architects, painters, and sculptors were working with restless activity in and for the churches, we hear at the beginning of the sixteenth century the bitterest complaints of the neglect of public worship and of these churches themselves.

> Templa ruunt, passim sordent altaria, cultus
> Paulatim divinus abit.[1]

It is well known how Luther was scandalised by the irreverence with which the priests in Rome said Mass. And at the same time the feasts of the Church were celebrated with a taste and magnificence of which Northern countries had no conception. It looks as if this most imaginative of nations was easily tempted to neglect every-day things, and as easily captivated by anything extraordinary.

It is to this excess of imagination that we must attribute the epidemic religious revivals, upon which we shall again say a few words. They must be clearly distinguished from the excitement called forth by the great preachers. They were rather due to general public calamities, or to the dread of such.

In the Middle Ages all Europe was from time to time flooded by these great tides, which carried away whole peoples in their waves. The Crusades and the Flagellant revival are instances. Italy took part in both of these movements. The first great companies of Flagellants appeared, immediately after the fall of Ezzelino and his house, in the neighbourhood of the same

[1] Bapt. Mantuan. *De Sacris Diebus*, l. v., and especially the speech of the younger Pico, which was intended for the Lateran Council, in Roscoe, *Leone X.* ed. Bossi, viii. p. 115. Comp. p. 121, note 3.

Perugia[1] which has been already spoken of (p. 482, note 2), as the head-quarters of the revivalist preachers. Then followed the Flagellants of 1310 and 1334,[2] and then the great pilgrimage without scourging in the year 1399, which Corio has recorded.[3] It is not impossible that the Jubilees were founded partly in order to regulate and render harmless this sinister passion for vagabondage which seized on whole populations at times of religious excitement. The great sanctuaries of Italy, such as Loreto and others, had meantime become famous, and no doubt diverted a certain part of this enthusiasm.[4]

But terrible crises had still at a much later time the power to reawaken the glow of mediæval penitence, and the conscience-stricken people, often still further appalled by signs and wonders, sought to move the pity of Heaven by wailings and scourgings, by fasts, processions, and moral enactments. So it was at Bologna when the plague came in 1457,[5] so in 1496 at a time of internal discord at Siena,[6] to mention two only out of countless instances. No more moving scene can be imagined than that we read of at Milan in 1529, when famine, plague, and war conspired with Spanish extortion to

[1] *Monach. Paduani Chron.* l. iii. at the beginning. We there read of this revival: 'Invasit primitus Perusinos, Romanos postmodum, deinde fere Italiæ populos universos.' Guil. Ventura (*Fragmenta de Gestis Astensium* in *Mon. Hist. Patr. SS.* tom. iii. col. 701) calls the Flagellant pilgrimage 'admirabilis Lombardorum commotio;' hermits came forth from their cells and summoned the cities to repent.

[2] G. Villani, viii. 122, xi. 23. The former were not received in Florence, the latter were welcomed all the more readily.

[3] Corio, fol. 281. Leon. Aretinus, *Hist. Flor.* lib. xii. (at the beginning) mentions a sudden revival called forth by the processions of the 'dealbati' from the Alps to Lucca, Florence, and still farther.

[4] Pilgrimages to distant places had already become very rare. Those of the princes of the House of Este to Jerusalem, St. Jago, and Vienne are enumerated in Murat. xxiv. col. 182, 187, 190, 279. For that of Rinaldo Albizzi to the Holy Land, see Macchiavelli, *Stor. Fior.* l. v. Here, too, the desire of fame is sometimes the motive. The chronicler Giov. Cavalcanti (*Ist. Fiorentine*, ed. Polidori, ii. 478) says of Lionardo Fescobaldi, who wanted to go with a companion (about the year 1400) to the Holy Sepulchre: 'Stimarono di eternarsi nella mente degli uomini futuri.'

[5] Bursellis, *Annal. Bon.* in Murat. xxiii. col. 890.

[6] Allegretto, in Murat. xxiii. col. 855 sqq. The report had got about that it had rained blood outside the gate. All rushed forth, yet 'gli uomini di guidizio non lo credono.'

reduce the city to the lowest depths of despair.[1] It chanced that the monk who had the ear of the people, Fra Tommaso Nieto, was himself a Spaniard. The Host was borne along in a novel fashion, amid barefooted crowds of old and young. It was placed on a decorated bier, which rested on the shoulders of four priests in linen garments—an imitation of the Ark of the Covenant[2] which the children of Israel once carried round the walls of Jericho. Thus did the afflicted people of Milan remind their ancient God of His old covenant with man; and when the procession again entered the cathedral, and it seemed as if the vast building must fall in with the agonised cry of 'Misericordia!' many who stood there may have believed that the Almighty would indeed subvert the laws of nature and of history, and send down upon them a miraculous deliverance.

There was one government in Italy, that of Duke Ercole I. of Ferrara,[3] which assumed the direction of public feeling, and compelled the popular revivals to move in regular channels. At the time when Savonarola was powerful in Florence, and the movement which he began spread far and wide among the population of central Italy, the people of Ferrara voluntarily entered on a general fast (at the beginning of 1496). A Lazarist announced from the pulpit the approach of a season of war and famine such as the world had never seen; but the Madonna had assured some pious people[4] that these evils might be avoided by fasting. Upon this, the court itself had no choice but to fast, but it took the conduct of the public devotions into its own hands. On Easter Day, the 3rd of April, a proclamation on morals and religion was published, forbidding blasphemy, prohibited games, sodomy, concubinage, the letting of houses to prostitutes or panders, and the opening of all shops on feast-days, excepting those of the bakers and

[1] Burigozzo, *Arch. Stor.* iii. 486. For the misery which then prevailed in Lombardy, Galeazzo Capello (*De Rebus nuper in Italia Gestis*) is the best authority. Milan suffered hardly less than Rome did in the sack of 1527.

[2] It was also called 'l' arca del testimonio,' and people told how it was 'conzado' (constructed) 'con gran misterio.'

[3] *Diario Ferrarese*, in Murat. xxiv. col. 317, 322, 323. 326, 386, 401.

[4] 'Ad uno santo homo o santa donna,' says the chronicle. Married men were forbidden to keep concubines.

greengrocers. The Jews and Moors, who had taken refuge from the Spaniards at Ferrara, were now compelled again to wear the yellow O upon the breast. Contraveners were threatened, not only with the punishments already provided by law, but also 'with such severer penalties as the Duke might think good to inflict,' of which one-fourth in case of a pecuniary fine was to be paid to the Duke, and the other three-fourths were to go to some public institution. After this, the Duke and the court went several days in succession to hear sermons in church, and on the 10th of April all the Jews in Ferrara were compelled to do the same.[1] On the 3rd of May the director of police—that Zampante who has been already referred to (p. 50)—sent the crier to announce that whoever had given money to the police-officers in order not to be informed against as a blasphemer, might, if he came forward, have it back with a further indemnification. These wicked officers, he said, had extorted as much as two or three ducats from innocent persons by threatening to lodge an information against them. They had then mutually informed against one another, and so had all found their way into prison. But as the money had been paid precisely in order not to have to do with Zampante, it is probable that his proclamation induced few people to come forward. In the year 1500, after the fall of Ludovico Moro, when a similar outbreak of popular feeling took place, Ercole[2] ordered a series of nine processions, in which there were 4,000 children dressed in white, bearing the standard of Jesus. He himself rode on horseback, as he could not walk without difficulty. An edict was afterwards published of the same kind as that of 1496. It is well known how many churches and monasteries were built by this ruler. He even sent for a live saint, the Suor Colomba, shortly before he married his son Alfonso to Lucrezia Borgia (1502). A

[1] The sermon was especially addressed to them; after it a Jew was baptised, 'ma non di quelli' adds the annalist, 'che erano stati a udire la predica.'

[2] 'Per buono rispetto a lui noto e perchè sempre è buono a star bene con Iddio,' says the annalist. After describing the arrangements, he adds resignedly: 'La cagione perchè sia fatto et si habbia a fare non s' intende; basta che ogni bene è bene.'

special messenger[1] fetched the saint with fifteen other nuns from Viterbo, and the Duke himself conducted her on her arrival at Ferrara into a convent prepared for her reception. We shall probably do him no injustice if we attribute all these measures very largely to political calculation. To the conception of government formed by the House of Este, as indicated above (p. 46, sqq.), this employment of religion for the ends of statecraft belongs by a kind of logical necessity.

[1] He is called 'Messo del Cancellieri del Duca.' The whole thing was evidently intended to appear the work of the court only, and not of any ecclesiastical authority.

CHAPTER III.

RELIGION AND THE SPIRIT OF THE RENAISSANCE.

But in order to reach a definite conclusion with regard to the religious sense of the men of this period, we must adopt a different method. From their intellectual attitude in general, we can infer their relation both to the Divine idea and to the existing religion of their age.

These modern men, the representatives of the culture of Italy, were born with the same religious instincts as other mediæval Europeans. But their powerful individuality made them in religion, as in other matters, altogether subjective, and the intense charm which the discovery of the inner and outer universe exercised upon them rendered them markedly worldly. In the rest of Europe religion remained, till a much later period, something given from without, and in practical life egoism and sensuality alternated with devotion and repentance. The latter had no spiritual competitors, as in Italy, or only to a far smaller extent.

Further, the close and frequent relations of Italy with Byzantium and the Mohammedan peoples had produced a dispassionate tolerance which weakened the ethnographical conception of a privileged Christendom. And when classical antiquity with its men and institutions became an ideal of life, as well as the greatest of historical memories, ancient speculation and scepticism obtained in many cases a complete mastery over the minds of Italians.

Since, again, the Italians were the first modern people of Europe who gave themselves boldly to speculations on freedom and necessity, and since they did so under violent and lawless political circumstances, in which evil seemed often to win a splendid and lasting victory, their belief in God began to waver, and their view of the government of the world became fatalistic. And when their passionate natures refused to rest in the sense of uncertainty, they made a shift to help themselves out with ancient, oriental, or mediæval superstition. They took to astrology and magic.

Finally, these intellectual giants, these representatives of the Renaissance, show, in respect to religion, a quality which is common in youthful natures. Distinguishing keenly between good and evil, they yet are conscious of no sin. Every disturbance of their inward harmony they feel themselves able to make good out of the plastic resources of their own nature, and therefore they feel no repentance. The need of salvation thus becomes felt more and more dimly, while the ambitions and the intellectual activity of the present either shut out altogether every thought of a world to come, or else cause it to assume a poetic instead of a dogmatic form.

When we look on all this as pervaded and often perverted by the all-powerful Italian imagination, we obtain a picture of that time which is certainly more in accordance with truth than are vague declamations against modern paganism. And closer investigation often reveals to us that underneath this outward shell much genuine religion could still survive.

The fuller discussion of these points must be limited to a few of the most essential explanations.

That religion should again become an affair of the individual and of his own personal feeling was inevitable when the Church became corrupt in doctrine and tyrannous in practice, and is a proof that the European mind was still alive. It is true that this showed itself in many different ways. While the mystical and ascetical sects of the North lost no time in creating new outward forms for their new modes of thought and feeling, each individual in Italy went his own way, and thousands wandered on the sea of life without any religious guidance whatever. All the more must we admire those who attained and held fast to a personal religion. They were not to blame for being unable to have any part or lot in the old Church, as she then was; nor would it be reasonable to expect that they should all of them go through that mighty spiritual labour which was appointed to the German reformers. The form and aim of this personal faith, as it showed itself in the better minds, will be set forth at the close of our work.

The worldliness, through which the Renaissance seems to offer so striking a contrast to the Middle Ages, owed its first origin to the flood of new thoughts, purposes, and views, which transformed the mediæval conception of nature and man. This spirit is not in itself more hostile to religion than that 'culture' which now holds its place, but which can give us only a feeble notion of the universal ferment which the discovery of a new world of greatness then called forth. This worldliness was not frivolous, but earnest, and was ennobled by art and poetry. It is a lofty necessity of the modern spirit that this attitude, once gained, can never again be lost, that an irresistible impulse forces us to the investigation of men and things, and that we must hold this enquiry to be our proper end and work.[1] How soon and by what paths this search will lead us back to God, and in what ways the religious temper of the individual will be affected by it, are questions which cannot be met by any general answer. The Middle Ages, which spared themselves the trouble of induction and free enquiry, can have no right to impose upon us their dogmatical verdict in a matter of such vast importance.

To the study of man, among many other causes, was due the tolerance and indifference with which the Mohammedan religion was regarded. The knowledge and admiration of the remarkable civilisation which Islam, particularly before the Mongol inundation, had attained, was peculiar to Italy from the time of the Crusades. This sympathy was fostered by the half-Mohammedan government of some Italian princes, by dislike and even contempt for the existing Church, and by constant commercial intercourse with the harbours of the Eastern and Southern Mediterranean.[2] It can be shown that in the thirteenth century the Italians recognised a Moham-

[1] See the quotations from Pico's *Discourse on the Dignity of Man* above, pp. 354–5.

[2] Not to speak of the fact that a similar tolerance or indifference was not uncommon among the Arabians themselves.

medan ideal of nobleness, dignity, and pride, which they loved to connect with the person of a Sultan. A Mameluke Sultan is commonly meant; if any name is mentioned, it is the name of Saladin.[1] Even the Osmanli Turks, whose destructive tendencies were no secret, gave the Italians, as we have shown above (p. 92, sqq.), only half a fright, and a peaceable accord with them was looked upon as no impossibility. Along with this tolerance, however, appeared the bitterest religious opposition to Mohammedanism; the clergy, says Filelfo, should come forward against it, since it prevailed over a great part of the world and was more dangerous to Christendom than Judaism was;[2] along with the readiness to compromise with the Turks, appeared the passionate desire for a war against them which possessed Pius II. during the whole of his pontificate, and which many of the humanists expressed in high-flown declamations.

The truest and most characteristic expression of this religious indifference is the famous story of the Three Rings, which Lessing has put into the mouth of his Nathan, after it had been already told centuries earlier, though with some reserve, in the 'Hundred Old Novels' (nov. 72 or 73), and more boldly in Boccaccio.[3] In what language and in what corner of the

[1] So in the *Decameron.* Sultans without name in Massuccio nov. 46, 48, 49; one called 'Rè di Fes,' another 'Rè di Tunisi.' In *Dittamondo*, ii. 25, we read, 'il buono Saladin.' For the Venetian alliance with the Sultan of Egypt in the year 1202, see G. Hanotaux in the *Revue Historique* iv. (1877) pp. 74–102. There were naturally also many attacks on Mohammedanism. For the Turkish woman baptized first in Venice and again in Rome, see Cechetti i. 487.

[2] *Philelphi Epistolae*, Venet. 1502 fol. 90 *b.* sqq.

[3] *Decamerone* i. nov. 3. Boccaccio is the first to name the Christian religion, which the others do not. For an old French authority of the thirteenth century, see Tobler, *Li di dou Vrai Aniel*, Leipzig, 1871. For the Hebrew story of Abr. Abulafia (b. 1241 in Spain, came to Italy about 1290 in the hope of converting the Pope to Judaism), in which two servants claim each to hold the jewel buried for the son, see Steinschneider, *Polem. und Apol. Lit. der Arab. Sprache*, pp. 319 and 360. From these and other sources we conclude that the story originally was less definite than as we now have it (in Abul. e.g. it is used polemically against the Christians), and that the doctrine of the equality of the three religions is a later addition. Comp. Reuter, *Gesch. der Relig. Aufklärung im M. A.* (Berlin, 1877), iii. 302 sqq. 390.

Mediterranean it was first told, can never be known; most likely the original was much more plain-spoken than the two Italian adaptations. The religious postulate on which it rests, namely Deism, will be discussed later on in its wider significance for this period. The same idea is repeated, though in a clumsy caricature, in the famous proverb of the 'three who have deceived the world, that is, Moses, Christ, and Mohammed.'[1] If the Emperor Frederick II., in whom this saying is said to have originated, really thought so, he probably expressed himself with more wit. Ideas of the same kind were also current in Islam.

At the height of the Renaissance, towards the close of the fifteenth century, Luigi Pulci offers us an example of the same mode of thought in the 'Morgante Maggiore.' The imaginary world of which his story treats is divided, as in all heroic poems of romance, into a Christian and a Mohammedan camp. In accordance with the mediæval temper, the victory of the Christian and the final reconciliation among the combatants was attended by the baptism of the defeated Islamites, and the Improvisatori, who preceded Pulci in the treatment of these subjects, must have made free use of this stock incident. It was Pulci's object to parody his predecessors, particularly the worst among them, and this he does by those appeals to God, Christ, and the Madonna, with which each canto begins; and still more clearly by the sudden conversions and baptisms, the utter senselessness of which must have struck every reader or hearer. This ridicule leads him further to the confession of his faith in the relative goodness of all religions,[2] which faith, notwithstanding his professions of orthodoxy,[3] rests on an essentially theistic basis. In another point too he departs widely from mediæval conceptions. The alternatives in past centuries were: Christian, or else Pagan and Mohammedan;

[1] *De Tribus Impostoribus*, the name of a work attributed to Frederick II. among many other people, and which by no means answers the expectations raised by the title. Latest ed. by Weller, Heilbronn, 1876. The nationality of the author and the date of composition are both disputed. See Reuter, op. cit. ii. 273–302.

[2] In the mouth, nevertheless, of the fiend Astarotte, canto xxv. str. 231 sqq. Comp. str. 141 sqq.

[3] Canto xxviii. str. 38 sqq.

orthodox believer or heretic. Pulci draws a picture of the Giant Margutte[1] who, disregarding each and every religion, jovially confesses to every form of vice and sensuality, and only reserves to himself the merit of having never broken faith. Perhaps the poet intended to make something of this —in his way—honest monster, possibly to have led him into virtuous paths by Morgante, but he soon got tired of his own creation, and in the next canto brought him to a comic end.[2] Margutte has been brought forward as a proof of Pulci's frivolity; but he is needed to complete the picture of the poetry of the fifteenth century. It was natural that it should somewhere present in grotesque proportions the figure of an untamed egoism, insensible to all established rule, and yet with a remnant of honourable feeling left. In other poems sentiments are put into the mouths of giants, fiends, infidels, and Mohammedans which no Christian knight would venture to utter.

Antiquity exercised an influence of another kind than that of Islam, and this not through its religion, which was but too much like the Catholicism of this period, but through its philosophy. Ancient literature, now worshipped as something incomparable, is full of the victory of philosophy over religious tradition. An endless number of systems and fragments of systems were suddenly presented to the Italian mind, not as curiosities or even as heresies, but almost with the authority of dogmas, which had now to be reconciled rather than discriminated. In nearly all these various opinions and doctrines a certain kind of belief in God was implied; but taken altogether they formed a marked contrast to the Christian faith in a Divine government of the world. And there was one central question, which mediæval theology had striven in vain to solve, and which now urgently demanded an answer from

[1] Canto xviii. str. 112 to the end.

[2] Pulci touches, though hastily, on a similar conception in his Prince Chiaristante (canto xxi. str. 101 sqq., 121 sqq., 145 sqq., 163 sqq.), who believes nothing and causes himself and his wife to be worshipped. We are reminded of Sigismondo Malatesta (p. 245).

the wisdom of the ancients, namely, the relation of Providence to the freedom or necessity of the human will. To write the history of this question even superficially from the fourteenth century onwards, would require a whole volume. A few hints must here suffice.

If we take Dante and his contemporaries as evidence, we shall find that ancient philosophy first came into contact with Italian life in the form which offered the most marked contrast to Christianity, that is to say, Epicureanism. The writings of Epicurus were no longer preserved, and even at the close of the classical age a more or less one-sided conception had been formed of his philosophy. Nevertheless, that phase of Epicureanism which can be studied in Lucretius, and especially in Cicero, is quite sufficient to make men familiar with a godless universe. To what extent his teaching was actually understood, and whether the name of the problematic Greek sage was not rather a catchword for the multitude, it is hard to say. It is probable that the Dominican Inquisition used it against men who could not be reached by a more definite accusation. In the case of sceptics born before the time was ripe, whom it was yet hard to convict of positive heretical utterances, a moderate degree of luxurious living may have sufficed to provoke the charge. The word is used in this conventional sense by Giovanni Villani,[1] when he explains the Florentine fires of 1115 and 1117 as a Divine judgment on heresies, among others, 'on the luxurious and gluttonous sect of Epicureans.' The same writer says of Manfred, 'His life was Epicurean, since he believed neither in God, nor in the Saints, but only in bodily pleasure.'

Dante speaks still more clearly in the ninth and tenth cantos of the 'Inferno.' That terrible fiery field covered with half-opened tombs, from which issued cries of hopeless agony, was peopled by the two great classes of those whom the Church had vanquished or expelled in the thirteenth century. The one were heretics who opposed the Church by deliberately

[1] Giov. Villani, iv. 29, vi. 46. The name occurs as early as 1150 in Northern countries. It is defined by William of Malmesbury (iii. 237, ed. Londin, 1840): 'Epicureorum . . . qui opinantur animam corpore solutam in aerem evanescere, in auras effluere.'

spreading false doctrine; the other were Epicureans, and their sin against the Church lay in their general disposition, which was summed up in the belief that the soul dies with the body.[1] The Church was well aware that this one doctrine, if it gained ground, must be more ruinous to her authority than all the teachings of the Manichaeans and Paterini, since it took away all reason for her interference in the affairs of men after death. That the means which she used in her struggles were precisely what had driven the most gifted natures to unbelief and despair was what she naturally would not herself admit.

Dante's loathing of Epicurus, or of what he took to be his doctrine, was certainly sincere. The poet of the life to come could not but detest the denier of immortality; and a world neither made nor ruled by God, no less than the vulgar objects of earthly life which the system appeared to countenance, could not but be intensely repugnant to a nature like his. But if we look closer, we find that certain doctrines of the ancients made even on him an impression which forced the biblical doctrine of the Divine government into the background, unless, indeed, it was his own reflection, the influence of opinions then prevalent, or loathing for the injustice that seemed to rule this world, which made him give up the belief in a special Providence.[2] His God leaves all the details of the world's government to a deputy, Fortune, whose sole work it is to change and change again all earthly things, and who can disregard the wailings of men in unalterable beatitude. Nevertheless, Dante does not for a moment loose his hold on the moral responsibility of man; he believes in free will.

The belief in the freedom of the will, in the popular sense of the words, has always prevailed in Western countries. At all times men have been held responsible for their actions,

[1] See the argument in the third book of Lucretius. The name of Epicurean was afterwards used as synonymous with freethinker. Lorenzo Valla (*Opp.* 795 sqq.) speaks as follows of Epicurus: 'Quis eo parcior, quis contentior, quis modestior, et quidem in nullo philosophorum omnium minus invenio fuisse vitiorum, plurimique honesti viri cum Graecorum, tum Romanorum, Epicurei fuerunt.' Valla was defending himself to Eugenius IV. against the attacks of Fra Antonio da Bitonto and others.

[2] *Inferno*, vii. 67–96.

as though this freedom were a matter of course. The case is otherwise with the religious and philosophical doctrine, which labours under the difficulty of harmonising the nature of the will with the laws of the universe at large. We have here to do with a question of more or less, which every moral estimate must take into account. Dante is not wholly free from those astrological superstitions which illumined the horizon of his time with deceptive light, but they do not hinder him from rising to a worthy conception of human nature. 'The stars,' he makes his Marco Lombardo say,[1] 'the stars give the first impulse to your actions,' but

> Light has been given you for good and evil
> And free volition ; which, if some fatigue
> In the first battles with the heavens it suffers,
> Afterwards conquers all, if well 'tis nurtured.

Others might seek the necessity which annulled human freedom in another power than the stars, but the question was henceforth an open and inevitable one. So far as it was a question for the schools or the pursuit of isolated thinkers, its treatment belongs to the historian of philosophy. But inasmuch as it entered into the consciousness of a wider public, it is necessary for us to say a few words respecting it.

The fourteenth century was chiefly stimulated by the writings of Cicero, who, though in fact an eclectic, yet, by his habit of setting forth the opinions of different schools, without coming to a decision between them, exercised the influence of a sceptic. Next in importance came Seneca, and the few works of Aristotle which had been translated into Latin. The immediate fruit of these studies was the capacity to reflect on great subjects, if not in direct opposition to the authority of the Church, at all events independently of it.

In the course of the fifteenth century the works of antiquity were discovered and diffused with extraordinary rapidity. All the writings of the Greek philosophers which we ourselves possess were now, at least in the form of Latin translations, in

[1] *Purgatorio*, xvi. 73. Compare the theory of the influence of the planets in the *Convito*. Even the fiend Astarotte in Pulci (*Morgante*, xxv. str. 150) attests the freedom of the human will and the justice of God.

everybody's hands. It is a curious fact that some of the most zealous apostles of this new culture were men of the strictest piety, or even ascetics (p. 273). Fra Ambrogio Camaldolese, as a spiritual dignitary chiefly occupied with ecclesiastical affairs, and as a literary man with the translation of the Greek Fathers of the Church, could not repress the humanistic impulse, and at the request of Cosimo de' Medici, undertook to translate Diogenes Laertius into Latin.[1] His contemporaries, Niccolò Niccoli, Giannozzo Manetti, Donato Acciajuoli, and Pope Nicholas V.,[2] united to a many-sided humanism profound biblical scholarship and deep piety. In Vittorino da Feltre the same temper has been already noticed (p. 213 sqq.). The same Matthew Vegio, who added a thirteenth book to the 'Æneid,' had an enthusiasm for the memory of St. Augustine and his mother Monica which cannot have been without a deeper influence upon him. The result of all these tendencies was that the Platonic Academy at Florence deliberately chose for its object the reconciliation of the spirit of antiquity with that of Christianity. It was a remarkable oasis in the humanism of the period.[3]

This humanism was in fact pagan, and became more and more so as its sphere widened in the fifteenth century. Its representatives, whom we have already described as the advanced guard of an unbridled individualism, display as a rule such a character that even their religion, which is sometimes professed very definitely, becomes a matter of indifference to us. They easily got the name of atheists, if they showed themselves indifferent to religion, and spoke freely against the Church; but not one of them ever professed, or

[1] Comp. Voigt, *Wiederbelebung*, 165–170.

[2] *Vespasiano Fiorent.* pp. 26, 320, 435, 626, 651. Murat. xx. col. 532.

[3] In Platina's introd. to his Life of Christ the religious influence of the Renaissance is curiously exemplified (*Vitæ Paparum*, at the beginning): Christ, he says, fully attained the fourfold Platonic 'nobilitas' according to his 'genus': 'quem enim ex gentilibus habemus qui gloria et nomine cum David et Salomone, quique sapientia et doctrina cum Christo ipso conferri merito debeat et possit?' Judaism, like classical antiquity, was also explained on a Christian hypothesis. Pico and Pietro Galatino endeavoured to show that Christian doctrine was foreshadowed in the Talmud and other Jewish writings.

dared to profess, a formal, philosophical atheism.[1] If they sought for any leading principle, it must have been a kind of superficial rationalism—a careless inference from the many and contradictory opinions of antiquity with which they busied themselves, and from the discredit into which the Church and her doctrines had fallen. This was the sort of reasoning which was near bringing Galeottus Martius[2] to the stake, had not his former pupil, Pope Sixtus IV., perhaps at the request of Lorenzo de' Medici, saved him from the hands of the Inquisition. Galeotto had ventured to write that the man who walked uprightly, and acted according to the natural law born within him, would go to heaven, whatever nation he belonged to.

Let us take, by way of example, the religious attitude of one of the smaller men in the great army. Codrus Urceus[3] was first the tutor of the last Ordelaffo, Prince of Forli, and afterwards for many years professor at Bologna. Against the Church and the monks his language is as abusive as that of the rest. His tone in general is reckless to the last degree, and he constantly introduces himself in all his local history and gossip. But he knows how to speak to edification of the true God-Man, Jesus Christ, and to commend himself by letter to the prayers of a saintly priest.[4] On one occasion, after enumerating the follies of the pagan religions, he thus goes on: 'Our theologians, too, fight and quarrel "de lana caprina," about the Immaculate Conception, Antichrist, Sacraments, Predestination, and other things, which were better let alone than talked of publicly.' Once, when he was not at

[1] On Pomponazzo, see the special works; among others, Ritter, *Geschichte der Philosophie*, bd. ix.

[2] Paul. Jovii, *Elog. Lit.* p. 90. G. M. was, however, compelled to recant publicly. His letter to Lorenzo (May 17, 1478) begging him to intercede with the Pope, 'satis enim poenarum dedi,' is given by Malagola, Codro Urceo, p. 433.

[3] *Codri Urcei Opera*, with his life by Bart. Bianchini; and in his philological lectures, pp. 65, 151, 278, &c.

[4] On one occasion he says, 'In Laudem Christi:'

Phoebum alii vates musasque Jovemque sequuntur,
At mihi pro vero nomine Christus erit.

He also (fol. x. *b*) attacks the Bohemians. Huss and Jerome of Prague are defended by Poggio in his famous letter to Lion. Aretino, and placed on a level with Mucius Scaevola and Socrates.

home, his room and manuscripts were burnt. When he heard the news he stood opposite a figure of the Madonna in the street, and cried to it: 'Listen to what I tell you; I am not mad, I am saying what I mean. If I ever call upon you in the hour of my death, you need not hear me or take me among your own, for I will go and spend eternity with the devil.'[1] After which speech he found it desirable to spend six months in retirement at the house of a wood-cutter. With all this, he was so superstitious that prodigies and omens gave him incessant frights, leaving him no belief to spare for the immortality of the soul. When his hearers questioned him on the matter, he answered that no one knew what became of a man, of his soul or his body, after death, and the talk about another life was only fit to frighten old women. But when he came to die, he commended in his will his soul or his spirit[2] to Almighty God, exhorted his weeping pupils to fear the Lord, and especially to believe in immortality and future retribution, and received the Sacrament with much fervour. We have no guarantee that more famous men in the same calling, however significant their opinions may be, were in practical life any more consistent. It is probable that most of them wavered inwardly between incredulity and a remnant of the faith in which they were brought up, and outwardly held for prudential reasons to the Church.

Through the connexion of rationalism with the newly born science of historical investigation, some timid attempts at biblical criticism may here and there have been made. A saying of Pius II.[3] has been recorded, which seems intended to prepare the way for such criticism: 'Even if Christianity were not confirmed by miracles, it ought still to be accepted on account of its morality.' When Lorenzo Valla calls Moses

[1] 'Audi virgo ea quae tibi mentis compos et ex animo dicam. Si forte cum ad ultimum vitae finem pervenero supplex accedam ad te spem oratum, ne me audias neve inter tuos accipias oro; cum infernis diis in aeternum vitam degere decrevi.'

[2] 'Animum meum seu animam'—a distinction by which philology used then to perplex theology.

[3] Platina, *Vitae Pontiff.* p. 311: 'Christianam fidem si miraculis non esset confirmata, honestate sua recipi debuisse.' It may be questioned whether all that Platina attributes to the Pope is in fact authentic.

and the Evangelists historians, he does not seek to diminish their dignity and reputation; but is nevertheless conscious that in these words lies as decided a contradiction to the traditional view taken by the Church, as in the denial that the Apostles' Creed was the work of all the Apostles, or that the letter of Abgarus to Christ was genuine.[1] The legends of the Church, in so far as they contained arbitrary versions of the biblical miracles, were freely ridiculed,[2] and this reacted on the religious sense of the people. Where Judaising heretics are mentioned, we must understand chiefly those who denied the Divinity of Christ, which was probably the offence for which Giorgio da Novara was burnt at Bologna about the year 1500.[3] But again at Bologna in the year 1497 the Dominican Inquisitor was forced to let the physician Gabrielle da Salò, who had powerful patrons, escape with a simple expression of penitence,[4] although he was in the habit of maintaining that Christ was not God, but son of Joseph and Mary, and conceived in the usual way; that by his cunning he had deceived the world to its ruin; that he may have died on the cross on account of crimes which he had committed; that his religion would soon come to an end; that his body was not really contained in the sacrament, and that he performed his miracles, not through any divine power, but through the influence of the heavenly bodies. This latter statement is most characteristic of the time, Faith is gone, but magic still holds its ground.[5]

[1] Preface to the *Historia Ferdinandi I.* (*Hist. Ztschr.* xxxiii. 61) and *Antid. in Pogg.* lib. iv. *Opp.* p. 256 sqq. Pontanus (*De Sermone*, i. 18) says that Valla did not hesitate 'dicere profiterique palam habere se quoque in Christum spicula.' Pontano, however, was a friend of Valla's enemies at Naples.

[2] Especially when the monks improvised them in the pulpit. But the old and recognised miracles did not remain unassailed. Firenzuola (*Opere*, vol. ii. p. 208, in the tenth novel) ridicules the Franciscans of Novara, who wanted to spend money which they had embezzled, in adding a chapel to their church, 'dove fusse dipinta quella bella storia, quando S. Francesco predicava agli uccelli nel deserto; e quando ei fece la santa zuppa, e che l' agnolo Gabriello gli portò i zoccoli.'

[3] Some facts about him are to be found in Bapt. Mantuan. *De Patientia*, l. iii. cap. 13.

[4] Bursellis, *Ann. Bonon.* in Murat. xxiii. col. 915.

[5] How far these blasphemous utterances sometimes went, has been

A worse fate befell a Canon of Bergamo, Zanino de Solcia, a few years earlier (1459), who had asserted that Christ did not suffer from love to man, but under the influence of the stars, and who advanced other curious scientific and moral ideas. He was forced to abjure his errors, and paid for them by perpetual imprisonment.[1]

With respect to the moral government of the world, the humanists seldom get beyond a cold and resigned consideration of the prevalent violence and misrule. In this mood the many works 'On Fate,' or whatever name they bear, are written. They tell of the turning of the wheel of Fortune, and of the instability of earthly, especially political, things. Providence is only brought in because the writers would still be ashamed of undisguised fatalism, of the avowal of their ignorance, or of useless complaints. Gioviano Pontano[2] ingeniously illustrates the nature of that mysterious something which men call Fortune by a hundred incidents, most of which belonged to his own experience. The subject is treated more humorously by Æneas Sylvius, in the form of a vision seen in a dream.[3] The aim of Poggio, on the other hand, in a work written in his old age,[4] is to represent the world as a vale of tears, and to fix the happiness of various classes as low as possible. This tone became in future the prevalent one. Distinguished men drew up a debit and credit of the happiness and unhappiness of their lives, and generally found that the latter outweighed the former. The fate of Italy and the Italians, so far as it could be told in the year 1510, has been described with dignity and an almost elegiac pathos by Tristano Caracciolo.[5] Applying this

shown by Gieseler (*Kirchengeschichte*, ii. iv. § 154, anm.) who quotes several striking instances.

[1] Voigt, *Enea Silvio*, iii. 581. It is not known what happened to the Bishop Petro of Aranda who (1500) denied the Divinity of Christ and the existence of Hell and Purgatory, and denounced indulgences as a device of the popes invented for their private advantage. For him, see *Burchardi Diarium*, ed. Leibnitz, p. 63 sqq.

[2] Jov. Pontanus, *De Fortuna*, *Opp.* i. 792–921. Comp. *Opp.* ii. 286.

[3] Æn. Sylvii, *Opera*, p. 611.

[4] Poggius, *De Miseriis Humanae Conditionis.*

[5] Caracciolo, *De Varietate Fortunae*, in Murat. xxii., one of the most valuable writings of a period rich in such works. On Fortune in public processions, see p. 421.

general tone of feeling to the humanists themselves, Pierio Valeriano afterwards composed his famous treatise (pp. 276–279). Some of these themes, such as the fortunes of Leo, were most suggestive. All the good that can be said of him politically has been briefly and admirably summed up by Francesco Vettori; the picture of Leo's pleasures is given by Paolo Giovio and in the anonymous biography;[1] and the shadows which attended his prosperity are drawn with inexorable truth by the same Pierio Valeriano.

We cannot on the other hand, read without a kind of awe how men sometimes boasted of their fortune in public inscriptions. Giovanni II. Bentivoglio, ruler of Bologna, ventured to carve in stone on the newly built tower by his palace, that his merit and his fortune had given him richly of all that could be desired[2]—and this a few years before his expulsion. The ancients, when they spoke in this tone, had nevertheless a sense of the envy of the gods. In Italy it was probably the Condottieri (p. 22) who first ventured to boast so loudly of their fortune.

But the way in which resuscitated antiquity affected religion most powerfully, was not through any doctrines or philosophical system, but through a general tendency which it fostered. The men, and in some respects the institutions of antiquity were preferred to those of the Middle Ages, and in the eager attempt to imitate and reproduce them, religion was left to take care of itself. All was absorbed in the admiration for historical greatness (part ii. chap. iii., and above, *passim*). To this the philologians added many special follies of their own, by which they became the mark for general attention.

[1] *Leonis X. Vita Anonyma*, in Roscoe, ed. Bossi, xii. p. 153.

[2] Bursellis, *Ann. Bonon.* in Murat. xxiii. col. 909: 'Monimentum hoc conditum a Joanne Bentivolo secundo patriae rectore, cui virtus et fortuna cuncta quæ optari possunt affatim praestiterunt.' It is still not quite certain whether this inscription was outside, and visible to everybody, or, like another mentioned just before, hidden on one of the foundation stones. In the latter case, a fresh idea is involved. By this secret inscription, which perhaps only the chronicler knew of, Fortune is to be magically bound to the building.

[According to the words of the chronicle, the inscription cannot have stood on the walls of the newly built tower. The exact spot is uncertain. —L.G.]

How far Paul II. was justified in calling his Abbreviators and their friends to account for their paganism, is certainly a matter of great doubt, as his biographer and chief victim, Platina, (pp. 231, 331) has shown a masterly skill in explaining his vindictiveness on other grounds, and especially in making him play a ludicrous figure. The charges of infidelity, paganism,[1] denial of immortality, and so forth, were not made against the accused till the charge of high treason had broken down. Paul, indeed, if we are correctly informed about him, was by no means the man to judge of intellectual things. He knew little Latin, and spoke Italian at Consistories and in diplomatic negotiations. It was he who exhorted the Romans to teach their children nothing beyond reading and writing. His priestly narrowness of view reminds us of Savonarola (p. 476), with the difference that Paul might fairly have been told that he and his like were in great part to blame if culture made men hostile to religion. It cannot, nevertheless, be doubted that he felt a real anxiety about the pagan tendencies which surrounded him. And what, in truth, may not the humanists have allowed themselves at the court of the profligate pagan, Sigismondo Malatesta? How far these men, destitute for the most part of fixed principle, ventured to go, depended assuredly on the sort of influences they were exposed to. Nor could they treat of Christianity without paganising it (part iii. chap. x.). It is curious, for instance, to notice how far Gioviano Pontano carried this confusion. He speaks of a saint not only as 'divus,' but as 'deus;' the angels he holds to be identical with the genii of antiquity;[2] and his notion of immortality reminds us of the old kingdom of the shades. This

[1] 'Quod nimium gentilitatis amatores essemus.' Paganism, at least in externals, certainly went rather far. Inscriptions lately found in the Catacombs show that the members of the Academy described themselves as 'sacerdotes,' and called Pomponius Lætus 'pontifex maximus;' the latter once addressed Platina as 'pater sanctissimus.' Gregorovius, vii. 578.

[2] While the plastic arts at all events distinguished between angels and 'putti,' and used the former for all serious purposes. In the *Annal. Estens.* Murat. xx. col. 468, the 'amorino' is naively called 'instar Cupidinis angelus.' Comp. the speech made before Leo X. (1521), in which the passage occurs: 'Quare et te non jam Juppiter, sed Virgo Capitolina Dei parens quæ hujus urbis et collis reliquis præsides, Romamque et Capitolium tutaris.' Greg. viii. 294.

spirit occasionally appears in the most extravagant shapes. In 1526, when Siena was attacked by the exiled party,[1] the worthy canon Tizio, who tells us the story himself, rose from his bed on the 22nd July, called to mind what is written in the third book of Macrobius,'[2] celebrated mass, and then pronounced against the enemy the curse with which his author had supplied him, only altering 'Tellus mater teque Juppiter obtestor' into 'Tellus teque Christe Deus obtestor.' After he had done this for three days, the enemy retreated. On the one side, these things strike us an affair of mere style and fashion; on the other, as a symptom of religious decadence.

[1] Della Valle, *Lettere Sanesi*, iii. 18.

[2] Macrob. *Saturnal.* iii. 9. Doubtless the canon did not omit the gestures there prescribed. Comp. Gregorovius, viii. 294, for Bembo. For the paganism thus prevalent in Rome, see also Ranke, *Päpste*, i. 73 sqq. Comp. also Gregorovius, viii. 268.

CHAPTER IV.

MIXTURE OF ANCIENT AND MODERN SUPERSTITION.

But in another way, and that dogmatically, antiquity exercised a perilous influence. It imparted to the Renaissance its own forms of superstition. Some fragments of this had survived in Italy all through the Middle Ages, and the resuscitation of the whole was thereby made so much the more easy. The part played by the imagination in the process need not be dwelt upon. This only could have silenced the critical intellect of the Italians.

The belief in a Divine government of the world was in many minds destroyed by the spectacle of so much injustice and misery. Others, like Dante, surrendered at all events this life to the caprices of chance, and if they nevertheless retained a sturdy faith, it was because they held that the higher destiny of man would be accomplished in the life to come. But when the belief in immortality began to waver, then Fatalism got the upper hand, or sometimes the latter came first and had the former as its consequence.

The gap thus opened was in the first place filled by the astrology of antiquity, or even of the Arabians. From the relations of the planets among themselves and to the signs of the zodiac, future events and the course of whole lives were inferred, and the most weighty decisions were taken in consequence. In many cases the line of action thus adopted at the suggestion of the stars may not have been more immoral than that which would otherwise have been followed. But too often the decision must have been made at the cost of honour and conscience. It is profoundly instructive to observe how powerless culture and enlightenment were against this delusion; since the latter had its support in the ardent imagination of the people, in the passionate wish to penetrate and determine the future. Antiquity, too, was on the side of astrology.

At the beginning of the thirteenth century this superstition suddenly appeared in the foreground of Italian life. The Emperor Frederick II. always travelled with his astrologer Theodorus; and Ezzelino da Romano[1] with a large, well-paid court of such people, among them the famous Guido Bonatto and the long-bearded Saracen, Paul of Bagdad. In all important undertakings they fixed for him the day and the hour, and the gigantic atrocities of which he was guilty may have been in part practical inferences from their prophecies. Soon all scruples about consulting the stars ceased. Not only princes, but free cities[2] had their regular astrologers, and at the universities,[3] from the fourteenth to the sixteenth century, professors of this pseudo-science were appointed, and lectured side by side with the astronomers. It was well known that Augustine and other Fathers of the Church had combated astrology, but their old-fashioned notions were dismissed with easy contempt.[4] The Popes[5] commonly made no secret of their star-gazing, though Pius II., who also despised magic, omens, and the interpretation of dreams, is an honourable ex-

[1] *Monachus Paduan.* l. ii. ap Urstisius, *Scriptt.* i. pp. 598, 599, 602, 607. The last Visconti (p. 37) had also a number of these men in his service (Comp. Decembrio, in Murat. xx. col. 1017): he undertook nothing without their advice. Among them was a Jew named Helias. Gasparino da Barzizzi once addressed him: 'Magna vi astrorum fortuna tuas res reget.' G. B. *Opera*, ed. Furietto, p. 38.

[2] E.g. Florence, where Bonatto filled the office for a long period. See too Matteo Villani, xi. 3, where the city astrologer is evidently meant.

[3] Libri, *Hist. des Sciences Mathém.* ii. 52, 193. At Bologna this professorship is said to have existed in 1125. Comp. the list of professors at Pavia, in Corio, fol. 290. For the professorship at the Sapienza under Leo X., see Roscoe, *Leone X.* ed. Bossi, v. p. 283.

[4] J. A. Campanus lays stress on the value and importance of astrology, and concludes with the words: 'Quamquam Augustinus sanctissimus ille vir quidem ac doctissimus, sed fortassis ad fidem religionemque propensior negat quicquam vel boni vel mali astrorum necessitate contingere.' 'Oratio initio studii Perugiæ habita,' compare *Opera*, Rome, 1495.

[5] About 1260 Pope Alexander IV. compelled a Cardinal (and shamefaced astrologer) Bianco to bring out a number of political prophecies. Giov. Villani, vi. 81.

ception.[1] Julius II., on the other hand, had the day for his coronation and the day for his return from Bologna calculated by the astrologers.[2] Even Leo X. seems to have thought the flourishing condition of astrology a credit to his pontificate,[3] and Paul III. never held a Consistory till the star-gazers had fixed the hour.[4]

It may fairly be assumed that the better natures did not allow their actions to be determined by the stars beyond a certain point, and that there was a limit where conscience and religion made them pause. In fact, not only did pious and excellent people share the delusion, but they actually came forward to profess it publicly. One of these was Maestro Pagolo of Florence,[5] in whom we can detect the same desire to turn astrology to moral account which meets us in the late Roman Firmicus Maternus.[6] His life was that of a saintly ascetic. He ate almost nothing, despised all temporal goods, and only collected books. A skilled physician, he only practised among his friends, and made it a condition of his treatment that they should confess their sins. He frequented the small but famous circle which assembled in the Monastery of the Angeli around Fra Ambrogio Camaldolese (p. 463). He also saw much of Cosimo the Elder, especially in his last years; for Cosimo accepted and used astrology, though probably only for

[1] *De Dictis, &c. Alfonsi, Opera*, p. 493. He held it to be 'pulchrius quam utile.' Platina, *Vitae Pontiff.* p. 310. For Sixtus IV. comp. Jac. Volaterran. in Murat. xxiii. col. 173, 186. He caused the hours for audiences, receptions, and the like, to be fixed by the 'planetarii.' In the *Europa*, c. 49, Pius II. mentions that Baptista Blasius, an astronomer from Cremona, had prophesied the misfortunes of Fr. Foscaro 'tanquam prævidisset.'

[2] Brosch, *Julius II.* (Gotha, 1878), pp. 97 and 323.

[3] P. Valeriano, *De Infel. Lit.* (318–324) speaks of Fr. Friuli, who wrote on Leo's horoscope, and 'abditissima quæque anteactæ ætatis et uni ipsi cognita principi explicuerat quæque incumberent quæque futura essent ad unguem ut eventus postmodum comprobavit, in singulos fere dies prædixerat.'

[4] Ranke, *Päpste*, i. 247.

[5] *Vespas. Fiorent.* p. 660, comp. 341. *Ibid.* p. 121, another Pagolo is mentioned as court mathematician and astrologer of Federigo of Montefeltro. Curiously enough, he was a German.

[6] Firmicus Maternus, *Matheseos Libri* viii. at the end of the second book.

objects of lesser importance. As a rule, however, Pagolo only interpreted the stars to his most confidential friends. But even without this severity of morals, the astrologers might be highly respected and show themselves everywhere. There were also far more of them in Italy than in other European countries, where they only appeared at the great courts, and there not always. All the great householders in Italy, when the fashion was once established, kept an astrologer, who, it must be added, was not always sure of his dinner.[1] Through the literature of this science, which was widely diffused even before the invention of printing, a dilettantism also grew up which as far as possible followed in the steps of the masters. The worst class of astrologers were those who used the stars either as an aid or a cloak to magical arts.

Yet apart from the latter, astrology is a miserable feature in the life of that time. What a figure do all these highly gifted, many-sided, original characters play, when the blind passion for knowing and determining the future dethrones their powerful will and resolution! Now and then, when the stars send them too cruel a message, they manage to brace themselves up, act for themselves, and say boldly: 'Vir sapiens dominabitur astris'—the wise man is master of the stars,[2] and then again relapse into the old delusion.

In all the better families the horoscope of the children was drawn as a matter of course, and it sometimes happened that for half a lifetime men were haunted by the idle expectation of events which never occurred. The stars[3] were questioned

[1] In Bandello, iii. nov. 60, the astrologer of Alessandro Bentivoglio, in Milan, confessed himself a poor devil before the whole company.

[2] It was in such a moment of resolution that Ludovico Moro had the cross with this inscription made, which is now in the Minster at Chur. Sixtus IV. too once said that he would try if the proverb was true. On this saying of the astrologer Ptolemæus, which B. Fazio took to be Virgilian, see Laur. Valla, *Opera*, p. 461.

[3] The father of Piero Capponi, himself an astrologer, put his son into trade lest he should get the dangerous wound in the head which threatened him. *Vita di P. Capponi*, *Arch. Stor.* iv. ii. 15. For an instance in the life of Cardanus, see p. 334. The physician and astrologer Pierleoni of Spoleto believed that he would be drowned, avoided in consequence all watery places, and refused brilliant positions offered him at Venice and Padua. Paul. Jov. *Elog. Liter.* pp. 67 sqq. Finally he threw himself

whenever a great man had to come to any important decision, and even consulted as to the hour at which any undertaking was to be begun. The journeys of princes, the reception of foreign ambassadors,[1] the laying of the foundation-stone of public buildings, depended on the answer. A striking instance of the latter occurs in the life of the aforenamed Guido Bonatto, who by his personal activity and by his great systematic work on the subject[2] deserves to be called the restorer of astrology in the thirteenth century. In order to put an end to the struggle of the Guelphs and Ghibellines at Forli, he persuaded the inhabitants to rebuild the city walls and to begin the works under a constellation indicated by himself. If then two men, one from each party, at the same moment put a stone into the foundation, there would henceforth and for ever be no more party divisions in Forli. A Guelph and a Ghibelline were selected for this office; the solemn moment arrived, each held the stone in his hands, the workmen stood ready with their implements, Bonatto gave the signal and the Ghibelline threw down his stone on to the foundation. But the Guelph hesitated, and at last refused to do anything at all, on the ground that Bonatto himself had the reputation of a Ghibelline

into the water, in despair at the charge brought against him of complicity in Lorenzo's death, and was actually drowned. Hier. Aliottus had been told to be careful in his sixty-second year, as his life would then be in danger. He lived with great circumspection, kept clear of the doctors, and the year passed safely. H. A. *Opuscula* (Arezzo, 1769), ii. 72. Marsilio Ficino, who despised astrology (*Opp.* p. 772) was written to by a friend (*Epist.* lib. 17): 'Praeterea me memini a duobus vestrorum astrologis audivisse, te ex quadam siderum positione antiquas revocaturum philosophorum sententias.'

[1] For instances in the life of Ludovico Moro, see Senarega, in Murat xxiv. col. 518, 524. Benedictus, in Eccard, ii. col. 1623. And yet his father, the great Francesco Sforza, had despised astrology, and his grandfather Giacomo had not at any rate followed its warnings. Corio, fol. 321, 413.

[2] For the facts here quoted, see *Annal. Foroliviens.* in Murat. xxii. col. 233 sqq. (comp. col. 150). Leonbattista Alberti endeavoured to give a spiritual meaning to the ceremony of laying the foundation. *Opere Volgari*, tom. iv. p. 314 (or *De Re Ædific.* l. i.). For Bonatto see Filippo Villani, *Vite* and *Della Vita e delle Opere di Guido Bonati, Astrologo e Astronomo del Secolo Decimoterzo, raccolte da R. Boncompagni*, Rome, 1851. B.'s great work, *De Astronomia*, lib. x. has been often printed.

and might be devising some mysterious mischief against the Guelphs. Upon which the astrologer addressed him: 'God damn thee and the Guelph party, with your distrustful malice! This constellation will not appear above our city for 500 years to come.' In fact God soon afterwards did destroy the Guelphs of Forli, but now, writes the chronicler about 1480, the two parties are thoroughly reconciled, and their very names are heard no longer.[1]

Nothing that depended upon the stars was more important than decisions in time of war. The same Bonatto procured for the great Ghibelline leader Guido da Montefeltro a series of victories, by telling him the propitious hour for marching.[2] When Montefeltro was no longer accompanied by him[3] he lost the courage to maintain his despotism, and entered a Minorite monastery, where he lived as a monk for many years till his death. In the war with Pisa in 1362, the Florentines commissioned their astrologer to fix the hour for the march,[4] and almost came too late through suddenly receiving orders to take a circuitous route through the city. On former occasions they had marched out by the Via di Borgo S. Apostolo, and the campaign had been unsuccessful. It was clear that there was some bad omen connected with the exit through this street against Pisa, and consequently the army was now led out by the Porta Rossa. But as the tents stretched out there to dry

[1] In the horoscopes of the second foundation of Florence (Giov. Villani, iii. 1. under Charles the Great) and of the first of Venice (see above, p. 62), an old tradition is perhaps mingled with the poetry of the Middle Ages.

[2] For one of these victories, see the remarkable passage quoted from Bonatto in Steinschneider, in the *Zeitschr. d. D. Morg. Ges.* xxv. p. 416. On B. comp. *ibid.* xviii. 120 sqq.

[3] *Ann. Foroliv.* 235–238. Filippo Villani, *Vite.* Macchiavelli, *Stor. Fior.* l. i. When constellations which augured victory appeared, Bonatto ascended with his book and astrolabe to the tower of San Mercuriale above the Piazza, and when the right moment came gave the signal for the great bell to be rung. Yet it was admitted that he was often wide of the mark, and foresaw neither his own death nor the fate of Montefeltro. Not far from Cesena he was killed by robbers, on his way back to Forli from Paris and from Italian universities where he had been lecturing. As a weather prophet he was once overmatched and made game of by a countryman.

[4] Matteo Villani, xi. 3; see above, p. 508.

had not been taken away, the flags—another bad omen—had to be lowered. The influence of astrology in war was confirmed by the fact that nearly all the Condottieri believed in it. Jacopo Caldora was cheerful in the most serious illness, knowing that he was fated to fall in battle, which in fact happened.[1] Bartolommeo Alviano was convinced that his wounds in the head were as much a gift of the stars as his military command.[2] Niccolò Orsini Pitigliano asked the physicist and astrologer Alessandro Benedetto[3] to fix a favourable hour for the conclusion of his bargain with Venice (1495). When the Florentines on June 1, 1498, solemnly invested their new Condottiere Paolo Vitelli with his office, the Marshal's staff which they handed him was, at his own wish, decorated with pictures of the constellations.[4] There were nevertheless generals like Alphonso the Great of Naples who did not allow their march to be settled by the prophets.[5]

Sometimes it is not easy to make out whether in important political events the stars were questioned beforehand, or whether the astrologers were simply impelled afterwards by curiosity to find out the constellation which decided the result. When Giangaleazzo Visconti (p. 12) by a master-stroke of policy took prisoners his uncle Bernabò, with the latter's family (1385), we are told by a contemporary, that Jupiter, Saturn, and Mars stood in the house of the Twins,[6] but we cannot say if the deed was resolved on in consequence. It is also probable that the advice of the astrologers was often determined by political calculation not less than by the course of the planets.[7]

[1] Jovian. Pontan. *De Fortitudine*, l. i. See p. 511 note 1, for the honourable exception made by the first Sforza.

[2] Paul. Jov. *Elog.* sub v. Livianus, p. 219.

[3] Who tells it us himself. Benedictus, in Eccard, ii. col. 1617.

[4] In this sense we must understand the words of Jac. Nardi, *Vita d' Ant. Giacomini*, p. 65. The same pictures were common on clothes and household utensils. At the reception of Lucrezia Borgia in Ferrara, the mule of the Duchess of Urbino wore trappings of black velvet with astrological figures in gold. *Arch. Stor. Append.* ii. p. 305.

[5] Æn. Sylvius, in the passage quoted above p. 508; comp. *Opp.* 481.

[6] Azario, in Corio, fol. 258.

[7] Considerations of this kind probably influenced the Turkish astrologers who, after the battle of Nicopolis, advised the Sultan Bajazet I. to consent to the ransom of John of Burgundy, since 'for his sake much

All Europe, through the latter part of the Middle Ages, had allowed itself to be terrified by predictions of plagues, wars, floods, and earthquakes, and in this respect Italy was by no means behind other countries. The unlucky year 1494, which for ever opened the gates of Italy to the stranger, was undeniably ushered in by many prophecies of misfortune[1]—only we cannot say whether such prophecies were not ready for each and every year.

This mode of thought was extended with thorough consistency into regions where we should hardly expect to meet with it. If the whole outward and spiritual life of the individual is determined by the facts of his birth, the same law also governs groups of individuals and historical products—that is to say, nations and religions; and as the constellation of these things changes, so do the things themselves. The idea that each religion has its day, first came into Italian culture in connexion with these astrological beliefs, chiefly from Jewish and Arabian sources.[2] The conjunction of Jupiter with Saturn brought forth, we are told,[3] the faith of Israel; that of Jupiter and Mars, the Chaldean; with the Sun, the Egyptian; with Venus, the Mohammedan; with Mercury, the Christian; and the conjunction of Jupiter with the Moon will one day bring forth the religion of Antichrist. Checco d' Ascoli had already blasphemously calculated the nativity of Christ, and deduced from it his death upon the cross. For this he was burnt at the stake in 1327, at Florence.[4] Doctrines of this sort ended by simply darkening men's whole perceptions of spiritual things.

So much more worthy then of recognition is the warfare

Christian blood would be shed.' It was not difficult to foresee the further course of the French civil war. *Magn. Chron. Belgicum*, p. 358. *Juvénal des Ursins*, ad. a. 1396.

[1] Benedictus, in Eccard, ii. col. 1579. It was said of King Ferrante in 1493 that he would lose his throne 'sine cruore sed sola fama'—which actually happened.

[2] Comp. Steinschneider, *Apokalypsen mit polemischer Tendenz*, D. M. G. Z. xxviii. 627 sqq. xxix. 261.

[3] Bapt. Mantuan. *De Patientia*, l. iii. cap. 12.

[4] Giov. Villani, x. 39, 40. Other reasons also existed, e.g. the jealousy of his colleagues. Bonatto had taught the same, and had explained the miracle of Divine Love in St. Francis as the effect of the planet Mars. Comp. Jo. Picus, *Adv. Astrol.* ii. 5.

which the clear Italian spirit waged against this army of delusions. Notwithstanding the great monumental glorification of astrology, as in the frescos in the Salone at Padua,[1] and those in Borso's summer palace (Schifanoja), at Ferrara, notwithstanding the shameless praises of even such a man as the elder Beroaldus,[2] there was no want of thoughtful and independent minds to protest against it. Here, too, the way had been prepared by antiquity, but it was their own common sense and observation which taught them what to say. Petrarch's attitude towards the astrologers, whom he knew by personal intercourse, is one of bitter contempt; [3] and no one saw through their system of lies more clearly than he. The novels, from the time when they first began to appear—from the time of the 'Cento novelle antiche,' are almost always hostile to the astrologers.[4] The Florentine chroniclers bravely keep themselves free from the delusions which, as part of historical tradition, they are compelled to record. Giovanni Villani says more than once,[5] 'No constellation can subjugate either the free will of man, or the counsels of God.' Matteo Villani [6] declares astrology to be a vice which the Florentines had inherited, along with other superstitions, from their pagan ancestors, the Romans. The question, however, did not remain one for mere literary discussion, but the parties for and against disputed publicly. After the terrible floods of 1333, and again in 1345, astrologers and theologians discussed with great minuteness the influence of the stars, the will of God, and the

[1] They were painted by Miretto at the beginning of the fifteenth century. Acc. to Scardeonius they were destined 'ad indicandum nascentium naturas per gradus et numeros'—a more popular way of teaching than we can now well imagine. It was astrology 'à la portée de tout le monde.'

[2] He says (*Orationes*, fol. 35, 'In Nuptias') of astrology: 'haec efficit ut homines parum a Diis distare videantur'! Another enthusiast of the same time is Jo. Garzonius, *De Dignitate Urbis Bononiae*, in Murat. xxi. col. 1163.

[3] Petrarca, *Epp. Seniles*, iii. 1 (p. 765) and elsewhere. The letter in question was written to Boccaccio. On Petrarch's polemic against the astrologers, see Geiger. *Petr.* 87–91 and 267, note 11.

[4] Franco Sacchetti (nov. 151) ridicules their claims to wisdom.

[5] Gio. Villani, iii. x. 39. Elsewhere he appears as a devout believer in astrology, x. 120, xii. 40.

[6] In the passage xi. 3.

justice of his punishments.[1] These struggles never ceased throughout the whole time of the Renaissance,[2] and we may conclude that the protestors were in earnest, since it was easier for them to recommend themselves to the great by defending, than by opposing astrology.

In the circle of Lorenzo the Magnificent, among his most distinguished Platonists, opinions were divided on this question. That Marsilio Ficino defended astrology, and drew the horoscope of the children of the house, promising the little Giovanni, afterwards Leo X., that he would one day be Pope,[3] as Giovio would have us believe, is an invention—but other academicians accepted astrology. Pico della Mirandola,[4] on the other hand, made an epoch in the subject by his famous refutation. He detects in this belief the root of all impiety and immorality. If the astrologer, he maintains, believes in anything at all, he must worship not God, but the planets, from which all good and evil are derived. All other superstitions find a ready instrument in astrology, which serves as handmaid to geomancy, chiromancy, and magic of every kind. As to morality, he maintains that nothing can more foster evil than the opinion that heaven itself is the cause of it, in which case the faith in eternal happiness and punishment must also disappear. Pico even took the trouble to check off the astrologers inductively, and found that in the course of a month three-fourths of their weather prophecies turned out false. But his main achievement was to set forth, in the Fourth Book—a positive Christian doctrine of the freedom of the will and the government of the universe, which seems to have made a greater impression on the educated classes throughout Italy than all the revivalist preachers put together. The latter, in fact, often failed to reach these classes.

[1] Gio. Villani, xi. 2, xii. 58.

[2] The author of the *Annales Placentini* (in Murat. xx. col. 931), the same Alberto di Ripalta mentioned at p. 241, took part in this controversy. The passage is in other respects remarkable, since it contains the popular opinion with regard to the nine known comets, their colour, origin, and significance. Comp. Gio. Villani, xi. 67. He speaks of a comet as the herald of great and generally disastrous events.

[3] Paul. Jov. *Vita Leonis* xx. l. iii. where it appears that Leo himself was a believer at least in premonitions and the like, see above p. 509.

[4] Jo. Picus Mirand. *Adversus Astrologos*, libri xii.

The first result of his book was that the astrologers ceased to publish their doctrines,[1] and those who had already printed them were more or less ashamed of what they had done. Gioviano Pontano, for example, in his book on Fate (p. 503), had recognised the science, and in a great work of his own,[2] the several parts of which were dedicated to his highly-placed friends and fellow-believers, Aldo Manucci, P. Bembo, and Sandazaro, had expounded the whole theory of it in the style of the old Firmicus, ascribing to the stars the growth of every bodily and spiritual quality. He now in his dialogue 'Ægidius,' surrendered, if not astrology, at least certain astrologers, and sounded the praises of free will, by which man is enabled to know God.[3] Astrology remained more or less in fashion, but seems not to have governed human life in the way it formerly had done. The art of painting, which in the fifteenth century had done its best to foster the delusion, now expressed the altered tone of thought. Raphael, in the cupola of the Cappella Chigi,[4] represents the gods of the different planets and the starry firmament, watched, however, and guided by beautiful angel-figures, and receiving from above the blessing of the Eternal Father. There was also another cause which now began to tell against astrology in Italy. The Spaniards took no interest in it, not even the generals, and those who wished to gain their favour[5] declared open war

[1] Acc. to Paul, Jov. *Elog. Lit.* sub tit. Jo. Picus, the result he achieved was 'ut subtilium disciplinarum professores a scribendo deterruisse videatur.'

[2] *De Rebus Caelestibus*, libri xiv. (*Opp.* iii. 1963–2591). In the twelfth book, dedicated to Paolo Cortese, he will not admit the latter's refutation of astrology. Ægidius, *Opp.* ii. 1455–1514. Pontano had dedicated his little work *De Luna* (*Opp.* iii. 2592) to the same hermit Egidio (of Viterbo?)

[3] For the latter passage, see p. 1486. The difference between Pontano and Pico is thus put by Franc. Pudericus, one of the interlocutors in the dialogue (p. 1496): 'Pontanus non ut Johannes Picus in disciplinam ipsam armis equisque, quod dicitur, irrumpit, cum illam tueatur, ut cognitu maxime dignam ac pene divinam, sed astrologos quosdam, ut parum cautos minimeque prudentes insectetur et rideat.'

[4] In S. Maria del Popolo at Rome. The angels remind us of Dante's theory at the beginning of the *Convito.*

[5] This was the case with Antonio Galateo who, in a letter to Ferdinand the Catholic (Mai, *Spicileg. Rom.* vol. viii. p. 226, ad a. 1510), disclaims astrology with violence, and in another letter to the Count of Potenza

against the half-heretical, half-Mohammedan science. It is true that Guicciardini[1] writes in the year 1529: 'How happy are the astrologers, who are believed if they tell one truth to a hundred lies, while other people lose all credit if they tell one lie to a hundred truths.' But the contempt for astrology did not necessarily lead to a return to the belief in Providence. It could as easily lead to an indefinite Fatalism.

In this respect, as in others, Italy was unable to make its own way healthily through the ferment of the Renaissance, because the foreign invasion and the Counter-Reformation came upon it in the middle. Without such interfering causes its own strength would have enabled it thoroughly to get rid of these fantastic illusions. Those who hold that the onslaught of the strangers and the Catholic reactions were necessities for which the Italian people was itself solely responsible, will look on the spiritual bankruptcy which they produced as a just retribution. But it is a pity that the rest of Europe had indirectly to pay so large a part of the penalty.

The beliefs in omens seems a much more innocent matter than astrology. The Middle Ages had everywhere inherited them in abundance from the various pagan religions; and Italy did not differ in this respect from other countries. What is characteristic of Italy is the support lent by humanism to the popular superstition. The pagan inheritance was here backed up by a pagan literary development.

The popular superstition of the Italians rested largely on premonitions and inferences drawn from ominous occurrences,[2] with which a good deal of magic, mostly of an innocent sort, was connected. There was, however, no lack of learned humanists who boldly ridiculed these delusions, and to whose attacks we partly owe the knowledge of them. Gioviano Pontano, the author of the great astrological work already

(*ibid.* p. 539) infers from the stars that the Turks would attack Rhodes the same year.

[1] *Ricordi*, l. c. n. 57.

[2] Many instances of such superstitions in the case of the last Visconti are mentioned by Decembrio (Murat. xx. col. 1016 sqq.). Odaxius says in his speech at the burial of Guidobaldo (*Bembi Opera*, i. 598 sqq.), that the gods had announced his approaching death by thunderbolts, earthquakes, and other signs and wonders.

mentioned (p. 280), enumerates with pity in his 'Charon,' a long string of Neapolitan superstitions—the grief of the women when a fowl or a goose caught the pip; the deep anxiety of the nobility if a hunting falcon did not come home, or if a horse sprained his foot; the magical formulæ of the Apulian peasants, recited on three Saturday evenings, when mad dogs were at large. The animal kingdom, as in antiquity, was regarded as specially significant in this respect, and the behaviour of the lions, leopards, and other beasts kept by the State (p. 293 sqq.) gave the people all the more food for reflection, because they had come to be considered as living symbols of the State. During the siege of Florence, in 1529, an eagle which had been shot at fled into the city, and the Signoria gave the bearer four ducats, because the omen was good.[1] Certain times and places were favourable or unfavourable, or even decisive one way or the other, for certain actions. The Florentines, so Varchi tells us, held Saturday to be the fateful day on which all important events, good as well as bad, commonly happened. Their prejudice against marching out to war through a particular street has been already mentioned (p. 512). At Perugia one of the gates, the 'Porta eburnea,' was thought lucky, and the Baglioni always went out to fight through it.[2] Meteors and the appearance of the heavens were as significant in Italy as elsewhere in the Middle Ages, and the popular imagination saw warring armies in an unusual formation of clouds, and heard the clash of their collision high in the air.[3] The superstition became a more serious matter when it attached itself to sacred things, when figures of the Virgin wept or moved the eyes,[4] or when public calamities were associated with some alleged act of impiety, for which the

[1] Varchi, *Stor. Fior.* l. iv. (p. 174); prophecies and premonitions were then as rife in Florence as at Jerusalem during the siege. Comp. *ibid.* iii. 143, 195; iv. 43, 177.

[2] Matarazzo, *Archiv. Stor.* xvi. ii. p. 208.

[3] Prato, *Arch. Stor.* iii. 324, for the year 1514.

[4] For the Madonna dell' Arbore in the Cathedral at Milan, and what she did in 1515, see Prato, l. c. p. 327. He also records the discovery of a dead dragon as thick as a horse in the excavations for a mortuary chapel near S. Nazaro. The head was taken to the Palace of the Triulzi for whom the chapel was built.

people demanded expiation. In 1478, when Piacenza was visited with a violent and prolonged rainfall, it was said that there would be no dry weather till a certain usurer, who had been lately buried at San Francesco, had ceased to rest in consecrated earth. As the bishop was not obliging enough to have the corpse dug up, the young fellows of the town took it by force, dragged it round the streets amid frightful confusion, offered it to be insulted and maltreated by former creditors, and at last threw it into the Po.[1] Even Politian accepted this point of view in speaking of Giacomo Pazzi, one of the chief of the conspiracy of 1478, in Florence, which is called after his name. When he was put to death, he devoted his soul to Satan with fearful words. Here, too, rain followed and threatened to ruin the harvest; here, too, a party of men, mostly peasants, dug up the body in the church, and immediately the clouds departed and the sun shone—'so gracious was fortune to the opinion of the people,' adds the great scholar.[2] The corpse was first cast into unhallowed ground, the next day again dug up, and after a horrible procession through the city, thrown into the Arno.

These facts and the like bear a popular character, and might have occurred in the tenth, just as well as in the sixteenth century. But now comes the literary influence of antiquity. We know positively that the humanists were peculiarly accessible to prodigies and auguries, and instances of this have been already quoted. If further evidence were needed, it would be found in Poggio. The same radical thinker who denied the rights of noble birth and the inequality of men (p. 361 sqq.), not only believed in all the mediæval stories of ghosts and devils (fol. 167, 179), but also in prodigies after the ancient pattern, like those said to have occurred on the last visit of

[1] 'Et fuit mirabile quod illico pluvia cessavit.' *Diar. Parmense* in Murat. xxii. col. 280. The author shares the popular hatred of the usurers. Comp. col. 371.

[2] *Conjurationis Pactianae Commentarius*, in the appendices to Roscoe's *Lorenzo.* Politian was in general an opponent of astrology. The saints were naturally able to cause the rain to cease. Comp. Æneas Sylvius, in his life of Bernadino da Siena (*De Vir. Ill.* p. 25): 'jussit in virtute Jesu nubem abire, quo facto solutis absque pluvia nubibus, prior serenitas rediit'

Eugenius IV. to Florence.[1] 'Near Como there was seen one evening 4,000 dogs, who took the road to Germany; these were followed by a great herd of cattle, and these by an army on foot and horseback, some with no heads and some with almost invisible heads, and then a gigantic horseman with another herd of cattle behind him.' Poggio also believes in a battle of magpies and jackdaws (fol. 180). He even relates, perhaps without being aware of it, a well-preserved piece of ancient mythology. On the Dalmatian coast a Triton had appeared, bearded and horned, a genuine sea-satyr, ending in fins and a tail; he carried away women and children from the shore, till five stout-hearted washer-women killed him with sticks and stones.[2] A wooden model of the monster, which was exhibited at Ferrara, makes the whole story credible to Poggio. Though there were no more oracles, and it was no longer possible to take counsel of the gods, yet it became again the fashion to open Virgil at hazard, and take the passage hit upon as an omen[3] ('Sortes Virgilianae'). Nor can the belief in dæmons current in the later period of antiquity have been without influence on the Renaissance. The work of Jamblichus or Abammon on the Mysteries of the Egyptians, which may have contributed to this result, was printed in a Latin translation at the end of the fifteenth century. The Platonic Academy at Florence was not free from these and other neoplatonic dreams of the Roman decadence. A few words must here be given to the belief in dæmons and to the magic which was connected with this belief.

The popular faith in what is called the spirit-world was

[1] *Poggi Facetiae*, fol. 174. Æn. Sylvius (*De Europa*, c. 53, 54, *Opera*, pp. 451, 455) mentions prodigies which may have really happened, such as combats between animals and strange appearances in the sky, and mentions them chiefly as curiosities, even when adding the results attributed to them. Similarly Antonio Ferrari (il Galateo), *De Situ Iapygiae*, p. 121, with the explanation: 'Et hae, ut puto, species erant earum rerum quæ longe aberant atque ab eo loco in quo species visae sunt minime poterant.'

[2] *Poggi Facetiae*, fol. 160. Comp. Pausanias, ix. 20.

[3] Varchi, iii 195. Two suspected persons decided on flight in 1529, because they opened the Æneid at book iii. 44. Comp. Rabelais, *Pantagruel*, iii. 10.

nearly the same in Italy as elsewhere in Europe.[1] In Italy as elsewhere there were ghosts, that is, reappearances of deceased persons; and if the view taken of them differed in any respect from that which prevailed in the North, the difference betrayed itself only in the ancient name 'ombra.' Nowadays if such a shade presents itself, a couple of masses are said for its repose. That the spirits of bad men appear in a dreadful shape, is a matter of course, but along with this we find the notion that the ghosts of the departed are universally malicious. The dead, says the priest in Bandello,[2] kill the little children. It seems as if a certain shade was here thought of as separate from the soul, since the latter suffers in Purgatory, and when it appears, does nothing but wail and pray. To lay the ghost, the tomb was opened, the corpse pulled to pieces, the heart burned and the ashes scattered to the four winds.[3] At other times what appears is not the ghost of a man, but of an event —of a past condition of things. So the neighbours explained the diabolical appearances in the old palace of the Visconti near San Giovanni in Conca, at Milan, since here it was that Bernabò Visconti had caused countless victims of his tyranny to be tortured and strangled, and no wonder if there were strange things to be seen.[4] One evening a swarm of poor people with candles in their hands appeared to a dishonest guardian of the poor at Perugia, and danced round about him; a great figure spoke in threatening tones on their behalf—it

[1] The imaginations of the scholars, such as the 'splendor' and the 'spiritus' of Cardanus, and the 'dæmon familiaris' of his father, may be taken for what they are worth. Comp. Cardanus, *De Propria Vita*, cap. 4, 38, 47. He was himself an opponent of magic; cap. 39. For the prodigies and ghosts he met with, see cap. 37, 41. For the terror of ghosts felt by the last Visconti, see Decembrio, in Murat. xx. col. 1016.

[2] 'Molte fiate i morti guastano le creature.' Bandello, ii. nov. 1. We read (Galateo, p. 177) that the 'animæ' of wicked men rise from the grave, appear to their friends and acquaintances, 'animalibus vexi, pueros sugere ac necare, deinde in sepulcra reverti.'

[3] Galateo, l. c. We also read (p. 119) of the 'Fata Morgana' and other similar appearances.

[4] Bandello, iii. nov. 20. It is true that the ghost was only a lover wishing to frighten the occupier of the palace, who was also the husband of the beloved lady. The lover and his accomplices dressed themselves up as devils; one of them, who could imitate the cry of different animals, had been sent for from a distance.

was St. Alò, the patron saint of the poor-house.[1] These modes of belief were so much a matter of course that the poets could make use of them as something which every reader would understand. The appearance of the slain Ludovico Pico under the walls of the besieged Mirandola is finely represented by Castiglione.[2] It is true that poetry made the freest use of these conceptions when the poet himself had outgrown them.

Italy, too, shared the belief in dæmons with the other nations of the Middle Ages. Men were convinced that God sometimes allowed bad spirits of every class to exercise a destructive influence on parts of the world and of human life. The only reservation made was that the man to whom the Evil One came as tempter, could use his free will to resist.[3] In Italy the dæmonic influence, especially as shown in natural events, easily assumed a character of poetical greatness. In the night before the great inundation of the Val d'Arno in 1333, a pious hermit above Vallombrosa heard a diabolical tumult in his cell, crossed himself, stepped to the door, and saw a crowd of black and terrible knights gallop by in armour. When conjured to stand, one of them said: 'We go to drown the city of Florence on account of its sins, if God will let us.'[4]

[1] Graziani, *Arch. Stor.* xvi. i. p. 640, ad a. 1467. The guardian died of fright.

[2] *Balth. Castilionii Carmina;* Prosopopeja Lud. Pici.

[3] Alexandri ab Alexandro, *Dierum Genialium*, libri vi. (Colon. 1539), is an authority of the first rank for these subjects, the more so as the author, a friend of Pontanus and a member of his academy, asserts that what he records either happened to himself, or was communicated to him by thoroughly trustworthy witnesses. Lib. vi. cap. 19: two evil men and a monk are attacked by devils, whom they recognise by the shape of their feet, and put to flight, partly by force and partly by the sign of the cross. Lib. vi. cap. 21: A servant, cast into prison by a cruel prince on account of a small offence, calls upon the devil, is miraculously brought out of the prison and back again, visits meanwhile the nether world, shows the prince his hand scorched by the flames of Hell, tells him on behalf of a departed spirit certain secrets which had been communicated to the latter, exhorts him to lay aside his cruelty, and dies soon after from the effects of the fright. Lib. ii. c. 19, iii. 15, v. 23: Ghosts of departed friends, of St. Cataldus, and of unknown beings in Rome, Arezzo and Naples. Lib. ii. 22, iii. 8: Appearances of mermen and mermaids at Naples, in Spain, and in the Peloponnesus; in the latter case guaranteed by Theodore Gaza and George of Trebizond.

[4] Gio. Villani, xi. 2. He had it from the Abbot of Vallombrosa, to whom the hermit had communicated it.

With this, the nearly contemporary vision at Venice (1340) may be compared, out of which a great master of the Venetian school, probably Giorgione, made the marvellous picture of a galley full of dæmons, which speeds with the swiftness of a bird over the stormy lagune to destroy the sinful island-city, till the three saints, who have stepped unobserved into a poor boatman's skiff, exorcised the fiends and sent them and their vessel to the bottom of the waters.[1]

To this belief the illusion was now added that by means of magical arts it was possible to enter into relations with the evil ones, and use their help to further the purposes of greed, ambition, and sensuality. Many persons were probably accused of doing so before the time when it was actually attempted by many; but when the so-called magicians and witches began to be burned, the deliberate practice of the black art became more frequent. With the smoke of the fires in which the suspected victims were sacrificed, were spread the narcotic fumes by which numbers of ruined characters were drugged into magic; and with them many calculating impostors became associated.

The primitive and popular form in which the superstition had probably lived on uninterruptedly from the time of the Romans,[2] was the art of the witch (Strega). The witch, so long as she limited herself to mere divination,[3] might be

[1] Another view of the Dæmons was given by Gemisthos Pletho, whose great philosophical work οἱ νόμοι, of which only fragments are now left (ed. Alexander, Paris, 1858), was probably known more fully to the Italians of the fifteenth century, either by means of copies or of tradition, and exercised undoubtedly a great influence on the philosophical, political, and religious culture of the time. According to him the dæmons, who belong to the third order of the gods, are preserved from all error, and are capable of following in the steps of the gods who stand above them; they are spirits who bring to men the good things 'which come down from Zeus through the other gods in order; they purify and watch over man, they raise and strengthen his heart.' Comp. Fritz Schultze, *Gesch. der Philosophie der Renaissance*, Jena, 1874.

[2] Yet but little remained of the wonders attributed to her. For probably the last metamorphosis of a man into an ass, in the eleventh century under Leo IX., see Giul. Malmesbur. ii. 171.

[3] This was probably the case with the possessed woman, who in 1513 at Ferrara and elsewhere was consulted by distinguished Lombards as to future events. Her name was Rodogine. See Rabelais, *Pantagruel*, iv. 58.

innocent enough, were it not that the transition from prophecy to active help could easily, though often imperceptibly, be a fatal downward step. She was credited in such a case not only with the power of exciting love or hatred between man and woman, but also with purely destructive and malignant arts, and was especially charged with the sickness of little children, even when the malady obviously came from the neglect and stupidity of the parents. It is still questionable how far she was supposed to act by mere magical ceremonies and formulæ, or by a conscious alliance with the fiends, apart from the poisons and drugs which she administered with a full knowledge of their effect.

The more innocent form of the superstition, in which the mendicant friar could venture to appear as the competitor of the witch, is shown in the case of the witch of Gaeta whom we read of in Pontano.[1] His traveller Suppatius reaches her dwelling while she is giving audience to a girl and a servant-maid, who come to her with a black hen, nine eggs laid on a Friday, a duck, and some white thread—for it is the third day since the new moon. They are then sent away, and bidden to come again at twilight. It is to be hoped that nothing worse than divination is intended. The mistress of the servant-maid is pregnant by a monk; the girl's lover has proved untrue and has gone into a monastery. The witch complains: 'Since my husband's death I support myself in this way, and should make a good thing of it, since the Gaetan women have plenty of faith, were it not that the monks baulk me of my gains by explaining dreams, appeasing the anger of the saints for money, promising husbands to the girls, men-children to the pregnant women, offspring to the barren, and besides all this visiting the women at night when their husbands are away fishing, in accordance with the assignations made in day-time at church.' Suppatius warns her against the envy of the monastery, but she has no fear, since the guardian of it is an old acquaintance of hers.[2]

[1] Jovian. Pontan. Antonius.

[2] How widespread the belief in witches then was, is shown by the fact that in 1483 Politian gave a 'praelectio' 'in priora Aristotelis Analytica cui titulus Lamia' (Italian trans. by Isidore del Lungo, Flor. 1864) Comp. Reumont, *Lorenzo*, ii. 75–77. Fiesole, according to this, was, in a certain sense, a witches' nest.

But the superstition further gave rise to a worse sort of witches, namely those who deprived men of their health and life. In these cases the mischief, when not sufficiently accounted for by the evil eye and the like, was naturally attributed to the aid of powerful spirits. The punishment, as we have seen in the case of Finicella (p. 469), was the stake; and yet a compromise with fanaticism was sometimes practicable. According to the laws of Perugia, for example, a witch could settle the affair by paying down 400 pounds.[1] The matter was not then treated with the seriousness and consistency of later times. In the territories of the Church, at Norcia (Nursia), the home of St. Benedict, in the upper Apennines, there was a perfect nest of witches and sorcerers, and no secret was made of it. It is spoken of in one of the most remarkable letters of Æneas Sylvius,[2] belonging to his earlier period. He writes to his brother: 'The bearer of this came to me to ask if I knew of a Mount of Venus in Italy, for in such a place magical arts were taught, and his master, a Saxon and a great astronomer,[3] was anxious to learn them. I told him that I knew of a Porto Venere not far from Carrara, on the rocky coast of Liguria, where I spent three nights on the way to Basel; I also found that there was a mountain called Eryx in Sicily, which was dedicated to Venus, but I did not know whether magic was taught there. But it came into my mind while talking that in Umbria, in the old Duchy (Spoleto), near the town of Nursia, there is a cave beneath a steep rock, in which water flows. There, as I remember to have heard, are witches (striges), dæmons, and nightly shades, and he that has the courage can see and speak to ghosts (spiritus), and learn magical arts.[4] I have not seen it, nor taken any trouble

[1] Graziani, *Arch. Stor.* xvi. i. p. 565, ad a. 1445, speaking of a witch at Nocera, who only offered half the sum, and was accordingly burnt. The law was aimed at such persons as 'facciono le fature overo venefitie overo encantatione d' ommunde spirite a nuocere,' l. c. note 1, 2.

[2] Lib. i. ep. 46, *Opera*, p. 531 sqq. For 'umbra' p. 552 read 'Umbria,' and for 'lacum' read 'locum.'

[3] He calls him later on: 'Medicus Ducis Saxoniæ, homo tum dives tum potens.'

[4] In the fourteenth century there existed a kind of hell-gate near Ansedonia in Tuscany. It was a cave, with footprints of men and animals in

about it, for that which is learned with sin is better not learned at all.' He nevertheless names his informant, and begs his brother to take the bearer of the letter to him, should he be still alive. Æneas goes far enough here in his politeness to a man of position, but personally he was not only freer from superstition than his contemporaries (pp. 481, 508), but he also stood a test on the subject which not every educated man of our own day could endure. At the time of the Council of Basel, when he lay sick of the fever for seventy-five days at Milan, he could never be persuaded to listen to the magic doctors, though a man was brought to his bedside who a short time before had marvellously cured 2,000 soldiers of fever in the camp of Piccinino. While still an invalid, Æneas rode over the mountains to Basel, and got well on the journey.[1]

We learn something more about the neighbourhood of Norcia through the necromancer who tried to get Benvenuto Cellini into his power. A new book of magic was to be consecrated,[2] and the best place for the ceremony was among the mountains in that district. The master of the magician had once, it is true, done the same thing near the Abbey of Farfa, but had there found difficulties which did not present themselves at Norcia; further, the peasants in the latter neighbourhood were trustworthy people who had practice in the matter, and who could afford considerable help in case of need. The expedition did not take place, else Benvenuto would probably have been able to tell us something of the impostor's assistants. The whole neighbourhood was then proverbial. Aretino says somewhere of an enchanted well, 'there dwell the sisters of the sibyl of Norcia and the aunt of the Fata Morgana.' And about the same time Trissino could still celebrate the place in his great epic[3] with all the

the sand, which whenever they were effaced, reappeared the next day. Uberti. *Il Dittamondo*, l. iii. cap. 9.

[1] *Pii II. Comment.* l. i. p. 10.

[2] Benv. Cellini, l. i. cap. 65.

[3] *L' Italia Liberata da' Goti*, canto xiv. It may be questioned whether Trissino himself believed in the possibility of his description, or whether he was not rather romancing. The same doubt is permissible in the case of his probable model, Lucan (book vi.), who represents the Thessalian witch conjuring up a corpse before Sextus Pompejus.

resources of poetry and allegory as the home of authentic prophecy.

After the famous Bull of Innocent VIII. (1484),[1] witchcraft and the persecution of witches grew into a great and revolting system. The chief representatives of this system of persecution were German Dominicans; and Germany and, curiously enough, those parts of Italy nearest Germany were the countries most afflicted by this plague. The bulls and injunctions of the Popes themselves[2] refer, for example, to the Dominican Province of Lombardy, to Cremona, to the dioceses of Brescia and Bergamo. We learn from Sprenger's famous theoretico-practical guide, the 'Malleus Maleficarum,' that forty-one witches were burnt at Como in the first year after the publication of the bull; crowds of Italian women took refuge in the territory of the Archduke Sigismund, where they believed themselves to be still safe. Witchcraft ended by taking firm root in a few unlucky Alpine valleys, especially in the Val Camonica;[3] the system of persecution had succeeded in permanently infecting with the delusion those populations which were in any way predisposed for it. This essentially German form of witchcraft is what we should think of when reading the stories and novels of Milan or Bologna.[4]

[1] *Septimo Decretal*, lib. v. tit. xii. It begins: 'Summis desiderantes affectibus' &c. I may here remark that a full consideration of the subject has convinced me that there are in this case no grounds for believing in a survival of pagan beliefs. To satisfy ourselves that the imagination of the mendicant friars is solely responsible for this delusion, we have only to study, in the Memoirs of Jacques du Clerc, the so-called trial of the Waldenses of Arras in the year 1459. A century's prosecutions and persecutions brought the popular imagination into such a state that witchcraft was accepted as a matter of course and reproduced itself naturally.

[2] Of Alexander VI., Leo X., Hadrian VI.

[3] Proverbial as the country of witches, e.g. *Orlandino*. i. 12.

[4] E.g. Bandello, iii. nov. 29, 52. Prato, *Arch. Stor.* iii. 409. Bursellis, *Ann. Bon.* in Murat. xxiii. col. 897, mentions the condemnation of a prior in 1468, who kept a ghostly brothel: 'cives Bononienses coire faciebat cum dæmonibus in specie puellarum.' He offered sacrifices to the dæmons. See for a parallel case, Procop. *Hist. Arcana*, c. 12, where a real brothel is frequented by a dæmon, who turns the other visitors out of doors. The Galateo (p. 116) confirms the existence of the belief in witches: 'volare per longinquas regiones, choreas per paludes dicere et dæmonibus cnogredi, ingredi et egredi per clausa ostia et foramina.'

That it did not make further progress in Italy is probably due to the fact that elsewhere a highly developed 'Stregheria' was already in existence, resting on a different set of ideas. The Italian witch practised a trade, and needed for it money and, above all, sense. We find nothing about her of the hysterical dreams of the Northern witch, of marvellous journeys through the air, of Incubus and Succubus; the business of the 'Strega' was to provide for other people's pleasure. If she was credited with the power of assuming different shapes, or of transporting herself suddenly to distant places, she was so far content to accept this reputation, as her influence was thereby increased; on the other hand, it was perilous for her when the fear of her malice and vengeance, and especially of her power for enchanting children, cattle, and crops, became general. Inquisitors and magistrates were then thoroughly in accord with popular wishes if they burnt her.

By far the most important field for the activity of the 'Strega' lay, as has been said, in love-affairs, and included the stirring up of love and of hatred, the producing of abortion, the pretended murder of the unfaithful man or woman by magical arts, and even the manufacture of poisons.[1] Owing to the unwillingness of many persons to have to do with these women, a class of occasional practitioners arose who secretly learned from them some one or other of their arts, and then used this knowledge on their own account. The Roman prostitutes, for example, tried to enhance their personal attractions by charms of another description in the style of Horatian Canidia. Aretino[2] may not only have known, but have also told the truth about them in this particular. He gives a list of the loathsome messes which were to be found in their boxes

[1] For the loathsome apparatus of the witches' kitchens, see *Maccaroneide*, Phant. xvi. xxi., where the whole procedure is described.

[2] In the *Ragionamento del Zoppino*. He is of opinion that the courtesans learn their arts from certain Jewish women, who are in possession of 'malie.' The following passage is very remarkable. Bembo says in the life of Guidobaldo (*Opera*, i. 614): Guid. constat sive corporis et naturae vitio, seu quod vulgo creditum est, actibus magicis ab Octaviano patruo propter regni cupiditatem impeditum, quarum omnino ille artium expeditissimus habebatur, nulla cum femina coire unquam in tota vita potuisse, nec unquam fuisse ad rem uxoriam idoneum.'

—hair, skulls, ribs, teeth, dead men's eyes, human skin, the navels of little children, the soles of shoes and pieces of clothing from tombs. They even went themselves to the graveyard and fetched bits of rotten flesh, which they slily gave their lovers to eat—with more that is still worse. Pieces of the hair and nails of the lover were boiled in oil stolen from the ever-burning lamps in the church. The most innocuous of their charms was to make a heart of glowing ashes, and then to pierce it while singing—

> Prima che 'l fuoco spenghi,
> Fa ch' a mia porta venghi;
> Tal ti punga mio amore
> Quale io fo questo cuore.

There were other charms practised by moonshine, with drawings on the ground, and figures of wax or bronze, which doubtless represented the lover, and were treated according to circumstances.

These things were so customary that a woman who, without youth and beauty, nevertheless exercised a powerful charm on men, naturally became suspected of witchcraft. The mother of Sanga,[1] secretary to Clement VII., poisoned her son's mistress, who was a woman of this kind. Unfortunately the son died too, as well as a party of friends who had eaten of the poisoned salad.

Next come, not as helper, but as competitor to the witch, the magician or enchanter—'incantatore'—who was still more familiar with the most perilous business of the craft. Sometimes he was as much or more of an astrologer than of a magician; he probably often gave himself out as an astrologer in order not to be prosecuted as a magician, and a certain astrology was essential in order to find out the favourable hour for a magical process.[2] But since many spirits are good[3] or indifferent, the magician could sometimes maintain a very tolerable reputation, and Sixtus IV. in the year 1474, had

[1] Varchi, *Stor. Fior.* ii. p. 153.

[2] Curious information is given by Landi, in the *Commentario*, fol. 36 *a* and 37 *a*, about two magicians, a Sicilian and a Jew; we read of magical mirrors, of a death's-head speaking, and of birds stopped short in their flight.

[3] Stress is laid on this reservation. Corn. Agrippa, *De Occulta Philosophia*, cap. 39.

to proceed expressly against some Bolognese Carmelites,[1] who asserted in the pulpit that there was no harm in seeking information from the dæmons. Very many people believed in the possibility of the thing itself; an indirect proof of this lies in the fact that the most pious men believed that by prayer they could obtain visions of good spirits. Savonarola's mind was filled with these things; the Florentine Platonists speak of a mystic union with God; and Marcellus Palingenius (p. 264), gives us to understand clearly enough that he had to do with consecrated spirits.[2] The same writer is convinced of the existence of a whole hierarchy of bad dæmons, who have their seat from the moon downwards, and are ever on the watch to do some mischief to nature and human life.[3] He even tells of his own personal acquaintance with some of them, and as the scope of the present work does not allow of a systematic exposition of the then prevalent belief in spirits, the narrative of Palingenius may be given as one instance out of many.[4]

At S. Silvestro, on Soracte, he had been receiving instruction from a pious hermit on the nothingness of earthly things and the worthlessness of human life; and when the night drew near he set out on his way back to Rome. On the road, in the full light of the moon, he was joined by three men, one of whom called him by name, and asked him whence he came. Palingenius made answer: 'From the wise man on the mountain.' 'O fool,' replied the stranger, 'dost thou in truth believe that anyone on earth is wise? Only higher beings (Divi) have wisdom, and such are we three, although we wear the shapes of men. I am named Saracil, and these two Sathiel and Jana. Our kingdom lies near the moon, where dwell that multitude of intermediate beings who have sway over earth and sea.' Palingenius then asked, not without an inward tremor, what they were going to do at Rome. The answer was: 'One of our comrades, Ammon, is kept in servitude by the magic arts of a youth from Narni, one of the attendants of Cardinal Orsini; for mark it, O men, there is proof of your own immortality

[1] *Septimo Decretal*, l. c.
[2] *Zodiacus Vitae*, xv. 363–549, comp. x. 393 sqq.
[3] *Ibid.* ix. 291 sqq.
[4] *Ibid.* x. 770 sqq.

therein, that you can control one of us; I myself, shut up in crystal, was once forced to serve a German, till a bearded monk set me free. This is the service which we wish to render at Rome to our friend, and we shall also take the opportunity of sending one or two distinguished Romans to the nether world.' At these words a light breeze arose, and Sathiel said: 'Listen, our messenger is coming back from Rome, and this wind announces him.' And then another being appeared, whom they greeted joyfully and then asked about Rome. His utterances are strongly anti-papal: Clement VII. was again allied with the Spaniards and hoped to root out Luther's doctrines, not with arguments, but by the Spanish sword. This is wholly in the interest of the dæmons, whom the impending bloodshed would enable to carry away the souls of thousands into hell. At the close of this conversation, in which Rome with all its guilt is represented as wholly given over to the Evil One, the apparitions vanish, and leave the poet sorrowfully to pursue his way alone.[1]

Those who would form a conception of the extent of the belief in those relations to the dæmons which could be openly avowed in spite of the penalties attaching to witchcraft, may be referred to the much read work of Agrippa of Nettesheim on 'Secret Philosophy.' He seems originally to have written it before he was in Italy,[2] but in the dedication to Trithemius he mentions Italian authorities among others, if only by way of disparagement. In the case of equivocal persons like Agrippa, or of the knaves and fools into whom the majority of the rest may be divided, there is little that is interesting in the system they profess, with its formulæ, fumigations, ointments, and the rest of it.[3] But this system was filled with quotations

[1] The mythical type of the magician among the poets of the time was Malagigi. Speaking of him, Pulci (*Morgante*, canto xxiv. 106 sqq.) gives his theoretical view of the limits of dæmonic and magic influence. It is hard to say how far he was in earnest. Comp. canto xxi.

[2] Polydorus Virgilius was an Italian by birth, but his work *De Prodigiis* treats chiefly of superstition in England, where his life was passed. Speaking of the prescience of the dæmons, he makes a curious reference to the sack of Rome in 1527.

[3] Yet murder is hardly ever the end, and never, perhaps, the means. A monster like Gilles de Retz (about 1440) who sacrificed more than 100 children to the dæmons, has scarcely a distant counterpart in Italy.

from the superstitions of antiquity, the influence of which on the life and the passions of Italians is at times most remarkable and fruitful. We might think that a great mind must be thoroughly ruined, before it surrendered itself to such influences; but the violence of hope and desire led even vigorous and original men of all classes to have recourse to the magician, and the belief that the thing was feasible at all weakened to some extent the faith, even of those who kept at a distance, in the moral order of the world. At the cost of a little money and danger it seemed possible to defy with impunity the universal reason and morality of mankind, and to spare oneself the intermediate steps which otherwise lie between a man and his lawful or unlawful ends.

Let us here glance for a moment at an older and now decaying form of superstition. From the darkest period of the Middle Ages, or even from the days of antiquity, many cities of Italy had kept the remembrance of the connexion of their fate with certain buildings, statues, or other material objects. The ancients had left records of consecrating priests or Telestæ, who were present at the solemn foundation of cities, and magically guaranteed their prosperity by erecting certain monuments or by burying certain objects (Telesmata). Traditions of this sort were more likely than anything else to live on in the form of popular, unwritten legend; but in the course of centuries the priest naturally became transformed into the magician, since the religious side of his function was no longer understood. In some of his Virgilian miracles at Naples,[1] the ancient remembrance of one of these Telestæ is clearly preserved, his name being in course of time supplanted by that of Virgil. The enclosing of the mysterious picture of the city in a vessel is neither more nor less than a genuine, ancient Telesma; and Virgil the founder of Naples is only the officiating priest, who took part in the ceremony, presented in another dress. The popular imagination went on working at these

[1] See the treatise of Roth 'Ueber den Zauberer Virgilius' in Pfeiffer's *Germania*, iv., and Comparetti's *Virgil in the Middle Ages*. That Virgil began to take the place of the older Telestæ may be explained partly by the fact that the frequent visits made to his grave even in the time of the Empire struck the popular imagination.

themes, till Virgil became also responsible for the brazen horse, for the heads at the Nolan gate, for the brazen fly over another gate, and even for the Grotto of Posilippo—all of them things which in one respect or other served to put a magical constraint upon fate, and the first two of which seemed to determine the whole fortune of the city. Mediæval Rome also preserved confused recollections of the same kind. At the church of S. Ambrogio at Milan, there was an ancient marble Hercules; so long, it was said, as this stood in its place, so long would the Empire last. That of the Germans is probably meant, as the coronation of their Emperors at Milan took place in this church.[1] The Florentines[2] were convinced that the temple of Mars, afterwards transformed into the Baptistry, would stand to the end of time, according to the constellation under which it had been built; they had, as Christians, removed from it the marble equestrian statue; but since the destruction of the latter would have brought some great calamity on the city—also according to a constellation—they set it upon a tower by the Arno. When Totila conquered Florence, the statue fell into the river, and was not fished out again till Charles the Great refounded the city. It was then placed on a pillar at the entrance to the Ponte Vecchio, and on this spot Buondelmente was slain in 1215. The origin of the great feud between Guelph and Ghibelline was thus associated with the dreaded idol. During the inundation of 1333 the statue vanished for ever.[3]

But the same Telesma reappears elsewhere. Guido Bonatto, already mentioned, was not satisfied, at the refounding of the walls of Forli, with requiring certain symbolic acts of reconciliation from the two parties (p. 511). By burying a bronze or stone equestrian statue,[4] which he had produced by astro-

[1] Uberti, *Dittamondo*, l. iii. cap. 4.

[2] For what follows, see Gio. Villani, i. 42, 60, ii. 1, iii. 1, v. 38, xi. He himself does not believe such godless superstitions. Comp. Dante, *Inferno*, xiii. 146.

[3] According to a fragment given in Baluz. Miscell. ix. 119, the Perugians had a quarrel in ancient times with the Ravennates, 'et militem marmoreum qui juxta Ravennam se continue volvebat ad solem usurpaverunt et ad eorum civitatem virtuosissime transtulerunt.'

[4] The local belief on the matter is given in *Annal. Forolivens.* Murat. xxii. col. 207, 238; more fully in Fil. Villani, *Vite*, p. 33.

logical or magical arts, he believed that he had defended the city from ruin, and even from capture and plunder. When Cardinal Albornoz (p. 102) was governor of Romagna some sixty years later, the statue was accidentally dug up and then shown to the people, probably by the order of the Cardinal, that it might be known by what means the cruel Montefeltro had defended himself against the Roman Church. And again, half a century later, when an attempt to surprise Forli had failed, men began to talk afresh of the virtue of the statue, which had perhaps been saved and reburied. It was the last time that they could do so; for a year later Forli was really taken. The foundation of buildings all through the fifteenth century was associated not only with astrology (p. 511) but also with magic. The large number of gold and silver medals which Paul II. buried in the foundations of his buildings [1] was noticed, and Platina was by no means displeased to recognise an old pagan Telesma in the fact. Neither Paul nor his biographer were in any way conscious of the mediæval religious significance of such an offering.[2]

But this official magic, which in many cases only rests on hearsay, was comparatively unimportant by the side of the secret arts practised for personal ends.

The form which these most often took in daily life is shown by Ariosto in his comedy of the necromancers.[3] His hero is one of the many Jewish exiles from Spain, although he also gives himself out for a Greek, an Egyptian, and an African, and is constantly changing his name and costume. He pretends that his incantations can darken the day and lighten the darkness, that he can move the earth, make himself invisible, and change men into beasts; but these vaunts are only an advertisement. His true object is to make his account out of unhappy and troubled marriages, and the traces which he leaves behind him in his course are like the slime of a snail,

[1] Platina, *Vitae Pontiff.* p. 320: 'Veteres potius hac in re quam Petrum, Anacletum, et Linum imitatus.'

[2] Which it is easy to recognise e.g. in Sugerius, *De Consecratione Ecclesiae* (Duchesne, *Scriptores*, iv. 355) and in *Chron. Petershusanum*, i. 13 and 16.

[3] Comp. the *Calandra* of Bibiena.

or often like the ruin wrought by a hail-storm. To attain his ends he can persuade people that the box in which a lover is hidden is full of ghosts, or that he can make a corpse talk. It is at all events a good sign that poets and novelists could reckon on popular applause in holding up this class of men to ridicule. Bandello not only treats the sorcery of a Lombard monk as a miserable, and in its consequences terrible, piece of knavery,[1] but he also describes with unaffected indignation[2] the disasters which never cease to pursue the credulous fool. 'A man hopes with "Solomon's Key" and other magical books to find the treasures hidden in the bosom of the earth, to force his lady to do his will, to find out the secrets of princes, and to transport himself in the twinkling of an eye from Milan to Rome. The more often he is deceived, the more steadfastly he believes . . . . Do you remember the time, Signor Carlo, when a friend of ours, in order to win the favour of his beloved, filled his room with skulls and bones like a churchyard?' The most loathsome tasks were prescribed—to draw three teeth from a corpse or a nail from its finger, and the like; and while the hocus-pocus of the incantation was going on, the unhappy participants sometimes died of terror.

Benvenuto Cellini did not die during the well-known incantation (1532) in the Coliseum at Rome,[3] although both he and his companions witnessed no ordinary horrors; the Sicilian priest, who probably expected to find him a useful coadjutor in the future, paid him the compliment as they went home of saying that he had never met a man of so sturdy a courage. Every reader will make his own reflections on the proceedings themselves. The narcotic fumes and the fact that the imaginations of the spectators were predisposed for all possible terrors, are the chief points to be noticed, and explain why the lad who formed one of the party, and on whom they made most

[1] Bandello, iii. nov. 52. Fr. Filelfo (*Epist. Venet.* lib. 34, fol. 240 sqq.) attacks nercromancy fiercely. He is tolerably free from superstition (*Sat.* iv. 4) but believes in the 'mali effectus,' of a comet (*Epist.* fol. 246 *b*).

[2] Bandello, iii. 29. The magician exacts a promise of secrecy strengthened by solemn oaths, in this case by an oath at the high altar of S. Petronio at Bologna, at a time when no one else was in the church. There is a good deal of magic in the *Maccaroneide*, Phant. xviii.

[3] Benv. Cellini, i. cap. 64.

impression, saw much more than the others. But it may be inferred that Benvenuto himself was the one whom it was wished to impress, since the dangerous beginning of the incantation can have had no other aim than to arouse curiosity. For Benvenuto had to think before the fair Angelica occurred to him; and the magician told him afterwards that love-making was folly compared with the finding of treasures. Further, it must not be forgotten that it flattered his vanity to be able to say, 'The dæmons have kept their word, and Angelica came into my hands, as they promised, just a month later' (cap. 68). Even on the supposition that Benvenuto gradually lied himself into believing the whole story, it would still be permanently valuable as evidence of the mode of thought then prevalent.

As a rule, however, the Italian artists, even 'the odd, capricious, and eccentric' among them, had little to do with magic. One of them, in his anatomical studies, may have cut himself a jacket out of the skin of a corpse, but at the advice of his confessor he put it again into the grave.[1] Indeed the frequent study of anatomy probably did more than anything else to destroy the belief in the magical influence of various parts of the body, while at the same time the incessant observation and representation of the human form made the artist familiar with a magic of a wholly different sort.

In general, notwithstanding the instances which have been quoted, magic seems to have been markedly on the decline at the beginning of the sixteenth century,—that is to say, at a time when it first began to flourish vigorously out of Italy; and thus the tours of Italian sorcerers and astrologers in the North seem not to have begun till their credit at home was thoroughly impaired. In the fourteenth century it was thought necessary carefully to watch the lake on Mount Pilatus, near Scariotto, to hinder the magicians from there consecrating their books.[2] In the fifteenth century we find, for

[1] Vasari, viii. 143, *Vita di Andrea da Fiesole.* It was Silvio Cosini, who also 'went after magical formulæ and other follies.'

[2] Uberti, *Dittamondo*, iii. cap. 1. In the March of Ancona he visits Scariotto, the supposed birthplace of Judas, and observes: 'I must not here pass over Mount Pilatus, with its lake, where throughout the summer the guards are changed regularly. For he who understands magic comes up hither to have his books consecrated, whereupon, as the people of the

example, that the offer was made to produce a storm of rain, in order to frighten away a besieged army; and even then the commander of the besieged town—Nicolò Vitelli in Città di Castello—had the good sense to dismiss the sorcerers as godless persons.[1] In the sixteenth century no more instances of this official kind appear, although in private life the magicians were still active. To this time belongs the classic figure of German sorcery, Dr. Johann Faust; the Italian ideal, on the other hand, Guido Bonatto, dates back to the thirteenth century.

It must nevertheless be added that the decrease of the belief in magic was not necessarily accompanied by an increase of the belief in a moral order, but that in many cases, like the decaying faith in astrology, the delusion left behind it nothing but a stupid fatalism.

One or two minor forms of this superstition, pyromancy, chiromancy[2] and others, which obtained some credit as the belief in sorcery and astrology were declining, may be here passed over, and even the pseudo-science of physiognomy has by no means the interest which the name might lead us to expect. For it did not appear as the sister and ally of art and psychology, but as a new form of fatalistic superstition, and, what it may have been among the Arabians, as the rival of astrology. The author of a physiognomical treatise, Bartolommeo Cocle, who styled himself a 'metoposcopist,'[3] and whose science, according to Giovio, seemed like one of the most respectable of the free arts, was not content with the prophecies which he made to the many clever people who daily consulted him, but wrote also a most serious 'catalogue of such

place say, a great storm arises.' (The consecration of books, as has been remarked, p. 527, is a special ceremony, distinct from the rest.) In the sixteenth century the ascent of Pilatus near Luzern was forbidden 'by lib und guot,' as Diebold Schilling records. It was believed that a ghost lay in the lake on the mountain, which was the spirit of Pilate. When people ascended the mountain or threw anything into the lake, fearful storms sprang up.

[1] *De Obsedione Tiphernatium*, 1474 (Rer. Ital. Scrippt. ex Florent. codicibus, tom. ii.).

[2] This superstition, which was widely spread among the soldiery (about 1520), is ridiculed by Limerno Pitocco, in the *Orlandino*, v. 60.

[3] Paul. Jov. *Elog. Lit.* p. 106, sub voce 'Cocles.'

whom great dangers to life were awaiting.' Giovio, although grown old in the free thought of Rome—'in hac luce romana'—is of opinion that the predictions contained therein had only too much truth in them.[1] We learn from the same source how the people aimed at in these and similar prophecies took vengeance on the seer. Giovanni Bentivoglio caused Lucas Gauricus to be five times swung to and fro against the wall, on a rope hanging from a lofty winding staircase, because Lucas had foretold to him the loss of his authority.[2] Ermes Bentivoglio sent an assassin after Cocle, because the unlucky metoposcopist had unwillingly prophesied to him that he would die an exile in battle. The murderer seems to have derided the dying man in his last moments, saying that the prophet had foretold to him that he would shortly commit an infamous murder. The reviver of chiromancy, Antioco Tiberto of Cesena,[3] came by an equally miserable end at the hands of Pandolfo Malatesta of Rimini, to whom he had prophesied the worst that a tyrant can imagine, namely, death in exile and in the most grievous poverty. Tiberto was a man of intelligence, who was supposed to give his answers less according to any methodical chiromancy than by means of his shrewd knowledge of mankind; and his high culture won for him the respect of those scholars who thought little of his divination.[4]

Alchemy, in conclusion, which is not mentioned in antiquity till quite late under Diocletian, played only a very subordinate part at the best period of the Renaissance.[5] Italy went through the disease earlier, when Petrarch in the fourteenth century confessed, in his polemic against it, that gold-making was a general practice.[6] Since then that particular kind of faith, devotion, and isolation which the practice of alchemy

[1] It is the enthusiastic collector of portraits who is here speaking.

[2] From the stars, since Gauricus did not know physiognomy. For his own fate he had to refer to the prophecies of Cocle, since his father had omitted to draw his horoscope.

[3] Paul. Jov. l. c. p. 100 sqq. s. v. Tibertus.

[4] The most essential facts as to these side-branches of divination, are given by Corn. Agrippa, *De Occulta Philosophia*, cap. 57.

[5] Libri, *Hist. des Sciences Mathém.* ii. 122.

[6] 'Novi nihil narro, mos est publicus' (*Remed. Utr. Fort.* p. 93), one of the lively passages of this book, written 'ab irato.'

required became more and more rare in Italy, just when Italian and other adepts began to make their full profit out of the great lords in the North.[1] Under Leo X. the few Italians who busied themselves with it were called 'ingenia curiosa,'[2] and Aurelio Augurelli, who dedicated to Leo X., the great despiser of gold, his didactic poem on the making of the metal, is said to have received in return a beautiful but empty purse. The mystic science which besides gold sought for the omnipotent philosopher's stone, is a late northern growth, which had its rise in the theories of Paracelsus and others.

[1] Chief passage in Trithem. *Ann. Hirsaug.* ii. 286 sqq.

[2] 'Neque enim desunt,' Paul. Jov. *Elog. Lit.* p. 150, s. v. 'Pomp, Gauricus;' comp. ibid. p, 130, s. v, Aurel, Augurellus, *Maccaroneide.* Phant. xii.

CHAPTER V.

GENERAL DISINTEGRATION OF BELIEF.

WITH these superstitions, as with ancient modes of thought generally, the decline in the belief of immortality stands in the closest connection.[1] This question has the widest and deepest relations with the whole development of the modern spirit.

One great source of doubt in immortality was the inward wish to be under no obligations to the hated Church. We have seen that the Church branded those who thus felt as Epicureans (p. 496 sqq.). In the hour of death many doubtless called for the sacraments, but multitudes during their whole lives, and especially during their most vigorous years, lived and acted on the negative supposition. That unbelief on this particular point must often have led to a general scepticism, is evident of itself, and is attested by abundant historical proof. These are the men of whom Ariosto says: 'Their faith goes no higher than the roof.'[2] In Italy, and especially in Florence, it was possible to live as an open and notorious unbeliever, if a man only refrained from direct acts of hostility against the Church.[3] The confessor, for instance, who was sent to prepare a political offender for death, began by inquiring whether the

[1] In writing a history of Italian unbelief it would be necessary to refer to the so-called Averrhoism, which was prevalent in Italy and especially in Venice, about the middle of the fourteenth century. It was opposed by Boccaccio and Petrarch in various letters, and by the latter in his work: *De Sui Ipsius et Aliorum Ignorantia.* Although Petrarch's opposition may have been increased by misunderstanding and exaggeration, he was nevertheless fully convinced that the Averrhoists ridiculed and rejected the Christian religion.

[2] Ariosto, *Sonetto*, 34: 'Non credere sopra il tetto.' The poet uses the words of an official who had decided against him in a matter of property.

[3] We may here again refer to Gemisthos Plethon, whose disregard of Christianity had an important influence on the Italians, and particularly on the Florentines of that period.

prisoner was a believer, 'for there was a false report that he had no belief at all.'[1]

The unhappy transgressor here referred to—the same Pierpaolo Boscoli who has been already mentioned (p. 59)—who in 1513 took part in an attempt against the newly restored family of the Medici, is a faithful mirror of the religious confusion then prevalent. Beginning as a partisan of Savonarola, he became afterwards possessed with an enthusiasm for the ancient ideals of liberty, and for paganism in general; but when he was in prison his early friends regained the control of his mind, and secured for him what they considered a pious ending. The tender witness and narrator of his last hours is one of the artistic family of the Della Robbia, the learned philologist Luca. 'Ah,' sighs Boscoli, 'get Brutus out of my head for me, that I may go my way as a Christian.' 'If you will,' answers Luca, 'the thing is not difficult; for you know that these deeds of the Romans are not handed down to us as they were, but idealised (con arte accresciute).' The penitent now forces his understanding to believe, and bewails his inability to believe voluntarily. If he could only live for a month with pious monks, he would truly become spiritually minded. It comes out that these partisans of Savonarola knew their Bible very imperfectly; Boscoli can only say the Paternoster and Avemaria, and earnestly begs Luca to exhort his friends to study the sacred writings, for only what a man has learned in life does he possess in death. Luca then reads and explains to him the story of the Passion according to the Gospel of St. Matthew; the poor listener, strange to say, can perceive clearly the Godhead of Christ, but is perplexed at his manhood; he wishes to get as firm a hold of it 'as if Christ came to meet him out of a wood.' His friend thereupon exhorts him to be humble, since this was only a doubt sent him by the Devil. Soon after it occurs to the penitent that he has not fulfilled a vow made in his youth to go on pilgrimage to the Impruneta; his friend promises to do it in his stead. Meantime the confessor—a monk, as was desired, from Savonarola's monastery—

[1] *Narrazione del Caso del Boscoli*, *Arch. Stor.* i. 273 sqq. The standing phrase was 'non aver fede;' comp. Vasari, vii. 122, *Vita di Piero di Cosimo.*

arrives, and after giving him the explanation quoted above of the opinion of St. Thomas Aquinas on tyrannicide, exhorts him to bear death manfully. Boscoli makes answer: 'Father, waste no time on this; the philosophers have taught it me already; help me to bear death out of love to Christ.' What follows—the communion, the leave-taking and the execution—is very touchingly described, one point deserves special mention. When Boscoli laid his head on the block, he begged the executioner to delay the stroke for a moment: 'During the whole time since the announcement of the sentence he had been striving after a close union with God, without attaining it as he wished, and now in this supreme moment he thought that by a strong effort he could give himself wholly to God.' It is clearly some half-understood expression of Savonarola which was troubling him.

If we had more confessions of this character the spiritual picture of the time would be the richer by many important features which no poem or treatise has preserved for us. We should see more clearly how strong the inborn religious instinct was, how subjective and how variable the relation of the individual to religion, and what powerful enemies and competitors religion had. That men whose inward condition is of this nature, are not the men to found a new church, is evident; but the history of the Western spirit would be imperfect without a view of that fermenting period among the Italians, while other nations, who have had no share in the evolution of thought, may be passed over without loss. But we must return to the question of immortality.

If unbelief in this respect made such progress among the more highly cultivated natures, the reason lay partly in the fact that the great earthly task of discovering the world and representing it in word and form, absorbed most of the higher spiritual faculties. We have already spoken (p. 490) of the inevitable worldliness of the Renaissance. But this investigation and this art were necessarily accompanied by a general spirit of doubt and inquiry. If this spirit shows itself but little in literature, if we find, for example, only isolated instances of the beginnings of biblical criticism (p. 465), we are not therefore to infer that it had no existence. The sound of it was only overpowered by the need of representation and creation in all departments—that is, by the artistic instinct; and it was further checked, whenever it tried to express itself theoretically, by the already existing despotism of the Church. This spirit of doubt must, for reasons too obvious to need discussion, have inevitably and chiefly busied itself with the question of the state of man after death.

And here came in the influence of antiquity, and worked in a twofold fashion on the argument. In the first place men set themselves to master the psychology of the ancients, and tortured the letter of Aristotle for a decisive answer. In one of the Lucianic dialogues of the time [1] Charon tells Mercury how he questioned Aristotle on his belief in immortality, when the philosopher crossed in the Stygian boat; but the prudent sage, although dead in the body and nevertheless living on, declined to compromise himself by a definite answer—and centuries later how was it likely to fare with the interpretation of his writings? All the more eagerly did men dispute about his opinion and that of others on the true nature of the soul, its origin, its pre-existence, its unity in all men, its absolute eternity, even its transformations; and there were men who treated of these things in the pulpit.[2] The dispute was warmly carried on even in the fifteenth century; some proved that Aristotle taught the doctrine of an immortal soul;[3] others complained of the hardness of men's hearts, who would not believe that there was a soul at all, till they saw it sitting down on a chair before them;[4] Filelfo in his funeral oration on Francesco Sforza brings forward a long list of opinions of ancient and even of Arabian philosophers in favour of immortality, and closes the mixture, which covers a folio page and a half of

[1] Jovian. Pontan. *Charon*, *Opp.* ii. 1128–1195.

[2] *Faustini Terdocei Triumphus Stultitiae*, l. ii.

[3] E.g. Borbone Morosini about 1460; comp. Sansovino, *Venezia* l. xiii. p. 243. He wrote 'de immortalite animæ ad mentem Aristotelis.' Pomponius Lætus, as a means of effecting his release from prison, pointed to the fact that he had written an epistle on the immortality of the soul. See the remarkable defence in Gregorovius, vii. 580 sqq. See on the other hand Pulci's ridicule of this belief in a sonnet, quoted by Galeotti, *Arch. Stor. Ital.* n. s. ix. 49 sqq.

[4] *Vespas. Fiorent.* p. 260.

print,[1] with the words, 'Besides all this we have the Old and New Testaments, which are above all truth.' Then came the Florentine Platonists with their master's doctrine of the soul, supplemented at times, as in the case of Pico, by Christian teaching. But the opposite opinion prevailed in the instructed world. At the beginning of the sixteenth century the stumbling-block which it put in the way of the Church was so serious that Leo X. set forth a Constitution [2] at the Lateran Council in 1513, in defence of the immortality and individuality of the soul, the latter against those who asserted that there was but one soul in all men. A few years later appeared the work of Pomponazzo, in which the impossibility of a philosophical proof of immortality is maintained; and the contest was now waged incessantly with replies and apologies, till it was silenced by the Catholic reaction. The pre-existence of the soul in God, conceived more or less in accordance with Plato's theory of ideas, long remained a common belief, and proved of service even to the poets.[3] The consequences which followed from it as to the mode of the soul's continued existence after death, were not more closely considered.

There was a second way in which the influence of antiquity made itself felt, chiefly by means of that remarkable fragment of the sixth book of Cicero's 'Republic' known by the name of Scipio's Dream. Without the commentary of Macrobius it would probably have perished like the rest of the second part of the work; it was now diffused in countless manuscript copies,[4] and, after the discovery of typography, in a printed form, and edited afresh by various commentators. It is the description of a transfigured hereafter for great men, pervaded by the harmony of the spheres. This pagan heaven, for which many other testimonies were gradually extracted from the writings of the ancients, came step by step to supplant the

[1] *Orationes Philelphi*, fol. 8.

[2] *Septimo Decretal.* lib. v. tit. iii. cap. 8.

[3] Ariosto, *Orlando*, vii. 61. Ridiculed in *Orlandino*, iv. 67, 68. Cariteo, a member of the Neapolitan Academy of Pontanus, uses the idea of the pre-existence of the soul in order to glorify the House of Aragon. Roscoe, *Leone X.* ed. Bossi, ii. 288.

[4] Orelli, ad Cic. *De Republ.* l. vi. Comp. Lucan, *Pharsalia*, at the beginning.

Christian heaven in proportion as the ideal of fame and historical greatness threw into the shade the ideal of the Christian life, without, nevertheless, the public feeling being thereby offended as it was by the doctrine of personal annihilation after death. Even Petrarch founds his hope chiefly on this Dream of Scipio, on the declarations found in other Ciceronian works, and on Plato's 'Phædo,' without making any mention of the Bible.[1] 'Why,' he asks elsewhere, 'should not I as a Catholic share a hope which was demonstrably cherished by the heathen?' Soon afterwards Coluccio Salutati wrote his 'Labours of Hercules' (still existing in manuscript), in which it is proved at the end that the valorous man, who has well endured the great labours of earthly life, is justly entitled to a dwelling among the stars.[2] If Dante still firmly maintained that the great pagans, whom he would have gladly welcomed in Paradise, nevertheless must not come beyond the Limbo at the entrance to Hell,[3] the poetry of a later time accepted joyfully the new liberal ideas of a future life. Cosimo the Elder, according to Bernardo Pulci's poem on his death, was received in heaven by Cicero, who had also been called the 'Father of his country,' by the Fabii, by Curius, Fabricius and many others; with them he would adorn the choir where only blameless spirits sing.[4]

But in the old writers there was another and less pleasing picture of the world to come—the shadowy realms of Homer and of those poets who had not sweetened and humanised the conception. This made an impression on certain temperaments. Gioviano Pontano somewhere attributes to Sannazaro the story of a vision, which he beheld one morning early while half awake.[5] He seemed to see a departed friend, Ferrandus

[1] Petrarca, *Epp. Fam.* iv. 3, iv. 6.

[2] Fil. Villani, *Vite*, p. 15. This remarkable passage is as follows: 'Che agli uomini fortissimi poichè hanno vinto le mostruose fatiche della terra, debitamente sieno date le stelle.'

[3] *Inferno*, iv. 24 sqq. Comp. *Purgatorio*, vii. 28, xxii. 100.

[4] This pagan heaven is referred to in the epitaph on the artist Niccolò dell' Arca:

'Nunc te Praxiteles, Phidias, Polycletus adorant,
Miranturque tuas, o Nicolae, manus.'

In Bursellis, *Ann. Bonon.* Murat. xxiii. col. 912.

[5] In his late work *Actius*.

Januarius, with whom he had often discoursed on the immortality of the soul, and whom he now asked whether it was true that the pains of Hell were really dreadful and eternal. The shadow gave an answer like that of Achilles when Odysseus questioned him. 'So much I tell and aver to thee, that we who are parted from earthly life have the strongest desire to return to it again.' He then saluted his friend and disappeared.

It cannot but be recognised that such views of the state of man after death partly presuppose and partly promote the dissolution of the most essential dogmas of Christianity. The notion of sin and of salvation must have almost entirely evaporated. We must not be misled by the effects of the great preachers of repentance or by the epidemic revivals which have been described above (part vi. cap. 2). For even granting that the individually developed classes had shared in them like the rest, the cause of their participation was rather the need of emotional excitement, the rebound of passionate natures, the horror felt at great national calamities, the cry to heaven for help. The awakening of the conscience had by no means necessarily the sense of sin and the felt need of salvation as its consequence, and even a very severe outward penance did not perforce involve any repentance in the Christian meaning of the word. When the powerful natures of the Renaissance tell us that their principle is to repent of nothing,[1] they may have in their minds only matters that are morally indifferent, faults of unreason or imprudence; but in the nature of the case this contempt for repentance must extend to the sphere of morals, because its origin, namely the consciousness of individual force, is common to both sides of human nature. The passive and contemplative form of Christianity, with its constant reference to a higher world beyond the grave, could no longer control these men. Macchiavelli ventured still farther, and maintained that it could not be serviceable to the state and to the maintenance of public freedom.[2]

[1] Cardanus, *De Propria Vita*, cap. 13: 'Non pœnitere ullius rei quam voluntarie effecerim, etiam quæ male cessisset;' else I should be of all men the most miserable.

[2] *Discorsi*, ii. cap. 2.

The form assumed by the strong religious instinct which, notwithstanding all, survived in many natures, was Theism or Deism, as we may please to call it. The latter name may be applied to that mode of thought which simply wiped away the Christian element out of religion, without either seeking or finding any other substitute for the feelings to rest upon. Theism may be considered that definite heightened devotion to the one Supreme Being which the Middle Ages were not acquainted with. This mode of faith does not exclude Christianity, and can either ally itself with the Christian doctrines of sin, redemption, and immortality, or else exist and flourish without them.

Sometimes this belief presents itself with childish naïveté and even with a half-pagan air, God appearing as the almighty fulfiller of human wishes. Agnolo Pandolfini [1] tells us how, after his wedding, he shut himself in with his wife, and knelt down before the family altar with the picture of the Madonna, and prayed, not to her, but to God that he would vouchsafe to them the right use of their property, a long life in joy and unity with one another, and many male descendants: 'for myself I prayed for wealth, honour, and friends, for her blamelessness, honesty, and that she might be a good housekeeper.' When the language used has a strong antique flavour, it is not always easy to keep apart the pagan style and the theistic belief.[2]

This temper sometimes manifests itself in times of misfortune

[1] *Del Governo della Famiglia*, p. 114.

[2] Comp. the short ode of M. Antonio Flaminio in the *Coryciana* (see p. 269):

Dii quibus tam Corycius venusta
Signa, tam dives posuit sacellum,
Ulla si vestros animos piorum
    Gratia tangit,

Vos jocos risusque senis faceti
Sospites servate diu; senectam
Vos date et semper viridem et Falerno
    Usque madentem.

At simul longo satiatus ævo
Liquerit terras, dapibus Deorum
Lætus intersit, potiore mutans
    Nectare Bacchum.

with a striking sincerity. Some addresses to God are left us from the latter period of Firenzuola, when for years he lay ill of fever, in which, though he expressly declares himself a believing Christian, he shows that his religious consciousness is essentially theistic.[1] His sufferings seem to him neither as the punishment of sin, nor as preparation for a higher world; they are an affair between him and God only, who has put the strong love of life between man and his despair. 'I curse, but only curse Nature, since thy greatness forbids me to utter thy name. . . . Give me death, Lord, I beseech thee, give it me now!'

In these utterances and the like, it would be vain to look for a conscious and consistent Theism; the speakers partly believed themselves to be still Christians, and for various other reasons respected the existing doctrines of the Church. But at the time of the Reformation, when men were driven to come to a distinct conclusion on such points, this mode of thought was accepted with a fuller consciousness; a number of the Italian Protestants came forward as Anti-Trinitarians and Socinians, and even as exiles in distant countries made the memorable attempt to found a church on these principles. From the foregoing exposition it will be clear that, apart from humanistic rationalism, other spirits were at work in this field.

One chief centre of theistic modes of thought lay in the Platonic Academy at Florence, and especially in Lorenzo Magnifico himself. The theoretical works and even the letters of these men show us only half their nature. It is true that Lorenzo, from his youth till he died, expressed himself dogmatically as a Christian,[2] and that Pico was drawn by Savonarola's influence to accept the point of view of a monkish ascetic.[3] But in the hymns of Lorenzo,[4] which we are tempted to

[1] Firenzuola, *Opere*, iv. p. 147 sqq.

[2] Nic. Valori, *Vita di Lorenzo*, *passim*. For the advice to his son Cardinal Giovanni, see Fabroni, *Laurentius*, adnot. 178, and the appendices to Roscoe's *Leo X.*

[3] *Jo. Pici Vita*, auct. Jo. Franc. Pico. For his 'Deprecatio ad Deum,' see *Deliciae Poetarum Italorum.*

[4] *Orazione*, Roscoe, *Leone X.* ed. Bossi viii. 120 (Magno Dio per la cui costante legge); hymn (oda il sacro inno tutta la natura) in Fabroni,'

regard as the highest product of the spirit of this school, an unreserved Theism is set forth—a Theism which strives to treat the world as a great moral and physical Cosmos. While the men of the Middle Ages look on the world as a vale of tears, which Pope and Emperor are set to guard against the coming of Antichrist; while the fatalists of the Renaissance oscillate between seasons of overflowing energy and seasons of superstition or of stupid resignation, here, in this circle of chosen spirits,[1] the doctrine is upheld that the visible world was created by God in love, that it is the copy of a pattern pre-existing in Him, and that He will ever remain its eternal mover and restorer. The soul of man can by recognising God draw Him into its narrow boundaries, but also by love to Him itself expand into the Infinite—and this is blessedness on earth.

Echoes of mediæval mysticism here flow into one current with Platonic doctrines, and with a characteristically modern spirit. One of the most precious fruits of the knowledge of the world and of man here comes to maturity, on whose account alone the Italian Renaissance must be called the leader of modern ages.

Laur. adnot. 9; *L'Altercazione*, in the *Poesie di Lor. Magn.* i. 265. The other poems here named are quoted in the same collection.

[1] If Pulci in his *Morgante* is anywhere in earnest with religion, he is so in canto xvi. str. 6. This deistic utterance of the fair pagan Antea is perhaps the plainest expression of the mode of thought prevalent in Lorenzo's circle, to which tone the words of the dæmon Astarotte (quoted above p. 494) form in a certain sense the complement.

THE END.

INDEX.

L.

M.

N.

R.

S.